J. B. Martin. A. B. Ritchie.

JOHN MARSHALL LL.D.

J Marshall

SKETCHES

OF THE

LIVES AND JUDICIAL SERVICES

OF THE

CHIEF-JUSTICES

OF THE

SUPREME COURT OF THE UNITED STATES.

BY

GEORGE VAN SANTVOORD.

NEW YORK:
CHARLES SCRIBNER, 145 NASSAU STREET.
1854.

STEREOTYPED BY
CHARLES W. BENEDICT,
10 Spruce Street.

TO THE

HON. SAMUEL NELSON,

ONE OF THE ASSOCIATE-JUSTICES OF THE SUPREME COURT OF THE UNITED STATES.

SIR,—I do not know to whom I can more appropriately dedicate this work than to yourself. For more than twenty years, as Circuit-Judge, as Associate-Justice, and as Chief-Justice of the New York Supreme Court, your learning illustrated, and your virtues adorned, the judicial records of our State. Appointed to the elevated position you now occupy, as the successor of a THOMPSON, and a LIVINGSTON, you carried with you the unanimous verdict of the profession that the ermine of those illustrious judges could not have fallen on one more worthy to receive it; and a service there of nearly ten years has rendered it abundantly evident that posterity will not seek to set that verdict aside.

As the only present member of the Court from our own State, whose bench and bar you may, therefore, be said to represent in the Federal Judiciary, there seems to be such a peculiar fitness in inscribing your name on these pages, that I esteem it not only an honor, but a privilege, in being allowed to make this dedication. Permit me then to express the lively gratification I feel in having your permission to inscribe this work to you.

With sincere respect, I have the honor to be your obliged and humble servant,

G. VAN SANTVOORD.

TROY, N. Y., *August 1st*, 1854.

CONTENTS.

PREFACE.

Of the five eminent Jurists who have successively filled the elevated station of Chief-Justice of the United States, only one—the first Chief-Justice, Jay—has hitherto been the subject of anything like a complete biography. So far as I know, with this exception, and except also an occasional sketch, or an obituary notice—such as that pronounced on Marshall, by his brother Judge Story, before the Suffolk bar—no attempt has been made to preserve in a connected narrative, even the public history and career, to say nothing of the professional life and judicial services, of these distinguished men, three of whom were prominent and active leaders among the statesmen of the Revolution. I have seen it stated some years since, that a son-in-law of Judge Ellsworth was preparing an extensive and complete biography of that gentleman, containing his speeches, extracts from his writings, and many interesting facts in regard to him, but, for some cause which I have not seen explained, the promised memoir has not made its appearance. It might indeed seem a singular, and unaccountable neglect, that one so eminent and distinguished in our civil and diplomatic, as well as our judicial annals, should not hitherto have had a place assigned him in our biographical literature, were not the same unaccountable neglect manifest in the case of his immediate predecessor, as well as in that of his illustrious successor, on the bench of the Supreme Court. Surely the rich mine of American biography cannot be nearly exhausted when such treasures as the lives of Rutledge, Ellsworth, and Marshall lie still undeveloped and comparatively neglected.

The plan of these memoirs, which are now submitted with unaffected diffidence to the public, is such, as necessarily to restrict that part of them which may properly be called biographical, within very narrow limits. They do not pretend to the minuteness of the full and complete biography, and I have not, therefore, assumed to dignify them with a higher title than simply that of "sketches." My object has been rather to trace the judicial history and follow the professional career of these illustrious jurists, than to write what may properly be called their biographies. Still, I have endeavored not to neglect entirely the essential requisites of biography, but have attempted, so far as the limits prescribed will permit, to present an accurate and connected view of the public and official life of each of them before coming to the bench.

Without further remark I might here submit this volume to the judgment of the reader, and leave it to speak for itself. But a single additional observation seems proper and necessary. I am aware that the review of judicial decisions, which I have given somewhat at length, is a wide departure from the ordinary course of biographical writing. I have not entered upon it, however, without due reflection and design. A main object in undertaking this work has been to trace something like a history of the United States Supreme Court, and to present a brief and succinct, but connected, view of the Constitutional jurisprudence of the United States; and I knew of no more agreeable and interesting mode of doing this than by combining it with sketches of the public and professional lives of those eminent men who have from time to time presided in the Supreme Federal tribunal. I have attempted thus to unite judicial and constitutional history with biography. This has enabled me to take a wider and more general view of the entire subject; to embrace within these sketches not only those matters which are properly the subject of the memoirs of a life, but also to trace the history of the Federal judiciary from its earliest beginnings; to consider the facts and results connected with the adoption of the Federal Constitution, and to review, or notice, more or less fully, most of the important Constitutional questions which have been discussed in the Supreme Court from the foundation of the government to the present time.

There are those, perhaps, who may consider such a work as too *professional*, to claim a place within the sphere of general literature, and to regard such an analysis of legal cases as has been incorporated into it, as incompatible with the legitimate objects of popular biography. Perhaps such a criticism may be just. It is not, however, for the author to anticipate it. If he has misjudged in this respect, he has at least, the satisfaction of knowing that the general plan of his work has been considered with favor by friends in whose judgment he has confidence; and should its success not meet their expectations he can but attribute it to its imperfect manner of execution, and not to any want of public interest in that branch of the subject alluded to; —a subject which can never be indifferent to the American citizen—the constitutional history and jurisprudence of his country.

JOHN JAY.

JOHN JAY.

HISTORY is not always just in its discriminations, or correct in its estimate of individual character and of the true worth and merit of public services. There is something so attractive to the historian in tracing successful results in administration, and brilliant achievements on the field of battle, that he is apt to lose sight of the less striking but no less valuable labors of the discreet statesman in the legislature, the jurist on the bench, and the ambassador in the field of foreign diplomacy. Thus it happens in regard to our revolutionary struggle, that while the popular admiration centres round the more prominent actors on the scene, there is a class of men, standing comparatively in the background, whose characters have never been fully appreciated, and to whose memories history has not yet done entire justice. These are the men of the Continental Congress and of the Federal and State Conventions—the Livingstons, the Rutledges, the Morrises, the Ellsworths—the men who aided, not only in achieving the American Revolution, but in laying broad and deep the foundations of liberty, and in reconstructing our political institutions. Without their aid, however successful the contest, it must have ended in ultimate defeat. The battle might have been won, but the fruits of victory never obtained. The arm of the conqueror would have fallen, paralyzed, in the moment of his triumph; for the experience of history shows that the civilian and the statesman are as necessary as the soldier to the successful issue of a revolution.

One of these men was John Jay—a man of modest virtue and unpretending merit, who quietly, faithfully, and ably discharged the most important duties in the sphere he was called upon to fill. There are those who played a more imposing and brilliant part than he in the revolutionary drama, and whose names posterity has been inclined to inscribe higher on the scroll of fame; but there are few who are more deserving the respect and veneration of their countrymen. His signature, it is true, is not found with those of Jefferson and Adams, affixed to the Declaration of Independence; nor with Hamilton and Madison did he assist in raising the fabric of the Federal Constitution. But no man rendered a more zealous and energetic support to the one, and none contributed more efficiently to sustain and carry out the other. And whatever in our day may be thought of the correctness of some of his political views, no American will fail to render a ready homage to that active zeal, courage, and devotion to the common cause, as well as to that honesty of purpose and moral rectitude which characterized the public, as it did the private life of one of the purest men of the Revolution.

The name of John Jay should be especially venerated by the American lawyer;—indeed it is a name that cannot soon be forgotten. The first Chief-Justice of the Supreme Court of the State of New York—the first Chief-Justice of the Supreme Court of the United States under the Federal Constitution, he occupied a position which of itself, and without the aid of that learning, and those varied accomplishments which adorned his mind, would have left a memory that could not soon have faded from the records of American jurisprudence.

I shall have occasion in attempting a sketch of the life and services of the first Chief-Justice of the United States, to consider him in the character of a lawyer and a judge, as well as in those more public capacities, legislative, diplomatic and executive, which he filled during the greater portion of his active life. It is not only as a statesman, but as a jurist, that John Jay ought to be known to his countrymen. For it is from the record of his judicial labors, as well as from the history of his political career, that we are to draw a true estimate of his character, and of the extent and value of the services he rendered his country.

JOHN JAY was born in the city of New York, on the 12th day of December, 1745. He was descended on the father's side from French ancestry. His mother's ancestors were from Holland. His paternal grandfather, Pierre Jay, was an opulent merchant at Rochelle. A Protestant, he was obliged to leave France on the revocation of the edict of Nantz, and take refuge in England. One of his three sons, Augustus, emigrated to New York, and married a daughter of Balthazar Bayard, whose ancestors, like those of Mr. Jay, had been Protestants, and had been obliged to emigrate from France to Holland. Three daughters and one son were the fruits of this union. The son, in honor of the Rochelle merchant, was named Peter. In 1728 Mr. Peter Jay married Mary Van Cortlandt, the daughter of Jacobus Van Cortlandt, a gentleman belonging to one of the oldest families of the Dutch colonists who settled Manhattan Island. Peter Jay had ten children, of whom the subject of this sketch, JOHN, was the eighth. The family, we are told, removed to the town of Rye, on Long Island Sound, about twenty-five miles distant from New York, and John was carried there in his nurse's arms.

At the age of six or seven years, his father remarks of him, that he is "of a very grave disposition, and takes to learning exceedingly well;" and again, "My Johnny gives me a very pleasing prospect. He seems to be endowed with a very good capacity, is very reserved, and quite of his brother James' disposition for books." At the age of eight John was sent to a grammar-school at New Rochelle, kept by the Rev. Mr. Strope, pastor of the French church at that place. At fourteen he entered King's College, in the city of New York, over which Dr. Samuel Johnson then presided. Egbert Benson, Peter Van Schaack, Richard Harrison, Gouverneur Morris and Robert R. Livingston, all of whom, like Mr. Jay, subsequently pursued with distinction the legal profession, were among his college acquaintances. He graduated on the 15th May, 1764, with the highest collegiate honors, having been selected to speak the Latin salutatory.

The father and grandfather of Mr. Jay had been merchants. That honorable pursuit, however, did not agree with the tastes and inclinations of the young graduate. The choice of a profession being left to him, he selected that of the law, and entered the office of

Mr. Benjamin Kissam, an eminent practitioner in the city of New York.

We have no very accurate account of the incidents attending the clerkship and preparatory studies of the future Chief-Justice—they were probably much the same as those which are familiar to the experience of every student. It must be recollected, that in those days, a preparation for the legal profession was not, as it often is at present, an agreeable recreation. It was a real labor, and often a drudgery. Printed blank forms were unknown, and every thing was written, even the argument of questions of law. The labors of a clerkship were consequently very arduous, and a large portion of the time of the student was occupied in attention to office duties. Nor were elementary treatises—those ready and convenient aids in acquiring the elements of the profession—so plenty then as now. Finch's Law, Wood's Institutes, or Coke upon Littleton were the books usually placed in the hands of the student at the commencement of his clerkship, each of which, to use the words of Lord Mansfield, applied to Coke, may be called "an uncouth, crabbed author, who has disappointed and disheartened many a tyro." The first volume of Blackstone's Commentaries was published in England in 1765, the second part some three years later. Up to this time the difficulty of selecting the book which should initiate the student in the elementary principles of law, is admitted by Lord Mansfield. "Till of late," he says, "I could never with any satisfaction to myself answer that question, but since the publication of Mr. Blackstone's Commentaries, I can never be at a loss." In entering upon his clerkship, however, Jay had not the advantage of this admirable treatise, and, therefore, unlike those students who have succeeded him, could not, *ab initio*, "imbibe imperceptibly (quoting again the words of Lord Mansfield,) the first principles upon which our excellent laws are founded." To him, as to others in those times, the labor was tedious and toilsome; but at the same time it was a healthy intellectual exercise, and a vigorous mental discipline.*

* The reader may be curious to learn the course of legal study which in Jay's time was recommended to the student. The following extracts are made from an old manuscript manual in my possession, bearing date 1768. It is in the hand-

Between Mr. Jay and the estimable gentleman in whose office he read law, the most entire confidence existed, which gradually ripened into familiarity and friendship. This is attested by several letters written by Mr. Kissam to Mr. Jay. In one of these, dated soon after Jay was admitted to the bar, Mr. Kissam, in a tone of playful and friendly familiarity, compliments his pupil upon having successfully tried several causes for him, which, he says, was done "by a kind of inspiration." Alluding to one cause in which Jay was opposed to him, Mr. Kissam remarks, "As to the cause about Captain's Island, this, tell Mr. Morris, must go off; because as you are concerned *against me*, I can't tell where to find another into whose head the cause can be infused in the miraculous way of inspiration, and without this it would be rather too intricate for any one to manage from my short hints."

writing and was the property of a cotemporary of Mr. Jay, then a student-at-law in the office of William Smith, the historian of New York.

"But now I bring our student home to the studies of his profession of the law, and I would advise him to read these books, in the following order:

"First, for the knowledge of the law in general:

"1. The treatise of laws in Wood's Institutes of the Civil Law, or in Domat, which are both the same.

"2. *Puffendorf de Officio Hominis et Civis*, or an English translation of it called "The Whole Duty of Man according to the Law of Nature," or the abridgment of Puffendorf, in two volumes, by Spavin."

And before entering further into the law of Nature and Nations and the Civil Law, the writer advises a general study of the elements of the Common Law, in the following order:

"Hall's History of the Common Law.

"Fortescue's Practice of the Laws of England.

"Sir Thomas Smith's *De Republica Anglorum.*

"The first book of Doctor and Student, *De Fundamentum Legum Angliæ.*

"The second part of Bacon's Elements.

"Wood's Institutes of the Common Law."

After recommending a farther and more extensive reading of the Law of Nature and Nations and the Civil Law, he remarks:

"Then to fill up and enlarge your ideas you may read Bacon's Abridgment of the law, which it is presumed will all be soon published. In reading this Abridgment, which is contrived *so as to be read pleasantly*, I would advise that you constantly refer from the Abridgment to Wood, and from Wood to the Abridgment, because I would have *these books the basis or foundation* of all your studies."

Mr. Kissam and Mr. Jay were frequently opposed to each other in the trial or on the argument of a cause. On one of these occasions, being hard pressed in the argument, the former remarked, "I have brought up a bird to pick out my own eyes." "Not so," retorted Jay, "not to pick out, but to open your eyes."*

On entering upon the practice of the law, Mr. Jay associated himself with his relative, Robert R. Livingston, the future chancellor, but the connection was soon dissolved. From his *debut* as an advocate in the colonial courts, it is said he entered upon a lucrative practice, and continued it down to the period of the revolutionary war. I have not been able, however, to draw from the imperfect record of colonial jurisprudence any very satisfactory information respecting his forensic career,† or even of the more important causes in which he was engaged. The race of reporters did not exist in those days, and the colonial decisions and adjudged cases with which the names of Jay, Livingston, Benson, Morris, Duane and their cotemporaries were identified must remain for us a lost and comparatively forgotten record.‡ Suffice it then to say that the practice of Mr. Jay during these six or eight years was extensive and lucrative, that he exhibited professional ability of the highest order, and that he acquired an eminent and proud position as an advocate at the New York bar.

* Life of John Jay, by his son, William Jay.

† It may be mentioned as a fact interesting to the legal profession, that in 1770 the young lawyers of New York formed a club called "The Moot," at which legal questions were discussed and argued in form. Some of the records of this club are still preserved. Its decisions acquired great authority, and the questions discussed and decided were considered as professionally settled. Among the junior members of the club were Jay, R. R. Livingston, James Duane, Egbert Benson, Gouverneur Morris, and Peter Van Schaack. The older members of the bar also regularly attended and participated in these discussions and arguments, and among them are found the names of those veteran lawyers, William Smith, Samuel Jones, William Livingston, Benjamin Kissam, John M. Scott, and Richard Morris.

‡ The author of the Life of William Livingston thinks we have lost very little in this respect. "An examination of Mr. Livingston's registers and business letters," he says, "would much tend to diminish any regret which may be felt for the want of colonial reports. A great number of the cases are suits for the collection of debts owned by English merchants; and causes under the complex law of ejectment, now so happily exploded, form another large class."—*Sedgwick's Life of Livingston*, p. 71.

But the quiet and peaceful course of professional life was about to be broken. The contest between the colonies and the mother country commenced. The young lawyer was summoned from his briefs and his cases, from his books and his precedents, to a nobler and more enlarged field of action. Nor did John Jay turn an unwilling ear to the summons. While others hesitated and wavered, while some of his own friends and intimate associates counselled submission or passive non-resistance, his voice was raised among the first in opposition to the arbitrary measures of Great Britain. On the 16th of May, 1774, Mr. Jay attended the first meeting of the citizens of New York called to "consult on measures proper to be pursued in consequence of the late extraordinary advices received from England." The result of that meeting was the appointment of a committee of fifty, of which Jay was one, and a subsequent report, said to be from his pen, which recommended the convocation of a *Congress of deputies* from the thirteen colonies.

The recommendation was adopted. A Congress was called and convened at Philadelphia, on the 5th of September, 1774. Jay was elected a member from New York, and took his seat on the first day of the session. Though one of the youngest members of the Congress, being then only in his twenty-ninth year, he was placed upon the committee to draft an address to the people of Great Britain. That celebrated address is from his pen. It had been composed and written by Jay in the room of an obscure tavern. It was reported to Congress by Mr. Livingston, and adopted as the work of the entire committee, and its paternity was not immediately known.

Jefferson attributed it to Gov. Livingston, by whom it had been reported, as chairman of the committee, and told that gentleman that he regarded it as "the production of the finest pen in America." The author of the life of Jefferson states, that this coming to the ears of Mr. Jay, he was at some pains to set Jefferson right in the matter and assert his own claims to its authorship.

Of the proceedings of this Congress it is not necessary now to speak. It was composed of fifty-five members. Among them were the distinguished orators from Virginia, Patrick Henry and Richard Henry Lee.* The debate was opened by Mr. Henry in a speech of

* Prof. Tucker remarks in his Life of Jefferson, that though Henry and Lee

matchless power and eloquence—a vivid and glowing description of which has been drawn by the graphic pen of Mr. Wirt. Richard Henry Lee followed, and charmed with his graceful eloquence an audience that had been spell-bound by the more potent declamation of his colleague. As he closed, Mr. Chase, a delegate from Maryland, whispered into the ear of one of his colleagues, "we may as well go home; we cannot legislate with these men." The whole assembly seemed to acknowledge their superiority. Lee was made chairman of the committee to prepare the address to the People of Great Britain; and Henry of the committee to prepare the address to the King. It soon became apparent, however, that their superiority consisted in powers of eloquence alone. The address of Lee fell far short of the high expectations that had been raised. Its reading disappointed the whole assembly. "After all," remarked Mr. Chase, with that quick perception and ready boldness which so strongly characterized his mind, "they are but men, and *very common men, too*."* After some faint and equivocal compliments, the address was laid on the table, and Gov. Livingston and John Jay were appointed upon the committee. The result was, as we have seen, the production of an address which the Congress adopted—an address worthy of the men and of the occasion, and fully equal to the crisis which called it forth.

Mr. Jay was now actively and warmly enlisted in the cause of the Colonies. A full review of his career from the time when he first took his seat as a delegate in Congress to the period when he accepted the Spanish mission, would comprise a record of the history of the Colonial struggle. The limits of the present sketch will not permit a detail, much less a discussion of these stirring events, and all that can be admitted here, is to indicate generally and briefly, the part taken in them by the subject of this memoir.

The first Revolutionary Congress, after a brief session, adjourned to meet again on the 10th of May in the following year. Accordingly, at that time, the Congress assembled at Philadelphia. It continued its session, with the exception of a brief recess in the month of

bore the palm for eloquence in debate, yet "for that of the pen, the first place must unquestionably be awarded to Mr. Jay, of New York."

* Wirt's Life of Patrick Henry.

August, during the remainder of the year. The decisive action which attended the deliberations of this Congress is well-known. The crisis was now at hand—the battle of Lexington had been fought—the alternative presented was armed resistance, or abject submission and slavery. A new set of ideas seemed to have been developed. The revolutionary mind had been ripened and matured in a day. A profound lesson of experience had been learned, and a vast stride taken in the direction of Colonial independence. It was no longer, as at the opening of the first Congress, a question of non-importation—of peaceable remonstrance. The aspect of affairs had changed, and it had become a question, which might well have made the boldest hesitate, of armed, open, determined, and manly resistance. But the men of the Continental Congress did not falter. The crisis was met, boldly and manfully ; an army was organized ; Washington appointed commander-in-chief ; subordinate officers nominated, among whom, on motion of Mr. Jay, John Sullivan, a modest and unobtrusive delegate from New Hampshire, was commissioned a Brigadier-General in the American army.

The important part taken by Mr. Jay in the deliberations of this Congress must be passed hastily over, and I can barely allude to a few prominent public acts in which he was engaged. His active and vigorous pen was almost ceaselessly at work, and his voice was frequently heard in the deliberations of the assembly. He was a member of the committee which prepared the DECLARATION setting forth the causes and necessity of the Colonies taking up arms.* He was also upon the committee appointed to carry out the measure originated by himself, of presenting a petition to the sovereign to redress the grievances of the Colonies, the rejection of which left no alternative but armed resistance. By direction of Congress he prepared an address to the people of Canada. He also wrote the celebrated address to the people of Jamaica and Ireland, in which he depicted in vivid colors the injuries which the Colonies had suffer-

* Mr. Jefferson and Mr. Dickinson were subsequently added to this committee. The address of the committee was drawn by Jefferson, but being considered "too bold," it was remodelled by Mr. Dickinson. It is a remarkable fact that this address, though reported only a year before the Declaration of Independence, disclaims all design to dissolve the union between Great Britain and the Colonies.

ed, and traced the origin of their rights and the grounds of their resistance.

Though a less prominent member of this Congress than some of his distinguished compatriots—though neither a Henry, a Rutledge, nor an Adams, in the rare gifts of an impassioned eloquence—still it is not claiming too high a distinction for the zeal, patriotism, ability, and modest worth of John Jay, to place him in the very front rank of those illustrious men who laid the foundations of the Republic.

The Continental Congress, it is well known, was a mere convention of delegates, a body, organized, it is true, but without specific objects, real authority, or definite powers. The Congress was of itself neither a sovereignty nor the representative of a sovereignty. The union of the colonies was little more than a league, and even after the declaration of independence it was a league scarcely of independent states, for though social institutions remained, yet the political fabric had been swept away by revolution, and the labor of organization and reconstruction was yet to be done. This was the work of some of the best and wisest men in the respective states of the confederacy. In the State of New York it was eminently the work of John Jay.

While yet a delegate in Congress, Mr. Jay had been elected, in the month of April, 1776, to the New York Colonial Convention. He took his seat in that body on the 25th of May, without resigning his commission as a member of Congress. It seems to have been his intention to return, but the New York Convention required his attendance, and, as he informs his colleague, Mr. Duane, "directed me not to leave them till further orders." And thus he was deprived of the honor of affixing his signature to the DECLARATION OF INDEPENDENCE. But while his name is not attached to that noble instrument, the records of the New York Provincial Convention attest the warmth and ardor of his approval of the act. From the committee to which it was referred in the Convention, Mr. Jay as chairman reported immediately the following resolution, which was unanimously adopted:

"*Resolved, unanimously,* That the reasons assigned by the Continental Congress for declaring these united Colonies free and independent States, are cogent and conclusive, and that while we lament the cruel necessity which has rendered that measure unavoidable, we approve the same, and will at the risk of our lives and fortunes, join with the other colonies in supporting it."

This resolution was adopted on the day of the opening of the Convention, July 9th, 1776. It is somewhat remarkable that though Chancellor Livingston was a member of the committee which drafted the Declaration of Independence, of which Jefferson was chairman, yet his name is not found attached to that instrument. The fact is, that though the declaration purports to be "the *unanimous* declaration," &c., yet the Chancellor and some other members of the Congress thought it premature. Indeed the whole New York delegation asked and obtained leave to retire, on the ground, that having been appointed when a reconciliation with Great Britain was possible, they did not regard themselves as empowered to sign this important manifesto. None of the New York members signed it until *after it was approved* by the New York Convention ; and it was not until the 15th of July that their signatures were actually placed to the Declaration. To John Jay, therefore, though his name does not appear attached to that celebrated instrument, is justly due the credit of having promptly and boldly taken the first official step toward the recognition by the State of New York of American Independence.

The new State Convention was called in pursuance of a resolution of the Continental Congress, recommending to the respective Colonies the adoption of independent governments. The former Assembly, to which Mr. Jay had been summoned from his seat in Congress, having been convened while the Colony was yet under the government of the Crown, had been established for the sole purpose of opposing the encroachments of the British parliament, and not with a view of declaring the Colony independent, and establishing a new form of government. To remove all doubts whether the Assembly was invested with authority to deliberate and act on these important questions, the Colonial assembly, on the 31st May, had, on motion of Mr. Jay, called a Convention to constitute and establish a new government. This body met at White Plains on the 9th July, 1776, and, as has been noticed, immediately ratified and confirmed unanimously the Declaration of the Independence of the Colonies. This first decisive step having been taken, nothing remained but to establish a constitution and organize the new government.

The Convention comprised a large share of the best intellect and worth of the Colony. Mr. Jay found himself associated with such men as Philip Livingston and James Duane of New York, Robert R. Livingston of Dutchess, the future Chancellor, Leonard Gansevoort and Robert Van Rensselaer of Albany, Gouverneur Morris, Pierre Van Cortlandt and Lewis Morris of Westchester. It is certainly no small compliment to the ability and character of Mr. Jay, still a young man, but little more than thirty years of age, that in a Convention numbering among its members such men as the Livingstons, the Morrises, and their illustrious associates, he should have been selected as the delegate to be charged with the responsible and arduous duty of drafting a Constitution for the new Commonwealth. Being assigned this duty and placed at the head of the committee created for that purpose during the first month of the Convention, he at once directed the whole power of his mind, and the resources of his political experience and judicial learning to attain the great end in view, namely the drafting of a Constitution fit to be established as the fundamental law of a free people.

It may here be remarked, that the idea of a *written Constitution*, emanating from and sanctioned by the people, as the basis of government and political and social rights, if not entirely a novel idea, was at least, practically, an untried experiment, prior to the formation of the State Constitutions. It had been hinted at and partially developed by some of the liberal writers and statesmen during, and subsequent to, the period of the English Revolution. Vane, Sidney, and Locke, had successively entertained the subject as an abstract political truth, and the latter had even attempted its practical development.* But it is not too much to say that it remained a theory only, and that hitherto no successful instance of a written

* In the Carolina colonies. This curious Constitution, almost as elaborate, unique and original in its way as that remarkable instrument which more than a century afterward Sieyes presented to Bonaparte, was adopted by the Proprietaries, but after a few years wasted in attempting to put it into practical operation it proved itself a miserable failure, and was abandoned.

constitution or fundamental law had existed in Christendom. The Bill of Rights, the charters of some of the Colonies, and particularly those established in one or two of the proprietary governments, such, for example, as the "Concessions of the proprietors of New Jersey with the people who might settle or plant there," approximated this idea of a written Constitution, but did not wholly realize it. The Bill of Rights was in the nature of a compact between king and people; the Colonial charters were royal grants, not resting upon, but independent of the popular sovereignty; the proprietary governments were what they claimed to be, *concessions* to the people, not original and elementary popular rights. It remained for the Colonists to put in successful operation this new political experiment, in the formation and organization of the State sovereignties—an experiment, destined, a few years later, to be crowned with complete success in the adoption of the Federal Constitution.

The first Constitution of the State of New York was mainly the work of John Jay. It was reported on the 6th of March, 1777, and adopted the 20th of April of the same year, at the village of Kingston, to which place the Convention had removed. This Constitution, which contained for nearly half a century the fundamental law of the State, is a monument to the memory of its illustrious author more lasting than a monument of brass or marble. I do not mean to assert that the Constitution was all that it *might have been*—that it was a perfect production—that it contained no imperfections and no errors. On the contrary, experience demonstrated the necessity of amendment; a trial of forty-five years proved that it was susceptible of material alterations; the progress of the age and the march of liberal ideas opened the door to improvement; but it is not too much to say that in the circumstances under which this Constitution was promulgated, and in view of the habits, customs, and ideas of the age, it was an original and vigorous, as well as a successful innovation, and it stamped its author as a bold and radical but judicious reformer.

All the guarantees of English liberty secured in the Bill of Rights were carefully preserved in this Constitution,—the trial by jury, the habeas corpus, and the privilege of the accused to defend by counsel. All political power was declared to be derived from the people. In addition to this, the free exercise and enjoyment of religious worship was established,* and the right of the people to bear arms in their own défence recognized and secured. Ten years afterwards, in the Federal Convention, Hamilton proposed, and sustained, in a speech of surpassing power, the project of appointing an executive and Senate, to hold for life or during good behavior. But Jay, even at this early day, comprehended the more correct idea of popular government. The New York Constitution provided for the election of an executive to hold office for three years, a Senate for four years, and an annual Assembly. The voting by ballot was not definitely established; it was left to be determined by the Legislature, a provision which may be regarded as the effect of excessive caution and prudence, if not of timidity, but one which the state of the times and the novelty of the experiment at that day might justify. So too in regard to the property qualification attached to the elective franchise, and the qualifications for office, the provisions of the Constitution fell far short of what we now regard as the correct and legitimate rule of political action, but at that day, when the colonists were just emancipated from British tutelage, and aristocratic customs and notions of hereditary right still prevailed, this section of the Constitution was a sensible reform, if not a radical revolution. The provision that "a wise and discreet freeholder of this State shall be, by ballot, elected Governor, by the freeholders of this State, qualified as before described, to elect Senators"—that is possessing a freehold of forty pounds, or renting a tenement of the yearly value of forty shillings,—was but a step from asserting the great principle of UNIVERSAL SUFFRAGE, which was established by the Constitution of 1821 as the basis of representative democracy.

As to the social institutions of the State, the Constitution left

* In regard to this clause, Mr. Jay, in his celebrated charge to the Grand Jury, at Kingston, uses these noble and dignified expressions. "Every man is permitted to consider, to adore, and to worship his Creator in the manner most agreeable to his conscience. No opinions are dictated, no rules of faith prescribed, no preference given to one sect to the prejudice of others." * * * "In a word, the Convention by whom that Constitution was formed, were of opinion that the Gospel of Christ, like the ark of God, would not fall, though unsupported by the arm of flesh; and happy would it be for mankind if that opinion prevailed more generally."

them very nearly in the position it found them. The revolution was purely political. The Convention did not undertake to meddle with the laws of property, the domestic relations, or indeed in any other respect with the judicial polity of the State. Accordingly, the Constitution re-enacted and established as the law of the State, the COMMON LAW of England, and such parts of prior statutes, both acts of Parliament, and acts of the Colonial Legislature, as were applicable and not repugnant to the Constitution, with the restriction, that all such parts thereof as might be construed "to establish or maintain any particular denomination of Christians or their ministers, or concern allegiance heretofore yielded to," &c., be abrogated and rejected.

Such were the main features of the Constitution of 1777. It may be remarked that Jay himself was not entirely satisfied with it. The vote on its final passage was taken during his temporary absence from the Convention, and some additional sections had been added which he disapproved ; what these sections were, does not clearly appear. He intended also, he says, to have moved several amendments, one for the support of literature, one against the continuance of slavery in the State, and one requiring all persons taking office to swear allegiance to the government, and renounce all allegiance to foreign kings, princes and states in all matters, *ecclesiastical as well as civil.*

Approving, however, the main features of the new Constitution, Mr. Jay devoted his best efforts to the task of setting it practically in operation. In the organization of the courts under it, the Convention tendered him the place of Chief-Justice of the Supreme Court, which he at once accepted, Livingston being at the same time appointed Chancellor. The Convention then adjourned, after appointing a "Council of Safety," of which Jay was a member, in whose hands was vested the absolute sovereignty of the State during the interim between the adjournment and the organization of the new government. This Committee was armed with plenary and unlimited power. It was indeed an arbitrary dictatorship. The crisis was such as seemed to demand it, for the darkest hour of the revolution had come. That power was exercised vigorously, but wisely and discreetly. It was wielded with tremendous effect, but not abused. It was the power which in a similar case was lodged by the French Convention in the hands of the Committee of Public Welfare, but it was used for wiser and better ends, for there were no Couthons and Robespierres upon the New York Council of Safety. The measures adopted against the royalists were such as the exigency of the times demanded. They were vigorous, stringent, severe. The jails and churches were filled with prisoners. Banishment and confiscation became the order of the day. But these measures, though harsh and rigorous were tempered with as much mildness as the nature of the case would admit. No member of that Committee, and least of all John Jay, is liable to the charge of wielding political power for the purposes of individual oppression.

One of the finest traits in the character of Jay was the warmth of his social feelings, and the constancy of his friendships. Adversity never separated him from his early associates, nor did political differences cause him to forget the attachments of other days. It was during the administration of the Council of Safety that the formidable invasion of Burgoyne threatened the safety of New York. General Philip Schuyler at that time had command of the army of the north. Jay was the friend of Schuyler; he knew and appreciated the worth, the patriotism, the chivalric honor, of that brave officer and gallant gentleman. In a moment of weakness, Congress, yielding either to false and malicious representations, or a timid policy, recalled Schuyler at the very moment when victory was within his grasp, and placed Gates in command. Schuyler felt the indignity, but with the generous magnanimity of his character, sacrificing every personal feeling to the cause of his country, cheerfully co-operated with the plan of the campaign, and aided Gen. Gates to reap the laurels which justly belonged to himself. Among the friends who adhered through good report and through evil report to Schuyler, and who never failed to vindicate his reputation, none was truer or more faithful than Jay. Sharing the same ancestral blood, the blood of the early Dutch settlers of the colony, and satisfied with the entire correctness of Schuyler's conduct, as well as the purity of his motives, Jay did not conceal his indignation at this act of injustice. In a letter to Mr. Duane, then in Congress, he expresses what he conceives to be the true reason. "General Schuyler is recalled," he says, " to *humor the eastern people*, who declare that their militia will not fight under his command." The warmth of his friendship, and the delicacy of his sympathy, are beautifully expressed in two or three letters to Schuyler himself about this period. In one of these, written some months after the victory of Saratoga, and while the laurels were yet fresh and green upon the brow of the commanding general, Jay, with his accustomed delicacy of expression, ventures to predict what the future has fully realized, and posterity cordially admits. " Justice will yet take place, and I do not despair of seeing the time when it will be confessed that the foundation of our success in the northern department was laid by the present commander's predecessor."

Not only to political associates, but even to political opponents, did Jay evince the kindliness of a generous nature ; and he never failed to respond to the recollections of early attachments. Few among the revolutionary leaders originated, advocated, and carried out more stringent and effective measures against the royalists and the disaffected, and yet he was never deaf to the voice of private friendship, and never disregarded the appeal of one to whom he had been kindly attached in other days. To his old classmate at King's College, Peter Van Schaack, who had from conscientious motives declined taking a part with the colonists, he writes with a feeling of the liveliest interest ; and the cordial intercourse is renewed when one is the honored representative of his country, and the other an exile in a foreign land. To Col. De Lancey, who had taken arms in the royal cause, and who was a prisoner on parole, he writes during the troubles of 1778 : " The friendship which subsisted between us is not forgotten ; nor will the good offices formerly done by yourself and family cease to excite my gratitude. How far you may be comfortable and easy I know not. It is my wish, and shall be my endeavor, that it be as much so as may be consistent with the interest of that great cause to which I have devoted every thing I hold dear in this world."

John Jay was a revolutionist, but no terrorist. He was resolute, stern, and inflexible, but not proscriptive. His was the uncompromising action based upon principle, not prompted by personal enmity. He had not a grain of bitterness in him, not a drop of malice, not the slightest tincture of vindictiveness. Firm, resolute, and unbending, but equable, magnanimous, generous and just, a man to suffer, rather than do a wrong, like Aristides he would have calmly written his own name upon the shell, and without a regret or a sigh, have retired into banishment.

The new State government went into operation in September, 1777. Jay having refused to be a candidate for Governor, George Clinton was elected to that office, and Pierre Van Cortlandt Lieutenant-Governor. Walter Livingston was chosen speaker of the Assembly. The Legislature promptly re-appointed Mr. Jay Chief-Justice of the Supreme Court, and Robert R. Livingston Chancellor.

It was but a few days before this re-appointment that the Chief-Justice held the first court under the State Constitution. It met at the village of Kingston, on the 9th of September, 1777. The circumstances under which it had convened were peculiar. The independence of the State had been declared, but that independence had not been established. A powerful army under Burgoyne was approaching Albany; another army was preparing to advance up the Hudson to effect a junction with the first, and in a few weeks after, actually destroyed the very village in which the court was assembled. To administer justice under the authority of the State was a crime and a treason against the British government, still claiming jurisdiction. It required, therefore, a portion of that same unflinching resolution, and sublime moral courage, which nerved the men who declared the independence of the colonies, to carry out fully and effectually this novel undertaking. The Chief-Justice was equal to the task. He did not hesitate, he did not doubt. He had entire faith in the success of the revolution; faith in the people; faith in the new Constitution which had been adopted; faith in the ultimate issue of the contest. He presided during the session of the court with a calm dignity, an intrepid courage, a confident assurance of rectitude which did not fail to impress itself upon the people. His charge to the Grand Jury was such as it might have been if the independence of the State had been already acknowledged, and the foot of the enemy no longer desecrated American soil. The following passages are worthy of remark:

"It affords me, gentlemen, very sensible pleasure to congratulate you on the dawn of that free, mild, and equable government which now begins to rise and break from amid those clouds of anarchy, confusion, and licentiousness which the arbitrary and violent domination of Great Britain had spread in greater or less degree throughout this and the other American states. This is one of those signal-instances in which Divine Providence has made the tyranny of princes instrumental in breaking the chains of their subjects, and rendered the most inhuman designs productive of the best consequences to those against whom they were intended.

"The infatuated sovereign of Great Britain, forgetful that kings were the servants, not the proprietors, and ought to be the fathers, not the incendiaries of their people, hath, by destroying our former constitutions, enabled us to erect more eligible systems of government on their ruins; and by unwarrantable attempts to bind us in all cases whatever, has reduced us to the happy necessity of being free from his control in any.

"Whoever compares our present with our former Constitution, will find abundant reason to rejoice in the exchange, and readily admit that all the calamities incident to this war will be amply compensated by the many blessings flowing from this glorious revolution—a revolution which in the course of its rise and progress is distinguished by so many marks of the Divine favor and interposition that no doubt can remain of its being finally accomplished."

The Chief-Justice, after commenting upon several features of the new Constitution in terms of unqualified approbation, particularly that relative to the rights of conscience and private judgment in matters of religion, and freedom of religious worship, remarks:

"But let it be remembered, that whatever marks of wisdom, experience, and patriotism there may be in your Constitution, yet like the beautiful symmetry, the just proportion, and elegant forms of our first parents before their Maker breathed into them the breath of life, it is yet to be animated, and till then may indeed excite admiration, but will be of no use. From the people it must receive its spirit, and by them be quickened. Let virtue, honor, the love of liberty and of science be and remain the soul of this Constitution, and it will become the source of great and extensive happiness to this and future generations. Vice, ignorance, and want of vigilance will be the only enemies able to destroy it. Against these be forever jealous."

Mr. Jay retained the office of Chief-Justice of the Supreme Court two years. He did not, however, actively discharge its duties during the whole of this period On the 10th November, 1778, the Legislature elected him a delegate to represent the State in Congress. By the Constitution, a Judge of the Supreme Court was prohibited from holding any other office, except that of delegate in Congress, on a *special occasion.* The controversy respecting the "New Hampshire Grants" having arisen, this was voted a *special occasion*, and the Chief-Justice was delegated to Congress without vacating his seat on the bench. On the 10th of December, three days after he took his seat, he was chosen President of Congress. Conceiving his continued residence at Philadelphia inconsistent with the discharge of the duties of Chief-Justice of the Supreme Court of New York, Mr. Jay during the following year resigned his Judicial office. Governor Clinton at first refused to receive the resignation. Mr. Jay, however, persisted; and, after some delay, the resignation was accepted; thenceforth he devoted his entire services to the duties connected with his attendance in Congress.

Mr. Jay retained his place as President of Congress nearly a year, during which time he discharged its duties with a dignity, an urbanity, and an impartiality, which commanded universal respect. The subject of the currency, and the emission of bills of credit, at that time, attracted the serious attention of Congress. The depreciation of the currency and the prostration of public credit were appalling. Congress was literally bankrupt, and the means of continuing the contest seemed no where to be found. Besides the sum of nearly forty millions of dollars borrowed abroad, Congress had put in circulation bills to the enormous amount of $160,000,000, for the payment of which the public faith was pledged. This paper currency had become absolutely worthless, so much so that it was literally true, as was remarked at the time, that a cart-load of provision could be purchased only with a cart-load of money. In this emergency, Congress, feeling the necessity of at once replenishing the public treasury and restoring the public confidence, passed a resolution that no more bills should be issued than sufficient to make the entire sum $200,000,000. A resolution was also passed calling upon the states for supplies by state loans and taxes, and the President, Mr. Jay, was directed to prepare an address to the people of the respective states of the confederacy, in regard to these objects. That celebrated and justly admired paper, the "Circular letter from Congress to their Constituents," bears date on the 13th September, 1779, and is signed by Jay as President of the Congress. It is a clear and forcible statement of the condition of affairs, particularly with reference to the question of finance, and a most ardent and earnest appeal to the people and the states, to stand by, assist, and sustain the honor of the confederacy. Not the least noticeable feature in this admirable address is the bold and courageous spirit, the tone of calm, well-grounded confidence as to the ultimate success of the struggle, pervading it. Not for an instant does the author intimate a doubt as to the ability of the states to maintain the independence they had so boldly declared. "That the time has been," he remarks, "when honest men might, without being charged with timidity, have doubted the success of the present revolution we admit; but that period is past. The independence of America is now as fixed as fate, and the petulant efforts of Britain to break it down are as vain and fruitless as the raging of the waves which beat against her cliffs." The appeal to the people of the States to sustain the honor of the Confederacy, to provide for continuing the revolutionary army in the field, and at least to share with France the glory of achieving American independence, is eloquent, impassioned, and spirit-stirring; in short, is worthy the classic and vigorous pen of John Jay. The following are its closing sentences:

"The war, though drawing fast to a successful issue, still rages. Disdain to leave the whole business of your defence to your ally. Be mindful that the brightest prospects may be clouded, and that prudence bids us be prepared for every event. Provide, therefore, for continuing your armies in the field till victory and peace shall lead them home; and avoid the reproach of permitting the currency to depreciate in your hands, when, by yielding a part to taxes and loans, the whole might have been appreciated and preserved. Humanity, as well as justice, makes this demand on you. The complaints of ruined widows, and the cries of fatherless children, whose whole support has been placed in your hands, and melted away, have doubtless reached you; take care that you ascend no higher. Rouse, therefore; strive who shall do most for his country; rekindle that flame of patriotism, which at the mention of disgrace and slavery, blazed throughout America, and animated all her citizens: determine to finish the contest as you began it, honestly and gloriously. Let it never be said that America had no sooner become independent than she became insolvent, or that her infant glories and growing fame were obscured and tarnished by broken contracts and violated faith, in the very hour when all the nations of the earth were admiring and almost adoring the splendor of her rising."

Mr. Jay was now about to enter upon a different, and if possible, a more arduous and responsible sphere of action. Tried in the revolutionary cause, and in every branch of legislative and executive service, he had been found true, active, discreet, and courageous. But a more difficult, and a new and untrodden field now lay before him. He was called upon to enter upon it. It was no enviable post, no tempting task; it promised few honors and less emoluments. His private interests and his feelings prompted him to shun the employment. But his country demanded the sacrifice, and it seemed to him the path of public duty. Jay did not hesitate as to the course he should pursue. He accepted the Spanish mission. His instructions were received on the 16th October, 1779, and four days after he sailed, in company with the French Minister, M. Gerard, for Europe. The object of this mission was two-fold. It was first to draw Spain into the Confederacy against Britain, pursuant to a secret clause in the treaty between France and the United States, and secondly, to raise money either by a loan or guaranty from Spain. It is highly probable that the latter was the more immediate and pressing object. It was, however, all the same to Jay. He had enlisted in the service of his country from the purest, the most elevated motives, and was ready to serve her wherever he could be most useful.

Upon the threshold of his theatre of operations in Spain, the American envoy encountered difficulties that would have discouraged and baffled a man of less moral courage and resolution. He encountered too, annoyances, humiliations and petty vexations that would have exhausted the patience of a man of a less equable temper of mind. But Jay bravely faced every difficulty, withstood all things, endured, conquered all. On his landing at Cadiz, the Spanish government invited him to Madrid, but refused to recognize him, in a formal character. "Pains were taken," he says in a letter to a friend, "to prevent any conduct towards me that might savor of an admission or knowledge of American independence." It seemed to be the policy of Spain rather to amuse than to aid the United States. She desired to injure Great Britain, and would, therefore, at the right time and on the proper occasion, render such assistance to the revolted colonies as might accomplish that result, but such aid was to be rendered only for a *consideration.* Certain concessions were required to be made, among which was the right of the United States to navigate the Mississippi. This Jay peremptorily declined, acting on the advice given by Franklin, then in France:—"Poor as we are, yet as I know we shall be rich, I would rather agree with them to buy at a great price the whole of their right on the Mississippi than sell a drop of its waters. A neighbor might as well ask me to sell my street door." In this Franklin manifested his accustomed good sense. Alluding to Jay's discouragements and difficulties in Spain, he counsels him to continue "the even good temper you have hitherto manifested." "Spain," remarks the philosopher, in his usual sententious style, "*owes* us nothing; therefore, whatever friendship she shows us in lending money or furnishing clothes, &c., though not equal to our wants and wishes, is, however, *tant de gagne.*"

But, in the mean time, how were the hopes, the wishes, nay the absolute expectations, prompted by inevitable necessity, of Congress to be realized! Money must be had somewhere. The supplies from the states did not come in; the continental currency continued rapidly to depreciate; the military chest was empty. Without money, without resources, without credit, absolute bankruptcy was staring them in the face. In this emergency Congress took an extraordinary step which nothing but desperation could have prompted. Without the slightest surmise of what might be Jay's reception or prospects of success in Spain, nay, without even apprising him of the step taken, it was resolved to draw upon him bills to the amount of half a million, payable in six months. The Spanish government, after authorizing the acceptance of these bills to the amount of a few thousand dollars, informed Mr. Jay that no more would be paid unless America agreed to furnish ships of war as an equivalent, or cede to Spain the sole right of navigating the Mississippi, but offered to guaranty the payment of $150,000 in three years, if Mr. Jay could effect such a loan. The conditions imposed by Spain were rejected ; Jay attempted to effect the loan, but failed. In this emergency, he resolved upon a step of extraordinary boldness, it might be called rashness, a step, however, not hastily determined on, but one which his calm judgment dictated, and his reason approved. Without any present prospect of meeting these demands as they fell due, but with unshaken confidence in himself, his country, and its cause, he resolved *to accept all bills presented to him, at his own risk.* Prudence and caution were eminently characteristics of the mind of John Jay ; a wise and cool discretion marked his general conduct in life, but when the crisis occurred which demanded prompt, bold, and daring action, few men were more ready to step resolutely forward and assume the responsibility. In him, that caution which usually governed his actions, was not the result of timidity ; it tempered but did not impair the higher qualities of a resolute and courageous mind.

The result of this bold and daring act fully justified his best expectations. The first cheering intelligence he received, was the arrival of $25,000 from Dr. Franklin, at Paris. This, however, did not nearly equal the amount of his acceptances. Still he continued to accept every bill that was presented, and still he pressed his importunities upon the Spanish Government. At length in December, 1780, the sum of $150,000 was promised him ; but the money was not paid, and the American envoy was not yet relieved from his financial embarrassments.

In April of the following year we find him writing to Dr. Franklin at Paris, and inclosing him a statement of the desperately hopeless condition of affairs. Not more than $35,000 of the Spanish loan had been paid in. He had then outstanding acceptances to the amount of $231,000, the largest portion of which must be paid in two months. His situation, he says, was a cruel one. It was rendered more annoying from the fact that he had never received a dollar of salary from America, and at one of the proudest courts in Europe was obliged to contract debts and live on credit. Still, however, Jay bore manfully up, and continued zealously and faithfully his labors at the Spanish court. By dint of almost superhuman exertions, he was enabled for a long time to meet his liabilities, and sustain the credit of the country. At length, in the month of March, 1782, the inevitable crisis came. The Spanish Government, after the payment of the $150,000, agreed to guaranty to a banker the amount necessary to liquidate the remainder of the bills accepted by Mr. Jay ; but the transaction was not completed, through the want of faith, it is believed, of the Government itself ; and Jay was subjected to the mortification of seeing the bills protested, and his own and his country's credit annihilated.

The misfortune, however, was soon retrieved. During the next month Jay received from Franklin the following welcome letter :

" PASSY, *April* 22, 1782.

" DEAR SIR—I have undertaken to pay all the bills of your acceptance that have come to my knowledge, and I hope in God no more will be drawn upon us but when funds are first provided. In that case your constant residence at Madrid is no longer necessary. You may make a journey either for health or pleasure, without retarding the progress of a negotiation not yet begun. Here you are greatly wanted, for messengers begin to come and go, and there is much talk of a treaty proposed, but I can neither make nor agree to propositions of peace without the assistance of my colleagues. Mr. Adams, I am afraid, cannot just now leave Holland. Mr. Jefferson is not in Europe, and Mr. Laurens is a prisoner, though abroad upon parol. I wish, therefore, you would resolve upon the journey, and render yourself here as soon as possible. You would be of infinite service. Spain has taken four years to consider whether she would treat with us or not. *Give her forty, and let us in the mean time mind our own business.* I have much to communicate to you, but choose rather to do it *viva voce* than trust it to letters.

" I am ever, my dear friend, yours most affectionately,

" BENJAMIN FRANKLIN."

The foregoing letter explains itself. Mr. Jay's mission to Spain was about to end. It had been fruitless in respect to the proposed treaty, although Congress, to the astonishment and mortification of Jay, had some time before passed a resolution instructing him to yield the claim to the navigation of the Mississippi. And he had drawn up and presented a treaty to that effect. A longer residence at the Spanish court was therefore unnecessary. He repaired to France to act in conjunction with Franklin, Adams, Jefferson, and Laurens, the commissioners appointed by the United States in negotiating a peace.

This commission was extremely distasteful to Mr. Jay, not on account of the difficulty and responsibility attending it, but by reason of what he conceived to be the humiliating conditions attached to it. At the instigation of the French minister, Mr. Adams, who had been appointed American plenipotentiary, had been instructed in negotiating a peace, "to make the most candid and confidential communications upon all subjects to the ministers of our generous ally the King of France; to undertake nothing in the negotiations for peace or truce without their knowledge or concurrence," &c. Subsequently, at the requisition of the French minister, the additional commissioners were appointed, and the following added to their instructions: "*And ultimately to govern yourselves by their* (the ministers of the King of France) *advice and opinion.*" It was in reference to these instructions that Mr. Jay protested, in a dignified letter to the President of Congress, in which, while reluctantly accepting the commission, he entreated to be relieved of it as soon as practicable. The following are the concluding sentences of this letter:

"Thus circumstanced, and at such a distance from America, it would not be proper to decline this appointment. I will, therefore, do my best endeavors to fulfil the expectations of Congress on this subject; but as for my own part, I think it improbable that serious negociations for peace will soon take place, I must entreat Congress to take an early opportunity of relieving me from a station where, in character of their minister, I must necessarily receive and obey (under the name of *opinions*) the directions of those on whom I really think no American minister ought to be dependant, and to whom, in love for our country, and zeal for her service, I am sure that my colleagues and myself are at least equal."

Jay accordingly repaired to Paris, where he arrived on the 23d June, 1782. Here he met Dr. Franklin, and these two mainly conducted the negotiations on the part of the United States. Jefferson was detained in America; Adams did not arrive till the 26th of October, after the preliminary articles were agreed upon between the Americans and Mr. Oswald, the British commissioner; and Col. Laurens reached Paris the 29th November, the day before the preliminary articles were signed.

It is not my design here to sketch the progress of this negotiation, or to discuss its merits. It has become a part of the history of the country, and is familiar to every one versed in the diplomatic events of that period. We are doing but justice to Mr. Jay in claiming for him a large share in the successful results of the negotiation—results upon which Jefferson himself in the warmest language congratulated him;—"The terms obtained for us," he remarks in the confidence of a friendly letter, "are indeed great, and are so deemed by your countrymen, a few ill-designing debtors excepted." Hamilton, also, highly complimented him. "The peace," he says, "which exceeds in the goodness of its terms the expectations of the most sanguine, does the highest honor to those who made it." These terms, however, and this successful negotiation, were not achieved without the most painful anxiety and difficult labor. England was of course prepared to grant but few concessions to her revolted colonies, and France, "our generous ally," had her own designs to subserve, and was as dangerous to America in diplomacy as she had been formidable to England in war. At the outset, too, Mr. Jay had the misfortune to differ with his then sole colleague, Dr. Franklin. The British commissioner, Mr. Oswald, had been authorized to treat with any commissioner or commissioners appointed by the thirteen *colonies* or plantations in North America. Jay regarded the independence of the colonies as already a fact not to be controverted even by implication; and he refused to treat with the British commissioner except upon terms of equality. The French minister, Vergennes, urged a compliance; Franklin himself thought "it would do;" but nothing could shake the firmness and sense of propriety of Mr. Jay; he assured the British envoy that he would under no circumstances take part in any negotiation in which the United States were not treated as an independent nation; and at Mr. Oswald's request he drew the draft of such a commission as would be satisfactory. A courier was dispatched with this to London, and finally, on the 27th September, returned with a commission to Mr. Oswald, authorizing him to treat with the commissioners of THE UNITED STATES OF AMERICA.

The draft of the preliminary articles is in the handwriting of Mr. Jay. Mr. Adams subsequently arriving in Paris, concurred in sentiment with him on all points, and assisted in completing the negotiations;—and finally, on the 30th November, 1782, they were signed by the four American commissioners, and by Mr. Oswald on behalf of the British Government. The success of the negotiation was handsomely complimented by the Spanish ambassador, the Count Aranda, whom Jay characterizes as the ablest Spaniard he had met. Meeting Mr. Jay the next day after the preliminaries were signed, he tapped him familiarly on the shoulder and remarked, "*Eh bien, mon amie, vous avez tres bien fait.*"

While these general results, however, were highly flattering, and greatly added to the credit of the ministers who had negotiated the treaty, it is not to be denied that there was much dissatisfaction manifested, and that too in the highest quarters, in regard to the *manner* in which the business had been conducted. The conduct of the envoys in violating their instructions, as was alleged, by proceeding in a separate and secret manner with respect to our ally, France, and confidentially with respect to the British commissioner, was severely criticised in Congress, and particularly by Mr. Mercer, a member from Virginia, who in a very warm speech denounced their conduct in meanly stooping, as he remarked, "to lick the dust from the feet of a nation whose hands were still dyed with the blood of their fellow-citizens."* Other members, though without using the same severity of language, concurred in these sentiments. The separate article in the treaty with Great Britain was peculiarly obnoxious to the charge of its being made in violation of our faith with France, and it must be confessed that the complaints of the French

* Madison Papers, Vol. I. p. 390.

minister of the manner in which the American commissioners had proceeded in that respect, without the advice and concurrence of the Government of France, were not entirely without foundation.

Indeed, we find Mr. Hamilton himself, in this same debate in Congress, while advising "coolness and circumspection," yet "disapproving highly of the conduct of our ministers in not showing the preliminary articles to our ally before they signed them, and still more so of their agreeing to the separate article." Mr. Hamilton also observed "particularly with respect to Mr. Jay, that although he was a man of profound sagacity and pure integrity, *yet he was of a suspicious temper*, and that this trait might explain the *extraordinary jealousies* which he professed."*

Jay's defence of his course of action in departing from his instructions was, in substance, that they had been given for the benefit of America, not of France, and that America alone had a right to complain. "Moreover," he remarks in a letter to the Secretary of Foreign Affairs, "as the French Minister did not consult us about his articles, nor make us any communication about them, our giving him as little trouble about ours did not violate any principle of reciprocity." John Rutledge, in the debate in Congress on this subject, placed the defence of the Ministers on higher and bolder grounds; they had done right, he maintained, in violating their instructions, because "instructions *ought to be disregarded when the public good requires it*."†

The definitive treaty of peace, though the preliminary articles had been signed in the autumn of 1782, was not executed until the

* Madison Papers, Vol. I. pp. 395, 396. This language of Hamilton is the more remarkable, inasmuch, as, *by profession*, at least, he afterwards so warmly approved the conduct of Mr. Jay. I have already quoted his complimentary language in regard to the treaty. In a letter to Jay, a few months subsequent, he says: "I have been witness with pleasure to every event which has had a tendency to advance you in the esteem of your country; and I may assure you, with sincerity, that it is as high as you could possibly wish. All *have united in the warmest approbation of your conduct*. I cannot forbear telling you this, because my situation has given me access to the truth, and I gratify my friendship for you in communicating what cannot fail to gratify your sensibility."

The debates in Congress, it will be recollected, were *not public*.

† See subsequent sketch. Life of Rutledge.

third of September, 1783. Mr. Jay thereupon went to England, where he remained a few months, and then returned to Paris. The Court of Spain had invited him to visit that country once more and resume negotiations. This was before the conclusion of the treaty, and Mr. Jay had determined to accept. But it seems the state of affairs in Paris, and ill-health, induced him to abandon this design. After the signing of the treaty he determined to resign his commission, and return to his native country. His name having been mentioned as a fit person to be appointed Minister at the Court of London, he expressly declined such an appointment in a letter to the Secretary for foreign affairs, refusing to be a competitor with Mr. Adams for the place in question. His motives in resigning his commission are best expressed in his own words, as found in a letter written to Gouverneur Morris from Paris, on the 10th February, 1784.

"You suppose that ill-health induces me to resign. You are mistaken. It seldom happens that any measure is prompted by one single motive, though one among others may sometimes have a decisive weight and influence. Many motives induce me to resign; but of those many there is one which predominates, and that is:— When I embarked in the public service, I said very sincerely, that I quitted private life with regret, and should be happy to return to it when the object which called me from it, should be attained. You know what those objects were, and that on the peace they ceased to operate. To be consistent, therefore, I must retire. The motive is irresistible. Superadded to this, are the education of my son, the attention I owe to the unfortunate part of my family, and the happiness I expect from rejoining my friends. Pecuniary considerations ever held a secondary place in my estimation. I know how to live within the limits of any income, however narrow; and my pride is not of a nature to be hurt by returning to the business which I formerly followed. But professions of this sort are common, and facts only can give unequivocal evidence of their sincerity."

Such were the views of Mr. Jay in returning to private life. Expressed in the unreserved confidence of an intimate friendship, their sincerity cannot be questioned. They were not, as is so often the case, *professions* merely, intended to catch the public ear and excite the popular applause; but they were actual *sentiments*, real, living rules of action. He had quitted private life with regret, he was about to return to it with pleasure, for the objects in view had been attained. The same elevated motive which prompted Washington to gird on his sword in the revolution, and to lay it aside when that revolution had been accomplished, had also prompted the actions of Jay. Ten years before, he had left the profession in which he had been educated; during that time he had filled the highest offices in the gift of his countrymen—Chief-Justice, President of Congress, Plenipotentiary at foreign courts—and now with the calm hope of a lofty purpose, and the serenity of a true philosophy, he expressed his determination to decline further public honors, and resume the labors of an arduous profession as the means of obtaining a livelihood for himself and family. His pride, he declares, will not be hurt at this, and he had learned to live "within the limits of any income." Passages like these beautifully illustrate the simplicity and purity of Jay's character. They impress upon it the stamp of a high moral worth, nay, of a true GREATNESS, which may suggest a comparison with the best examples of Roman virtue.

On the 24th day of July, 1784, Mr. Jay arrived in New York. He was received with the most distinguished marks of respect and public confidence. The public authorities presented to him an address accompanied by the freedom of the city in a gold box. His old friends hastened to congratulate him upon his safe arrival, and on every side he received those marks of attention which are due to eminent worth and distinguished and successful public services.

It had been his intention, on his return from Europe, to resume the practice of the law. Since his entrance in public life, ten years before, he had been almost entirely withdrawn from the active duties of his profession, yet he had never ceased to give his attention, when not diverted by public employment, to matter connected with his former practice at the bar. Even after his return from Europe his time was frequently occupied in applications of this kind. In a letter to Chancellor Livingston, after arriving at New York, he mentions this as a reason why he is prevented from making him a visit. He says he has so many applications about papers and business respecting causes in which he was formerly concerned, that he is obliged to pass a fortnight or three weeks in New York. In the same letter he alludes to his intention of again returning to the practice of his profession.

This intention, however, was frustrated. Congress, on learning Mr. Jay's design of returning to America, tendered him the appointment of Secretary for Foreign Affairs, a place formerly filled by Chancellor Livingston, but which by the resignation of the Chancellor had been vacant during the past year. Mr. Jay hesitated to accept this appointment. The Legislature of his native State, in the mean time, appointed him again a delegate in Congress. The session was held at Trenton. On the 23d of December Congress adjourned to New York, which it was determined should be its future seat; and having, in the mean time, granted permission to Mr. Jay to select the clerks of his department, he accepted the office of Secretary for Foreign Affairs, and entered upon his duties early in the following year.

Mr. Jay remained in the discharge of the duties of this responsible position until after the meeting of the Convention which adopted the Federal Constitution. Of that body he was not a member, it being impossible for him at the same time to attend its deliberations, and to discharge the duties of his present place. It is not necessary here to detail his official services in the capacity of Foreign Secretary to the confederacy, or to dwell upon this portion of his public career. It may, however, be remarked, that he resumed the negociations for a treaty with Spain, through the Spanish ambassador, and prescribed to that functionary the forms and etiquette to be observed in his introduction to Congress. The negociations resulted in nothing. Mr. Jay, in a speech to Congress, recommended as the basis of a treaty, the abandonment, for a specific number of years, of the navigation of the Mississippi below the Southern boundary. The recommendation gave great, and perhaps, deserved umbrage to the Southern members of Congress; but the northern members supported the Secretary, and voted down a resolution to terminate his powers of negociation.

During this period, Jay was again solicited to become a candidate for the office of Governor of New York, there having been some discontent expressed at the course and proceedings of Governor

Clinton. He however again refused, mainly upon the ground of the obligations he was under and the services he owed Congress, and his unwillingness to exchange his present for a more honorable and lucrative position, without the consent and sanction of that body. In a letter addressed to his old friend, General Schuyler, he strongly enforces this view, adding that if *real* disgust and discontent had spread through the country, and a change had became not only proper but *necessary*, he would have felt bound to make his personal feelings yield to public considerations.

The necessity of a change in the articles of confederation, and the establishment of a general government, was very early felt. Almost all the public men of America concurred in this opinion. It is scarcely necessary to add that Mr. Jay was among the very first to express his sentiments upon the propriety and necessity of such a change. It is well known, too, that his opinions, from the start, were strongly federal. With Hamilton and Adams he inclined decidedly to centralization, and favored the establishment of an energetic national government. The federal system, as actually adopted, and especially as it was subsequently construed by Jefferson and Madison, seemed never to have harmonized entirely with his views, or to have met his ideas of a perfect government, though we find him warmly defending the new Constitution as a plan of government infinitely preferable, in all respects, to the old Confederation. It is not my purpose, however, to point out what might be regarded as the errors of Mr. Jay's theory, or to criticise his speculative opinions on government. Those opinions were shared by some of the wisest, ablest, and may we not add best, of the public men of that day. That they were erroneous is evident from the workings of the admirable system which was subsequently adopted as a sort of compromise between the extreme views of the ultra Federalists on the one hand, and on the other the doctrine of absolute state sovereignty, and the more radical and democratic element of popular government. It is, nevertheless, but doing justice to the most high-toned Federalist of that period to say, that however erroneous may have been his views, and widely as we at this day may differ from these doctrines of consolidation, and a strong central government, yet that these very doctrines, as society then stood, were a progressive step in the science of government, and even a struggle against a worse and more arbitrary system. At the present day, we are too apt to lose sight of the fact, that the opinions, customs, and habits of the monarchy had not yet lost their hold upon the people. Washington himself, in a letter to Jay, before the meeting of the Convention, uses the following language: "I am told that even respectable characters speak of a monarchical form of government without horror. From thinking proceeds speaking; thence to action is often but a single step. But how irrevocable and tremendous! What a triumph for the advocates of despotism, to find that we are incapable of governing ourselves, and that systems founded on the basis of equal liberty are merely ideal and fallacious! Would to God that wise measures may be taken in time to avert the consequences we have but too much reason to apprehend." These apprehensions of Washington were shared by Jay, and, it is believed, by most of the prominent Federalists. They honestly and zealously endeavored to avert the threatened evil. The result was, that even the plan of Hamilton, of an executive and Senate for life, was repudiated, and the present Federal Constitution adopted.

Jay was neither a monarchist nor in favor of an aristocratic government. There is no evidence that his sympathies and inclinations were not from the start in favor of pure republican, though not strictly democratic institutions. It is clear, however, that he never gave in his adhesion to the Jeffersonian construction of the Constitution, or thoroughly comprehended what we have been accustomed to regard as the true theory of democratic progress. Thus he says in a letter to General Washington: "The mass of men are neither wise nor good, and the virtue, like the other resources of a country, can only be drawn to a point and exerted by *strong circumstances, ably managed*, or a *strong government, ably administered*." So too in regard to the great principle of free suffrage, he hesitated to trust the masses; it was a favorite maxim with him, says his son, in writing his memoirs, that those who *own the country* (i. e. the land-holders,) should govern it.

The views of Mr. Jay upon the great question of the formation of a national Constitution, were freely expressed in letters to his friends, and show very clearly the force of his convictions in favor of a consolidated and energetic central government. So early as the spring of 1785, he writes to a friend as follows :

" It is my first wish to see the United States assume and merit the character of ONE GREAT NATION, whose territory is divided into different states merely for more convenient government, and the more easy and prompt administration of justice ; just as our several states are divided into counties and townships for the like purposes."

The same sentiments are repeated a year after in a letter to John Adams at London, in which he expresses as one of the first wishes of his heart, the desire "to see the people of America become one nation in every respect ; for, (he continues,) as to the separate legislatures, I would have them considered, with relation to the confederacy, in the same light in which counties stand to the State of which they are parts, viz., merely as districts to facilitate the purposes of domestic order and good government."

And in a long letter to General Washington, just before the Convention, he intimates the same thing : "What powers should be granted to the Government so constituted," he remarks, " is a question which deserves much thought. *I think the more the better ;* the states retaining only so much as may be necessary for domestic purposes, and all their principal officers, civil and military, being commissioned and removable by the national Government." In the same letter Mr. Jay, though expressing himself against a monarchy, goes so far as to suggest a Congress divided into an upper and lower house, *the former appointed for life*, and the latter annually ; and a Governor-General, limited in prerogative and duration. At the same time, however, he never for a moment loses sight of the true basis of popular rights, and the cardinal doctrine of republican government ; for his letter closes with the declaration, that no alteration in the government should be made "unless deducible from the only source of just authority—THE PEOPLE."

In like manner the general principle of the Federal union, as subsequently adopted, was already a familiar idea to the mind of Jay, for in a letter to Jefferson, at Paris, alluding to the weakness of the confederacy, and the necessity for a better and a stronger union, he thus sketches the main features of what he conceives to be the true plan which ought to be adopted : "To vest legislative, judicial, and executive powers in one and the same body of men, and that too in a body daily changing its members, can never be wise. In my opinion those three great departments of sovereignty should be forever separated, and so distributed as to serve as checks on each other."

These extracts will suffice to show Mr. Jay's opinions upon the subject of the proposed Federal Constitution. It has been before remarked that he was not a member of the Convention which framed it, being prevented from accepting a nomination by the pressing nature of the duties of the office he then held and the necessity of his attending the sittings of Congress. But no sooner was the Constitution agreed upon and submitted to the States for ratification, than Jay stepped forward, its zealous and earnest advocate. Public opinion was divided in regard to it. An active opposition was at once manifested : or if not a direct opposition, an earnest and determined effort to secure a larger concession to popular rights and state sovereignty. Perhaps in no State in the union was the opposition more strenuous and determined than in New York. The city, indeed, not then as now the metropolis of the country, but then as now, the loyal and devoted friend of the American union, was decidedly favorable to the proposed plan. But a strong feeling existed in the country in favor of a larger concession of popular rights and a less extensive delegation of power to the General Government. The people were jealous of their liberties, and hesitated to ratify an instrument which called for a surrender of some of the most important powers of State sovereignty. Some were unconditionally and unalterably opposed to the adoption of the proposed instrument ; others would adopt it conditionally, and others still, merely desired its amendment in a variety of particulars. The ranks of the anti-Federalists comprised all these different shades of opinions, and certainly the power of numbers seemed to be clearly with them. But the weight of the intellect of the State was on the side of the Federalists, and prominent among them stood those distinguished advocates and champions of the proposed Constitution, Livingston, Hamilton, and John Jay.

The first decided impression made by the Federalists upon the people was through the public press. Jay united with Hamilton and Madison in writing and publishing that celebrated series of papers, which has since been known by the name of the FEDERALIST, the first number of which appeared in the month following the adjournment of the Federal Convention. Three such minds have been rarely combined in the elucidation of any political system, or the discussion of any question, whether practical or theoretical, of politics or government. It is not surprising then that this publication should have impressed itself deeply upon the public mind, and exercised a wide-spread and powerful influence; nor that the Federalist should have been ever since regarded by the American statesman and jurist* as the most valuable commentary ever written upon the American Constitution. In this production Jay does not lay claim to an equal share with his illustrious coadjutors. He contributed, it is believed, but five papers, four of which immediately followed the opening number of the series. The remainder is the work of Hamilton and Madison.†

The Federalist was followed by a pamphlet, written by Mr. Jay, but published anonymously, addressed to the people of New York. This pamphlet discussed with great candor as well as ability, the three following questions, with reference to the proposed Constitution.

1. Is it probable a better plan can be obtained?
2. If attainable, is it likely to be in season?
3. What would be our condition, if, rejecting this, all efforts to obtain a better should prove fruitless?

* Chancellor Kent speaks of the Federalist in the following terms: "No Constitution of government ever received a more masterly and successful vindication. I know not indeed of any work on the principles of free government that is to be compared in instruction and intrinsic value to this small and unpretending volume of the *Federalist;* not even if we resort to Aristotle, Cicero, Machiavel, Montesquieu, Milton, Locke, or Burke. It is equally admirable in the depth of its wisdom, the comprehensiveness of its views, the sagacity of its reflections, and the fearlessness, patrotism, candor, simplicity and elegance with which its truths are uttered and recommended."—1 *Kent. Com.*, p. 241, *note.*

† Mr. Jay would doubtless have been a larger contributor to the Federalist, but for the occurrence of a serious accident, which interrupted his labors. While endeavoring with other citizens of New York, under the lead of Col. Hamilton, to quell a riot, he was struck with a stone on the temple, and taken up for dead. He recovered only in time to write the sixty-fourth number of the series.

In the argument of these questions, Jay starts with the admission that the proposed Constitution is imperfect. It is not such as he and the friends of a strong federal government desired. Their views had been clearly expressed and eloquently advocated by Col. Hamilton upon the floor of the Convention, but these views had not been adopted by that body. Unlike the opponents of the proposed Constitution, however, Mr. Jay avows himself prepared to submit, and to yield his cordial and unqualified support to the projected plan of union. The first two questions as above stated are accordingly answered in the negative. The third is discussed with an earnestness, a candor, and a power of argument, which leave no room to doubt the author's thorough conviction of the truth of the propositions he advocates, and his entire confidence in the ultimate success of the Constitution. Washington took occasion to compliment him upon the "good sense, forcible observation, temper, and moderation with which the pamphlet is written;" and Franklin deemed it advisable that Jay should give it additional weight by attaching to it his name; but the habitual modesty of the author impelled him to decline this suggestion, and prompted the characteristic reply: "If the reasoning in the pamphlet you allude to is just, it will have its effect on candid and discerning minds;—if weak and inconclusive, my name cannot render it otherwise."

The assent of New York to the new Constitution was felt by the Federalists to be an indispensable requisite to its success. The great battle of the Constitution, as has been well observed, was fought in New York. A Convention of delegates of the people was called by the Legislature. The strongest men in the State were proposed as candidates on either side. The election was held in April, 1788. In the city of New York the Federalists carried it their own way. Jay was put in nomination for that city and elected.* He had for his colleagues the Chief-Justice, Richard Morris, Chancellor Livingston, Alexander Hamilton, James Duane, Richard Harrison, Judge John Sloss Hobart, Isaac Roosevelt and Nicholas Low—an array of worth, character, and talent, that has never been surpassed, if equalled, by any delegation ever elected to represent that city.

In the country, however, the elections were strongly against the

* Out of a poll list of nearly 3000, he received all but about 100 votes.

Federalists. Most of the members returned were opposed to the ratification of the Constitution, except upon condition, or with some important amendments. Nor where the anti-Federalists, as they were called, deficient either in influence, activity, or ability. Prominent among the list stood the formidable name of that able and experienced leader, Governor Clinton, who was elected President of the Convention. Mr. John Lansing of Albany, afterwards for many years Chancellor, a gentleman of sound judgment and cultivated intellect, as well as a most adroit and active parliamentarian,* Mr. Melancthon Smith of Dutchess, one of the most fluent and ready debaters, perhaps under all circumstances the best, next to Hamilton, in the house, Mr. Treadwell, Mr. Williams, and Mr. G. Livingston, may be mentioned as among the most prominent of the opposition.

On the first day of the session Chancellor Livingston opened the deliberations in an elaborate speech, at the close of which he moved the consideration of the Constitution by sections, which was adopted. The motion was a wise and discreet one, had there been, as was alleged, a desire on the part of the majority to defeat the ratification entirely. It seems, however, from the cause of the debates, that this was not seriously intended, and that the design was merely to secure the adoption of some very important amendments, together with a declaration, or bill of rights, to be attached to the Constitution, a matter which had been singularly enough omitted.† Of the more important amendments desired were those in regard to taxa-

* Mr. Lansing had been a member of the Convention which framed the Constitution. He retired with his colleague, Mr. Yates, before the Constitution was agreed upon, leaving Hamilton the sole representative from New York.

† This had been Jefferson's main objection to the Constitution. In a letter to Washington, Mr. Jefferson, alluding to the charge (which he attributed to Hamilton) that he (Jefferson) had written letters from Europe to his friends to oppose the Constitution, says: "The charge is most false. I approve as much of the Constitution as most persons, and more of it was disapproved by my accuser than by me, and of its parts most vitally republican. My objection to the Constitution was the want of a bill of rights—Col. Hamilton's that it wanted a king and House of Lords. The sense of America has approved my objection, and added the bill of rights, and not the king and lords."

Mr. Jefferson was in favor also of making the presidential term six years, and not renewable.

tion, one for increasing the number of the representatives, and one moved by Mr. G. Livingston, and sustained with great ability and force of argument by Messrs. Lansing and Smith, to authorize the *recall* of a Senator by the State Legislature, and prohibiting his re-election for the six years immediately succeeding the expiration of his term. All these amendments, as well as the important one embraced in the bill of rights subsequently moved by Mr. Lansing, and which was substantially adopted and ratified by the requisite majority of the States, and thus became a part of the Constitution, were prompted not by hostility to a plan of union among the States, or even to an energetic federal government, but by a well-grounded jealousy of the encroachments of power, and a vigilant care for the rights and liberties of the people. Much injustice has been done the *anti-Federalists* of the Convention in this respect, and their views are not at this day correctly understood. No one will question the sincerity of Governor Clinton, who is regarded as standing at their head; and Governor Clinton himself stated in the Convention, "I solemnly declare that I am a friend to a strong and efficient government. But, sir, we may err in this extreme; we may erect a system that will destroy the liberties of the people. * * * Because a strong government was wanted during the late war, does it follow that we should now be obliged to accept a dangerous one? I even lamented the feebleness of the Confederation," &c. &c.

Similar views were expressed by all the prominent members, inasmuch as Mr. Jay himself remarked in his place: "Sir, it seems to be on all sides agreed, that a strong, energetic, federal government is necessary for the United States." Mr. Melancthon Smith, the confidential friend of Clinton, and one of the most ardent and uncompromising advocates of popular rights and State sovereignty on the floor, and Mr. G. Livingston, who moved the amendment authorizing the State to recall their senators at pleasure, are both found voting in favor of an absolute, and against a conditional ratification; and if the name of Mr. Lansing is found in the negative, it is no more than happened in Virginia, where the names of Patrick Henry and James Monroe appear in opposition to that of James Madison, on the final question of ratification.

That the majority of the Convention were in favor of some sort of ratification, is apparent from the description given of the members by Jay himself, in a letter to Washington :

"The leaders in opposition seem to have more extensive views than their adherents, and until the latter perceive that circumstance, they will probably continue combined. *The greater number are, I believe, averse to a vote of rejection.* Some would be content with *recommendatory* amendments ; others wish for *explanatory* ones, to settle constructions which they think doubtful ; others would not be satisfied with less than *absolute* and *previous* amendments, and I am mistaken if there be not a few who prefer a separation from the union to any national government whatever. They suggest hints of the importance of the State, of its capacity to command terms, of the policy of its taking its own time, and fixing its own price, &c. They intimate that an adjournment may be expedient, and that it might be best to see the operation of the new government before they receive it."

Mr. Jay, of course, was one of those who desired the *absolute* and *unconditional* ratification of the Constitution. His influence in bringing this about was no doubt great, though from the sketch of the debates it does not appear that he took any very active or prominent part in the discussions of the Convention. He was not a frequent speaker ; indeed he was never a very ready and skillful debater. He was better adapted to the committee room, or perhaps the chair, than the floor of a deliberative body. His strength, like Mr. Jefferson's in that respect, lay rather in his pen than in oral speech. As a pamphleteer and political essayist, he had few equals ; as a parliamentary orator he had many superiors, and some, too, upon the floor of the Convention itself. The efforts of Mr. Jay cannot compare with the clear, calm, logical, comprehensive speeches of Livingston, much less with the bold, rapid, impetuous harangues of Hamilton, alike brilliant as declamations, and convincing as arguments. These two were therefore regarded as in some sense the parliamentary leaders of the Federalists ; but Mr. Jay in point of real influence was inferior to neither, and doubtless contributed as much as any man in the Convention, by his well-directed efforts, and the weight of his character and acknowledged ability, to bring these deliberations to a successful issue. Occasionally too he mingled in the debates, and expressed his opinions upon the more important questions raised with freedom and frankness. He spoke upon the question of representation in reply to Mr. M. Smith, and while avowing himself in favor of a large representation, yet was satisfied with the matter as the Convention had left it, and urged a general acquiescence. He spoke also upon the important question of revenue, and the power of Congress to levy taxes, advocating the propriety of investing the General Government with the command of the national resources, in opposition to the amendment proposed of limiting this power by reserving to the States the right in certain cases of regulating the supplies. The speeches of Mr. Jay are characterized by great simplicity and candor, as well as force of expression and cogency of argument.

On the 11th of July, Mr. Jay moved the unconditional ratification of the Constitution, and that such amendments as might be deemed expedient, ought to be *recommended*. He was ably supported by Chancellor Livingston and Chief-Justice Morris, and opposed by Mr. Smith. On the 15th July, the latter gentleman moved, as an amendment, that the Constitution ought to be ratified, *on condition* that certain amendments specified, should be made. This was the test question, and the serious struggle in the Convention now occurred.* A proposition to adjourn, was made and voted down.

* Ten of the states had already adopted the Constitution before it was ratified by New York. The order in which it was ratified by the respective states and the votes thereon, are as follows:

Delaware,	December 3,	1787	unanimously.
Pennsylvania,	December 13,	1787	46 to 23.
New Jersey,	December 19,	1787	unanimously.
Georgia,	January 7,	1788	unanimously.
Connecticut,	January 9,	1788	140 to 128.
Massachusetts,	February 6,	1788	187 to 168.
Maryland,	April 28,	1788	63 to 12.
South Carolina,	May 23,	1788	149 to 73.
New Hampshire,	June 21,	1788	57 to 46.
Virginia,	June 25,	1788	89 to 79.
New York,	July 25,	1788	30 to 27.

North Carolina and Rhode Island came into the Union after the new government went into operation. The former ratified the Constitution on the 21st November, 1789; the latter not till the 29th May, 1790.

A resolution, by Mr. Lansing, reserving the right to New York to withdraw from the union, in like manner passed in the negative. The absolute ratification would probably have been also rejected if the timely amendment moved by Mr. Jones had not been adopted, changing the words *on condition*, into the words *in full confidence*. Among the affirmative votes were, Mr. Smith, Mr. G. Livingston, Mr. Williams, &c. In this shape the resolutions passed on the 25th July, by a vote of 30 to 27, and New York assumed a place among her sister states in the federal union.

The new government was to go into operation on the 4th March, 1789. Congress was summoned to meet on that day at the city of New York, when the votes for President and Vice-President were to be counted. On the appointed day, however, it was found that a quorum was not in attendance, and the two houses adjourned. The House of Representatives was the first to organize ; the Senate continued to adjourn from day to day for want of a quorum, until the 6th of April. On that day a quorum of both houses being present, the electoral vote for President and Vice-President was counted, when it appeared that George Washington, having received the whole number of votes cast, sixty-nine,* was elected President, and John Adams having received a majority of all the votes, was elected Vice-President. Mr. Jay received the votes of Delaware and New Jersey, for the Vice-Presidency.

The election of General Washington having been announced, and he having signified his acceptance of the trust, it was thought proper to make the necessary arrangements for the accommodation of the President at New York. These arrangements were not immediately completed, and in the mean time Jay wrote to Washington, tendering the hospitalities of his house, and with a sincerity and delicacy that could not fail to be appreciated. "As the measures that were in contemplation on this subject," he says, "would have given an earlier invitation the appearance of a mere compliment, it was

* These comprised the electoral votes of ten of the States only. Rhode Island and North Carolina had not yet adopted the Constitution, and New York did not vote. At the opening of the Congress no member from New York appeared in either house. Rufus King took his seat in the Senate on the 25th of July, and Gen. Schuyler two days after.

omitted. Considering all circumstances, I really think you would experience at least as few inconveniences with me as in any other situation here. Your reluctance to give trouble will doubtless suggest objections. Apprised of this, we shall be particularly careful to preserve such a degree of simplicity in our domestic arrangements as will render you easy on that. In a word you shall be received and entertained exactly in the way which, if in your place, I should prefer, viz., with plain and friendly hospitality." The completion of the public arrangements for the reception of Gen. Washington prevented his acceptance of this invitation. He arrived in New York soon after, and delivered his inaugural address on the 30th April. At his request Mr. Jay continued to act as Foreign Secretary until the arrival of Mr. Jefferson from Europe.

The Constitution provided that the judicial power of the United States should be vested in a Supreme Court and in such inferior courts as Congress might from time to time establish. At the first session of Congress the organization of the federal judiciary engaged the early and constant attention of that body. The judiciary bill, organizing the new courts, approved the 24th September 1789, will be more particularly noticed in the succeeding sketch of Chief-Justice Ellsworth, then a senator in Congress, from the State of Connecticut. By its provisions a Chief-Justice and five Associate-Justices, were to constitute the Supreme Court of the United States.

On the very day of the approval of the Judiciary bill, the President sent in to the Senate the name of John Jay for the office of Chief-Justice, and the names of the following gentlemen for the offices of Associate-Justices of the Supreme Court ;—John Rutledge, of South Carolina ; William Cushing, of Massachusetts ; Benjamin H. Harrison, of Maryland ; James Wilson, of Pennsylvania ; and John Blair, of Virginia ; who were immediately confirmed. Edmund Randolph was at the same time appointed Attorney-General. Mr. Harrison resigned, and James Iredell, of North Carolina, was subsequently appointed in his place.

General Washington had been earnestly desirous of securing the services and well-known ability of Mr. Jay in support of the new government ; and the position in which he was now placed was the one which Jay himself had preferred, as most in accordance with his tastes, his previous studies, and habits of life.*

The first term of the Supreme Court was held in New York, in February, 1790. The Chief-Justice, and Justices Cushing, Wilson, and Blair, appeared,† constituting a quorum. Very little seems to have been done except the adoption of three or four rules of court, one relative to the seal of the Supreme and Circuit Courts; another in regard to the admission of attorneys and counsellors, and another directing that all process of the court should be in the name of "the President of the United States." At the next term, in August of the same year, the commission of Judge Iredell was read, who was sworn in, and took his seat, soon after which the Court adjourned. No case of special importance seems to have been argued before the Court until the August term, 1792, when the first motion was made in the case of the State of Georgia *vs.* Braislford and others; and the important case of Chisholm *vs.* Georgia, which will be presently noticed, was also brought on for argument.

The Chief-Justice, in the mean time, regularly rode the circuit twice a year, in company with one of his associates. The Eastern circuit, to which he was assignd, comprised the New England States and New York. The Judiciary bill provided that two Circuit Courts a year should be held in each district, by two Justices of the Supreme Court and the District Judge.

The Chief-Justice held his first circuit in New York, on the 4th April, 1790, assisted by one of his associates and the District Judge, James Duane, Esq., an eminent and able lawyer of that time.‡ His charge to the grand jury was carefully prepared, temperate, and

* Jay's appointment as Chief-Justice, in preference to Chancellor Livingston, it has been intimated, was the real cause of the Chancellor's abandonment of the Federal party, and his subsequent opposition to Jay's election. The authority for this assertion, however, seems somewhat questionable. See *Hammond's Political History of New York*, p. 107.

† Judge Rutledge did not take his seat. He resigned the next year, and the commission of Thomas Johnson, bearing date 7th November, 1791, was read at the August term 1792, when that gentleman took his seat. See following sketch of Rutledge.

‡ See Sketch of Duane, by Hon. Samuel Jones, in 4th Vol. *Documentary History of New York.*

discreet, and withal thoroughly conservative. "It cannot be too strongly impressed on the minds of all," he remarked, "how greatly our individual prosperity depends on our national prosperity, and how greatly our national prosperity depends on a *well-organized, vigorous government*, ruling by wise and equal laws faithfully executed. Nor is such a government unfriendly to liberty—to that liberty which is really estimable. On the contrary, nothing but a strong government of laws, irresistibly bearing down arbitrary power and licentiousness, can defend it against these two formidable enemies."

Immediately after the close of this Court the Chief-Justice commenced his first circuit through New England, and was everywhere received with the most flattering marks of respect. In those primitive days it was deemed no improper civility, or extraordinary occurrence, to lavish upon the head of the federal judiciary the somewhat tumultuous demonstrations of popular applause. Thus the citizens of New Haven and the citizens of Portsmouth honored him with "a public entry" into these towns; and even the staid people of Boston were moved from their propriety in a similar manner. A year or two later we find him fêted and toasted at public dinners—crossing the Hudson at Albany under the roar of artillery—"attended for twelve miles on his journey by a body of cavalry"—entering the village of Hudson on "Independence Day," amid the ringing of bells and roar of cannon; and, finally, received by a deputation of citizens eight miles from New York, who carried him in triumph into the bosom of his native city. But these latter demonstrations, it must be confessed, were political, and not in compliment to his judicial character.

In April, 1791, the Chief-Justice, with Justice Cushing and the District Judge, Duane, held the circuit at New York, and made a very important decision, involving the jurisdiction and powers of the Justices of the Supreme Court. Congress had passed an act to regulate, among other things, the claims to invalid pensions. Under this act certain duties were assigned to the Circuit Courts; but the decisions of the courts thereon were made subject, first to the consideration and suspension of the Secretary of War, and then to the revision of Congress. It speaks well for the independence and firmness of the Supreme Court, even at that early day, to observe the Judges standing up boldly to resist a constitutional encroachment. The Chief-Justice and his associates refused to perform judicially the duties imposed by the act. They declared that, by the Constitution, neither the Secretary of War, nor any other executive officer, nor the Legislature itself, was authorized to sit as a court of errors on the judicial acts or opinions of the Court. They regarded the act therefore as appointing the judges commissioners merely, which appointment they might accept or decline at their option. In this case, as they desired to manifest in every proper manner their respect for the national Legislature, they would execute the act, not as a court, but in the capacity of commissioners. Similar views were taken of the act in the Circuit Court of Pennsylvania by Justices Wilson and Blair, and Peters, District Judge, who united in representing their opinions in a joint letter addressed to the President.

At the August term of the Supreme Court, 1792, a motion was made by the Attorney-General for a *mandamus*, directed to the Circuit Court of Pennsylvania, commanding it to proceed on the petition of William Heyburn, as an invalid pensioner. The Attorney-General made an elaborate argument upon the merits of the case and the refusal of the Judges to carry the law into effect. The Court held the case under advisement until the next term; but no decision was ever pronounced, as Congress, in the mean time, provided for the relief of pensioners by another law.

At this same term was brought on for argument the first motion in the important case of the State of Georgia *vs.* Braislford et al. The case presented several novel questions connected with the Constitution jurisprudence of the country, and is remarkable as being the only case in which a special trial by jury has ever been had before the Supreme Court. The State of Georgia had passed an act of confiscation, whereby it was claimed that the debt in controversy—a bond made by Kelsey and Spalding to Braislford and others, whom it was alleged were aliens—had been sequestrated to the State. Notwithstanding their alienage and the act of confiscation, Braislford and his co-partners had brought an action on the bond against Kelsey and Spalding in the Circuit Court of

Georgia. The State of Georgia applied to be admitted to assert her claim, but was refused, and judgment passed for the plaintiffs. The State now filed a bill in equity and moved that an injunction might issue to stay further proceedings in the Circuit Court, and also to the Marshal of the Georgia district to stay money levied on any execution that might have come to his hands. This motion was made and argued by Alexander J. Dallas, of Pennsylvania,* one of the most eminent, as he was decidedly one of the most accomplished and able lawyers of that day, and was opposed by the Attorney-General, Mr. Randolph. The Court, after argument, delivered their opinions *seriatim.*

Justice Johnson was of the opinion that if the State had a right to the debt in question, it might be enforced at common law, and that an injunction should not issue. Justice Cushing was of a similar opinion. On the other hand, Justices Blair, Iredell, and Wilson, thought that a temporary injunction should issue till the Court should be enabled by a full inquiry to decide upon the whole merits of the case ; though the latter was inclined to think that the more proper course would have been for Georgia to have sued out a writ of error, rather than have asked for an injunction. In these views the Chief-Justice concurred, and accordingly an injunction issued.

* Alexander J. Dallas was a native of the Island of Jamaica, and born on the 1st day of June, 1759. He was educated in Europe, and emigrated to Philadelphia in 1783. Two years after his arrival he was admitted to the bar. In a few years he acquired a distinguished reputation as a lawyer ; and on the organization of the Federal judiciary we find him engaged in nearly all the important causes in the Supreme Court, and the criminal trials of these days. Mr. Dallas was several years Secretary of the Commonwealth of Pennsylvania. He published the four volumes of the Reports which bear his name, containing the earlier decisions of the Pennsylvania and the Federal Courts. He also published an edition of the laws of Pennsylvania, which he illustrated with notes and references.

In 1801 Mr. Dallas was appointed by Mr. Jefferson District Attorney for the Eastern District of Pennsylvania, and in 1808 he was invited to a place in the Cabinet as Secretary of the Treasury. He continued in the Cabinet until 1816, a part of which time he performed the duties of Secretary of War. Returning again to the bar, on his resignation of this office, he resumed an extensive and brilliant practice, which was, however, interrupted the next year by an untimely death. He died on the 16th January, 1817, in the 58th year of his age.

At the following term, February, 1793, the case was again brought before the Court on a motion by the Attorney-General to dissolve the injunction and dismiss the bill. Justices Iredell and Blair were still of opinion that the injunction ought to be sustained, but the rest of the Court coincided in the opinion delivered by the Chief-Justice that if Georgia had a right to the debt, it was a right to be pursued at common law, and it was ordered that the injunction should stand until the next term, when it would be dissolved, unless Georgia instituted her action at common law. An amicable action was accordingly entered, in which an issue was made up whether the debt and the right of action belonged to the State of Georgia, or to the original creditors. This issue was brought to trial before a jury at the February term, 1794. The question was argued with great ability, and learning, by Dallas and Ingersoll for the State, and by William Bradford, who had been appointed Attorney-General in place of Randolph, for the defendants. The cause went to the jury under the charge of the Chief-Justice, who declared it as the unanimous opinion of the Judges, that the act of Georgia did not vest the debt in the State at the time of passing it ; that it was subjected not to *confiscation*, but only to *sequestration*, and the owner's right to recover it revived at the peace. The jury, under this charge, of course, returned a verdict against the State, and the injunction was accordingly dissolved.*

At the February term of the Court, 1793, held at Philadelphia, the celebrated case of Chisholm Executors *vs.* Georgia, was brought on for argument.† This great case excited an unusual degree of attention, both on account of the novelty of the questions raised, and the important political consequences that were supposed to be involved in the decision. The doctrine of State sovereignty, and State rights, was for the first time brought before the Court, for discussion. The question was, whether a state was amenable to the jurisdiction of the Supreme Court, at the suit of a citizen of another state, a question which might, in the language of Judge Wilson, ultimately resolve itself into another no less radical than this, "Do the United States constitute a nation?" Chisholm, a citizen of South Carolina,

* See this case reported, 2 Dallas, 403, 415. 3 Dallas, 1.

† 2 Dallas, 419.

had brought an action against the State of Georgia by service of process upon the Governor and Attorney-General of that State. Georgia refused to appear, and now the Attorney-General of the United States moved that unless Georgia caused her appearance to be entered by the next term, judgment should be rendered against her by default, and a writ of inquiry issue. No case of a similar kind had yet been regularly brought before the Court for adjudication. In a case against Maryland, the Attorney-General of the State had voluntarily appeared. In a case against the State of New York a motion had been made to compel an appearance on the part of the State, but while the Court held the motion under advisement the suit had been discontinued.* The question was now brought up on the motion of Mr. Randolph, the Attorney-General, who delivered a lucid and most masterly argument, the analysis of which, gives us the highest opinion of the forensic talents, and profound legal attainments of that gentleman. The State of Georgia refused to recognize the jurisdiction even so far as to appear upon the argument, but presented by Mr. Dallas and Mr. Ingersoll, an eminent lawyer of the Philadelphia bar,† a written remonstrance and protestation on behalf of the State. Under these circumstances this important question was considered by the Judges, who, after advisement and careful deliberation, pronounced their opinions *seriatim.*

* Oswald *vs.* State of New York, 2 Dall. 401. But see same case, 2 Dall. 415, where default against the State was ordered to be taken at the next term, unless appearance was entered.

† Jared Ingersoll was at that time Attorney-General of Pennsylvania, a post which he held from 1791 to 1800, and again from 1811 to 1816. He was born in New Haven in 1750, was educated to the bar, and in 1773 was sent to London to complete his education at the Temple. Mr. Ingersoll left England after the Declaration of Independence, and went to France, where he remained for some time, after which he returned to Philadelphia to the practice of the law. His success was immediate, and he was soon at the head of his profession, "in the midst," says a judicious writer, "of the well-known formidable competition of a day when the bar of Philadelphia by concession led the Union, and gave birth to a proverb which has been handed down to present times." Mr. Ingersoll declined the place offered him of Judge, on the organization of the Circuit Court, for New Jersey, Pennsylvania and Delaware, in 1801. He presided, however, for a short time preceding his death, in the District Court at Philadelphia. In 1812 Mr. Ingersoll was a candidate for Vice-President. He died in 1822, at the age of seventy.

The opinion of the Chief-Justice in this case, is by far the most elaborate, perhaps the most able, delivered by him while on the bench. It occupies over ten pages of the printed report of the case. He makes no reference to cases, for the reason given by him that he knows of none which are not distinguishable from this case. Unlike the learned, and somewhat scholastic opinion of his associate, Justice Wilson, in the same case, he does not attempt an analysis and comparison of other forms of government and social institutions, nor does he undertake to discuss the opinions of writers on government and the rights of man, or show the harmony of their views with the principles which governed his own judgment. He discusses the question purely as a practical, constitutional question ; he examines it in three separate propositions. 1st, In what sense Georgia is a sovereign State ? 2d, Whether suability is compatible with such sovereignty ? 3d, Whether the Constitution authorizes such an action against her ? To the first proposition he applies those strong federal views and ideas of nationality, which he was always known to entertain, going to the very opposite extreme of the doctrine of state rights and state sovereignty. A corporation was an aggregate of individuals, and so was a state. The citizens of Philadelphia, numbering forty thousand, in their corporate capacity, were suable by a single citizen, and there was no reason why the fifty thousand citizens, of Delaware should not be. He distinguishes, it is true, between the case of a suit against the United States, and a suit against a state, because the national courts being supported by the arm of the Executive power of the United States, that power could not be exercised against itself. The sovereignty of Georgia was therefore not absolute, but subordinate to the nationality of the United States. There was nothing incompatible with such sovereignty, in a public arraignment in a court of law at the suit of a citizen of another state, in an action of assumpit for the breach of a contract ; and moreover, the Constitution, to which Georgia had acceded, authorized such a suit.*

*In reference to this decision Chancellor Kent observes in his commentaries : " It is a little *remarkable* that the Court, in one of its earliest decisions, should have assumed a jurisdiction which the authors of the Federalist had a few years before declared to be without *a color of foundation.*

These views were not concurred in by Judge Iredell, who delivered a dissenting opinion. That able jurist considered the question also in a Constitutional point of view, and as a question of strict construction. With great force of reasoning, and admirable precision and clearness of illustration, he analyzed the argument of the Attorney-General, and arrived at exactly the opposite conclusion. His opinion was, that no part of the existing law applied to this case ; and even if the Constitution would admit of the exercise of such a power, a new law was necessary to carry the power into effect, and that assumpsit at the suit of a citizen would not lie against a state. One can scarcely arise from a careful perusal of this able opinion without being sensibly impressed with the force of the reasoning of the learned Judge, and the accuracy of his deductions ;—lucid, logical, compact, comprehensive, it certainly compares very favorably with that of the Chief-Justice, in every respect, and as a mere legal argument must be admitted to be far superior.* The majority of the Court, however, concurred with the Chief-Justice and granted the motion.

This decision created much excitement in the public mind at the time. The subject was at once brought before several of the State Legislatures, and an amendment of the Constitution proposed.

* Judge Iredell may be regarded as one of the ablest of the many distinguished jurists who have graced the bench of the Supreme Court. He had been a delegate to the Constitutional Convention of the State of North Carolina, and was appointed to the Bench of the Supreme Court, in place of Mr. Harrison of Maryland, one of the originally commissioned judges, who declined. As a constitutional lawyer, Judge Iredell had no superior upon the bench. His judicial opinions are marked by great vigor of thought, clearness of argument, and force of expression. He did not always concur with the majorityof his brethren in their constitutional constructions, and on such occasions rarely failed to sustain his positions by the strictest legal, as well as logical deductions. In the interesting case of Ware *vs.* Hylton, 3 Dallas 199—(referred to in sketch of Ch. J. Marshall)—his dissenting opinion exhibits uncommon research, learning and ability. As a legal argument it may be regarded as one of the best specimens that have been preserved of the old Supreme Court. In the case of Wilson *vs.* Daniels, 3 Dallas 401, (referred to in the subsequent sketch of Chief-Justice Ellsworth,) he also dissented, and his views relative to jurisdiction on a writ of error were subsequently adopted by the Court overruling the prevailing opinion in that case. Judge Iredell died in 1799, and was succeeded by Hon. Alfred Moore of North Carolina.

The advocates of state rights viewed the decision as a direct attack upon the sovereignty of the States. Georgia openly defied the federal authority, and refused to enter her appearance. The Supreme Court, however, stood firm. At the February term, 1794, judgment was rendered against the State by default, and a writ of inquiry awarded. Where the controversy would have ended, it is impossible to conjecture, had not the question been put at rest by a speedy amendment of the Constitution, which declared that the jurisdiction of the Supreme Court should not extend to suits against a state by citizens of another state, or subjects of a foreign state. This amendment having been adopted, it was unanimously determined by the Court, at the February term, 1798, that no farther jurisdiction could be exercised, in any case, past or future, wherein a state should be sued by citizens of another state.

This is not a proper place, perhaps, to enter upon a review of that series of exciting political trials which grew out of the foreign relations of the United States, and commenced during the latter period of Mr. Jay's service on the bench. I may allude, however, to one of the earliest and most celebrated of these trials,—that of Henfield, an American citizen, tried on an indictment for enlisting in a French privateer—as well on account of the extraordinary interest and novelty of the case itself, as for the purpose of bringing to view a most important principle advanced by the Chief-Justice, with the direct or tacit concurrence of nearly all his associates. The principle alluded to is, that by the common law, independent of any statute, the federal courts have power to punish offences against the federal sovereignty—a doctrine which seems to have grown out of the political emergencies of the times, but which has been shaken by subsequent decisions, and it is believed, is now finally abandoned. This doctrine is found laid down in a charge delivered by the Chief-Justice to the first federal grand jury ever impannelled, at Richmond, in the State of Virginia. He had been summoned, it appears, to hold this Court for this express purpose, and his charge, though not delivered to the particular grand jury by which Henfield was indicted, had been prepared with great deliberation and care, for the purpose of settling the law generally as applicable to this class of offenders. This charge (which was deemed of so much consequence as to be printed by order of the government, for the purpose of explaining abroad the position of the United States,) very clearly and explicitly enunciated the principle that any American citizen who should violate the neutrality recently proclaimed by the President, was to be deemed guilty of a violation of the laws of the United States, and liable to a prosecution in the federal courts, under an indictment at common law, for disturbing the peace; or, to quote the very language of the Chief-Justice, "That the United States are in a state of neutrality relative to all the powers at war, and that it is their duty, their interest, and their disposition, to maintain it; that, therefore, they who commit, aid, or abet hostilities against these powers, or either of them, offend against the laws of the United States, and ought to be punished; and consequently, that it is your duty, gentlemen, to inquire into, and prevent all such of these offences, as you shall find to have been committed within this district."*

Under the rule of law thus laid down, and as subsequently applied and amplified by Judge Wilson, in one of his learned and scholastic discourses to the grand jury, two months after at Philadelphia, Gideon Henfield, a citizen of the United States, was indicted for enlisting on the "Citizen Genet," an armed vessel, commissioned by the French Revolutionary Government, then at war with England and other European states.

We may read in our day with a feeling of astonishment the proceedings on an indictment, deliberately found, gravely argued, and even sustained by the Court, on common-law principles, against a single individual, for an alleged offence against the law of nations, defined by no statute of the United States, and which, if a crime, under the law of nations, was precisely such an one as had been committed by Lafayette, Kosciusko, and Dekalb, in defence of American Independence. The case, of course, at once aroused party spirit, and political feeling. The fiercest invectives from both sides were launched by the respective partisans and opponents of the French republic at their adversaries. The English minister had demanded the arrest of Henfield; the French minister, after his arrest, demanded his release. The government was determined to sustain, in its full force, the procla-

* See the whole of this charge published in Wharton's State Trials, p. 49.

mation of neutrality, and for that purpose, as we have seen, the aid of the Supreme Court had been invoked. It was not to be disguised that the contest would be formidable. There was among the American people a deep, and wide-spread sympathy with the young republic of France, struggling in what appeared to be its death agony, in a contest with that unhallowed coalition which Europe, under the lead of England, had raised to crush democracy in its cradle. The generous instincts of the American people were all for freedom. The great mass of the people did not reason upon, perhaps did not comprehend, the question of *policy* involved in the declaration of neutrality, and they could not, therefore, be made to understand the *crime* of Henfield in enlisting on a French cruiser, under the tri-color flag of liberty. Popular sympathy was strong in his favor. Brought to trial, all the formidable power of the Court, consistent with a fair and impartial hearing of the case, was arrayed against him, but all to no effect. The well known ability of the Attorney-General, united with the legal acumen and forensic skill of the District-Attorney of Pennsylvania, Mr. Rawle,*

* WILLIAM RAWLE was born in Philadelphia in 1759, and was descended from an old and respectable family of the early settlers. Having commenced his legal studies in New York, he crossed the Atlantic, and was entered a student in the Middle Temple. Returning to America he entered upon his profession, but found his progress slow, so much so, that at one time he resolved to abandon it. Ten years passed before he could be assured of success. As to that success, it is enough to say, that for more than twenty years his business was very large, and he occupied, deservedly, a front rank at the Philadelphia bar. Mr. Rawle was much engaged in the political trials of that period. He never held but one public office, that of District-Attorney of Pennsylvania, which he received at the hands of Washington. His thoughts, habits, and feelings were all professional, and to his profession he devoted the best and most valuable part of a long life. In 1794, Mr. Rawle, together with Hamilton, accompanied George Washington into the western part of the State of Pennsylvania, for the purpose of quelling the insurrection which there broke out. In this expedition he formed one of the family, and shared the tent of Washington. Subsequently he was engaged in his official capacity, as the representative of the government in the prosecution of these offenders. Mr. Rawle was the author of a "treatise on the Constitution of the United States." He was also a member of the commission appointed in 1830, to revise and digest the civil code of Pennsylvania. He died in April, 1836. "His mind," says a writer, "was eminently clear and discriminating, and his arguments and speeches simple, strong, earnest and impressive." His amiability of temper, and kind and

was exerted in vain. In vain did the Court lay down with the most scrupulous and minute exactness, the doctrines of law, as settled by the charge of Chief-Justice Jay. The jury rendered a verdict of "not guilty," and "citizen Henfield" retired in triumph amid the plaudits and acclamations of the crowd.* The verdict was regarded by the popular party as a substantial triumph over the government, as well as the Court. In some sense it was so, for it undoubtedly impeded the vigorous execution of the proclamation of neutrality, so far as the acts of individuals were concerned, though it did not of itself impair the doctrines laid down by the Chief-Justice, and the federal courts. Henfield was not acquitted on the ground of any misdirection as to the law of the case, but on the ground that the crime was not knowingly and wilfully committed, and therefore, as Mr. Jefferson observed in a letter to Mr. Morris, then in England, the jury did no more than the Constitutional authority might have done.

The doctrine of a common law jurisdiction, in criminal cases, seemed to be thus an established principle in the federal courts. Chief-Justice Jay held the April session of the Circuit Court, in 1794, for the Pennsylvania district, and had occasion again to apply the same principle. Joseph Ravara, a Consul of Genoa, was brought to trial before him on an indictment for sending threatening letters to the British minister, and others, with a view of extorting money. Ravara's counsel, Messrs. Dallas, Lewis,† and Heatley, seem to

courteous deportment at the bar, are mentioned as among the most pleasing traits of his character and manners.

* So elated was the French minister, Genet, at this triumph over the Court, that he immediately issued cards to a grand dinner party to meet "citizen Henfield," and that patriotic personage was formally taken under the protection of the French republic. It may be interesting to the reader to know that sallying out soon after on a new excursion, he was captured by a British cruiser, and thus "citizen Henfield" passes from the stage.

† William Lewis was born in Chester County, Pennsylvania, in 1751, on a small farm, in a family whose stringent Quakerism, it is said, held a liberal, and especially a professional education to be inconsistent both with common sense and religious duty. His early education was therefore deficient, nor did he in after life reach any considerable degree of literary attainment. His learning was almost exclusively confined to his profession, and though several times elected to Legislative bodies, and for a brief period, under Washington's administration, holding the

have placed his defence mainly upon the ground, that the act complained of was not a crime at common law, nor was it made such by any positive law of the United States. Judge Jay, in his charge to the jury, ruled otherwise, and sustained the indictment on common law principles. The prisoner was convicted, but was afterwards pardoned on surrendering his commission and *exequatur*.

It only remains to be added, on this subject, that this doctrine, so positively asserted, and rigorously applied by the Chief-Justice and most of his associates in the Supreme Court, was a few years after unsettled, and may now be considered as entirely overthrown. The keen, bold, and penetrating mind of Judge Chase, gave it the first blow on the trial of Worrall, at Philadelphia, in 1798, when in the face of the known opinions of all his associates, and as a very judicious writer remarks, "with that quick perception of the spirit of the Constitution, for which his clear intellect was so conspicuous"—he abruptly and boldly denied that the federal courts possessed any such common law Jurisdiction.* Soon after, Judge Wash-

office of District-Judge of Pennsylvania, yet it is as a lawyer, and mainly as an advocate at the bar, that he is best and most favorably known. Lewis commenced his practice in 1773, and though his business was interrupted during the Revolution, yet it again revived at the close of the war, and owing in some degree to his supposed partiality for the royal cause during the Revolution, he at once succeeded in obtaining a most extensive and lucrative practice among the Quaker loyalists of Pennsylvania. Mr. Lewis was engaged in some of those celebrated criminal trials which began to occupy the attention of the community, soon after Mr. Jay left the bench. He was the leading counsel in the trial of the western insurgents, and it is said, that his pride of conscious superiority at the bar was so much wounded by the request of the defendants' friends to admit Mr. Dallas as his associate, that he expressed himself with such asperity and superciliousness iu regard to Mr. Dallas, as called out from the latter gentleman a challenge. This Lewis accepted, but the difficulty was amicably arranged, and both gentlemen afterwards appeared as counsel for Fries, the first of the insurgents who was brought to trial.

Mr. Lewis continued at the bar, in the practice of his profession, with increasing reputation and unabated ability, until the time of his death, which occurred on the 15th August, 1819.

* The District-Attorney, Mr. Rawle, was in the midst of his argument in reply to Mr. Dallas, discussing the question of jurisdiction in another point of view, when to his utter dismay, and the astonishment of the whole bar, Judge Chase interrupted him with the question: "Do you mean, Mr. Attorney, to support this indictment solely at common law? If you do, I have no difficulty upon the subject;

ington, at the circuit, coincided in the opinion of Judge Chase. He was followed by that eminent jurist, Chief-Justice Marshall, who in more than one case, advances the same opinion; and the question was finally put to rest by the decision of the Supreme Court, in United States *vs.* Hudson,* in which there appears to be no dissent from the opinion delivered by the Court, that a common law offence, not specified by statute, is not indictable in the federal courts.†

It was while the Chief-Justice and Judge Iredell, with the District Judge of Virginia, were holding the Circuit Court at Richmond, in 1793, that the great case of Ware, Administrator, *vs.* Hylton and others, relative to the right of British creditors to collect debts of American citizens, contracted before the war, came on for trial. This case called out a display of forensic talent, eloquence and learning, that hitherto had been without a parallel in the courts of Virginia, and placed the bar of that State, in the opinion of the federal judges, according to Mr. Wirt's account, ahead of all others in the Union. The cause was originally tried in 1791, and was now brought on a second time before the Chief-Justice and his associates. Among the array of counsel for the defendants, the American debtors, were Patrick Henry and John Marshall. Mr. Wirt, in his life of Henry, gives a very graphic and animated description of this celebrated trial, and a copious sketch of the speech of the great Virginian orator, which is said to have required three days for its delivery. He was followed by Marshall, who brought the heavy batteries of his logic to bear upon the breach made by the powerful

the indictment cannot be maintained!" The question, it was supposed, had been long since put at rest, and beyond all hopes of a resurrection at the hands of the "metaphysical Virginia lawyers," as they were called by an eminent Federalist of that day.

* 7 Cranch Rep. 32. See also U. S. *vs.* Coolidge, 1 Wheaton, 415.

† The principle is considered too well settled to be again shaken. Justice McLean in his late opinion in the Wheeling Bridge case, says: "It is admitted that the federal courts have no jurisdiction of common law offences." And Chief-Justice Taney, in his dissenting opinion says: "It has been settled since the beginning of this government, that the courts of the United States, as such have no common law jurisdiction, civil or criminal, unless conferred upon them by act of Congress."—State of Pennsylvania *vs.* Wheeling Bridge Co., 13 Howard, 519.

eloquence of his associate. Alexander Campbell and Col. Innis, two of the most distinguished orators at the bar of Virginia, took the floor on the same side—and the counsel for the plaintiff followed in reply.* Some idea of the effect of this magnificent exhibition of forensic skill, this grand and imposing display of eloquence, may be obtained from the impression left upon the mind of Judge Iredell, who in his written opinion, after the argument, declares with more warmth and enthusiasm than usually belongs to the unimpassioned judicial mind, that the arguments in the case displayed an ingenuity, a depth of investigation, and a power of reasoning, equal to anything he ever witnessed, and that some of them had been "adorned with a splendor of eloquence surpassing what I have ever felt before."†

Chief-Justice Jay presided for the last time at the term of the Supreme Court, in February, 1794. It was at this term that the issue in the case of Georgia *vs.* Braislford, which I have already alluded to, was tried. At the same term the case of Glass *vs.* The Sloop Betsey,‡ presenting one of the earliest questions raised in the Supreme Court on the subject of admiralty jurisdiction, was argued and decided. The Betsey was a Swedish vessel, the cargo of which was owned jointly by Americans and Swedes. She had been captured by the "Citizen Genet," a French privateer, and sent into Baltimore. The owners of the Betsey filed a libel in the District Court of Maryland, claiming restitution, and the captors (who had undertaken to proceed before the French Consul for a condemnation of the vessel) pleaded to the jurisdiction, that the federal courts had no power to take cognizance in the case of a captured vessel, belonging to a foreign and neutral power. After an elaborate and exhausting argument, Chief-Justice Jay delivered the unanimous decision of the court, wherein, without assigning any reasons, he overruled the plea as insufficient, and reversed the decision of the District Court. In respect to the admiralty jurisdiction claimed to be exercised within the limits of the United States by the consuls of France, it was determined by the court that no such power could be exercised, inasmuch as none was reserved or conferred upon these

* See notice of this trial in the following sketch of Chief-Justice Marshall.

† See opinion of Judge Iredell in the Report, 3 Dallas, 275.

‡ 3 Dallas Rep. 6.

functionaries by the treaty. This important case established the admiralty jurisdiction of the federal courts in cases of prize and captures on the high seas.

At the expiration of this term of the court, Judge Jay, as has been mentioned, presided at the April session of the Circuit Court at Philadelphia, and it was during this session that Ravara was tried. About the same time he was commissioned as Minister to England, and although he accepted this appointment without vacating his seat on the bench, yet he never afterwards acted in a judicial capacity. On his return to America, in 1795, having in the mean time been elected Governor of New York, he resigned the office of Chief-Justice of the United States.

No portion of the public career of Mr. Jay has been the subject of more unsparing criticism, than that upon which he was now about to enter. A full history of it involves the discussion of political questions, happily long since laid at rest, and revives the memories of party controversies, which for animosity and bitterness of feeling, have never been surpassed in this country or Europe. Such a review would be fruitless and unprofitable. Without entering upon it in detail, therefore, I shall allude to these events only so far as may be necessary, in order to trace the history of the mission to England, and to sketch, briefly, the part sustained in it by Judge Jay.

On the execution of Louis XVI., England joined the European coalition, and commenced hostilities against the French republic. Up to this period, and even long afterwards, and as late as the overthrow of the republic by Bonaparte, the popular feeling in America was warmly enlisted on the side of France, and the prominent republican leaders did not hesitate to express their sympathy with the progress of popular principles in Europe.* A class of public men in America, however, like Mr. Pitt, Mr. Burke, and their adherents in England, never could be brought to regard with satisfaction the rapid progress of the democratic principle in Europe, as developed in the startling drama of the French Revolution. At the head of

* At a public dinner in New York, in 1796, Chancellor Livingston gave the following toast:

"May the present coolness between France and America produce, like the quarrels of lovers, a renewal of love."

these stood the acknowledged chiefs of the Federal party, Hamilton, Adams, and Gouverneur Morris,* and with these, doubtless, Jay concurred in sentiment on this subject. So strong was this bias against the French Revolution on the mind of Hamilton, that with all his clear, far-seeing sagacity, and practical statesmanship, he doubted whether it would be proper for the United States to receive a minister from the French republic, or whether, if *a regent,* pretending to represent the monarchy beyond the boundaries of France, should send a rival ambassador, the United States ought not to receive *both!* This grave doubt Hamilton proposes in a letter to Jay, but the question did not for a moment perplex the latter. The Chief-Justice entertained a too clear and just conception of international law, and of the principles which should regulate the intercourse of nations, to hesitate for a moment, and he accordingly advises against receiving "any minister from a regent, until he was regent *de facto.*"†

The arrival of Genet in America, as minister from the French republic, and the imprudent and exceptionable conduct of that personage, contributed to fan the flames of party spirit, and to open wider the breaches between the Republicans and the Federalists. Washington held with a firm and steady hand the reins between the two factions, turning neither to the right hand nor to the left, but

* The journal of Gouverneur Morris—an acute observer, as well as an accomplished gentleman—during his stay in Paris, exhibits his strong conservative, perhaps we may say, monarchical, sentiments. Mr. Morris had no faith in the revolution from the outset. He sided with the King, on all occasions, against the liberals. He sneered at Sièyes, disputed constantly, and always warmly, with that "strong-minded woman," Madame De Stael, in her own drawing-rooms, and almost quarrelled with Lafayette at his own dinner table. Mr. Morris denounced the Constitution of 1791 as "a wretched piece of paper"—the same Constitution which Lafayette regarded as the perfection of wisdom, and that liberal and enlightened British statesman, Mr. Fox, pronounced "the most stupendous and glorious edifice of liberty which has been erected on the foundation of human integrity, in any age or country."

† When this question was submitted by Washington to his Cabinet, Hamilton and General Knox thought that the French minister ought to be received *with qualifications.* The sound judgment of the President, however, acceded to the reasoning of Mr. Jefferson, with whom the Attorney-General, Randolph, agreed that the French Minister should be received without any qualifications.

rigidly and impartially adhering to the principles of neutrality which he had proclaimed, with the unanimous advice and assent of his Cabinet, including Jefferson himself. It was a position of no ordinary embarrassment and difficulty. The Republicans were loud and earnest in expressing their sympathy for republican principles in Europe, and their desire for a closer union with France against the natural enemies of liberty; the Federalists were no less earnest, nay were bitter and vindictive, in their denunciations of jacobinism and "French principles." On the one hand the British minister, Mr. Hammond, uttered the complaints of his Government against the United States for discriminating against British subjects and British interests, in violation of treaty stipulations; on the other, the republican envoy, Genet, reproached the public authorities for the ingratitude of America, and threatened to appeal from the Government to the people.

The conduct of England was such, indeed, as to cause deep and wide-spread indignation among all classes of our citizens. England had never yet carried out, either according to its spirit or its letter, the treaty of peace. British troops still garrisoned several posts on our frontiers, and within the jurisdiction of the United States. American citizens were excluded from navigating the great lakes; and Great Britain had neglected to make compensation for negroes carried away by the British fleet, after the war.* These violations of the treaty of peace were admitted by Great Britain, but justified on the ground that the United States had not fulfilled her engagements under the same treaty—a charge specifically made and urged at length by Mr. Hammond, the British minister, but triumphantly answered and conclusively refuted, in a very elaborate and most able communication from Mr. Jefferson, the American Secretary of State.†

Other causes of differences, and grievances growing out of the belligerent attitude of England towards France, served, soon after, to widen the breach between her and this country. Under the British Orders in Council, the last of which authorized the capture by Brit-

* Letter of Mr. Jefferson, Secretary of State, to Mr. Hammond, the British minister, Dec. 15th, 1791, American State Papers, Vol. I. p. 179.

† See this correspondence in Vol. I. American State Papers.

ish cruisers of all vessels carrying supplies to any French colony, or laden with its produce, numerous American vessels were seized and sent to England for "legal adjudication." The right of search was claimed, and American sailors were torn from the decks of American vessels, under pretence of their being British subjects. These and other outrages committed upon our commerce and maritime rights, for some time previous to the spring of 1794, justly excited the indignation of the popular party, who loudly demanded of Congress the adoption of vigorous and energetic war measures. It required all the firmness and prudence of Washington, barely sustained in the Senate, and with a small majority against the Federal policy in the lower house, to stem the current of popular passion, and avert the threatened storm. The excitement of party gradually reached such a point as to overstep the bounds of propriety, and even decency; and the clamors of mob violence invaded the habitation of the President himself. According to the statements, perhaps too highly colored, of Mr. Adams, "innumerable multitudes" surrounded the President's house from day to day, "hurraing, demanding war with England, cursing Washington, and crying success to the French patriots and virtuous republicans."*

The Democratic party in Congress were in favor of prompt and immediate action against England, looking mainly toward commercial restriction. Steps were taken to increase the military force; an embargo was laid for thirty days on all vessels bound to foreign ports; and a resolution was introduced to suspend commercial intercourse with Great Britian till indemnity should be made for the losses sustained under her orders in council, and until she surrendered the military posts agreeably to the treaty of peace.

It was at this moment, when the public mind was in the highest state of ferment, and a speedy rupture seemed inevitable, that Washington determined to make another effort to reconcile the differences between the two countries, and preserve peace. He resolved upon sending a special envoy to England, and he selected for that purpose the Chief-Justice of the United States. As in the case of the

* The "innumerable multitudes" of Mr. Adams have been discredited, on good authority. Perhaps the rest of the statement is also to be taken with considerable abatement.

Spanish mission, the appointment was one in no way to be coveted or desired, and indeed was repugnant to all Mr. Jay's ideas of personal convenience. But in this as in almost every act of his public life, he demonstrated that his conduct was governed by a high and exalted sense of duty, and not by mere personal considerations; and the rule of action which he had marked out for himself did not suffer him to shun the responsibility or decline the appointment. "There is here," he remarks in a letter to Mrs. Jay, on the 15th April, 1794, "a serious determination to send me to England, if possible to avert a war. The object is so interesting to our country, and the combination of circumstances such, that I find myself in a dilemma between personal considerations and public ones." And again, a few days after, "So far as I am personally concerned, my feelings are very far from exciting wishes for its taking place. No appointment ever operated more unpleasantly upon me; but the public considerations which were urged, and the manner in which it was pressed, strongly impressed me with a conviction that to refuse it would be to desert my duty for the sake of my ease and domestic concerns and comfort."

The Chief-Justice was at this time holding the Circuit Court at Philadelphia. The nomination was sent in, and acted upon by the Senate, on the 19th April, 1794. It appears that the object of the mission was distasteful to the party in opposition in the Senate. Some of the members, among whom was Mr. Burr, refused to sanction it, on personal grounds, alleging the impropriety of the nomination itself. It was, however, confirmed by a decisive vote, 18 to 8. Two days afterwards the House passed a bill, prohibiting, at the end of a limited period, the importation of articles of British growth or manufacture into the United States—a bill that of course would have rendered Mr. Jay's mission nugatory. Its passage in the Senate was only prevented by the casting vote of the Vice-President.

Within a month after his appointment Mr. Jay sailed from New York, accompanied by his son, and Col. Trumbell, as Secretary of Legation. Coming as the envoy of the peace party in the United States, and charged directly to negotiate a treaty between the two countries, he was of course received with every proper mark of respect and attention. His negotiations and intercourse with Lord

Grenville, the Secretary of Foreign Affairs, were of the most friendly and agreeable character ; and so far as appears, tended to create in each a mutual respect for the other. With this gentleman, mostly in friendly and unreserved intercourse, and by oral communication, Mr. Jay negotiated and finally settled upon the terms of that celebrated treaty, the promulgation of which in the United States brought down upon the head of its author such a tempest of popular indignation.

The terms of this treaty, and the policy or impolicy of its ratification, were fully discussed at that day, and with great vigor of argument. Indeed it became for a time the dividing line of political sentiment, upon which those two distinguished leaders, Jefferson and Hamilton, representing the rival political parties of the country, irrevocably separated. Hamilton, with his accustomed ardor, ably defended the treaty in some papers under the signature of 'Curtius' and 'Camillus.' Jefferson, in a letter to Governor Rutledge of South Carolina, pronounced it an "execrable thing," and nothing more than "a treaty of alliance between England and the Anglo-men of this country, against the Legislature and the people." In a letter to Madison, he says, alluding to Hamilton's pamphlet: "Hamilton is really a Colossus to the anti-republican party ;—without numbers, he is a host in himself." * * * "In truth when he comes forward there is nobody but yourself who can meet him." * * * * "For God's sake take up your pen and give a fundamental reply to 'Curtius' and 'Camillus.'" This Mr. Madison did, and very ably replied to the argument of Hamilton.

As to the merits of the treaty itself, very few, I believe, at this day, will undertake to defend it on *principle*, whatever may be said of it on the score of *policy*. Mr. Jay declares, and doubtless with truth, that it was based upon the very best terms that could have been obtained ; yet Washington himself hesitated to give it his approval, and it was only by a close vote that it escaped the ordeal of the Senate. As a commercial treaty the advantages were altogether on the side of Great Britain. There was no reciprocity in it.* It was a treaty between a strong and a

* In this respect it compares very unfavorably with the treaty with France subsequently negotiated by Ellsworth and his associates, which Hamilton and some of the Federalists severely censured. See subsequent sketch of Ellsworth.

weak power, where the former insisted upon much and yielded little, and where the latter agreed to receive that little in order to purchase the boon of future peace and security. Great Britain, it is true, agreed to surrender the military posts, but this she was already bound to do by the treaty of peace twelve years before ; she also agreed to pay for property which her subjects had illegally captured, after a failure to recover of the captors in due course of law. But with the exception of these two points, she yielded little or nothing that it was an object to her to retain. The treaty did not even settle existing disputes, for while providing for the more easy and certain collection of British debts in the United States, it gave no indemnification for the negroes carried away by the British troops at the close of the war ; nor did it contain any concessions in regard to the right of search and privateering claimed and exercised by British armed vessels on the high seas.

Mr. Jay had been instructed by his government to procure a direct trade with the West Indies in our own vessels, "of certain defined burdens." The part of the treaty which was negotiated under these instructions, is perhaps the most objectionable, and indeed was most warmly attacked at the time. The manner in which they were carried out seems scarcely reconcilable with their *spirit*, even if it actually came up to the *letter*. True, the treaty did provide that England should open these ports, but only to vessels, or, as a member of the House of Representatives* ex-

* Mr. Lyman. In the debate on the treaty in the House of Representatives, alluding to its want of reciprocity, he remarks: "In Europe we are told we may freely enter her (Great Britain's) ports. In the West Indies we are *to sail in canoes of seventy tons burthen*. In the East Indies we are not to settle or reside without leave of the local government. In the sea ports of Canada and Nova Scotia we are not to be admitted at all, while all our rivers and countries are opened without the least reserve. Yet surely our *all* was as dear to us as the all of any other nation, and ought not to have been parted with but on equivalent terms."

Mr. Madison spoke in opposition to the treaty in the same debate. He took particular exceptions to that portion of it which permitted aliens to hold lands in perpetuity. Other portions of the treaty he found equally objectionable. "With respect to the great points in the law of nations comprehended in the stipulations of the treaty," he remarks, "the same want of real reciprocity, and the same sacrifice of the interests of the United States are conspicuous."

pressed it, "canoes" of the burthen of seventy tons;—and as a restriction upon this slight relaxation of the British colonial system, and perhaps as an *equivalent* for it, the American minister consented to insert the stipulation that all cargoes taken in such vessels should be landed in the United States; and further that the United States should ship no molasses, sugar, coffee, cocoa, or cotton to any other part of the world! It may seem surprising at this day that so shrewd and able a negotiator as Chief-Justice Jay should have consented, under any circumstances, and in view of any possible consequences, to accede to such humiliating restrictions. The explanation is to be found in two facts: First, that a weak power always treats under disadvantageous terms with a strong one. Second, the disadvantage in the present case was increased because the negotiator was known to the British minister to be ardently desirous of procuring peace, and the friendship and good will of Great Britain. On the latter point the remarks of Prof. Tucker, in his Life of Jefferson,* are so discriminating and just, that no apology is necessary in presenting the reader with the following passage. While awarding to the distinguished negotiator of the treaty, in the execution of his trust, the highest talents as well as zeal and patriotism, Prof. Tucker remarks: "But the misfortune was, that Mr. Jay left the United States under the firm belief, generally entertained by his party, that peace with England, the prevention of a closer fraternity with the French, and the continued ascendancy of the Federalists, all depended on his making a treaty. Every thing then which could interest either his patriotic or party feelings, (and neither were lukewarm,) was hazarded on this single step. The moral necessity under which he acted was as well known to the British ministry, as it was felt by himself; and they naturally profited by it to insist on every thing which he could venture to give, and to concede nothing which they could decently refuse."

Without entering upon a further review or criticism of this celebrated treaty, I dismiss the subject with the single remark, that containing such a provision as that in regard to the West India trade, and securing peace and friendship with England without corresponding reciprocal commercial advantages, it is not at all remark-

* Life of Jefferson, vol. I. page 507.

able that the treaty should have been exceedingly distasteful to the republican party. Nor is it a matter of surprise that such men at the south as Pinckney and Rutledge should have denounced it in unmeasured terms; that Madison should have censured it in the strongest language on the floor of the House of Representatives; and that Jefferson himself, should for the moment have been ruffled in the serenity of his philosophic temper, and even have forgotten the ordinary courtesies of language, in giving expression to his dissatisfaction.*

A few days after Jay's arrival in America, the Senate assembled, and the treaty was submitted by the President. On the 24th of June the Senate advised the ratification of the treaty, except the article relating to the West India trade. Soon after, and while its consideration was still before the Senate, it was made public by a senator from Virginia.† At once the public was in a blaze of excitement, or, to use the language of the biographer of Mr. Jay, the torch was applied to that mass of combustibles which had long been collecting, and the intended explosion instantly followed. In a free country no one has a right to object to the free and unrestrained expression of public opinion;—but at the same time, while the people have a right to make known their sentiments without reserve in regard to public men and public measures, this liberty ought not to be abused, or be suffered to degenerate into licentiousness. On this occasion, though unquestionably much might be excused to the intensity of public feeling, yet no one will undertake to justify the violence of language and action employed by some of those who denounced the treaty. It was doubtless unpopular. It was such as a large portion of the people of the country did not and could not approve. But to look beyond the treaty itself, and attack the character and motives of the negotiator, was both illiberal and unjust. Some few even of the Democratic societies, transcended the bounds of decency as well as propriety, and talked of the GUILLOTINE, and of bringing JOHN JAY to trial and justice;—while the mob did not hesitate, in following the example, to parade the effigy of Jay through

* In one of his letters Jefferson calls the negociator of the treaty *a rogue of a pilot*, who had run the vessel of state into an enemy's port.

† James T. Mason.

the streets, labelled, "Come up to my price, and I will sell you my country;" and publicly to burn the obnoxious treaty in front of his own house.* These details, however, are not necessary to be dwelt upon, and it is gratifying to know that such proceedings were neither shared in, nor approved, by temperate and intelligent political opponents, nor by the great mass of the Republican party.

Washington deliberated carefully and hesitated a long time before he signed the treaty. His habitual prudence, and his earnest desire to preserve the peace of the country, finally overcame his scruples and determined his conduct; and on the 15th August, 1795, he gave it his official sanction, and it thus became the law of the land. The treaty, however, had still a narrow escape in the House of Representatives the following spring, on the question of passing the laws necessary to carry it into effect. The sum of $90,000 was to be appropriated for this purpose, and a determined opposition was manifested. On a question taken in the House, it was found that the vote was equally divided, and the chairman, though opposed to the treaty, gave his casting vote in favor of its execution. Soon after the necessary laws were passed, and the treaty went into full effect.

It has already been mentioned that Chief-Justice Jay had been elected Governor of the State of New York during his absence, and had been put in nomination without even his knowledge or consent. Three years before, while still holding his seat on the bench of the Supreme Court, he had consented to be put in nomination for this office against Governor Clinton. The election had been unusually

* It is but simple justice to say that the commission of outrages like these was not confined to the Republicans. Similar acts were perperatedg by the other party. Jefferson was subsequently treated in the same manner in New England; and during the absence of Mr. Gerry in France, his unoffenging wife and family were subjected to unheard of insults. "On several occasions," says Mr. Austin, in his life of Gerry, "the morning sun shone upon a model of a guillotine erected in the field before her windows, smeared with blood, and having the effigy of a headless man. Savage yells were uttered in the night time to disturb the sleep of this family of females, and the glare of blazing faggots suddenly broke upon its darkness to terrify them with the apprehensions of immediate conflagration." —2 *Austin's Life of Gerry*. 267.

close and animated. Mr. Jay received the greatest number of votes, but owing to an informality in the vote of the counties of Otsego, Tioga, and Clinton, these ballots had been rejected, and Mr. Clinton was declared by the canvassers duly elected Governor by a majority of 108. It was in this election that Mr. Jay's old friend, Chancellor Livingston, left the ranks of the Federal party, and allied himself to the Republicans, assuming an attitude of decided hostility to Mr. Jay's election. The decision of the canvassers was the subject of much dissatisfaction to the party which had supported Mr. Jay, and an investigation was had thereon at the ensuing session of the Legislature, but the house of Assembly, by a majority of only four votes, resolved that the canvassers had not conducted themselves with impropriety in the execution of their trust, and Mr. Clinton accordingly continued to discharge the duties of the office. These considerations doubtless influenced the party which had supported Mr. Jay, to present his name again for the same office, and that too without his knowledge, and before his arrival from Europe. Mr. Clinton declined a re-election, and the Chief-Justice, Mr. Yates, was selected as the opposing candidate. Jay was elected by a large majority, and he was welcomed by his friends with this flattering announcement on his arrival at New York, only two days after the result had been officially ascertained.

The author of the Political History of New York thinks, and perhaps very correctly, that if the British treaty had been published on the 1st of April instead of the 1st of July, Jay could not have been elected Governor. In proof of this assertion he alludes to the fact, that although up to that time the city of New York had been almost unanimously Federal, and even De Witt Clinton, then a young man just entering public life, had failed of an election to the Legislature at the time of Jay's election, yet the very next year Edward Livingston, a decided Republican, was elected to Congress from that city. Be this as it may, it is certain that Mr. Jay came into office with a very flattering popular vote. The elections had generally been in favor of the Federalists, and the Governor found himself supported by a decided majority in both branches of the Legislature. The late venerable Chief-Justice Ambrose Spencer, *Clarum et venerabile nomen,* was the same year elected to the

State Senate. Though then comparatively a young man, but thirty years of age, his great talents were known and appreciated, and he at once assumed a position of commanding influence in support of the administration. Besides Mr. Spencer, the Governor found himself sustained in the Senate by many other gentlemen of great ability and influencé, among whom may be mentioned Gen. Schuyler, Mr. Cruger, and Mr. Ph. Livingston.

The Legislature convened in the city of New York on the 6th of January, 1796. The new Governor, as was usual at that period, met the two houses, and delivered a speech at the opening of the session, which though neat and appropriate, contained nothing very striking or remarkable. He declared his determination "to regard all his fellow-citizens with an equal eye, and to cherish and advance merit, *wherever found.*" If this declaration referred to the dispensing of executive patronage, it was a declaration which, however honestly intended, was not, and probably could not, have been consistently carried out. Jay had been elected as a Federalist, and opposed by the Republicans, and his fidelity to his political friends, it is believed, has never been questioned. And although, in those primitive days, offices were not yet regarded as the "spoils of victory," and removals for opinion sake were comparatively unknown, yet when an office had become vacant by resignation or otherwise, it was generally filled by the appointment of a political friend, rather than of a political opponent. The course of Mr. Jay was no exception to this rule. Indeed, it had heretofore been made a cause of perhaps just complaint against him and Generals Hamilton and Schuyler, that, through their controlling influence with the President, most of the appointments under the Federal Government had been made from the ranks of the political opponents of Gov. Clinton and the Republicans. Nor does it appear that Gov. Jay ever urged upon the council of appointment the nomination of an anti-Federalist to office on the ground of superior merit alone.

The answer of the two houses to the Governor's speech was highly laudatory, going even beyond the bounds of ordinary compliment. "The evidence of ability, integrity and patriotism," it says, "which have been *invariably* afforded by your conduct in the discharge of the variety of arduous and important trusts, authorize us to anticipate an administration conducive to the welfare of your constituents." The word "*invariably*" was not contained in the original draft. It was inserted by the Senate, on motion of Mr. Spencer, by a vote of 11 to 6, "thus repelling in unequivocal terms"—remarks the son and biographer of Mr. Jay—"the calumnies with which the opposers of the British treaty had found it convenient to assail the minister who negociated it." Such, no doubt, was the object of Mr. Spencer's motion, and so far as a party vote in a legislative body may be said to reflect public sentiment, it was successful. It may be thought surprising that Mr. Spencer himself did not always continue to yield the same unqualified approbation to Mr. Jay's political actions. Before the close of the next gubernatorial term, we find him enrolled with the Republicans, and in connection with De Witt Clinton and another opposition member of the Council, sending in to the Assembly a paper, in which the character and conduct of the Governor are criticised with much asperity. This disagreement grew out of the contest between the Governor and Messrs. Clinton and Spencer, then in opposition, and members of the council of appointment, relative to the right of nominations to office—the Governor claiming an exclusive right of nomination, and the council, which consisted of four Senators, three of whom were in opposition, claiming a concurrent right.*

* From this it appears that notwithstanding Gov. Jay's declaration in his opening speech, his practice was uniformly to dispense official patronage among his political friends. Mr. William Jay, in his memoirs of his father, does not, indeed, claim that the Governor ever appointed anti-Federalists to office, but regards the fact that he made no removals, as evidence of the sincerity of his intention "to dispense his patronage for the good of the whole, and not of his friends." The explanation, it must be confessed, is not entirely satisfactory. It ought not, certainly, to be claimed as a peculiar merit in Governor Jay, that he declined to make removals, at a day when—as Mr. Barnard remarks in his able discourse on Chief-Justice Spencer—removal from office on account of political opinions, was unknown. Nor, can it be regarded as a fulfilment of the declaration made by the Governor, of his intention to "advance merit *wherever found.*" In declining to make removals, Gov. Jay is entitled to no more, and no less, credit than his distinguished opponent, Gov. Clinton, who, on being again reinstated in office, says Mr. Barnard, utterly refused to give the practice the sanction of his name, and even caused his solemn protest to be entered on the journals of the Council, against some of the removals.

It was during this year that the purpose of Washington to decline a re-election and to retire to private life, became known. Jay had been one of his warmest personal and political friends. No man in the State of New York, not even Hamilton, enjoyed in a higher degree the esteem and confidence of the first President. In his annual speech to the Legislature, at their meeting in November, 1796, the Governor, alluding to the fact of Washington's purpose to retire from public life, delivered a very beautiful eulogium upon the character of that great and good man. It may here be mentioned as an instance of the friendship and unreserved confidence existing between them, that General Washington submitted to Jay and Hamilton the draft of his celebrated farewell address, for revision and approval. The subject has excited some attention, from the fact of a copy of this address having been found in the hand-writing of General Hamilton, from which circumstance its authorship was attributed to him. Many years after, Governor Jay, in a letter to a friend, explained the circumstance as follows: Washington sent the draft to Hamilton with a request that he would confer with Jay on the subject, and suggest any alterations that might occur. The conference took place at the house of Jay. Several additions and modifications were proposed, and, at the suggestion of Jay, instead of interlining and mutilating the original draft, Hamilton copied it entire, incorporating into it the proposed alterations. This was sent to General Washington, Hamilton probably retaining the copy, which was subsequently found among his papers.

The vote of the State of New York, at this Presidential election, as is well known, was cast for Adams and Pinckney, for President and Vice-President of the United States. That remarkable man, whose name has become a sinister omen in the political history of the country, Aaron Burr, was sustained by the Republicans for Vice-President, with Mr. Jefferson for President. Burr was then a member of the Senate of the United States. His term of service expired in the spring of 1797, and the Legislature being strongly Federal, General Schuyler was elected to succeed him. Burr returned to New York and immediately offered himself as a candidate for member of Assembly. The Republican ticket was elected in the city by about a thousand majority, and at the ensuing session Colonel Burr appeared in the Legislature with De Witt Clinton,* as one of his colleagues from New York, to organize a vigorous and active opposition to the administration of Governor Jay.

This session of the Legislature commenced at the city of Albany, on the 2d of January, 1798. The speech of the Governor was mild and judicious, avoiding any allusion to political matters, and being confined mainly to the domestic affairs of the State. It was well received by both houses, and a respectful answer returned. Nevertheless, a vigorous opposition was manifested in the Legislature, under the lead of Burr and other prominent Republicans, although no measure of any great political importance was discussed, except the bill to abolish slavery in the State, which passed the Assembly, but was lost in the Senate—a bill, it must be added, which Governor Jay warmly approved.

The first term of the Governor was drawing to a close. The election was to take place in April, of this year, and the campaign was carried on with great vigor during the winter session, outside as well as in the Legislature. The Republican party had been gradually gaining strength, and was directed by able and resolute leaders. It had life, activity, energy, character, talent, and withal the popular sympathy to invigorate and sustain it. It marshalled itself under the lead of those experienced and veteran statesmen, Chancellor Livingston and George Clinton. It availed itself of the indefatigable exertions of that able, adroit, clear-headed, and not over-scrupulous politician, Aaron Burr. It numbered among its younger members, such men as Edward Livingston, whose name and reputation have since become national, De Witt Clinton, whom General Hamilton, it is said, at one time thought would become a Federalist, and Ambrose Spencer, who had just enrolled himself in the Republican ranks. With such an array of influence, energy, and talent on its side, the Republicans might well hope for success; but the Federal party stood firm, and indeed seemed invincible so long as it was sustained by the exalted character and wide-spread personal popularity of John Jay, and guided by the colossal intellect of Alexander Hamilton.

The election was held in April. Each party selected, perhaps,

* This was the first appearance of De Witt Clinton in public life. He was then about 28 years of age.

under all the circumstances, its strongest candidate. The Republicans supported Chancellor Livingston ; the Federalists again rallied around Gov. Jay. We are told by his son that he would gladly have retired from the contest. It was peculiarly disagreeable to him to have for a rival and opponent, his old friend and relative, the Chancellor ; but, remarks Mr. William Jay, " his fellow-citizens still claimed his services, and he resolved not to abandon the helm when the lowering clouds portended a storm."

The result is well known. Gov. Jay was elected, and by a large majority.* The Federalists were every where successful, and carried the Legislature. But, from the smoke of the contest, some of the opposition leaders emerged triumphantly, and among these Spencer and De Witt Clinton were elected to the Senate, and to the Assembly, that name of evil omen to the Federal party, Aaron Burr !

The Governor called the Legislature together in an extra session in August, of this year, for the purpose of making preparations for the immediate defence of the State, in prospect of a war with France, resulting from the unsuccessful mission of Messrs. Pinckney, Gerry, and Marshall. For the moment, says the biographer of Governor Jay, the voice of faction was drowned in a loud and vehement burst of indignation against the insulting cupidity of the French Directory, and the Legislature unanimously voted a patriotic address to the President, pledging the support of the State of New York in his endeavors to maintain the rights and honor of the nation. An act was passed appropriating money for the erection of fortifications and the purchase of arms, at the discretion of the Governor. Little of a party nature, however, transpired, except the election of a United States Senator, James Watson, a Federalist, in place of Gen. North, who had been temporarily appointed to fill a vacancy.

At the regular session, commencing on the 2d of January, 1799, the strife of parties again commenced. Under the vigorous and skillful opposition of Burr, and others in the Legislature, the Republicans were fast organizing that powerful party which two years later carried the State, and placed Jefferson in the presidential chair. This seemed now to be the main object entertained by the opposition

* His majority was 2,380. Two years before, the whole number of legal voters in the State was returned at 66,000.

in New York, at least of all save one—for who shall undertake to fathom the mysterious and inscrutable mind of Aaron Burr?—and every effort was directed to this end. Burr himself co-operated with the other Republican leaders, and brought to the common cause all the craft of his singularly subtle intellect, and the tact of a wily and experienced politician.

Matters, however, did not appear very auspicious for the Repub licans. The elections in April, 1799, were decidedly against them. Burr, himself, at the head of the Republican ticket for the Assembly in New York, was defeated, and the Legislature in both its branches, still remained with the administration. It was at this session, in January, 1800, that the Governor, in his opening speech to the Legislature, had occasion to allude to the recent national affliction which had occurred in the death of Washington. His language, as usual, was chaste, beautiful, and strictly appropriate. "You will, I am persuaded," he said, "join with me in regretting that the topic which naturally rises first into view on this occasion, is the afflicting and unexpected death of that virtuous and great man who, both in the field and in the cabinet, in public and private life, attracted such an uncommon degree of merited esteem, confidence, and admiration. His memory will be cherished by the wise and good of every nation; and truth triumphing over her adversaries, will transmit his character to posterity in all its genuine lustre." How fully and accurately has the prediction been fulfilled!

The Legislature cordially responded to these sentiments and adopted resolutions suitable to the occasion.

Both the present house of Assembly and the Senate, as has been observed, were strongly Federal. The next Legislature were to choose electors of President and Vice-President of the United States. It was supposed by the Federalists that they would carry a majority of the members of Assembly at the election in April, 1800, and thus secure all the presidential electors. Accordingly on a bill introduced at this session to divide the State into election Districts, and provide for *the choice of presidential electors by the people in the respective districts*, the Assembly divided upon this important question, the Federalists opposing and the Republicans sustaining the measure. This bill was finally lost by a party vote, 55 to 47. The fact it is necessary to state in order properly to appreciate a circumstance which will be presently alluded to, and which may be regarded as one of the finest and most characteristic passages in the life of Governor Jay.

The Federalists, however, were sadly disappointed in their hope of carrying the election in this memorable spring of 1800. The great tact and superior management of Colonel Burr, were peculiarly manifested in the selection of the Republican candidates in the city of New York, where the year before there was nearly a thousand Federal majority. Somewhat unpopular himself, from his connection with a local question,* he was not a candidate for the city, but was nominated and elected in the county of Orange. The New York nominees, thirteen in number, were men who, says Mr. Hammond, "in wealth and talents, and weight of character, were probably greater than any other equal number of Republicans then to be found in the city, or perhaps, any other equal number of citizens." Among them may be mentioned Governor Clinton, Brockholst Livingston, (afterwards Judge of the Supreme Court,) Gen. Horatio Gates, Henry Rutgers, and Col Burr's particular friend and adherent, John Swartwout. The result was a decisive Republican triumph. A large and controlling majority in the Assembly, and the reduction of the Federal majority in the Senate to seven, gave the choice of the twelve presidential electors to the Republicans, and it was supposed insuring the election of Mr. Jefferson by a majority of three in the electoral college.

The Federalists now saw their mistake in defeating the bill to divide the State into electoral districts; for, the choice of Federal electors from only a few of the districts, would, it was thought, entirely change the aspect of the presidential election. The bill, however, had been opposed and defeated, not strictly as a political measure, but on *constitutional* grounds, as stated at the time by that able and distinguished lawyer, John V. Henry, the Federal leader in the Assembly, and there appeared, therefore, no remedy.

In this emergency, as soon as the result was known, the bold and impetuous mind of Hamilton conceived a project to defeat the elec-

* The charter of the Manhattan Company, which, after it had passed the Legislature, was found to contain banking powers.

tion of Mr. Jefferson, which may be properly characterized as a mean between a daring *coup d'etat,* and a questionable political finesse. It was nothing less than the immediate convening of the *existing Legislature,* in an extra session, for the purpose of passing the very bill to divide the State into electoral districts, which his own friends in the Legislature had defeated on constitutional grounds! This proposition he actually made, and urged with much earnestness in a letter to Governor Jay, dated May 7th, 1800.* "In times like these," remarks the writer, "it will not do to be *over scrupulous.* It is easy to sacrifice the substantial interests of society, by a strict adherence to ordinary rules." And again, "I shall not be supposed to mean that anything ought to be done which integrity will forbid; but merely that the *scruples of delicacy and propriety,* as relative to a common course of things, ought to yield to the extraordinary nature of the crisis."

But John Jay did not so understand the code of political ethics. Not only was he guided by "scruples of delicacy and propriety," but by a sense of justice and of right, that never suffered him to sacrifice a principle to a temporary expediency, or swerve a hair's breadth from the line of what he regarded as his duty. He kept his official robes as Governor of the State, pure and unsullied, as he had preserved the judicial ermine. The Chief-Magistrate of New York was no less upright and single-minded in his official actions, than the Chief-Justice of the United States had been. His errors, if he committed any, were errors of position, not of design—errors resulting from opinion, which every liberal mind can understand and tolerate, and not errors knowingly committed. In the present case, it appears that even the highest political considerations could not induce him to adopt a course of questionable propriety. He shunned the very appearance and suspicion of evil, and avoided even a constructive wrong. The letter of Hamilton was found among his papers endorsed "*Proposing a measure for party purposes which I do not think it becomes me to adopt.*"

Governor Jay, as has been remarked, was no lukewarm politician; he believed, and no doubt with all the sincerity of a thorough convic-

* This letter is published at length in the life of Jay, by his son, but without the signature of Hamilton, vol. I. page 412.

tion, that the ascendancy of the Republican party in the State and nation was dangerous to the political institutions he had assisted in establishing. Yet with him, political success was never regarded as the sole measure of right and wrong. He was governed by higher and nobler, and more controlling considerations. Thus, when Jefferson was elected President, and some of the political friends with whom Gov. Jay acted, were counselling indiscreet, if not intemperate action, the same hand which had endorsed the above words upon the letter of Gen. Hamilton, penned a letter to the freeholders of New York, containing this wise, dignified, and temperate advice: "I take the liberty, therefore, of suggesting whether the patriotic principles on which we profess to act, do not call upon us to give (as far as may depend upon us) fair and full effect to the known sense and intention of a majority of the people in every constitutional exercise of their will, and to support every administration of the government of our country, which may prove to be intelligent and upright, of whatever party the persons comprising it may be."

These simple and unobtrusive passages in the history of a life, however unimportant they may at first sight appear, are noticeable facts, and should never be lost sight of when we come to measure the moral worth of the individual. They are strongly characteristic. They lay open to us the mind, the heart, the inner life of the man. They indicate the salient features of his character; they serve to measure his sincerity and truth; they point out the secret springs which prompt his action—the motives which regulate his conduct—and by them we can estimate the moral worth, and just value of the man. The passages I have alluded to, beautifully illustrate the character of John Jay—his uprightness of conduct—his sincerity of purpose—his purity of mind. They show him, down to the close of his political career, the John Jay of the Revolution, of the Continental Congress, and of the New York Provincial Assemblies.

The close of his official career was rendered less dignified perhaps, certainly less agreeable, by that political contest between the Governor and his council of appointment, which has been alluded to on a former page. Not that it detracted from the personal dignity of Gov. Jay, but, that it placed him in an unenviable and awkward position;—he, a veteran statesman, just about to retire forever from

6

public life, drawn thus by the force of circumstances, and an honest regard for the preservation of his constitutional rights and official dignity, into a contest with two of the ablest, most energetic and ambitious of those young Republican politicians, who were yet children at school, at a period when Jay had earned for himself a reputation as a statesman.

It may well be imagined that there must have been something ludicrous, notwithstanding the gravity and earnestness of their deliberation, in these two or three meetings of the council, in the winter of 1800 and 1801. On the one side sat Spencer, De Witt Clinton, and Roseboom : on the other the Governor, (for the first time during his official career, in a minority,) with his solitary adherent. Eight different nominations for a Sheriff of the county Dutchess were made by the Governor at the first meeting—and each time was the nominee rejected by the council. A few other nominations were then suffered to pass the ordeal, and the council adjourned. At the next meeting the Governor yielded the sheriff of Dutchess and nominated a Republican, who was approved. A third and final meeting was held on the 24th of February. The Republican members of the Council determined to approve no Federal nominee for the office of sheriff, in either of the counties of Orange or Schoharie. Gov. Jay proceeded as usual, to nominate for Sheriff of the county of Orange. A single affirmative responded to the nomination, and three resolute and determined voices were heard in the negative. Again and again were different individuals named for the office, but with the same result. It was evident that nothing could be done unless his excellency should yield, which did not seem to be at all probable. At this juncture the Governor was startled by a very bold and novel procedure. "*I* nominate John Blake, Jr.," said Clinton, in the firm tone of a man assured of his position. The meeting had in a moment been transformed from a Council into a deliberative assembly ! Jay hesitated an instant, but refused to entertain the motion or put the question. "I nominate John Nicholson," he then said ; Clinton, Spencer, and Roseboom refused to vote ; matters had come to a stand still, and the business of the Council was at an end. Gov. Jay, thereupon stating that he desired time for deliberation, adjourned the Council, and never convened it again, leaving the vacant offices unfilled. Thereupon he sent in a communication to the Assembly, asking its direction, which that body refused to give, on the ground that it was a constitutional question, not to be decided by them. He also addressed the Chancellor and Judges of the Supreme Court, but they, too, declined giving an opinion, on the ground that it was not within the scope of their official duties.

The term of office of Governor Jay expired on the 1st of July, 1801. It seems that he had for some time contemplated a final withdrawal from public life. The determination had been formed with deliberation, and it was adhered to with rigid firmness. To the committee who waited upon him soliciting him to accept a nomination for a third term, he replied : "The period has now nearly arrived, at which I have for many years intended to retire from the cares of public life, and for which I have been for more than ten years preparing." Mr. Jay had become weary of the toils and cares of public life ; perhaps, too, the example of Washington in declining to serve a third term, may not have been without its influence upon his mind ; at all events he seems to have adopted the resolution as a matter of choice, and not from any anticipation of a possible adverse result at the election. No public inducements were able to tempt him to resign the retirement he had voluntarily chosen. A short time after he thus declined a third nomination for Governor, the President, Mr. Adams, unexpectedly informed him, that he had been appointed, and confirmed to his old office of Chief-Justice of the United States. "It appeared to me," remarks Mr. Adams, in explaining to Jay the cause of his nomination, "that Providence had thrown in my way an opportunity, not only of marking to the public the spot where, in my opinion, the greatest mass of worth remained collected in one individual, but of furnishing my country with the best security its inhabitants afforded against the increasing dissolution of morals." Jay, however, declined the appointment, and six weeks before the close of his term of office, removed to his family estate, at Bedford, a quiet and retired part of Westchester county, about fifty miles from the city of New York, where he continued to reside to the day of his death.

The public career of this eminent man was now closed—closed at a period of life, (for he was but 56 years of age,) when many of our public men have not reached midway their course of usefulness. And yet what an active, and busy, and eventful life had been his; and what a startling chapter in the history of America, and of the world, had been written during the quarter of a century which had elapsed since he first entered the service of his country! With the events of that period, whose results have been so grand and stupendous, his name, as we have seen, is intimately associated, and without it the history of the times cannot be written. He now finally passed from the stage, and during the next quarter of a century lived in the unbroken seclusion of a quiet and contemplative retirement, a silent, but not an indifferent spectator to the course of public events, and to the development of those institutions which his hands had helped to raise.

Little remains to be added to this imperfect sketch of Gov. Jay's career. The remainder of his life, as his son remarks, being entirely passed in the bosom of his family, and in the peaceful and unostentatious discharge of the duties of religion and benevolence, affords but few instances for the biographer. It was the life of the upright and just man—the faithful public servant, who has discharged his whole duty—whose conscience is void of offence, and who feels the pleasing satisfaction that his work is done. His time was principally passed in those agreeable employments, which were so much in accordance with his natural tastes, the pursuits of agriculture. His amusements and recreations were few and simple. He found the most of them within the bosom of his family, or in the resources of his own mind. A work of benevolence or charity would sometimes occupy his attention—the building of a church, or the interests of an educational or religious society. At rare intervals, a journey to New York or Albany, on a visit to some member of his family—often on horseback, exercising in open air—frequently conversing, as he says, with the "mighty dead," of whom Cicero was his favorite, or reading the Scriptures—now and then a letter to an old friend—these and kindred employments went to make up the routine of his daily life. To the question how it was possible for him to occupy his mind in the seclusion of his retirement, he replied with a smile," I have a long life to look back upon, and an eternity to look forward to." If the character of this eminent man is beautiful in its simplicity and its moral purity, it becomes still more interesting when regarded as a bright example of Christian virtue. The tone of his mind was always serious. He regarded religious meditation and worship as no unimportant part of the duties of life. He, himself, in his own family, regularly led the family devotions both morning and evening; and though courtesy to guests might sometimes postpone the customary early hour for retiring, yet the presence of company never postponed nor suspended the family worship.* Death invaded his quiet retreat within a twelvemonth after he entered it, and snatched away the wife of his bosom, who for so many years had been his companion and counsellor. Jay endured the afflicting dispensation, not merely with the calmness of a philosopher, but with that better resignation and nobler fortitude which Christianity inspires.

The retirement of Mr. Jay was seldom broken in upon, and he regarded the political dissensions of the day, with the philosophic gaze of a mere spectator. It is not true, however, as has been stated, that he took no interest in politics, and would not even peruse political newspapers. On the contrary, he constantly read the news of the day, and at times took papers of opposite politics, that he might obtain more full information of passing events. He also made it a point of duty to vote at every election.†

The manner of his life, we are told, was simple and regular. He rose with, or before, the sun, read prayers, breakfasted, aud then spent the greater portion of the day in the open air, often on horseback. He conscientiously devoted himself to the duties of a private life; he improved his paternal acres; he rebuilt the mansion of his fathers; he was kind to his dependents, useful to his equals. He busied himself with all the interesting occupations of a country life; was a promoter of, and a member of societies for the diffusion of knowledge and religion, and instructed his relations and servants in those

* Life by Wm. Jay, vol. I. p. 444.

† Letter of Judge William Jay to Mr. Hammond, note D, Political History of New York.

Christian principles which had always been the guide of his own course.*

Such were the occupations and manner of life of this venerable patriot and statesman, for the period of more than a quarter of a century. The evening of his life was serene and quiet, and he went down to the tomb full of years and honors. On the 14th of May, 1829, having retired to his bed in the enjoyment of his customary health, he was seized with palsy, from which he never recovered. He died on the 17th of the same month in the 84th year of his age.

Mr. Jay was married in April, 1774, to Sarah Van Brugh Livingston, daughter of William Livingston, who had recently removed from New York to New Jersey, and was subsequently for many years Governor of the latter State. He was also a member with Mr. Jay of the Continental Congress of 1775. By this marriage, Mr. Jay had several children, among whom were the late Peter A. Jay, an eminent lawyer of New York, and Judge William Jay, of Westchester county, who still continues to occupy the family mansion in the town of Bedford.

The prominent features of Gov. Jay's character are plainly indicated in his various official and public actions, as well as in his quiet and unostentatious discharge of the duties of private life. He was not, perhaps, what may be called a great man. He was not gifted with those shining qualities of genius, which at once astonish and dazzle mankind; nor was he endowed with those creative faculties, that originality of thought, that vigorous grasp of intellect which stamp their possessor with the impress of greatness. And yet, though laying claim to none of these, his was far from a mediocrity, much less an inferiority, of intellect. Jay was decidedly an able man—a man of extensive attainments and erudition—a vigorous writer, and a sound thinker. He was more—he had a healthy, temperate, and well-balanced mind—a clear, sound, and comprehensive judgment—an admirable prudence and caution. And withal he was a conscientious and a just man—just to his neighbours, as well as to his family, just to his political opponents, as well as to his

* Prof. Renwick's Sketch of Jay, p. 134.

friends. The caution of Jay was a quality not resulting from timidity or irresolution. Few men were capable of acting a bolder or more determined part, when occasion demanded. Thus we have seen that when Livingston and the New York members hesitated to sign the Declaration, Jay stepped boldly forward in the Convention, and assumed the responsibility of recommending its approval ; and thus, too, while on his mission in Spain, without any present prospect of meeting the payment of the heavy amounts drawn upon him, he accepted all bills at his own risk—an act which some might call temerity and rashness. But the prudent conduct of Jay was rather the result of that innate love of justice, that desire on all occasions of standing publicly upon the clearest and most defensible issues, that effort to avoid every controversy, unless under the most obvious claim of right. Thus it was, that even after the humble petition of the first Congress to the King had been treated with the most insulting neglect, Jay originated and carried through, in the next Congress, against the most determined opposition, the proposition to send another "petition" to the King, which in like manner was "spurned from the foot of the throne." He desired to place the action of the Congress upon the highest, the clearest and most indisputable basis of right, and to leave no cause for cavil, even on the part of the friends of the British cause. It was the suggestion, not of prudence merely, but of wisdom, for it placed in the hands of Congress, a moral power which nothing else could give. The same calm, deliberate, but firm judgment, tempered always with prudence and caution, is observable in all his actions. And yet he was deficient neither in quickness of determination, vigor and boldness of design, nor tenacity of purpose. Indeed, in some respects he might be called an obstinate man—tenacious of what he believed to be the right—never conceding a point of conscience, and never yielding a principle.

The virtues of such a man might still be remembered and sung in lyric strains by the Roman bard—

Justum et tenacem propositi virum,

though the republic no longer existed, and the last bright exemplar of those virtues had passed away. The same virtues lived and were exemplified in the early ages of our republic, and in the character of John Jay. Just and firm of purpose, neither the idle clamor of the populace, nor the countenance of the tyrant could avail to shake his solid temper ; and these virtues, though perchance they may not be breathed in the numbers of some future lyric song, will be remembered in history, even though America should follow the example of the proud republic of antiquity.

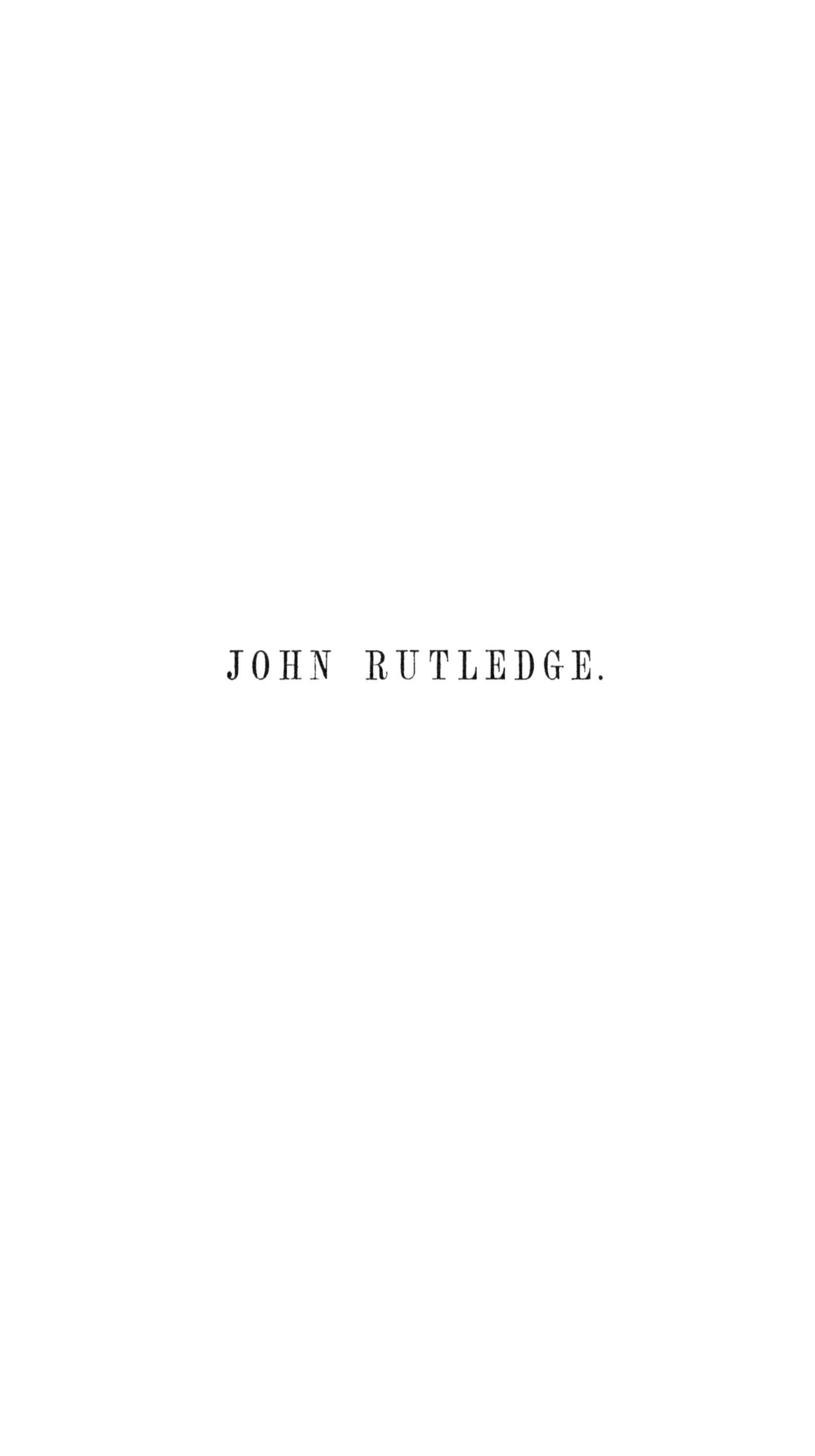

JOHN RUTLEDGE.

JOHN RUTLEDGE.

THE practical sagacity of Washington, and his almost intuitive knowledge of character, rarely failed him in that most difficult branch of executive duty, appointments to places of official trust and responsibility. In the administration of government, as well as upon the theatre of military operations, he was not only quick in discerning real merit, but correct in estimating the true worth of a man and his fitness for the discharge of a specific duty. The same penetrating glance which discovered under the modest garb of General Greene a military genius fit to direct the operations of the southern army, discovered also, not the ability and worth only, but the precise sphere of action suited to the capacity and genius of the men he called around him to fill the highest executive and judicial stations under the Federal Government. Thus it was that, on the resignation of Chief-Justice Jay, trusting to the instincts of his own mind, and relying upon his own discriminating judgment, in opposition to the advice of perhaps the most trusted of his counsellors, he passed by such able jurists as Ellsworth and Livingston, Cushing and Paterson, and promptly tendered the vacant Chief-Justiceship to JOHN RUTLEDGE, of South Carolina.

It is much to be regretted that no complete biography of this eminent statesman and jurist has been written, and that so little is now known of one of the earliest, and ablest, and firmest friends of American independence.

John Rutledge was a man of mark and of note in his day ;—at once the Adams and the Patrick Henry of South Carolina—chief among the South Carolina revolutionary leaders—first in station, in influence, in talent, amid the brilliant galaxy of patriots whose names adorn the revolutionary annals of his native State. It is true that the main facts of his public career remain to us, forming, as they do, a part of the history of his native State and the country. Here and there may also be discovered traces of his judicial life, in the few and not very fully stated cases found in the earlier South Carolina reports; but it is to be feared, that now, after the lapse of more than half a century, the real John Rutledge of the Continental Congress and of the Revolution—the John Rutledge as he lived and acted in private as well as in public life—as he appeared upon the bench and to his cotemporaries of the bar—has passed away, and that it will be difficult, if not impossible to revive any considerable portion of those private memoirs and personal reminiscenses which go to make up the most suggestive and interesting portion of biography. A late writer has alluded to the difficulty of drawing a faithful sketch of Rutledge's career, and remarks: "This now can only imperfectly be done. The private records are wanting. There are no family memorials, or very few. The voluminous correspondence of Mr. Rutledge, as President of the colony of South Carolina, Governor of the State, its representative in Congress, and Chief-Justice of the United States, seems now to be irrecoverable, and but a few letters remain to us which are yet unpublished."* I shall, however, avail myself of such materials as can now be obtained, to give some account of the life, public services, and judicial career of the second Chief-Justice of the United States.

The father of John Rutledge was a physician. He emigrated from Ireland with his brother Andrew about the year 1735. The two brothers settled in South Carolina, where John commenced the practice of medicine, and Andrew the practice of the law. Two or three years after his arrival, Dr. John Rutledge married Miss Hexe, a young lady not yet fifteen years of age, who in 1739 gave birth to a son, the subject of this memoir. John was the oldest of seven

From an interesting sketch of the life of Rutledge, by the author of "The Partisan," "The Yemassee," &c., &c., published in the American Review for 1847. In this sketch Dr. Simms has presented us with some curious original correspondence of Rutledge during the war, from which I have taken the liberty to make a few brief extracts. See *Post*, pp. 134–140.

children. The celebrated Edward Rutledge, one of the signers of the Declaration of Independence, of whom I shall hereafter have occasion to speak, was the youngest of these children. He was born in 1749, soon after which Dr. Rutledge died, leaving to his young widow the care and training of her large family. We are told she was a woman of great energy, and of more than ordinary endowments. How she accomplished the task thus devolved upon her, the future history of her distinguished sons will speak for itself.

The early education of young Rutledge was the best that the colony of Carolina at that day afforded. He was placed under the tuition of David Rhind, an eminent and successful teacher of the classics. Having made what progress he could in the institutions of Charleston, his mother, who was possessor in her own right of an ample fortune, and spared no pains in the education of her children, sent him to England to complete his preliminary studies. Here, after a time, having determined to follow the profession of the law, he was entered a student of the Temple, in London, and was in due time licensed a barrister-at-law. The same course was subsequently pursued by his younger brother, Edward.*

Mr. Rutledge returned to Charleston, where he commenced the practice of the law in 1761. He was then twenty-two years of age. He entered upon his profession under the *prestige* of a reputation for ability, attainments and eloquence second to that of no young man in the colony. Unlike many others, however, who have commenced life under equally favorable auspices, but whose attainments have been brilliant and precocious, rather than solid, young Rutledge did *not* disappoint the high expectations that had been formed of him. It has been said of him with truth that he rose in his profession at a bound, and that his was no tedious probation. Cotemporary accounts still preserve the memory of his first effort at the bar,† an effort in which the vehemence and power of his diction, the splendor of his declamation, the brilliancy of his eloquence, confounded his adversa-

* This was the course usually followed by young gentlemen of fortune and family at that day in South Carolina. Rutledge's three colleagues who signed the declaration, Heyward, Lynch, and Arthur Middleton, all young men like himself, completed their academic studies at the English universities ; and so also did the Pinckneys, William Henry Drayton, and others.

† See Sketch of Rutledge by Dr. Ramsay, 2 History of South Carolina.

ries, and carried away the judgment and feelings of the jury. It was in an action for damages for a breach of promise to marry—an action of very infrequent occurrence at the south, and one which was well calculated to excite the interest and fix the attention of the public. His successful debut in this suit was but the prelude to a brilliant career at the bar. It gave him at once position among his brethren of the profession. How Mr. Rutledge maintained that position is shown by his future forensic triumphs. Business accumulated rapidly on his hands; that description of business which furnishes the best test of professional ability and success, a test which is to be found in the importance and character of the cases submitted to the care of the advocate, and the liberal compensation with which his services are rewarded. It became customary, says the writer I have quoted, to think that his clients were necessarily to be successful, and no doubt a foregone conclusion of this sort did much towards the further conviction of judge and jury. Such a conviction could not readily have been reached until repeated triumphs had impressed the popular mind with the most perfect assurance of his powers.

The same writer,* speaking of Rutledge's characteristics as a lawyer, remarks: "He had shown himself equal at once to the boldest flights of passion and fancy, and to the strictest and severest processes of ratiocination. His reason and his impulse wrought happily together. His enthusiasm was never suffered to cripple his induction, nor the severity of his analysis to stifle the ardor of his utterance. A happy combination of all the essentials of the lawyer and the orator were soon acknowledged to be in his possession."

And again, at a later period, in speaking of his qualifications as a judge: "He was born a lawyer. His studies in his profession had been pursued *con amore.* He had wrestled with the law as one wrestles with a mistress, and had taken her to his heart as well as to his lips. His knowledge of principles was profound—his appreciation of details accurate and immense; and that large grasp of judgment, that comprehensive reach of vision, which enabled him to take in at a glance, not merely the central proportions, but all its several relations and dependencies, eminently fitted him for the new career before him. With the facts fairly within his survey, his

* Dr. Simms' Sketch of the Life of Rutledge, American Review.

coup d'œil was instantaneous. His mind seemed to leap to its conclusions at a bound. He loved pleading—could listen with rare delight to the eloquence of the specious advocate ; but while these gratified his sense of the ingenious and beautiful, they failed to persuade his fancy or to mislead his judgment. His sense of justice was invincible. He threaded with ease the most difficult avenues of litigation—speedily resolved the subtleness of special pleading—steadily pursued, and finally grasped the leading principle of the case, and rendered his judgments so luminously and forcibly, as in most cases to satisfy even those who suffered from his decision."

Such was Rutledge as he afterwards appeared in the character of a judge. And indeed such was he in these the earlier years of his professional life. But a higher eulogium is paid him, and a better testimonial afforded of his splendid professional success, in the fact which has become matter of history, that within four years from his debut at the bar, he had reached so high a public standing, and acquired so large a share of the public confidence, that he was appointed a delegate, with General Christopher Gadsden and Thomas Lynch, to represent the province of South Carolina in the first Congress of the colonies.

This Congress assembled in 1765, soon after the passage of the memorable Stamp Act. It convened on the proposition of the province of Massachusetts, and was the first step taken toward a permanent political organization and union among the colonies. The people of South Carolina were among the first to respond to the call of their New England brethren. The question, however, was not decided without great and violent opposition. There was a feeling of deep-rooted loyalty among the people of the colony—the descendants of the cavaliers of England—and they looked with suspicion and alarm upon this proposition for a union. But the leading intellect of the province, the men of real talent and influence, were mostly in favor of a vigorous assertion of colonial rights. Among these was Christopher Gadsden, who perhaps contributed more than any other man to awaken the spirit of the colony and to excite the people to prompt and vigorous action. The year previous, the royal Governor had refused to administer the oath to General Gadsden as member of Assembly, and he thus became virtually disfranchised on account of the freedom of his political opinions. The Assembly, with much spirit, protested against this high-handed act, and the usurpation of the royal representative was vigorously denounced, both in and out of the legislative body. Among the boldest, the most earnest, and most eloquent in their denunciations was John Rutledge. It was his first step upon that brilliant political career which the colonial struggle laid open before him—a career which he entered with all the fire of youth, all the zeal of an impassioned temper, and the ardor of a bold and impetuous mind.

This circumstance doubtless contributed much to shape the future course of Rutledge, and to give that strong and decided tone to his opinions in regard to colonial rights which he ever afterwards entertained and avowed. His was one of those unconquerable wills, one of those firm and unyielding tempers, which opposition and resistance serve only to strengthen and confirm in its purpose. His eye was never accustomed to look back, nor his foot to retrograde. From that day down to the close of the struggle, he was the firm, vigorous, and uncompromising champion of the rights of the colonies, always in advance of the popular movement, always the advocate of the boldest measures, and always the formidable opponent of the royal authority. He was doubtless among the first who contemplated the independence of America; and when the rupture actually occurred, he would have been the last to consent to a reconciliation.

The Stamp Act was followed by the proposal of Massachusetts to the provincial Assemblies to send delegates to a common Congress. Christopher Gadsden, as has been already mentioned, at once came down in support of the measure. He was vigorously and ably sustained by Rutledge, who went into the contest with his accustomed spirit and zeal. Tradition still preserves to us the memory of that vehement and impassioned eloquence which brought home to the minds and the hearts of the people of South Carolina a conviction of the importance and necessity of the proposed measure;—but it is the memory alone, faint and dim in the distance of the past, and while the imperishable result stands out a notable and prominent historical fact, the breathing thoughts and burning words of the orator which so largely contributed to bring about that result, passed away, finding no record in the present, and no life in the future.

It is sufficient to say that the efforts of Rutledge and Gadsden were successful. After a vigorous opposition in the Colonial Assembly,* the measure passed by a small majority, and three deputies were appointed to represent the province in the General Congress. Their names are JOHN RUTLEDGE, CHRISTOPHER GADSDEN, and THOMAS LYNCH, the father of the signer of the Declaration of Independence. South Carolina was the first province south of New England which responded to the call; indeed, with the exception of Maryland and Delaware, she was the only southern province which appeared in the first American Congress. The royal authority was yet too strong for the popular party in North Carolina, Georgia, and even Virginia herself.

When the Congress assembled in the city of New York, twenty-eight delegates, representing nine of the colonies,† appeared. It was the most important body that had yet convened—in some respects the most important that had ever convened in America. A quaint writer has styled it "the very *ovum reipublicæ*." It contained the germ of those great ideas, and the elements of those popular principles which were about to burst forth and shape the political and social destiny of a continent. It was composed generally of men of great ability and worth; and yet it is somewhat remarkable that among these twenty-eight delegates are to be found very few of the future prominent statesmen of the Revolution. It is true Robert R. Livingston of New York was there, and so was James

* When the measure was first proposed, it was treated with ridicule. One member made a very humorous speech, and described in a ludicrous manner the heterogeneous and discordant materials of which such a body would be composed. "New England will throw in fish and onions," he remarked; "the middle states flax-seed and flour; Maryland and Virginia will add tobacco; North Carolina pitch, tar and turpentine; South Carolina rice and indigo, and Georgia will sprinkle the whole composition with saw-dust." A country member retorted that he would not choose the gentleman for his cook, but nevertheless if the colonies proceeded judiciously, they would prepare a dish fit to be presented to any crowned head in Europe.

† The three southern colonies above mentioned, and New Hampshire, were unrepresented.

7

Otis of Massachusetts, and Cæsar Rodney of Delaware. But Franklin and Hancock, Roger Sherman, Samuel Adams, and Robert Morris were none of them present; nor (except Rutledge himself,) were any of those celebrated revolutionary orators who ten years later electrified the country with an eloquence whose trumpet tones have been borne on the wings of the flying years, to the ears of a second and a third generation of men. Virginia's gifted sons were absent from the Convention. The silvery tones of Lee, whose classic diction and copious eloquence won for him the title of the Cicero of America, were not heard in that body, nor the voice of Henry,

——" the forest-born Demosthenes,
Whose thunder shook the Philip of the seas."

Nor was John Adams there, equal in intellect to either, and perhaps superior to both in powers of sarcasm and of bitter, scathing, terrible denunciation. Hamilton was scarcely out of his nurse's arms, and Edward Rutledge was yet a boy at school; Ellsworth was in his senior year at College; Jay was quietly engaged in reading law at New York, and Jefferson was angling in Virginia, or perhaps dreaming in his office at *Devils-burg*,* upon metaphysics or political philosophy.

In the midst, then, of these twenty-eight steady, solid, unpretending representatives of the colonies, John Rutledge, at the age of twenty-six, and the youngest member of the body, stood up in this first Continental Congress, foremost among the opponents of the arbitrary measures of Great Britain. What was his precise share in the deliberations of this body, we have now no means of determining. The official journal, which has been published, is little more than a brief minute of the daily proceedings of the Congress. Enough appears from it, however, and from other sources, to justify the conclusion that he was one of the most prominent as well as one of the ablest members of the Convention. Of the three committees which were appointed, he was made chairman of the one charged with the duty of preparing an address to the Lords in Parliament. This duty was promptly performed, and the address, it is believed, is from his pen.

The Congress commenced its session on the 7th, and closed on the

* The name he applied to the ancient metropolis of Virginia.

24th of October, 1765. Rutledge shared largely in all its deliberations. The brilliancy of his genius, the boldness of his ideas, the extent and variety of his information, and the beauty and power of his diction, all together made a deep impression upon the body of which he was a member. He had come among them unheralded and unknown; he left behind him a reputation of which any man might be proud. "The members of the distant provinces were surprised at the eloquence of the young member from South Carolina," says Dr. Ramsey. Nothing great, "neither wit nor wisdom," from that province, it seems, had been expected, and their surprise was complete at witnessing the surpassing ability of one of its delegates, and he too the youngest member of the Congress. In short, Rutledge made a *sensation* at this first meeting of the colonial delegates, as he did upon all occasions, and in all public bodies, whenever and wherever he chose to mingle in debate.

From the accounts that have been left us by his cotemporaries, we may gain something of an idea of his mode of speaking, and his style as a debater. It would seem from these accounts that he had a tinge of that haughty manner, and all that rapid and vehement impetuosity—that passionate and earnest emphasis—which characterized the later efforts of the great Maryland advocate, William Pinkney; but his action was less violent and his gesture more graceful. He had a copious flow of language at command, and much too of that quick repartee and lively play of fancy and wit which occasionally broke like a gleam of sunshine over the gorgeous but closely woven web of one of Wirt's forensic arguments. Dr. Ramsay, a cotemporary, and who must have heard him frequently, both at the bar and in the Legislature, thus describes him:

"In both capacities he was admired as a public speaker. His ideas were clear and strong, his utterance rapid but distinct; his voice, action, and energetic manner of speaking forcibly impressed his sentiments on the minds and hearts of all who heard him. At reply he was quick—instantly comprehending the force of an objection—and saw at once the best mode of weakening or repelling it. He successfully used both argument and wit for invalidating the observations of his adversary. By the former he destroyed or weakened their force; by the latter he placed them in so ludicrous a point of light that it often convinced, and scarcely ever failed of conciliating and pleasing his hearers. Many were the triumphs of his eloquence at the bar and in the Legislature ; and in the former case probably more than strict impartial justice would sanction ; for judges and jury, counsel and audience, hung upon his accents." The same excellent authority notices the distinction in oratorical power between the two brothers, John and Edward : "Demosthenes seemed to be the model of the one," he remarks, "Cicero of the other. The eloquence of the elder, like a torrent, bore down all opposition, and controlled the passions of the hearer ; that of the younger was soothing, persuasive, and made willing proselytes."*

Rutledge returned to Charleston at the close of this brief session

* The following extract relative to Mr. Edward Rutledge is from Garden's Anecdotes of the Revolution :

"If the Demosthenian eloquence of John Rutledge was more impetuous and commanding, the Ciceronian style of Edward was more persuasive. There was a suavity in his manner, and conciliating attraction in his arguments, that had frequently the effect of subduing the prejudices of the unfriendly, and which never failed to increase the ardor and inflexibility of steady friends. The eloquence of John Rutledge was as a rapid torrent ; that of Edward as a gentle and smoothly gliding stream—the first hurried you forward to the point it aimed at with powerful impetuosity—the last conducted to it with fascinations that made every progressive step appear enchanting. Civil occupations engaged the attention of the elder brother. The younger, in the field, as well as in the cabinet, obtained celebrity. In the well-contested action on Port Royal Island, he had the command of one of the field pieces which essentially contributed to the victory, and justly received the thanks of the General who commanded. After the capture of Charleston, the influence both of his talents and example did not escape the penetration of the British commanders. They plainly saw how much a man of such superior ability would be looked up to by the suffering multitude ; and to destroy the effect, by an act of as great tyranny as ever was exercised, removed him to St. Augustine. The cheerfulness of his natural disposition, his conciliating attention to his companions in this situation of unmerited persecution, contributed in no trifling degree to cherish hope, and oppose intrepid resistance to every encroachment of despondency. After his exchange and freedom from captivity, he was elected a member of the Legislature of the State ; and at the conclusion of the war served in the Council, aiding the administration of Governor Mathews."

Mr. E. Rutledge was one of the signers of the Declaration of Independence, and served with distinction through several sessions of the Continental Congress. He was elected Governor of South Carolina in 1798, and died two years afterwards, universally regretted as he was beloved by the people of his native State.

of the first Congress, with a reputation greatly enhanced. He returned to continue the practice of his profession, in which he had already laid the sure foundation for success and eminence. The Stamp Act repealed, he mingled no farther in politics, except so far as to discharge the duties of a member of the provincial Assembly, in which station he had been placed by the suffrages of his fellow citizens. His professional success continued to grow upon him, and his reputation to increase with years. At the opening of the Revolution, when he was again called to relinquish his business, he stood confessedly at the head of the South Carolina bar. It is to be regretted that we have so few data for supplying this portion of Rutledge's career. Like the other colonies, the records of South Carolina colonial jurisprudence are few and meagre. Reports of cases were not commenced until some time after the Revolution, and the opinions of courts, if any were written at that day, with the arguments of counsel, have all passed away. It appears that in Rutledge's time there were no courts, judges, or juries beyond the limits of Charleston. A single provost marshal was charged with the service of process over the whole province. The intolerable inconvenience to the people in the back country of attending courts at such a distance, led them frequently to take the law into their own hands, and inflict summary punishment upon outrageous offenders. This evil, however, was remedied in a measure by the passage of an act in 1769, creating seven new district courts. The organization of these new courts, while relieving suitors, of course added greatly to the labors of the practicing advocate, who was obliged to ride the circuit in his attendance upon them. Business, doubtless, increased in a corresponding degree, and to such members of the profession as Rutledge, neither fees nor clients were ever wanting. Still, notwithstanding the increase of courts, at that early day in South Carolina, the amount of litigation was quite limited. The greatest number of judgments ever entered up in Charleston in any one year before the Revolution, was 390, and the average of seven years immediately preceding the Revolution, 236. These included *all* the judgments entered up in the colony ; for although new courts were organized by the act of 1769, yet they were not courts of original jurisdiction or of record, and all the judgments obtained in the country districts were entered up in Charleston.* This statement, therefore, shows very correctly the extent of legal business in the colony during the period of Rutledge's practice. From his great abilities and success as a *nisi prius* lawyer, he no doubt participated to a large degree in all the business of the courts, and was probably engaged, on one side or the other, in every important litigated suit. Many of these questions would no doubt now be of peculiar interest, as exhibiting the state of colonial jurisprudence at that time, and the manner of Rutledge's demeanor at the bar. It seems, however, impossible to revive them, except through the dim and uncertain light of traditionary accounts; I therefore take leave of Rutledge as an advocate at the bar, doing so with the less regret, as we are now about to follow him upon that broad and extended theatre of public usefulness which the Revolution opened before him, and in which the most shining qualities of his genius were exhibited.

The revolutionary movements in South Carolina may be said to date from that general Convention of the citizens of the colony which assembled at Charleston on the 6th July, 1774. At this Convention the proceedings of the parliament of Great Britain against the province of Massachusetts were considered, and strong resolutions passed in favor of sustaining the rights of the colonies against the unjust pretensions of the crown. In order to lay the foundation for a permanent organization, the Convention appointed a general committee of ninety-nine persons, to act as a committee of correspondence, and with full powers to do every thing necessary to carry into effect the resolutions then passed. The Convention also appointed five delegates "to meet the deputies of the several colonies in North America in General Congress." These delegates were John Rutledge, Edward Rutledge, Henry Middleton, Christopher Gadsden, and Thomas Lynch. They of course acted under no legal and constitutional authority, but simply as the representatives of a Convention of the people which doubtless indicated the public sentiment of the colony. Of this Convention the Rutledges had been members. Upon the motion to appoint delegates to the General Congress, an effort was made to instruct them as to the extent

* 1 Ramsay Hist. South Carolina, p. 158.

to which they might go in pledging the support of their colony to the Bostonians. This proposition was vigorously and successfully combatted by John Rutledge. He desired the South Carolina delegates to go into the Congress untrammelled by instructions, and unlimited in powers. These views he enforced in a speech of transcendant ability—one of those impetuous and soul-stirring harangues which, like the impassioned appeals of the great Virginia orator, infused a new courage into the hearts of the people, and opened their minds to a full comprehension of those great issues which were now to be encountered. It was the first blast of the revolutionary trumpet from South Carolina—not merely a feeble re-echo of those warlike notes which were wafted on every breeze from the provinces of Massachusetts and Virginia—but a bold and hearty response, ringing out loud and clear, like the clarion notes with which the knight as he entered the tournament responded to the challenge of his adversary. Rutledge clearly saw that the crisis had arrived when it was necessary to act, and to act with vigor and firmness. The proposal to limit the powers of the delegates he believed would defeat the object of their appointment. He was satisfied that a Congress of the colonies for *consultation* merely would amount to nothing. It was necessary therefore that the delegates should have plenary power to act, limited by nothing but their own discretion, as the emergency might require. These views he enforced in a speech of overwhelming eloquence and unanswerable argument. He infused his own daring spirit into those who had hitherto been timorous and wavering. He silenced, if he did not convince, every opponent. On that day, undoubtedly, John Rutledge gave its first impulse to the Revolution in South Carolina; and perhaps it may be added, that on that day, too, he placed himself at its head. "What shall be done with the delegates if they betray their constituents, and pledge the colony to a course inconsistent with the public interests?" demanded an opponent. Rutledge turned upon him, and with a passionate gesture, and an eye flashing indignation, exclaimed, "*Hang them! hang them!*" It was idle to resist such appeals, or to combat an energy and resolution like this. The views of Rutledge prevailed, and the delegates, of whom he was one, were appointed under no instructions, or pledge of fidelity whatever, and with unlimited powers. The resolution of appointment clothed them "with full power and authority, in behalf of us and our constituents, to concert, agree to, and effectually to prosecute such legal measures (by which we for ourselves and them most solemnly engage to abide,) as in the opinion of the said deputies and of the deputies so to be assembled shall be most likely to obtain a repeal of the said acts, and a redress of these grievances."

A few days after this, Rutledge and his associates sailed for Philadelphia. On their arrival they were joined by deputies from the other provinces, clothed with similar powers, and soon after the memorable Congress of 1774 commenced its session. The proceedings of this body are matters of history, and it is not necessary to detail or discuss them here. It was in every sense an extraordinary body of men. Most of them were still strangers to each other, and the great majority of them had not yet acquired even a provincial reputation. Only nine of the delegates to the Congress of 1765 had been returned, namely Eliphalet Dyer, of Connecticut, Philip Livingston, of New York, John Dickinson and John Morton, of Pennsylvannia, Cæsar Rodney and Thomas M'Kean, of Delaware, and Gadsden, Rutledge and Lynch, of South Carolina. But in the list of the new members were numbered some whose names were destined to become famous in the history of their country. Among the delegates from Virginia was a modest and unobtrusive gentleman, in whom the penetrating eye of Patrick Henry had detected "the GREATEST MAN on the floor"—Col. George Washington. HENRY himself was already a man of note, and had acquired more than a provincial reputation;—and among his colleagues was one who might in some degree claim to dispute with him the palm of eloquence, RICHARD HENRY LEE. In the delegation from Massachusetts Bay was an active, resolute, ambitious man—a man of extensive information, great energy, and indefatigable industry—JOHN ADAMS—destined to act no inconsiderable part in the grand drama that was about to open. THOMAS JOHNSON, subsequently a Justice of the Supreme Court of the United States, was a member of the Maryland delegation; and from the same State another future Justice of the Supreme Court, that able and singularly gifted, but wayward and erratic genius, SAMUEL CHASE. New York had sent among her eight delegates, a young man who was thought to possess some talent, and now made his *debut* in public life—JOHN JAY—the future Chief-Justice ; and among the five delegates from South Carolina another still younger man appeared, EDWARD RUTLEDGE, then only twenty-five years of age, who had come with his brother John from Charleston, to assist in these serious deliberations, and who proved himself, in real capacity and influence, as well as in eloquence of speech, inferior to few men in that assembly. The name of ROGER SHERMAN appeared in the list of the Connecticut delegates—that of SAMUEL ADAMS from Massachusetts, JOHN SULLIVAN from New Hampshire, and WILLIAM LIVINGSTON form New Jersey.

Such were the men with whom John Rutledge now found himself associated. To assume and maintain a commanding position in a body composed of materials like this, required no ordinary ability. But Rutledge was fully equal to the effort. As an orator and a statesman, few men attained a prouder position in that body. In the language of Patrick Henry, "he shone with superior lustre." His powers of eloquence are vouched for by no meaner authority than Mr. Henry himself. Being questioned, on his return to Virginia, relative to the character of the Congress, and of the individuals composing it, and particularly whom he thought its greatest man, he replied, "If you speak of *eloquence*, John Rutledge of South Carolina is the greatest orator ; but if you speak of information and sound judgment, Col. Washington is unquestionably the greatest man on the floor." * Such was the estimate of Rutledge's powers by the great orator of Virginia ; and the accuracy of Mr. Henry's judgment upon a matter of this kind cannot be questioned. To be assigned by him the first place in a body containing such parliamentary orators as Adams and Lee, is no common praise ;—and the tribute is the more valuable, inasmuch as it was frankly and freely offered to one who, if not already, might some day, perhaps, become a rival. It is Cicero speaking the praises of Crassus.

At the close of the deliberations of this Congress, Rutledge and his associates returned to South Carolina. In the mean time, the Executive Committee had summoned the first provincial Congress

* Wirt's Life of Patrick Henry. Garden's Anecdotes.

of the colony, composed of representatives elected by the people in every parish and district. This Assembly of course had no *legal* or *constitutional* existence. It was entirely revolutionary in its character, but as representing the great mass of the people, its acts and proceedings were regarded as of the highest authority. It met on the 11th January, 1775, and immediately took into consideration the proceedings of the Continental Congress at Philadelphia. It was upon this occasion that Rutledge and his associates appeared before the Assembly to render an account of their proceedings. Some objections had been taken to a clause in the non-intercourse act with Great Britain, excepting from the operation of the act the exporting of rice to Europe. Rutledge, who with three of his associates had voted in favor of this exception, now undertook the defence of himself and colleagues, and explained the object and design of the exception. His speech upon this occasion was very able and ingenious, and withal was attended with the most gratifying results. The assembly, without a dissenting voice, returned public thanks to their late delegates, approved their proceedings, and resolved to carry them into execution. The Assembly also re-appointed Rutledge and his four associates to represent South Carolina in the next General Congress.

The autobiography of Mr. John Adams shows that Rutledge, even at this early period, was the warm advocate of measures tending toward colonial independence, and far in advance of most of his colleagues. On the 2nd of June, 1775, the President laid before Congress a letter from the provincial Convention of Massachusetts, requesting Congress, among other things, to favor them with "explicit advice respecting the taking up and exercising the powers of civil government," &c. The vigorous and impulsive mind of John Adams had already anticipated the subject. In his opinion, Congress ought at once to recommend *to the people of every colony* to call conventions of representatives immediately, and set up governments of their own, under their own authority; for THE PEOPLE, he thought, were the source of all authority, and ORIGINAL OF ALL POWER. "These were new, strange, and terrible doctrines," he remarks, "to the greatest part of the members; but not a very small number heard them with apparent pleasure, and none more than Mr. John

Rutledge of South Carolina, and Mr. John Sullivan of New Hampshire." *

John Adams was no half-way revolutionist ; he had the ring of the true metal in him ; while others lagged in the rear, he pressed forward to the van, in the very front rank of this revolutionary movement ; and by his side stood John Rutledge of South Carolina. Let us observe the further proceedings upon this project for "independent colonial governments," brought forward in Congress more than a year before the Declaration of Independence.

The next day a committee was appointed on the Massachusetts memorial, of which Rutledge was chairman. They had several conferences with the Massachusetts delegates, and reported on the 7th of June, in substance, that in their opinion the royal Governor and Lieutenant-Governor ought to be considered as absent, and that it be recommended to the provincial Congress of Massachusetts to take measures for choosing an assembly or council to exercise the powers of Government, until "a Governor of his majesty's appointment *will consent to govern the colony according to its charter*." Rutledge entered fully into all these views. He had frequent conferences with Adams on the subject, and they fully discussed together the important question as to what form of government it was proper to adopt, as the government of a free State. "Not long after this," says Mr. Adams, "Mr. John Rutledge returned to South Carolina, and Mr. Sullivan went with Gen. Washington to Cambridge, so that I lost two of my able coadjutors. But we soon found the benefit of their co-operation at a distance."

On the return of Rutledge to Congress the subject was again agitated. An animated debate sprang up, October 26th, on the question of instructing the New Hampshire delegation, namely, that Congress should direct "a method for our administering justice and regulating our civil police." In this discussion Adams and Rutledge took the lead, and were ably sustained by Lee, Gadsden, Sherman, and Dyer. At the close of the debate a committee of five was appointed, of which Rutledge was chairman, and Adams a member, which reported, November 3d, recommending the establishment of an independent government by New Hampshire during

* Life and Works of John Adams, Vol. III. p. 16.

"the continuance of the present dispute." Rutledge, who, says Adams, was now "completely with us in our desire *of revolutionizing all the governments*," immediately brought forward some representations from his own State, which were referred to a select committee of five. This committee reported the next day, recommending a course precisely similar to that which had been recommended in the case of New Hampshire.* Let us now see how this revolutionary movement, instituted by Rutledge in the Continental Congress, was carried out in his own State.

No revolution was ever effected with greater unanimity, or with more order and regularity than the revolution in South Carolina; and the reason assigned is that the leading men in every part of the province, from the first moment of the contest, exerted themselves in the cause of their country, and very few of them took sides with the royalists. Thus, it appears that the Constitutional Assembly, under the royal government, in 1774, without a dissenting voice, sanctioned the appointment of Rutledge and his associates as delegates to Congress. In the spring of 1775 his majesty's justices made their last circuit, on which occasion William Henry Drayton, the only one of the judges born in America, in charging the grand jury, distinctly avowed the sentiments of the popular leaders.† Indeed it may be said that after the reception of the news of the battle of Lexington, in the spring of 1775, there was no longer any royal government or royal authority in South Carolina. The revolution was already accomplished. And although the royal Governor, Lord William Campbell, refused to recognize the Provincial Congress, and returned the haughty answer to their address, "I know of no representatives of the people of this province, except those constitutionally convened in the General Assembly," yet the Provincial Congress was none the less *de facto* the ruling authority in the province.

On the reception of the news of the battle of Lexington, the Pro-

* Life and Works of John Adams. Vol. III. p. 20–22.

† Soon after this, the other judges, having refused to sign the articles of association, were put under arrest; the doors of the courts of justice were thereupon closed, and so remained for a twelvemonth, and until re-opened by Judge Drayton under the authority of the new Constitution.

vincial Congress was summoned by the committee to meet in twenty-three days. On the second day after their meeting, the delegates passed a resolution wherein they declared that they united themselves "under every tie of religion and honor" in defence of their country—" hereby solemnly engaging, that whenever our continental or provincial councils shall decree it necessary, we will go forth, and be ready to sacrifice our lives and fortunes to secure her freedom and safety." The character of the men who engaged in this work was the best guaranty of its final accomplishment. Nearly every prominent man in the colony pressed forward into actual service. The Council of Safety was composed of such distinguished citizens as Henry Laurens, Charles Pinckney, Arthur Middleton, William Henry Drayton, and others of equal worth and ability. When it was proposed to raise two regiments of foot and a regiment of rangers, for the public defence, many gentlemen of the first families in Carolina pressed forward for commissions, and the applicants were four times as numerous as could be employed. The well known names of Gadsden, Moultrie, and Sumpter, appear in the list of colonels commissioned by this Congress, and among the captains, Francis Marion, Thomas Pinckney, Charles Cotesworth Pinckney, Thomas Lynch, Jr., and Francis Huger. Thus it was that by imperceptible degrees the whole authority of the State, legislative and judicial, as well as executive, was transferred to the Provincial Congress, and a new government introduced, by the common consent of the people.

The ancient forms of the royal Constitution, however, were still preserved, but the impropriety of this soon became manifest. Accordingly, in the spring of 1776, South Carolina, acting upon the recommendation which, as we have just seen, had already been given by Congress, threw off the shackles of colonial servitude, and adopted an independent Constitution and form of government—thus virtually asserting her own independence some months before the declaration of July 4th, 1776.

In this great work, John Rutledge acted a most important part. Early in the spring he had returned with two of his colleagues from attending the American Congress in Philadelphia. The Provincial Congress, then in session, welcomed the three delegates with the most flattering marks of attention ; and the President, Judge Drayton, was directed to address them in the name of the Congress, and present its thanks for their important services. Rutledge thereupon took his seat in this Assembly, and immediately directed his attention to the formation of the proposed plan of government.

The measure was not carried without a warm and spirited struggle. A desire for a reconciliation was still openly professed by all, and doubtless sincerely entertained by many. Some denied the necessity of any independent Constitution ; some were willing to establish a temporary government, as recommended by Congress ; while the bolder and more ardent popular leaders advocated a total and permanent change. While the measure was yet under consideration, new acts of aggression on the part of Great Britain turned the scale, and silenced all opposition. An independent Constitution was resolved on. Rutledge was placed upon the committee of eleven charged to prepare and report a plan. Still the more moderate men and friends of a reconciliation achieved a partial triumph, for it was decided after a long and exciting debate, that the new government should be temporary merely, and should exist only "till a reconciliation between Great Britain and the colonies should take place."

On the 24th of March, Rutledge made a final report upon the subject in charge of the committee, and two days after, the new Constitution was adopted. It is said, with truth, doubtless, that to Mr. Rutledge's activity and grasp of mind, his political acuteness and great legal knowledge, the people of South Carolina were indebted for most of the provisions of this first Constitution. The preamble, in which are set forth at length the grievances of the Colonies, and the causes inducing the Assembly to adopt the new Constitution, is entirely the production of his pen. "It is remarkable," says a writer, "not less because of its compactness and comprehensiveness, than because it embodies in nearly the same order, and sometimes in the same phraseology, the very matter which in a more condensed form, was subsequently employed by Mr. Jefferson in the famous Declaration." It closes with the following compact and nervous sentences : "And whereas the judges of the courts of law here have refused to exercise their respective functions, so that it is become indispensably necessary that during the present situation of American affairs, and until an accommodation of the unhappy differences between Great Britain and America can be obtained, (an event which, though traduced and treated as rebels, we still earnestly desire,) some mode should be established by common consent, and for the good of the people, THE ORIGIN AND END OF ALL GOVERNMENT, for regulating the internal polity of this colony;—the Congress being vested with powers competent for the purpose, and having fully deliberated touching the premises, do therefore resolve," &c.

The legislative authority under the new government consisted of three branches—an Assembly elected every two years by the people, a legislative Council, consisting of thirteen members, elected out of their own body by the Assembly, and a privy Council, together with a president and commander-in-chief, elected by the Assembly and legislative Council from among themselves or the people at large. The executive authority was vested in the president, with the right to appoint all officers in the army and navy, except field-officers in the army and captains in the navy. This extensive authority was subsequently, as we shall see, enlarged in the hands of President Rutledge into complete dictatorial powers—powers which, though wielded by him with characteristic energy, were never perverted or abused.

The Constitution provided that the existing Congress should be the first General Assembly of South Carolina, and accordingly the new government went immediately into operation. Rutledge was chosen President without opposition, and Col. Henry Laurens Vice-President. William Henry Drayton was, at the same time, elected Chief-Justice, with Thomas Bee, John Mathews and Henry Pendleton, Esqrs., Associate-Justices. An Admiralty Court was organized by the appointment of HUGH RUTLEDGE, a younger brother of the President, as judge;* and the Vice-President of the colony, with

* "The talents of Mr Hugh Rutledge were not perhaps equally brilliant, nor of so distinguished a cast as those of his brothers; but for solidity of judgment and strong manly sense, he was not inferior to either of them; and as a firm and intrepid patriot was pre-eminently distinguished by the cheerful performance of every duty to his country. He, too, like his brother Edward, was deemed of

the privy council, among whom were Judge Drayton and Charles Pinckney, exercised for the time being the powers of a court of Chancery.

Mr. Rutledge being present, as a member of the Assembly, when elected president and commander-in-chief, immediately delivered the following brief extemporaneous address :

"GENTLEMEN—The very great, unsolicited and unexpected honor which you have been pleased to confer on me, has overwhelmed me with gratitude and concern. Permit me to return you my most sincere thanks, for so distinguishing and unmerited a mark of your confidence and esteem. I have the deepest sense of this honor. The being called by the free suffrages of a brave and generous people, to preside over their welfare, is in my opinion the highest any man can receive. But dreading the weighty and arduous duties of this station, I really wish that your choice had fallen upon one better qualified to discharge them ; for, though in zeal and integrity I will yield to no man, in abilities to serve you I know my inferiority to many. Since, however, this, gentlemen, is your pleasure, although I foresee that by submitting to it I shall be ranked by our enemies amongst ambitious and designing men, by whom, they say, the people have been deceived and misled, yet as I have always thought every man's best services due to his country, no fear of slander or of difficulty or danger shall deter me from yielding mine. In so perilous a season as the present I will not withhold them ; but in her cause every moment of my time shall be employed. Happy indeed shall I be if those services answer your expectations, or my own wishes. On the candor of my worthy countrymen I rely to put the most favorable construction, as they hitherto have done, upon my actions. I assure myself of receiving, in the faithful discharge of my duty, the support and assistance of every good man in the colony ; and my most fervent prayer to the omnipotent Ruler

sufficient consequence to be made an object of peculiar persecution ; and being sent into exile, supported all the trials of long confinement and irritating restrictions with unshaken constancy. After his exchange, he filled the speaker's chair in the Legislature, greatly to the satisfaction of its members, and finally advanced to the Chancery bench, closed a life of usefulness with the applause and sincere regrets of his grateful country."—*Garden's Anecdotes.*

of the universe is, that under his gracious Providence the liberties of America may be forever preserved."

The president immediately, in presence of both houses, took the constitutional oath to sustain the new form of government, adding thereto the solemn asseveration that he would "cause law and justice in mercy to be executed, and to the utmost of my power maintain and defend the laws of God, the protestant religion, and the liberties of America."

Alluding to this in his speech to the legislative body, two weeks afterwards, when the session closed, President Rutledge remarks:

"On my part a most solemn oath has been taken for the faithful discharge of my duty. On yours a solemn assurance has been given to support me therein. Thus a public compact between us stands recorded. You may rest assured that I shall keep this oath ever in my mind; the Constitution shall be the invariable rule of my conduct; my ears shall be always open to the complaints of the injured; justice in mercy shall neither be denied nor delayed; our laws and religion, and the liberties of America, shall be maintained and defended to the utmost of my power. I repose the most perfect confidence in your engagements."

The speech from which the foregoing extract is taken contained a *resumé* of the various matters in dispute between the colonies and Great Britain, and an earnest appeal to the people, through their representatives. It was printed at the time, by order of the Assembly, in handbills, and circulated throughout the colony. The criticism passed upon it by the writer of the sketch of Rutledge, heretofore alluded to, seems, however, quite just; that the speech, reduced to writing, is not such a performance as would command attention now. Nor can it be compared for a moment with that forcible, spirit-stirring and masterly statement with which, under the form of a charge to the grand jury, Judge Drayton, a few days afterwards, opened the provincial courts under the authority of the Legislature, after they had been closed for a period of twelve months.*

* Judge William Henry Drayton was born at Drayton Hall, South Carolina, in September, 1742. At the age of eleven his father sent him to England, under the care of Charles Pinckney, for the purpose of prosecuting his studies with Mr. Pinckney's two sons, Charles Cotesworth and Thomas Pinckney. In the autumn

In the foregoing extract from President Rutledge's address, he speaks of the "solemn assurance" given by the Legislature to sustain him in his office. This assurance was contained in the address of both houses, presented a few days after his inauguration. It is curious to observe, however, that in this address the "accommodation with Great Britain" is still prominently put forward.

"We firmly trust you will make the Constitution the great rule of your conduct;"—it says—"and in the most solemn manner, we do assure your Excellency, that in the discharge of your duties under that Constitution, which looks forward to an accommodation with Great Britain (an event which, though traduced and treated as rebels, we still earnestly desire), we will support you with our lives and fortunes." President Rutledge, it appears, did not at this period look forward so anxiously toward this "accommodation," nor esteem it to be any part of his executive duties to bring it about. His language upon this subject is cautious and guarded: "Be persuaded that no man would embrace a just and equitable accommodation with Great Britain more gladly than myself; but until so desirable an object can be obtained, the defence of my country, and

of 1761 young Drayton entered Oxford, where he continued his studies nearly three years. Being obliged to return to America before the completion of his studies, he turned his attention, it is said, to law and politics. In 1771 he was appointed a privy councillor for the province of South Carolina, and on the decease of Judge Murray was commissioned, in January, 1774, by Lieutenant-Governor Bull, an assistant judge of the province until his Majesty's pleasure should be known thereon. Soon after the Continental Congress met at Philadelphia, and Judge Drayton, who had warmly espoused the cause of the colonists, addressed a very able pamphlet to the deputies in Congress, in which he stated the grievances of America, and drew up a bill of rights. This brought down upon him an accusation of the Chief-Justice, Gordon, and one of the Associate-Justices, before the Council, and Judge Drayton was finally superceded in March, 1775. The next year he was appointed Chief-Justice, under the Revolutionary government. In this capacity he re-opened the courts, and in various charges to the Grand Jury sustained the cause of the colonies with great boldness, vigor and ability. Judge Drayton was a member and President of the Provincial Congress of South Carolina. Subsequently, in 1778, he was elected a delegate to the Continental Congress. He died at Philadelphia, in September, 1799, while still a member of Congress, and Chief-Justice of South Carolina, in the thirty-seventh year of his age. "He was a statesman," says Dr. Ramsay, "of great decision and energy, and one of the ablest political writers South Carolina has produced."

the preservation of that Constitution, which from a perfect knowledge of the rights, and a laudable regard to the happiness of the people you have so wisely framed, shall engross my whole attention." The most sagacious intellects in the State had no doubt already begun to realize the momentous truth which a few months latter was demonstrated in the action of the Continental Congress, that accommodation with Great Britain was impossible. Thus Judge Drayton did not hesitate to express it in his celebrated charge to the Grand Jury, to which I have alluded. "The Almighty created America to be independent of Britain," he remarked ; "let us beware of the impiety of being backward to act as instruments in the Almighty hand, now extended to accomplish his purpose."

Installed as President and Commander-in-chief of the colony, Rutledge was soon called upon to exhibit his zeal and courage in the defence of his people. Up to this time South Carolina had been exempt from the presence of the enemy, and with the exception of a few royalists scattered here and there over the colony, very little opposition had been manifested to the new government. The royal Governor, Lord William Campbell, after vain efforts to excite the royalists to opposition, had some months previous to this time abandoned the government, and taken refuge on board a British sloop-of-war in the harbor of Charleston. He had promised his adherents before his departure that "his Majesty was determined to send out troops" to reduce the rebels to submission ; but for several months he awaited in vain the arrival of the expected aid. At length early in June, 1776, it was announced. The citizens of Charleston were suddenly aroused from their repose by the intelligence that a British fleet of forty or fifty vessels was at anchor about six leagues to the north of Sullivan's Island, carrying a formidable and overwhelming force under the command of Sir Henry Clinton, for the reduction of the rebellious province. Instantly the alarm was given, and every thing was in commotion in the colony. The President and Commander-in-chief was upon the scene of action ; and the firmness, decision and energy with which he guided public affairs at this critical moment, caused the superiority of his genius to be known and acknowledged by all. He immediately summoned the militia of the county to repair to Charleston ; he ordered the regiments already formed into active service; he exerted his authority to the utmost to arm, equip and supply the troops. His efforts were nobly seconded by the officers under his command. In the course of a few days five or six thousand men were assembled for the defence of Charleston. Congress, unable at that particular juncture to furnish any thing more valuable, sent the southern people a very experienced, and, as it was then supposed, a very able and skilful general, the eccentric Charles Lee, whose subsequent exploits by no means equalled his great reputation. It has been well remarked that it was fortunate for South Carolina at that juncture that she had placed at the head of her affairs a man so resolute and prompt, and a statesman so sagacious as John Rutledge. Without him, and with no councils to guide but those of General Lee, Charleston would most probably have fallen, and the royal Governor, Lord Campbell, have been reinstated in his authority, under the guns of the British squadron and the bayonets of Sir Henry Clinton's army.

One of the main points of defence to the city was upon Sullivan's Island, six miles nearer the sea than the neck of land on which Charleston stands, and so near the channel as to be a convenient post for annoying ships approaching the town. A rude fort had been erected on this island, constructed of timber of the Palmetto tree. This fort, subsequently known by the name of Fort Moultrie, from its heroic defender, with its little garrison of three hundred and forty-four men, was condemned by General Lee on his arrival, who declared it to be a "slaughter-pen," and advised President Rutledge to order its immediate abandonment. This Rutledge promptly declined, and heroically replied that "while a soldier remained alive to defend it, he would never give his sanction to such an order." "They will knock your fort about your heads in half an hour," remarked Gen. Lee to Moultrie, and actually proposed to diminish the number of troops on the island.* But Rutledge, taking counsel from the inspiration of his own courage, rather than from the skill of his experienced adviser, persisted in his resolution, and directed Moultrie to defend the fort to the last extremity.

* In a despatch to Moultrie, Gen. Lee, alluding to the force of about one thousand regulars and militia under Cols. Clark, Thompson and Horry stationed on the east end of Governor's Island, says: "I would order the whole body off the island, but apprehend it would make your garrison uneasy."

The attack on Fort Moultrie was made on the 28th of June. The British fleet consisted of ten vessels, two of which were fifty gun ships, and four frigates of twenty-eight guns each. The heroic and successful defence of the fort by Col. Moultrie constitutes a proud chapter in the revolutionary annals of South Carolina. For a moment, however, in the midst of that terrible cannonade, as the flag of the fortress fell to the beach, it seemed that Lee's prediction would be verified; that the fort would be battered down, and the garrison annihilated. But it was for a moment only. The same anxious eye that saw through the distance and the smoke of the battle, the flag-staff fall from the merlon, the next moment gazed upon a sight that caused every heart to thrill with exultation. A sergeant of grenadiers leaped from one of the embrasures of the fort upon the beach, into the open fire of the British guns, seized the fallen banner, and bearing it back amid a shower of balls, planted it once more upon the American works in triumph. This gallant soldier was Sergeant Jasper. Rutledge appropriately acknowledged his heroism after the battle, by presenting him with his own sword, in presence of the garrison, and tendering him a commission in the regiment.*

General Lee, it seems, could not be convinced, even after the battle had been raging two hours, that it was possible to beat off the British frigates. The following is his dispatch to Moultrie during the battle:

"DEAR COLONEL—If you should unfortunately expend your ammunition without beating off the enemy, or driving them on ground, *spike your guns, and retreat with all the order possible.*"

But the gallant Moultrie had no thought of retreat. The inspiration of courage was with him the inspiration of hope, and the assurance of success. Not even the positive command of Lee would

* Jasper proudly accepted the sword, but declined the commission. "Were I made an officer," he modestly said, "my comrades would be constantly blushing for my ignorance, and I should be unhappy, feeling my own inferiority. I have no ambition for higher rank than that of a sergeant." Mr. Garden says, in his Anecdotes, that the subsequent conduct of Jasper was exemplary—but in the details which he had seen carried too much the air of romance to be dwelt upon. He fell, mortally wounded, while vainly endeavoring to plant the colors of his regiment on the walls of Savannah.

have drawn him from his post while a single cannon remained mounted, or one palmetto log lay upon another. He had in his pocket the directions of his own commander-in-chief—received on the morning of the battle—and they coincided too closely with his own determined bravery to be disregarded. These directions were given in the following laconic and characteristic sentences :

"General Lee wishes you to evacuate the fort. You will not do so without an order from me. *I would sooner cut off my hand than write one.*" J. RUTLEDGE."

During the whole of the engagement, President Rutledge was in active duty among the citizens and soldiers, who had crowded to their various posts of defence in the city, with arms in their hands, determined to fight every inch of ground from the waters' edge, if the enemy should finally overpower the fort and garrison, and effect a landing. While Lee was talking of retreat, Rutledge was devising means to supply the garrison with ammunition. At the height of the engagement he sent in a quantity of powder, with the following despatch to Moultrie :

"I send you five hundred pounds of powder. You know our collection is not great. Honor and victory, my good sir, to you and our worthy countrymen with you. Do not make too free with your cannon. *Cool and do mischief.*"

The advice was followed to the letter. The officers from the fort managed the guns with such skill, that nearly every shot took effect. The Thunder Bomb, after discharging sixty shells, was disabled. The Acteon was so crippled that after the action she was abandoned and blew up. The Bristol, fifty gun ship, had every man on her quarter-deck killed or wounded, and with the Experiment, the other fifty gun ship, sustained a loss of sixty-three killed and one hundred and forty-seven wounded. Finally, after a cannonade of eight or ten hours without intermission, the squadron slipped its cables and retired, bearing away Lord William Campbell mortally wounded. Thus ended the threatened invasion of South Carolina.

Congress returned a vote of thanks to *General Lee*, and Colonels Moultrie and Thomson, for their good conduct on this memorable day. The result of that day was of the utmost importance to South

Carolina. It removed the foot of the invader from her soil, and gave her peace and tranquillity for a period of nearly three years.

On the fourth of July, 1776, six days after the battle, President Rutledge officially visited the garrison on Sullivan's Island, for the purpose of returning thanks to them for their gallant conduct in defence of the fortress. It was upon this occasion that, looking around him with an eye beaming with exultation, and kindling with pride, he broke forth into one of those fiery and impassioned harangues to which the inspirations of genius, warmed into life by the glow of passionate feeling, can alone give utterance. Pointing to the azure banner which now floated in triumph over one of the bastions of the fortress, he singled out from the ranks the gallant soldier who had planted it there amid the fire of the British cannon, and after pronouncing a beautiful encomium upon his heroism, gracefully presented him the sword which he ungirded from his own side.

A cotemporary of Rutledge * had the good fortune to meet him many years afterwards, on this very spot, and he has recorded the words he then uttered—his eye kindling with delight, and his voice trembling with emotion, as the recollections of other days clustered thick around him. "I remember," he exclaimed, "the engagement, as if it were fought but yesterday! I remember my perfect confidence in Moultrie! I have all the scene before me, too, when I visited the post to express the thanks of the country to the heroes who defended it. *There* stood Moultrie—*there* Motte—*there* Marion, Horry, and the intrepid band whom they commanded. I addressed them with an energy of feeling that I had never before experienced; and if ever I had pretensions to eloquence, it was at that moment." The same gentleman who has given this account, adds, that Rutledge, becoming animated as he spoke, as though his old companions in arms and in council were immediately before him, "delivered himself in an eloquent and impressive strain of eulogy, so perfectly fascinating, that had his first address but borne a shadow of resemblance to it, there could not have been a man among his auditors who would not have been proud to die for liberty and his country."

On the very day that Rutledge visited Fort Moultrie to express

* Mr. Alexander Garden. See his Anecdotes of the Revolution.

the thanks of a grateful country to its heroic defenders, the American Congress at Philadelphia, declared the colonies FREE AND INDEPENDENT STATES. The news of this great event arrived in Charleston at a most auspicious period. It found the minds of the people fully prepared for it. There was no longer any talk of an "accommodation" with Great Britain. The threatened invasion of South Carolina, and the glorious defence of Fort Moultrie, had rendered accommodation impossible. The declaration was received with every demonstration of joy, amid the firing of cannon and the ringing of bells, and was publicly read to the troops under arms. In transmitting it to the Legislature, Governor Rutledge said, "It is an event which necessity had rendered not only justifiable, but absosolutely unavoidable. It is a decree now worthy of America. We thankfully receive the notification of, and rejoice at it; and we are determined at every hazard to endeavor to maintain it, that so, after we have departed, our children and their latest posterity may have cause to bless our memory." In response to the President's address, the General Assembly expressed "the joy and satisfaction" with which they had received the intelligence, and their hearty approval of the Declaration of Independence.

The General Assembly was dissolved on the 21st of October of this year, and a new election held, agreeably to the Constitution. The result of the election was the return of nearly all the old members. The Assembly met on the 5th December, and soon after re-elected Rutledge President of the State, and Col. Laurens Vice-President.

During the period of a year and upward, in which he continued to discharge the duties of this office, but little of interest occurred in South Carolina. A formidable Indian invasion was briskly met and successfully repelled, and the savages, attacked on all sides, sued for peace. A treaty between them and the State was soon after signed, by which the Indians ceded a considerable part of their territory, and the frontier settlement thereafter continued to remain in undisturbed tranquillity. Throughout the entire State business revived, and agriculture flourished. Commerce increased. Rutledge's administration was everywhere successful and fortunate. So much tranquillity reigned in every part of South Carolina, says Dr.

Ramsay, that after the departure of the British fleet and army, in July, and the termination of the Cherokee expedition, in October, 1776, the bulk of the people was scarcely sensible of any revolution, or that the country was at war.

But this tranquillity was about to be broken. A more formidable invasion was preparing against the southern states than the futile attempt in 1776, and the people of South Carolina were about to experience in its most fearful and appalling shape, the horror of civil war. Before entering upon this narrative, however, it is proper to glance at the change which, in the mean time, occurred in the form of the new State government, inasmuch as the subject is intimately connected with Mr. Rutledge's history.

The temporary Constitution, as has been observed, was ratified in March, 1776. It was designed to last only until an "accommodation of the differences between Great Britain and America should take place." The Declaration of Independence rendered it necessary to adopt a new and permanent Constitution and form of government. This was the work of the deliberative branches of the Legislature during part of the year 1777, and having been completed, it was finally passed into a law in March, 1778, and presented to the President for his ratification. Rutledge disapproved the proposed plan of government, and refused to give it his assent. Unwilling, however, to obstruct the wishes of the people as expressed through their delegates, he tendered his resignation as President, leaving the Legislature to choose another executive magistrate to carry out their demands by the approval of the proposed Constitution.

The reasons of his refusal to approve this measure were expressed in a speech of some length, delivered to both houses on the occasion of his resignation. These reasons do not appear to be entirely satisfactory, and would probably fail to convince any one at this day of the correctness of his position. The new form of government differed from the old in some important particulars. Not to mention the change in the appellation of the commonwealth from colony to State, and of the chief-magistrate from President to Governor, there were some essential and fundamental alterations proposed. Thus the legislative body was reduced from three to two branches. The second branch, instead of being elected by the Assembly from their own body, were to be elected by the people ; and a rotation was established in the office of Governor and the other principal offices of the State. Rutledge refused his assent to the bill on the ground first of a want of power to pass it ;* and secondly, admitting the power, that the system itself was objectionable. He thought the people "preferred the present mode of electing a legislative council to that which is offered for electing a senate, probably because it appeared more likely that persons of the greatest integrity, learning and abilities, should be chosen by and from amongst these representatives when assembled, than by electors in their several districts." Remarking upon the policy of the change proposed, he says : "Certain it is that systems which in theory have been much admired, on trial have not succeeded ; and that projects and experiments relative to government are of all schemes the most dangerous and fatal. The people having adopted such a Constitution as appeared to them most perfect, when it is not even surmised that any grievance or inconvenience has arisen from it, and when they are satisfied with and happy under it (which I firmly believe they are), if we had authority, I should conceive it neither politic, expedient, nor justifiable to change this form for another, especially as I think that the one proposed will not be better than, or so good as what we now enjoy ; and whether it would or not, is a speculative point which time only can determine."

Rutledge thereupon resigned his office of President, and recommended the election of some person who would be able to give the necessary assent and ratification to the new Constitution. The Legislature accepted his resignation, and immediately elected Hon. Rawlins Lowndes, President, who soon after gave his assent to the Constitution, which thus became the fundamental law of the State.

Mr. Rutledge now retired for a brief period from the public service, although we are assured on good authority that his resignation did not in the least "diminish his popularity." This is evident in

* There is some force in this objection. The Legislature was certainly not elected with a view of framing a new Constitution. But the difference between a mere legislative act, and the passage of a fundamental law or Constitutional provision, was not so well understood at that day as it is now.

the fact that soon after, in a time of real danger, when a formidable invasion threatened the State, and when gloom and darkness overspread the whole country, he was recalled, and again replaced at the helm.

In this time of general alarm, says the historian of South Carolina, John Rutledge, by the almost unanimous voice of his countrymen, was called to the chair of government. Although he had opposed the adoption of the new system, he did not hesitate for a moment to accept the trust, and as Governor of the State took the oath of fidelity to the Constitution. With characteristic promptness and energy he immediately set about devising means for the defence of the country. The British General, Prevost, with two thousand men, had crossed over into Carolina, while General Lincoln, with the main body of the American army, was commencing offensive operations in Georgia. A small force under General Moultrie lay at Black Swamp, between Prevost and the capital of South Carolina. Rutledge, in the capacity of Governor and commander-in-chief, summoned the State militia to his camp at Orangeburgh, near the centre of the State, and put himself at their head, prepared to march wherever the public exigencies required. From this camp he dispatched Col. Simmons, with a thousand men, to reinforce Moultrie. Before the juncture was effected, Moultrie retreated to Tulifinny Bridge, keeping between the advancing British army and Charleston. Prevost followed, apparently with the design of attacking Charleston, and Rutledge thereupon set his whole force in motion, with the view of joining Moultrie at Tulifinny, and disputing with the British the possession of the capital. On the second day of his march he received advices that Moultrie had abandoned his post and was slowly retreating before a superior British force toward Charleston. This intelligence changed the plan of Gov. Rutledge, who immediately marched with all the forces under his command to the defence of the capital.

Moultrie and Rutledge reached Charleston about the same time, the 9th and 10th of May. Their arrival gave hopes of a successful defence, particularly as by the efforts of Lieutenant-Governor Bee and the Council, the town had been placed in a respectable state of defence on the land side. This confidence was increased a day or two after by the arrival of the gallant Pulaski, with his legionary corps, almost at the same moment that the advance guard of the British appeared on Charleston neck.

The American forces, however, were far inferior to the British, and it seems doubtful whether they would have been able to sustain an assault upon their lines. It was supposed that General Lincoln, with the main army, was in pursuit of Prevost, but his position was entirely unknown. In this emergency it was of the utmost importance to the Americans to gain time, and accordingly a conference was opened with General Prevost on the subject of a capitulation. The British General offered "peace and protection" to the inhabitants, and, to such as declined to submit, that they should be received as prisoners of war. This was refused by the garrison as dishonorable, and an interview between the officers of the army proposed to confer on terms. It is somewhat surprising to find at this conference, the officers of the garrison proposing "a neutrality during the war between Great Britain and America; and that the question whether the State shall belong to Great Britain, or remain one of the United States, be determined by the treaty of peace between these powers." It seems a confession on the part of South Carolina of utter inability to contribute to the general defence of the States. Still more surprising is it to find this proposition rejected by General Prevost, who claimed that "as the garrison was in arms, they must surrender prisoners of war." This was refused, and the garrison and citizens of Charleston determining to defend their works to the last extremity, prepared to sustain an immediate assault. All night the garrison stood to their guns, and the people remained in a state of suspense, expecting each moment an attack by the enemy. The morning relieved their apprehensions. The cry of "the enemy is gone," resounded along the lines, and Prevost was seen in full retreat. Intelligence had probably been received by him of the arrival of Lincoln, and the threatened assault was abandoned. Count Pulaski pursued the retreating British with his cavalry, but they crossed the Ashley river before he came up with them. The capital was again for a brief period rescued from the hands of the enemy.

The unsuccessful attempt of Prevost was followed the next year by a more systematic and formidable attack. The capture of Charleston was now threatened in earnest. Sir Henry Clinton, sailing from New York with a powerful and well-appointed army of twelve thousand men, landed on the 11th of February, 1780, within thirty miles of Charleston. Gov. Rutledge, with an insufficient garrison, under the command of Lincoln, was at his post for the defence of the town. The militia came in slowly ; supplies were far from abundant ; the aid ordered by Congress for the defence of Charleston had not arrived ; every thing seemed favorable for the enemy ; and had Sir. Henry Clinton on his arrival marched at once upon the town, it would doubtless have fallen at a blow.

In this emergency the assembly, then in session, acted with much spirit. They resolved unanimously that Charleston should be defended to the last extremity. Soon after it was determined to clothe the Governor and his Council with an *absolute dictatorship,* and accordingly they delegated "till ten days after their next session, to the Governor, John Rutledge, Esq., and such of his Council as he could conveniently consult, a power to do every thing necessary for the public good, except the taking away the life of a citizen without a legal trial ;" after which the Assembly adjourned. Armed with this formidable power, the Governor immediately placed himself in co-operation with the military authority in command of the town. He ordered the militia to rendezvous, but the call was disregarded. Thereupon he issued a proclamation requiring "such of the militia as were regularly drafted, and all the inhabitants and owners of property in the town, to repair to the American standard, and join the garrison immediately, on pain of confiscation." But the proclamation produced as little effect as the former order. The approach of the British army seemed to have chilled the hopes and paralyzed the minds of the inhabitants.

Rutledge and Lincoln, however, did not yet despair. What men could do was done by them. The lines were increased and strengthened—a citadel erected, and works thrown up on all sides of the town. But it seemed to be manifest even before the batteries of the British were opened, that resistance was hopeless. Notwithstanding every exertion to reinforce the garrison, only four thousand troops could be collected within the lines. They were too few to defend the extensive works around the city; the works themselves were weak and badly served with artillery, and the fall of Charleston seemed certain. Then it was that on the pressing solicitation of Lincoln, it was decided that in order to preserve the civil and executive authority of the State, in the event of the fall of the capital, Governor Rutledge and three of his Council should retire, and Lieutenant-Governor Gadsden with the other five of that body should remain within the lines. It was thought that the presence of the Governor, clothed as he was with dictatorial power, was necessary in the country, not only to raise levies for the relief of the capital, but to organize a new resistance in the event of its fall. Accordingly on the 12th April, Gov. Rutledge, with Messrs. Charles Pinckney, Daniel Huger, and John L. Gervaise, left Charleston. On the same day the British batteries were opened; and on the 12th May, General Lincoln, after a stout resistance, surrendered.

The wisdom of the Assembly in delegating plenary power to Rutledge and such of his council as he "could conveniently consult," was now apparent. It was the sole power, executive, legislative, or judicial, left remaining of the new government; and although for some time after the fall of Charleston it was scarcely anything more than the shadow of a name, yet it was still a rallying point for the patriots, or at least it might become such at some future and more auspicious day. Rutledge endeavored to collect the militia and march to the relief of Charleston. Failing in this, he attempted to make a stand on the north side of the Santee, and rally forces in sufficient numbers to renew the struggle for the dominion of the State. Several parties of Americans, including three hundred Continentals of the Virginia line, under Colonel Buford, had advanced into the northern part of the State, but after the fall of the capital, and the rapid approach of the British northward, they retreated toward North Carolina. Tarleton's brigade having overtaken Buford's command, barbarously massacred the greater portion of it, after a feeble resistance, and even after the men had sued for quarter, and surrendered. On every side the royalists were triumphant—not a single company of Americans was in the field—and the war in South Carolina was apparently at an end.

But even in this gloomy crisis the restless and indomitable spirit of John Rutledge, unbroken by defeat, and still hopeful of success, was meditating new plans for the defence of the country. Driven, with scarcely an escort, by Tarleton's dragoons, beyond the frontiers of his native State, he hastened with all despatch to solicit succor from the States of North Carolina, Virginia, and from Congress. A detachment of fourteen hundred Continentals was already on its march towards the South, under the command of the brave and chivalrous De Kalb. The appeals of Gov. Rutledge to North Carolina and Virginia, seem to have been successful, for each of those States detailed a body of militia to co-operate with the Continental army; and on the 15th of August, Gen. Gates, who had been assigned to the Southern department, found himself near Camden at the head of an army of three thousand five hundred effective men. The forces under Lord Cornwallis, who had been left in command of the British after Sir Henry Clinton's departure, were far inferior in point of numbers, but admirably disciplined, and flushed with victory. Gates, in the full *prestige* of his late triumph at Saratoga, rashly confident in himself and in his own fortune, risked a battle and lost it. His defeat was total. It was more than a defeat—it was a rout—almost an annihilation. Such a terrible overthrow had not been sustained by any American General during the war.* Gates fled from Camden to Hillsborough in North Carolina, where he attempted to rally the wreck of this unfortunate army. Here, it seems, he was met by Governor Rutledge. The appearance of the American army—the army which Rutledge had so fondly hoped was destined to effect the liberation of South Carolina, was pitiable in the extreme. Nothing but the mere wreck, the *tristes reliquiæ*, of that army, remained; and in its destruction Rutledge witnessed the ruin of those hopes he had so warmly and so ardently cherished. But the eager reproach, if he had any to make, must have died upon his lips as he encountered the commanding general. The pride

* The main error of Gen. Gates seems to have consisted in his rashness in risking a battle without taking the necessary precautions in case of disaster. His arrangements on the field appear to have been skillfully made, and it was certainly no fault of his that he could not make the Virginia militia stand fire, or the North Carolina militia face the British bayonet. Had his whole force consisted of Delaware and Maryland Continentals, the issue of that unfortunate day would have been far different.

of Gates had been crushed—the iron had entered his soul—he was a humbled and a broken man. He had seen in a day the laurels of victory wither upon his brow ; he had rashly reached out his hand to pluck the tempting fruit, and it had turned to ashes upon his lips. Gates, in his little camp at Hillsborough, was an object of sympathy, not of reproach. The conqueror of Burgoyne, who had returned laden with the spoils of Saratoga, had become the fugitive of Camden. It was the spectacle of the vanquished Hector :

> *Hei mihi! qualis erat! quantum mutatus ab illo*
> *Hectore, qui redit exuvias indutus Achillis.*

Immediately after the defeat of Gates at Camden, news of a fresh disaster reached the ears of Rutledge. This was the surprise and dispersion of the corps of General Sumpter, who for some time past had carried on a successful partisan warfare against the British and tories in South Carolina. That gallant officer, on hearing of Gates' defeat, began a rapid retreat up the Wateree river, with three hundred prisoners and a quantity of captured stores. But he was unable to escape the march of Tarleton, who had been dispatched from the victorious British army in pursuit. The Americans, having been four days without sleep or provisions, were surprised at Fishing Creek, and completely dispersed. The three hundred prisoners were liberated, and all the stores recaptured. South Carolina again lay prostrate and powerless beneath the foot of the invader.

These repeated disasters would have overcome a man of less firmness and courage than Rutledge. But he did not despair—he did not cease to hope and to labor. Placing himself in communication with the remains of Gates' army, he applied all his energies and influence to the task of re-organizing that army, and keeping it in the field. His services, in this respect, were invaluable ; and their worth was duly estimated by the penetrating judgment of General Greene, on his taking the command, as I shall presently have occasion to notice.

The admirable discernment and sagacity of Rutledge were displayed in a remarkable degree, in his estimate of the character and ability of others. His keen glance penetrated through the ranks of the army, and selected for the highest trusts those active and vigorous partisan leaders, who, by means of their own indomitable energy and unaided resources, revived the war against the enemy, brought hope to the minds of the despairing, and contributed, in no small degree, to the final triumph. By virtue of his authority as governor and commander-in-chief, he commissioned SUMPTER, as a brigadier-general, when, after the fall of Charleston, that indefatigable and gallant soldier, penetrating into the thickets and swamps of South Carolina, with his handful of adherents, entered upon that successful and active career which we have seen checked, but by no means closed, by his misfortune at Fishing Creek. He conferred, also, the same elevated rank upon PICKENS and upon FRANCIS MARION, the most famous partisan leader in our revolutionary annals, whom we have seen commencing his service as a captain in one of the first regiments raised in South Carolina, and between whom and Rutledge the most intimate confidence subsequently existed. The same quick perception of high military endowments led him to discover the great capacity of Col. Morgan, and to urge successfully upon Congress the claims of that gallant officer to be made a Brigadier-General. These claims were recognized ; the commission was issued ; Greene, on his arrival at the southern camp, found Morgan at the head of his riflemen in Gates' army ; and, dividing his forces, entrusted him with a separate command. The glorious victory of the Cowpens followed, in which the haughty Tarleton, at the head of a superior force, for the first time was made to bite the dust. The result was highly honorable to the American arms, and while it covered Morgan and his troop with renown, furnished proof of the wisdom and discernment of both Rutledge and the commanding General.

It appears that Gov. Rutledge remained with the army after the defeat of Gates on the 16th of August, 1780, up to the time of the arrival of the new commander, General Greene. Heretofore the selection of a commander-in-chief in the southern department had been made by Congress. General Lee had been assigned to this post in 1776 ; General Lincoln, a brave, experienced, and meritorious officer, took the command during the campaign which resulted in the unfortunate capitulation of Charleston ; and Gen. Gates, the most distinguished officer in the service, succeeded him in that unfortunate campaign which ended in the rout at Camden. The duty of selecting a commander-in-chief in the southern department was now imposed by Congress on Washington. It was observed at the commencement of this sketch that the wisdom and sagacity of Washington were never displayed in a more striking manner than in his appointments to places of high official trust and responsibility. Upon the present occasion, his discriminating judgment amounted almost to prescience. His choice fell upon Nathaniel Greene, an officer whose subsequent brilliant career merited the handsome compliment passed upon him by the officers of the army in a series of resolutions, expressing the articles of their faith, one of which was to the effect, that "Nathaniel Greene was born a General."

The American army had moved down from Hillsborough to Charlotte, and Greene arrived at head-quarters on the 2d of December, 1780. Here, it seems, he met Rutledge. Each of these distinguished men, at a glance, appreciated and comprehended the other. Each looked upon the other as a man of commanding genius and great capacity, and the confidence of mutual esteem and respect was at once established between them. To Greene, Rutledge appeared "the first character" he had ever met with; and to Rutledge, the commanding general was from the outset, as he afterwards officially expressed it, "the great and gallant General Greene."

It required, however, all the energies and resources of these two distinguished men to reassure the troops, to furnish them food and clothing, and, in short, to reconstruct from nothing, the southern army. Offensive operations seemed to be desperate and chimerical. The entire force of the American army at the south was but about two thousand men, continentals and militia. They were without pay and almost without clothing; to say nothing of ammunition. The procuring of provisions was of itself a most difficult matter. Impressment seemed to be the only source; and the country had been so ravaged that all which could be obtained, even in that way, was far from sufficient. In order to carry on the business in the least offensive way, and not to alienate the people, the duty of impressment was transferred from the military to the civil authority.

In this emergency, the assistance of Rutledge was of the highest importance. Greene expresses his indebtedness to him soon after the battle of the Cowpens, in one of his communications, from which I extract the following passage: "The situation of these States is wretched, and the distress of the inhabitants beyond all description. Nor is the condition of the army more agreeable. We have but few troops that are fit for duty, and all those are employed upon different detachments, the success of which depends upon time and chance. We are obliged to subsist ourselves by our own industry, *aided by the influence of Governor Rutledge, who is one of the first characters I ever met with.* Our prospects are gloomy," &c.

Notwithstanding this almost desperate condition of affairs, Greene took the field during the winter of 1780, with his almost naked troops, without food, without clothing, marching without shoes over frozen and flinty roads, which gashed the feet of his soldiers, marking with blood every step of their progress, and commenced that series of masterly and brilliant movements which finally resulted in the liberation of South Carolina, and the capture of Cornwallis in Virginia.* The great qualities of Greene were coolness, courage, and caution. He entered into action with no arrogant confidence of success, nor without counting the cost of disaster, and making preparations for retreat. Unlike his predecessor at Camden, he never went into battle without leaving his baggage and stores a sufficient distance in the rear. Hence defeat never disconcerted or disheartened him; though beaten, he was never vanquished; at every overthrow, he arose, Antæas-like, prouder and stronger from the fall. I shall not follow him during that toilsome and terrible campaign, which, ending with the brilliant battle of Eutaw Springs, virtually destroyed the British power in the South, and liberated the State of South Carolina. It comprised a series of marches, battles, and military maneuvres, where success would have done credit to the genius of the most skilful and veteran commander.

Rutledge, it seems, was at the camp at Haw River, March 8th,

* After the battle at Guilford Court House, though Lord Cornwallis was ostensibly the victor, he retreated to Wilmington, and from thence, instead of returning to South Carolina, retired into Virginia, where he remained until captured at Yorktown.

1781. From this point, he addresses a letter to General Marion, declaring his intention of proceeding to Philadelphia in a few days, with a view of procuring, if possible, some supplies of clothing for the militia, whose distress for want of it gave him great concern.* This mission was undoubtedly undertaken at the urgent request of General Greene, and was the more readily undertaken, because he says his remaining could be of little service to the State, inasmuch as it had become impracticable to return immediately into South Carolina, or even if that were possible, to re-establish a civil government there, for some time. His watchful care over the provincial militia is also manifest in this communication. He speaks of sending to Marion some blank commissions, and, in the mean time, authorizes him to give brevets, and in order to maintain sufficient authority over the officers in his brigade, empowers him to remove any of them, and appoint others in their stead. He has sent, he says, some linen, to be distributed among Marion's, Sumpter's, and Pickens' brigades, as a free gift from the States, and requests Marion to send him, by express to Gen. Greene, a list of such articles of clothing as he may need, with a view of obtaining them at Philadelphia.

On the retreat of Cornwallis to Virginia, General Greene at once marched into South Carolina, and, in conjunction with those active partisan leaders, Marion, Sumpter, and Pickens, commenced offensive operations against the British and tories. His efforts during the spring and summer were crowned with great success, and the enemy were dispossessed of most of their posts in the upper country, and driven back into the vicinity of Charleston. The time had now arrived for Rutledge to return, and again establish civil government over the wasted and desolate country. Clothed with ample power for that purpose, he set about this important work with his characteristic ability and energy; and sustained as he now was by the

* His mission to Philadelphia seems to have been not entirely unsuccessful. The following is an extract from the Journal of Congress, of June 20th, 1781: "On motion of Mr. Matthews, seconded by Mr. Bee, Resolved, that the board of war be directed to furnish Governor Rutledge with four wagons for transporting clothing to the State of South Carolina, which wagons, when discharged by the said Gov. Rutledge, to be delivered over to the orders of the commanding general of the Southern army."

strong arm of a military force, his proclamations and ordinances contributed greatly to the re-establishment of order and law among the citizens of the State.

His first proclamation is issued under the great seal of the State, from the high hills of the Santee, on the 5th of August, 1781, and is directed against those marauders, who, under pretence of indemnifying themselves for losses of property, or that such property belonged to tories or the enemies of the State, had committed and continued to commit "most wanton and rapacious acts of plundering." In case such plundered property is not immediately restored, or these practices are repeated, he threatens "speedy and effectual punishment" on the offenders ; and he charges the civil officers of the State to bring all such culprits to justice, and commands the military officers to lend their aid to the civil power. By such timely and vigorous measures, Rutledge in a short time succeeded in re-establishing order and security in such parts of the State as had been recovered from the enemy. Magistrates were appointed,* property secured, and confusion and anarchy gave place to order and regular government.

Some of the measures of Rutledge, at this period, were harsh and severe, but necessarily and justly so. Clothed with an arbitrary and dictatorial power, he retaliated with a heavy hand upon the royalists. Nor did he shrink from bringing odium upon his own authority, among the friends of the State, by resorting to impressment, when necessary, to sustain his lieutenants in the field, or the army of Greene in its now successful career against the enemy. In order to raise money and means, he had undertaken, on his return from Philadelphia, to put in operation the ideas he had obtained from that able financier, Robert Morris, in relation to the establishment of a bank ; † but his route lying through a tract of country where the inhabitants were little acquainted with commerce, he unfortu-

* So early as the 13th August, 1781, and before the battle of Eutaw, he writes to Marion, expressing his intention of appointing *Ordinaries* in each District, to prove wills, grant letters testamentary, and transact other business within the jurisdiction of such officers ; and requests Marion to recommend suitable persons who will undertake the offices of Ordinary for the Georgetown, Cheraw, and Charleston Districts.

† See subsequent sketch of Chief-Justice Ellsworth.

nately, as Greene informed Morris, "met with none who were willing to interest themselves in a bank." Money or its equivalent, however, must be had,* and Rutledge did not hesitate to resort to the law of extreme necessity. We find him soon after, directing the seizure of a large quantity of indigo, and placing it to the credit of the army. "I have appointed Captain Richardson," he writes to Marion, "to procure indigo and specie for public use, and request that you will give him every assistance in your power, to aid him in this business. If he should want an escort, or any military aid, you will be pleased to furnish him." In regard to reprisals upon the British and royalists, his course was no less decided and bold. It was, however, always governed by motives of public policy, and never by a spirit of wanton revenge. He scorned to imitate the barbarities of Tarleton, or that cold-blooded act of cruelty which disgraces the memory of Lord Rawdon, the murderer of the gallant Hayne. That "last and stinging outrage," as it has been justly called, might well have caused the flame which had been kindled in Rutledge's bosom to "burst forth with consuming energy." But we look in vain for any "comprehensive system of reprisals," or act of retaliation, which is not strictly justified by the laws of war, as well as in accordance with an enlarged and liberal policy. Thus, just before the battle of Eutaw, when the British ordered the wives and families of the prisoners who had been taken at the capitulation of Charleston, to withdraw from the State, Rutledge retaliated by sending the families of the loyalists and adherents of Britain, within the enemy's lines at Charleston. "Justice to our friends," he remarks in a letter to Marion, "whose wives and families the enemy have sent out of the State, and *policy* require that we should send into the enemy's lines the wives and families of all such men as are now with and adhere to the British." And although the death of Hayne had already taken place, and Rutledge himself had witnessed the horrible outrages committed by the infu-

* The utter destitution of the army and the great scarcity of money are shown in a letter from Rutledge to his favorite lieutenant, Marion, in charge of one of the military districts of the State. It is dated soon after Rutledge's return: "I entirely forgot, when I saw you last," he says, "to mention what I intended before we met, that if a little *hard money, 30 or 35 guineas*, would be useful for getting information, or other service, I have this sum ready for you."

riated royalists, yet he immediately adds : "I lament the distresses which many innocent women and children may probably suffer by this measure, but they must follow the fate of their husbands and parents. Blame can only be imputed to the latter, and to the British commanders, whose conduct, on the principle of retaliation, justifies this step, which, all circumstances considered, is an indispensable one." He then directs Marion to give the necessary orders to enforce the measure within the district of his brigade.

The impressments ordered by Rutledge, in virtue of his supreme civil authority in the State, were carried out with as much leniency and system as the nature of the case allowed. This authority he held in his own hand, and never suffered it to be executed except under his own warrant. Accordingly, we find him sharply rebuking Col. Horry, who, it seems, attempted to execute such a power beyond the instructions he had received. "I know of no authority," he says in a subsequent letter to Marion, "that any continental officer, or any other person, whoever he may be, has to impress in this State. Gen. Greene, it is true, did, before my return, direct him (Col. Horry) to impress, but he has never (I believe, and indeed I am well persuaded of it) since my return, give any such power to any one. He knows better." Rutledge then laments the abuse of this power, which furnished so just a cause of complaint to the people, and directs Marion, with whom he seems to be constantly advised, and in whose judgment he reposed the most unlimited confidence, to correct this abuse, as far as it might be practicable, within his district: "I find every authority may be abused, and perhaps that which I have given on this head may be, also. Therefore, to cut the matter short, wherever you find that it is wantonly exercised, and an oppressive and improper use is made of it, within the district of your brigade, I give you full authority to order the officer attempting to impress such subjects to cease from it, or to have them restored, if impressed. It would give me great pleasure to redress every encroachment on the liberties of the people ; and I shall certainly do so as far as my power extends, in any of the cases which you say you will mention to me when we meet."

The celebrated battle of Eutaw was fought on the 8th of September, 1781. Governor Rutledge was present in this engagement, and acted in the staff of General Greene. The good conduct of the South Carolina militia and State troops on that day, was a matter of pride and satisfaction to their commander-in-chief. The militia, under the orders of Marion and Pickens, formed a portion of the front line, and the eye of Rutledge lighted up with exultation as it witnessed the courage and firmness with which they advanced under the fire of the British, delivering seventeen rounds before falling back for support upon the second line, formed of the Maryland and Virginia Continentals. The South Carolina State Corps, under the gallant Colonel Henderson, covered the left, and behaved with equal spirit and gallantry. Their good conduct on that day was such as to deserve a special notice in the resolutions of Congress, one of which expressed thanks "to the State corps of South Carolina, for the zeal, activity and firmness by them exhibited, throughout the engagement." It must be added, that the North Carolina militia, forming also a portion of the front line, on this occasion, behaved with great gallantry and spirit.*

* It is scarcely possible to account for the defection and shameful conduct of the provincial militia in some of the actions during the Revolution. At the unfortunate battle of Camden, the North Carolina militia were placed in the centre and the Virginia militia, under the gallant General Stevens, on the left. As Stevens was leading his brigade to the attack and had advanced within fifty paces of the British column, the latter charged with a cheer, and the Virginians, throwing down their arms, fled in the utmost disorder. The greater part of the militia of North Carolina followed, without firing a shot, leaving the Maryland and Delaware Continentals to sustain the brunt of the battle. At the battle of Guilford Court House the same mortifying circumstance took place. Greene had formed three lines, placing the North Carolina militia in the front, the Virginia militia in the second, and that ever reliable and heroic corps of Maryland Continentals, with the Virginia Continentals, in the rear. As the British advanced, and while yet distant 140 yards, the North Carolina militia gave way, most of them without firing a shot. The Virginia militia behaved better, perhaps under the good influence of the precaution taken by General Stevens, who had posted some riflemen twenty paces in the rear of his brigade, with orders to shoot every man who should leave his post.

The Continentals, on the other hand, always behaved with the utmost gallantry and spirit. They fought with the discipline of veterans, and the heroism of men worthy to be free. It may with truth be said, that no better soldiers were ever mustered into any service than those fourteen hundred gallant troops of the Maryland and Delaware line which marched under Baron De Kalb to the South, and so

This decisive action forced back the enemy to their lines at Charleston, extended the jurisdiction of the Americans over nearly every other portion of the State, and may be considered as closing the war in South Carolina. The civil government, represented in the person of Rutledge on the field, was literally re-established in South Carolina, at the cannon's mouth, and amid the smoke and carnage of battle.

Though the greater part of the State was thus rescued from British dominion, yet for some time after this, no other civil government was established than the authority vested in Rutledge's hands as Governor and commander-in-chief. His proclamations had all the force and effect of laws, and they were sustained, as far as was possible in those unsettled times, by the military. Thus a few days after the battle of Eutaw, we find him sending to Marion copies of three proclamations, which he promises to have printed "as soon as a press can be got to work." He directs Marion to deliver to each colonel copies, with orders to read them at the head of his regiment, and circulate through the district. The same course was no doubt pursued in regard to the other districts of the State, and in this manner these proclamations or temporary laws were promulgated. One of the proclamations referred to directed a suspension of the acts making Continental and State money a lawful tender, and directing in future all fines to be paid in specie. The worthlessness of the paper currency, it seems, had rendered fines nugatory, and the public exigencies demanded that where the law directed a penalty it should be rigorously enforced.

About the same time also he writes to Marion for counsel and advice in regard to a very important subject, namely, as to the policy of offering a free pardon to such as had joined the enemy, with

nobly sustained themselves after the flight of the militia on the fatal field of Camden. Every man was a hero, and those who fell, like the slaughtered Athenians at Marathon, deserved their names inscribed upon a monument erected on the field. "You may judge of the virtues of our small army," writes Baron De Kalb a day or two before the battle, "from the following fact: we have for several days lived on nothing but peaches, and I have not heard a complaint. There has been no desertion." Such men, equally armed, under a general like De Kalb or Greene, on a fair field, would have proved invincible to any thing but superior numbers.

liberty to them and their families to return and occupy their possessions, on certain conditions. "This is a nice point," he observes, "and I don't know how it will be relished by our friends. You know mankind generally judge of the propriety of measures from events." The advice of Marion seems to have been favorable to the proposed measure. The proclamation was issued under the great seal of State, at the American camp, at the high hills of Santee, on the 27th of September, 1781. It is a bold, but calm and dignified production, setting forth frankly the condition of affairs in the State, and alluding with confidence, but without arrogance, to the prosperous condition of the American cause, and the certainty of its ultimate triumph. It offers full and free pardon for the offence of bearing arms with, or adhering to the enemy, on condition that the persons accepting shall within thirty days from date surrender them selves, and engage to serve six months in the militia of the State—excepting, however, those who had signed the congratulatory addresses to Clinton and Cornwallis, those who held civil or military commissions under the British government, and some others. The proclamation closes with the following noble and dignified expressions: "At a juncture when the force of the enemy in this State, though lately considerable, is greatly reduced by the many defeats which they have suffered, and particularly at the late important action at Eutaw; when they are dispossessed of every post and garrison except Charleston; when the formidable fleet of his most Christian Majesty in Chesapeake Bay, and the combined armies of the King of France and of the United States, under the command of his Excellency General Washington, in Virginia, afford a well-grounded hope that by the effort of their armies, this campaign will be happily terminated, and the British power in every part of the confederate states soon totally annihilated; it is conceived that the true and real motive of the offer hereby made will be acknowledged. It must be allowed to proceed not from timidity, to which the enemy affect to attribute every act of clemency and mercy on our part, but from a wish to impress with a sense of their error, and to reclaim misguided subjects, and give them once more an opportunity of becoming valuable members of the community, instead of banishing them, or forever cutting them off from it; for even the most disaffected cannot suppose that the brave and determined freemen of this State have any dread of their arms.

"With the persons to whom this pardon is thus offered, the choice still remains, either to return to their allegiance, and with their families, be restored to the favor of their country, and to their possessions, or to abandon their properties in this State forever, and go with their wives and children, whither, for what purpose, on whom to depend, or how to subsist, they know not—most probably to experience in some strange and distant country, all the miseries and horrors of beggary, sickness, and despair. This alternative is now for the last time submitted to their judgment. It will never be renewed."

In a few weeks several hundred of the royalists come out of the British lines upon this proclamation, and greatly reinforced the American militia.

The time was now approaching when Rutledge was to surrender his dictatorship into the hands of those who had conferred it. No General Assembly had convened in the State since the fall of Charleston. The time was auspicious for summoning together the legislative body. Most of the civil officers of the State, and members of the Legislature, who had either fled or been captured, had now found their way back, and the American army lay posted within thirty-six miles of Charleston, the last stronghold of British power in the State. Rutledge accordingly issued writs for an election of members to a General Assembly, appointed by him to convene on the 8th of January, 1782, at Jacksonborough, a small village on the Edisto river, about thirty-five miles from Charleston. A letter to Marion, of the 23d of November, relates to this subject, and encloses some of these writs for distribution. They were probably distributed in the same manner through the other districts. The Governor himself, by virtue of his extraordinary authority, prescribed the mode of holding these elections, and the qualifications of the voters. The polls were directed to be held in "the usual places," where it was practicable, and in other cases as near as safety and other circumstances would permit. None were allowed to vote but such as had never taken British protection, or having taken it, had rejoined their countrymen on or before the 27th of September, 1781. All others were excluded from the elective franchise.

Not only did Rutledge discharge the duty of convening this Assembly, but the care of making provision for *its subsistence* seems also to have exclusively rested upon him. In these primitive and revolutionary days, members of the legislative body were doubtless relieved from all concern of mind in regard to their *per diem*, but the question whether they would be able to get any thing to eat or not, might certainly become one of much more serious import. The providence of Rutledge had guarded against any misfortune in this respect. His mind was admirably adapted to the details of business —small or great, he suffered none to escape him. In a letter to Marion two or three weeks before the opening of the Jacksonborough Assembly, he writes: "I wish to procure *twelve barrels of rice for the use of the Assembly*, at their intended meeting on the 8th of next month. Be pleased to have that quantity procured as high up Santee River as it can be got, and let me know as soon as possible where it is, that I may order wagons down to fetch it from thence to Camden in time." The idea of keeping members of the Legislature on an allowance of rice, may perhaps excite a smile in our day, but no doubt the gentlemen for whom this provision had been made were abundantly satisfied. The revolutionary fire had swept over the harvest fields of South Carolina, and to the civilian as to the soldier, the certainty of obtaining rations at all was of vastly more importance than their kind or quality.* The men of Marion and Sumpter had fared much worse in their hiding-places in the woods and swamps. De Kalb's gallant army had uttered no complaint while marching under arms without any food, except half-ripe fruit, for several days before the battle of Camden. Greene's soldiers had penetrated into South Carolina with little to eat, and almost as naked as they were born—having green moss about their loins and shoulders, to protect them from the galling effect of their belts and knapsacks. Perhaps we shall see these rice-fed members of the

* If the twelve barrels constituted the entire supply, their contents without doubt would have measured the duration of the session with an accuracy as unerring as those ingenious constitutional provisions in some of the states which stop the pay of the members after a limited number of days.

South Carolina Assembly conducting themselves, in their legislative capacity, with the same spirit which marked the action of the half-starved, half-clothed troops of Greene and De Kalb, and the men of Sumpter and Marion.

The Assembly convened at the appointed day and place. It presented, says a writer, the appearance of a parliament of feudal barons. Many of its members, like Gen. Marion, were drawn from the army, and most of them had seen service in the camp and the field. Their deliberations were carried on under the protection of the American cannon, for the army of Greene had been set in motion to take a position between the place of their meeting and a British post below. Rutledge met the two houses soon after the opening of the session, and addressed them in a speech of some length, in which, with rather more than his natural warmth of language and asperity of temper, he alluded to the unprovoked outrages committed by the enemy, the desolation which lawless violence and rapine had brought upon the land, and the proud triumph which had finally been achieved. Looking abroad as he did at the wide-spread ruin and devastation around him—over a land thickly strewn with the ashes of hamlets and villages destroyed, and still wet with the blood of its sons, his natural impetuosity broke forth into something like the language of bitter denunciation, and indeed we can well understand the burning indignation which prompted such sentences as these :

"Regardless, therefore, of the sacred ties of honor, destitute of the feelings of humanity, and determined to extinguish, if possible, every spark of freedom in this country, they, with the insolent pride of conquerors, gave unbounded scope to the exercise of their tyrannical disposition, infringed their public engagements and violated their most solemn capitulations. Many of our worthiest citizens were, without cause, long and closely confined, some on board of prison ships, and others in the town and castle of St. Augustine,* their properties disposed of at the will and caprice of the enemy, and their families sent to a different and distant part of the continent,

* His two brothers, Edward and Hugh Rutledge, with Lieutenant-Governor Gadsden and most of the civil and military officers, prisoners on parole, after the fall of Charleston, had been seized by order of Cornwallis and transported to St. Augustine.

without the means of support. Many who had surrendered as prisoners of war, were killed in cold blood ; several suffered death in the most ignominious manner, and others were delivered up to savages, and put to tortures under which they expired. Thus the lives, liberties and properties of the people were dependent solely on the pleasure of British officers, who deprived them of either, or all, on the most frivolous pretences. Indians, slaves, and a desperate banditti of the most profligate characters, were caressed and employed by the enemy to execute their infamous purposes. Devastation and ruin marked their progress and that of their adherents, nor were their violences restrained by the charms or influence of beauty and innocence. Even the fair sex, whom it is the duty of all, and the pleasure and pride of the brave, to protect, they, and their tender offspring, were victims to the inveterate malice of an unrelenting foe. Neither the tears of mothers, nor the cries of infants could excite in their breasts pity or compassion. Not only the peaceful habitations of the widow, the aged and the infirm, but the holy temples of the Most High, were consumed in flames, kindled by their sacrilegious hands. They have tarnished the glory of the British arms, disgraced the profession of a British soldier, and fixed indelible stigmas of rapine, cruelty, perfidy and profaneness on the British name. But I can now congratulate you, and I do so most cordially, on the pleasing change of affairs, which, under the blessing of God, the wisdom, prudence, address, and bravery of the great and gallant General Greene, and the intrepidity of the officers and men under his command, has been happily effected—a general who is justly entitled, from his many signal services, to honorable and singular marks of your approbation and gratitude. His successes have been more rapid and complete than the most sanguine could have expected. The enemy, compelled to surrender or evacuate every post which they held in the country, frequently defeated and driven from place to place, are obliged to seek refuge under the walls of Charleston, and on islands in its vicinity. We have now the full and absolute possession of every other part of the State ; and the legislative, executive and judicial powers are in the free exercise of their respective authorities."

The whole of the address from which the foregoing extract is taken, breathes the same spirit. He speaks with confidence of the preservation of the independence of the State, but earnestly urges the raising and equipping of a respectable permament force. He also calls the attention of the Legislature to the necessity of a thorough organization of the militia, to the state of the currency, and some other matters of interest, among which, is the treatment proper to be adopted toward such of the royalists as refused to come in under the proclamation. "It is with you," he says, "whether the forfeiture and appropriation of their property should now take place." But at the same time adds his opinion, that if such should be the determination of the Assembly, "it will redound to the reputation of this State to provide a becoming support for the families of those whom you may deprive of their property."

This part of the suggestion in the Governor's speech, was promptly acted upon. A law was introduced for confiscating the estates and banishing the persons of the most active friends of the British Government, and for amercing the estates of others, as a substitution for those personal services of which the country had been deprived. Though the law was opposed by Gen. Gadsden, and other influential members, it passed by a large majority. It included two hundred and thirty-seven persons and estates in the first class, and forty-eight in the last. This arbitrary and severe measure, though perhaps strictly justifiable by the laws of war, has been generally disapproved since that time Rutledge was taxed by *Cassius*, a political writer, with being the author of the act; but from the testimony of one who was on the spot at the moment the bill passed,* there is every reason to believe that, though approved, it certainly did not originate with him. It is proper to add, that though the law was in the first instance executed, yet its harsh features were afterwards relaxed. In conformity to the treaty of peace and the recommendation of Congress, the Legislature permitted the greater part of the exiles to return. Thirty-one were fully restored to their property and citizenship, thirty-three were disqualified from holding any place of trust within the State for seven years, and they, with sixty-two others, were relieved from total confiscation, by paying twelve per cent. on the equitable value of their property.

* Mr. Alexander Garden. See his Anecdotes of the American Revolution.

The Senate and the House of Representatives returned separate addresses to the Governor, responding in the warmest terms to the sentiments contained in his speech. Each of these addresses contained, also, a flattering personal compliment, in the assurance which it conveyed of the entire approbation with which his conduct was regarded by the representatives of the people. Upon this point there seemed to be no dissenting voice.* "It is with peculiar pleasure," says the address of the Senate, "that we take the earliest opportunity to present to your Excellency our unfeigned thanks for your unwearied zeal and attention to the real interests of this country, and to testify our entire approbation of the good conduct of the Executive since the last meeting of the General Assembly." The language of the House of Representatives was no less flattering. After alluding to the happy re-establishment of law and government, it adds: "This auspicious change is in a great degree owing to the prudence, firmness, and good conduct of your Excellency. If anything can add to the sublime and refined enjoyment, which must arise from your Excellency's own reflections on your persevering, unabated, and successful exertions towards rescuing your country from the iron hand of oppression, be pleased, sir, to accept the most sincere and unfeigned thanks of your grateful fellow-citizens."

The term for which Rutledge had been elected Governor had now expired. By an unfortunate provision of the Constitution, no person was eligible to the office of Governor for more than two years out of a period of six, and the State was therefore deprived, at this important juncture, of his services, in an office in the discharge of whose duties he had displayed such great capacity. The Legislature thereupon proceeded to elect Christopher Gadsden, but that veteran patriot, who had served the State in various stations for thirty years, declined, on account, as he alleged, of the increasing infirmities of old age, and being satisfied that the times required the vigor and activity of the prime of life. He would cheerfully, he said,

* "Above every other trait of character, it must redound to the honor of John Rutledge, possessing dictatorial powers, that the justice and equitable current of his administration, never engendered the slightest murmur, nor gave birth to a single complaint. So mild, indeed, and conciliating were all his actions, that obedience went hand in hand with command, and the ardor of zeal seemed rather to solicit service than seek the means of avoiding it."—*Garden's Anecdotes.*

make one of a forlorn hope in an assault on the lines of Charleston, if it was probable that with the certain loss of his life, the citizens of South Carolina would be reinstated in the possession of their capital. But he declined an office in which he feared he could render no good service. Thereupon, the Assembly chose the Honorable John Mathews, who was subsequently one of Rutledge's colleagues on the bench, to the office of Governor. They also filled up the vacancies in the different departments, and re-established civil government in all its branches.

Mr. Rutledge was not permitted to retire from the service of the State. On the termination of his Executive duties, he was at once elected a member of Congress, and took his seat in that body on the 2d of May, 1782. In this situation, he was immediately called upon to perform an extraordinary duty. The surrender of Cornwallis at Yorktown terminated the war of Independence; so, at least, it seemed to the people and governments of the different States, and very little further effort was made to carry on the contest. Such, however, was not the opinion of Congress, who manifested much solicitude on the subject. Fearing that the general apathy would encourage Great Britain to recommence the contest, they delegated certain members of their body to make a proper representation of the public danger to the respective States. To this duty John Rutledge was assigned, on the 22d of May, 1782, and in conjunction with George Clymer, he was instructed "to make such representations to the several States southward of Philadelphia, as were best adapted to their respective circumstances and the present situations of public affairs, and as might induce them to carry the requisitions of Congress into effect with the greatest despatch." Under these instructions, it seems, the delegates were permitted to address the Virginia Assembly. The duty of course devolved upon Rutledge, and, to use again the language of Dr. Ramsay, he "drew such a picture of the United States, and of the danger to which they were exposed by the backwardness of the particular States to comply with the requisitions of Congress, as produced a very happy effect. The addresser acquitted himself with so much ability, that the Virginians, who, not without reason, are proud of their statesmen and orators, began to doubt whether their

Patrick Henry or the South Carolina Rutledge was the most accomplished public speaker." This speech, so highly eulogized, like almost every other public effort of its author, has been lost. It seems to have been premeditated, for Mr. Rutledge, in alluding to some fact in regard to it, during the session, remarked that it was delivered from "notes," which he had prepared for the occasion, but that he had destroyed these notes immediately afterwards, as was always his custom.

Rutledge and Clymer set out on this mission somewhere about the 1st June. It is probable that they did not go further south than Virginia, or perhaps North Carolina. Their instructions excused them from visiting the States of South Carolina and Georgia, unless they might "deem the public exigencies required." But previous to leaving Philadelphia they were directed to make representations to the State of Pennsylvania, which no doubt was done. What was the success of this mission we believe remains unknown. The delegates were back again in their seats, June 27th, and on that day a brief entry appears in the Journal, thus: "Mr. Rutledge and Mr. Clymer having returned, made a report of their proceedings." No action seems to have been taken upon it. The important case of the State of Pennsylvania against the State of Connecticut, was then occupying the attention of Congress. Mr. Rutledge appeared in his seat in time to take a part in the deliberation of this question, and to discountenance by his vote the principle that the representatives of either State should be allowed to sit during the argument and decision of the case.*

It was in this Congress that Rutledge first met Oliver Ellsworth, then delegate from the State of Connecticut. Here, too, for the first time, he met another gentleman, who subsequently became still more celebrated—James Madison of Virginia. Hamilton of New York, was also a member of this Congress, and Wilson of Pennsylvania. Besides these gentlemen, he found here three or four members of the old Congress, which published the Declaration of Independence; namely, Dyer of Connecticut, Clark of New Jersey, Floyd of New York, and Clymer of Pennsylvania. The renewal

* This case was subsequently referred to a commission of judges appointed by Congress, on which Rutledge was named, but he declined serving.

of friendly acquaintance and intercourse with men like these, must have been highly gratifying to Gov. Rutledge. They had labored together at the commencement of the struggle, and now, at its close, found themselves again united in the common cause. They could look back with a calm and serene satisfaction over the fearful struggles and perils of the past, for the day was at length breaking, and the distant port might be seen, far off, through the angry clouds and over the raging sea.

But the danger was not yet passed. The port was not yet gained. Every nerve must be strained, every rag of canvas set, every man fit for duty summoned to the pumps, to keep the disabled and half-wrecked vessel afloat until she could reach the harbor of safety. Dropping the figure, it is sufficient to remark here that the confederacy rarely passed through a more critical period than during this session of 1782 and 1783. It is true, actual hostilities had ceased with the capture of Cornwallis, but the treaty of peace was not concluded till long afterward. Every thing was confusion, doubt and discouragement. The confederacy was utterly bankrupt, and its credit annihilated. The public creditors were unpaid and clamorous. The army, so long in arrear of pay, almost in a state of open mutiny;—and that able and indefatigable financier, Robert Morris, whose genius in the darkest days of the revolution had from nothing created resources to supply a bankrupt treasury and an empty army chest, was now, in despair, about to resign the superintendence of what was called the *finances.*

This gloomy position of affairs served to give a more than ordinary degree of importance and interest to the deliberations of this Congress; and when Rutledge took his seat, he found staring him and his associates full in the face, this great and momentous question—a question overshadowing all others—one which must be met and could not be avoided—the question of the PUBLIC CREDIT.

In the deliberations upon this subject, Mr. Rutledge, in conjunction with Madison and Hamilton, acted a very prominent and influential part; and although his views differed from those of the two gentlemen last mentioned in many respects, yet he finally concurred in the general plan agreed upon as a compromise, and submitted by

Congress to the States. A very brief statement will serve to explain his position and views on this important subject.

The articles of the confederation provided that the general treasury should be supplied "by the several States in proportion to the value of all land within each State," &c.; but the States had not complied with the requisitions, and it had been, as we have seen, an object of Rutledge's mission to the South, to induce the States to carry out the requisitions of Congress. It had been found troublesome, also, if not impossible to settle the proportion of contribution of each State in this scale of land valuation; and the whole matter had occasioned much warm debate and anxious deliberation in Congress. The subject of the land valuation was now referred to a grand committee of one from each State, of which Rutledge was a member. While the majority of the committee were convinced of the utter impracticability of retaining this scale of contribution, Mr. Rutledge seems to have favored it, and even to have sustained it with some degree of pertinacity, until finally overruled by numbers. The utter hopelessness of affairs, and the necessity of some step to avert the dissolution of the confederacy, is evident from some of the proceedings before this "grand committee." Mr. Peters proposed the almost desperate expedient of making "further applications for loans in Europe," remarking that money "must, if possible, be procured for the army." Mr. Madison seconded it, adding that "it was expedient to make the trial, because, if it failed, *our situation could not be made worse.*" A deputation from the army appeared before the committee, who communicated the startling fact that unless some provision was speedily made there was reason to dread that a mutiny would ensue; and General McDougal, one of the deputies, remarked that "the army were verging to that state which, we are told, will make a wise man mad."* The deliberations of the committee seem to have resulted in very little beyond the appointment of a sub-committee, consisting of Hamilton, Madison and Rutledge, to report arrangements. These various conferences and discussions were continued from time to time with no definite result. On the 27th January, 1783, on Rutledge's motion, Congress went into committee of the whole to consider the most effectual means of

* Madison Papers, Vol. I. pp. 256, 257.

restoring the public credit. After a long and animated debate, and a variety of propositions had been suggested, Rutledge moved a resolution recommending to the several States to lay and collect a duty of five per cent. *ad valorem* on all foreign goods, and a like duty on prizes and prize goods condemned; such revenue to be applied to the payment of the foreign debt, the arrears of the army, and the future support of the war, and no other purpose whatever; and that the said duties so paid by any State into the treasury be passed to the *credit of such State on account of its quota of contribution.* This was something definite and positive; and if not the basis, was at least suggestive of the plan finally agreed to for restoring the public credit by obtaining from the States the right for Congress to levy and collect a tariff on foreign imports. The latter part of the resolution was of course warmly opposed, and finally voted down. The remaining part of the resolution, with some modifications and additions, was, after a debate of more than a month, reported to Congress by a select committee of five, to whom the whole matter had been referred. The report was made on the 6th of March. Mr. Rutledge was a member of this important committee. The plan agreed upon to raise funds sufficient to restore the public credit was that Congress should be empowered to lay an *ad valorem* duty of five per cent. on certain foreign goods, as originally proposed by Mr. Rutledge—also a specific duty on salt, sugars, teas, wines, &c.; the avails of which should be applied to no other purpose than the discharge of the debts contracted by the United States for the support of the war. And the respective States were also recommended to provide some "substantial and effectual revenue" to supply their proportion of $1,500,000 annually for twenty-five years, for a similar purpose. This plan of revenue, with some slight amendments, passed on the 18th of April, 1783, with the unanimous concurrence of all the States except Rhode Island, and the vote of Mr. Hamilton of New York, who was indissolubly wedded to a plan of his own, which he supposed more perfect.

As respects the *proportion* in which the States were to contribute, a very important amendment was proposed to the articles of confederation. The *land valuation*, which we have seen Mr. Rutledge strongly favored, was abandoned, and population adopted as the basis of contribution. This amendment is not the least interesting part of this important act of legislation, inasmuch as it exhibits the origin of that liberal compromise between the North and South in regard to population and representation, which was subsequently embodied in the federal Constitution. Instead of the land valuation as the basis of contribution, the amendment proposed that the charges which had been incurred for the common defence should be defrayed out of a common treasury, supplied by the several states "in proportion to the whole number of white and other free citizens and inhabitants, of every age, sex and condition, including those bound to servitude for a term of years, *and three-fifths of all other persons* not comprehended in the foregoing description, except Indians not paying taxes in each State."*

* The history of this amendment is somewhat curious. The original report of the committee on the subject of revenue, made on the 9th of March, 1783, proposed that contributions from the States, instead of being in proportion to the *value of the land*, should be in proportion to the *whole number of inhabitants of every age, sex or condition*, except Indians. This of course was opposed by the Southern States, and the compromise of three-fifths finally agreed to. In the debate on this subject, March 27th and 28th, Mr. Wilson of Pennsylvania stated that the ratio of land valuation, instead of population, had been agreed to in the articles of confederation, because of the impossibility of compromising the ideas of the eastern and southern States as to the value of slaves compared with the whites. Mr. Clark of New Jersey, who had been present at that time, stated that the southern States would have agreed to numbers in preference to the value of land, if half their slaves only should be included; but that *the eastern States would not agree in the proposition.*

The clause having been recommitted, the next morning after this discussion the committee reported that two blacks be rated as one freeman. The report being read, Mr. Wolcott was for rating them as four to three. Mr. Carroll as four to one. Mr. Higginson, Mr. Holton and Mr. Osgood. as four to three. Mr. Rutledge said, for the sake of the object, he would agree to rate slaves as two to one, but he sincerely thought three to one would be a juster proportion. A question for rating them as three to two was then put and lost, and the paragraph was thereupon postponed, it appearing to be the general opinion, says Mr. Madison in his minutes, that no compromise would be agreed to. Subsequently Mr. Madison remarked, that in order to give a proof of the sincerity of his professions of liberality, he would propose that slaves be rated as *five to three.* Mr. Rutledge seconded the motion. Mr. Wilson said he would sacrifice his opinion on this compromise, and the question for five to three passed in the affirmative by a vote of all the States except Rhode Island and Connecticut, and Massachusetts divided.

Madison Papers, Vol. I. p. 421–4.

Notwithstanding Rutledge's partiality to the land valuation, we find him, on this occasion, actuated by those comprehensive and statesmanlike views of policy, and that liberal spirit of concession which marked all his actions, assenting to the proposition as thus agreed upon, and cordially sustaining the act as matured by the committee. I have said that it was a mutual concession and a compromise, and the original of that other compromise which in almost identical language is found embodied in the federal Constitution. The committee appointed to prepare an address to the States to accompany the act, consisting of Madison, Hamilton, and Ellsworth, so also viewed it, as appears by the following passage in their address: "The only material difficulty which attended it in the deliberations, of Congress was to fix the proper difference between the labor and industry of *free inhabitants*, and of *all other inhabitants*. The ratio ultimately agreed on was the effect of *mutual concessions;* and if it should be supposed not to correspond precisely with the fact, no doubt ought to be entertained that an equal spirit of accommodation among the several legislatures, will prevail against little inequalities which may be calculated on one side or the other." Thus we see at this early period the representatives of the North uniting almost unanimously with the representatives of the South, in a spirit of "mutual concession," and with the most elevated, liberal, and patriotic views, agreeing upon a rule of contribution between the different States founded upon the ratio of population, which was subsequently adopted into the federal Constitution as the basis of representation.

During this session of Congress, the treaty of peace with Great Britain was communicated to the House. The conduct of the commissioners in violating, as it was alleged, their instructions, was severely criticised, particularly by Mr. Mercer, a member from Virginia, who declared that he "felt inexpressible indignation at their meanly stooping, as it were, to lick the dust from the feet of a nation whose hands were still dyed with the blood of their fellow citizens." Rutledge stoutly defended the ministers, and maintained that the separate article, which was especially complained of, did not concern France, and therefore there was no necessity for communicating it to the French minister. The debate was warm and animated, and was renewed from day to day for several days. On a subsequent occasion Rutledge assumed bolder grounds. He insisted that the ministers had done right, and had maintained the honor of the United States after Congress had given it up—placing their justification upon a principle which no other man on the floor, perhaps, would have had the courage and independence to avow, namely that *instructions ought to be regarded only when the public good requires it.* As for himself, he remarked, he would never be bound by them when he thought them improper.*

Mr. Rutledge shared very largely and efficiently in all the business of this Congress. He was a member of nearly every important committee, and his name appears frequently with those of Hamilton, Madison, or Ellsworth, on the same committees. The journals show also that scarcely any question was decided, upon which his vote is not recorded. He seems to have served in this Congress until about the middle of June, 1783, when Mr. Jacob Read having appeared as a delegate from South Carolina, he returned home. A few days after this period, Congress was surrounded and threatened by the mutinous soldiers from Lancaster, and the authorities of Philadelphia being unable to protect that body, it was abruptly adjourned, to meet again at Trenton, in New Jersey.

Rutledge was elected Judge of the South Carolina Court of Chancery in the year 1784. His associates were John Mathews† and Richard Hutson. This was under the new organization of the Court. Indeed, up to the year 1784, there had been no regular Courts of Equity in South Carolina. They had been originally held by the council of proprietors, and subsequently by the representatives of the royal authority. It is somewhat remarkable, that on the formation of the new Constitution in 1776, this feature of mon-

* Madison Papers, Vol. II. p. 410.

† This true patriot and upright judge was one of the earliest and most devoted friends of the liberty of his native State and country. He served with distinction in the Continental Congress, and was a member while the subject was contemplated, if not agitated, of purchasing peace with Great Britain by the sacrifice of the Carolinas and Georgia. This intrigue was strenuously and effectually opposed by Mr. Mathews, supported by his colleagues, Mr. Bee and Col. Eveleigh.

At the expiration of Rutledge's term as Governor, Mr. Mathews was elected to that office, and served with great credit to himself and profit to the State. His selection as Chancellor was a proper and deserved compliment to exalted worth and disinterested services.

archy was preserved. By that instrument the Lieutenant-Governor and Privy Council were vested with equity jurisdiction. This state of things continued until the year 1784, when, by the passage of a bill reorganizing Courts of Equity, jurisdiction in all cases in equity was vested in a Chancellor and two associates. This bill was drawn by Rutledge. It provided that each of the three judges, or Chancellors, should hold a court for the hearing of causes in equity, with the right to any party to appeal from a decree to the three Chancellors in banc. This constitution of the Courts of Equity continued until the year 1808, when two more judges were added to the Court, giving the right of appeal from a single judge to a full bench of five, whose decision was final.

The first term of the Court was held at Charleston, on the 14th day of June, 1784. All three of the judges were present. Many petitions were presented, and some business transacted, but no causes were heard, and no decisions made which involved any principle of importance. At the next term, held in September, many important cases were brought on for argument. At that time, however, it appears that decretal orders were made without stating the reasons of the Court in writing, or the grounds of the decision, so that very little information can be drawn from a number of the earlier cases.* The proceedings seem to have been conducted very much in the ordinary form, and upon similar principles with the English Courts of Equity. From the outset, the business of the Court was transacted with the utmost dignity and decorum, and participated in by the ablest members of the South Carolina bar. A very remarkable case, which created much interest, both on account of the high character of the parties, and the novelty of the questions presented, was brought to argument before a full bench, at the March term 1785. About the year 1766, Ralph and John Izard, two young men, heads of collateral branches, sprung from a common ancestor, who early settled the country, entered into an agreement that in case either of them died without issue, he should bequeath the other the sum of five thousand pounds sterling, for the purpose of keeping up the name and consequence of the family. John Izard died without issue, and made no such provision in his

* 1 Desaussure's Ch. Rep. 107.

will, but left the bulk of his property to his sister Mary, the wife of Arthur Middleton. Thereupon, Ralph Izard * filed a bill against Arthur Middleton as executor of John Izard, praying a performance of the agreement, and the payment of the five thousand pounds.

This novel case was argued with consummate ability on both sides, and by the most eminent lawyers of the State. William Drayton and Judge Bee, Edward Rutledge and Charles Cotesworth Pinckney, were the counsel engaged upon it, but neither the argument nor any portion of the evidence has been preserved. Chancellor Mathews pronounced the unanimous opinion of the Court, dismissing the bill, partly for the reason that such a promise not being reduced to writing was not binding, and partly, as it seems from a note of the reporter, because the alleged agreement to make mutual and corresponding wills was not fully made out by sufficient positive and legal proof.†

The reported cases, in the decision of which Rutledge participated, are mainly collected in the first volume of Desaussure's Chancery Reports of South Carolina, and extend only through about eighty pages of the volume. I do not find any written opinion or decision by Rutledge, or indeed, of any of the other judges, with the exception of three or four which appear to have been taken from Chancellor Mathews' notes. Rutledge, however, seems to have been present on the bench, and to have participated in all these decisions up to the year 1790, except during the period of his absence at the Convention in Philadelphia. The questions argued before him were precisely of the same nature as those which usually occupy the attention of other Courts of Equity—questions of fraud, of trust, of the rights of infants and married women, the construction of wills, agreements, and other written instruments, the conveyance and title of lands, and indeed almost every other question involved in that extensive system of equity jurisprudence which had grown up under the English Chancellors, and had been transferred in its full maturity to the colony of South Carolina.

* This gentleman was a delegate in the Continental Congress, with Rutledge, in 1782-3. The defendant, Mr. Middleton, was also a member of the same delegation in Congress.

† 1 Desaussure's Reports, 114.

At the new organization of the Courts of law and equity, in the month of February, 1791, Rutledge was elected Chief-Justice of the Supreme Courts of Judicature of the State, thereby vacating his seat on the Equity bench. His associates were Ædanus Burke,* John F. Grimke, Thomas Waties, and Elihu Hall Bay, the accomplished reporter of the Court, all of them gentlemen of distinguished legal attainments, and of the very highest character and moral worth. In this respect, there was a striking contrast between the judiciary under the State government, and the Colonial bench under the appointment of the crown. When Rutledge was at the bar, prior to the revolution, the judges were mostly foreigners, holding

* Throughout the whole of the Revolution, says Mr. Garden, Judge Burke acted a very conspicuous part. He was a steady and inflexible patriot and zealous supporter of the laws. The people had not an advocate more ready to maintain their just rights, nor a more prompt opponent whenever they manifested the slightest disposition to licentiousness. He always meant well, though he frequently took an awkward way of showing it, and secured confidence by his unremitted endeavors to deserve it.

Mr. Garden relates several anecdotes of this eccentric gentleman, some of which exhibit a keen but rough and unpolished wit. Sending a challenge to a person who had grossly insulted him, he thus expressed himself: "Sir, I must insist upon your giving me immediate satisfaction for having so far imposed on me as to make me believe for a single moment that you were a man of honor or a gentleman."

In those primitive days when Burke first came to the bench, society, in the back settlements, tolerated the practice of biting, gouging out eyes, &c. Burke, while travelling his circuits, was in the habit of carrying pistols of extraordinary size and calibre. Being asked the reason, he replied: "As the best specific for the preservation of my *eye-sight*—country frolics too frequently producing blindness."

On the day before his death, being tapped for the dropsy, he asked his physician—"Well, Irvine, what am I to expect; is the decree life, or death?" "Life, my good fellow," said Irvine; "you are an Irishman, and will yet last a long time." "Then, by ——," said Burke, "I shall be the first thing that ever lasted long in this house, after being once put on tap."

Burke was the writer, who, under the signature of Cassius, attacked the proscriptive act of the Jacksonborough Assembly, and accused Rutledge of being its author. He was a strenuous opponent of the Federal Constitution, but subsequently abandoned his opposition and gave it his full support. In 1799 he was appointed to the Chancery bench, on filling up the vacancies occasioned by the death of Chancellor Hutson and the resignation of Chancellor Mathews.

their commissions from the King. At the opening of the Revolution, William Henry Drayton was the only native South Carolinian on the bench, and he, it seems, was there only by the temporary appointment of the Lieutenant-Governor, and was actually superseded about the commencement of the troubles by an Englishman, named Gregory.* Prior to 1769 the Judges received no fee or reward, and the character of the bench, composed as it was mainly of gentlemen of good fortunes and estates, was comparatively good. But subsequently to that period, and up to the time of the Revolution, with some few exceptions, the Judges were utterly unfitted for the station, either in character, talent, or learning. It is stated of Chief-Justice Shinner, that he never opened a law book until he was actually on his passage to America. Mr. Garden, in his Anecdotes, relates an occurrence which gives us some idea of the qualifications and characters of these English judges. One of them, Mr. Justice Futerel, having sacrificed too freely to Bacchus, at a dancing assembly, lay extended on a bench, confused with liquor, when, observing a gentleman pulling off his coat for the purpose of changing a waistcoat that had been accidentally soiled, he leaped up, and putting himself in a boxing attitude, exclaimed, "Oh, damn you, if you are for that sport, I'm at home—come on."

The character of the South Carolina judiciary was redeemed when her native sons were called to the bench. That pure and inflexible patriot and able jurist, William Henry Drayton, as we have seen, was the first Chief-Justice under the revolutionary government. In the discharge of his duties, justice was administered with "discerning eyes," as well as "clean hands." Nor did the judicial ermine lose in the slightest degree its purity when, falling from him and others who had worn it after him, without spot or blemish, it rested upon the shoulders of John Rutledge.

The first case adjudicated by Judge Rutledge and his associates, after his appointment as Chief-Justice of the law courts, was in the Common Pleas, at the February session, 1791. It was a prosecution for forgery against a man named Welch, indicted under the assumed name of Washington. The punishment of the offence by the laws of South Carolina, was death, and the case, apart from the nature

* Drayton's Memoirs, p. 151.

of the legal questions involved, attracted very great interest. The prisoner, after a long and deliberate trial, had been found guilty; whereupon his counsel gave notice to the Attorney-General that they intended to move in arrest of judgment. On the 9th March, 1791, the motion was brought on before the Chief-Justice, Mr. Justice Bay and Mr. Justice Grimke, the two former of whom on that day, for the first time, took their seats upon the bench. The guilt of the prisoner had been established by the verdict, and the questions, of course, were purely technical ones, turning mainly upon the sufficiency of the indictment. An analysis of the very able argument in this case has been preserved in the report,* but involving, as it did, questions of law merely, and as such interesting to the legal profession alone, I shall not undertake to follow or review it in this place. On the part of the prisoner, the argument was conducted by Messrs. Holmes, Lowndes and Hall. It being a capital case, and very great public expectations having been raised, and no gentleman of the bar being willing to volunteer against the prisoner, the Attorney-General, Alexander Moultrie, applied to the Governor to have counsel assigned, whereupon his excellency appointed Col. Read, who, with the Attorney-General, argued the case on behalf of the people. The Chief-Justice delivered the opinion of the Court, and it is on the whole, perhaps the best specimen we have of his legal acumen and his mode of treating a purely technical question. He meets and examines each point taken by the counsel for the defence with the utmost care and attention, and withal with lawyerlike precision and accuracy, and shows, by a chain of unanswerable reasoning, and of the clearest illustration, that the objections raised are untenable. The opinion, in which the rest of the Court concurred, is amply fortified by references to the sources of the common law, and a copious analysis and comparison of adjudged cases. It was more full and circumstantial than was usual with the Chief-Justice, but being, as he remarked, a case of great importance to the prisoner, and the public at large, he considered it proper " to state thus fully the reasons upon which our decision is founded." It is scarcely necessary to add, that the motion was overruled, and the prisoner adjudged to undergo the full penalty of the law. The Chief-

* 1 Bay's South Carolina Reports, 120.

Justice passed sentence of death upon him in a very "affecting address," as the reporter remarks, recommending him in "a very pathetic manner to employ that little interval of life which remained, in making his peace with that God whose law he had offended."

I shall not undertake to follow the course of Judge Rutledge through the four years of his judicial service in the law courts of South Carolina. His demeanor was dignified, and his manner, though somewhat distant and haughty, was courteous to the bar as well as to his brethren of the bench. His judgments were strictly impartial, and most of them, so far as we can now form an opinion from such of the cases as were decided in banc and have been reported, were in accordance with the principles of the common law. Such, for example, was the judgment in one of the last cases discussed before him—the case of the creditors of Scott *vs.* Scott—decided in the spring of 1795, and argued with very great learning and ingenuity by Col. Read, on the one side, and Charles Cotesworth Pinckney on the other. The question in the case was whether commissioners in a writ of dower could assign a widow the whole of one of several tracts, or whether they were not bound to give her one-third of each separate tract. Rutledge delivered the opinion of the Court in this case, and by a very careful examination of old authorities and the strictest legal deductions, arrived at the conclusion, which was concurred in by his associates, that the assignment of dower must be by metes and bounds, and of each tract of land in severalty.

Most of the reported cases decided by the courts during this period involved questions of this nature—questions of common law, the decision of which was to be governed by established legal maxims, and the principles of which were to be sought in the common law of England as it stood at that time. Occasionally, however, questions of a more novel and original character arose, in which the court was left without the light of established principles, and the authority of ancient precedents.

Thus, at the May term, 1791, in the case of Eden *vs.* Legaré,* we find Rutledge laying down the rule, that calling a man a mulatto is a slander, *per se*, and actionable. The reason assigned is, that if

* 1 Bay's South Carolina Reports, 174.

true, "the party would be deprived of all civil rights, and moreover would be liable to be tried in all cases under the negro act, without the privilege of a trial by jury."

The bar, as well as the bench, at this period, comprised gentlemen of unusual ability and eminence in their profession. At the head of these stood Charles Cotesworth Pinckney* and Edward Rutledge, who are found opposed in almost every case of importance argued in the Superior Courts. The latter of these gentlemen continued his brilliant and honorable career at the bar, down to the period of his election as chief-magistrate of the State. In addition to these may be mentioned the names of those eminent and able lawyers, whose talents and learning illustrate the judicial records of South Carolina—Read, Pringle, Desaussure, Lowndes, Moultrie, Harper and Holmes. With the advantage of the experience, the learning and the abilities of such advocates at the bar, the labors of

* This distinguished gentleman was the son of Charles Pinckney, who twenty years prior to the Revolution was a Judge of the Colonial Courts in South Carolina. Resigning his seat on the bench, Judge Pinckney took his two sons, Charles Cotesworth and Thomas Pinckney, to England, for the purpose of completing their education. Returning to America, and being admitted to the bar, Charles C. Pinckney entered upon the practice of his profession. The revolutionary movements found in him a warm and decided advocate. He was chosen captain in the first South Carolina regiment, and was afterwards promoted to the command of it. Subsequently joining General Washington, he was received into the family of the Commander-in-chief as one of his aids, and was present at the battles of Brandywine and Germantown. Returning to South Carolina on the second invasion of Sir Henry Clinton, he was entrusted with the command of Fort Moultrie; and having been taken prisoner at the fall of Charleston, was, with many of the most distinguished sons of South Carolina, sent into exile at St. Augustine.

As an enlightened statesman and able lawyer, General Pinckney ranks unquestionably among the first men of the country. He was an influential member of the Convention which framed the Federal Constitution, and afterwards of the State Convention of South Carolina which ratified it. To the efforts of Pinckney and Rutledge may be attributed, in a great measure, the success of the Constitution in the State of South Carolina. Gen. Pinckney was appointed, with Marshall and Gerry, to negociate with France in 1798. At the election of 1800, he was one of the candidates for President and Vice-President of the United States. By consenting to unite his name with that of Jefferson, he would probably have secured the vote of his State, which would have elected him to one of these distinguished stations. As it turned out, however, the vote of South Carolina was given to Mr. Burr, who thereupon was elected Vice-President.

the bench was rendered far less arduous. Every important question was the subject of full and accurate discussion, and was in turn subjected to the most rigid and severe examination by the judges; and it may be added that the authority of these earlier decisions in the State Courts of South Carolina, has always been received and treated with the highest respect.

During the period of his service as one of the Chancellors of the State, and without resigning his place upon the bench, Rutledge consented to serve as a delegate from South Carolina in the Convention which framed the Constitution of the United States. His colleagues were Charles Pinckney, Charles Cotesworth Pinckney, and Pierce Butler. The Convention, although called for the second Monday in May, 1787, did not organize until the 25th of that month. On that day, a majority of the States being represented, George Washington was unanimously chosen President of the Convention, and was conducted to the chair by Robert Morris and John Rutledge,* when having delivered his brief and modest introductory address, the business of the Convention commenced.

It is impossible to look over the list of the members comprising this august body, without being deeply impressed with its exalted character, its great dignity, and its commanding ability. With some notable exceptions, such as Jefferson of Virginia, the Livingstons, Clinton and Jay of New York, and the Adamses of Massachusetts, most of the prominent statesmen and civilians of that day were members.† Among the list are the names of three out of the five Associate-Justices of the Supreme Court originally nominated by Washington, namely, Rutledge of South Carolina, Wilson of Pennsylvania, and Blair of Virginia—the first Attorney-General of the United States, Edmund Randolph, and the third Chief-Justice, Oliver Ellsworth. Besides these eminent and able jurists, the American bar

* Mr. Rutledge seconded the motion of Mr. Morris, nominating Gen. Washington President of the Convention. He expressed the hope that the choice would be unanimous. The presence of General Washington, he observed, forbade any remarks in regard to him, which on another occasion would be proper. Washington was thereupon unanimously chosen, by ballot, to preside over the Convention.

† Some of them, however, never attended, among whom was Patrick Henry of Virginia.

was represented on the floor of that Convention by such men as Chancellor Wythe of Virginia, the Pinckneys of South Carolina, Paterson of New Jersey, Luther Martin of Maryland, and Jared Ingersoll of Pennsylvania.

The general proceedings of this Convention, forming so prominent a part of the history of the country, and so deeply interesting to every American, are tolerably familiar to the public, through the journal of its proceedings, the brief minutes of Mr. Yates, and the published papers of Mr. Madison. It is to be regretted that, the Convention having sat with closed doors, no extended report of its proceedings from day to day was taken, and thus so few of these deeply interesting discussions remain.

It appears from the Journal, as well as from other sources, that Mr. Rutledge was not only an active, but one of the most influential members of the Convention, and that many of his views were adopted in the final compromise of the Constitution. I shall, however, allude to the proceedings of this body, only so far as may be necessary to indicate the general nature of Mr. Rutledge's services, and the views which he entertained and advocated.

Immediately on the organization of the Convention, Edmund Randolph, of Virginia, offered a set of resolutions embodying his idea of the leading principles which should be established as the basis of the new government. He accompanied them with an elaborate speech, in which he admitted that they were not intended for a Federal Government, but meant a strong *consolidated union*, in which the idea of States should be *nearly* annihilated. Upon this point the main and formidable struggle in the Convention subsequently occurred, namely, as between a Federal Union of the States and a Consolidated Government. Randolph's plan provided for a national Legislature to consist of two branches, the first to be elected by the people of the States in proportion to the quota of contribution, or the number of free inhabitants, and the second to be elected by the first branch out of persons nominated by the individual legislatures. It provided also for a national Executive with a Council of Revision, and a national Judiciary.

At the same time the draft of a plan of Government was submitted by Mr. Charles Pinckney of South Carolina. This plan, it is presumed, had received the approbation of Rutledge, and the rest of the South Carolina delegation, although it professed to express the individual views of Mr. Pinckney alone. It was more specific, and went more into detail than the propositions of Mr. Randolph, and though Mr. Pinckney declared it was based on similar principles, yet there were some essential points of difference. Thus it defined and specified the powers which should be vested in the new government—and this enumeration of powers was subsequently, with some additions and modifications, grafted upon the new Constitution. It provided also for the election of an executive magistrate, with the title of President of the United States, to serve for a term of years, and be reëligible, and contained various other provisions which the Convention subsequently approved. Like the Virginia plan, however, it contemplated the election of a Senate by the house of delegates, the senators to be taken from among the citizens of the respective States, although not nominated by the legislatures thereof. Each State was to be represented in the Senate as well as in the popular branch, in proportion to the ratio of its population. Upon this point, that is to say, the *equality of representation* in the national legislature, the serious struggle in the Convention occurred, the large States insisting upon a representation in both branches according to population, or wealth, or both, and most of the smaller States contending as strenuously for an equal representation on the part of the States. Upon this question South Carolina voted with the larger States.

Previous to its decision, however, the question as to the mode of election, the term of service, &c., came up. On the 7th of June, on motion of Rutledge, the Convention went into consideration of the mode of electing the second branch of the Legislature. Mr. Dickinson of Delaware, moved that they be chosen by the legislatures of the States, which after some debate was carried unanimously. Two or three days after, the question came up as to the mode of appointing the first branch of the national Legislature. Roger Sherman was of the opinion that they should be chosen in proportion to the whole number of inhabitants in each State. Thereupon Rutledge moved as an amendment, "that the proportion of representation ought to be according to and in proportion to the contribution of each

State." This motion was subsequently postponed, and one by Judge Wilson adopted, namely, that the representation of each State ought to be from the number of its free inhabitants and three-fifths of all other persons, except Indians not paying taxes. The proposition prevailed by a vote of nine States to two—New Jersey and Delaware voting in the negative.* In regard to the period of service of the members of the first branch, Mr. Sherman moved one year, Mr. Rutledge two years, and Mr. Jenifer, with whom Madison coincided, three years. The latter motion was carried, and it was so contained in the resolutions subsequently reported to the House from the Committee of the Whole.

Immediately on the determination of the question relative to the ratio of representation in the popular branch of the national Legislature, it seems from the Journal, that Mr. Sherman, seconded by Mr. Ellsworth, moved "that in the second branch of the national Legislature each State have a vote." The motion was negatived by a vote of six States to five. Thereupon Mr. Wilson, seconded by Mr. Hamilton, moved "that the right of suffrage in the second branch of the national Legislature ought to be according to the rule established for the first." This was adopted by precisely the same relative vote.† Thus, upon the start, the advocates of a strictly Federal Government, which should preserve the unity, identity and influence of the respective States, were overpowered, and the friends of a consolidated national Government, in which, to use the language of Mr. Randolph, "the idea of States should be nearly annihilated," carried the day. In this manner a series of resolutions were elaborated in Committee of the Whole, and reported to the House as the basis of the plan of a Federal Government. They were altered, amended and modified from time to time, but without essentially changing their complexion, until, on Saturday the 30th June, the question again came up on the troublesome resolution—

* Rhode Island appointed no delegates to the Convention, and the New Hampshire members had not yet arrived.

† The following is the vote on Mr. Wilson's motion: *Yeas*—Massachusetts, Pennsylvania, Virginia, North Carolina, South Carolina, Georgia—6.

Nays—Connecticut, New York, New Jersey, Delaware, Maryland—5. Hamilton, of New York, favored the motion, but his two colleagues, Yates and Lansing, who were opposed, cast the vote of the State.

"That in the second branch of the Legislature of the United States, each State should have an equal vote." Upon this a stormy and highly exciting discussion arose. Judge Wilson contended with great earnestness against the proposition. It was sustained by Ellsworth with an equal degree of zeal and ardor, and moreover with a closer logic. But the Connecticut delegate encountered a more formidable opposition in the clear and pointed reasoning of Madison, and the practical and plain common sense of Franklin. "A joiner," said Franklin, resorting as usual to one of his homely illustrations, "when he wants to fit two boards, takes off with his plane the uneven parts from each side, and thus they fit. Let us do the same—we are all met to do something." He then proposed the singular expedient that in the passage of general laws in the second branch of the national Legislature, each State should have a right of suffrage in proportion to the sums they respectively contributed, but in all acts of authority and sovereignty the vote should be equal.

The debate grew warm and animated, nay, even stormy. Mr. Bedford of Delaware took the floor, and amid the most intense excitement, launched the arrows of his scathing invective and bitter sarcasm on every side against the opponents of an equal representation. "Even the diminutive State of Georgia," he exclaimed, turning to the now hesitating delegation from that State, "has an eye to her future wealth and greatness. South Carolina, puffed up with the possession of her wealth and negroes, and North Carolina, are all, from different views, united with the great States. And these latter, although it is said they can never, from interested views, form a coalition, we find united in one scheme of interest and ambition, notwithstanding they endeavor to amuse us with the purity of their principles and the rectitude of their intentions, in asserting that the General Government must be drawn from an equal representation of the people. Pretences to support ambition are never wanting." * * * * * "*I do not trust you, gentlemen.*" He continued with increased vehemence—"Where is your plighted faith? Will you crush the smaller States, or must they be left unmolested? Sooner than be ruined, *there are foreign powers who will take us by the hand.*"*

The excitement was now intense. The period appeared to have

* See Yates' Minutes.

approached when the Convention was about to be dissolved. As Mr. Luther Martin subsequently remarked to the Maryland Legislature, it now seemed "scarce held together by the strength of a hair." It was a critical moment in the history of the country; on the change of a single vote the most stupendous issues were suspended. In the midst of the confusion and excitement of the debate, the Convention adjourned without taking the question. Fortunately an intervening Sunday afforded time for reflection and cool deliberation. At the reassembling on Monday morning the vote was taken on Mr. Ellsworth's proposition for an equality in the second branch. One of the two delegates from Georgia wavered, not from any change of view, but because of his fear that the Convention would dissolve without further action, changed his vote, and thus divided the State. The result was five States in favor of the proposition, five against it, and Georgia divided. "There was," says Mr. Martin, "a total stand, and we did not seem very likely to proceed any further."

At this critical moment there was found in the Convention a sufficient number of men of enlarged and liberal views, to change the aspect of affairs. South Carolina, generously and magnanimously, stepped forward as the mediator between the large and small States, and proposed a compromise. Gen. Pinckney moved a select committee of one from each State, to take into consideration both branches of the Legislature. The extreme men on both sides hung back.

"It is attempted again to compromise!" exclaimed Mr. Martin. "You MUST give each State an equal suffrage, or our business is at an end." Judge Wilson was equally obstinate and dogmatical on the other side, and did not approve of the motion for a committee; and even Madison observed that "committees only delay business," and thought the matter might be decided on the spot. But Roger Sherman believed a committee was "necessary to set us right." Gov. Randolph was in favor of its appointment, but considering the warmth of debate exhibited on Saturday, confessed "no great hopes that any good will arise from it;" and Mr. Gerry, believing that accommodation was absolutely necessary, and that the world at large expected something from the Convention, was desirous of seeing "if no concession could be made."

The motion to appoint the committee was carried, and the members balloted for on the spot. John Rutledge was chosen on behalf of the State of South Carolina. Its composition was, in other respects, also, singularly fortunate. The members selected from the three large States, Gerry from Massachusetts, Franklin from Pennsylvania, and Mason from Virginia, were among the most moderate, liberal, and conciliatory members of the Convention. The former of these was chosen Chairman, and the committee immediately commenced its deliberations, the Convention having in the mean time adjourned.

Mr. Yates of New York was a member of this committee of conference, and has briefly described its proceedings in his minutes. Both sides, it seems, at first adhered to their original positions; Mr. Yates thereupon gave his views in detail, he being, as is well known, opposed to a consolidated, and in favor of a strictly federal union. These remarks, he says, gave rise to the motion of Dr. Franklin for the compromise which was subsequently agreed upon, and has become the foundation and corner-stone of the union of these States. In the first branch of the national Legislature each State should be allowed one member for every forty thousand inhabitants, this branch to have the sole right of originating all money bills; in the second branch, each State should have an equal vote. Such was, substantially, the report of the committee. It was, says Mr. Madison, *barely acquiesced in* by the members of the committee who opposed an equality of votes, and it was evidently considered by members on the other side to be a gaining of their point. As a compromise it was certainly the most obvious one that could have suggested itself, and perhaps the only one that could have been adopted. The principle of representation according to population and numbers established in regard to the first branch, secured the larger States; while the equality of votes in the second branch preserved the identity and sovereignty of all the States. And yet the compromise, as has usually been the case in regard to all the compromises of great national questions, failed at first to satisfy the extreme men of either division. The report of the committee was received with many marks of dissent. "The committee has exceeded its powers!" exclaimed Judge Wilson. Gouverneur Morris also warmly and earnestly opposed it. It is somewhat surprising to find Mr. Madison on the same side; he was only restrained from "animadverting on the report," by the respect he had for the members of the committee. He could "see nothing of concession in it." * On the other hand some of the advocates of State sovereignty and an equality of representation in both branches, were far from satisfied. Of this number was Mr. Luther Martin of Maryland; while so great was the disgust of Messrs. Yates and Lansing, that they left the Convention and returned home, convinced, as they remark in their letter to Governor Clinton, that no alteration was to be expected in the proposed system to conform it to their ideas of expediency and safety, and that their "further attendance would be fruitless and unavailing." New York was therefore left for the remainder of the session without a quorum on the floor of the Convention.

Happy was it for the country that these extreme counsels did not prevail;—that the Convention numbered among its members such men as Franklin and Washington,† Sherman and Ellsworth, Mason and Rutledge—men who were determined to complete the great work for which they had assembled, and not to separate until that work was done.‡ How and in what manner it was accomplished are matters of history. Though intimately connected with the pub-

* See Yates' Minutes of the Convention.

† Mr. Luther Martin, in his address to the Maryland Legislature, complains somewhat sharply of the conduct of both Washington and Franklin. "During this struggle to prevent the large States from having all power in their hands," he says, "which had nearly terminated in a dissolution of the Convention, it did not appear to me that either of those illustrious characters, the honorable Mr. Washington, or the President of the State of Pennsylvania, was disposed to favor the claims of the smaller States, against the undue superiority attempted by the large States; on the contrary, the honorable President of Pennsylvania was a member of the committee of compromise, and there advocated the *right* of the large States to an inequality in both branches, and only ultimately conceded it in the second branch, on the principle of conciliation, when it was found no other terms would be accepted. This, sir, I think it my duty to mention, for the consideration of those who endeavor to prop up a dangerous and defective system by great names," &c.

‡ Mr. Mason of Virginia, declared in his place, that instead of returning home to attend to his private affairs, "he would bury his bones in this city rather than expose his country to the consequences of a dissolution of the Convention without any thing being done."

lic life of the subject of this memoir, a minute detail of this history would lead me beyond the limits and object of the present sketch. The general posture of affairs in the Convention at this most critical period, has been glanced at for the purpose of indicating the position occupied by Rutledge therein, and his share in the adjustment of this momentous question. Having done thus much, I shall follow no further the regular proceedings of the Convention, but confine myself to a brief review of the particular services rendered by Chancellor Rutledge in the Convention, and the opinions entertained by him in regard to some of the more important subjects which, from time to time, were brought up for discussion.

We have seen that he was a member of the committee of eleven, which reported the compromise in regard to the representation of the States in the national Legislature. The high confidence reposed by the Convention in his abilities and character, led to his being selected also to serve on several others of the most important committees of the House. A series of resolutions having been agreed to, after a protracted discussion, as the basis of the proposed Constitution, it was determined to refer them to a select committee of five, for the purpose of drafting a Constitution. Rutledge was chosen chairman of this committee. His associates were Randolph of Virginia, Gorham of Massachusetts, Ellsworth of Connecticut, and Wilson of Pennsylvania. On the 6th of August, 1787, Rutledge had the honor of reporting to the Convention the first draft of a Constitution for the United States. I am not aware that it can now be determined that the whole of this draft, or if not the whole, what particular part, is from his pen. It is not, indeed, the Constitution as it was finally adopted—many changes and modifications having been made, in the discussions which subsequently took place—but the outlines and substantial parts are there. The preamble is rather remarkable. It is in precisely the words of the draft originally submitted by Mr. Charles Pinckney: "We the people OF THE STATES of New Hampshire, Rhode Island, &c., do ordain, declare and establish the following Constitution, for the government of ourselves and our posterity." It is worthy of remark that on the questions, separately taken, of agreeing to this preamble, it passed *unanimously in the affirmative.** Subsequently, when the terms of

* See Journal of Convention, August 7th, 1787.

the Constitution had been fully discussed and agreed on, a committee of five was appointed to revise the style, and arrange the articles of the Constitution. This committee consisted of Mr. Johnson, Mr. Hamilton, Mr. Gouverneur Morris, Mr. Madison, and Mr. King.* It is said that the style and finish, of the Constitution are to be attributed in a great degree to the elegant pen of Mr. Morris ; to the same source, perhaps, may also be attributed the change of phraseology in the preamble. Instead of the preamble of Mr. Rutledge's draft : " *We, the people of the States,*" &c., which, we have seen, passed unanimously in the affirmative, the committee of revision reported the preamble : " *We, the people of the United States,* in order to form a more perfect union, to establish justice, insure domestic tranquillity," &c.†

The Constitution, as reported by Mr. Rutledge, provided for the election of a President of the United States by the national Legislature, by ballot, to hold office for seven years, and not to be eligible a second time. This was a favorite proposition with Mr Rutledge, except that instead of electing the Executive by the Legislature, he wished him to be elected by the second branch or Senate alone. Upon this subject he avowed his opinions in the Convention at a very early day. When the question in regard to the Executive first came up, there seemed to be an unwillingness on the part of members to express their opinion, and the resolution was about to be put without debate. Rutledge thereupon arose and animadverted on the shyness of gentlemen upon this and other subjects. It looked, he said, as if they supposed themselves precluded, by having frankly disclosed their opinions, from afterwards changing them, which he did not take to be at all the case. He then frankly avowed that he was in favor of a single person as Executive, though he was not for giving him the power of war and peace.‡ Subsequently, on the same day, he moved that the Executive be elected by the second branch

* Journal of Constitution, September 8th, 1787.

† Was this alteration regarded at the time in any other light than as a mere revision of the language, and verbal alteration? It has been since thought significant in its application to the great question of power as between the federal Government and the States.

‡ Madison Papers, vol. ii. p. 762. Gov. Randolph strenuously opposed a unity in the Executive magistracy.

of the Legislature. Mr. Sherman was for the appointment by the Legislature ; Mr. Wilson for an election by the people of the States through the medium of electors ; Mr. Ellsworth of electors appointed by the State Legislatures ; Mr. Gerry was opposed to all these plans, and offered one of his own, which is certainly remarkable for its novelty. He was for giving to the Legislatures of the States the right to *nominate* candidates, and to the electors chosen by the people the power of *appointment* ; he was, however, not clear that the people ought to act directly, even in the choice of electors.* The question of the appointment excited much discussion in the Convention, and much change of opinion was manifested in regard to it. Mr. Rutledge, it seems, did not press his proposition of an election by the second branch, but adhered strenuously to the appointment by the national Legislature, and the ineligibility of the Executive for a second term. The Convention at first sanctioned this mode by a unanimous vote. The vote was subsequently reconsidered, and it was resolved that the national Executive should be appointed by electors, chosen by the State Legislatures. This resolution was also reconsidered, and the Convention again resolved to elect the Executive by the national Legislature ; that he should serve for seven years, and be ineligible a second time. In this shape it went to the committee of detail, and was reported in Rutledge's draft of a Constitution. But the plan was again altered by the Convention, which finally agreed to the mode of election as it now stands, namely, by electors appointed in each State, in the manner its Legislature shall direct.

Rutledge was also in favor of limiting the power of the Executive, not only in regard to the question of his right to make peace and declare war, but also to some extent in regard to his authority to

* Madison Papers, vol ii. p. 770. Mr. Gerry may be called the Sièyes of the Convention. His mind was active and acute, but somewhat too fond of refinements and abstractions. His plan, though less artificial than the ingenious system which was offered to Bonaparte by Sièyes, was still such as might have originated in the brain of that famous philosopher, who to use his own expression, had "carried the science of politics to perfection."

Mr. Gerry, though opposed to both monarchy and aristocracy, was in favor of having the members of the first branch appointed by the State Legislatures, from a certain number of persons nominated by the people in the respective districts.

appoint to office. Thus, he contended that the appointment of the national Judiciary should never be entrusted to one person; "the people," he remarked, "will think we are leaning too much to monarchy." In his opinion, the Judiciary should be chosen by one, or both branches of the Legislature. He thought, too, that there was no necessity for establishing any national tribunal, except a single supreme one, as a kind of appellate court, the State tribunals deciding in all cases in the first instance.*

But perhaps the opinion of which he was the most tenacious, and which he advocated with the greatest earnestness and the utmost sincerity of conviction, was that the proportion of representation of each State in the national Legislature, should not be based upon population, but should be in accordance with the quota of its contribution. In sustaining this proposition Mr. Rutledge advanced a very extraordinary doctrine, namely, that property was the *principal object of society*, and, therefore, the most correct and just basis of representation. This doctrine had been first broached on the floor of the Convention by Gouverneur Morris, a gentleman of great brilliancy and acuteness of mind, as well as versatility of talent, who leaned strongly to the side of aristocratic institutions and government.† "Life and liberty," said Mr. Morris, "were generally said to be of more value than property. An accurate view of the matter would, nevertheless, prove that property was the main object of society. The savage state was more favorable to liberty than the civilized, and sufficiently so to life. *It was preferred by all men who had not acquired a taste for property*, &c. If property, then, was the main object of government, certainly it ought to be one measure of the influence due to those who were to be affected by the government." To this conclusion Mr. Rutledge, in a measure, assented, remarking that "The gentleman last up had spoken some of his sentiments precisely. *Property was certainly the principal object of society*," &c. He thereupon moved that the suffrages of the States be proportioned by the sums paid toward the general revenue by each

* Madison Papers, vol. ii. p. 792.

† Mr. Morris did not hesitate to avow "that his creed was that there never was, nor ever will be a civilized society without an aristocracy."—*Debates in Convention, Madison Papers*, vol. ii. p. 1043.

State respectively. The proposition, however, found but little favor in the Convention, and was negatived by a decisive vote, South Carolina alone being in the affirmative.*

The views of Rutledge were freely and fully expressed, upon nearly every question of importance which was raised in the Convention. They were always frank, bold and independent. However erroneous may have been some of these impressions, no one will deny that they were the honest convictions of a mind which endeavored to bring every proposition to the test of truth. No narrow and partial views governed his course of action. He opposed with as much earnestness the motion of a friend and colleague, when he believed it wrong, as if the proposition had proceeded from a part of the confederacy whose interests were in direct conflict with his own. Thus when Mr. Pinckney moved to clothe the national Legislature with power, "to negative all laws passed by the several States, interfering, in the opinion of the Legislature, with the general interests and harmony of the Union," Rutledge warmly opposed the proposition. "This alone, if nothing else," he exclaimed, "will damn, and ought to damn the Constitution. Will any State ever agree to be bound hand and foot in this manner? It is worse than making mere corporations of them, whose by-laws would not be subject to this shackle."† And so, too, when the same gentleman proposed an amendment, "that no act of the Legislature, for the purpose of regulating the commerce of the United States with foreign powers, or among the several States, should be passed without the assent of two-thirds of the members of each house," Rutledge, rising superior to mere sectional considerations and the interests of the present moment, opposed the motion. A navigation act, he thought, would bear hard for a little while on the southern States, but as the Convention was laying the foundation for a great empire, it ought to take a permanent view of the subject, and not look at the present moment only.‡

It is, however, due to candor and the truth of history to say that Rutledge stood firm and unyielding to what he esteemed the sub-

* Debates in Convention—Madison Papers, vol. ii. p. 1035.

† Madison Papers, vol. iii. 1411.

‡ Madison Papers, vol. iii. p. 1454.

stantial interests of his section of the confederacy. Thus, though assenting to the compromise proposed on the question of representation, he refused to yield to the proposal for the immediate prohibition of the importation of slaves. The people of North Carolina, South Carolina and Georgia, he declared, will never agree to the proposed Constitution, unless their right to import slaves be untouched; and the true question, therefore, he thought, was whether the southern States should, or should not, be parties to the Union. Finally, he acceded to the proposition that the importation of slaves should not be prohibited prior to the year 1808; and when Mr. Madison moved the consideration of a proposition for making amendments to the Constitution, Rutledge offered to add the provision, which was adopted by the Convention, that no amendments which should be made prior to 1808, should in any way affect the clause of the Constitution relative to this subject.*

The labors of the Convention were brought to a close on the 17th of September, 1787. On that day, we are told, Dr. Franklin rose with a written speech in his hands, which his friend, Mr. Wilson, read to the Convention. It was highly conciliatory. The object was to induce the Convention unanimously to agree to the Constitution as formed, or at least to sanction it, *pro forma*, by the signature of their names; and in order to avoid the scruples of any tender consciences, he proposed the following ambiguous form: "Done in Convention by the unanimous consent of *the States* present," &c. The motion was adopted by all the States except South Carolina, Gen. Pinckney and Mr. Butler dissenting, which divided the vote of that State. Notwithstanding this equivocal expression of assent, three of the members, Messrs. Gerry of Massachusetts, and Randolph and Mason of Virginia, refused to sign.† All the rest of the members present, including the whole of the South Carolina delegation, then affixed their names, and the Convention adjourned *sine die*.

* Madison Papers, vol iii. p. 1536.

† Messrs. Yates and Lansing, it will be recollected, had left the Convention. Besides these there were eleven other members of the Convention who had attended during the session, whose names do not appear affixed to the instrument. Among these are Oliver Ellsworth and Luther Martin, the former of whom, however, was accidentally absent, as it is well known he was warmly in favor of the Constitution.—*See subsequent sketch of Ellsworth.*

Rutledge and his associates returned to South Carolina, the firm and ardent champions of the new Constitution. Their labors and influence contributed doubtless, in a very great degree, to its ratification on the part of that State. On the 16th of January following, the subject was brought before the Legislature, on a resolution to call a convention of the people to consider the Constitution. A long and interesting debate followed—a debate characterized by as much ability, perhaps, as any which occurred in either of the States on this momentous question. The South Carolina Legislature, at that period, was a body of the most exalted character. Nearly every distinguished and eminent citizen of the State was a member. Among them were the three Rutledges, John, Edward and Hugh, the Pinckneys, Rawlins Lowndes, Pierce Butler, Robert Barnwell, Dr. Ramsay, Thomas Bee, Judges Grimke and Burke, Chancellor Mathews, and many others of equal respectability. The debate was opened by Mr. Charles Pinckney, in an elaborate and masterly speech, explanatory of the principal features of the new Constitution. The discussion which followed soon developed the fact that the majority, comprising most of the intellect and talent of the State, was decidedly in favor of the ratification of the Constitution. The Honorable Rawlins Lowndes was the only gentleman of any considerable distinction, who as the representative of a minority, strong in point of numbers, opposed the Constitution. He conducted the discussion with much ability on his side, but was successfully met and answered by Mr. Charles Pinckney, Charles Cotesworth Pinckney, Edward Rutledge, Robert Barnwell, and Chancellor Mathews, who mainly conducted the debate on the other side. Of course it was not to be expected that with such an overwhelming force against him, Mr. Lowndes could make a successful stand. He pressed his points, however, with great shrewdness, and the utmost pertinacity. Chancellor Rutledge did not mingle in these debates to any considerable extent, believing the convention to be the proper place for a full discussion of the question. He took up the argument, however, against Mr. Lowndes, in regard to the treaty-making power vested by the Constitution in the Senate, and showed very clearly that no solid reasons could be given to justify the fears expressed by his opponent, that this power might be used to the subversion of the laws of the country and the public liberty. Mr. Lowndes, far from yielding the point, reiterated his proposition, and attempted to sustain it by additional arguments. This again called out Chancellor Rutledge, who, after declaring the pleasure with which he had often heard the gentleman, expressed astonishment at his perseverance on the present occasion. His obstinacy, he remarked, brought to his recollection a friend to his country, once a member of that house, who said: "It is generally imputed to me that I am obstinate; this is a mistake; I am not so, *but hard to be convinced.*" Mr. Lowndes had declared that his own sentiments were so opposed to the voice of his constituents, that he did not expect to be a member of the Convention. Alluding to this, and the preference which Mr. Lowndes had declared for the confederation, the Chancellor expressed the hope that his opponent would be appointed, adding that he "did not hesitate to pledge himself to prove demonstrably, that all those grounds on which he dwelt so much, amounted to nothing more than mere declamation; that his boasted confederation was not worth a farthing, and that if Mr. Chairman was intrenched in such instruments up to his chin, they would not shield him from one single national calamity." Mr. Lowndes, however, does not appear to have been a member of the Convention, and if Rutledge redeemed his pledge, it must have been to some person other than that gentleman.

Notwithstanding the great preponderance of talent and influence in favor of the Constitution, the resolution calling the Convention was passed in the Legislature by a very close vote—only one majority—and it is also worthy of remark, that Mr. Lowndes himself, voted in the affirmative.*

The Convention assembled at Charleston on the 12th of May, 1788. Rutledge was a member, with both his associates on the bench, and nearly every gentleman of distinction and talent in the State. The assembly was composed of upwards of two hundred members, and the Governor of the State, Thomas Pinckney, was elected to preside over it. Mr. Charles Pinckney appropriately opened the deliberations, as one of the delegates to the Federal Convention. His speech, upon this occasion, was a philosophical and statesman-like exposition of the nature of government in general, a

* See Elliott's Debates on the Federal Constitution, vol. iv. p. 303.

comprehensive review of the governments of the various States and the principles established therein, and a clear and forcible application of the subject to that new and untried system which the Federal Convention had agreed upon.* The discussion thus opened continued more than a week, and it is unnecessary to add that here, as in every other proper place and on all suitable occasions, Chancellor Rutledge was the eloquent advocate, and the firm, unwavering, steadfast champion of the Constitution, substantially as it came from the hands of its framers.

On the 21st of May, General Sumpter, who was opposed to the Constitution, moved an adjournment of the Convention until the 20th of October, in order to give time for *further consideration.* This motion, after considerable debate, was rejected by a large majority. Two days afterwards the vote was taken on the question of ratification, and carried in the affirmative by a majority of 76. South Carolina accepted the Federal Constitution and took her place in the Union. She was thus assigned a position speedily to realize the prediction of her distinguished and devoted son, John Rutledge, who had declared in reply to the doubts and fears of his opponents, that "so far from thinking that the sun of this country was obscured by the new Constitution, he did not doubt but that whenever it was adopted, the sun of this State, united with twelve other suns, would exhibit a meridian radiance astonishing to the world."†

On the organization of the Federal Government, Chancellor Rutledge was handsomely complimented by his native State, in receiving its electoral vote for the office of Vice-President of the United States —the vote of the State being cast unanimously for Gen. Washington for President. This circumstance, of itself, is sufficient to show the high place occupied by Rutledge in the estimation of his fellow-citizens, and that he was regarded then, as he had been for years previous, and as he continued to be for years subsequent, as among the foremost men in America. A higher compliment, if possible, certainly one more honorable to his judicial character, was his appointment by the President, and unanimous confirmation by the Senate, as an Associate-Justice of the Supreme Court of the United States, imme-

* Elliott's Debates, vol. iv. pp. 305 to 317.

† Elliott's Debates, vol. iv. p. 299.

diately on its organization, in September, 1789. The name of Rutledge is next in the order of commission to that of the Chief-Justice.* Indeed, it has been intimated that the President only assigned the Chief-Justiceship to Mr. Jay, "after some deliberation."† This, however, I think is incorrect. The "Act to establish the Judicial Courts of the United States" was approved on the 24th September, 1789, and the President sent into the Senate, on the very same day, his list of nominations for Judges of the Court. There is very little doubt that Jay, above all others, was Washington's first choice for the Chief-Justiceship, and without any "deliberation;" and as little doubt, perhaps, that if Jay had declined, the office would then have been tendered to Rutledge; in which event, it is more than probable that Chancellor Livingston would have been the selection from New York for a seat upon the bench of the Supreme Court.

Mr. Rutledge was, as we have seen, at the time of his appointment, one of the Chancellors of the State of South Carolina. In the introduction to Desaussure's Chancery Reports, it is stated that he continued to hold this office till his appointment in February, 1791, to the Chief-Justiceship of South Carolina. If this be so he must have held the Chancellorship and his appointment under the Federal Government concurrently, for it does not appear that he resigned his office as Associate-Justice of the Supreme Court, until after his appointment to the Chief-Justiceship of South Carolina. Thomas Johnson of Maryland, who succeeded Judge Rutledge on the bench of the United States Supreme Court, was appointed and took his seat at the August term, 1791, so that the latter must have held this place up to that time. During the short time, however, which elapsed between his appointment and resignation—a period of less than two years—it is not probable that he performed much active service. The courts where then in the process of organization, and very little business could have been transacted at this early period, either at the Circuits or in the Supreme Court. We have seen that Judge

* By the Judiciary Act, the Judges were to take precedence according to the dates of their respective commissions. The commission of Judge Rutledge is dated the 26th of September; that of Judge Cushing the 27th; Judge Harrison the 28th; Judge Wilson the 29th, and Judge Blair the 30th.

† See Preliminary Notes to Wharton's State Trials.

Rutledge was not present at the organization of the Supreme Court, February term, 1790,* nor indeed does it appear that he was present at either of the two following terms. It is not unlikely that, with the assistance perhaps of Judge Iredell, he held the Circuit Courts for the southern circuit, comprising the States of South Carolina and Georgia, and North Carolina on the accession of that State to the confederacy;—but I do not find any thing of special importance relative to this portion of his judicial career. If, as Mr. Desaussure states, Judge Rutledge continued to hold the office of Chancellor during this period, he must have held it nominally, merely, and without rendering any active duties. The last case I can find, in which he sat on the bench as Chancellor, is at the December term, in the year 1789. Every other reported case down to the period of his resignation, seems to have been decided in his absence by his associates, Chancellors Hutson and Mathews.

The politics of Judge Rutledge had been of the Federal stamp; that is to say, he had been, as we have already seen, ardently and zealously in favor of the Federal Union, upon the principles embodied in the Constitution;—and he had been also classed with the leading Federalists of that day, who sustained the administration of President Washington. He was now to separate from his party upon a vital and important question. It was in regard to the celebrated treaty of Mr. Jay, which I have alluded to in the preceding sketch of that gentleman. The course taken by Rutledge in this matter, is by no means remarkable. His prompt, fearless, and independent action in opposing the treaty, was precisely what might have been expected from a haughty but chivalric temper, and a mind not slow to forget a wrong or resent an injury. Two opposite sentiments—passions they might be called—had taken deep root in his breast, and strongly influenced, if they did not absolutely control his political views and actions; namely, antipathy to England, nourished as it was by the bitter and undying memory of past wrongs, and love for his own people and the gallant State of his birth. And surely no man ever had cause to love England less, or South Carolina more. It is no wonder, therefore, that Rutledge should have opposed and denounced with passionate earnestness, this treaty, regarding it as he did both as

* See Life of Jay, *ante*, page 47.

an unworthy concession to the grasping policy of England, and as an unjust sacrifice of the rights and interests of that portion of the confederacy to which he belonged. The opposition of such men as Rutledge and Pinckney struck the friends of the treaty with astonishment and dismay. Nor was it a lukewarm opposition ; he entered into it as he had done into the revolutionary struggle in his native State, with all the warmth and ardor, all the energy and impetuosity of his temper. This is manifest from the strong language used by some of the prominent Federalists of the day, in opposition to his appointment as Chief-Justice. Oliver Ellsworth remarks in a letter to Mr. Wolcott: "That E. R. (Edward Rutledge) should not act at all, is less surprising than that J. R. (John Rutledge) should act like the *devil.* I wait for the unravelling, when more is to be known."

But the composure and firmness of Washington raised him above all party and personal considerations.* Sustained by the majestic strength of his own character, and relying with a just confidence upon the suggestions of his own judgment and the instincts of his own noble nature, he stood unmoved amid the war of faction, and was deaf alike to the dark hints, and the open remonstrances, of those who desired to defeat the nomination. Without a moment's hesitation, and with scarcely an intimation of his purpose to his cabinet, on the resignation of Judge Jay, he tendered to Rutledge the vacant Chief-Justiceship. His letter of appointment is both cordial and respectful ; and bears honorable testimony alike to the greatness of the mind that conceived it, and the character of the man to whom it was addressed. It bears date at Philadelphia, July 1, 1795, and is as follows :

"Dear Sir :—Your private letter of the 18th ultimo, and Mr. Jay's resignation of the office of Chief-Justice of the United States, both came to my hands yesterday. The former gave me much pleasure, and without hesitating a moment, after knowing you would accept the latter, I directed the Secretary of State to make you an

* President Adams very complacently contrasts his own policy in regard to appointments to office with that of Washington. In a letter to Wolcott he says: "Washington appointed a multitude of Democrats and Jacobins of the deepest dye. *I have been more cautious in this respect,*" &c.

official offer of this honorable appointment; to express to you my wish that it may be convenient and agreeable to you to accept it; to intimate, in that case, my desire, and the advantages that would attend your being in this city the first Monday in August, at which time the next session of the Supreme Court will commence; and to inform you that your commission as Chief-Justice will take date on this day, July 1st, when Mr. Jay's will cease, but that it would be detained here to be presented to you on your arrival.

"I shall only add that the Secretary will write to you by post and by a water conveyance also, if there be any vessel in this harbor which will sail for Charleston in a few days, and that with much sensibility for your good wishes, and an assurance of the sincerest esteem and regard, I am, my dear sir," &c.

Rutledge accepted the appointment so handsomely tendered, and immediately set out for Philadelphia. He arrived in time to take his seat as Chief-Justice in the Supreme Court at the commencement of the August term of the same year.

In the mean time rumors of the appointment had got abroad, and the leading Federalists who were enlisted in carrying through the Jay treaty did not scruple to express their dissatisfaction. "To my astonishment," writes the Secretary of the Treasury, Wolcott, to Hamilton, July 28, 1795: "To my astonishment I am recently told that John Rutledge has had the tender of the office of Chief-Justice. By the favor of Heaven the commission is not tendered, and now I presume it will not be; *but how near ruin and disgrace has the country been!*" A sentiment in which Hamilton very cordially concurred, as is evident from his reply a few days after: "I find it is true that John Rutledge has been invited to be Chief-Justice, but he is not commissioned, and I must presume he will not be after his late conduct." Indeed to such an extent did party feelings carry that uncompromising Federalist, Wolcott, that he does not hesitate in one of his letters to Hamilton to stigmatize Rutledge as "a driveller and a fool," and even to cast obliquely a reflection on the President himself.* Others of the Federalists, however, were more

* The same gentleman characterizes one of Edward Livingston's finest speeches in the House of Representatives as "rant." The high terms in which Chief-Justice Marshall speaks of Rutledge's abilities are in strong contrast with the

moderate in the expression of their opinion. Mr. Ellsworth, who disapproved the appointment merely, remarks: "With regard to Mr. Rutledge, it certainly was difficult, after he had come, not to commission him. If the evil is without remedy, we must, as in other cases, make the best of it."

A leading Federal member of Congress* about the same time writes:—"Many of the advocates for the present measures are hurt by Mr. Rutledge's appointment, and are unable to account for it, but impute it to want of information of his hostility to the government, or some hidden cause which justifies the measure. We shall be loth to find that faction is to be courted at so great a sacrifice of consistency." Remarks like these, from comparatively moderate men, alike unjust to the motives of the President, and to the character of Judge Rutledge, will serve to show the state of party feeling at the time. It must be added that the appointment had not been made in consequence of a "want of information." Rutledge's position in regard to the treaty was well known; indeed it is said that Washington had from the outset fully weighed the objections that would be made, had anticipated the opposition of members of his cabinet, and therefore had given them no intimation of his intentions. He certainly could not have anticipated the extraordinary course subsequently taken by those claiming to be the peculiar friends of his administration in the Senate, and who undertook to *correct his error*, by refusing to confirm the nomination.

The newspapers of the day in the Federal interest, in like manner, censured the appointment in the strongest terms. Rutledge's opposition to the Jay treaty was no secret. It was a public, bold, and energetic opposition, and from the character and standing of the man, it attracted the attention of the whole country. About the time his appointment as Chief-Justice became known, the news was received at the North of a large and enthusiastic meeting held at Charleston, July 16, 1795, to denounce the treaty. General Gadsden, Judge Mathews, and other eminent citizens took the lead

petulant and contemptuous language of Wolcott. He call him "a gentleman of vigor and talents:" a gentleman of great talents and decision," &c. See 1 Marshall's *Washington*, p. 72–297.

* Chauncey Goodrich.

at this meeting, and among others Rutledge addressed it with more than his usual animation and vehemence in condemnation of the treaty.* A pretended report of this speech found its way into the papers, and some expressions in it were criticised with great severity. Nor was this all. There were those who did not hesitate, under the protection of anonymous newspaper publications, to attack not only the political, but the private character of the Chief-Justice. In the "Columbian Centinel," a Federal paper published at Boston, an anonymous letter appeared, August 26, 1795, under the signature of "A real Republican," addressed to Judge Rutledge, and filled with the most bitter and violent denunciation. This letter alludes to his "mounting a hogshead, haranguing a mob assembled purposely to reprobate the treaty and insult the Executive of the United States." In regard to his office of Chief-Justice, the writer very considerately advises him, "if he would save himself from disgrace," to decline the appointment. After some severe, and even savage, comments upon his pecuniary situation and financial embarrassments, the author of this letter, apparently stimulated by his own passions to redoubled virulence, insinuates, "from common report," charges against Rutledge's morals and habits too gross to be here repeated. An able and candid vindication by "a South Carolinian," who describes himself as differing from the Chief-Justice in opinion upon the treaty, appeared, a few days after, in the same paper. If Judge Rutledge is embarrassed in his affairs, the writer says, it is because his fortune had been freely sacrificed in the service of his country; but the Constitution does not demand fortune as a qualification for the Chief-Justiceship. The great legal ability, and the eminent fitness of Judge Rutledge for the office, are dwelt upon with force and becoming

* It was in reference to this speech, doubtless, that his name is mentioned in the "elegant lines" (as they are called by a Federal newspaper of the day) which introduce a summing up, or peroration of "the Echo," published at the time in the Connecticut "Courant," commencing thus:

"Oh, Washington! how stands thy dauntless breast?
Do scenes like these disturb thy mighty rest?
Though Charleston mob, like lice in Egypt, swarms;
Though RUTLEDGE rages, and though PINCKNEY storms;
Though *thieves* and LIVINGSTONS with patriot ire
Commit the accursed paper to the fire," &c., &c.

dignity. It is but justice also to add that while the writer assumes that "his private character has nothing to do with his official uprightness," yet he indignantly remarks, "even *that* defies the tongue of calumny, although 'a Real Republican' would hint at, he says not what, to excite a suspicion against it."*

These attacks, however, as is usual in such cases, appear to have produced very little or no impression. Nor did they operate in that quarter toward which perhaps they were more especially directed—the mind of the President. The confidence of Washington seems to have continued unabated. During Rutledge's stay in Philadelphia, at the August session of the Supreme Court, he was invited to dine with the President; and this circumstance is mentioned even by the "Centinel" as "evincive of cordiality between these two distinguished characters, notwithstanding any difference of political sentiment between them." But a stronger evidence that the mind of Washington was not influenced by these combined assaults, and that his confidence in the fitness and capacity of the Chief-Justice remained unshaken, is found in the fact that notwithstanding this outside pressure, he resolutely adhered to his original purpose, and on the opening of Congress sent in the name of Judge Rutledge to the Senate for confirmation in the office of Chief-Justice.

Chief-Justice Rutledge presided in the Supreme Court at the August term, 1795. There are only two reported cases at this term. In the decision of both of them the Chief-Justice took part, but in neither of them does he assign the reasons upon which his judgment is based. Each of these cases involved a question of jurisdiction. The first † was a motion for a prohibition to the District Court of Pennsylvania, restraining that Court from assuming jurisdiction in the case of a libel filed for damages against the *Cassius*, an armed vessel belonging to the French republic, which had captured an American vessel on the high seas. The vessel which had been captured by the Cassius had not been brought within the jurisdic-

* The reply to this vindication in the "Centinel" of Sept. 5, 1795, seems to disclose the real motive of this personal attack on Rutledge. It evidently came from a warm and indiscreet friend of Jay, of whom Rutledge was said to have spoken very harshly in his Charleston speech.

† United States *vs.* Peters, District Judge, 3 Dallas, 120.

tion of the United States; but had been sent to St. Domingo and condemned there as a prize. The question, argued by Mr. Dallas in support of the motion, was whether under such circumstances the District Court had cognizance of the matter. In granting the motion the Chief-Justice delivers his opinion in his usual terse and laconic style, stating simply the conclusion arrived at without assigning any reason for the decision. "We have consulted together on this motion, and though a difference of sentiment exists, a majority of the Court are clearly of the opinion that the motion ought to be granted. Therefore let a prohibition issue."*

A more important question was brought before the Court in the case of Talbot *vs.* Jansen† which was argued at the same term.

A brief statement of the facts will be necessary to show the points at issue in this interesting controversy. Ballard, an American citizen, was in command of a vessel called *L' Ami de la Liberté*, pretending to be a French cruiser, but which had been illegally fitted out in the United States. Talbot, also an American citizen, but who produced French naturalization papers, was in command of another armed vessel called *L'Ami de la point a Petre*, sailing under a French commission. Ballard captured a Dutch vessel, and being soon after joined by Talbot, the latter took possession of the prize, and in company with Ballard, both having put prize masters on board, brought the captured vessel into the port of Charleston. The Dutch captain claimed restitution, which the District Court of Charleston decreed, and the Circuit Court of Charleston confirmed the decree. From this decision Talbot, the captain of the French vessel, appealed. The argument turned mainly upon the questions whether the capture under such circumstances was in

* The case of "The Cassius" has been, subsequently, approved in the Supreme Court by the decision in the case of "The Invincible," 1 Wheaton, 238; and also in the opinion pronounced by Justice Story in the case of "The Santissima Trinidad," 7 Wheaton, 288. The seizure of "The Cassius" was made an accusation against the American government by Talleyrand, in his correspondence with the American envoys, Messrs. Marshall, Pinckney, and Gerry. In his reply to Talleyrand, General Marshall very clearly states the case on the other side; and refers to the decision of the Supreme Court, refusing to take jurisdiction, as a complete vindication of the United States. See American State Papers.

† 3 Dallas' Reports, 133.

violation of the treaty with Holland; and if so whether the United States courts could take jurisdiction of the case consistently with the treaty between America and France. But another question of the gravest character and highest importance was also raised and discussed for the first time in the Federal courts—a question upon which the judicial mind remained unsettled for years subsequently, and which in some respects may still be considered a *questio vexata* —namely, whether the common law doctrine as to allegiance and expatriation was to be regarded in America as a rule of municipal law. It had been made a point in the argument against the legality of the capture, that Talbot's French naturalization was unavailing, and that he remained still a citizen of the United States. This, of course, opened the way for a full discussion of the doctrine of perpetual allegiance, but no decision was pronounced upon it, the case being finally disposed of upon other principles. The question, however, was considered by Judges Paterson and Iredell in their carefully written opinions, the latter of whom seemed inclined to hold the doctrine subsequently laid down by Judge Ellsworth, and applied with such strictness in the trial of Williams,* that a citizen does not possess the right of voluntary expatriation without the permission of his own government. Judge Rutledge carefully avoided expressing an opinion on the subject. "The doctrine of expatriation is certainly of great magnitude," he remarks, "but it is not necessary to give an opinion upon it in the present cause, there being no proof that Captain Talbot's admission as a citizen of the French republic, was with a view to relinquish his native country; and a man may at the same time enjoy the rights of citizenship under two governments." Upon the merits of the case the Chief-Justice concurred entirely with his associates in sustaining the decree of the District Court, which awarded the Dutch vessel to its rightful owners. In pronouncing the judgment of the court, which he does with more than his usual economy of language, he disposes of the pretensions of Capt. Talbot in the following decisive and summary manner: "The capture was a violation of the law of nations, and of the treaty with Holland. The Court has a clear jurisdiction of the cause.

* See remarks on the trial of Williams in subsequent sketch of Judge Ellsworth.

Every motive of good faith and justice must induce us to concur with the Circuit Court in awarding restitution."

The dignified bearing of Chief-Justice Rutledge on the bench has been spoken of, on the authority of traditionary accounts, in the highest terms of praise. It was graceful and courtly, though tinged, it is said, with that haughtiness which in later years had marked him. In these closing scenes of his judicial career, and of his public life, it was remarked that his natural impetuosity had been subdued by the approach of age, the weight of long public service, and the anxiety of a position, the intrigues of which, he soon became conscious, admonished him was but too insecure.*

The appointment of Rutledge had been made during the recess of Congress. He was yet to pass the ordeal of the Senate. The Jay treaty had been approved by the President, and there seemed now no controlling reason for opposing his confirmation, unless, perhaps, on account of the affirmative action still required of Congress to carry out some of the provisions of the treaty. Nevertheless so great was the chagrin of the dominant party in the Senate, that notwithstanding their avowed respect for the President, they determined to carry out the extraordinary measure of opposing him in this nomination. The subject was entertained among prominent men some time before it was acted upon by the Senate, as is evident from a letter of the elder Wolcott, dated Nov. 23, 1795. "I hope we may rely upon the firmness of the Senate," he says. "The virtuous motives which have induced the treating with regard men who avow and act upon principles inconsistent with the preservation of order, to influence them to a more just conduct, have been and will be ineffectual. I hope, therefore, however disagreeable it may be to imply an error of judgment in the President in appointing Mr. Rutledge, that he will not be confirmed in his office."

The hope thus expressed was destined to no disappointment. On the 15th December, 1795, the Senate, by a small majority, refused to confirm the nomination, and thus the "error in judgment" of the President was corrected by his own professed personal and political friends. It was well understood that the vote of the Senate was

* Notes to Wharton's State Trials.

governed mainly by political considerations.* This is very clearly evident from an expression in a letter from Jefferson to Madison written at the time. "The rejection of Rutledge by the Senate," he says, "is a bold thing, because they cannot pretend any objection to him but his disapprobation of the treaty."

But, whatever may have been the reasons and motives which influenced the action of the Senate, the rejection of Rutledge was in many respects fortunate both for himself and his friends. Even if he had been confirmed, he would probably never again have taken his seat on the bench. For, while his nomination was yet pending in the Senate, that strong and vigorous mind was becoming unsettled, and the light of that brilliant intellect was fading into darkness and night. The Senate had scarcely set its seal of disapprobation upon the nomination of Rutledge when rumors reached Philadelphia that he was becoming insane. "The fact," says a correspondent from that city, "is daily corroborated. I have it from authority which mingles the tears of pity and commiseration."

The malady which prostrated Rutledge and overclouded the latter years of his life was in a measure the result of diseases brought upon him many years before by sufferings and exposure in the service of his country. I am assured by a connection of the family that the mother and wife of Rutledge were frequently heard to say that a fever taken at an unhealthy season of the year, in a swampy district of country, at the time the British troops were overrunning the colony, had laid the seeds of that disorder which broke down his constitution while he was yet in the prime of life, and from which he never recovered.

Just before his rejection by the Senate—though that body does not seem to have had at the time of the vote any definite knowledge of the true state of the case—he experienced a renewed and violent attack of sickness which it appears ended in insanity. A letter from Charleston, under date of December 1st, 1795, conveys the first inti-

* Hamilton hints at other reasons, in a letter to Rufus King, so late as December 14th, and speaks of the reports which had been circulated to Mr. Rutledge's discredit. "If there were nothing in the case," he remarks, "but his imprudent sally upon a certain occasion, I should think the reasons for letting him pass would outweigh those for opposing his passage."—*Hamilton's Works*, vol. VI. p. 76.

mation of his illness: "By a gentleman who left Camden on Wednesday last, we are informed that the Chief-Justice of the United States left that place on the Saturday preceding on his way to hold the Circuit Court in North Carolina; that on the evening of that day he reached Evans's tavern on Lynch Creek, which he left the next morning. A few hours after he was taken so unwell that he was obliged to return to Mr. Evans'. When the account came away he was so much indisposed as to make it doubtful whether he would be able to proceed in time to hold the court in North Carolina."*

Three days afterwards, a paragraph in the same paper announces: "By a southern paper we learn that Judge Rutledge is so disordered in his intellect, as to render it necessary to have him constantly guarded, he having threatened and even attempted his own destruction."†

And here the scene closes upon the life of Rutledge. Nothing remains to be added. The remnant of his life is a blank and a void. It was passed in the fluctuations of a disease which prostrated alike body and mind. The strong man had fallen, and the light of a great intellect had become dimmed. To borrow the striking imagery of oriental imagination, the silver cord was loosened, the pitcher broken at the fountain, and the wheel broken at the cistern. He died in the summer of 1800, about six months after the decease of his brother, Gov. Edward Rutledge, and was interred in St. Michael's churchyard, in his native city of Charleston.

Mr. Rutledge was married in the year 1763, to Miss Elizabeth Grimké. He left a family of five sons and two daughters, all of whom are now dead. His descendants, however, are numerous, many of them residing in the city of Charleston. His eldest son, John Rutledge, jun., a gentleman of fine talents and effective eloquence, was a leading member of Congress, during a part of the administrations of Adams and Jefferson; retaining his place in that body as long as the Federal party was in the ascendancy in South Carolina.‡

* Boston "Centinel," January 2, 1796.

† The "Aurora" announces on the authority of a letter from a gentleman of Charleston, of Dec. 31, 1795, that "Chief-Justice Rutledge, on Saturday last, attempted to drown himself, but was taken out of the water by some negroes. It is said he has discovered symptoms of derangement for some weeks past."

‡ He took a prominent part in the discussions of that body, and particularly

There were many traits in the character of Judge Rutledge calculated to attract the popular admiration. He was bold, open, frank and ardent in temper and disposition, and was gifted with those captivating conversational powers which rarely fail to find their way to the sympathies and hearts of his fellows. But independent of this he possessed many of those higher and more sterling qualities which stamp the man of real superiority of mind. I am doing no injustice to others in claiming for Rutledge a place among the very ablest and greatest of the revolutionary leaders.* He exhibited abilities of the most striking character in every position in which he was placed. He was eminent, not merely as an orator—in the eloquence of language and of action—but as a statesman, a legislator, a jurist. His administrative talents were of the first order. He was a man of action, of energy, of resources—a man of a powerful grasp of intellect, of liberal views, and of original impressions. He possessed the qualities of decision and firmness in a remarkable degree and in their best sense, and he was endowed with an indomitable will which adversity could not shake, nor misfortune crush. The courage of Rutledge was of the highest character; he exhibited every degree of it—from the courage of the grenadier to that of the statesman—from mere physical composure and intrepidity in the midst of danger, to that more exalted species of courage which shrinks not to incur a responsibility, or boldly avow an unpopular principle in the face of the world. His public career is full of instances of courageous action and fearless independence. No public man of the times acted under less restraint from the shackles of party. His independence was not a mere semblance, but a reality—a full, genuine, unfettered independence of thought, word, and action. He scorned alike to conceal an opinion, and to abandon a principle, no matter at what cost to himself, or what personal sacrifice.

If to these superior qualities were added some which may be sup-

distinguished himself in the celebrated debates on the change of the judiciary system in January, 1802. He also participated effectively in the animated discussions on the extradition of Nash, in the year 1800.

* "He was the soul of every council and enterprise," says an intelligent gentleman of his native State in a letter now before me, "and his energy and genius went far in the conduct of the war in this section of the country."

posed to detract in a measure from his greatness, it merely proves the general imperfection of all human excellence. If it be true that he was proud and haughty, imperious in manner, and hasty and obstinate in temper—if it be true even, as his enemies insinuated, that he was not entirely exempt from those frailties which social custom in his day tolerated, if it did not encourage,—it affords but another evidence of the fact which all history demonstrates and experience confirms, that mankind furnish few, if any, examples of perfect character. But there was in Rutledge so much of real superiority and genuine greatness, that these imperfections, though perhaps they ought not to be entirely overlooked, may be passed by in silence. To the American people, and especially the people of his own State, he must always appear, as he appeared to General Greene, "one of the first characters" in our annals. Such a distinction he honorably and nobly won, and surely no one better deserves to wear it than he.

In the hall of the Supreme Court at the Capitol in Washington may be seen, upon their marble pedestals, the busts of Jay, of Ellsworth, and of Marshall. The eye of the stranger naturally seeks the bust of the distinguished Carolinian also, in that august tribunal over which he too, though for a brief period, presided;—but it seeks it in vain. No product of the sculptor's chisel, amid that silent but impressive marble group, recalls the memory of John Rutledge. And the thought naturally arises in the mind, why is it that his place is vacant? Surely there might be found at least some niche in the judicial temple by the side of his predecessor, and his successors, on the bench, for the second Chief-Justice of the United States.

OLIVER ELLSWORTH.

OLIVER ELLSWORTH.

Oliver Ellsworth was a Senator in Congress from the State of Connecticut at the time the Senate refused to confirm Mr. Rutledge in the office of Chief-Justice. As a member of the Federal party he of course contributed to defeat the nomination of his predecessor; but no one has ventured to question the purity of motive which prompted his action on that occasion. From his known reluctance to accept the vacant place, it is probable that he himself was the last member of the Senate who could have anticipated that the judicial robe was about to fall from Judge Rutledge's shoulders on his own.

Chief-Justice Ellsworth brought to that high tribunal, over which, for a brief period, he presided, a valuable experience both as a lawyer and a judge. Called to the bar a few years previous to the revolution, he had attained a respectable professional position before his business was interrupted by those great political events which summoned him into the public service; and when, at the close of the revolution, he returned to his native State, it was to take his seat upon the bench of the Connecticut Superior Courts, in which station he continued until the Federal Convention, and the organization of the new government opened to him a wider and more extended field of usefulness. He came to the bench of the Federal Courts, therefore, under the most favorable auspices; for he added the experience of the statesman to that of the advocate and the jurist. He possessed, in a felicitous combination, remarks a very judicious writer, "those qualities which make up a great judge, and which afterwards, through a much longer career, were displayed by his eminent successor. His mind, naturally exact and comprehensive, had been disciplined by severe study and by the exercises of an extended practice. He went into public life just at that period, when the intellect, not yet so settled in the professional mold as to lose its natural malleability, is able to adapt itself to its new and more liberal pursuits with tenacity and precision, but without the stiffness attendant on long service at the bar." * He remained, it is true, but a few years on the bench of the Supreme Court; but, like his predecessor, Jay, he retired with honor, and left the impress of his mind upon the early history of the federal judiciary.

I have not been able to collect materials for any very detailed account of the early years of Mr. Ellsworth's life. In this respect, indeed, he has but little the advantage of the great majority of his brethren of the old Supreme Court, of whom scarcely a notice remains. Nor, perhaps, could this be expected. The life of a plain New England lawyer must have glided on smoothly and quietly enough until broken in upon by the stormy scenes of the revolution; and whatever of local interest may have attached to it, we could scarcely hope, even were it possible to retrace the record, to meet with many of those personal recollections which serve at once to illustrate the character, and to indicate the temper and talents of the future judge. Nor should we expect to find in these earlier years of his life a narrative replete with those striking incidents or great enterprises, which sometimes sparkle on the page of biography, and never fail to attract the public gaze. There is nothing of this in the early history of Oliver Ellsworth. Indeed, that history may be said to commence with his appointment to the Continental Congress in 1777. With little to interest, and nothing to excite previous to this period, we shall, thenceforth, on every hand, encounter interesting traces of the labors and services of the pains-taking and judicious statesman, and the discreet and careful judge, in the various departments of civil life which he filled, legislative, diplomatic, and judicial. From this point then I shall take up the narrative; first, however, presenting the reader with a summary of the earlier years of his life, as it is sketched by the graceful pen of one who seems to have thoroughly understood and appreciated the character of his subject.†

* Notes to Wharton's Am. State Trials, p. 37.

† From an original memoir of Chief-Justice Ellsworth, published in the Ana-

" Oliver Ellsworth was born at Windsor, a village in the interior of Connecticut, April 29th, 1745, of respectable, but not very wealthy parents. He was brought up in the simple, regular, and frugal mode of life which at that time universally prevailed throughout the province, and which is still, although in a less degree, a striking characteristic of the domestic manners of Connecticut.

" The state of manners and of education in New England about this period, was, perhaps, of all others, the best calculated to rear up men fitted to struggle through the toils, the difficulties, and the dangers of a great revolution, without endangering the safety of those republican institutions for which they contended, either by turbulent violence, or unprincipled ambition. A greater proportion of the whole population of the country had received a liberal education, than was probably the case in any other part of the civilized world. Thus, in addition to the number of men, not, indeed, profoundly learned, but competently instructed for any ordinary purpose of active life, a great mass of general information was diffused, and a universal activity of mind excited throughout the whole community. The bigotry and fanaticism which occasionally disgraced the elder puritan settlers had died away ; much, too, of their rigid virtue and high-toned principle had gradually decayed with them ; but enough was left to keep up a very general regard to moral and religious character, and an habitual reference to principle, in the conduct and opinions of the great body of the people. Above all, the peculiar state of the country, which had just emerged from the hardships of a new and half-peopled colony, while it excluded most of the luxuries and many of the refinements of civilized life, had a strong tendency to train up the youth in those habits of simplicity and privation, of personal independence, and of constant activity of mind and body, which, however ill the parallel may accord with the magnificent illusions of classical prejudice—in fact constituted the most essential part of that education which formed the heroes and patriots of republican antiquity. *Sanctos illis, horrida, mores—tradidit domus, ac veteres imitata Sabinas.*

" In this state of society was Mr. Ellsworth's character formed, and the early impressions of his youth may be traced through the whole

lectic Magazine for 1814, Vol. III. page 382, and republished a few years since in Vol. III. American Law Journal.

uniform tenor of his public and private life. His youth was passed alternately in agricultural labors, and in the elementary studies of a liberal education. At the age of seventeen he entered Yale College; but after some residence there, in consequence of a boyish disgust or irregularity, he removed to Princeton, where he completed his academic course, and received the degree of A.B. in 1766.

"His standing as a student was sufficiently respectable; but he is said to have been much more remarkable for his shrewdness and adroit management in all the little politics of the College, than for any uncommon proficiency in science or literature. Within two or three years after his leaving college, he was admitted to the bar in Connecticut, and commenced the practice of his profession in the county of Hartford.* The jurisprudence of Connecticut, after a long period of darkness and uncertainty, had, a very short time before Mr. Ellsworth's entrance upon professional life, assumed a regular form.

"The common law, after overcoming many doubts, and some strenuous opposition, was fully received; a regular mode of practice, not very formal, but sufficiently accurate for every ordinary purpose, was now settled; and the decisions of Lord Mansfield and the other great English Judges, who had introduced light and order into the scholastic refinements and nice technical distinctions of the ancient law, and gradually adapted it to the necessities of an enlightened age, and a commercial people, were at length familiarly cited at the Connecticut bar. This amelioration of the legal system was accompanied or preceded by a corresponding improvement in literature and taste, and public speakers

* I find the following anecdote related of his early practice at the bar. "His father presented him with a small farm, situated in the south-western corner of Windsor, and in the management of this and the few suits with which his acquaintances and friends entrusted him, his ardent and active mind was forced for a time to content itself. As often as the session of the Court occurred at Hartford, leaving his farm and revolving his cases in his mind, he travelled thither on foot, and back again in the same manner, when the season was over. Soon, however, a suit was committed to his management, of trivial importance, indeed, so far as concerned the pecuniary interest at stake, but at the same time involving the decision of a legal principle of the deepest moment. Young Oliver proved himself equal to the emergency; and by the ability and skill he exhibited in the conduct of the suit, at once established his reputation on a permanent basis, and he took his stand among the most promising and talented of the younger members of his profession at the Hartford bar.

and advocates found themselves compelled to pay a much greater attention to correctness, and even elegance, of language, than the public taste had ever before required. With this era of legal and intellectual light Mr. Ellsworth commenced his professional career. He had not laid a very deep foundation either of general or professional learning; but the native vigor of his mind supplied every deficiency; the rapidity of his conceptions made up for the want of previous knowledge; the diligent study of the cases which arose in actual business, stored his mind with principles: whatever was thus acquired was firmly rooted in his memory; and thus, as he became eminent, he grew learned.

"The whole powers of his mind were applied with unremitted attention to the business of his profession, and those public duties in which he was occasionally engaged. Capable of great application, and constitutionally full of ardor, he pursued every object to which he applied himself with a strong and constant interest which never suffered his mind to flag or grow torpid with listless indolence. But his ardor was always under the guidance of sober reason. His cold and colorless imagination never led him astray from the realities of life to wanton in the gay visions of fancy; and his attention was seldom attracted by that general literary curiosity which so often beguiles the man of genius away from his destined pursuit, to waste his powers in studies of no immediate personal utility. At the same time his unblemished character, his uniform prudence and regularity of conduct acquired him the general confidence and respect of his fellow-citizens—a people in a remarkable degree attentive to all the decorum and decencies of civilized life. He very soon rose into high reputation and lucrative practice; and before he had been long at the bar received the appointment of State's Attorney for the district of Hartford, an office at that time of very considerable emolument. This he continued to hold during the greater part of the revolutionary war. From the very commencement of that contest he declared himself resolutely on the side of his country; and on two or three occasions, when Connecticut was harrassed by the incursions of the enemy, went out with the militia of his country into actual servive, more, however, for the sake of example, than from any particular inclination to military life. For several sessions in the years immediately preceding the declaration of independence, he represented the town in which he resided in the general Assembly of the State, with great reputation, and took a large share, not only in the ordinary business of the House, but also in all those public acts and declarations which were called forth by the peculiar circumstances of the times. About the commencement of the war he presided for a short time at the *pay-table*, as it was called, or office of public accounts of the State of Connecticut.

* * * * * * *

"Mr. Ellsworth was now fairly entered upon his career, and with a character and talents so admirably adapted to the state of society around him, he was enabled, without trick or artifice, or the sacrifice of principle, to take at the flood that *tide which leads to fortune*."

Such is the modest and unpretending history of Mr. Ellsworth's life up to the period of his entry upon that broader theatre of action which the revolution laid open before him. By the force of his talents and industry he had risen to an honorable position at the bar of his native province—a bar which could boast the names of such men as Johnson, Hosmer, Law, and Huntingdon, to stand side by side with whom might surely be an object worthy the ambition of the young aspirant after professional fame. This Ellsworth speedily accomplished, and if he did not outstrip, he at least soon equalled his older competitors. His talents as an advocate are said to have been unrivalled. He excelled especially as a *nisi prius* lawyer, in the conduct and management of causes, at the trial table ;—cool, adroit, cautious, and endowed with an admirable self-possession, and felicity of temper, he came to the trial of his cases, not only with perfect self-reliance on his own talents, but with that confidence which a thorough knowledge of the facts, as well as the law, and a careful and laborious preparation, never fail to inspire.

It is stated that when he took his seat in Congress in 1778, he abandoned a practice the most lucrative in Connecticut. The expression, I apprehend, is not strictly correct, as it does not appear that he actually abandoned his professional avocations during the war, although undoubtedly the business of the courts in that State, as well as in others, was much impeded at this period.* Ellsworth, like the

* That Ellsworth continued in the active practice of his profession up to the

rest of the Connecticut delegates, was not constant in his attendance upon the deliberations of Congress. That State usually commissioned seven delegates annually, not less than two nor more than four of whom were to attend at any one time at the charge of the State. The consequence of this arrangement was, that the delegates were alternately relieved by their colleagues, and thus were enabled to return home at intervals to attend to their private affairs and business avocations. Though Mr. Ellsworth was commissioned in the autumn of 1777, yet he did not actually take his seat until the 8th of October of the following year, Connecticut having been meanwhile represented alternately by his colleagues, Roger Sherman, Hosmer, A. Adams, and others.

In the mean time he had been assigned to the discharge of a difficult as well as delicate duty. On the very day when his name was placed on the commission as a deputy from the State of Connecticut to Congress, that body had named him as one of a committee of five to examine into, and report, the causes of the late failure of the expedition against Rhode Island. Ellsworth, with two of his associates, entered upon the discharge of this duty during the latter part of the next winter and spring, and, having taken a mass of testimony, reported the same to Congress. Nothing, however, seems to have been done beyond a mere entry of the fact upon the journal ; perhaps Congress deemed it a matter of more consequence to make provision for the success of new expeditions, than to waste its time in investigating the causes of the failure of old ones.

When Ellsworth took his seat in Congress, in October, 1778, that body consisted of about thirty members. It numbered some of the best, and ablest, and wisest men whom the revolution produced. Besides Ellsworth's colleague, Roger Sherman, the roll of its members contained the names of Samuel Adams, and Elbridge Gerry, of Massachusetts ; the two Morrises, Robert and Gouverneur ; Dr. Witherspoon, of New Jersey ; Richard Henry Lee, of Virginia ; Laurens, Drayton, and Mathews, of South Carolina ; and, soon after, John Jay, of New

period of his appointment as Judge of the Connecticut Superior Court, is evident from the fact which appears by the reports, that several important cases, in which he had been engaged as counsel, came before the Court for review, Judge Ellsworth, of course, taking no part in the decision.

York. It was a grave, discreet, dignified body of men, and its deliberations in the main were all characterized by order, moderation, firmness, and wisdom. The serious character of some of these deliberations would no doubt provoke idle criticism, if not ridicule, in our day. Only two or three days had elapsed after Ellsworth took his seat, when he was called upon to vote (and it is unnecessary to say that his vote was in the affirmative) upon the following resolutions, whose stern and rigid morality attest their genuine New England origin.

"Whereas, true religion and good morals are the only solid foundations of public liberty and happiness:

"*Resolved*—That it be, and it hereby is, earnestly recommended to the several States, to take the most effectual measures for the encouragement thereof; and for the suppressing theatrical entertainments, horse-racing, gaming, and such other diversions as are productive of idleness, dissipation, and a general depravity of principles and manners.

"*Resolved*—That all officers in the army of the United States be, and hereby are, strictly enjoined to see that the good and wholesome rules provided for the discountenancing of profaneness and vice, and the preservation of morals among the soldiers, are duly and punctually observed."

It may be added, that every New England vote is found recorded in the affirmative; and that the resolutions passed almost unanimously, one or two of the Southern States only dissenting.*

The deliberations of the Congress, it is well known, were secret, and we cannot, therefore, at this period of time, determine what may have been Ellsworth's precise share in the discussions of that body. Enough appears, however, from the Journal, to show that he was a prominent and active, as well as an efficient member, and that

* Journal of Congress, October 12th, 1778. Only a few days after, the following still more stringent resolutions were passed:

"WHEREAS, frequenting play-houses and theatrical entertainments has a fatal tendency to divert the minds of the people from a due attention to the means necessary for the defence of their country, and the preservation of their liberties:

"*Resolved*—That any person holding an office under the United States who shall act, promote, encourage, or attend such plays, shall be deemed unworthy to hold such office, and shall be accordingly dismissed."—*Journal of Congress*, Oct. 16th, 1778.

his services were peculiarly valuable upon the various important committees on which he was placed. Sitting, as it did, with closed doors, Congress exercised the double functions of a secret executive council, and of a supreme legislative body, and even added to these, at times, functions of a judicial character. It wielded the entire sovereignty of the confederacy—the powers of war and peace—and gave directions, through its committees and otherwise, to the finances, to foreign intercourse, and all naval and military operations. It may readily be supposed that the talents of Mr. Ellsworth were admirably adapted to this sphere of action. Indeed, his great administrative capacity was known and appreciated from the moment he entered the halls of Congress. The day after he took his seat, it appears, from the Journal, that he was appointed a member of one of the most important committees in the House—that on marine affairs*—a committee which acted as a Board of Admiralty, and had the general superintendence and control of naval affairs. This committee continued with extensive powers until toward the close of the next year, when it was superseded by the establishment of a Board of Admiralty.

Ellsworth was also appointed a member of the committee of appeals soon after taking his seat in Congress.† The functions of this committee were entirely judicial. It was vested with power by Congress to hear and determine appeals brought from the Admiralty Courts of the respective States, in cases of prize and captures on the seas. The history of this committee is one of the most curious parts of the history of the old Congress. We may trace in it distinctly the very earliest idea of a federal judiciary, clothed with appellate powers; and, were I writing the history of the Supreme Court of the United States, I should begin at the period of the establishment by the old Congress of this committee of appeals in Admiralty cases. It is worthy of remark that the necessity of an appellate judicial tribunal was felt from the very first hour of the confederacy, and even before the Declaration of Independence. So early as November 25th, 1775, Congress, by resolution, recommended to the several legislatures to erect Courts for the purpose of determining concerning captures, and providing that an appeal should be allowed to Congress from such decisions. Originally each appeal was referred to a separate committee;

* Jour. of Congress, Oct. 9th, 1778.

† Jour. of Congress, Oct. 26th, 1778.

but these becoming more frequent, a permanent COMMITTEE of APPEALS —that is to say, a judicial tribunal—was appointed on the 30th January, 1777, to hear and determine cases of appeal from sentences of the respective State Courts in Admiralty. The committee was always composed of the ablest lawyers in the House; and its decisions in several of the earlier cases were received with respect, and acquiesced in by the State Courts. A question, however, soon arose which brought with it a conflict of jurisdiction.

In the Journal of Congress of November 28th, 1778, the entry appears, "An appeal from the judgment of a Court of Admiralty for the State of Pennsylvania, on a libel, 'Thomas Houston *versus* Sloop Active,' was lodged with the secretary, and referred to the committee on appeals."

Mr. Ellsworth and his then associates in the committee sat upon the hearing of this appeal.

The facts the case were these:—Gideon Olmstead and others, citizens of Connecticut, had been captured by the British and carried to Jamaica, where they were put on board an enemy's vessel, the sloop Active, (bound for New York with supplies for the British,) as navigators to assist in the management of the vessel. During the voyage they rose upon the master and crew of the sloop, confined them to the cabin, took command of the vessel, and steered for Egg Harbor, in the State of New Jersey. When in sight of that harbor the American brig Convention, belonging to the State of Pennsylvania, Captain Houston commander, took possession of the Active, and brought her to the port of Philadelphia. Captain Houston libelled the vessel as lawful prize of the Convention, and Olmstead for himself and others, interposed a claim to the cargo and vessel, as their exclusive prize. The State Court of Admiralty, the cause having been tried before a jury, adjudged Olmstead and his companions entitled to only one-fourth part, and decreed the residue to the other claimants. From this decree Olmstead for himself and others appealed.

This appeal was heard by the Committee of Appeals, of which Ellsworth was at that time a member, on the 15th December, 1778. After full argument of the case, which, as will be seen at a glance, was really one of no small importance, involving some novel and interesting questions of public and prize law, the committee reversed the judgment of the State Court, and adjudged that the Active should be condemned as lawful prize for the use of the appellants Olmstead and his companions, and remanded the cause to the State Court, with directions to carry the decree into execution.

The Pennsylvania Judge refused to obey, and a conflict of jurisdiction of course ensued. I believe it is the earliest case on record of a collision between the judicial authorities of the confederation and of a State. The result was, that Congress found itself without an adequate remedy, and powerless. The Committee of Appeals, on the motion of Olmstead's counsel, issued an injunction to the Marshal to restrain him from paying into Court the money arising from the sale of the vessel. The Marshal disregarded the injunction, and paid the money to the Judge, who gave a receipt for it. Whereupon the committee, pursuing the course dictated by discretion, and perhaps by necessity, declined to take any proceedings for contempt, lest consequences might ensue, as they declare, "dangerous to the public peace of the United States;" and caused an entry to be made on their minutes that they would proceed no further in the matter, nor hear any appeal, "until the authority of the Court be so settled as to give full efficacy to their decrees and process."

The matter was subsequently brought before Congress, who unanimously—with the exception of the State of Pennsylvania, and one vote from New Jersey—passed a series of resolutions vindicating their right to the exercise of this appellate power over the State Admiralty Courts.*

* Journal of Congress, March 6th, 1779. The extent of the power claimed by Congress will be seen by the following extract from these resolutions:

"That no Act of any one State can or ought to destroy the right of appeal to Congress in the sense above declared:

"That Congress is by these United States invested with the supreme sovereign power of war and peace:

"That the power of executing the law of nations is essential to the sovereign supreme power of war and peace:

"That the legality of all captures on the high seas must be determined by the laws of nations.

"That the authority ultimately and finally to decide on all matters and questions touching the law of nations, does reside and is vested in the sovereign supreme power of war and peace:

"That a control by appeal is necessary, in order to complete a just and uniform execution of the law of nations."

It may be added, that the jurisdiction claimed to be exercised by Congress in these cases was subsequently fully recognized by the Supreme Court of the United States. Nearly thirty years afterwards, in Chief-Justice Marshall's time, the decision of the Committee of Appeals in this very case was confirmed, and under it the right of the original captors, Olmstead and others, to the proceeds of the sale of the Active fully established.*

I do not find that Ellsworth took part in any further proceedings before the Committee of Appeals after the case of the "Active." Before the passage of the resolutions referred to, March 6th, 1779, vindicating the authority and jurisdiction of Congress over the subject, he had leave of absence and returned home. He was appointed, as usual, among the delegates to Congress from Connecticut for the ensuing year, but did not take his seat until the middle of December. Soon after, he was chosen to his old position upon the Committee of Appeals, in place of Mr. Paca, of Maryland, who at that time was absent.† The functions of this committee, however, were about drawing to a close. The case of the "Active" had demonstrated the necessity of a more thoroughly organized and vigorous tribunal. In January, 1780, Congress passed resolutions for the establishment of a Court of Appeals in cases of capture, consisting of three judges, appointed and commissioned by Congress; and in May following, the Court being then fully organized, by a resolution of Congress all mat-

* United States *vs.* Judge Peters, 5 Cranch Reports, 115. The validity of the powers exercised by the Court of Appeals, under the articles of Confederation, and by the Committee of Appeals under the old Continental Congress, had been established by a former decision of the Court, made just before Ellsworth came to the bench. In the case of Penhallow, et. al. *vs.* Doane's administrators, Feb. Term, 1795, 3 Dallas Reports, 54, Judge Paterson, delivering the opinion of the Court, fully sanctions the resolutions of Congress in the case of the "Active," remarking that they contain "a course of reasoning which, in my opinion, is cogent and conclusive." In the opinion of that learned Judge the supreme sovereignty claimed to be exercised by the Continental Congress even before the article of Confederation, was a necessary attribute, and grew out of its revolutionary character. And he remarks in a somewhat lofty and imposing figure of speech—"As to war and peace, and their necessary incidents, Congress, by the unanimous voice of the people, exercised exclusive jurisdiction, and stood, like Jove, amidst the deities of old, paramount and supreme."

† Journal of Congress, January 5th, 1780.

ters respecting appeals in cases of capture, then pending before the Committee of Appeals, were transferred to the new Court.* Under the articles of Confederation, adopted by all the States, March 1st, 1781, this tribunal was re-organized, and it continued to exercise its functions till superseded by the Supreme Court of the United States.

Mr. Ellsworth remained constantly in attendance upon Congress from the time of his return in December, 1779, until the following summer. The post of a delegate in Congress was certainly not at that time to be coveted. The first burst of enthusiasm which greeted the opening of the Revolution had subsided; there was no longer an *éclat* attending a service in the councils of the Confederacy; the prominent statesmen who had set in motion the ball of the revolution were mostly engaged in other spheres of action; the great orators who had sounded the first blast upon the revolutionary trumpet had passed away; there were no more laurels to be won; no honors to be gained; nothing to be encountered but toil, responsibility, anxiety, embarrassment. The delegate, setting out on horseback from his rural New England residence, to pursue his weary and tedious journey, perhaps alone, to Philadelphia, surely exhibited a courage as lofty and a temper as steady as that which sustained the half-fed and half-clothed soldier of Washington in his winter encampment at Valley Forge. And it was fortunate for the country that at this most perilous crisis, such men were found as Ellsworth and his associates—men of solid, steady, resolute energy of purpose, and unshaken firmness of mind, who, when ambition no longer offered her glittering prizes, and fame held out no more her tempting rewards, could listen calmly and earnestly to the voice of principle and duty. Without such men in council, as well as in the field, the contest must have closed; for the darkest hour of the revolution had arrived. The army was now upon the brink of dissolution. The Continental treasury was bankrupt. Congress, in despair, had resolved to issue no more bills of credit; and the States were unable to advance their respective quotas of contribution.

It was at this moment that Ellsworth again took his seat in Congress. A resolution had just been adopted, changing the mode of supplying the army from purchases, to requisitions of specific articles on the several States. As preliminary to this system a committee

* Journal of Congress, May 24th, 1780.

was appointed to make the estimates, and to introduce every practicable reform in the expenditures. On this important committee Ellsworth was placed the very next day after his arrival. His labors here were no doubt great; but as to their extent we have little means of judging. The subject was kept under deliberation until the 25th of February, the committee in the mean time having made their report, which Congress adopted substantially as it came from their hands, apportioning among the respective States their various quotas of supplies.*

Among the important labors of Mr. Ellsworth during this session, one other should be here properly mentioned, inasmuch as it is highly honorable to all parties connected with it. When that patriotic and true-hearted American, Robert Morris, brought forward his scheme for the establishment of a BANK, no one co-operated more cordially and efficiently with the proposed plan than Oliver Ellsworth. On the 21st June, 1780, a letter from the Board of War informed Congress that a "number of patriotic persons" had formed a plan for the establishment of a Bank whose object should be the public service, and desired a committee appointed to confer with them on the subject. Whereupon a committee of three was chosen, of whom Ellsworth was chairman. The next day he laid before Congress the plan of the Bank, which, after some discussion, was adopted. Its sole object was to establish a credit by means of which, without the least pecuniary advantage to the stockholders, relief could be furnished to a suffering and almost disbanded army. They proposed on their own credit to transport three millions of rations and three hundred hogsheads of rum for the use of the army, the public credit being pledged only for their ultimate reimbursement. Morris himself headed the subscription-list of stock with the sum of £10,000; and others, through his influence, augmented it to the sum of £315,000. And thus, when every other expedient had well nigh failed, the genius of one man, united with the well-timed efforts of those who promptly and efficiently sustained him, kept the American army on foot, and gave a new impulse to the war of independence. A successful result in finance, in the public estimation, of course, sinks into insignificance in comparison

* This system, like some others adopted by Congress, rather from desperation than choice, was soon found to be utterly inefficient. It never, from the start, seems to have had the concurrence of General Washington.

with the brilliant efforts of the statesman in the Senate, or the prowess of the commanding general on the field; and yet the genius of the Philadelphia banker at that moment was of more consequence to the American cause than the tongues of the best orators in Congress, or the swords of half the general officers in the army. What the country needed then were supplies and credit, rather than men; and as an historical fact, the establishment of Morris's bank may be regarded as not secondary in importance to the battle of Trenton. Had this taken place in Rome, remarks the biographer of Morris, even in her most virtuous age, posterity would justly have considered it as adorning one of the fairest and most splendid eras of her histories.*

It may be added, that Ellsworth was continued chairman of the standing committee to confer with the officers of the Bank, as occasion might require; but, leaving Congress soon after, his place was filled by the appointment of Mr. Adams.

Mr. Ellsworth was re-appointed, as usual, one of the delegates to Congress from Connecticut, for the ensuing year. He did not resume his place, however, until the 4th June, 1781, when he appeared with his colleague, Roger Sherman, and immediately entered upon the discharge of the important duties assigned him. From the scanty records of the Congressional Journal of that period, it is now impossible to ascertain with precision not only what were the specific duties assigned to individual members, but even in some cases what were the daily subjects of the deliberations of Congress. It appears, however, that Congress was laboring with unabated energy to restore the public credit, and to organize measures of public defence. Robert Morris had been placed at the head of the finances; and Ellsworth was now,

* Many anecdotes are related of this eminent man, honorable alike to his practical sagacity, as well as his disinterested patriotism. One of the most characteristic of these anecdotes is that stated by Marshall, in a note to the Life of Washington, as coming from the lips of Morris himself,—of his keeping a secret agent in the army of Gen. Greene, with instructions to advance certain drafts and sums of money to Greene, when every hope of supplies had failed. Thus Greene, in ignorance of the character of this secret agent, was constantly kept upon his own resources until the very last moment, and then, by an almost miraculous interposition, was relieved from impending ruin without the slightest idea of the quarter from whence the timely assistance came. Mr. Morris was one of the first senators of the United States from the State of Pennsylvania. He died in 1806, aged seventy-three years.

as he had been on the occasion of the establishment of the Pennsylvania Bank, one of his most ardent and efficient coadjutors. We find about this time a variety of resolutions passed to facilitate the operations of Mr. Morris, all of which Ellsworth concurred in, if he did not originate. One day the disposition and management of the public money granted by his most Christian Majesty to the United States, and the unsold Bills of Exchange drawn on Jay, Franklin, and Laurens, are committed to the superintendent of finances, to be applied and disposed of;* at another time he is directed to take order for discharging the debt due from the United States to the Pennsylvania Bank;† and that the Board of Admiralty assign him the shares of the United States in certain prizes to enable him speedily to launch and equip for sea the ship "America" on the stocks at Portsmouth;‡ and again, that he be furnished with an account of the several requisitions of money and supplies from the States, and that he take measures for calling upon them, and pressing a compliance with the said requisitions.§

It appears also from the Journal, that notwithstanding these united efforts of Congress in the common cause of the country, yet no little diversity of opinions, and even jealousies, were at times manifested in regard to the burdens to be borne by, and the distribution of supplies among, the respective States. Candor and truth require it to be said that on such occasions Ellsworth was generally found standing up firmly, and, perhaps, with a too unyielding pertinacity, for the interests of his own State. On a motion, that the Board of War forward to North Carolina three thousand stand of arms *for the use of the militia of that State*, Ellsworth voted to strike out the latter words, and insert "to be disposed of as the commanding officer of the Southern department shall direct;" and the motion being lost, he voted in favor of one made by his colleague, Mr. Sherman, giving the commanding officer, General Greene, instead of the State authorities, the disposition of these arms among the State militia.|| A few days after, his vote is recorded in the negative on a proposition recommending the

* Journal of Congress, June 4th, 1781.

† Journal of Congress, June 22d, 1781.

‡ Journal of Congress, June 23rd, 1781.

§ Journal of Congress, June 28th, 1781.

|| Journal of Congress, July 7th, 1781.

States to loan money for the relief of the exiled inhabitants of South Carolina and Georgia, and guaranteeing by Congress the repayment of such money so loaned.* So too, on a proposition that certain supplies furnished by the States for their respective troops should be accredited to such States respectively as so much advanced on their respective quotas of taxes, the name of Ellsworth, with that of every other New England member, except Mr. Sullivan, of New Hampshire, is found in the affirmative.†

It would be doing injustice, however, to Mr. Ellsworth, to suppose that his action on these questions was influenced by any contracted or illiberal sectional feeling. Of this he seems to have been incapable, as his conduct on various occasions shows. Thus, soon after the vote on the supplies, we find him at the head of a committee, of which Madison also was a member, devising the means of defraying out of the public treasury the expenses of the delegates from North Carolina, South Carolina, and Georgia, who were shut out by the events of the war, from receiving remittances from their respective States, and recommending suitable provisions for that purposes, which Congress promptly adopted.‡

Ellsworth remained in attendance upon Congress during the whole summer, and rendered good service in various capacities, particularly upon the executive committees on which he was placed, a sphere in which his industry, his practical good sense, and his sound, discriminating judgment eminently fitted him for usefulness. Returning home toward the latter part of August, he remained absent more than a year, though in the mean time re-chosen at the annual session of the Assembly one of the seven delegates from Connecticut to Congress.

He took his seat again in Congress on the 20th of December, 1782, and with the exception of a month or two, during the winter, remained in constant attendance until after the removal, or rather flight, of that body from Philadelphia to Princeton, in the latter part of June in the following year. This was the last period of Mr. Ellsworth's service in Congress. And it was a period, perhaps, more interesting to the

* Journal of Congress, July 21st, 1781.

† Journal of Congress, July 23rd, 1781.

‡ Journal of Congress, July 30th, 1781.

civilian and statesman than any which had preceded it. The confederation had now reached the turning point of its destiny. The war of the revolution had been brought to a close; but the grand result was still a problem, and the issue of the struggle lay darkly concealed in the future. The great work of organization was now to be done; the elements of empire lay scattered all around, and these were to be gathered up, and brought together, and moulded in symmetrical form; political institutions were to be reared; social rights secured; and civil liberty consolidated upon the basis of republican institutions. Such, in its broadest view, was really the labor devolving on the men who represented the sovereignty of the Confederation at the close of the revolutionary war, when Ellsworth once more took his seat in Congress. Never, since he had been a member of that body, had it exhibited a greater degree of intellectual vigor. Its deliberations were now influenced, if not guided, by the splendid talents of a Madison, a Rutledge, and a Hamilton, and around these, who might justly be said to stand *primi inter pares*, were gathered Wilson, Carroll, Lee, Bland, Dyer, Gorham, Ramsay, and others, whose names are equally entitled to an honorable mention in history.

In the preceding sketch of Judge Rutledge I have alluded to some of the important subjects which occupied the attention of Congress at this period. Though Ellsworth did not participate in the discussions growing out of these subjects so prominently as some of his associates, yet he occasionally mingled in the debates, and always with effectiveness and force. On the overshadowing question of the PUBLIC CREDIT, and the raising of a revenue, he differed essentially from Hamilton, Wilson, and Madison. These gentlemen were strongly desirous of providing for a general and permanent revenue instead of State contributions; but the mode of raising it and enforcing the collection was the main difficulty in question. The favorite proposition of Hamilton was, that it should be "collected under the authority of Congress." But this excited the jealousy of Ellsworth, who, even at this early period, viewed with disfavor any encroachments of the Federal power upon the complete and absolute sovereignty of the States. "On the one side," he remarked, "he felt the necessity of Continental funds for making good the Continental engagements; but on the other desponded of a unanimous concurrence of the States in such an establishment.

He observed that it was a question of great importance how far the Federal Government *can, or ought, to exert coercion against delinquent members of the Confederacy;* and that without such coercion no certainty could attend the Constitutional mode which referred every thing to the unanimous punctuality of thirteen different councils. Considering, therefore, a continental revenue as unattainable, and periodical requisitions from Congress as inadequate, he was inclined to make trial of the middle mode of *permanent State funds,* to be provided at the recommendation of Congress, and appropriated to the discharge of the common debt." *

This brought out Hamilton, who, with that impetuous boldness which marked his character, scorning everything that looked like concealment in attack as well as defence, avowed as an additional reason for wishing the revenue to be collected by the government, that "as the energy of the Federal Government was evidently short of the degree necessary for pervading and uniting the States, it was expedient to introduce the influence of officers deriving their emoluments from, and consequently interested in, supporting the power of Congress." A general smile from those members who concurred with Ellsworth, greeted these remarks of Hamilton. Mr. Madison himself regarded them as "imprudent and injurious to the cause," observing that some of the members took notice in private conversation that Hamilton had let out the secret.†

Soon after this, Mr. Rutledge introduced his scheme for raising revenue by an impost of five per cent. *ad valorem,* with the proviso that the money arising from such duties, and paid by any State, should be passed to the credit of such State on account of its quota of the debt of the United States. Ellsworth was favorable to this mode of raising revenue; but strongly opposed the proposition that each State should be credited for the duties collected within its ports, as a proposition eminently unjust to his own State, which did not import one-fiftieth part of the merchandise consumed within it. He was opposed also to Hamilton's plan of the appointment of collectors by Congress; but was willing to compromise, provided the respective States had the nomination of these officers. "He concurred," he said, "in the expe-

* Madison Papers, Vol. I. 291.

† Madison Papers, Vol. I. p. 291, *note.*

diency of new modeling the scheme of the impost by defining the period of its continuance; by leaving to the States the nomination, and to Congress the appointment of collectors, or *vice versa,* and by a more determinate appropriation of the revenue. The first object to which it ought to be applied was, he thought, the foreign debt. This object claimed a preference, as well from the hope of facilitating further aids from that quarter, as from the disputes into which a failure may embroil the United States. The prejudices against making a provision for foreign debts which should not include domestic ones was unjust, and might be satisfied by immediately requiring a tax, in discharge of which loan-office certificates should be receivable. State funds, for the domestic debts, would be proper for subsequent consideration," &c.*

The history of these discussions in regard to the public revenue, has been briefly traced, and the result indicated, in the preceding sketch of Rutledge,† which renders it unnecessary to pursue the subject farther in this place. To the final compromise Ellsworth gave his cordial assent. Immediately afterwards he was placed on a committee with Hamilton and Madison to draft an address to the people of the States, recommending the sanction and adoption of the proposed measure. The admirable address of the committee is from the pen of Madison.‡ It was submitted to Congress, and unanimously ratified by that body on the 26th of April following.

In the interval of the debates on the Public Credit, Congress found time for a moment to revert to the great work of organizing the civil departments of the Government, and to the arrangements necessary to be taken in consequence of the peace. A committee was ordered whose object was "to provide a system for foreign affairs, for Indian affairs, for military and naval establishments, and also to carry into execution the regulation of weights and measures, and other articles of the Confederation not attended to during the war." It was scarcely possible to entrust to any committee a more important charge than this, embracing as it did the organization of some of the most essential departments of civil administration. The selection of the committee,

* Madison Papers, Vol. I. pp. 309, 310.

† *Ante,* pages 148 to 151.

‡ Madison Papers, Vol. I. Appendix, No. 2.

too, indicates something of the sense entertained by Congress of the pre-eminent talents and capacity of the members chosen to fill it. They were Madison, Ellsworth, and Hamilton. It is worthy of remark, that no committee of special importance was ordered by Congress while these gentlemen were members of that body, without the appointment of some one or more of them to serve upon it. With Rutledge, who is frequently found their associate upon committees and otherwise, they may be regarded as the leading and controlling minds of that Congress. It would have been idle to seek in the body, of which they were members, or any other legislative body of the times, men whose characters were stamped with a more striking and marked individuality, and who were endowed with a wider diversity of talents and faculties; yet, they seem to have been admirably adapted to unite in harmonious effort, each strong in his own sphere of thought and action, and apparently eliciting by contact of mind, a more full and vigorous development of the peculiar talent possessed by the other.

The session of Congress was abruptly terminated on the 21st June, 1783. On that day a small body of mutinous soldiers from Lancaster, who had marched into the city the day before for the avowed purpose of obtaining a settlement of their accounts, surrounded the State House where Congress had assembled. Although no act of violence was committed, yet the soldiers remained in their position around the hall, occasionally uttering abusive words, and wantonly pointing their muskets to the windows of the State House. The revolutionary days of Paris and the scenes of the French Convention were thus, on a less formidable scale, anticipated by these disgraceful outrages of a mutinous soldiery. But Congress acted with firmness and spirit. A committee was appointed, consisting of Hamilton, Ellsworth, and Peters, to confer with the executive magistrates of Pennsylvania on the practicability of taking effective measures to put down the mutiny, and support the public authorities. The conference, however, was unsatisfactory. It disclosed the humiliating fact that the authorities of Pennsylvania were not capable of protecting Congress in its deliberations. They could not, as they alleged, induce their militia to act, nor did they believe any exertions were to be looked for from them, except "in case of *actual violence* to personal property." A fresh conference was ordered on the evening of the 21st, the committee being instructed, in case it was unsuccessful, to advise the President to adjourn Congress, and summon the members to meet at Princeton or Trenton, in New Jersey. This new conference produced only a repetition of the doubts respecting the disposition of the militia to act; and it was even questioned whether a renewal of the insult to Congress would be a sufficient provocation. The committee being convinced that there was "no satisfactory ground to expect prompt and adequate exertions on the part of the Executive of the State for supporting the public authorities," on receiving the final answer of the Council, advised the President, pursuant to their instructions, to adjourn Congress, which was thereupon done, the members being notified verbally, and also summoned by proclamation to meet at Princeton.

On the re-assembling of Congress at Princeton, June 30th, Ellsworth and Hamilton made a report from their committee, giving a detailed account of their conferences with the authorities of Pennsylvania, and its unsuccessful result. They also made a report from another committee on which they had been appointed, with Mr. Bland, recommending that General Howe march to Pennsylvania with such force as might be necessary to put down the mutiny, and bring the mutineers to trial and punishment. The report was unanimously adopted. General Washington, who keenly felt the mortification of this disgraceful outrage, had already taken prompt and efficient measures to put down the mutiny and restore order. This was promptly effected without bloodshed, and most of the insurgents subsequently accepted furloughs under the resolution of Congress to that effect.*

Ellsworth remained a member of Congress but a short time after that body removed to Princeton. His name is found on the Journal as late as July 11th, 1783, soon after which period he was relieved by the arrival of two of his colleagues, and returned home. It was his last service in the councils of the Confederacy. For, though chosen again by the Connecticut Legislature at the annual election, as he had been for six years previous, he declined to serve, and a successor was accordingly appointed. The following year Congress conferred upon him the appointment of commissioner of the Board of Treasury. This

* See Journals of Congress, June 30th and July 1st, 1783. Madison Papers, Vol. I. p. 467.

also he declined. The period had arrived when his private affairs imperatively demanded his attention. Now that the crisis was over, and the danger had passed, he thought that a long, and arduous, and faithful public service entitled him to an honorable discharge. Besides, he considered his first fealty to be due to his native State, and a place of honorable usefulness, if not of inviting ambition, was urged upon him in a branch of her legislative council, and upon her supreme judicial bench, which he did not feel at liberty to decline.

It was as a member of the Supreme Court of Errors, into which he came on its organization in 1784, that the first judicial service of Mr. Ellsworth was rendered. This court consisted of the Lieutenant-Governor and the twelve assistants, or upper house of the Legislature,* and sat as an appellant court to review the judgments of the Superior Court.† Judge Ellsworth remained in it only a short time. The following year an act was passed prohibiting the same person from holding the office of Judge of the Superior Court and of the Supreme Court of Errors at the same time; whereupon Ellsworth resigned the latter place, as did also three of his associates, namely, the Chief-Justice Richard Law, Roger Sherman, and William Pitkin, all of whom retained their seats on the bench of the Superior Court. The remaining member of the court was Eliphalet Dyer, one of the signers of the Declaration of Independence, and a gentleman who had distinguished himself by various important civil services during the period of the revolutionary war.

The Superior Court of Connecticut had an extended, and indeed, almost unlimited jurisdiction. It embraced suits in equity as well as at law, an appellate jurisdiction over the county courts, and an exclusive jurisdiction of all criminal cases relating to life, limb and banishment. At the time when Ellsworth came to the bench, the jurisprudence of Connecticut was in a very unsettled state. It was indeed still a question, how far the common law was to be regarded as

* In 1794, an act was passed, making the Governor also a member of the court. The court continued in existence until 1807, when its powers were transferred to the nine Judges of the new Supreme Court.

† Ellsworth had been a member of the Council for several years, having been first elected in 1780.

a rule of decision by the courts ;* and some years later we find Judge Root himself, in the preface to his reports, discussing the question, whether there is any "common law in Connecticut ;" denying that the English common law was ever applicable to the colony, and broadly asserting that their own was "derived from the *law of nature* and *revelation*."† Some of the earlier decisions, indeed, seem to sustain this position. Thus, in a case decided about the time of Ellsworth's admission to the bar, it was held, that the English doctrine of survivorship between joint tenants was exploded, and was not regarded as the law in Connecticut ; and Judge Root adds, that the principle so established, had never since, to his knowledge, been contradicted or shaken.‡ So, too, among the earliest cases decided by Ellsworth in the Superior Court are some which directly contravene established common law principles ; as for example, in the case of Horsford *vs.* Wright,§ which holds that the damages on a breach of covenant of warranty in a deed, are to be ascertained by the value of the land, and not, as by the English rule, which gives the consideration of the deed, &c.

On the other hand, it is clearly evident, from the whole current of these early Connecticut decisions, that not only was the common law recognized in their courts, but that in some cases it was applied with strict and technical precision. An instance of this is to be found in the case of Hart *vs.* Smith,‖ at the September term of the court, 1786, wherein the majority of the court laid down the rule, that assumpsit would not lie to recover back money paid *by mistake* in the settlement of an account. It was intimated, that if the mistake ap-

* "Our courts were still in a state of embarrassment," says Kirby, "sensible that the common law of England, though a highly improved system, was not fully applicable to our situation."

† In Fitch *vs.* Brainerd, 2 Day's Reports, 189, decided in 1805, the Court of Errors, though denying that the common law of England, *as such*, ever had any force in Connecticut, admits that it had become "necessary, in order to avoid arbitrary decisions, and for the sake of *rules*, which habit had rendered familiar, as well as the wisdom of ages matured, to make that law our own by practical *adoption*—with such exceptions as a diversity of circumstances, and the incipient customs of our own country required."

‡ Phelps *vs.* Jepson, 1 Root's Reports, 48. § Kirby's Reports, 3.

‖ Kirby's Reports, 127.

peared upon the face of the account, the party aggrieved might have his remedy, but this remedy could be only by *special action on the case*.

It seems somewhat surprising that such a distinction, based upon the merest technicality, should have made an impression upon a mind so eminently practical as that of Roger Sherman ;* and that, sitting in a court with both equity and common law jurisdiction, he should have

* ROGER SHERMAN is less known as a lawyer and a judge, than as a statesman and staunch revolutionary patriot. Born in 1721, of humble parents, he was apprenticed in his youth to a shoemaker, and continued to work at his trade for a livelihood for some time after he arrived at age. But the cobbler's bench was not the appropriate sphere of action for a mind like Sherman's. His active intellect, thirsting for knowledge, soon rose superior to circumstances; and, in a few years, by dint of untiring labor and perseverance, he exhibited, for the emulation of his own age and posterity, an example of one of the most thoroughly "self-made men" that America has produced. In 1743, we find the shoemaker on his bench with a book fixed before him, engaged in studying the elementary mathematics over his work; a year or two later he is employed in surveying, having mastered the principles of that science; in 1748, he is making "astronomical calculations for an almanac;" soon after we find him studying law, and in 1754, admitted an attorney, commencing a career of honorable and successful practice. Sherman served in the Connecticut General Assembly for many years prior to the Revolution. As is well known, he was one of the signers of the Declaration, and served in Congress during nearly the whole period of the Revolutionary war. He was a member of the Convention which framed the Federal Constitution, and of the State Convention which ratified it. He was a member of the first House of Representatives of the United States, and on the resignation of Dr. Johnson, was elected to the Senate, of which body he was a member at the time of his death, in 1793.

Sherman had practised five years at the bar, when, in 1759, he was appointed a Judge of the Litchfield County Court. Two years afterwards, on removing to New Haven, he received a similar appointment in that county. In 1766, he was elevated to the bench of the Superior Court, which office he held until his election to Congress in 1789, a period of twenty-three years. During nineteen years of this period, he was also an assistant, or member of the council (annually elected), and resigned his place there, with Ellsworth, on the passage of the law prohibiting the same person from serving as a Judge of the Superior Court and the Supreme Court of Errors. Mr. Sherman, besides his judicial duties, rendered valuable service to his State in 1783, by revising, with the assistance of Judge Law, the whole body of the Connecticut statutes. Throughout life he sustained an unblemished reputation; and at the time of his death enjoyed an enviable reputation as one of the ablest and soundest jurists whom Connecticut has produced. The modest inscription upon his tomb is a just tribute to his character and

insisted with such unbending rigor in preserving the boundaries which limited the jurisdiction of each, and maintaining the line of demarcation between them. Ellsworth dissented from this judgment, and applied to the case what seems to us at this day, the more liberal, as well as more correct principle. He thought it was an established proposition of law, founded on the most approved justice, that an action would lie for money paid by mistake, whether in the settlement of an account, or in any other way, and no matter whether the mistake appear upon the face of the account or not. It was sufficient that there had been a settlement and a mistake, and that the defendant had received money of the plaintiff which he ought not in conscience to retain. This point settled, he applies the equitable principle to a common law action, holding that the plaintiff might recover in assumpsit. Under the issue in this action, the defendant might disprove the facts set up by the plaintiff, or establish other and independent facts to rebut the equity of the plaintiff's demand.

So much of the labors of Ellsworth, while a Judge of the Superior Courts of Connecticut, as have been preserved, may be found in Kirby's Report, a single volume, containing the adjudged cases from 1785 to 1788. This was the first attempt, in Connecticut, to preserve the *lex non scripta*. Up to 1785, the decisions of the courts had been oral, and of course were not preserved. In that year the Legislature passed an act requiring the Judges to render written reasons for their decisions, when the pleadings closed in an issue of law. "This," remarks the reporter, "was a great advance towards improvement." Still the business was but half accomplished, for the arguments of the Judges, without a history of the case, as he also, somewhat *naïvely*, remarks, "could not be intelligible." In other words, the services of a reporter were essential to rescue from oblivion the learning of the judiciary, as well as to render their judgments "intelligible." This was the task of Mr. Kirby—a task undertaken *con amore*, diligently prosecuted, and faithfully executed. The result, whatever may be thought of it in a practical and utilitarian sense, is certainly a matter of curious interest to the legal antiquarian. Like the renovated tombstones of the Cameronian martyrs, under the pious chisel of Old

virtues:—"A man of approved integrity, a cool, discerning Judge, a prudent, sagacious Politician, a true, faithful, and firm Patriot."

Mortality, these relics of the past, under the revivifying touch of Mr. Kirby, stand out legible monuments of the early jurisprudence of Connecticut.

Few of the reported cases in Kirby would attract attention in our day, either on account of their novelty or importance. I may allude in this place, however, to one of them, as it affords a fair sample—the best, on the whole, which remains—of Judge Ellsworth's method in the examination of a legal question, and his mode of reasoning. It is the case of Adams *vs.* Kellogg,* at the November term of the court, 1786. The point involved was, whether a married woman might devise her real estate to her husband; and it brought up for discussion the very interesting question, which has been debated with great learning and skill since that time, whether the right to devise by will, was or was not, a natural right, which might be exercised independent of statute. The opinion of Judge Ellsworth upon this point is different from some conclusions that have been arrived at in our day; I shall not, however, undertake to aver that it is less correct, but leave him to speak for himself. His opinion in the case,—which is on all points adverse to the right of a *feme covert* to devise—is preserved in the appendix to the report. It seems to be a very carefully considered, compact, and logical exposition of his views, bearing upon it the impress of a strong, and well disciplined, but cautious mind; a mind not keenly suggestive, or strongly original, but constitutionally adverse to innovations, preferring to follow the conservative doctrines of society, and to stand with Lord Kenyon *super antiquas vias*, in the well-beaten paths of the law. Without attempting a full analysis, the following brief *resumé* will serve to indicate the general scope of the argument:

A married woman has neither a natural right to devise, nor a right at common law, nor by statute.

1st. The right to direct the succession of estates by will is not a natural but a municipal right.

2d. Even if it is a natural right, it does not follow that a *feme covert* has it.

3d. It is a common law and not a statute disability that she is under.

4th. The statute (by examination) furnishes as little authority for

* Kirby's Reports, 195.

a *feme covert* to make a will as the law of nature or the common law had done before.

5th. Considerations of policy serve to confirm the opinion that she has no power to devise.

"The possession of this power," he remarks, "would be as *inconvenient* for a *feme covert*, as *unnecessary*, because it would expose them to endless teasings and to dangerous coercions, placed in the power of a husband whose solicitations they cannot resist, and whose commands in all that is lawful, it is their duty to obey;"—a wholesome doctrine that perhaps might properly be recommended to the attention of our modern reformers; and he adds, as a final reason of policy, "Their wills, taken in a corner, and concealed from all the world, till they have left it, can afford but very uncertain evidence of the real wishes of their hearts."*

There are also a few cases, or rather brief memoranda and notes of cases of the old Superior Court, during Ellsworth's service, collected in the first volume of Judge Root's Reports. But the same remark may be generally made in regard to their novelty and value, as of the majority of the cases in Kirby. I do not find in them much worthy of notice, as connected with Ellsworth's judicial character, especially as the reasons for the judgments rendered are not given. Occasionally, however, we find something beyond the ordinary and beaten track of common law decisions, mainly growing out of that new class of cases, which the revolutionary troubles had excited. In the deci-

* Two years afterwards the Supreme Court of Errors reversed this judgment of the Superior Court, after an elaborate argument at the May term, and a further argument at the October term of the same year. That decision was followed by the subordinate courts, and the law was considered as settled. Numerous wills, made by *femes coverts*, by the advice of the best counsel in the State, were approbated by the Court of Probates. In 1805, the question again came before the Court of Errors, Judge Ellsworth being at that time a member of the court; and after a full and very learned argument, the court unanimously reversed the judgment, and came back to the principle established by the Superior Court in Adams *vs.* Kellogg. "That decision," says the court, alluding to the reversal of the judgment of Kellogg *vs.* Adams, by the Court of Error, "we are constrained to say, after much deliberation, was not law." A full report of this case, under the title of Fitch *vs.* Brainard, is to be found in 2 Day's Conn. Reports, 163–194. The reasoning of the court in delivering this judgment, proceeds upon similar principles with that of Judge Ellsworth, in Adams *vs.* Kellogg.

sion of such questions, Ellsworth and his associates were governed by the broadest and most liberal principles of public policy. Thus, for example, in one case, in an action against a deputy commissary for army purchases, the court held the defendant not liable, he having acted as the agent or servant of the public. In another, a negro slave having enlisted and served in the continental army, with his master's consent, is held to be manumitted by such service, and entitled to a discharge from imprisonment, on habeas corpus.*

In some of these cases, too, there seems to be a disposition to relax the strict severity of New England custom, as in Carpenter *vs.* Crane,† where the defence set up to a promissory note was, that it was executed on Saturday night, at about two o'clock, "which was Sunday, or Lord's day;" the note having been given to procure the release from prison of the defendant's brother; the court, under these circumstances, innovating upon the good old New England custom, declared the note to be valid, inasmuch as there was no statute expressly forbidding it, or declaring such note void.

In the discharge of his official functions, Judge Ellsworth, of course, had frequent occasion to administer the criminal law to all grades of offenders. It was a day when a principal object of legislation was still thought to be to suppress vice and immorality, by statutory enactment, as well as to restrain the commission of crime. The judicial edifice stood upon nearly the same foundation where the fathers of the colony had placed it; and the ruthless hand of modern innovation had not yet, to any great extent, impaired the ancestral structure. Crimes and misdemeanors were then *punished*, not merely by a beggarly fine, or a brief imprisonment, but by a genuine corporal punishment—whipping on the bare back, cropping, branding with a hot iron, exposure with a halter tied round the neck, &c. Some curious cases are

* This was the case of Jack Arabus, who was a member of a company of blacks mustered into the continental service, and attached to one of the Connecticut regiments of the line. After Jack was discharged, his master, Ives, claimed him as his servant. Jack fled to the eastward, and his master having pursued and overtaken him, brought him to New Haven, and lodged him in jail. Jack sued out a habeas corpus, and on a summary hearing before the Superior Court, was discharged, on the ground that he was a freeman, absolutely manumitted by his service in the army.—1 *Root's Reports*, 93.

† 1 Root's Reports, 98.

still to be met with, illustrative of the state of criminal jurisprudence in Connecticut, when Ellsworth administered the law as one of the judges of the Superior Court. Thus, for example, we find in a cotemporary newspaper, the following sentences, passed at a session of the Supreme Court, at Hartford, in January, 1785 : "Moses Parker, for horse-stealing, to sit on the wooden horse * half an hour ; to receive fifteen stripes ; pay a fine of £10 ; be confined in gaol and the work-house three months ; and every Monday morning, for the first month, to receive ten stripes, and sit on the wooden horse, as aforesaid."

"Moses Lusk, of Middletown, for counterfeiting treasurer's certificate, to receive twenty stripes ; pay a fine of £20, and be confined six months."

"Judah Benjamin, for polygamy (he having married a wife in Symsbury, when he had another living in Massachusetts), to receive ten stripes ; be branded with the letter A, and wear a halter about his neck during his continuance in this State ; and if ever found with it off, to receive thirty stripes."

The punishment of cropping and branding was not an uncommon sentence for crime at that time in Connecticut. Thus, in the case last mentioned, the branding was in the forehead with the letter A ; in the case of burglary, cropping and branding with the letter B ; of counterfeiting, whipping or branding with the letter C, or both, &c.

* The "wooden horse" seems to have been an *institution* peculiar to Connecticut, and an essential element in the administration of her penal laws. The execution of the sentence in this particular case is described in the "Connecticut Courant" of that day, in the following ludicrous manner : "One of the rogues was sentenced to ride the *wooden horse*, that wonderful refinement of punishment in our modern statutes. Accordingly, on Thursday last the terrible machine was prepared, consisting of one simple stick of wood, supported by four legs, and by order of the Sheriff placed in State House Square. Hither the prisoner was conducted, and being previously well booted and spurred by the officer, was mounted on the oaken steed. Here he continued for half an hour, laughing at his own fate, and making diversion for a numerous body of spectators, who honored him with their company. He took several starts for a race with the best horses in the city, and it was difficult to determine who were most pleased with the exhibition—the criminal or the spectators. After this part of the sentence had been legally and faithfully executed, the culprit was dismounted, and led to the whipping-post, where the duties made him more serious. The whole was performed with great order and regularity."

In Ellsworth's time, the offence of adultery, which the early laws of Connecticut punished with death,* subjected the offender to whipping on the naked body, branding the letter A on the forehead with a hot iron, wearing a halter on the neck over the garments as long as the convict remained in the State, and as often as found without such halter, to be whipped, not exceeding thirty stripes.† It might be thought that the ignominy of the punishment was sufficient either to restrain the commission of the offence entirely, or to prevent a conviction ; such, however, was not the fact ; as is evident in Benjamin's case. Another very curious case as reported in Kirby, was argued before Ellsworth and his associates at the August term of the Court 1786.‡ One William Green had been indicted under this statute and convicted on the verdict of a jury. The evidence showed that Green had been traced to the house of his neighbor Samuel Rossetar, and found in Rossetar's nuptial couch with "Tryphena, the wife of said Rossetar, at a little after ten o'clock in the evening,"—evidence which might be thought strongly circumstantial, and perhaps tolerably con-

* The early criminal code of Connecticut recognized twelve capital offences, to which two more were afterwards added, and all of which were founded on the strict precepts of the Levitical law. Some of them were of a savage and almost Draconian sternness, as for example :—

"If any man or woman be a witch, that is, hath or consulted with a familiar spirit, they shall be put to death." *Ex.* 22 : 18. *Levit.* 20 : 27. *Deut.* 18 : 10, 11.

"If any person shall blaspheme the name of God the Father, Son, or Holy Ghost, with direct, express, presumptuous, or high-handed blasphemy, or shall curse in the like manner, he shall be put to death."

The 13th of these laws provided that if a child above the age of sixteen should curse or smite his natural father or mother, he should be put to death ; founded on *Ex.* 21 : 15–17. *Levit.* 20 : 9.

And the 14th, the most singular, perhaps, of all, that a stubborn and rebellious son, "who will not obey the voice of his father, or the voice of his mother, and when they have chastened him, will not hearken unto them," might, if sixteen years of age, on complaint of the parents, be brought before the civil magistrate, and condemned to death. *Deut.* 20 : 18–21.

(See *Conn. Hist. Collections*, p. 16.

† This curious law remained on the Statute book, I believe, for some years after this period. In the revision of 1821, the punishment for this offence is, imprisonment in Newgate prison for the man, and in the county jail for the woman for a period not exceeding five, nor less than two years.

‡ The State *vs.* Green, Kirby's Report, 87.

clusive by a jury in our day. Not so, however, thought the ingenious counsel for the prisoner, who now moved to arrest the judgment on the ground that the *corpus delicti* had not been proved. There was another statute defining in terms exactly the offence which the evidence established, the punishment of which was simply whipping not exceeding thirty stripes ; and the efforts of the prisoner's counsel of course were to bring the case within the latter statute, and thus escape the branding and the wearing of the halter. After solemn argument and consideration, the Court overruled the motion on the perfectly obvious and strictly legal principle that the jury were the proper judges of the weight of the evidence on the whole circumstances of the case, and their verdict must therefore be regarded as conclusive. We hear no more of the unfortunate Mr. Green ; but he doubtless paid the full penalty of his transgression.

The proposition to appoint delegates to a Convention to frame a plan for a Federal Government, was acceded to with reluctance, and almost at the last moment, by Connecticut. The Anti-Federal party in that State was numerous and persevering, and up to within a few weeks of the meeting of the Convention it was doubtful what course the Assembly would adopt. "Of Connecticut alone doubts are entertained," writes Madison to Jefferson, in the latter part of April, 1787. These doubts however were soon after solved. The Assembly determined to appoint delegates to the Convention, and selected three of the most eminent citizens of the State, Oliver Ellsworth, Roger Sherman, and William Samuel Johnson.

Ellsworth took his seat in the Convention a few days after it was organized and just before the respective propositions of Randolph and Pinckney, were submitted. For some weeks he was a silent, but not inattentive listener to the interesting discussions which took place in that body. Indeed, though he subsequently mingled freely in the debates of the Convention, he never aspired to act a prominent and leading part in sketching out the plan of the new Government. It was a sphere not so well adapted perhaps to his talents as that which he had previously, and which he subsequently, filled. His mind was not inventive ; he was better adapted to aid in the execution, than in the construction, of a plan of government ;—to organize and carry out a system in detail, than to originate it. Hence the great work of framing the new Government, fell to the hands of others. But in the arrangement of its details, in harmonizing its various branches, and especially in preserving those checks and balances so necessary to the success of the projected Constitution, he rendered the most signal and valuable service. He came to the Convention with two ideas fixed and indelibly impressed on his mind. One of these was the preservation of the identity, the influence, and the sovereignty of the respective States : and the other, the engrafting upon the new system, as far as practicable, those simple democratic principles, which were embodied in the institutions and government of his native State. His entire course in the Convention seems to have been guided and influenced by these ideas. One of his earliest acts was to second a motion of his colleague Sherman, that the members of the first branch of the National Legislature be elected every year, in opposition to Mr. Rutledge, who proposed two years, and Mr. Madison, who was in favor of three ; the people, he said, were fond of frequent elections, and might be safely indulged in one branch of the Legislature.* Soon after, on the consideration of the resolution that " A national Government ought to be established, consisting of a Supreme Legislative, Executive, and Judiciary," he moved to strike out the word *national*, and retain the proper title, the *United States*. "He could not admit the doctrine," he remarked, " that a breach of any of the Federal articles could dissolve the whole. It would be highly dangerous not to consider the Confederation as still subsisting. He wished also the plan of the Convention to go forth as an amendment of the articles of the Confederation, since under this idea the authority of the Legislatures could ratify it. If they are unwilling, the people will be so too. If the plan goes forth to the people for ratification, several succeeding Conventions within the States, would be unavoidable. He did not like these Conventions. They were better fitted to pull down than to build up Constitutions." † For similar reasons he opposed the proposition to pay the representatives out of the national treasury, and moved to substitute payment by the States, in opposition to Hamilton, Madison, Wilson and others, remarking with much warmth : " If we are so exceedingly jealous of State Legislatures, will they not have reason to be

* Madison Papers, Vol. II. pp. 846, 929.

† Madison Papers, Vol. II. pp. 908, 909.

equally jealous of us? If I return to my State and tell them we made such and such regulations for a General Government, because we dared not trust you with very extensive powers, will they be satisfied? Nay, will they adopt your Government? And let it ever be remembered that without their approbation your Government is nothing more than a rope of sand." * On the question whether the members of the second branch should be chosen by the Legislatures of the States, Ellsworth was no less resolute and determined in his opposition to the advocates of a consolidated Government, and in support of the sovereignty of the States. He urged the necessity of maintaining the existence and agency of the State Governments; without their co-operation it would be impossible to support a republican government over so great an extent of country; an army could scarcely render it practicable: "If the principles and materials of our Government," he added, "are not adequate to the extent of these single States, how can it be imagined that they can support a single government throughout the United States? The only chance of supporting a general government lies *in grafting it on those of the individual States.*" †

Ellsworth's solicitude for the preservation of the rights and sovereignty of the States, was again exhibited in a striking manner in the discussions arising on the great question which agitated and divided the Convention, as to the ratio of State representation in the National Legislature. In these discussions he took a decided and prominent, and it may be added a controlling part, for upon him mainly rested the labor of sustaining the rights and interests of the smaller States against that splendid array of intellectual strength which had espoused the other side. The great capacity of Ellsworth on this occasion was exhibited to the best advantage. His coolness, his adroitness, his moderation, the weight and momentum of his attacks, the unyielding pertinacity and firmness of his resistance, formed altogether an invincible obstacle to the advocates of consolidation. It is not too much to say that to the resolute efforts and persevering energy of Oliver Ellsworth, more than to any other man in the Convention, is the country

* Yates' Minutes, Elliott's Debates, Vol. I. p. 478. He subsequently made an ineffectual effort to strike out the provision that Senators be paid out of the national treasury. Madison Papers, Vol. I. p. 970.

† Madison Papers, Vol. II. pp. 957, 958.

indebted for the final compromise of the Constitution which gave to each State an equality of representation in the Senate. Upon this point, having reluctantly yielded the equality of representation in the other branch, he stood firm and immovable. It was a point beyond which compromise itself was impossible ; nor could any efforts avail to move him a hair's breadth from the position he had taken in regard to it. The greatest names in the Convention were arrayed against him—Madison, Hamilton, Franklin, Randolph, Pinckney, Governeur Morris, Rufus King—a phalanx, that it might have been supposed, would have overwhelmed all opposition at a single charge. But Ellsworth stood firm and undismayed, and for two days bore up almost single-handed and alone in the unequal contest, aided only by the occasional interposition of his colleague Sherman, and one or two others, and the fiery philipics of Mr. Bedford, of Delaware, which served to divert the attacks if they did not materially weaken the strength of their opponents.

In the preceding sketch of Judge Rutledge,* I have briefly traced this animated and stormy debate as it is found preserved in the notes of Mr. Madison, who, himself, took a prominent part in it. It commenced on the 29th of June, on Ellsworth's motion that "the rule of suffrage in the second branch be the same as that established in the articles of Confederation"—that is, that each State have an equal vote, a contrary rule having just been adopted in regard to the first branch. In support of his motion Ellsworth observed : "He was not sorry, on the whole, that the vote just passed, had determined against this rule in the first branch. He hoped it would become a *ground of compromise* with regard to the second branch. We were partly national, partly Federal. The proportional representation in the first branch was conformable to the national principle, and would secure the large States against the small. An equality of voices was conformable to the Federal principle, and was necessary to secure the small States against the large. He trusted that on this middle ground a compromise would take place. He did not see that it could on any other, and if no compromise should take place, the meeting would be not only in vain, but worse than vain." He then proceeded in the discussion of the question with admirable felicity and directness of argument, and

* *Ante*, pages 163–167.

advanced his reasons for desiring to preserve the Federal principle in the Constitution of the national Senate, concluding with the earnest and stirring appeal: "Let a strong Executive, Judiciary, and Legislative, be created, but let not too much be attempted by which all may be lost. He was not in general a half-way man; yet he preferred doing half the good we could, rather than do nothing at all. The other half may be added when the necessity shall be more fully experienced." *

The next day the discussion was continued with renewed vigor, Judge Wilson opening the debate in opposition to Ellsworth. He maintained, with great plausibility of argument, that the Convention was framing a government for *men*, and not for the imaginary beings called *States*, and therefore, the proposed rule of representation would be unjust, as it would subject the majority to be ruled by the minority. Ellsworth again took up the argument, and replied to these positions, in a train of reasoning that no one who has witnessed the practical workings of the Federal system in our day, would be inclined to controvert. "The power is given to the few," he says, "to save them from being destroyed by the many. If an equality had been given to them in both branches, the objection might have had weight. Is it a novel thing that the few should have a check upon the many? Is it not the case in the British Constitution, the wisdom of which so many gentlemen have united in applauding? Have not the House of Lords, who form so small a proportion of the nation, a negative on the laws, as a necessary defence of their peculiar rights against the encroachments of the Commons? No instance of a confederacy has existed in which an equality of voices has not been exercised by the members of it. We are running from one extreme to another. We are *razing the foundations of the building, when we need only repair the roof*."†

As the discussion increased in warmth and intensity, Ellsworth found himself surrounded by a formidable and crushing opposition. The attack from the heavy batteries of Wilson's learning and logic, was followed by a combined onslaught from all sides. Every variety of weapon known to the practice of legitimate discussion was brought

* Madison Papers, Vol. II. pp. 996–998.

† Madison Papers, Vol. II. p. 1003.

to bear, to drive him and those who stood with him, from the position they maintained with such invincible firmness—the keen and unerring arrows drawn from the inexhaustible quiver of Madison's forensic skill; the blunt and homely, but ponderous weapons of Franklin's common sense; the rapid and effective artillery of Rufus King's gorgeous declamations;—but all in vain. The phalanx of the opposition stood firm, with Ellsworth at its head, armed at all points in proof. Madison, while complimenting the "admirable and close reasoning" of his opponent, endeavored in vain to weaken his position and overthrow his argument; Franklin hinted at a compromise that would have been substantially a victory, and enforced his views by a practical and characteristic illustration, but to no purpose; King attacked, with eloquent invective, the "phantom of State sovereignty," and endeavored to dispel "this wonderful illusion," without effect. Though the field of argument was exhausted, the Connecticut delegate still stood unconvinced and still unyielding. His answer to all his opponents was the earnest and emphatic announcement which conveyed the unalterable conviction of his mind: "What he wanted was domestic happiness. The National Government could not descend to the local objects on which this depended. It could only embrace objects of a general nature. He turned his eyes, therefore, for the preservation of their rights to the State governments. From that alone he could derive the greatest happiness he expected in this life. His happiness depended on their existence, as much as a new born infant on its mother for nourishment. If this reasoning was not satisfactory, he had nothing to add that could be so."*

The result of the day's discussion was the change of a single vote in Georgia, and the consequent division of that State, and of all the States upon the main question. A committee of conference was thereupon ordered, whose action has been noticed in another place.† Ellsworth was appointed a member of it, but for some cause, which I have not been able to ascertain, did not serve, his place being filled by his colleague, Mr. Sherman. With the every way fortunate result of the labors of that committee, however, he expressed himself fully satisfied. "Some compromise was necessary," he remarked, "and he saw none more convenient or reasonable."‡

* Madison Papers, Vol. II. p. 1014.

† *Ante*, pages 165–167

‡ Madison Papers, Vol. II. p. 1032.

A full review of the acts and services of Ellsworth, during the session of the Convention, would extend this sketch to undue limits, and I shall, therefore, in passing, barely glance at the more important matters with which his name is connected, and which may serve to illustrate the nature of his opinions.

He was appointed upon the committee of detail, of which Rutledge was chairman, and which prepared and reported to the Convention, the first official draft of a Constitution.

He participated in the debates on the constitution of the Executive office, and gave free expression to his views in regard to it. He moved that the Executive be appointed by electors chosen by *the Legislatures of the States*, in a certain specified ratio.* Subsequently, he moved that the Executive be appointed by the Legislature, except when the magistrate last chosen shall have continued in office the whole term for which he was chosen and be re-eligible ; in which case he should be chosen by electors appointed by the State Legislatures. This, he thought, would at once provide for the re-election of a deserving magistrate, and secure his independence of the Legislature.† He favored the motion of Mr. Wilson, which was also supported by Madison, that the Supreme National Judiciary should be associated with the Executive in the revisionary power‡—a proposition whose singular incongruity was not perceived by some of the best minds in the Convention, but which Rutledge pointed out in the brief but emphatic sentence, that "the Judges ought never to give their opinion on a law, till it comes before them."

He was opposed to the project of clothing the Executive with power to nominate the Judges. Though he was willing to leave with the Executive a negative on a nomination made by the Senate, yet he preferred to vest that body, absolutely, with the power of appointment. The Executive, he remarked, will be regarded by the people with a jealous eye ; and every project for augmenting, unnecessarily, his influence will be disliked.§

Ellsworth was a strenuous opponent of every attempt to confer on the National Legislature the power to interfere with the elective franchise in the States, or to impose unnecessary restrictions on the

* Madison Papers, Vol. II. p. 1149.

† Madison Papers, Vol. II. p. 1198.

‡ Ibid., Vol. II. p. 1162.

§ Ibid., Vol. II. p. 1173.

qualifications of its own members. To the suggestion of Gouverneur Morris, proposing a freehold qualification for electors, he remarks: "The right of suffrage is a tender point, and strongly guarded by most of the State Constitutions. The people will not readily subscribe to the National Constitution if it should subject them to be disfranchised. The States are the best judges of the circumstances and temper of their own people."* And, on a subsequent occasion, he earnestly and effectively opposed the proposition to require a freehold qualification for the offices of President, Judges, and members of Congress. It was better, he thought, to leave the whole matter to the discretion of the Legislatures than to insert a provision for it in the Constitution.† His views in regard to the qualification of aliens were of a similar nature. He disapproved the motion of Col. Mason making a residence of seven years a requisite of citizenship, and proposed in lieu of it a residence of one year, though expressing his willingness to assent to three.‡ In like manner he opposed Mr. Morris' proposition requiring a residence of fourteen years as a qualification for the Senatorship, believing, as he remarked, that it would discourage meritorious aliens from emigrating to this country.§

The simplicity of his views in regard to the organization of the government, and his partiality to those elementary democratic ideas which he had imbibed from the institutions of his native State, were also evinced on various other occasions. Not only did he contend that the members of Congress should be paid by the respective States, as has been already remarked, and that the members of the popular branch should be chosen annually, but he saw no difficulty in carrying out every branch of the Federal administration through the medium of frequent elections, and short periods of official service. He advocated also the ineligibility of members of Congress to any other office;‖ and even discountenanced the project of taking the yeas and nays in the Federal legislature, preferring, with his colleague Sherman, the primitive New England mode of determining a question

* Madison Papers, Vol. III. p. 1250.

† Madison Papers, Vol. III. p. 1284.

‡ Madison Papers, Vol. III. pp. 1258, 1259.

§ Madison Papers, Vol. III. p. 1273.

‖ Madison Papers, Vol. III. p. 1323.

by voices.* On the proposition to authorize Congress to emit bills on the credit of the United States, he thought a favorable moment had come to shut and bar the door forever against paper money. "Paper money," he remarked, "can in no case be necessary. Give the Government credit, and other resources will follow. The power may do harm, never good." And to that singular proposition, favored by Charles Pinckney and other influential members, whose object was to vest Congress with power to annul the laws of the States, he manifested a staunch and resolute resistance—a proposition which Wilson, carried away with the enthusiasm of the moment, considered "as the key stone wanted to complete the wide arch of government we are raising," but which the more penetrating intellect of Rutledge condemned as an act which of itself alone "would damn, and ought to damn, the Constitution."†

Mr. Ellsworth does not seem to have been present during nearly the whole of the last month of the Convention, nor is his name found attached to the Constitution as it came from the hands of its framers. The omission, however, is entirely accidental, as he was from the moment of its adoption, the firm and unswerving friend of the projected system. This is evident from his letter to the Governor of Connecticut, signed by himself and his colleague Sherman, enclosing a printed copy of the instrument and explaining its provisions. At the close of this letter, the delegates remark: "We wish it may meet the approbation of the several States, and be a means of securing their rights, and lengthening out their tranquillity."‡

The Connecticut Convention assembled about the 1st of January following. Ellsworth was of course a member, and upon him mainly devolved the duty of defending the new plan of government before that body. The task, however, was not a difficult one, for a large and controlling majority was favorable to the new Constitution.§

* Madison Papers, Vol. III. p. 1291.

† *Ante*, page 165. Madison Papers, Vol. III. p. 1411.

‡ 1 Elliot's Debates, p. 431.

§ From the final result in the several States it would seem that the compromise of the Constitution was regarded as a substantial triumph by the smaller States. The votes of New Jersey and Delaware were *unanimous* for the ratification, while those of the three larger States were comparatively close.

Ellsworth, however, relaxed no effort and spared no labor in presenting the subject fully and favorably to the Convention. As one of the delegates to the late assembly at Philadelphia, he appropriately opened the discussion. The outlines of this speech are preserved.* It is exceedingly plain, and without the slightest pretensions to rhetorical elegance, though certainly clear, forcible, and direct. The main argument is drawn from a consideration of the value and necessity of the Union, and its adaptation to the wants and interests of the State of Connecticut. This idea he enforces by a brief, though by no means striking reference to the histories of ancient and modern confederacies. It is not difficult, however, to see that he is more at home in the practical examination of the subject under the light of existing facts. As, for example, when, with true professional tact, and genuine New England shrewdness, he presses the argument on the score of interest and policy, and urges the necessity of the Union on the ground of economy as well as of safety. The small States, he urges, can alone be saved by the Union. Nothing but the Union can preserve Connecticut from the rapacity of her two grasping neighbors, Massachusetts and New York ;—and his reasoning loses not a particle of its point from the quaint and homely illustration with which he enforces it : "If divided, what is to prevent the large States from oppressing the small? What is to defend us from the ambition and rapacity of New York, when she has spread over that vast territory which she claims and holds? Do we not already see in her the seeds of an overbearing ambition? On the other side there is a large and powerful State. Have we not already begun to be tributaries? If we do not improve the present critical time—if we do not unite, shall we not be *like Issachar of old, a strong ass crouching down between two burdens*"?†

The debates of the Connecticut Convention, with the exception of brief sketches of some half dozen speeches collected from cotemporary publications, are lost. Of these speeches two are by Ellsworth, who seems to have been the acknowledged leader of the Convention. The first of these was his speech on opening the debate which has just been noticed, and the second, delivered a few days after, was on the power of Congress to lay taxes. The latter is by far the more happy effort,

* See 2 Elliot's Debates, pp. 189–193.

† 2 Elliot's Debates, 190.

and may be regarded as the best preserved specimen of its author's talent as a debater. He addresses himself to the subject with characteristic plainness of speech, but with admirable skill and force of reasoning, and conclusively refutes in detail each of the objections urged against vesting the general government with this power. The arguments of Ellsworth, cool, dispassioned, ingenious, and searching, were thoroughly adapted to the character of his audience ; and we can well conceive the truth of the remark which has been made of them, that they left a deeper impression upon the minds to which they were addressed than would have been produced by the brilliant efforts of Ames or the impassioned appeals of Hamilton.

The Constitution was ratified by a large majority. Out of one hundred and sixty-eight votes only forty are recorded in the negative, a result that might be considered complimentary either to the influence and talent of Ellsworth, or the good sense of the representatives of the Connecticut people.

As one of the foremost men in the State, Ellsworth, of course, could not be overlooked in the organization of the new government. He was chosen one of the senators of the United States, his colleague being William Samuel Johnson, lately appointed to an office which his father had filled before him, that of President of Columbia College. The first Congress met at "Federal Hall," in the city of New York, on the 4th of March, 1789 ; but to the mortification of the more zealous Federalists, says the historian, only eight senators and thirteen representatives made their appearance. Of these eight senators Ellsworth was one, and patiently waited, from day to day, with his colleagues, until the 6th April, when Mr. Richard Henry Lee appeared, making twelve senators in all, which formed a quorum ; the Senate then organized and proceeded to business.

Mr. Ellsworth's services in the Senate through the seven years which comprised the period of his connexion with that body, were of the most valuable character. It was indeed a field of laborious and important, as well as honorable service, and it required talents of a high order to enter upon it with success and the hope of usefulness. The whole machinery of the new government was to be put in motion ; the substantial frame work which the Federal Convention had raised, was to be elaborated by the National Legislature into the complete and perfect structure fit to subserve the useful purposes of its creation. The work of invention was now to give place to the labor of detail; theoretic ideas to practical results; the devising of systems and plans of government to the organization of the means of execution. Every thing was to be organized—the civil department, the diplomatic department, the judicial department, the treasury, the customs, the post-office, the army and navy, and, in short, all the departments of administration. And here Oliver Ellsworth found the true sphere of his usefulness. It was here that the practical value of such talents as he possessed was felt and known. Among all his associates, during the whole period of his service in the Senate, it would be difficult to point out one who may justly claim the possession of equal capacity in everything pertaining to the utilities of legislation. It has been remarked that in no portion of his career did he exhibit a greater degree of progressive improvement and a more continued and vigorous development of his intellectual faculties than during these years of his service in the Senate. His labors were arduous, often embarrassing; but he applied himself to them with that plodding perseverance and unwearied industry, which in his hands were the potent and sure weapons of success. Some of his mental labors, during this period, if the account that has come down to us be correct, were not only of a tedious but even of a painful character. To him a great intellectual achievement was not a sudden and happy inspiration of genius. The thought did not flash across his mind with the vividness and velocity of a sunbeam; it was produced only through the painful and toilsome process of mental travail. While engaged in these important investigations, we are told, he would pass whole days, and sometimes nights, in walking up and down his chamber, absorbed in mental labor. It was impossible to divert his attention toward any other object before he had thoroughly formed his conclusions on the subject which engaged him. When, at last, the question which had thoroughly excited him was finally determined, he appeared at once relieved from a weight of thought, and was left languid and exhausted, as if he had been wearied out by severe bodily labor.*

When the first Congress met, and, indeed, for four or five years afterwards, the Senate, which in its creation had excited such popular

* 3 Anal. Magazine. Sketch of Ellsworth.

jealousies and called out such violent attacks, was an entirely different body from what it subsequently became, and now is. A certain degree of mystery enshrouded its deliberations, and it maintained a distant formality and an aristocratic reserve which by no means contributed to conciliate the popular good will. One of its earliest disagreements with the other House arose upon a mere point of etiquette, namely, as to what title or style should be used in addressing the President of the United States. The title of "*His Excellency*" had been rejected as not sufficiently respectful, and a committee of three, of which Ellsworth was a member, subsequently reported that in their opinion it would be proper to address him as "*His Highness, the President of the United States, and Protector of their liberties*," which report the Senate seemed inclined to adopt. But the House of Representatives, staunch in its republican principles, refused to yield, or recognize any other title for the President than that "expressed in the Constitution." Before a committee of conference could report, the House had already addressed the Executive in the simple and appropriate form which has ever since been observed, "*To the President of the United States*;" a style of address which the Senate, though with some disgust, thought it expedient, "for the present," to adopt.

At this early period, too, the doors of the Senate Chamber were closed, and the debates were secret, which was another source of popular animadversion and jealousy. This continued during nearly the whole period of Ellsworth's service, and we are thus cut off from a vast deal of interesting information; for while the debates of the other branch remain in a tolerable state of preservation, nothing but the merest skeleton outline of the Senate's proceedings, as it appears in its journal, is left. We can therefore, do nothing more than conjecture what may have been the eloquence of such orators as Rufus King and Richard Henry Lee, the statesmanship of such tried patriots as Charles Carrol and Robert Morris, or the judicial wisdom of such lawyers as William Paterson and Oliver Ellsworth. The Senate continued to adhere to this secret session system for some time with blind and persevering tenacity. Mr. Monroe made an effort to have the sessions public, in the spring of 1791, but the motion was voted down, as a similar one had been the previous session, by a vote of nine to seventeen, Ellsworth being in the negative.* And it was not until four years afterwards that the doors were ordered to be opened, and the Senate became convinced that the deliberations of a free legislative body should be not only free but PUBLIC. From that day the Senate regained the public confidence, and continued to increase in the popular esteem, until it came to be regarded, as it now is, with marked and peculiar reverence, as the grand conservative balance-wheel of the Federal system.

The secret sessions of the Senate, and the meagre outlines of its history, which the journal presents, of course render it impracticable to determine what precise share Ellsworth is entitled to claim in most of the important public measures discussed before that body. Of one great act, however—the organization of the Federal Judiciary—an act intimately connected with his professional, as well as senatorial fame, we can speak with more certainty. Of this act Mr. Ellsworth is justly entitled to claim the chief paternity ; and for that reason, if no other, as one of his eulogists has very properly remarked, he ought to be spoken of with peculiar reverence by the American bar ; for, it is added, though with a latitude of expression somewhat too wide, the entire Federal system was made by him,—"the whole edifice, organization, jurisdiction, and process, was built by him as it now stands." †

The Constitution had barely sketched the outline of a Federal Judiciary ; it had marked out the ground and defined the fixed boundaries on which the superstructure was to stand ; but the edifice itself, was left to be reared by the Legislature. It declared that the judicial power of the United States should be vested in one Supreme Court, and in such inferior Courts as the Congress may from time to time ordain and establish,‡ thus leaving a wide margin for the action of the Legislature. No part of the system had been regarded with more distrust than this. It was thought to contain an element of power dangerous to the sovereignty and existence of the several States. The establishment of *inferior Courts* especially, had been resisted, even in the Federal Convention, as unnecessary,§ it being proposed to establish a Su-

* Ellsworth's vote is found recorded against a similar proposition in the old Congress, a proposition which was favored by Hamilton and Wilson.

† Notes to Wharton's State Trials, p. 41.

‡ Federal Constitution, Art. III. Section 1.

§ See Sketch of Rutledge, *ante*, p. 171.

preme Court simply as an appellate tribunal from the decisions of the State Courts, which latter, it was thought, might be appropriately invested with jurisdiction in offences against the United States, admiralty cases, &c. &c., as under the Confederation.

As an ultra States'-rights man, it might have been supposed that Ellsworth would have favored these notions in Congress, where they re-appeared and were urged with great force in the debate on the judiciary bill. This, however, was not the case. With the adoption of the Constitution his views seem to have become modified, and from standing upon the extreme of the States'-rights doctrine, he became the warm and consistent, but not ultra advocate of a liberal construction of all the provisions of the new system. It was not many years after the adjournment of the Convention, that he and Madison found themselves occupying in Congress precisely antagonist positions from those in which they formerly stood. His support of the Judiciary Act is one of the earliest and strongest evidences of his thorough adhesion to the new Federal system.

The early organization of the Courts seems to have been regarded by Congress as one of the most pressing necessities of the times. The next day after the opening of the Senate, and before the President's inaugural speech had been delivered, a committee of the Senate was appointed "to bring in a bill for organizing the Judiciary of the United States." * Ellsworth was placed at the head of this committee. It would, perhaps, be unjust to others, nor is it necessary for his reputation, to claim for him the entire and unaided construction of the judicial system; for that able lawyer, his future associate on the bench, Judge Paterson, was a member of the committee, and it is said that he was assisted also by the valuable aid of his colleague, Mr. Johnson. To Ellsworth, however, was assigned the chief share of the labor, and the draft of the bill is undoubtedly from his pen. The assiduous industry he brought to this duty, and the promptitude of its performance, are evidenced in the fact that within three weeks of the appointment of the committee, the outlines of the plan were matured. From the following letter of Ellsworth, to his former colleague, Chief-Justice Law, dated April 30th, 1789, the reader will perceive that the system as it was first sketched by the committee, and as it came from

* Senate Journal, April 7th, 1789.

their hands, was the same, substantially, as that which Congress finally adopted :

"The following," he says, "are outlines of a Judiciary system contemplating before a committee of the Senate.

"That the Supreme Court consist of six Judges, and hold two stated sessions annually at or near the seat of Government.

"That there be a District Court, with one Judge resident in each State, with jurisdiction in admiralty cases, smaller offences, and some other special cases.

"That the United States be divided into three circuits. That a court be holden twice annually in each State, to consist of two Judges of the Supreme Court and the District Judge. This Court to receive appeals in some cases from the District Court, to try high crimes, and have original jurisdiction in law and equity, in controversies between foreigners and citizens, and between citizens of different States, and where the matter in dispute exceeds five hundred dollars ; and to grant appeals to the Supreme Court except as to facts, where the matter in dispute exceeds two thousand dollars." *

The committee, through Mr. Richard Henry Lee, reported the bill to the Senate on the 12th of June. Though it encountered in that body a searching discussion, it had a comparatively easy passage. Of twenty votes recorded on taking the final question, six only are in the negative, and among these it is singular enough to find the name of Mr. Lee, himself.† But a vigorous and formidable opposition sprang up in the house, headed by Livermore, of New Hampshire, Jackson, of Georgia, and Burke, of South Carolina, which, for a time, at least, threatened to defeat the bill. The debate was characterized by great ability, and no small degree of warmth. The unaccountable jealousies entertained of the entire judicial system, were stimulated and excited, rather than soothed by discussion ; and we can read in our day with a feeling little short of astonishment such exaggerated expressions as those with which Mr. Livermore closed one of his ablest speeches : "For my part, I contemplate with horror the effects of the plan. I think I see a foundation laid for discord, civil war, and all its concom-

* This and the letter from which the subsequent extract is taken, are published from the original manuscript by Mr. Wharton, in his Notes to the State Trials.

† Journal of the Senate, July 17th, 1789.

itants. To avert these evils I hope the house will reject the proposed system." *

During this period of suspense, Ellsworth relaxed no effort to secure the final passage of the bill. On the fourth of August he writes to Judge Law : " I consider a proper arrangement of the judiciary, however difficult to establish, among the best securities the government will have, and question much if any will be found at once more economical, systematic and efficient, than the one under consideration. Its fate in the House of Representatives, or in the opinion of the public, I cannot determine. But being, after a long investigation, satisfied in my own mind of its expediency, I have not hesitated, nor shall I, to give it the little support in my power."

Fortunately, the majority in Congress entertained similar views. The bill as it came from the Senate was supported, not by the votes only, but by the active efforts of such men as Benson, Sedgwick, Ames, Madison, and Gerry. It passed the House of Representatives on the 17th September, and soon after, by the signature of the President, became a law. The judicial structure thus raised has stood the test of time from that day to this ; for it remains in its essential features the same that it came from the hands of its founders. The only substantial and radical change ever made in it was in the last year of Mr. Adams' administration, when a batch of new officials and tribunals was created, and the Judges of the Supreme Court, relieved of Circuit duty, were required simply to sit as an Appellate Court. But the change was temporary only. During the very next year, under the auspices of Jefferson's Administration, the law was repealed and the system restored to its original simplicity.

The scheme of Hamilton for funding the debt of the United States found in Ellsworth a vigorous and able auxiliary. He was upon the select committee to whom it was referred, and rendered valuable service in amending and perfecting the plan, until it had assumed the shape in which it finally passed the Senate. It appears, however, that he differed from Hamilton in one or two important particulars. He was of opinion that it was not expedient to attempt to fund the debt at a higher rate of interest than four per cent., as this would answer the expectations of the creditors and all the requirements

* Debates of Congress, Vol. I. p. 814.

of substantial justice. He was also dissatisfied with the Secretary's proposal of leaving one-third of the debt unfunded for ten years, as this measure he thought would tend to encourage speculations, and would leave, after ten years, a great burden upon the country, with little advantage to the creditors; and these opinions, we are told, were supported by him "with all that boldness and reason which gave him a predominant influence in the Senate;"* and also with so much of energy and success as finally to secure a compromise. It should be added, that he was warmly in favor of that part of Hamilton's plan, which proposed the funding of the debts of the States with the foreign debt, a proposition which had been rejected in the other house; and he pressed this matter with so much vigor that the Senate finally agreed, by a small majority, to unite such portion of State debts as should be assumed, in the general funding bill, and so consolidate the whole in one system.†

Mr. Ellsworth also seconded, and materially aided in carrying out, Hamilton's plan for the incorporation of a Bank of the United States. He was one of the select committee to whom the matter was originally referred, and which reported the bill. The plan, after some discussion, passed the Senate by a large majority.‡ But it encountered, in the House of Representatives, a powerful and determined opposition under the well directed lead of Madison,§ Giles, and Jackson, who demonstrated both the unconstitutionality and inexpediency of the institution. After one of the most animated and brilliant debates which had yet occurred in that body—enlivened by the splendid eloquence of Ames on the one side, and the logical reasoning of Madison

* Letter from Secretary Wolcott, July 20th, 1790. 1 Gibbs' Wol., 49.

† Journal of the Senate, July 16th, 1790.

‡ The Journal does nor show the exact vote on the passage of the bill. The motion to limit the term of incorporation to the year 1801 instead of 1811, probably exhibits the strength of the opposition—six to sixteen, Mr. Monroe being one of the minority. See Journal of January 20th, 1791.

§ Mr. Madison's views of strict construction on the subject of the Bank were no recent convictions. He had opposed Mr. Morris's Bank of North America, which he called "the child of necessity," on the ground that it was unauthorized by the articles of confederation. See Madison's Speech on the Bank, 2 Congressional Debates, 2011.

on the other—the advocates of the bank carried the day by a majority of nineteen votes.

Under the classification of Senators, as required by law, Ellsworth drew for the shortest term—the period of two years. At the expiration of that time he was again handsomely complimented by his native State, in a re-election to the Senate. He took his seat at the opening of the next session, and preserved his connexion with that body unbroken until his resignation in the Spring of 1796, on his appointment to the Chief-Justiceship.

The passage of the Bank Bill contributed in no inconsiderable degree, as we are assured on the highest cotemporary authority, to the complete organization of those distinct and visible parties, which, in their long and dubious conflict for power, have since shaken the United States to their centre.* It left the two most active intellects of the country, Jefferson and Hamilton, in permanent antagonism in the cabinet of Washington,† and it placed the name of Ellsworth in opposition to that of Monroe on the record of the Senate. The respective positions thus taken were never changed. Subsequent events, particularly those growing out of the French Revolution, served to render the line of division more definite and distinct. Ellsworth attached himself with all the ardor of a thorough conviction, but without that intemperance of party zeal which some of his associates exhibited, to the Federal party. With all their measures, during his continuance in the Senate, his name is prominently connected. He gave to Washington's administration a sober, but cordial and energetic support. He approved and sustained the proclamation of neutrality. He was one of those who dreaded what he called the "baleful ascendancy of French influence,"‡ and was ardently in favor of cultivating friendly relations with England.

* Marshall's Life of Washington, Vol. II. p. 206.

† It is scarcely necessary to remind the reader that the cabinet of Washington divided on the question of the constitutionality of the Bank, Hamilton and Knox being in favor, and Jefferson and Randolph opposed, the President siding with the former. Precisely the same division occurred on the question of the constitutionality of the bill apportioning the Representatives, with the exception that General Knox was rather undecided. This time, however, the President acceded to the views of Jefferson, and vetoed the bill.

‡ See his letter to Oliver Wolcott, sen,, April 5th, 1794. 1 Gibbs' Wolcott, 134.

He approved the mission of Mr. Jay, and even spoke of it with some degree of exaltation, as "a mortifying movement to those who have endeavored by every possible means to prevent a reconciliation between this country and Great Britain." * He also warmly approved the treaty itself, and voted for its confirmation, and even censured the delay of the President in ratifying it. "If the President decides wrong," he writes, in regard to this subject, "or does not decide soon, his good fortune will forsake him."† And again, a few days after, when it had become known that the President had approved the treaty: "I am glad the President has done at last what I am unwilling to believe he ever hesitated about, and the delay of which has not been without hazard and some mischief. The crisis admits not of the appearance of indecision, and much less of steering any course but one." ‡

As the warm and ardent friend of the Jay treaty, of course Ellsworth was one of those who disapproved the nomination of Rutledge to the vacant Chief-Justiceship of the Supreme Court. This nomination indeed had struck the leaders of the Federal party with astonishment and dismay. For a moment their confidence seemed to be shaken, not in the motives, but in the discretion and judgment of the President. The violence of language used, and the extreme action recommended, by some of his indiscreet friends, are certainly lamentable exhibitions of a blind and over-zealous party spirit. "A driviller and a fool appointed to be Chief-Justice!" exclaims a member of the President's cabinet. § "Faction is to be courted at so great a sacrifice of consistency!" responds another influential Federal politician, || and a third counsels the Senate to stand firm, and correct the President's "error of judgment," by rejecting the nominee.¶ It must be added that

* Letter to Wolcott, April 16th, 1794. 1 Gibbs' Wolcott, 135.

† Letter to Wolcott, jr., August 15th, 1795. 1 Gibbs' Wolcott, 225.

‡ Letter to Wolcott, Jr., August 20th, 1795. 1 Gibbs' Wolcott, 226. In this letter he congratulates his correspondent on the favorable prospects of the treaty in New England. As to New Hampshire, he remarks playfully, he infers, "that brother Langdon's argument, that ''tis a damned thing made to plague the French,' has by repetition lost its power."

§ Wolcott, Jr., letter to Hamilton, July 30th, 1795.

|| Chauncey Goodrich, letter to Wolcott, July 30th, 1795.

¶ See preceding sketch of Rutledge, pp. 180, 181–186

Ellsworth was by no means exempt from these warm party feelings, but he never suffered them to manifest themselves in violent action, or to drive him from that dignified propriety of language and conduct which governed his political as well as his private intercourse. "If the evil is without remedy," he quietly remarks, in a letter to Secretary Wolcott, about this time, "we must, as in other cases, make the best of it. Believe not, my dear sir, that I have feelings on this occasion which are not common to all well disposed friends of the government."*

Rutledge rejected, the confidence of the Federalists in the President returned; the *entente cordiale* was restored; it had become a matter of entire certainty on their part that the office would now be properly filled; no Jacobin, or opponent of the Jay treaty, no Democrat, or other disorderly or improper person, would be selected to fill the important station of Chief-Justice of the United States. At this time, it is to be recollected, the two great parties into which the country was divided had assumed distinct form and shape, and had entered fully armed into the political arena. Washington could be said strictly to belong to neither. He endeavored to hold, with a firm and steady hand, the balance equally poised between both; yet the close observer might even then see that the Federal scale slightly predominated. Like a parent, striving to govern, with wisdom and strict impartiality, two rebellious sons, he could not entirely conceal his partiality for the elder born. He selected, as President Adams rather strongly expresses it, "a multitude of Democrats and Jacobins" for office; but it was plain to be seen, that his most trusted officials were drawn from the opposite ranks. He conferred upon Monroe and Jay, almost at the same time, high diplomatic trusts, and though the former enjoyed his entire respect and esteem, the latter carried with him also his unreserved confidence. His judgment appreciated, as they deserved, the great abilities and valuable services of Jefferson in the cabinet, but it was not difficult to see that with Hamilton were lodged the affections of his heart.

The rejection of Rutledge, therefore, produced no permanent estrangement or misunderstanding between the President and his Federal friends, particularly as he soon after sent into the Senate the name of Mr. Cushing, the senior Judge in commission then on the

* 2 Gibbs' Wolcott, p. 226.

bench, for the office of Chief-Justice. The nomination was at once ratified with entire unanimity. But that excellent and exemplary gentleman declined to accept the presidency of the court, preferring to retain the less ambitious and less prominent post of an associate.*

* The first intimation Judge Cushing received of his appointment was at a diplomatic dinner given by the President. In seating the guests, Washington, with the stately etiquette of that day, bowed to Judge C., and pointing to a vacant place near him, said, "The Chief-Justice of the United States will please take the seat on my right." The next day he received his commission. This anecdote, I am informed by the friend who communicates it, has been preserved on the relation of Judge Cushing himself.

The fact that Judge C. actually presided in the Supreme Court, and was also tendered the commission of Chief-Justice, would have authorized me perhaps to assign him a more prominent place, and to introduce a more extended notice of him in this work. For the present, however, I must confine myself to the limits of the following brief, but interesting sketch, which has been kindly furnished me by Charles C. Paine, Esq., of Boston, a family connexion of Judge Cushing, and who has come into possession of his papers.

William Cushing was born in Scituate, Massachusetts, March 1, 1732. His family was of ancient and respectable English descent, and came over in 1636; this branch of it soon afterwards settled in Scituate on the estate on which he was born, and which he afterwards inherited. His father and grandfather were Judges of the Superior Court, and his great-grandfather an assistant of the colony of Plymouth, a Judge, and one of the commissioners for uniting the two colonies of Plymouth and Massachusetts.

He graduated at Harvard College in 1751, studied law with Jeremy Gridley, Attorney-General; commenced practice in Scituate, in 1760; was appointed Judge of Probate for Lincoln county, (now in Maine,) and removed to Pownalborough, on the Kennebec river and practiced there with great success. His brothers, Charles and Roland, also educated at Harvard College and to the bar, both practised in Maine.

In 1772, upon the resignation by his father of the office of Judge of the Superior Court, which he had held for over 28 years, he was appointed to the vacancy, and thereupon returned to Scituate, where he resided for the rest of his life.

From this time to the Revolution, in 1775, such were the dignity and amenity of his character that he enjoyed the respect and friendship of the principal men of both parties, his associates on the bench, the Governor, and others of the royalists, being friends of his father, while his relative, Thomas Cushing, the Speaker of the House, Robert Treat Paine, and others of the leading patriots, were his own friends. He was the only member of the bench who adhered to the American side, and upon the re-organization of the Supreme Court in 1775 was made Chief-Justice, which post he held till 1789, during the independent sovereignty of the

It was now exceedingly doubtful upon whom the choice of the President would fall. Wilson was the oldest Judge in commission after Judge Cushing, and it might have been supposed was next in the line of

State. In 1780 he was one of the committee for revising the laws of the State. In 1783, the great question, whether slavery was abolished in the State by the language of the Bill of Rights declaring that all men are born free and equal, came before the court on an indictment of the master for an assault on his slave; in his charge to the jury he held that it was so—and thus slavery in the State came to an end.

The interval from 1782 to 1788 was a period of constant difficulty and danger to the Judges. The people, unable to meet their debts and taxation, assembled in armed mobs around the court houses and endeavored to prevent the sittings of the courts, until, finally, Shay's rebellion broke out. The judges, on approaching the court houses, not unfrequently were obliged to pass through these infuriated masses, and the unflinching firmness with which they never failed to perform their duties was witnessed with admiration.

In 1785 he was requested to be a candidate for Governor, as he was again in 1794, but on both occasions he declined. In 1788 he was Vice-President of the Convention for ratifying the Constitution of the United States, presided most of the time, and gave his support to the adoption of it. Upon the organization of the Supreme Bench of the United States, in 1789, he was appointed judge of it, next to the Chief-Justice.

After Jay's departure for England in 1794, he presided in the Court, and in 1796, upon Jay's resignation, he was nominated by Washington as Chief-Justice, and at a time of great party exasperation was unanimously confirmed by the Senate. This appointment was made without his knowledge, and was an entire surprise to him.

After holding the commission for about a week he returned it, though Washington solicited him to keep it, and was never willing to appoint any other over him. He continued on the bench till his death.

He was of good height, graceful, and of great personal dignity; his purity and simplicity of character and urbanity of manners fascinated every one, and at the same time he had unbending firmness and an integrity which inspired universal confidence. He was always cheerful, and fond of social enjoyments. He possessed a remarkably strong and clear mind; was a man of great abilities and learning, and profoundly read in the law. As a judge he commanded the entire respect and confidence of the Massachusetts bar, while at the head of the State bench, and of the bar generally in the federal court. He was a great reader of works of history and literature, and a liberal and fervent Christian.

In 1774 he married Miss Hannah Phillips, of Middletown, Conn., a lady much younger than himself, and of great accomplishments, who was his constant companion in all his journeyings, and survived him many years.

succession. But public rumor seemed rather to point to Judge Paterson, though no one could venture, with certainty, to predict the final action of the President. "Mr. Paterson, of New Jersey, is thought of," writes Mr. Tracy to the senior Wolcott,* "but our President keeps his own counsel tolerably well till he acts officially."

The name of Ellsworth does not seem to have been mentioned in connection with the office, and it was, doubtless, with as much surprise to himself as to any other person, that he received the information that the choice of the President had fallen on him. His nomination was confirmed at once by the Senate with gratifying unanimity. It had not been sought by him, and it was accepted with reluctance. This is evident from his letter to Governor Wolcott, communicating the intelligence, and his resignation of the office of Senator. "It is, Sir, my duty to acquaint you," he says, "that I have, with some hesitation, accepted an appointment in the judiciary of the United States, which, of course, vacates my seat in the Senate. This step, I hope, will not be regarded as disrespectful to a State which I have so long had the honor to serve, and whose interests must forever remain precious to my heart."† The step was by no means regarded as disrespectful; on the contrary, the appointment was considered by the friends of Ellsworth as a deserved compliment to his abilities and integrity, and as a matter of just pride to the State. "Mr. Ellsworth's appointment," says Governor Wolcott to Trumbull, "will be satisfactory to all who are willing to be pleased. If our country shall be saved from anarchy and confusion, it must be by men of his character."‡

Chief-Justice Ellsworth's commission was dated on the 4th of March,

His brother, Roland, died young and unmarried. His brother Gen. Charles Cushing, removed to Boston, and married a sister of Governor Sumner, and a daughter married Charles Paine, son of Robert Treat Paine. In these families Judge and Mrs. Cushing enjoyed their chief society and intercourse when at home. Judge Cushing never had issue. He died on the 13th of September, 1810, in the 79th year of his age.

* 1 Gibbs' Wolcott, 299. This was not the only time Mr. Paterson was "thought of." In the appointment of a successor to Ellsworth it was supposed he would be nominated, and the President was censured for passing by "*old* friends," to reward "*dear* ones." See subsequent sketch of C. J. Marshall.

† 1 Gibbs' Wolcott, 306.

‡ 1 Gibbs' Wolcott, 322.

1796. He took his seat on the bench the 8th of the same month, and during the then February session of the court. The morning on which he was sworn into office, the argument of the important case of Hylton *vs.* the United States* was in progress, one of the earliest cases involving a question of constitutional law ever discussed in the Supreme Court. The point upon which the discussion turned was the constitutionality of the law of Congress of 1794, laying *duties* upon carriages for the conveyance of persons. It was maintained that this was a *direct tax*, and could not be laid except in proportion to the census, or enumeration of inhabitants of the United States. Alexander Hamilton maintained the constitutionality of the act with that power and originality and vigor of argument which he never failed to display on all great occasions;† and he succeeded by the unanimous vote of all the judges who participated in the decision, the Chief-Justice delivering no opinion, as he had not heard the whole of the argument. It is worthy of remark that the sole question submitted to the Court was, is the law of Congress *unconstitutional* and *void?* So Judge Chase himself considered it, although the Supreme Court had not yet decided that it possessed the power to declare an act of Congress void, and the same judge, in a subsequent case, four years after, doubted where the power resided to declare such an act void.‡

The case of Ware *vs.* Hylton *et. al.*§ was argued and determined at the same session of the court—a case deciding the important principle that a statute passed during the revolution, by the Virginia Legislature, confiscating the debts of British subjects, was annulled by the treaty of peace, so as to enable the foreign creditor to recover his debt in

* 3 Dallas Reports, 171.

† Hamilton was in truth at the bar, as Jefferson had declared him to be elsewhere, "a Colossus;" nor was his celebrated speech in the case of the People *vs.* Croswell, in the New York Supreme Court in 1804—which a competent critic has declared to have been "greater than any other man who ever lived in the State, was intellectually competent enough to make"—by any means a solitary example of that brilliant genius, and those inexhaustible intellectual resources with which he was endowed. His occasional efforts in the federal tribunals might compare favorably with it in all respects; and one of these was his argument in this very case of Hylton *vs.* the United States."

‡ Cooper *vs.* Telfair, 4 Dallas Reports, 14, and see note to case of Marbury *vs.* Madison, in subsequent sketch of Chief-Justice Marshall.

§ 3 Dallas' Reports, 199.

the federal courts, notwithstanding such debt had been paid into the loan office of Virginia, under authority of the State law. It was upon the argument of this case that Ellsworth's illustrious successor on the bench—then in the prime of vigorous manhood, and the full strength of his splendid intellectual faculties—appeared for the first time at the bar of that tribunal over which he subsequently, for so many years, presided, and in a single argument, whose masterly analysis, and powerful and comprehensive logic excited the admiration of the bench as well as the bar, achieved a fame as a lawyer that was exceeded only by that which he afterwards won as a judge.*

Many of the cases which engaged the attention of the Supreme Court during the period of Judge Ellsworth's service were Admiralty cases, involving not only nice and sometimes intricate questions of jurisdiction, but some of them also bringing up for discussion the gravest principles of international and prize law. It will be recollected that nearly twenty years before, Ellsworth, as a member of the Committee of Appeals of the Continental Congress, had participated in the judgments of the first judicial tribunal ever organized in America with appellate jurisdiction in Admiralty cases. The functions of that committee were now exercised, under a better system, and a more complete and thorough organization, by the Supreme Court ; and though a somewhat different class of cases now arose, growing out of the more extended commerce of the United States, and our peculiar attitude with regard to the belligerent nations of Europe, and particularly with France, yet the general principles applicable to the subject, were not entirely new to the mind of Ellsworth.

One of the earliest of these cases is that of *La Vengeance,*† decided the next term after the Chief-Justice took his seat, and which has always since been regarded as a leading case upon the important question of the nature and extent of the Admiralty jurisdiction conferred by the Constitution and judiciary act on the federal tribunals. In the case of Glass *vs.* The Sloop Betsey, decided in Chief-Justice Jay's time ‡ the jurisdiction of the Admiralty in cases of prize and captures

* See a more full notice of this interesting case in the subsequent sketch of Chief-Justice Marshall.

† United States *vs.* La Vengeance. 3 Dallas' Reports, 297.

‡ *Ante*, page 61.

on the high seas, was established.* The case of *La Vengeance* now established a like jurisdiction in cases of seizure within a port, and forfeiture for a violation of an act of Congress, the Court being unanimously of opinion that it was a civil cause, and therefore coming within the Admiralty and maritime jurisdiction conferred by the judiciary act. But another question of novelty, as well as of great practical importance, was raised, and one which has been frequently discussed since that time—namely, whether the Admiralty jurisdiction can extend to causes arising on navigable waters within the precincts of a county. The *La Vengeance* had been libelled in the District Court of New York for exporting arms from Sandy Hook, in the State of New Jersey, to a foreign country. The Attorney-General Lee, in a very ingenious and able argument, maintained that to make it a cause of Admiralty, cognizable by the federal tribunals, it must arise *wholly* upon the sea, and not in a bay, harbor, or water within the precincts of a county of a State. But the Chief-Justice and his associates ruled the contrary, and thus established the precedent which has never since been shaken, that the Admiralty and maritime jurisdiction of the Federal Courts extends as far as the ebb and flow of the tide.†

At the same term of the court the Chief-Justice rendered judgment in another interesting case of Admiralty, arising under the construction of our treaty with France, which allowed the privateers of that country to send into our ports their prizes captured of the enemy on the high seas. A French privateer had captured a British merchantman, the Phœbe Ann, and sent her into the port of Charleston. The British consul filed a libel, claiming restitution of the prize on the

* The jurisdiction in cases of prize is at least as ample, says Judge Story, as the Admiralty in England. Brown *vs.* United States, 8 Cranch, 110.

† The principle was fully recognized and sanctioned in the case of United States *vs.* The Schooner Betsey (4 Cranch, 443), by Chief-Justice Marshall; and has been carried still farther since his time, as I shall have occasion to show in the subsequent sketch of Chief-Justice Taney.

It should be added that the principle has been disapproved by jurists of the highest reputation. JUDGE WOODBURY, in his dissenting opinion in Waring *vs.* Clark, 5 Howard, 448, considers the decision in this case as "the parent of mistaken references;" and even Chancellor Kent remarks, "it may be doubted whether the case of *La Vengeance*, on which all the subsequent decisions of the Supreme Court have rested, was sufficiently considered." 1 Kent. Com. 376.

ground that the French privateer had been illegally fitted out in the United States. The evidence was, that the privateer had entered the port of Charleston for repairs, as she lawfully might do under the treaty; but there had been no *material augmentation* of her force. The Court, therefore, refused to decree restitution, leaving undecided, however, the important question, whether if there had been a *material augmentation*, it would have been an illegal fitting out within the meaning of the law. One thing, however, was clearly established by the decision—namely, that the Judges of the Federal Courts, notwithstanding any political prejudices they might have been supposed to entertain against the "regicide republic," were determined to carry out in good faith the provisions of existing treaties with France. The language of Judge Ellsworth, in delivering the opinion of the Court, is alike dignified and honorable. "Suggestions of policy and convenience," he says, "cannot be considered in the judicial determination of a question of right. The treaty with France, whatever that is, must have its effect." *

Various other cases of Admiralty and prize law, involving mainly questions as to the nature and extent of the jurisdiction of the Federal Courts, were brought before Chief-Justice Ellsworth both at the Circuit and in the Supreme Court; but as these are of interest to the professional reader alone, who has an opportunity of examining the reports for himself, and as I have already by the foregoing references indicated generally the nature of the questions discussed befo e the Chief-Justice arising on this branch of the law, I dismiss the subject without further remark.†

* Moodie *vs.* Ship Phœbe Ann. 3 Dallas' Reports, 319.

† One of the most novel and curious of these cases is that of McDonough *vs.* Delancey, 3 Dallas, 188, at the first term Judge Ellsworth came to the Bench. A British merchant ship had been captured by a French squadron on the high seas, and a prize-master and crew put on board. Soon after she was left by the prize-master and crew, after several ineffectual attempts to set her on fire. An American vessel fell in with her, and brought her into the port of Boston. The owners of the American vessel, the British consul, and the French consul, respectively set up their claims to the captured vessel and cargo. The District Court adjudged one-third part of the vessel and cargo as *salvage* to the owners and crew of the American ship, and the residue to remain in court for the British owners. The Circuit Court on appeal reversed the decree as to the residue, awarding it to th

It is to be observed, however, that these jurisdictional questions so much mooted in Ellsworth's time, were by no means confined to cases of Admiralty and prize law. They grew out of every branch of jurisprudence, and were presented in almost every form, being the necessary consequence of that new, and in some respects untried, system, which was introduced by the passage of the act organizing the courts. Under that system of course every case of doubtful jurisdiction was to be settled by judicial construction.

Thus, in Wiscart *et al. vs.* Dauchy,* decided at the same term with the case of *La Vengeance*, the Chief-Justice laid down a principle of vast importance to the profession, so much so, indeed, as to lead in a short time to a change in the judiciary act. It was an action on the Equity side of the Circuit Court; and the record, containing the statement of facts required by the law, had been brought by *Writ of Error* to the Supreme Court. The main question was, whether this statement of facts was conclusive;—that is, whether the Supreme Court had the right to look into the testimony for the purpose of readjudicating the facts, decided in the Court below. It was a question, as Judge Wilson, who delivered a dissenting opinion, very truly remarked, which would materially affect the jurisdiction of all the Courts in the United States; and as it extended not only to Equity, but to Admiralty and maritime cases, it became of the highest importance, inasmuch as it might affect the rights and pretensions of foreign nations, as well as our own citizens.

Judge Wilson thought that the Supreme Court had jurisdiction in all these cases to review the *fact* as well as the *law*. But the Chief-Justice and the majority of the Court did not so regard the subject. Ellsworth's opinion, which, it seems, as was usually the case with him, was oral, contains a brief but clear and pointed exposition of his views of the law, and must be admitted to be strictly legal, as well as logical. An *appeal*, he remarks, is a process of civil law origin, and removes a cause entirely, subjecting the fact as well as the law to a review and retrial. But a *writ of error* is a process of

French Republic.; and the Supreme Court affirmed the decision of the Circuit Court. The question of the jurisdiction of the District Court was raised on the appeal, but decided unanimously in favor of the jurisdiction.

* 3 Dallas' Reports, 321.

common law origin, and removes nothing for re-examination but the law. The judiciary act, he thinks, preserves this obvious distinction, but it had provided no other mode than a *writ of error* for removing a cause to the Supreme Court. The conclusion, therefore, follows, that no matter whether the evidence is returned or not, the Court is bound by the statement of fact. " The law may, indeed, be improper and inconvenient," he remarks; " but it is of more importance for a judicial determination to ascertain what the law is, than to speculate upon what it ought to be."

At the following term of the Court the same question was presented in a slightly different form. It was an Admiralty case,* and the record had been sent up with all the evidence, but without the *statement of fact* required by the law, the District Judge having died soon after decree. Mr. Tilghman, for plaintiff in error, thereupon endeavored to distinguish the case from Wiscart *vs.* Dauchy; and insisted upon going into the evidence, notwithstanding the abrupt and sarcastic remark of Judge Chase from the bench—" Even if the Court were to permit it, you would find little encouragement to enter into the merits; the evidence is too plainly against you!" But the Chief-Justice and his associates held the principle to be the same as in Wiscart *vs.* Dauchy, and adhered to their former decision, Mr. Justice Paterson remarking, " If there is no statement of facts, the consequence seems naturally to follow, that there can be no error." †

A question of no less professional interest relative to the appellate jurisdiction of the Supreme Court was decided by the well-known case of Wilson *vs.* Daniel, at the August term, 1798.‡ The case had been argued at the preceding term, in the absence of the Chief-Justice; the main question presented by the record being whether the "matter

* Jennings *vs.* The Brig Perseverance. 3 Dallas, 336.

† In the subsequent case of Blain *vs.* Ship Carter, 4 Dallas, 22, it was again held that whatever might be the nature of the suit, there was no mode of removing causes to the Supreme Court, except by *writ of error.* The inconvenience of the rule thus established, was felt to be so great, that Congress, by the act of March 3rd, 1803, provided for an *appeal* instead of a *writ of error*, in equity and Admiralty cases, thus subjecting the evidence, as well as the law, to review in the Supreme Court.

‡ 3 Dallas' Reports, 401.

in dispute" was of sufficient value to give the Court jurisdiction.* The judgment was in an action of debt for the penalty of £60,000; but the real and operative judgment of the Circuit Court was only for the sum due, amounting to $1800. Three of the Judges, CHASE, PATERSON, and CUSHING, concurred in considering the judgment as a judgment at common law for the full penalty; and therefore that the Court had jurisdiction. Judge WILSON dissented; and IREDELL declined taking a part in the decision. The argument was now renewed on this point before the Chief-Justice, by Tilghman on the one side, and by Lee and Ingersoll on the other. At the close of the discussion Ellsworth delivered the opinion of the Court, concurring with the majority of his brethren, that the Court had jurisdiction. The actual judgment, or verdict, he thought was not to be regarded as the rule for ascertaining the matter in dispute. But that to determine it, recurrence must be had to the foundation of the original controversy—to the matter in dispute (in this case the penalty of the bond) when the action was instituted.†

This was the last term of the service of Mr. JUSTICE WILSON‡ in

* By the judiciary act, there could be no removal of a civil cause from the Circuit Court to the Supreme Court unless the matter in dispute exceeds the value of $2000.

† Judge Iredell now delivered an opinion, agreeing with the positions taken by Judge Wilson on the previous argument. This dissenting opinion proved to be the correct construction of the law, as subsequently laid down by the Supreme Court in several cases. In Gordon *vs.* Ogden, 3 Peters, 33, Chief-Justice Marshall says, that notwithstanding Wilson *vs.* Daniels was decided by a divided court, he would have followed it, had not a contrary practice prevailed.

‡ JAMES WILSON was a native of Scotland. He was born about the year 1742, and at the age of twenty-one emigrated to America, and settled in Philadelphia. After a brief period passed as a teacher in the Philadelphia College, a position for which his eminent scholarship and learning admirably qualified him, he commenced the study of the law, and two years afterwards entered upon the practice of his profession at Reading, Pennsylvania. Removing from thence to Carlisle, and from Carlisle to Annapolis, he finally, about the year 1773, settled at Philadelphia, where he fixed his residence for life. Mr. Wilson early engaged with ardor in the revolutionary struggle; was a member of Congress during a part of the revolutionary war, and one of the signers of the Declaration of Independence. He was also, as is well known, a prominent and influential member of the Convention which framed the Federal Convention, in which body, as all his speeches and votes show, he was numbered among the most extreme of the advo-

the Supreme Court. He died during the year, at the house of his friend and colleague, Judge Iredell, at Edenton, North Carolina, while on a judicial circuit in that State. At the opening of the February term of the Court, 1799, the commission of his successor, BUSHROD WASHINGTON,* was read, who was then qualified, and took

cates of a strong consolidated government. On the organization of the Federal judiciary he was appointed to a seat on the Bench of the Supreme Court, which he continued to occupy until his death, in 1798. A law professorship having been established in the College of Philadelphia, Mr. Wilson, soon after his appointment as Judge, was chosen first Professor; and two years after, when the college was united with the University of Pennsylvania, and a professorship of a similar kind was established, he was appointed to fill it; thus, like one of the most eminent of his successors, he sat, during his judgeship, alternately in the Professor's chair and on the bench.

In this position the comprehensive and almost inexhaustible erudition of Judge Wilson fitted him to shine with no ordinary degree of lustre. It was a position, perhaps, better adapted to his attainments and capacity than his place in the Federal judiciary. And yet Judge Wilson exhibited no ordinary ability as a jurist and lawyer. While in active practice his reputation, it is said, was unsurpassed by any of the able members of the Philadelphia bar, at the head of which he confessedly stood. As a judge he is also entitled to high respect, not more on account of his great learning, than of his patient industry, his uprightness of character, and his dignified bearing on the bench. Some of his judicial opinions display a needless prolixity of learning, and bear upon them evident marks of the lecture-room. This may be said as well of his charges to juries, especially in criminal cases, as of his judgments pronounced from the bench. Among the former it is only necessary to instance his charge to the grand jury which indicted, and to the petit jury which acquitted Henfield, on whose trial Judge Wilson presided.

* BUSHROD WASHINGTON was the son of John A. Washington, of Westmoreland County, Virginia, the next eldest brother of General Washington. He received part of his classical education under a private tutor at the house of Richard Henry Lee, and his studies were afterwards continued and completed at William and Mary College, in Virginia. Here commenced his acquaintance with Marshall, an acquaintance which afterwards ripened into friendship and intimacy, and continued unbroken till the period of his death. At the time of the invasion of Virginia by Cornwallis, young Washington, just arrived at the age of manhood, joined a volunteer troop of cavalry, and served in the army under the command of Lafayette. The following winter he came to Philadelphia, and under the auspices and care of his uncle, General Washington, commenced the study of the law in the office of Judge Wilson, whom he afterwards succeeded on the bench of the Supreme Court of the United States. His studies completed, he returned to Virginia, where he practiced his profession with reputation and success. In 1787 he

his seat. It may be added that Judge Iredell died the following year, and was succeeded by ALFRED MOORE, of North Carolina, and

was chosen a member of the Virginia House of Delegates; and the following year served in the Convention which ratified the Constitution of the United States. During the period of his practice at the bar he reported the decisions of the Supreme Court of Virginia, a work in two volumes, which furnishes abundant indications of the talents, industry, and success of Judge Washington, as an advocate at the bar. He served as an Associate-Justice of the United States Supreme Court with unsullied reputation, and a constantly increasing fame, from his appointment in 1798 to the time of his death, a period of more than thirty years. He died on the 26th of November, 1829, in the sixty-eighth year of his age; his remains were deposited at Mount Vernon, in the same vault which contained the ashes of Gen. Washington, and his monument is now to be seen on the banks of the Potomac, by the side of the new tomb, where rest the ashes of the father of his country.

Judge Washington, it is well known, was the favorite nephew of General Washington, and the devisee of Mount Vernon; he left no issue, however, to inherit that estate after him. He was also one of the executors of General Washington, and came into possession of all his uncle's public and private papers, which he subsequently passed over into the hands of his friend, Chief-Justice Marshall, for the purpose of being used by him in his "Life of Washington." Judge Story, who sat with him during so many years on the bench, and who fully appreciated his worth and virtues, has left a brief but discriminating eulogy upon the character of Judge Washington, from which I select the following passages:

"His mind was solid rather than brilliant; sagacious and searching rather than quick or eager; slow, but not torpid; steady, but not unyielding; comprehensive, but at the same time cautious; patient in inquiry, forcible in conception, clear in reasoning. He was, by original temperament, mild, conciliating, and candid; and yet was remarkable for an uncompromising firmness. Of him it may be truly said that the fear of man never fell upon him; it never entered into his thoughts, much less was it seen in his actions. In him the love of justice was the ruling passion—it was the master-spring of all his conduct. He made it a matter of conscience to discharge every duty with scrupulous fidelity and scrupulous zeal. It mattered not whether the duty were small or great, witnessed by the world or performed in private; everywhere the same diligence, watchfulness, and pervading sense of justice were seen. There was about him a tenderness of giving offence, and yet a fearlessness of consequences in his official character, which it is difficult to portray. It was a rare combination which added much to the dignity of the bench, and made justice itself, even when most severe, soften into the moderation of mercy. It gained confidence when it seemed least to seek it. It repressed arrogance by overawing or confounding it. * * * * * * He was a learned judge. Not in that every-day learning which may be gathered up by a hasty reading of books and cases; but that which is the result of long-continued

these were the only changes made in the constitution of the Court during the period of Ellsworth's service. JUDGE CHASE came upon the bench at the same term the Chief-Justice took his seat; and JUDGES CUSHING and PATERSON * remained members of the Court until after Ellsworth's resignation.

laborious services, and comprehensive studies. He read to learn, not to quote; to digest and master, and not merely to display. He was not easily satisfied. If he was not as profound as some, he was more exact than most men. But the value of his learning was, that it was the keystone of all his judgments. He indulged not the rash desire to fashion the law to his own views, but to follow out its precepts with a sincere good faith and simplicity. Hence he possessed the happy faculty of yielding just and proper weight to authority; neither on the one hand surrendering himself to the dictates of other judges, nor on the other hand overruling settled doctrines upon his own private notions of policy or justice."

* WILLIAM PATERSON was one of the ablest jurists whom New Jersey has produced. He came later into public life than some of his associates, but he brought with him to the bench an extensive and valuable experience at the bar as well as in various departments of public life. He was first elected to Congress in 1780, and afterwards in 1786, having previously served in the provincial Congress of New Jersey. He was also appointed and served in the Convention which adopted the Federal Constitution. In this body Mr. Paterson, like Ellsworth, advocated a strictly federal, in opposition to a strong consolidated government. As a counter plan to those proposed by Randolph and Pinckney, he presented one of his own, which is known as the "New Jersey plan," being in the main a mere revision of the articles of Confederation, though proposing to establish a supreme Executive, composed of several persons, and also a Federal judiciary. This plan, after some discussion, was rejected, it receiving the support only of the delegates from New Jersey, Connecticut, Delaware, and in part of Maryland. On the organization of the government Mr. Paterson was appointed one of the senators in Congress from New Jersey. In that body he was placed with Ellsworth upon the committee which drafted the bill to organize the Federal judiciary. He served through two sessions of this Congress, when, being elected Governor of New Jersey, he resigned, and Mr. Philemon Dickinson was chosen to succeed him. On the death of Judge Johnson, of Maryland, Mr. Paterson was chosen to the vacant seat on the bench of the Supreme Court, and was commissioned, March 9th, 1793. He retained this place until his decease in 1806, and was succeeded by Brockholst Livingston, of New York. Judge Paterson was unquestionably one of the ablest jurists who sat upon the bench of the old Supreme Court. In most of those qualities which constitute a successful judge he was inferior to none of his colleagues, and perhaps was not equalled by any, save his brethren, Iredell and Chase. His intellect, though less accurate and logical than that of the former, and less bold and self-reliant than that of the latter, was original, comprehensive, discriminating,

Though, as before remarked, many of the cases brought into the Supreme Court in Ellsworth's time involved questions of jurisdiction, or other questions growing out of the peculiar structure of the federal system, yet occasionally matters were brought there for adjudication, as they frequently are now, the argument of which turned simply and purely upon points of common law or equity jurisprudence. The jurisdiction of the Court in some cases is determined by the character of the parties, as well as the subject matter of the suit. Then, as now, the citizen of one State could sue the citizen of another State in the Federal Courts, in any recognized form of action, thus laying open the whole field of legal and equitable jurisprudence. In short, the Judges of the Court were not strangers to the discussion of the most abstruse, and sometimes the most technical, questions, drawn from the musty recesses of the common law. Thus, in Brown *vs.* Barry, at the August term, 1797,* the controversy hinged upon the merest refinements of *special pleading*—presenting a point too minute and unsubstantial for any one but the practiced lawyer to appreciate. It was a motion to arrest the judgment after verdict; and the professional reader will readily perceive the delicate refinements of learning, and the technical precision of argument called forth in the discussion of propositions like these: That the declaration demands foreign money without stating the value thereof in the current money of the United States; that it is in the *debet*, as well as in the *detinet;* that it does not charge that the bill of exchange therein mentioned was protested for non-acceptance; that it does not charge that the said bill was presented to the persons on whom it was drawn for acceptance, or

and strong. Some of his judicial opinions are among the best specimens left us of the old Supreme Court. Judge Paterson presided with firmness and dignity, but with moderation, in several of those exciting criminal trials which took place during Adams' and the latter part of Washington's administrations. Among these were the trials of the Western Insurgents, the trial of Guinet, at Philadelphia, for illegal privateering; and the trial of Haswell, in the Vermont District, for a seditious libel.

The rigid discipline preserved by Judge Paterson in Court on some of these trials has been complained of. On the trial of Haswell, it is said, he even prevented the printer of the Vergennes Gazette from taking notes. His conduct, however, was generally marked by strict impartiality and a scrupulous regard for the rights and privileges of the accused.

* 3 Dallas' Reports, 365.

that they were ever required to accept it, &c. Judge Ellsworth brought to the examination of questions like these, the plain, and somewhat homely, but clear, and strong common sense, which characterized his practical mind. No one who reads his decision, in this day of legal quibbles, would be apt to call him a great lawyer—that is to say, one skilled in the refinements of legal metaphysics, and in that precise, but narrow and technical attorney-logic, with which the old books are filled. He, indeed, scarcely enters into the discussion at all. He adduces no authority, and cites no adjudged case ; and yet there is no lack either of shrewdness or masculine common sense in the manner in which he takes up, and considers, and *over-rules*, each objection, seriatim. The opinion which would have occupied at least fifty pages of a modern report, is condensed within two pages of the published case ; and yet it is one of the longest ever delivered by the Chief-Justice while presiding in the Supreme Court.

The case of Clark *vs.* Russell, at the February term, 1799,* presented the subject of a similar examination. From the report of this case, and the number of authorities cited by counsel, it would appear that the argument was conducted with a most exuberant profusion of learning, and an extraordinary display of ability ; nor could it well have been otherwise, when Ingersoll was the leading counsel on one side, and Dexter, of Massachusetts,† headed the array on the other,

* 3 Dallas' Reports, 415.

† Samuel Dexter is justly regarded as one of the brightest ornaments of the Massachusetts bar. His professional career was one of great success and brilliancy, and for a time he was regarded at the bar of the United States Supreme Court as the rival, and, perhaps, the sole rival, of Pinkney. The friends and admirers of each claimed the superiority over the other, and perhaps it was difficult to say to whom the forensic crown legitimately belonged. Judge Story, in one of his letters, contrasts the respective merits and style of these great advocates, in a manner certainly not unfavorable to Mr. Dexter, which must be esteemed the very highest compliment, when it is recollected that Story's admiration for Pinkney was unbounded. Subsequently, in the eulogy delivered on Mr. Dexter's death, as part of a charge to a grand jury, Story speaks of him in terms of almost exaggerated praise : "Mr. Dexter was a man of such rare endowments, that in whatever age or nation he had lived, he would have been in the first rank of professional eminence. It is unfortunate that he has left no written record of himself. The only monument of his fame rests in the frail recollections of memory, and can reach future ages only through the indistinctness of tradition or history.

The opinion of the Court, pronounced by the Chief-Justice, is even more brief and sententious than in the former case. The first question discussed, he thinks, had been already decided in Brown *vs.* Barry, and is summarily dismissed. On the second question, namely, whe-

His glowing thoughts, his brilliant periods, and his profound reasonings have perished forever." Judge Story adds that he rejoiced "to have lived in the same age with him, and to have been permitted to hear his eloquence, and to be instructed by his wisdom."

Dexter was born in the year 1761, and educated at Harvard University in 1781. Admitted to the bar, he rose rapidly into professional notice, and soon passed into the State Legislature, and from thence into Congress. He was a senator in Congress when Mr. Adams appointed him Secretary of War, in place of Mr. McHenry. On the accession of Mr. Jefferson he retired from the cabinet, and generally from political employments; and thenceforth devoted himself mainly to the labors of his profession, up to the time of his death, which happened in May, 1816. For several years previous to his death, Mr. Dexter was constant in his attendance upon the sessions of the Supreme Court at Washington, where, engaged in many of the most important causes, he held "his career in the foremost rank of advocates."

The brilliancy of his forensic arguments, and the effect of his eloquence, may be conceived by the account given of them by his eulogist, Judge Story, who so often, as he says, listened to him "with pride and pleasure" from the bench. "Rarely did he speak without attracting an audience composed of the taste, the beauty, the wit, and the learning, that adorned the city; and never was he heard without instruction and delight. On such occasions involuntary tears from the whole audience have testified the touching power of his eloquence and pathos. On others a profound and breathless silence, expressed, more forcibly than any human language, the riveted attention of a hundred minds." The same competent hand, in the eulogy alluded to, has sketched the character of Mr. Dexter's oratory, from which the limited space of a note enables me to select only the following passages: "His enunciation was remarkably slow, distinct and musical; though the intonations of his voice were sometimes too monotonous. His language was plain, but pure and well selected; and though his mind was stored with poetic images, he rarely indulged himself in ornaments of any kind. If a rhetorical illustration, or striking metaphor sometimes adorned his speeches, they seemed the spontaneous burst of his genius, produced without effort, and dismissed without regret. * * * * * * In the exordiums of his speeches he was rarely happy. It seemed like the first exercise of a mind struggling to break its slumbers, or to control the torrent of its thoughts. As he advanced, he became collected, forcible, and argumentative; and his perorations were uniformly grand and impressive. They were often felt when they could not be perceived."—*Story's Miscellanies.—Eulogy on Dexter.*

ther parol testimony might be admitted *to explain* certain letters introduced in evidence, he reverses the judgment, without examining the many learned references and authorities adduced in the argument; the main reason assigned for the reversal being, because the charge of the Judge, that such testimony might be admitted, without any qualifications or restrictions, "was too broad, and may have misled the jury."

The habitual brevity of Judge Ellsworth in the delivery of his judgments is observable in all these decisions. Indeed, taken together, they constitute but an imperfect record of his judicial career, and scarcely enable us to form a proper estimate of his capacity as a judge in the discussion of mere legal questions. He seems to have had a repugnance at all times to enter minutely into the examination of the subject under discussion, or to state fully the grounds of his decision. Though an accurate and ready speaker, he was never an easy or fluent writer. Hence, perhaps, his disinclination to elaborate an argument, and the reason why so few of his judgments attract attention, in comparison with those of his brethren on the bench;—with the bold and pointed reasoning of Chase, the keen, subtle, logical argumentation of Iredell, or even the learned, but florid and scholastic dissertations of Wilson. Indeed, it mattered very little what was the nature of the controversy before him, or how intricate the question under discussion might be;—the same studious and sententious brevity is apparent in his judgments, whether the point at issue was a mere technical question of practice, or involved the most recondite principles of the common law.

Thus the last case argued at this winter session of 1799—Sims *vs.* Irvine,* brought up for examination the effect of the treaty or compact between Virginia and Pennsylvania, and presented an important question in regard to the nature of the land titles in the latter State. The subject was discussed at great length, and with a profusion of learning, by some of the ablest counsel at the bar, as the reported analysis of the argument clearly shows. But the opinion of the Chief-Justice, affirming the judgment of the Circuit Court and the validity of the Pennsylvania land title, is compressed within a single page of the report. He decides that the survey of the land and payment, though without an actual patent issued, is a *legal title*, sufficient to

* 3 Dallas' Reports, 425.

maintain ejectment under the laws of property and tenures of Pennsylvania; and this law, notwithstanding the new distribution of judicial powers in the federal tribunals, must be regarded by them as a settled RULE OF DECISION, in regard to estates in Pennsylvania. Judge Iredell concurred in the judgment, but for different reasons, which he assigns at length in one of his best and most carefully written opinions. But from the habitual brevity of the Chief-Justice, we do not clearly see wherein he differs from Judge Iredell, nor in what manner by another mode of reasoning, he arrives at precisely the same conclusions.

Through the whole period of his official service, Judge Ellsworth regularly rode the circuits, as had previously been done by his predecessor Jay. The law requiring a Circuit Court to be held by two Justices of the Supreme Court, with the District Judge, had been modified so as to require the attendance of but one of the Supreme Court Justices; but the old practice of the allotment of circuits among the Judges, so that the same Judge, except by his own consent, should not be assigned to the same circuit until after it had been held by each of his associates successively, was still in force.* This, of course, increased the fatigue and labor of circuit duty, and, with the two regular sessions of the Court *in banc* at Philadelphia, rendered the office of Justice of the Supreme Court, in those days when steamboats and railroads were unknown, no sinecure.

As a Judge at *nisi prius*, Ellsworth has been spoken of in terms of the highest praise. Perhaps the temper of his mind, his habits of thought, and his past experience, better fitted him for the performance of this branch of his official duty than any other. He certainly brought to its discharge qualities of a very high order. A calm, discriminating, and well-balanced, if not original intellect; a solid, practical good sense, equally beyond the reach of influence from passion, imagination, or prejudice; powers of accurate and unerring, though not rapid, analysis; courtesy of manner, simplicity and dignity of deportment, an industry that knew no fatigue, and never courted repose, and an impartiality of judgment and uprightness of character, that none ever ventured to assail. His charges, particularly those delivered to grand juries, have been mentioned as deeply impressive, both in

* Act of April 13th, 1792.

matter and manner—breathing a lofty moral tone, and never failing to inculcate those elevated principles of legal ethics of which the judicial bench is so fitly the expositor.

In the discharge of his circuit duties, Judge Ellsworth did not entirely escape a participation in those criminal trials so celebrated at that period, some of which left their "fatal dowry" to his less fortunate brother, Judge Chase.* But, unlike that gifted, though indiscreet

* SAMUEL CHASE, the only son of a clergyman, was born in Somerset County, Maryland, on the 17th April, 1741. At the age of eighteen he commenced the study of the law, in Annapolis, and two or three years afterwards established himself there in the practice of his profession. For several years prior to the Revolution he was a member of the Colonial Legislature, where he distinguished himself by his ardent republicanism, his vehement temper, and his "uncourtly bearing to the court party." In the Continental Congress he performed good service, and by his resolute and persevering energy contributed in no small degree to bring about the Declaration of Independence. Though originally an opponent of the Federal Constitution, he was appointed by President Washington, in 1796, one of the Associate-Justices of the Supreme Court of the United States, an office which he continued to hold, notwithstanding the unhappy interruption of his official duties by his impeachment before the Senate, until the close of his life, in 1811.

The extraordinary capacity of Judge Chase has never been questioned or denied. It was such as almost to justify the remark said to have been made of him by a distinguished member of the Philadelphia bar—neither a personal nor a political friend—that he was the greatest judge he had ever seen. But the strength of these intellectual endowments was in a measure impaired by an unhappy mental constitution, and an impetuous, arbitrary temper, which fitted him rather for a partisan than a judge, and kept him at constant variance with the bar, and indeed all with whom he came professionally in contact; causing him, as it is expressed in his biography, "to be running perpetually with a mob at his heels."

The energy of his character and the fearlessness of his temper, were displayed in a very striking manner while holding the double office of Chief-Justice of the General Court, and Judge of the Criminal Court in Baltimore. Two persons of respectability had been brought before him charged with participating in a riot, on whose behalf the most overwhelming and violent popular sympathy was manifested. Refusing to give bail, they were ordered to prison. The sheriff, pointing to the mob in despair, declined to undertake the task. "Summon the *posse comitatus!*" exclaimed the Judge; but the sheriff replied that no one would obey the call. "Summon *me* then," replied the Judge, with determined emphasis; "I will be the *posse comitatus*, and I will take the prisoners to jail!" After some delay the prisoners yielded, and gave the required bail. Four months afterwards, when the grand jury refused to find a bill against them, he publicly censured the

Judge, he passed through the ordeal in safety, and came out of the furnace without the smell of fire upon his garments. I do not mean to say that his opinions escaped criticism, and severe, perhaps just,

sheriff for returning *so bad a jury.* Fired with indignation, they immediately found a presentment against the Judge for the offence of holding two incompatible offices at the same time. To this Chase took no exceptions, if they really believed it to be an offence, though he could not help observing, he said, that it seemed to flow from a supposed insult to themselves. "You will continue, gentlemen," he remarked with biting sarcasm, "to do your duty, and I shall persevere in mine; and rest assured that no mistaken opinion of yours, or resentment against me, will prevent my having a due respect for you—*as a jury.*" But it was in his administration of the criminal law on the bench of the Federal Courts that Judge Chase acquired the widest and most unenviable notoriety; not that it was characterised by ignorance, much less by actual injustice, for his keen and powerful intellect lifted him far above the one, and his bold independence and natural magnanimity of temper preserved him from the other. But Chase brought to the bench the feelings of a partisan; and, as a Judge, he enforced the criminal law, and those penal statutes, which even then, were widely unpopular, with the unrelenting sternness and severity of the inquisitor. Counsel as well as prisoner alike experienced his harshness of temper, and were forced to bear up under his abrupt, arbitrary, dictatorial manner. The "conduct directed by the Court" on the trial of Fries, drove Messrs. Dallas and Lewis out of the case. "You may think to embarrass the Court," he remarked to Mr. Dallas, "but you shall find yourself mistaken." And when the counsel had left the bar, turning to the prisoner, he observed that, "by the blessing of God, the Court would do him as much justice as the counsel who had been assigned him." On the trial of Cooper, at Philadelphia, for seditious libel, he exhibited a comparative moderation, for the reason, perhaps, that he found very little difficulty in obtaining a conviction; but all the daring of his temper and the dictatorial energy of his mind were called forth in the famous trial of Callender, which finally brought down on his devoted head the long pent up vials of the public indignation. Judge Chase started for Richmond on this trial with the declaration, as was stated at the time, that he would "teach the lawyers of Virginia the difference between the liberty and licentiousness of the press;" and so resolutely was his mind bent on obtaining a conviction, that, it is also said on the highest authority, he instructed the Marshal "not to put any of these creatures called democrats on the jury." During the whole trial the contest seems to have been mainly between the Court and the prisoner's counsel; and though the latter were among the most eminent lawyers at the Virginia bar—Nicholas, Hay, and Wirt—it must be confessed that the indomitable will, and arbitrary and overbearing temper of the Judge got the better of them. The excitement of the contest appeared to elevate his spirits, to augment his boldness, and even to sharpen his intellectual vigor. As Dryden described Shaftesbury, he was not only

animadversion ; but that while the judgment of the Court was deprecated, the person and character of the Judge were respected ; and

"Sagacious, bold, and turbulent of wit ;"

but he was also, as was fully exhibited on this trial—

"The daring pilot in extremity,
Pleased with the danger when the waves ran high."

The eminent counsel who defended the prisoner, foiled and brow-beaten, were filled with a just indignation. A determination to procure his impeachment, is said to have been avowed during the trial, and for a long time counsel refused to appear before him. At length, in 1804, Mr. Randolph moved the long expected charges against him in the House of Representatives, and the famous impeachment was subsequently tried by the Senate. His conduct on the trial of Fries formed the first charge, and on Callender's trial the next five charges in the indictment; and though a majority voted him guilty on one or two of these charges, such as for "rude and contemptuous conduct during the trial," &c., he was saved from conviction by the failure to obtain a two-third vote.

This unfortunate affair, as might well be imagined, subdued the impetuosity of his temper, and cast a shadow over the remaining years of his life. Thenceforth he discharged all the duties of his station with his usual ability, indeed, but with a calm and formal moderation, and a haughty decorum, which, though it might provoke criticism, could not bring down censure on his head. He had always been esteemed, in everything pertaining to the civil jurisdiction of the Courts, a wise, able, and impartial Judge, even during the most stormy portion of his career. His keen and bold intellect, his profound knowledge of legal principles, his comprehensive and accurate judgment, and his integrity and perfect independence of character, fitted him admirably for the discharge of these duties. With all the daring of Shaftesbury as a partisan—though without his other blemishes of character—he might be said to rival that unscrupulous, but capable minister, in almost his only redeeming trait—his wisdom and capacity as a Judge. The industry and application of Judge Chase were also great; and though, hurried away by the ardor of his temper in a season of excitement, he might come down from the Bench of the Supreme Court, even though his absence left it without a quorum, and canvass his State on the eve of a presidential election, in behalf of his friend, President Adams, "with such *éclat*," says Mr. Wharton, "that at his final harangue at Elk Ridge, nearly all Maryland was congregated to listen to a stump speech 'two hours long;'" yet he rarely failed at all other times in the punctilious and thorough discharge of every official engagement. In his private intercourse, though rough, he was not uncourteous in manner, and indeed seems to have favorably impressed all who approached him. Judge Story saw him late in life, and speaks with great respect both of his abilities and his unaffected courtesy. "I suspect he is the American Thurlow," says Story, in one of his letters, and adds, "I like him hugely."

while his supposed errors were condemned, his integrity of motive was neither aspersed nor suspected.

I have briefly alluded in the sketch of Chief-Justice Jay to one of the earliest of those criminal trials, which, from that time to the repeal of the sedition law, kept the country in a constant fever of excitement —namely, the case of Henfield. That trial laid down with circumstantial precision the doctrine of a common-law jurisdiction in the Federal Courts in criminal cases—a doctrine then, and subsequently, odious to the republican party, and denounced by some of their ablest men in unmeasured terms.* It is, perhaps, unnecessary to say that Ellsworth was a believer in this doctrine, which no Judge of the Federal Courts at that time, save Samuel Chase, had been bold enough to deny. The Chief-Justice, however, was but a follower over the beaten track which his predecessors had travelled, in holding the doctrine of a common-law jurisdiction ; and therefore, in a measure, might escape the censure with which they were visited. But another question now arose, involving a proposition of almost equal importance, and certainly of no less interest in its political aspects, in the establish-

The fact has also been mentioned as strikingly characteristic of Judge Chase, and illustrative of his bold and independent habits of thought, that he did not hesitate to differ from his brethren and his own party-associates on the most important questions, even though they might involve political considerations. While claiming to exercise as a Judge in criminal cases the most arbitrary powers, he was singularly averse to assuming any doubtful civil jurisdiction; thus he was the first to deny that the Court possessed a common-law jurisdiction, and the last to admit that it could pronounce an act of Congress void, as being repugnant to the Constitution.

* Says Jefferson, in a letter to Edmund Randolph, August 18th, 1799. "Of all the doctrines which have ever been broached by the Federal Government, the novel one of the common law being in force and cognizable as an existing law in these Courts, is to me the most formidable. All their other assumptions of ungiven powers have been in the detail. The bank law, the treaty doctrine, the sedition act, alien act, the undertaking to change the State laws of evidence in the State Courts by certain parts of the stamp act, &c., have been solitary, unconsequential, timid things, in comparison with the audacious, barefaced, and sweeping pretension to a system of law for the United States, without the adoption of their legislature, and so infinitely beyond their power to adopt." * * * "Great Heavens!" he exclaims, in the conclusion of this letter, "Who could have conceived in 1789 that, within ten years, we should have to combat such windmills!"—3 *Jefferson's Writings*, 425, 428.

ment of which Ellsworth was to be the pioneer, and the full responsibility of which he was to take on his own shoulders. This was the question, so often and so ably discussed since that time, whether the right of expatriation was to be recognized in the Federal Courts as a part of the municipal law of the country. The question came directly before the Chief-Justice in the trial of the noted privateer's man, Isaac Williams, for enlisting on board a French vessel in alleged violation of a clause in the treaty with Great Britain. The trial is sufficiently interesting to deserve a brief notice.*

Williams was indicted and tried at the Circuit Court for the Connecticut District, at Hartford, in September, 1799. The crime alleged against him was, that, being a citizen of the United States, he had accepted a commission as lieutenant on a vessel belonging to the French Republic, then at war with England, contrary to the treaty of amity and commerce between Great Britain and the United States. Williams admitted the act alleged against him, but claimed that he was a French citizen, offering to show French naturalization papers, and continued residence in France since 1792, except a period of not more than six months in 1796, when he returned to America on a visit to his relatives and friends. The case in its general features was similar to that of Henfield's, with the exception that Williams relied mainly on his character of a French citizen; and the question therefore turned entirely upon the point whether the common-law maxim, "no one can throw off his country, or abjure his allegiance," † was the law of the United States.

Judge Law, the District Judge of Connecticut, sat with the Chief-Justice on this trial, and was of the opinion that the evidence offered by the prisoner should be left to the consideration of the jury. But the Chief-Justice was decidedly of a contrary opinion. He boldly,

* The ruling of Judge Ellsworth upon this trial was very severely criticised, and particularly in two letters published in the "Examiner," under the title of "Aristogiton," said to have been written by Mr. Nicholas, of Virginia, in which the popular American doctrine is very ably and successfully maintained, and which "exposed completely," says the author of the suppressed history of Mr. Adams' Administration, "the fallacy of the arguments adduced by the Chief-Justice."

† *Nemo potest exuere patriam, nec debitum ligeantiæ ejurare.*

and without the slightest hesitation, met the question which Chief-Justice Rutledge and his associates in Talbot *vs.* Jansen* had avoided —and which for years after was cautiously avoided by his successors on the bench—and held that the English common-law doctrine as to perpetual allegiance, was a part of the municipal law of the land, and applicable to the case at bar. It is curious to observe, however, that while the English rule is to be traced to the feudal system, and is based exclusively on the feudal relation of lord and vassal, the American Judge, applying it in an American Court, deduces it solely from the comparatively modern doctrine of the *social compact* as the basis of government. All the members of a civil community, he remarks, in his address to the jury, are bound to each other by compact. The compact is, that the community will protect its members, and they on the other hand will at all times be obedient to the laws of the community, and faithful in its defence. It necessarily follows that the members cannot dissolve this compact, without the consent or default of the community, &c.

It had been argued with great pertinency and force by the prisoner's counsel, that the policy of the government and its practice in permitting the naturalization of foreigners,† were sufficient evidence of consent. Judge Ellsworth meets and answers this argument with the following propositions, the soundness of which I shall leave to the advocates of the doctrine of perpetual allegiance to defend.

"Consent has been argued from the acts of our government permitting the naturalization of foreigners. When a foreigner presents himself here, and proves himself to be of good moral character, well affected to the Constitution and Government of the United States, and a friend to the good order and happiness of civil society; if he has resided here the time prescribed by law, we grant him the privilege of a citizen. We do not inquire what his relation is to his own country; we have not the means of knowing, and the inquiry would be indelicate; we

* *Ante*, pages 184, 185.

† The alien is required on his naturalization to abjure his former allegiance. Chancellor Kent notices this glaring inconsistency between the doctrines sought to be established in the Federal Courts, and the policy of the government in its naturalization laws, which practically asserts the right of all mankind to emigrate from one country to another, and renounce their allegiance at will.—*See* 2 Kent's Com. p. 49, *note.*

leave him to judge of that. If he *embarrasses himself by contracting contradictory obligations, the fault and the folly are his own.* But this implies no consent of the government, that our own citizens should expatriate themselves. Therefore it is my opinion that these facts which the prisoner offers to prove in his defence, are totally irrelevant; they can have no operation in law; and the jury ought not to be embarrassed or troubled with them; but by the constitution of the Court the evidence must go to the jury."

Of course the jury, under this charge of the presiding judge, at once found a verdict of guilty. Williams was sentenced to four months' imprisonment, and to pay a fine of one thousand dollars. Pleading guilty to another indictment for a similar offence, a like sentence was passed upon him by the Court. "So much for naturalization acts," says a prominent Federalist of the day. "The jacobins are impudent and cross; they think they gain ground; they are mistaken." *

It is scarcely necessary here to remark, that the rule so decisively laid down by Ellsworth in Williams' case, was widely at variance with the popular doctrines of the day, and is in direct conflict with the whole policy and practice of the government since that time. It, indeed, goes far to justify the claims set up by Great Britain in the war

* Letter of Mr. Chauncey Goodrich to Wolcott, Sept. 28th, 1799. The republicans, on the other hand, were indignant at the sentence.

"Great God!" exclaims Aristogiton, "What must have been the feelings of Judge Ellsworth when he was depriving Williams of this natural right. But I will suppress the emotions which beat in my bosom upon the recollection of this hideous sentence, and I will proceed to examine coolly and dispassionately the question. If this alien had not a right to throw off his allegiance to his own country, then Congress, by making the law, have deprived foreign governments of one of their most essential rights, and have moreover been guilty of a crime which approaches very nearly to man-stealing."

In the further examination of the subject, the writer proceeds to put the Chief-Justice in a dilemma from which it is not easy to see how he can be extricated. "Such is the dilemma," he remarks, "in which he has placed himself. He must either admit that according to the principles of our naturalization laws our citizens have a right to expatriate themselves, or that the legislature of the United States, that body whose laws (when they are constituted) he is bound to expound and enforce, have been guilty of the most horrible of all crimes, and have given a sufficient cause of war to all the nations of the world."

of 1812, and if recognized by the government as a rule of international law, would strike at the foundation of the right asserted and exercised by the United States of protecting adopted citizens even against the wrongful acts of the government claiming their allegiance. This right has been ably and triumphantly vindicated since that time,* and may be regarded, so far as the intercourse of this country with foreign nations is concerned, as a settled principle of international law. It must be confessed, however, that the Courts have not fully sanctioned the doctrine ; but that on the contrary, though never applying it in its full extent, as it was laid down in Williams' case, they have in one or two instances been inclined to consider the common-law principle of perpetual allegiance as a part of the municipal law of the land. Such at least was the case in Shanks *vs.* Dupont,† where Judge

* See the masterly dispatches of Mr. Buchanan, Secretary of State under Mr. Polk's administration, in the case of Bergen ; and that of the present Secretary of State, Mr. Marcy, in the Kozsta case.

† 3 Peters' Reports, 242. It is worthy of remark that up to this time, though the question had been repeatedly argued by the ablest counsel at the bar, yet the Supreme Court of the United States had constantly avoided its decision. The case of Talbot *vs.* Jansen has already been mentioned. In the case of Murray *vs.* Charming Betsey, in 1804, 2 Cranch, 64, it was discussed at great length and with commanding ability ; but Chief-Justice Marshall, who delivered the opinion of the Court, avoided the decision with more than his usual caution. "Whether a person born within the United States," he says, "or becoming a citizen according to the established laws of the country, can divest himself absolutely of that character otherwise than in such manner as may be prescribed by law, is a question which it is not necessary now to decide." And four years later, in the case of McIlvaine *vs.* Coxe's Lessees, 4 Cranch, 209—though the whole question was again discussed at the bar with an accuracy of learning worthy the magnitude and importance of the subject, Judge Cushing, who pronounced the decision of the Court, declined expressing an opinion "upon the right of expatriation, as founded on the common law." In the celebrated case of the *Santissima Trinidad*, Judge Story in like manner declined examining the doctrine, though it had been much discussed at the bar, remarking that it would be "sufficient to ascertain its precise nature and limits, when it shall become a leading point of a judgment of the Court." A few years later, however, in the cases of Inglis *vs.* Sailors' Snug Harbor, 3 Peters, 156 ; and Shanks *vs.* Dupont, mentioned in the text, he recognizes the general doctrine to be, that allegiance by birth cannot be put off except by consent of the government. But it is to be remarked that even in the latter case the learned Judge, though stating "the general doctrine" of the common law, does not undertake "to ascertain its precise nature and limits;"

Story recognizes generally the existence of the principle, and Judge Johnson, in a dissenting opinion, sustains the same proposition in a very plausible and ingenious argument. If this is to be regarded as a judicial decision upon the precise question under consideration—which, however, is by no means clear—then the United States presents the singular spectacle of a nation administering in its Courts a rule of municipal law, which its government practically ignores in its intercourse with foreign nations, as a rule of public and international law. A position so inconsistent it will be difficult to maintain; and the question, if ever presented directly to the Court, must doubtless be decided in accordance with the more liberal doctrine, sanctioned by the practice of the government, which recognizes the right to change allegiance as a natural right, inseparably connected with a *bonâ-fide* and permanent change of domicil. Indeed, but for the opinions of the learned judges, in the case last-mentioned, it might even now be confidently asserted that the doctrine of perpetual allegiance as laid down by Ellsworth, had passed away even as a rule of municipal law, with the doctrine of a common law jurisdiction, as expounded by his predecessor. Applied as it was in the case of Williams, it certainly could not be sustained in our day. But it should be recollected that these were times of warm party strife and excitement, and to suppose that the opinions of the Chief-Justice were entirely untinged by his known political predilections, would be to suppose him elevated above human weaknesses and imperfections. It has been observed of a more profound lawyer than Ellsworth, and of a greater judge than Jay—none other than the illustrious Mansfield himself—that in those cases wherein political considerations mix themselves with the trial, and the result might be supposed to affect party interests or party prejudices, he was no longer the same *lex loquens*, the same living pattern of justice.* Nor is it discreditable either to Jay or Ellsworth,

even as a rule of municipal law; and the opinion of Judge Johnson, which, it must be admitted, is precise and definite upon the point, *was a dissenting* opinion. I cannot agree, therefore, with the author of the Notes to the "State Trials," that the case of Shanks *vs.* Dupont closed "the long circuit of doubts and reservations," and brought the Court "back again at the position of Williams' case, that allegiance without mutual consent is indissoluble."

* As for example, in questions of libel, that he leaned against the freedom of discussion, and favored those doctrines then current, which withdrew the cogni-

under similar circumstances, to attribute an honestly entertained, but erroneous judgment, to the insensible bias of warm party feelings and political prejudices, when the great mind of Mansfield himself could not entirely surmount them.

Though Judge Ellsworth received his appointment as envoy to France on the 27th of February, 1799, he did not proceed upon the mission until the following November, and in the mean time continued, without interruption, to discharge his judicial duties. It was during this interval that Williams was tried ; and, indeed, so late as October of the same year he was upon the point of setting out to hold the Vermont Circuit Court, in place of Judge Cushing, who had been suddenly taken ill ; but the recovery of that judge relieved him of this duty, and gave him, as he says, time "to sit down and think" before proceeding on the French mission.

He presided for the last time at a general term of the Court in August of that year, and among the cases decided at this session delivered the judgment in Turner *vs.* The Bank of North America,* in which the principle is settled that a cause in the Circuit Court must affirmatively, and upon the face of the pleadings, appear to be within the jurisdiction of the Court, otherwise the judgment will be reversed in the Supreme Court, as jurisdiction is never to be presumed. I mention this decision as exhibiting the marked aversion of Ellsworth to dispose of a cause otherwise than strictly upon the merits, without regard to technical defects. The objection to the record was, that the pleadings did not show the parties to be citizens of different States, or one of them an alien, a fatal jurisdictional defect, but one which he thought might better have been raised in the Court below. "It is to be exceedingly regretted," he says, "that exceptions which might be taken in abatement, and often cured in a moment, should be reserved to the last stage of a suit to destroy its fruits."

Not only did Judge Ellsworth continue in the discharge of his judicial functions down to the last moment, but he actually proceeded on his mission, as his predecessor Jay had done before him, without resigning his seat. At that period it was not deemed incompatible

zance of the question from the jury to vest it in the Court.—See Lord Brougham's "Sketch of Mansfield." Statesmen of Times of George III., Vol. I. p. 113.

* 4 Dallas' Reports, 8.

with the highest judicial station, to annex to it an appointment of a purely political character. Thus, not only did both Jay and Ellsworth hold the office of Chief-Justice and that of foreign minister at the same time, but even their successor, Marshall, continued for a short period to discharge the apparently inconsistent duties of Judge of the Supreme Court and Secretary of State.

The history of the second French mission, so celebrated in the annals of our diplomacy, is doubtless familiar to the reader. It seems necessary, however, in this connexion, to notice it briefly, as a part of Judge Ellsworth's public life, too important by far to be passed over entirely in silence.

The unsuccessful result of the negotiation of Marshall, Pinckney, and Gerry, and the treatment those gentlemen had received from the authorities of the French Republic (which will be noticed in another part of this work) had created a deep feeling of indignation throughout the whole country, and particularly among the friends of the Federal administration. It had called out the celebrated declaration of President Adams to Congress—" I will never send another minister to France without assurances that he will be received, respected, and honored, as the representative of a great, free, powerful, and independent people ;" a declaration that was greeted at the time with something like universal acclamation. The ultra-Federal leaders—those who subsequently comprised the Hamilton wing of the party, whom Mr. Adams did not hesitate afterwards to denounce with bitter and fierce invective, as the " British faction ;" * and who regarded all overtures for negotiation and all terms of friendship with " the regicide Republic " as incompatible with the national honor and safety—heard with ill-concealed disgust and dissatisfaction the announcement that the President had rather suddenly determined to send another embassy to France. Accordingly when the name of the envoy first proposed—William Vans Murray—was sent in to the Senate, it was strongly intimated that he would not be confirmed. " Some of the President's real

* In one of his famous Cunningham letters, Mr. Adams remarks, that he could not have lived through another year of " such labors and cares as were studiously and maliciously accumulated upon me, by the French faction, and the British faction ; the former aided by the republicans, and the latter by *Alexander Hamilton and his satellites.*"

friends," says the Secretary of State, in a letter to Murray, "endeavored to persuade him to withdraw the nomination. He was inflexible. They then determined *to put a negative upon it.*" Mr. Adams, with the characteristic promptness which so strongly marked all his actions, anticipated this design, and two days afterwards sent in the names of Oliver Ellsworth and Patrick Henry, with that of Mr. Murray, as joint envoys to the French Republic. The "President's real friends" thereupon thought better of the matter, and consented, though with some hesitation, to confirm the appointments. Mr. Henry, having declined on account of his age and infirmities, Governor Davie, of North Carolina, was substituted.

It was with unfeigned reluctance that Judge Ellsworth consented to accept this commission. It was extremely distasteful to him, not on personal considerations alone, but also no doubt because he was satisfied that it was viewed with disfavor by a large portion of the leading men of the party with whom he acted.* The editor of the Wolcott

* The French mission was the cause, if not of the original difficulty, at least of the final rupture between President Adams and the Hamilton branch of the Federal party, including three members of his own Cabinet, Pickering, McHenry, and Wolcott. The charges against Mr. Adams by his Federal friends—or perhaps more properly enemies—of his having violated the solemn declaration of his message to Congress of June 21st by nominating the embassy to France, do not appear to be just. He has himself ably and successfully vindicated his action in this respect in his celebrated "Cunningham Letters," to which it is scarcely necessary here to allude. "*Assurances*" certainly were given by the French government, and conveyed in perhaps as direct a manner as could have been reasonably expected. These *assurances* were received partly through Mr. Gerry on his return from France, but principally through Mr. Murray, the American Minister at the Hague. In Talleyrand's letter to the French Chargé at the Hague, the assurances required by Mr. Adams' message to Congress are made almost in identical words. "Whatever plenipotentiary the government of the United States might send to France to put an end to the existing differences between the countries, would be undoubtedly received with the respect due to the representatives of a free, independent, and powerful nation." He then charges him to communicate this to Mr. Murray that it might be transmitted to the government of the United States. "Carry therefore, citizen," he says, "to Mr. Murray, these *positive instructions*, in order to convince him of our sincerity, and prevail upon him to transmit them to his government." These overtures were considered by Mr. Adams to be substantially the "*assurances*" he had required as preliminary to *an appointment*, and accordingly on his own responsibility, and without consultation with his Cabinet,

papers—who has certainly made out a very ingenious case in favor of the Cabinet and against the President in his history of the Adams' Administration—states that Ellsworth would have refused to go but for the apprehension that Madison or Burr would have been sen't in his place. He alleges, also, but upon what authority it does not appear, that the Chief-Justice to the last *disapproved the mission.** This certainly seems to have been a mistake. Though Ellsworth had doubtless advised a suspension of the mission until "it could be better seen" to whom the envoys should be accredited, yet there is no evidence that he did not enter upon the duty with alacrity, and hopeful of success. Indeed, from the statements that have been given, it would seem that he even yielded his opinion as to the policy of suspending the mission.

In the early part of October President Adams called upon him at his seat in Windsor. Mr. Adams left the following statement of the interview: "He was perfectly candid. Whatever should be the determination, he was ready at an hour's warning to comply. If it was thought best to embark immediately, he was ready. If it was judged more expedient to postpone it for a little time, though that might subject him to a winter voyage, that danger had no weight

he sent in to the Senate the name of Mr. Murray as Minister to France, with whom Ellsworth and Davie were afterwards joined. It was not intended, however, as he remarked in his message to the Senate, that they should proceed on their mission until they had "received from the Executive Directory assurances, signified by their secretary of foreign relations, that they shall be received in character; that they shall enjoy all the prerogatives attached to their character by the law of nations; and that a minister or ministers of equal powers shall be appointed and commissioned to treat with them." This was communicated by Murray to Talleyrand, who promptly replied in his official character, giving unequivocally the assurances required. On receipt of this communication the envoys were directed to hold themselves in readiness, and their instructions were prepared. The further delay of two or three months which occurred was occasioned by the Revolution of the 30th Prairial. The French Directory, it was supposed, would soon fall to pieces, and this was deemed by the Cabinet a sufficient reason for an entire suspension of the mission. Mr. Adams, however, thought differently; and, after waiting a reasonable time, took upon himself the responsibility of sending off the envoys, contrary to the known wishes of his Cabinet advisers. This kindled the flame which during the remainder of his administration continued to blaze with intense energy and warmth.

* 2 Gibbs' Wolcott, 274.

with him. If it was concluded to defer it till the spring, he was willing to wait. In this disposition I took leave of him." This statement of Mr. Ellsworth's willingness to embark on the mission is corroborated by what took place a few days after at Trenton, where the President met Governor Davie and Ellsworth at dinner. An idea, strangely enough, seems to have been entertained at that time, that the first arrivals from Europe would bring what some of the Federal leaders called "the glorious news" that Louis XVIII. had been restored to the throne of France. Ellsworth, it appears, shared in this delusion, which failed, however, to deceive the keener and more experienced mind of Mr. Adams. "Is it possible, Chief-Justice," asked the latter, that you can seriously believe that the Bourbons are or will be soon restored to the throne of France?" "Why," said Ellsworth, smiling, "*it looks a good deal so.*" Mr. Adams was not afraid, he said, to stake his life upon it, that they would not be restored in seven years, if they ever were, and thereupon entered into a detail of the reasons of his opinion, which he declares convinced Ellsworth, who expressed himself satisfied and willing to embark as soon as the President pleased.*

That Ellsworth was not only willing to proceed on the mission, but actually assented to the policy which dictated it, and was hopeful of its success, is, I think, fully evident, from his subsequent conduct. Writing to Wolcott on the 1st of October, he says, "I think that the prospects of that distracted country (France) and of Europe, and of course our own, begin to brighten. Pray indulge in the same thought if you can, for *you certainly stand in need of it.*" † A short time after, he thoroughly disgusted both Pickering and Wolcott by repeating the President's remark, in answer to the argument that the French negociation would produce a war with England, "What if it does, England cannot hurt us." This remark was too much for Mr. Pickering. "I had not patience to hear more," he observes; ‡ and left Ells-

* See Mr. Adams' Cunningham Letters. This statement is not considered entirely reliable by Mr. Gibbs, who, in his anxiety to make out a strong case against President Adams, seems disposed almost to send Ellsworth on a compulsory mission.

† 2 Gibbs' Wolcott, 266.

‡ Letter to General Washington, October 24th, 1799.

worth, doubtless under the impression that he had become a backslider from that orthodox doctrine which regarded hostility to France and friendship for England as an essential element of political faith.

The truth is, Ellsworth did not sympathize with the friends of Hamilton in the cabinet in their opposition to this important measure of Mr. Adams' administration, which was doubtless then considered, as it has subsequently been characterized by an able advocate of their views, "the crowning effort of democratic skill and sagacity." * That opposition was based upon the theory that there was necessarily something jacobinical and democratical in everything which looked like a negotiation with the French Republic, and that this of course was to be avoided. "All deprecate the French mission," says Pickering, in a letter to General Washington, "as fraught with irreparable mischief." The Chief-Justice, however, seems to have risen superior to these narrow views of party policy. For a politician of those times he might have been considered a moderate partisan. He was one of those who had not yet learned to regard a Democrat as "out of the pale of social sympathy;" and, besides, he had the sagacity to perceive, what others, in the blindness of party zeal, were so prone to overlook—the importance of preserving peace with France as well as with England, and of extending by treaty the commercial intercourse of the country. With these statesmanlike views, Oliver Ellsworth, though a Federalist, and attached by strong ties to that party which regarded the measure with so much disfavor, set out with Governor Davie to negotiate a treaty with the French Republic.

The envoys left Newport on the 3rd of November for Lisbon, where they arrived on the 27th. Before they reached that place, however, a new and important phase was presented in the political horizon of France and Europe. The revolution of the 18th of Brumaire (November) 1799, was accomplished; the "five kings" had been driven out ignominiously from the Luxembourg; and the fortunate soldier of Lodi and Arcola had risen to the chief power in the State. A single day in Paris had overthrown the Republic;—one throe of the revolutionary earthquake had changed the face of Europe and the world.

These great events had transpired while the American envoys were yet tossed on the bosom of the Atlantic. Fate had destined that

* 2 Gibbs' Wolcott, 222.

they were not to place their credentials in the hands of the profligate Barras and his brethren of the Directory, nor, as Ellsworth had vainly conjectured, into those of the restored Bourbons. They arrived as the day was breaking over the new revolutionary chaos—a chaos already fast subsiding into order—and just in time to greet the rising star of Napoleon.

Doubtful whether their letters of credence would avail them with the new government, the envoys hesitated as to what course to pursue. Though slowly proceeding onward toward Paris, they took the precaution to send letters in advance to Talleyrand, who retained his office of minister for foreign affairs. Bonaparte had the sagacity to see, what the imbecile folly of the Directory caused them to overlook, the importance of a commercial treaty with the United States. The American envoys were promptly advised that the form of their letters would present no obstacle, and that they were "expected with impatience, and would be received with warmth." Ellsworth and Davie thereupon pushed on to Paris, which they reached on the 2nd of March, and there found their colleague, Mr. Murray, who had arrived from the Hague the day previous.

Six days after their arrival they were presented to the first consul in form, and they certainly had no cause then, or subsequently, to complain of any want of cordiality in their reception.* Bonaparte immediately appointed his eldest brother, Joseph, and two of his councillors of state, Fleurieu and Rœderer, to treat with them. Soon after the negotiations commenced, which finally ended in the treaty of the 30th September, 1800.

Almost at the outset of the negotiations a serious difficulty occurred. The American ministers had been instructed to insist upon indemnities for illegal captures made by privateers of the Republic. The French commissioners, on the other hand, insisted upon the restoration of the treaties of 1778 (which it was alleged the United States

* The audience was a public one in the Hall of the Ambassadors, at the palace of the Tuilleries, and was attended by the two other consuls, the ministers of the French government, the ministers of foreign powers, and other public functionaries; and the whole presented a striking contrast with the studied indignity with which the Directory had treated the late envoys from the United States.—*Life of Davie.* 25 *Sparks' Am. Biog.*

had violated), and the privileges guaranteed by the Convention of 1788.* Both parties were unwilling, and one, at least, unable to comply. A full renewal of the French treaties of alliance, &c., was impossible by reason of the engagements contracted by Mr. Jay's treaty with Great Britain. This was urged by the Americans; and on the other hand, the French commissioners replied "that their *real object* was to *avoid* indemnities, and that it was not in the power of France to pay them." † In other words, the French refused to pay indemnities for acts growing out of alleged infractions of the treaties, unless those treaties were restored, which certainly seems not to have been unreasonable; and the Americans very properly refused to accept indemnities, when by doing so they must "subject their country perpetually to the mischievous effects of these treaties." Here then the negotiations came to a stand; and here it was the opinion of the Hamilton Federalists they should have finally terminated. Not so, however, thought Ellsworth and his associates. Unable to agree upon these points, instead of throwing up their commissions in disgust, they took the wiser, more politic, and more statesmanlike course of negotiating a commercial treaty—favorable in all respects to their country—leaving those points which could not then be satisfactorily settled for a future "definite adjustment." ‡ The second article of the treaty, as finally agreed upon, provided that as to these subjects (the treaties and convention, and the indemnities) "the parties will negotiate further at a convenient time, and until they may agree upon these points the said treaties and convention shall have no operation, and the relation of the two countries shall be regulated as follows." §

* See remarks in regard to the origin of the difficulties with France in subsequent sketch of Marshall.—*Post*, page 332, and note.

† See a full account of this negotiation in a letter by the American Envoys to Secretary Marshall, October 4th, 1800.

‡ It is not a little remarkable that the same men who had so warmly sustained the incomplete treaty of Jay, should have so obstinately opposed that negotiated by Ellsworth and his associates, which certainly compares favorably with it in every respect. But it is to be recollected that the party politics of the day made a vast difference between a negotiation with France and one with England.

§ See U. S. Statutes at large, Vol. 8, p. 178. This article was struck out by the Senate and a provision inserted that the treaty should remain in force for the term of eight years. Bonaparte accepted the amendment with the further proviso

As to all other matters, the provisions of the treaty were ample and satisfactory, and honorable to both parties.* The debts due by the French government were covenanted to be paid as though no misunderstanding had taken place ; and under this provision, and the subsequent treaty of 1803, claims to the amount of twenty millions of francs were made good against France, so late as the administration of President Jackson.

The commercial relations of the United States were also amply provided for by the treaty. *Free ships* were to make *free goods*,† and

that "the two States should mutually renounce the respective pretensions which are the subject of this article." In this shape it was finally ratified by the Senate early in Mr. Jefferson's administration.

* The fortunate issue of these negotiations was celebrated by the French commissioners with some degree of pomp and *éclat*. Joseph Bonaparte gave an elegant entertainment at his beautiful seat at Monfontaine, at which all the ambassadors were present. "The first consul went there accompanied by a brilliant and numerous party. Elegant decorations set up in the mansion and gardens everywhere exhibited France and America united. Toasts suited to the occasion were drank. The first consul proposed, 'The names of the French and the Americans who died on the field of battle for the independence of the New World.' Lebrun proposed, 'The union of America with the northern powers, to enforce respect for the liberty of the seas.' Cambacérès gave for the third, 'The successor of Washington.'" —*Thiers' Cons. and Empire*, Book VII.

† The principle that free ships make free goods, that is to say that the property of belligerents, except articles contraband of war, shall not be liable to confiscation when found in neutral vessels, had been proclaimed by the Empress of Russia in 1780, and acceded to by all the great commercial powers, except Great Britain, which alone resisted, and from that time to the present has continued successfully to resist the introduction of the principle into the international code. America first obtained its recognition in the treaty with Prussia in 1785, which was closely followed by this treaty, negotiated by Ellsworth and his associates. The Baltic powers, about the same time, were attempting again to enforce those liberal commercial principles, so favorable to the commerce and prosperity of neutral nations ; but the maritime superiority of Great Britain soon dissolved the league, and put down the attempt at a forcible innovation upon what was regarded as the settled principles of international law. During the wars of the French Revolution our own government seems to have practically recognized the validity of the English rule, as appears by the correspondence of the state department and our diplomatic agents abroad. It was virtually conceded, under the provisions of the Jay treaty, and was subsequently repeatedly sanctioned by decisions of the Supreme Court. (See 1 Kent's Commentaries, 126 128. Case of the Nereide, &c.) The right of a belligerent power to search our vessels for enemy's goods seems not to have been made

the neutral flag to protect the cargo; and commerce between the two countries was made reciprocally free, and placed upon the footing of the most favored nations. Under these provisions the ships of the American merchants soon secured a large share of the carrying trade of the Atlantic, and the United States entered upon that career of commercial prosperity, which is unexampled in the history of the world.

The treaty was of course disapproved by those who originally opposed the mission, and who regarded its consummation as but another step in the downfall of the Federal policy. "It is now certain," says Wolcott, in a letter to Pickering,* "that the mission has proved as unfortunate as we considered it at the time it was instituted."

a point of controversy in the discussions which led to the war of 1812; the government merely denying that the right extended to search for seamen or subjects. Great Britain conceded nothing on the subject by the treaty of peace; nor has she done so in any subsequent treaty up to the present time. The recent events in Europe, however, appear to have rendered it evident to the British government that it can no longer maintain a doctrine so oppressive and unjust to the rights of neutral nations. The time has at length arrived when the voice of a majority of the nations of the civilized world will be able TO CHANGE an arbitrary rule of international law, even without the assent of that nation which so long and so perseveringly, and so successfully maintained it. America, as the leading neutral commercial power, is of course the first to assert the liberal principles of commercial freedom and reciprocity proclaimed by the Baltic league in 1801, and embraced in the Prussian treaty, and the French treaty, and if necessary will maintain and enforce them as the cardinal principles of a new and more enlightened code of international law. It is gratifying however to observe that England, though apparently reluctant to concede the principle, seems at last willing that it shall be practically applied as a part of the code of nations. "Her Majesty is willing *for the present*," says the recent proclamation of the Queen, "to waive a part of the *belligerent rights* appertaining to her by the law of nations." One of these *rights* which her Majesty declares herself thus willing to forego, is "the right of seizing enemy's property laden on board a neutral vessel, unless it be contraband of war." It may well be believed that this *right*, thus waived "for the present," will never again be recognized as resting upon any known principle of international law, certainly not by either the express or implied assent of this country, without which it would be somewhat difficult to revive an obsolete or abrogated principle of the international code. Henceforth the United States, as a neutral nation, will stand among the belligerents of Europe, on the broad and liberal principles of the treaty negotiated by Ellsworth and his colleagues, that free ships make free goods, and that the neutral flag shall protect the cargo.

* December 28th, 1800. 2 Gibbs' Wolcott, 461.

What seemed to strike them with most amazement was the participation of Ellsworth in this "unfortunate" business; and they could account for it only on the hypothesis that sickness had impaired or destroyed his intellect. In this same letter Wolcott remarks: "You will read the treaty which was signed with France with astonishment. I can account for it only on the supposition that the vigor of Mr. Ellsworth's mind has been enfeebled by sickness." And in another of about the same date, to Hamilton: "You will be afflicted on reading the treaty with France. Mr. Ellsworth's health, I fear, is destroyed." * Pickering replies in the same lugubrious strain: "The treaty with France, as you suppose, has excited my utter astonishment. Davie and Murray always appeared to me fond of the mission, and I supposed they had made the treaty; but when informed that our friend, our highly respected and respectable friend, Mr. E—— was *most urgent for its adoption*, my regret equalled my astonishment. The fact can be solved only on the ground you have suggested." †

Sedgwick entertained similar views. He thought the treaty plainly showed that "the mind, as well as body, of Mr. Ellsworth are rendered feeble by disease." ‡ Gunn thought the thing "detestable," and that its ratification "would be dishonorable." § Otis saw in it but "another chapter in the book of humiliation;" || and even John Marshall, though in favor of ratifying it, was "far, very far from approving it." ¶

Such was the general opinion entertained by Mr. Hamilton and his friends.** But, upon the other hand, to say nothing of the approval

* 2 Gibbs' Wolcott, 460.

† 2 Gibbs' Wolcott, 463.

‡ Sedgwick to Hamilton, Dec. 17th, 1800.—6 *Hamilton's Works*, 491.

§ Gunn to Hamilton, Dee. 18th and January 9th. Ibid. 492, 508.

|| Otis to Hamilton, Dec. 17th. Ibid. 490.

¶ Marshall to Hamilton, January 1st, 1801. Ibid. 502.

** Though Hamilton advised the ratification of the treaty, he did not hesitate to condemn it in his private letters to his friends. Writing to Sedgwick under date of December 22, 1800, he says: "The Convention with France is just such an issue as was to have been expected. *It plays into the hands of France* by the precedent of those principles of navigation which she is at this moment desirous of making the basis of *a league of the northern powers against England.*" —*Hamilton's Works*, Vol. 6, p. 495. Similar views are expressed in a letter to

of the republican party, let us hear Mr. Adams speak, whose opinion is certainly entitled to some weight. He considered it, he said, "the most disinterested, the most determined, and the most successful" action of his whole life. "Had it betrayed a single point of essential honor or interest," he exclaims, with his accustomed energy, "I would have sent it back as Mr. Jefferson did the treaty with England, without laying it before the Senate. If I had been doubtful, the Senate would have decided." * The Senate did decide, and, with the amendment of the second article, ratified the treaty.†

It may be added that Ellsworth himself, though not obtaining all he desired, was fully satisfied with the general results of his labor. "Be assured," he remarks, in a letter to Wolcott, "more could not be done without too great a sacrifice, and as the reign of Jaco-

Gouverneur Morris, to whom he points out as an objectionable feature the article of the treaty providing that *free ships* should make *free goods*, and that the flags of ships of war shall protect. They were features, he thought, which would not be pleasant to the British Cabinet, and therefore were "to be regretted at the present moment." Hamilton's reasons for urging the ratification of the treaty seem to have been, as expressed in these letters, to avert "the utter ruin of the Federal party;" and besides he thought it better "to close the thing where it is, than to leave it to a Jacobin administration to do worse." At the same time, he says, he wished his friends in the Senate to declare that they thought "the treaty liable to strong objections, and *pregnant with dangers to the interests of this country.*"

How, then, it might be asked, could Hamilton, with perhaps the same pen with which he had traced these private communications, *publicly* declare the treaty "an honorable accommodation"? In that caustic Review of "the public conduct and character of John Adams, Esq., President, &c.," which he published about this period, he remarks: "The final issue of the mission in *an honorable accommodation, may compensate* for the sacrifice of consistency, dignity, harmony, and reputation at which it was undertaken." In this same paper, Hamilton, in sustaining his position, and making out his case against his adversary, seems inclined to concede the main point in the argument of the opponents of the treaty. "When, afterwards, commissioners were appointed," he remarks, "I expressly gave it as my opinion that indemnification for spoliations should not be a *sine qua non* of accommodation."—7 *Hamilton's Works*, 714, 724.

* Cunningham Letters, No. XII.

† Gouverneur Morris thought with this amendment and the retrenchment of the third article, which provided for a mutual surrender of captured vessels of war, the treaty would be "no bad bargain," and so expresses himself in a letter to Hamilton.—6 *Hamilton's Works*, 503.

binism is over in France, and appearances are strong in favor of a general peace, I hope you will think it was better to sign a convention than to do nothing." And to Pickering: "My best efforts and those of my colleagues have not obtained all that justice required, or which the policy of France should have given. Enough is, however, done, if ratified, to extricate the United States from a contest, which it might be as difficult to relinquish with honor, as to pursue with a prospect of advantage." *

The moderation, wisdom, and sound sense of these views, and indeed, the whole conduct of Ellsworth in undertaking the French negotiations, strongly recommended him to moderate and enlightened men of both parties as a suitable candidate for the Presidency. A caucus of the moderate Federalists was held in the autumn of 1800, at which it was said this project was determined on in case Mr. Adams should withdraw. But the withdrawal of Mr. Adams was impossible in the then state of the feud between himself and Hamilton; and besides, that very moderation of sentiment which recommended Ellsworth to one portion of the Federal party, utterly estranged him from the other.

Meanwhile, Ellsworth, a stranger to all these intrigues, having completed his negotiations in France, and being unable on account of the state of his health to return immediately to America, was preparing to pass over into England. He had become wearied with his residence in Paris. A stranger to the language, as well as the customs and manners of the French people, with little taste for works of art, or the conversation of *savans* and *litterateurs*, and less for those light amusements and elegant frivolities which make up so large a segment of metropolitan life, and which, indeed, his rigid and austere New England morals did not suffer him to approve, he found but little pleasure, and no great degree of sympathy in the society which surrounded him. Nor, his mission being ended, was his a character or a reputation calculated to command those nameless attentions which might have served to render a longer residence in France agreeable. Unlike Franklin, who came to Versailles under the *prestige* of a reputation that drew upon him the favorable eye of royalty itself, the plain New England Judge had

* 2 Gibbs' Wolcott, 434, 463.

come to Paris unheralded and comparatively unknown.* In that brilliant circle of courtiers and soldiers which the first consul called around him, a mere civilian or jurist stood a fair chance of being entirely lost in the glittering crowd. Erskine himself experienced the truth of this a year or two later. Utterly eclipsed in the shadow of his celebrated countryman, Mr. Fox, the first consul brushed past the illustrious advocate with the abrupt and hasty question, "*Etes-vous légiste?*" † Nor could it be supposed that the simple manners and austere character of the American Judge would have attracted a greater degree of attention. Another, and perhaps a stronger motive for his leaving France was the hope of his obtaining some relief to the distressing malady which afflicted him, by the use of the mineral waters of England. His constitution had indeed become so shattered as to render it uncertain when he would be able to resume his judicial duties, and accordingly he sent over his resignation of the office of Chief-Justice before leaving France, to the regret, it is said, of his countrymen of all parties. "Sufferings at sea," he says, in a letter to Wolcott, from Havre,‡ "and a winter's journey through Spain,

* It is said that even during the continuance of the mission, Ellsworth, though at the head of the embassy, received less attention than one at least of his colleagues. The private Secretary of Governor Davie thought that "the imposing appearance" of that gentleman, his "dignified deportment," and what he calls "a slight degree of *hauteur*," attracted more consideration than the plainer and more homely manners of his colleague. "I could not but remark," says the Secretary, "that Bonaparte, in addressing the American legation at his levees, seemed for the time to forget that Governor Davie was *second* in the commission, his attention being more particularly directed to him."—*Life of Davie*, 25 Spark's Am. Biog. 125.

† 2 Roscoe's British Lawyers, 193.

‡ October 16th, 1800. 2 Gibbs' Wolcott, 434.

Mr. Jefferson seems to have drawn an unwarrantable inference from the fact, that the Chief-Justice remained in Europe after the treaty was signed. In a confidential letter to Madison he says: "Ellsworth remains in France for his health. He has resigned his office of Chief-Justice. Putting these two things together we cannot misconstrue his views. He must have had great confidence in Mr. Adams' continuance, *to risk such a certainty as he had.*" 3 *Jefferson's Writings*, 448. Jefferson speaks of the treaty in the same letter as "a bungling negotiation." Though in the main satisfied with it; he considered it as containing "some disagreeable features," and was of the opinion that it would "endanger the compromitting us with Great Britain."

gave me an obstinate gravel, which, by wounding the kidneys, has drawn and fixed my wandering gout to those parts. My pains are constant, and at times excruciating; they do not permit me to embark for America at this late season of the year; nor, if there, would they permit me to discharge my official duties. I have, therefore, sent my resignation of the office of Chief-Justice, and shall, after spending a few weeks in England, retire for winter-quarters to the south of France."

Prompted thus by *ennui*, by a desire to obtain some relief to his disease, and perhaps by a natural curiosity to visit the land of his forefathers, Ellsworth passed over to England. Here, it seems, he found his residence more agreeable, and he contrived to pass not only with profit, but with pleasure, a much longer period of time than he had intended. The name of the American Chief-Justice was not unknown to the English bench and bar; it had found its way into Westminster Hall; and on his arrival in England he was received with marked respect and attention, and was surrounded by a group of eminent lawyers and judges, by one or two of whom, it is said, he was asked some very curious and perplexing questions. On a visit to Westminster Hall he was invited to a seat by the side of Lord Kenyon, then sitting with Judge Le Blanc and Judge Grose in the King's Bench. Of that visit Mr. Wharton, in his entertaining notes to the American State Trials, has given the following lively and graphic description.

"It was, as is said, during the train of arguments, which are reported in the beginning of the first volume of Mr. East, that the American Chief-Justice visited Westminster Hall. The famous case of Rex *vs.* Waddington was then before the Court, in which all the leaders of the bar were retained, and at the inception of which a scuffle is said to have taken place near Mr. Garrows' Chambers, between the emissaries of the two contending interests, each seeking to be the first at the door of that eminent advocate. Mr. Law led off for the defendants in the proceedings in arrest of judgment, and was followed by Mr. Erskine, Mr. Garrow, and Mr. Scott. Notwithstanding Mr. Jay's previous appearance at the Court of St. James, and the contemporaneous presence there of Mr. King, the fame of their accomplishments had not reached the King's Bench, whose precincts they had probably never invaded; and it was, consequently, with great curiosity that the elder lawyers, whose notions of America had been derived from the kidnapping cases which were the only precipitate cast on the reports of the Privy Council, by the current of Colonial litigation, spied out the American Chief-Justice. Mr. Ellsworth's simple, but dignified carriage, so much like, as is said, that of his successor on the bench, was in happy contrast to the awkwardness of the English Chief-Justice ; and, as soon as it was discovered that, though his worn and marked features bore a stamp which had not then become familiar to the English eye, he was neither an Indian nor a Jacobin, two things regarded as equally beyond the limits of civilized sympathy, he was surrounded by a knot of lawyers, curious to know how the common law stood transplanting. Still, the obscurity which hung around the history of the American Republic, could not but produce some confusion ; and it was with this view of the supposed creolishness of the American people—a hybrid between the Englishman and the Indian, mingling the distinctive powers of each without that power of perpetuating them, which the old philosophers thought belonged only to unmixed races—that Judge Grose, with an air, it is said, of grave delicacy, inquired whether the obstruction of the course of descent had not turned fee simples into life estates. Perhaps to the same uncertainty may be traced the question which Mr. Garrow is said to have addressed to the American Judge, " Pray, Chief-Justice, in what cases do the half-blood in America take by descent ?"

The recreations of the Chief-Justice in England were diversified by travel ; and among his other employments he amused himself with tracing the records and traditions of his family. On a small stream, a few miles from Cambridge, he found a hamlet called Ellsworth. To his surprise he learned that many of the inhabitants of the hamlet bore the same name. Inquiring the origin of the name, he was told that being a famous place for eels, the inhabitants had called it *Eelsworth*—worth being the Saxon name for place. By a trifling alteration of the first syllable the name of Ellsworth is obtained. His ancestors had emigrated from that part of England a century and a half before.

On his return to America, in the spring of 1801, Ellsworth retired to his residence at Windsor, but the people of Connecticut were yet unwilling to allow him that repose in private life which he now courted. Though his health was feeble, and his constitution impaired by disease, still his intellect was active and vigorous as ever. It is true, he was no longer equal to the labor of the Federal judiciary, attended as it was by the toil and fatigue of circuit duty, but his wisdom and experience might yet be available in the legislative and judicial councils of his own State. Though the war-worn veteran was no longer fit for foreign service, he could still stand sentinel on the watch-towers at home and guard the domestic citadel. He was accordingly called, almost before the dust of foreign travel had been shaken from his feet, to take his place among the Assistants of the Connecticut Council, and as such *ex-officio* Judge of the Supreme Court of Errors of the State—a position which eighteen years before he had resigned, to hold his seat on the bench of the Superior Court.

Jonathan Trumbull, Governor of the State, presided in the Supreme Court of Errors at the time Ellsworth took his seat in it, in 1802, and continued to do so, down to the termination of its existence as a Court in 1807. The Governor, Lieutenant-Governor, and the twelve Assistants or Senators, at that time composed the Court. It met alternately at Hartford and New Haven, and, as I have already mentioned, sat as a Court of Review over the judgments rendered in the Superior Court. Its decisions are to be found collected in Day's Connecticut Reports, to which the professional reader is referred. Though comprising a great variety of questions, full of interest to the lawyer and jurist, they do not serve to throw much additional light upon Ellsworth's judicial career. The judgments delivered are generally reported as the opinions of the whole Court, without connecting them with the names of the particular member or members by whom they were drawn ; and we can, therefore, discover but few traces of individuality in these opinions, and of course cannot undertake to determine what particular portions of them may have been the emanations of Judge Ellsworth's mind. That which was delivered in the important case of Fitch *vs.* Brainerd,* holding a will of real estate executed by a *feme covert* to be void—a closely written and logically reasoned legal argument—might very well be supposed to be his. It sustained a

* 2 Day's Reports, 163–194.

former decision made by the Superior Court while he was a member of that tribunal, in the case of Adams *vs.* Kellogg, noticed on a preceding page,* which the Court of Errors on appeal had reversed.

As a member of the Council, and *ex-officio* Judge, Ellsworth, though subject to occasional fits of distressing illness, continued his annual attendance upon the Legislature and the Courts down to the close of the session of 1807. In May of that year the judiciary system of the State was changed—the Superior Court having been blended with the Court of Errors. Desirous of giving dignity to the new system by the appointment of a Chief-Justice of the highest character, Judge Ellsworth was selected to fill that place. He consented at first to accept, but before the close of the then session of the Legislature, feeling strong symptoms of a recurrence of his disease, and persuaded that he could not survive many more of its attacks, he declined the appointment.

Soon after he was seized with great violence, and for a time his life was despaired of. He partially recovered, however, and was so well in October as to be able to attend during part of the session of the General Assembly at New Haven. Returning to his seat at Windsor, he was again attacked, this time fatally ; and, after a severe illness of eight days, expired in the midst of his family, on the 26th of November, 1807, in the sixty-third year of his age.

His funeral was attended on Saturday the 28th. A sermon adapted to the melancholy occasion, says a cotemporary publication,† was preached by the Rev. Mr. Rowland, of Windsor, to a large assembly collected from that and the adjacent towns to pay the last duties to their deceased friend and fellow-citizen. He was interred in the burial-yard of the Congregational Church at Windsor, of which church, from early youth, he had been a sincere, an exemplary, and a consistent member.

Mr. Ellsworth was married in early life to Miss Abigail Wolcott, a daughter of William Wolcott, of East Windsor. He left a family of several sons and daughters. One of these sons is ex-governor Ellsworth of Connecticut, now living at Hartford, and a Judge of the Supreme Court of the State, a gentleman of estimable character, and of eminent worth and abilities.

* *Ante*, page 219.

† American Register for 1807.

Judge Ellsworth was endowed with a strong practical judgment, a vigorous common sense, a well-balanced temper, an accurate perception, and a clear and ready, if not a quick and ingenious understanding. Though he might not be called a great statesman, he was certainly an honest and useful one; and few of his New England cotemporaries may claim a more honorable niche in the temple of fame. If not a profoundly learned, he was an accurate and able lawyer. If not a brilliant orator, he was a ready, effective, and forcible debater. If not pre-eminently superior as a judge, he certainly brought to the bench judicial talents of a very high order, and while there sustained himself at all times creditably, and sometimes with well-merited distinction;—"dignified in demeanor, indefatigable in his attention to business, patient in the trial of causes, perspicuous and convincing in his charges to the jury."

And, above all, the moral character of Oliver Ellsworth was sustained through life without reproach, and it lifted him far above the miserable criminations of party strife, and even beyond the breath of suspicion itself. "In all the public stations which he ever filled with so much reputation," says the writer of a brief notice of the Chief-Justice at the time of his decease, "Mr. Ellsworth evinced an inflexible integrity, the purest morality, and the most unshaken firmness and independence. In the most intemperate periods of our national history, when the foul spirit of party, like the scythe of time, has mowed down virtue and talents, almost without discrimination, no person has attempted to blast the fame of Mr. Ellsworth." *

The public man who leaves behind him a record like this—a record which even the tongue of calumny itself cannot venture to impeach—need fear nothing at the hands of posterity. And such seems to have been the fortunate lot of Mr. Ellsworth. It is said of him, with truth perhaps, that in his later years he exhibited a degree of warmth and feeling in the political contests of the day scarcely consistent with the dignified repose of age, and the high character which he sustained. This no doubt resulted as well from the thoroughness of his own convictions as the ardor of his temper. His political opinions, whatever they were—and of which I am neither the advocate nor apologist—were sincerely entertained, and consistently and firmly carried out.

* American Register for 1807.

But his political action, decided and warm though it might have been, left no sting behind. In the language of his eulogist, " No person attempted to blast the fame of Mr. Ellsworth."

In social life, it is added, he was truly estimable,—just in his dealings, frank and sociable in his disposition, kind and obliging in his temper ; he was respected and beloved by his neighbors and acquaintances. His religious sentiments were strong and earnest. They tinged all his thoughts in later years, and imparted to his actions a seriousness sometimes bordering upon austerity. In his youth he had been designed for the ministry, and had actually pursued the study of theology with Rev. Dr. Bellamy, an eminent divine of Connecticut, the year before commencing the study of the law. Toward the close of his life his thoughts were fond of reverting to these grave subjects, and he devoted a considerable portion of his time to the examination and study of controversial divinity. But the seriousness of his mind never verged toward bigotry, nor in the strictness of his life was there a particle of asceticism. He preserved to the last his habitual liberality of thought, warmth of social sympathy, and serenity of temper.

The epitaph which the hand of affection, of ambition, or of pride traces upon the tomb of the departed, is too often the record of exaggerated praise or of fabulous virtue. Pointing to the dust of the sleeper beneath, it speaks in the language of fulsome eulogy, or of mocking sarcasm, and describes him

" Not as he was, but as he should have been."

Not so, however, the simple and modest inscription on the tomb of Oliver Ellsworth, in the Congregational church-yard at Windsor. It contains not a word of undeserved eulogy, not a syllable of exaggerated praise. Dictated by affection, but chastened by a severe criticism, it has fortunately anticipated the sober judgment of posterity : " Amiable and exemplary in all the relations of the domestic, social, and Christian character ; pre-eminently useful in all the offices he sustained ; whose great talents, under the guidance of inflexible integrity, consummate wisdom, and enlightened zeal, placed him among the first of the illustrious statesmen who achieved the independence, and established the Constitution of the American Republic."

JOHN MARSHALL.

JOHN MARSHALL.

In his brilliant speech at the trial of Lord George Gordon, Mr. Erskine speaks of the illustrious judge who, for thirty-two years, had presided in the Court of King's Bench, as "that great and venerable magistrate who had presided so long in this great and high tribunal, that the oldest of us do not remember him with any other impression than the awful form and figure of Justice!" What the celebrated English advocate could thus appropriately say of Lord Mansfield, the American lawyer, who, twenty years ago, frequented the Supreme Court at Washington, might with equal truth and propriety have said of the venerable judge then presiding in that august tribunal. The long and honorable career of Chief-Justice Marshall upon the bench of the Supreme Court; the purity and dignity of his character, and his eminent judicial services, naturally suggest a comparison with the great English jurist. Marshall has been called the American Mansfield. Such a comparison to almost any other jurist would be no ordinary compliment, for it implies the most exalted worth and the highest grade of judicial ability. But, to Marshall, the compliment, though just, cannot be deemed flattering. It is suggestive, at least, of an imitative greatness, and a borrowed and reflected lustre, and can add no new dignity to a character like his, of native, innate strength, and original independent greatness. Marshall is the American Mansfield, as Washington—greater than the noblest Roman of them all—is the American Cincinnatus. The skillful pen of some future Plutarch may run an ingenious parallel; bnt that parallel soon ends; for the antique virtue of the old Roman, though it may suggest a comparison with Washington, cannot measure the moral elevation of a nature like his.

"None but himself can be his parallel."

And so with the comparison between the American and the great English judge. Gifted with a more elegant intellect, and endowed with more profound learning and varied accomplishments—with a dignity of character that could rise superior to the assaults of Camden, and the bitter invective of Pitt—with a virtue whose panoply of proof could ward off the keen and glittering shafts of Junius himself—and with those stupendous and unrivalled powers of judicial investigation which have made his name a synonym for all that is great in jurisprudence—with all these, Mansfield himself is not the prototype, and does not furnish a standard by which to measure the full capacity of Marshall. The American Chief-Justice is something more than a Mansfield. Equally endowed with every moral as well as intellectual attribute which can adorn the highest judicial character, but with a firmer temper and a loftier courage, a more solid and compact intellect, a more robust and rugged manhood, he stands before us, if not superior as a judge, yet greater as a man. Erskine could say of Mansfield, not in the warm and glowing language of eulogy, but in the sober words of truth, that he was "a man of whom any country might be proud;" and in like manner could Pinkney—the Erskine of the American bar—say of the venerable Marshall, that he was "born to be the Chief-Justice of any country into which Providence should have cast him."

I approach the task of attempting to sketch the life and judicial services of this eminent man with much hesitation. I am sensible of its magnitude, and of the difficulty of executing it in an acceptable manner. His judicial career alone extends through a continuous period of thirty-five years. I believe, if not the longest, it is the most successful, the most brilliant, the most honorable of any on record. Its history is the history of the Supreme Court through this entire period. Its published decisions alone fill more than thirty volumes of Reports. Nothing, therefore, but a general survey, a mere glance at the judicial labors of Marshall will be practicable within the plan I have marked out. Independent of this, and before coming to the Bench of the Supreme

Court, he has a history of no ordinary interest—a life full of incident, full of honorable action, and intimately interwoven with the civil and diplomatic history of the times. This portion of his career I approach with the more confidence, for it is not entirely a new and untrodden path. The copious narrative * of a brother on the bench, who, for twenty-three years, sat by his side in the same high tribunal—a narrative drawn with a nicely discriminating pen, but all glowing in the warm sunshine of a sincere, a generous, a profound, an almost reverential admiration—will throw light upon that path, and enable me to pursue it with unerring certainty. This narrative of Judge Story bears the highest marks of authenticity ; most of its facts are evidently drawn from the lips of the Chief-Justice himself, and its estimate of Judge Marshall's judicial services and character is made with a personal knowledge derived from an intimate and unbroken friendship, and an almost daily association of a quarter of a century. I shall avail myself of its statements so far as it may be useful or proper to do so, supplying from authentic historical and other sources such details of Judge Marshall's public and political career as I have been able to obtain and the subject may require.†

The grandfather of Chief-Justice Marshall was a native of Wales. He settled in Westmorland County, Virginia, about the year 1730, where he married Elizabeth Markham, a native of England. This gentleman's eldest son, Thomas, the father of the Chief-Justice, inherited the family estate called "Forest," consisting of a few hundred acres of poor land in Westmorland. He removed from this county to Fauquier, soon after attaining the age of manhood, and having intermarried with Mary Keith, by which he became connected with the Randolphs, he seated upon a small farm at a place called Germantown, where John Marshall was born. The great proprietor of the Northern neck of Virginia, including Fauquier County, was at that time

* A Discourse before the Suffolk Bar on the Life, Character, and Services of Chief-Justice Marshall, by Joseph Story. October 15th, 1835.

† It may be remarked, that in 1828 Judge Story published a Sketch of Chief-Justice Marshall in the North American Review. This was subsequently retouched by him for the National Portrait Gallery, and became the basis of his more elaborate discourse before the Suffolk Bar. The latter may be found in Story's Miscellanies, edited by his son, and recently published.

Lord Fairfax, who gave George Washington the appointment of surveyor in the Western part of his territory. Washington employed Thomas Marshall in the same business. They had been near neighbors from birth, associates from boyhood, and were always friends.*

Thomas Marshall, though a planter of retired habits and narrow fortune, was a man of great energy of character and vigor of intellect. When Washington received the command of the American armies in the war of the Revolution, his friend and associate, Colonel Marshall, left his estate and his large family, and embarked in the same cause. He was placed in command of the third Virginia Regiment in the Continental establishment, and served with distinction under the immediate orders of Washington, during the darkest and most eventful period of the war. This regiment performed very severe duties during the campaigns of 1776 and 1777. It was present under the orders of Marshall at the battle of Trenton, and subsequently on the bloody field of Brandywine, where father and son served in different regiments, and each distinguished himself by good conduct and heroism.

Though without the advantages of an early education, Colonel Marshall was a man not only of great native endowments, but of considerable mental culture. He was a practical surveyor, adequately acquainted with the mathematics and astronomy, and familiarly conversant with history, poetry, and general literature, of which he possessed most of the standard works in the language; and these were the means, which, under his fostering attention, served to complete all the early education his distinguished son received.† The care and attention thus bestowed were neither lost nor forgotten. Long after that son had arrived at the high station which he so long adorned, he was accustomed, in private and familiar conversation, to speak of his father in terms of affectionate and reverential admiration. "My father," he would say, "was a far abler man than any of his sons. To him I owe the solid foundation of all my own success in life."

Such was the stock from which JOHN MARSHALL sprang. He was born at Germantown, Virginia, on the 24th of September, 1755, and was the eldest of a family of fifteen children. A few years after his

* Sketch of Chief-Justice Marshall, and eulogy by Horace Binney, delivered before the Councils of Philadelphia, Sept. 24th, 1835.

† Binney's Eulogy on Chief-Justice Marshall.

birth his father removed his family to the then frontier settlements, thirty miles further west, and located in the midst of the mountains east of the Blue Ridge, at a place called the "Hollow," in a country thinly peopled, and destitute of schools, but remarkable for the salubrity of its atmosphere and the picturesque beauty of its mountain scenery. It was a place admirable for the formation of a physical constitution, and for the development of its powers by athletic exercises and sports. Here the son remained until his fourteenth year, laying the foundation of that vigorous health which attended him through life, and deriving from his father all the training in letters which he received up to that period.

He developed even in his younger years, a remarkable aptitude for study. At an age when most children are engaged in those simple elementary tasks, which make up the routine of schoolboy life, he had already acquired, we are told, a taste for reading poetry and history, and was fond of amusing his leisure hours by a study of the old English authors. Though it may seem surprising in our day that the library of a plain, uneducated planter, in one of the back settlements of Virginia, before the revolution, should have been found to contain Milton and Shakspeare, Dryden and Pope, and the principal classic authors of the language, yet such, we are assured, was the fact, and the mind of young Marshall was thus from boyhood enabled to familiarize itself with the thoughts of those great masters of the poetic art. At the age of twelve he had transcribed the whole of Pope's Essay on Man, and some of his moral essays, and had committed to memory many of their most interesting passages.

Subsequent to this period, and before attaining the age of manhood, he yielded to the seductive influence of the muses, so far as to suffer his feet to stray into the flowery but hazardous paths of poetic composition. This taste for general literature, and especially for works of the imagination and poetry, remained with Marshall through life. Judge Story dwells upon the fact with peculiar satisfaction. He would read, he says, with intense interest all the higher literature of modern times, especially those departments which had been the favorite studies of his youth, and would kindle with enthusiasm at the names of the great novelists and poets of the age. These elegant amusements, Judge Story evidently seems to regard, with Sir James

Mackintosh, as the refuge of men of genius from "the vulgarity and irritation of business." The union of such a taste with that severe logic and closeness of thought which belong to the judicial character, he remarks, is "far less uncommon in the highest class of minds than slight observers are apt to suppose." It must be admitted that many illustrious examples, besides Marshall's, might be mentioned to verify the remark. Lord Mansfield, the friend of the poet Pope, was distinguished for his classic attainments and literary tastes. When he first came to town, according to Johnson, "he drank champagne with the wits;" and it is not certain but that he always preferred the society of scholars and men of genius, to that of his professional brethren.* A more striking example still is the case of Judge Story himself. He wrote and published a poem after he came to the bar, the success of which was probably not commensurate with its merits, or at least with the author's expectations, for we find him some years afterwards buying up and destroying all the copies that had escaped the hands of the trunk-makers. It is not improbable that, if "the Power of Solitude" had passed safely and successfully through the hands of the critics, the Commentaries on the Constitution might not have been written. Be this as it may, the muses still continued to bring its author "delicious dreams," long after he attained professional eminence; and he could never, not even after he had taken his seat by the side of Marshall on the bench, bring himself to confess that—

"The dreams of Pindus and the Aonian maid
Invite no more."†

* "Mr. Pope," says Warburton, "had all the warmth of affection for this great lawyer; and, indeed, no man ever more deserved to have a poet for his friend."

The poet handsomely compliments his friend in the well known lines ending

"Where Murray (long enough his country's pride)
Shall be no more than TULLY or than *Hyde*."

See Life of Mansfield. Roscoe's British Lawyers.

† Many years after we find Story writing to his wife as follows:

"When I have nothing else to do, in order to get rid of my own sad thoughts, I fly to poetry. I have written some lines to you since I have been here, which I intended to send to you in this letter. But the Chief-Justice requested me to give him a copy, and I shall retain the original until I can make one."

The lines referred to—which are somewhat didactic—are entitled "Sketches of Character," and are published in Story's "Life and Letters."

Young Marshall was sent from home at the age of fourteen, and placed under the tuition of a clergyman residing in Westmoreland, named Campbell, a gentleman of great respectability and learning. Here he remained a year, having for one of his fellow-students James Monroe, afterwards President of the United States. Returning home, he continued his studies another year under the care of a Scotch gentleman named Thompson, just settled in the parish as pastor, and who resided in his father's family. At the end of this year, we are told, he had just commenced reading Horace and Livy. These two years of classical instruction are all which the Chief-Justice ever received. He never graduated at a college, though by his own industry and with the aid of a grammar and dictionary, he subsequently managed to acquire a respectable knowledge of the Latin classics, and it has been well remarked that his attainments in learning were "nursed by the solitary vigils of his own genius."

But these vigils were soon broken in upon by the stirring events of the revolution. Young Marshall was entering his eighteenth year when the contest between the colonists and Great Britain commenced. It found him engaged in studying the classics and in reading by turns poetry and history, and the Commentaries of Blackstone. These pursuits, though congenial to the studious habits of his mind, were not suffered to engross his attention to the exclusion of the exciting political topics of the day. On the contrary, he entered into the controversy with a zeal which had not yet become tempered by the sober lessons of wisdom and experience. Nor did his zeal waste itself in noisy and boisterous declamation, or in the mere expression of speculative opinion; for he was among the first to set the example of prompt, energetic, and decisive action. The thrilling words of Patrick Henry—"*We must fight! An appeal to arms and the God of Hosts is all that is left us!*"—had scarcely fallen from the lips of the great orator, ere we find John Marshall, laying aside his Horace and Pope, his Lyttelton and Blackstone, to acquire the rudiments of military exercise, and actively engaged in training a militia company in the neighborhood. His first appearance after the intelligence of the battle of Lexington had been received, was as an officer of a militia company in Fauquier County, and is described by a venerable kinsman who was himself an eye-witness of the occurrences he relates; and this description is so graphic, and so full of interest, that I cannot refrain from transcribing it in the words in which it is written :*

"It was in May, 1775. He was then a youth of nineteen. The muster-field was some twenty miles distant from the Court house, and in a section of the country peopled by tillers of the earth. Rumors of the occurrences near Boston had circulated with the effect of alarm and agitation, but without the means of ascertaining the truth, for not a newspaper was printed nearer than Williamsburgh, nor was one taken within the bounds of the militia company, though large. The Captain had called the company together and was expected to attend, but did not. John Marshall had been appointed a lieutenant to it. His father had formerly commanded it. Soon after Lieutenant Marshall's appearance on the ground, those who knew him clustered about him to greet him, others from curiosity, and to hear the news.

"He proceeded to inform the company that the captain would not be there, and that he had been appointed lieutenant instead of a better ;—that he had come to meet them as fellow-soldiers who were likely to be called on to defend their country, and their own rights and liberties, invaded by the British ;—that there had been a battle at Lexington, in Massachusetts, between the British and Americans, in which the Americans were victorious, but that more fighting was expected ;—that soldiers were called for, and that it was time to brighten their fire-arms and learn to use them in the field ;—and that if they would fall into a single line he would show them the new manual exercise, for which purpose he had brought his gun—bringing it up to his shoulder. The sergeants put the men in line, and their fugleman presented himself in front to the right."

The same excellent authority goes on to describe the personal appearance and figure of Marshall, and the simple and familiar manner of his intercourse with the men whom he had undertaken to instruct in the "new manual exercise." The picture is striking and graphic ; I shall hereafter compare it with another, drawn by a different hand, of the same John Marshall as he appeared, not as lieutenant of militia, but as Chief-Justice of the United States :

"He was about six feet high, straight and rather slender, of dark complexion—showing little, if any, rosy red, yet good health, the out-

* From the Sketch of Marshall by Mr. Binney.

line of the face nearly a circle, and within that eyes dark to blackness, strong and penetrating, beaming with intelligence and good nature; an upright forehead, rather low, was terminated in a horizontal line by a mass of raven black hair of unusual thickness and strength. The features of the face were in harmony with this outline, and the temples fully developed. The result of this combination was interesting and very agreeable. The body and limbs indicated agility rather than strength, in which, however, he was by no means deficient. He wore a purple or pale blue hunting-shirt, and trowsers of the same material fringed with white. A round black hat, mounted with the buck's tail for a cockade, crowned the figure and the man.

"He went through the manual exercise by word and motion, deliberately pronounced and performed in presence of the company, before he required the men to imitate him; and then proceeded to exercise them with the most perfect temper. Never did man possess a temper more happy, or if otherwise, more subdued or better disciplined.

"After a few lessons the company were dismissed, and informed that if they wished to hear more about the war, and would form a circle around him, he would tell them what he understood about it. The circle was formed and he addressed the company for something like an hour. I remember, for I was near him, that he spoke, at the close of his speech, of the minute battalion about to be raised, and said he was going into it, and expected to be joined by many of his hearers. He then challenged an acquaintance to a game of quoits, and they closed the day with foot races, and other athletic exercises, at which there was no betting. He had walked ten miles to the muster field, and returned the same distance on foot to his father's house, at Oak Hill, where he arrived a little after sunset."

Such is the life-like picture which a cotemporary and kinsman has left of the Chief-Justice, as he appeared upon the threshhold of early manhood. One cannot help being struck with its truthfulness and simplicity;—a walk of ten miles from Oak Hill in a blue hunting-shirt and buck tail cockade—a frank, friendly, and hearty greeting with his comrades—a drill in the "manual exercise"—a familiar talk about the war—foot races, and a game at quoits at which "there was no betting," make up the prominent points of the picture. And it may here be added, that this admirable simplicity of manners—nay, the very tastes and habits of his early manhood, remained with him through life. Thus he never lost his fondness for those field sports and athletic exercises, which in youth laid the foundation of that robust health which he continued to enjoy to a green old age ; nor did he disdain his favorite game of quoits, even when he had been placed at the head of the Federal Judiciary. The Chief-Justice of the United States never ceased to be John Marshall.

Soon after this the Virginia Convention resolved to raise two regiments for the public defence. Marshall promptly enrolled himself in the "minute battalion," of which he had spoken, and in the summer of 1775 received the commission of lieutenant in one of the companies comprising it. The battalion to which he belonged was mustered into service on the first of September of the same year, and a few days after was ordered to march to the lower country, to defend it against a small predatory force under Lord Dunmore, the royal Governor of Virginia. This was his first active service, and the particulars of the expedition, from his own observation, are given by him in his life of Washington. Lord Dunmore, it appears, had proclaimed martial law in Virginia, and early in November had succeeded in collecting such a force of tories and negroes as to give him entire ascendancy in the southern part of the colony. Hearing of these transactions, the Virginia Convention ordered Colonel Woodford, with a regiment of regulars and about two hundred minute men, to advance to the defence of the inhabitants. Dunmore intrenched himself on the Elizabeth River, near the Great Bridge, where he erected a fort on a small piece of firm ground, surrounded by a marsh, which was accessible only by a long causeway. Being without artillery, the Virginians were unable to make any attempt upon these works ; they therefore stationed themselves at a village within cannon-shot of the enemy, and erected a breast-work at the extremity of the causeway. A few days passed without any action on either side. The royal Governor at length resolved to storm the works of the provincials. About sunrise on the 9th of December, Captain Fordyce, at the head of about sixty British grenadiers, advanced along the causeway. With fixed bayonets he entered the breast-work. The alarm, says Marshall, was immediately given ; and, as is the practice with raw troops, the bravest rushed to the works, where, regardless of order, they kept up a heavy fire on the front of the British column. Captain Fordyce, though received so warmly in front, and taken in flank by a party posted on a small eminence on his right, marched up with great intrepidity, until he fell dead within a few steps of the breast-work. The column immediately broke and retreated, but being covered by the artillery of the fort, was not pursued. In this first battle on the soil of Virginia—the Lexington it may be called of the old Commonwealth—the future Chief-Justice took an active part. Even at this distant day the imagination can paint the tall form of the young provincial lieutenant—not as it appeared more than half a century later, in its dignified repose on the bench, robed in the judicial gown and slightly bent with the weight of years—but, animated with the enthusiasm of the soldier, erect, vigorous, and athletic, rising above those frail breast-works, and urging on the "bravest of the troops" to defend their position to the last against the assault of the enemy. The result of the attack was disastrous to the British. Every grenadier, it is said, was either killed or wounded, while the Americans did not lose a single man. Lord Dunmore found himself obliged to evacuate the fort the following night and take refuge on board his vessels, and the provincials proceeded in triumph to take possession of Norfolk. The city was soon after cannonaded by the British ships and set on fire by a strong detachment of the enemy, landing under cover of the cannon of their vessels, and was afterwards entirely destroyed by order of the Committee of Safety, and the place evacuated.

As the war became more serious, the Virginia Convention determined to increase the number of their regiments from two to eleven, which were afterwards taken into the continental service. In July, 1776, Marshall was appointed first lieutenant in one of these Continental regiments. His father, Colonel Marshall, commanded the third regiment, which was with the army under Washington, in the campaign of 1776, as I have already mentioned, and performed very severe duty during the retreat through New Jersey.* After the close of this disastrous campaign, when the American army, broken and dispirited, had retired into winter-quarters in New Jersey, and the American

* President Monroe held the commission of Lieutenant in this regiment, and was wounded at the battle of Trenton.

cause, notwithstanding the brilliant successes at Trenton and Princeton, seemed almost hopeless, the regiment to which Lieutenant Marshall was attached was ordered to the North, to reinforce the Commander-in-chief in New Jersey. Marshall was soon after promoted to the rank of captain, and was at the head of his company when the army, the encampment at Morristown being broken up, took the field for the campaign of 1777. Though the new recruits had come in, and the total returns of the army at this time, exclusive of cavalry and artillery, amounted to eight thousand three hundred and seventy-eight men, yet of this number he states two thousand were sick, and the effective force of the Americans, rank and file, was something less than six thousand men. Of these troops more than one-half were unacquainted with the first rudiments of military duty and had never looked an enemy in the face, and yet with this insufficient force Washington took the field and attempted to make head against the enemy. For a month or two no decisive movement was made. Washington entrenched himself at Middlebrook, between the British General Howe and Philadelphia, closely watching every movement of the enemy, and prepared to dispute with him the possession of the American capital. In the mean time fresh recruits joined the army, its discipline was increased, its *materiel* augmented, and in a short time, though not nearly equal in point of effective strength to the British, it was in a condition to manœuvre, with some prospect of success, in presence of the enemy. The British General Howe, abandoning his design of forcing his way to Philadelphia by land, about the middle of July embarked at New York a force of eighteen thousand men, the destination of which was not at first known. On the 30th July the British fleet was seen off the capes of the Delaware, when orders were immediately given to the various detachments of the American army to assemble in the neighborhood of Philadelphia. General Howe having relinquished his design of attempting to carry the British fleet up the Delaware bay and river, entered the Chesapeake, which owing to unfavorable winds he did not reach till the 16th of August; and having sailed up that bay and entered Elk river, he landed his forces at the ferry on the 25th. The day before this landing the American army marched through Philadelphia and proceeded towards the Brandywine. Being united with the Pennsylvania militia under General

Armstrong, their numbers amounted to fifteen thousand ; but the effective force was far below this, and did not exceed, according to Marshall's own statement, eleven thousand men. Marshall's company, it appears, was attached to a corps of light infantry formed for the occasion, the command of which was given to General Maxwell. This corps was advanced to Iron Hill, about three miles in front of White Clay Creek. The opportunity was thus given to Captain Marshall of engaging in the first skirmish which preceded the battle of Brandywine. A column of British, led by Lord Cornwallis, moving forward to join Knyphausen, fell in with and attacked Maxwell, who retreated over White Creek with the loss of about forty men. Meanwhile the American army crossed the Brandywine and took a strong position behind that river at Chadd's Ford, determined at this place to dispute with the enemy the possession of Philadelphia. General Maxwell's corps, to which Marshall belonged, was advanced in front and placed advantageously on the hills south of the river, on the road leading over the Ford.* In this position, on the 11th September, about daybreak, the whole British army was seen advancing on the direct road leading over Chadd's Ford. The Americans were immediately under arms, and skirmishing commenced between the advanced parties, though without much loss on either side. By 10 o'clock Maxwell was obliged to give way and retreat over the Brandywine, below the Ford. Knyphausen paraded on the heights lately occupied by Maxwell, and both armies prepared for battle. The American troops were in good spirits, and even eager for action. This seems evident from the relation given by Marshall, in his Life of Washington, of a skirmish in which he himself was engaged. The British were divided from Maxwell's corps only by a skirt of woods and the river ; and it seems that so great was the ardor of the Americans, that small parties would leave their posts, and crossing over the stream, keep up a scattering fire against the enemy. One of these parties, commanded by Captains Waggoner and Porterfield, engaged the British flank guard closely, killed a captain with ten or fifteen privates, drove them out of the wood, and were on the point of taking a field-piece. The sharpness of the skirmish soon drew a large body of the British to that quarter, and the Americans were again driven over the Brandywine.

* Marshall's Life of Washington, Vol. I. p. 155.

The characteristic modesty of the author causes him to omit any mention of his own share in the engagement, and he merely adds in a note, that he was "an eye-witness of this skirmish."*

The battle of Brandywine was fought on the 10th September, 1777. The result was not decisive, though the Americans were defeated and driven from their position. They sustained a loss of nearly a thousand men killed and wounded, besides some prisoners. The British loss was about half that number. The same night Washington retreated in good order to Chester, and the next day to Philadelphia. In this hotly contested action the Virginia troops behaved with great gallantry. The elder Marshall, in command of the third regiment, greatly distinguished himself. He was stationed in a wood on the right, and though attacked by superior numbers, maintained his position without losing an inch of ground, until his ammunition was nearly exhausted and one-third of his soldiers killed or wounded. Colonel Marshall, whose horse had received two balls, then retired in good order to resume his position on the right of his division, but found it had already retreated.†

That the victory of General Howe, if it may be called such, was not decisive, is evident from the fact that four days afterwards Washington was on the Lancaster road in pursuit of the British General, for the purpose of bringing him to another engagement. On the 16th the two armies again met, and after a brief skirmish were separated by a heavy storm. Soon after Philadelphia fell into the hands of the enemy.

The battle of Germantown followed—a battle skilfully planned and gallantly contested, but like the battle of Brandywine, indecisive in its results. Captain Marshall was in this engagement, his company being attached to Woodford's brigade, which was stationed in the left wing immediately opposite the British right. This wing coming into action, gallantly attacked the British light infantry, and after a sharp contest drove it from the ground. While rapidly pursuing the flying enemy, the brigade to which Marshall belonged was arrested by a destructive fire of musketry from a large stone house into which some companies of British infantry had thrown themselves. Unable to return this fire with effect, the brigade was drawn off to the left by its commanding offi-

* Marshall's Life of Washington, Vol. I., p. 156. † *Ibid.* Vol. I., p. 158.

cers, and some field-pieces were brought up to play upon the house, but were found too light for effective service. The advance of the brigade was of course retarded, and the line broken, although one division pressed forward with such eagerness that it drove back part of the British right wing, and made a considerable number of prisoners.* This untoward accident, in conjunction with some other unforseen and unfortunate occurrences, snatched the victory from the hands of the Americans when it seemed to be already within their grasp. Washington found himself compelled to draw off his army, which he did in good order. The loss on both sides was about the same as in the former battle at the Brandywine. The Americans retreated a few miles from the field, but meeting with a reinforcement large enough to repair their losses they again advanced towards Philadelphia and encamped on Skippach Creek, and soon after took a strong position at White Marsh.

It was while the Americans lay encamped at White Marsh, and just before the army went into winter-quarters at Valley Forge, that General Howe marched out of Philadelphia with his whole army, with the design of forcing Washington from his position and driving him beyond the mountains. The attack, however, was never made. Some skirmishing ensued between the armies, and at one time a general action seemed inevitable. Upon this occasion Marshall alludes to the courage and spirit that were infused into the troops by the presence of Washington, who rode through every brigade, delivering his orders relative to the battle in person, exhorting the soldiers to rely principally on the bayonet, and animating them to a vigorous performance of their duty. It may well be imagined that such words and such a presence, were to the timid and wavering, powerful incentives to duty. But they were not necessary to inspire the courage or animate the zeal of the young captain of Virginia continentals. That zeal had been already proved and that courage tried. No officer of his grade in the service stood higher. He was deservedly esteemed and beloved by his comrades. His acquaintance with the officers of the army was extensive, more extensive, perhaps, because he was called upon frequently to act as Deputy Judge Advocate, in which position he acquired deserved reputation and influence. The feeling of affection

* 1 Marshall's Washington, p. 169.

which the officers of the army entertained for their young comrade, continued unabated to the last. Years afterwards it was a subject they delighted to speak of. "I myself," says Judge Story, "have often heard him spoken of by some of these veterans in terms of the highest praise. In an especial manner, the Revolutionary officers of the Virginia line appeared almost to idolize him, as an old friend and companion in arms, enjoying their fullest confidence." His acquaintance extended to officers of superior grades, and other regiments as well as his own. His discharge of the duties of Judge Advocate brought him in familiar intercourse with Col. Hamilton, and about the same time he made the personal acquaintance of that great man who then commanded in chief the American army, and for whose personal character, it is unnecessary to say, he never ceased to entertain the most profound reverence.

Captain Marshall went into winter-quarters with the army at Valley Forge, and shared the privations and sufferings of the troops during the whole of that terrible and ever memorable season. A cotemporary and eye-witness describes him as he appeared at this time among his brother officers of the regiment to which he belonged:—"When the writer of this article first saw him," he remarks, "he held the commission of captain in that regiment. It was in the trying severe winter of 1777–8, a few months after the disastrous battles of Brandywine and Germantown had tested his firmness, hardihood and heroism. The spot where we acquired our earliest information of him, was the famous hutted encampment at Valley Forge, about thirty miles from Philadelphia. By his appearance then we supposed him about twenty-two or twenty-three years of age. Even so early in life we recollect that he appeared to us *primus inter pares*, for amidst the many commissioned officers he was discriminated for superior intelligence. Our informant, Col. Ball, of another regiment in the same line, represented him as a young man, not only brave, but signally intelligent. Indeed, all those who intimately knew him, affirmed that his capacity was held in such estimation by many of his brother officers, that in many disputes of a certain description, he was constantly chosen arbiter; and that officers, irritated by differences, or animated by debate, often submitted the contested points to his judgment, which being given in writing, and accompanied, as it commonly was, by sound reasons in support of his decision, obtained general acquiescence." *

Marshall remained at the head of his company in the army, under the immediate command of Washington, during the two following campaigns, of 1778 and 1779. He was present, and participated in the celebrated battle of Monmouth, and at the expiration of that campaign, went with the army into winter-quarters. The following year he was again in the field, and formed one of the covering party detailed to sustain General Wayne in his daring, brilliant, and successful assault upon Stony Point. He was also concerned in the enterprise so admirably planned and successfully executed by Major Lee against the British post at Powles Hook.†

When the army went into winter-quarters at the close of the campaign of 1779, there being a superabundance of officers belonging to the Virginia line—the term of enlistment of most of the soldiers having expired—Marshall and many of his brother officers were directed to return home in order to take charge of such men as the State Legislature might raise for their command. In this interval of comparative repose and leisure, the first that he had known since the breaking out of the war, he applied himself with renewed ardor to a severe course of study. Chancellor Wythe was at that time professor of law in the College of William and Mary, and Mr. Madison, afterwards Bishop of Virginia, the President of that College. Marshall now found an opportunity to avail himself of the instructions of these eminent men, and attended a course of law lectures by the former, and a course of lectures on natural philosophy by the latter. He left the college in the summer vacation of 1780, and obtained a license to practice law.

But the license of the young lawyer availed him very little at this period. It was a time when men might fully realize the truth of the maxim, *inter arma silent leges.* The invasion of Virginia soon after shut up the courts of law, and they were not opened again until after the capitulation of Cornwallis. In the mean time Marshall returned to the army, and remained in the service under command of Baron Steuben

* See North American Review, January, 1828, p. 8.

† 1 Marshall's Life of Washington, pp. 311, 316.

until after the termination of Arnold's invasion.* There being still a redundance of officers in the Virginia line, he then resigned his commission, and thenceforth applied himself with unremitted diligence to the study of his future profession.

Immediately on the close of hostilities in Virginia, by the capture of Cornwallis, Mr. Marshall commenced the practice of the law, and soon rose to distinction at the bar. His placidity, moderation, and calmness, says one of his eulogists, irresistibly won the esteem of men and invited them to intercourse with him ;—his benevolent heart and his serene, and at times joyous temper, made him the cherished companion of his friends ;—his candor and integrity attracted the confidence of the bar ;—and that extraordinary comprehension and grasp of mind, by which difficulties were seized and overcome without effort or parade, commanded the attention and respect of the courts of justice. This is the traditionary account of the first professional years of John Marshall. He accordingly rose rapidly to distinction, and to a distinction which nobody envied, because he seemed neither to wish it, nor to be conscious of it himself.†

Marshall, it is said, attributed his early advancement and lucrative practice, not so much to his own merits, as to his extensive acquaintance with the officers of the army, who, by the termination of hostilities, had returned to their families, and were scattered over the States. Discerning friends, however, have not failed to trace it to what is doubtless its true source, namely, his own great talents and exertions.

Mr. Marshall's first appearance in political life was in the Virginia Legislature, of which he was elected a member in the spring of 1782. The following autumn he was chosen a member of the State Executive Council. This latter position he resigned in the spring of 1784, in order to devote himself more exclusively to his professional duties. He does not appear, however, to have found a seat in the Legislature incompatible with these duties, as we find him elected a member of that body from his native County of Fauquier, immediately after

* On the 10th of January, 1781, he was with the army near Hood's, when the British troops, on retiring to Portsmouth, sustained, in an ambuscade by the Americans, the only loss which on their part attended that incursion.

† Binney's Eulogy on Marshall.

resigning his seat in the Council. On the 3d of January, 1783, he married Miss Mary Willis Ambler, daughter of the then State Treasurer, to whom he had become attached before leaving the army. This was one of three events of his life which alone he deemed worthy of commemoration in the simple inscription, which two days before his death, his own hand wrote to be placed on his tomb—his birth, his marriage, and his death! With this lady he lived nearly fifty years, in the most devoted conjugal affection, and her death, says Judge Story, cast a gloom over his thoughts from which he never recovered.

About the same time Mr. Marshall took up his permanent residence in the city of Richmond, and was soon extensively engaged in the practice of the law. He also engaged with interest and ardor in the political questions of the day, particularly those in which his own State was more immediately interested. He was continued, by repeated elections, a member of the State Legislature during most of this period, up to the final adoption of the Constitution. Here he came in contact with such men as Henry, Lee, Tyler, Tazewell and Madison; the latter gentleman warmly sustained him in his enlightened advocacy of a union between the states and the establishment of an efficient federal government. Though at a subsequent period Marshall and Madison widely differed in their political views and constitutional constructions, yet the respect and friendship with which they mutually regarded each other, were continued to the close of their lives. "Nothing, indeed, could be more touching to an ingenuous mind," remarks Judge Story, "than to hear from their lips, in their latter years, expressions of mutual respect and confidence; or to witness their earnest testimony to the talents, the virtues, and the services of each other."

The questions occupying the attention of the Virginia Legislature during this period, were of the gravest character. Besides those which may be considered as more especially belonging to the internal affairs of the State, such as the administration of justice, the collection of taxes, the regulation of the currency, and the like, other questions relative to the external and federal relations of the State, were constantly brought up for discussion. And rising above and extending far beyond all in its magnitude and greatness, at the very threshold of these discussions, stood the formidable question, whether the union of the

States should or should not be preserved; and if preserved, under what form of confederation or government. Deeply interesting to the people of Virginia as was the discussion of all these questions, it is not necessary for the purposes of this sketch to inquire what particular part was sustained in them by Mr. Marshall; and I shall merely allude to the question last mentioned, for the purpose of indicating generally the nature of his views and opinions at this time.

The insufficiency of the old articles of confederation was seen at an early period in Virginia, as elsewhere, and discerning men were not slow to perceive that the cumbrous and unwieldy mechanism must soon fall to pieces. This being the case, the question occurred whether any further union should be attempted, and it is unnecessary to say that it was discussed in Virginia, as in other States, with no little warmth, and that it had its opponents as well as its advocates. Marshall was one of those who, in the Legislature, warmly seconded Madison, and the other friends of an effective federal union. His course was precisely such as might have been anticipated. And though taken under the enthusiastic impulses of youth, and, as he himself thought, governed in a great degree by circumstances, it was one which his mature and deliberate judgment in after years fully approved. Long afterwards, in a letter to a friend, he frankly intimates the reasons which he supposes influenced his early opinions on this subject:—

"When I recollect the wild and enthusiastic notions with which my political opinions of that day were tinctured, I am disposed to ascribe my devotion to the Union, and to a government competent to its preservation, at least as much to casual circumstances as to judgment. I had grown up at a time when the love of the Union, and the resistance to the claims of Great Britain, were the inseparable inmates of the same bosom; when patriotism and a strong fellow-feeling with our suffering fellow-citizens of Boston were identical; when the maxim 'United we stand, divided we fall,' was the maxim of every orthodox American. And I had imbibed these sentiments so thoroughly that they constituted a part of my being. I carried them with me into the army, where I found myself associated with brave men, from different states, who were risking life and everything valuable, in a common cause, believed by all to be most precious, and where I was confirmed in the habit of considering America as my country, and Congress as my government."

And in the same letter he adds: "My immediate entrance into the State Legislature opened to my view the causes which had been chiefly instrumental in augmenting those sufferings (of the army); and the general tendency of State politics convinced me that no safe and permanent remedy could be found but in a more efficient and better organized general government."

With these views Marshall firmly arrayed himself in the Legislature by the side of those whose efforts tended to secure the great object in view, a permanent and efficient union of the States under a federal government. He was not himself a member of the Convention which framed the Constitution; but the same year in which that body met, he was again elected to the Virginia house of delegates, from the county of Henrico, there to sustain and defend, so far as was requisite, and until the time arrived for more efficient action, the policy and measures of the Convention.

When the Constitution was submitted to the States for their decision, Marshall, who warmly advocated its adoption, became a candidate for election to the Virginia Convention. The majority of the voters in the county where he resided were opposed to the Constitution. He was assured that all opposition would be withdrawn if he would pledge himself to vote against its adoption, otherwise he would be strenuously resisted. Marshall, of course, refused the pledge, and determined to encounter the opposition. But no opposition could withstand his personal popularity and the high estimate in which his character and virtues were held in the community; and though the question at issue naturally excited the utmost warmth of feeling, yet, as he remarks himself, "parties had not yet become so bitter as to extinguish the private affections." The result of the canvass was his election by a triumphant majority.

The Virginia Convention assembled at Richmond on the 2d of June, 1788. EDWARD PENDLETON was chosen its president. The debates of this body have been preserved, and are published.* Though said to be loose and imperfect, and by no means to do full justice to the elo-

* They comprise the entire third volume of Elliott's Debates on the Federal Constitution.

quence and ability of the respective speakers, yet they are still, even in our day, worthy of careful perusal by the student of our constitutional history. The first orators and the ablest lawyers in Virginia—the greatest names in her civil and political annals—are found among the members of this body. Mr. NICHOLAS led off in these discussions in favor of the Constitution. PATRICK HENRY followed, in warm and earnest opposition. GOV. RANDOLPH succeeded MR. HENRY, and though he had refused to sign the instrument in the Federal Convention, he now brought to its support the timely aid of his vigorous and powerful eloquence;* and GEORGE MASON followed in a strong and searching argument on the other side. The debate thus opened was continued from day to day, with increased animation and interest, till the close of the Convention. By the side of Nicholas and Randolph were ranged Madison, Pendleton, Wythe, Innis, Blair, Bushrod Washington, and Marshall; and with Henry and Mason on the other side, stood Bland, Grayson, Tyler, and Monroe.

It appears from the debates that Mr. Marshall delivered three speeches during the Convention. The first of these was in reply to Patrick Henry, in which he enters upon a full and somewhat general discussion of the proposed plan of government, and very ably vindicates it against the various objections raised and urged with so much force and eloquence by that celebrated orator. The second is more brief, and relates exclusively to the organization of the militia; and the third is a clear, lucid, and powerful argument in favor of the judiciary clause of the Constitution, and in reply to Mr. George Mason. I cannot refrain from transcribing a single passage in this admirable speech, in reference to that celebrated constitutional question, which

* Mr. Randolph's last words in the Convention are reported as follows:—"The suffrage which I shall give in favor of the Constitution will be ascribed by malice to motives unknown to my breast. But although for every other act of my life I shall seek refuge in the mercy of God—for this I request his *justice* only. Lest, however, some future annalist should, in the spirit of party vengeance, deign to mention my name, let him recite these truths—that I went to the Federal Convention with the strongest affection for the Union; that I acted there in full conformity with that affection; *that I refused to subscribe, because I had, as I still have, objections to the Constitution,* and wished a free inquiry into its merits; and that the accession of eight States reduced our deliberations to the single question of Union or no Union."—3 *Elliott's Debates,* 587.

was discussed in Chief-Justice Jay's time, in the case of Chisholm *vs.* The State of Georgia, namely, whether a State was liable to answer in the Federal courts at the suit of a citizen of another State. The wide difference between the views of Marshall and those subsequently advanced by Jay and his associates, including Justice Blair, who was himself a member of the Convention, is worthy of notice :—

"With respect to disputes between a State and the citizens of another State, its jurisdiction has been decried with usual vehemence. I hope that no gentleman will think *that a State will be called at the bar of the Federal court.* Is there no such case at present? Are there not many cases in which the Legislature of Virginia is a party, and yet the State is not sued? It is not rational to suppose *that the sovereign power shall be dragged before a court.* The intent is to enable states to recover claims of individuals residing in other states. *I contend this construction is warranted by the words.* But say they, there will be a partiality in it, if a State cannot be defendant—if an individual cannot proceed to obtain judgment against a State, though he may be sued by a State. It is necessary to be so, and cannot be avoided. I see a difficulty in making a State defendant which does not prevent its being plaintiff. If this be only what cannot be avoided, why object to the system on that account? If an individual has a just claim against any particular State, is it to be presumed that on application to its Legislature he will not obtain satisfaction? But how could a State recover any claim from a citizen of another State without the establishment of these tribunals?"

The session of the Convention lasted twenty-five days. From its commencement to its close it was attended by crowds of citizens of all ages and conditions, attracted both by the intense interest everywhere felt in the subject under discussion, and by the splendid displays of eloquence which it elicited. Wirt's glowing and animated description of this distinguished body—the most illustrious perhaps and ablest that ever assembled in Virginia—is no doubt familiar to the reader. Still I am tempted to embellish my own imperfect sketch with a touch of the warm and rich coloring which never failed to follow the pencil which that master hand guided over the canvass.

"Day after day, from morning till night, the galleries of the house were continually filled with an anxious crowd, who forgot the inconvenience of their situation in the excess of their enjoyment; and, far from giving any interruption to the course of the debate, increased its interest and solemnity by their silence and attention. No bustle, no motion, no sound, was heard among them, save only a slight movement, when some new speaker arose, whom they were all eager to see as well as to hear; or when some master-stroke of eloquence shot thrilling along their nerves, and extorted an involuntary and inarticulate murmur. Day after day was this banquet of the mind and of the heart spread before them, with a delicacy and variety which could never cloy. There every taste might find its peculiar gratification—the man of wit—the man of feeling—the critic—the philosopher—the historian—the metaphysician—the lover of logic—the admirer of rhetoric—any man who had an eye for the beauty of action or an ear for the harmony of sound, or a soul for the charms of poetic fancy—in short every one, who could see, or hear, or feel, or understand, might find in the wanton profusion and prodigality of that Attic feast, some delicacy adapted to his peculiar taste. Every mode of attack and defence of which the human mind is capable, in decorous debate—every species of weapon and armor, offensive and defensive, that could be used with advantage, from the Roman javelin to the Parthian arrow, from the cloud of Æneas to the shield of Achilles—all that could be accomplished by human strength, and almost more than human activity, was seen exhibited on that celebrated floor."*

At the close of the debates in the Virginia Convention, it was known that eight States had already ratified the Constitution. The accession of Virginia was all that was now required in order to complete the confederacy and put the new government into operation. Yet, notwithstanding the great ability and influence of the friends of the Constitution in the Convention, it had a narrow escape on its final passage. A resolution, that a bill of rights, together with amendments to its most objectionable parts should be submitted, previous to its ratification, to a convention of the States, was negatived by a bare majority of eight votes; and, on the final question of ratification, the vote stood 89 to 79. Mr. Marshall was appointed on the committee to prepare a form of ratification. He was also a member of the committee, of which Chancellor Wythe was chairman, appointed to pre-

* Life of Patrick Henry, p. 311.

pare and report a bill of rights and such amendments as were deemed necessary to be recommended to the consideration of Congress. The report was made on the 27th July, the bill of rights and the amendments proposed by the committee adopted, and the Convention thereupon adjourned *sine die.* On that day the Constitution received its vitality and the American Republic the charter of its liberties.

Mr. Marshall continued a member of the State Legislature at intervals for some years after the adoption of the Federal Constitution. During this period nearly all those important measures consequent upon the organization of the government which I have alluded to in another part of this volume,* were discussed in the Virginia Legislature with great warmth and freedom. It is unnecessary to say that Marshall mingled prominently in these debates, and adopting a large and liberal view of public policy, cordially and efficiently co-operated, so far as his position enabled him to do, in sustaining, the national government in what he conceived to be its true spirit. It was here, perhaps, that he first applied himself to a close and critical study of the constitutional compact, and his mind became settled in those convictions and views of constitutional construction which his subsequent legal opinions so clearly elucidated. The opposition to the adoption of the Constitution in Virginia, as elsewhere, had been mainly upon the ground of its strong tendency to consolidation, and to destroy the separate existence and independence of the States. It therefore manifested itself at an early period in a jealous vigilance against any construction not warranted by the strict terms of the instrument itself, and insisted upon the closest abridgement of its powers. On the other hand, most of those, who, like Marshall, had been warm and ardent friends of an efficient federal union from the beginning, were in favor of giving full effect to all the necessary measures of government by a more liberal construction. Madison, it is well known, adopted the former of these opinions; and Marshall, in a few years, found himself in an antagonistic position to this gentleman, with whom he had stood side by side fighting the battle of the Constitution on the floor of the Virginia Convention. In common with the great mass of the Federal party, he did not yield his assent to Madison's famous resolution of 1798; much less to those said to have been drafted by Jeffer-

* Sketch of Ellsworth, *ante*, pages 240–243.

son and known by the name of the Kentucky resolutions. And these opinions he entertained even at the early period of which I am now speaking. Thus, when the funding system of Hamilton was attacked with great acrimony in the Virginia Legislature, and the constitutionality of that part of it assuming the State debts denied, Marshall came to its support, and with his accustomed clearness, vigor and force undertook to demonstrate its constitutionality. In the same spirit he examined other constitutional questions and measures of public policy, and, his ideas once matured and his convictions settled, he rarely failed to silence, if he did not convince his adversaries. In powers of clear, calm, logical discussion, he stood unrivalled, and was confessedly one of the leaders of the Virginia Legislature.

But it was to the labors of his profession during these years that he devoted the best portion of his intellect and his energies. Nothing was suffered to divert his attention, or turn him from the steady pursuit of this object. Indeed in 1792, he retired from the Legislature altogether, for the purpose of devoting himself more exclusively to the bar. His professional reputation at this period was very high. He found himself engaged in all the leading causes in the State and national tribunals; and by a course of profound study and culture, of severe mental training, and of successful practice at the bar, he gradually matured and developed those great powers which shed lustre around that higher and more honorable career on the bench upon which he was about to enter.

Some idea of the extent of Marshall's practice, as well as of his eminent ability in forensic argument, may be obtained by glancing at the Virginia reports of this period, especially the two volumes by Washington of cases adjudged in the Courts of Appeals. The latter of these volumes in particular, embracing a period of three years, from 1794 to 1797, is replete with the learning, and may well be considered a proud monument to the professional fame of the future Chief-Justice. His name is found as counsel, on one side or the other, in the great majority of the cases reported—indeed it may be added in every case of any degree of importance. However high might be the reputation of a counsel engaged in a cause of great difficulty, or of great magnitude, he considered it no disparagement to call to his aid the ponderous strength, and avail himself of the close logic of

Marshall. And this, it must be remembered, was at a day, when to occupy a front rank amid such an array as the bar of Virginia then presented, was no empty honor. Patrick Henry indeed was about passing away; but that bar could boast of such bright ornaments as Campbell, and Lee, and Ronald, and Wickham, and Warden, and Baker, and Randolph, and Washington—a bar possessing every element of forensic greatness—learning, eloquence, intellect, culture—all that can adorn and dignify the professional mind. And above them all Marshall towered a Colossus in intellectual strength—or, perhaps, if the figure be not too bold, a majestic pillar in this temple of Themis, standing out like the massive Doric shaft amid a clustre of luxuriant Corinthian columns,

"Nobly plain and unadorned,"

the emblem of simplicity combined with majestic strength, and the type of a primeval age.

The professional reader will see, by these reports, what was the character of the more important cases which enlisted the abilities of Marshall while an advocate at the bar. He will see, too, how wide and deep the common law had struck its roots into the soil of Virginia, nor will he fail to admire the research, the learning, the ingenuity, and the professional acumen which distinguished not only the arguments at bar, but the judgments pronounced from the bench in the highest tribunal of the State. The most abstruse and perplexing questions of the law of real property were involved in some of these cases, and in their discussion the whole field of common-law learning was explored, and the subtlest distinctions, the most ingenious analogies, and the most recondite principles were often brought to bear upon the argument. Nor were the Virginia lawyers, and even Marshall himself, unskilled in the use of those keen and glittering weapons of law logic, which, like the sword of Saladin, are formidable mainly from the dexterity with which they are wielded. But these were never the favorite weapons of Marshall. He preferred the ponderous battle-axe, to the Turkish scimitar; he could apply with admirable felicity, but he never delighted in discussing, a mere technical principle; if he did, it was with him technical in the best and highest sense of the term—a something which pertained to the *ars juridica*—not a mere verbal distinction or quibble of logic.

Questions like these, however, were not of frequent occurrence. Indeed, their discussion would seem to have been out of place in that august tribunal, over which the venerable Edmund Pendleton presided. Accordingly we find that by far the greater number of these cases reported by Judge Washington, involved high and important, and some of them, the most profound legal principles. Were I to select from them one, the argument of which might be taken as a fair specimen of the whole, and as exhibiting also in a high degree the accurate learning, the close logic, and splendid abilities of Marshall, it would be the case of Roy *vs.* Garnett,* argued at the autumn term of the Court of Appeals in 1794. It was a case turning upon some of those abstruse principles on which the law governing real property is built, the very enunciation of which would be incomprehensible to the non-professional reader. On account of the great difficulty of the questions involved, as well as of the importance of the matter in controversy, it had been continued from a preceding term in order to be argued before, and decided by, a full bench. On either side a formidable array of counsel appeared. Campbell opened the discussion with more than his usual energy and impressive power. Warden, Bushrod Washington, and Wickham followed in opposition. It was reserved for Marshall to make the reply which was to close the argument. The analysis of that reply is preserved in the report. It may be referred to as an admirable specimen of the style and manner of Marshall's reasoning—clear in its statements, simple in its processes, strong and irresistible in its conclusions. Thoroughly versed in the principles of the law of real property, and fond of tracing those principles to their source, he makes no ostentatious display of black-letter learning ; a master of the entire subject in controversy, and familiar with the whole range of the debate, he does not seek to confound his adversaries or perplex the court by that hair-splitting logic, and those metaphysical abstractions in which some of his brethren in Westminster Hall, even at that day, were fond of indulging. Every thing is direct, clear, simple, logical, strong—every thing, in short, characteristic of the mind of Marshall. Though his argument failed to convince the judgment of the court, no one who reads it, even in the imperfect

* 2 Washington's Reports, 9.

analysis presented by the report, can hesitate to admit its matchless power, and the almost irresistible force of its conclusions.

I had designed, in this connection, to allude to a few of the more interesting cases in which the Chief-Justice was engaged while an advocate at the bar ; but in doing so it would become necessary to abridge the brief notice contemplated of those grave constitutional questions which passed under his review while on the bench, and the design is therefore the more willingly abandoned. Justice to the subject, however, will require some notice of one of these cases, as well on account of its own intrinsic importance, and the great interest it excited in Virginia, as of the splendid forensic effort of Marshall in its final argument—an argument which deservedly placed him on an equality with the very ablest advocates who had ever appeared at the American bar. I allude to the great case of Ware, Administrator, &c., *vs.* Hylton and others, which decided the right of British creditors under the treaty of peace, to recover debts contracted before the war, which had been sequestrated during the war by an act of the State Legislature.

This suit was instituted in the United States Circuit Court for the District of Virginia, in 1791, and was terminated only by its final adjudication in the Supreme Court of the United States in the winter of 1796. The facts presented were briefly these. The defendants, Hylton and others, citizens of Virginia, had, before the war of the revolution, executed their bond to the plaintiff, William Jones, a subject of Great Britain, (who dying *pendente lite*, his administrator, Ware, was substituted,) in the penal sum of £2976 11s. 6d. Under the Virginia act of sequestration, passed in 1777, the defendants paid into the Virginia loan office part of their debt, and took a certificate from the commissioners and a receipt from the Governor and Council in discharge thereof, pursuant to the provisions of the act. Notwithstanding this discharge, the plaintiff, after the treaty of peace, brought a suit to recover the whole debt, claiming a right thereto under the treaty, one article of which expressly provided that "creditors, on either side, shall meet with no *lawful impediment* to the recovery of the full value, in sterling money, of all *bona fide* debts heretofore contracted." The question, therefore, was, whether the payment of the debt to the State, pursuant to its sequestration law was an absolute discharge to the creditor ; and whether the treaty of peace could annul a legislative act of one of the States, and destroy rights acquired by, or vested in, individuals by virtue of such acts. The case originally came on for trial at the Circuit Court of the United States at Richmond, in November, 1791, before Judges Johnson and Blair of the Supreme Court, and Griffin, District Judge, and afterwards, in 1793, before Chief-Justice Jay and Judge Iredell, and the same District Judge. Marshall was one of the counsel for the defendants, the American debtors, having for his colleagues Patrick Henry, Alexander Campbell, and Col. Innis, the Attorney-General of Virginia. They were opposed by Mr. Ronald, Mr. Baker, Mr. Wickham, and Mr. Starke. Such an array of counsel, on either side, would never have been retained, except in a cause of the very greatest magnitude and difficulty. The question was, indeed, one of the highest interest to the people of Virginia, involving as it did the honor of the State, and the fortunes of many of her citizens. Mr. Wirt, in his life of Patrick Henry, has given a full sketch of the speech of that celebrated orator in this case—a speech which occupied three days in its delivery, and which he considers to be "his most distinguished display of professional talents." * Marshall followed Mr. Henry, and was succeeded by Campbell and Innis, both of them men of rare powers of forensic eloquence. The discussion in this great case seems to have been one of the most brilliant exhibitions ever witnessed at the bar of Virginia, and to have been carried on, in the language of Mr. Wirt, "with so much learning, argument, and eloquence, as to have placed that bar, in the estimation of the federal judges, above all others in the United States." That this eulogy is not too highly colored, is evident from the language of Judge Iredell, as it is found embodied in the opinion pronounced by him in the case. "The cause," he says, "has been spoken to, at the bar, (alluding to the trial before him,) with a degree of ability equal to any occasion. However painfully I may at any time reflect on the inadequacy of my own talents, I shall as long as I live, remember with pleasure and respect the arguments which I have heard in this case. They have discovered an ingenuity, a depth of investigation, and a power of reasoning fully equal to any thing I have

* Judge Iredell, on hearing Henry's speech, is said to have exclaimed on the bench : "Gracious God! He *is* an *orator* indeed!"

ever witnessed, and some of them have been adorned with a splendor of eloquence surpassing what I have ever felt before. Fatigue has given way under its influence, and the heart has been warmed, while the understanding has been instructed." * If Henry is justly entitled to so much of the above compliment as refers to the "splendor of eloquence" exhibited on that occasion, Marshall may fairly claim his full share of that which speaks of a "depth of investigation and a power of reasoning" equal to any thing which that eminent and experienced judge had ever before witnessed.

On the trial at the Circuit, the court sustained the main positions taken by the defendants; and from this judgment the plaintiffs appealed to the Supreme Court. When the cause came on for argument in the winter of 1796, (Mr. Henry in the mean time having retired from the bar,) Marshall appeared as the leading counsel for the defendants, with his associate, Campbell, a man of whom Wirt says, that "for mere eloquence, his equal has never been seen in the United States." They were opposed by three of the most eminent lawyers at the Pennsylvania bar, Tighlman, Lewis and Wilcocks. The case has been fully reported,† with the opinions of the court and a brief sketch of the argument of counsel. The report, however, by no means does justice to the masterly and every way triumphant effort of Marshall, being little more than a *resumé*, or mere summary, of his argument. In order to gain an idea of its astonishing force, and the wonderful effect it produced, we must turn away from the reports and consult cotemporary accounts, as handed down in the traditionary annals of the bar. Though Marshall was upon the losing side of the question, yet this circumstance detracted not the least from the eclat of his brilliant effort. He had reached, at a bound, the proudest eminence of professional fame. He stood among his brethren an intellectual giant, and the public gaze was fixed upon him in admiration. His reputation was no longer provincial, it had become a part of the reputation of the American bar.

In one of those familiar and agreeable letters which Wirt was accustomed to write to his friends, he alludes to this great argument, years afterwards, with that feeling of admiration for the Chief-Justice,

* See Opinion of Judge Iredell in this case, 3 Dallas Reports.

† 3 Dallas Reports, pages 195 to 285.

which he habitually cherished ; and contrasts its massive strength with the brilliant and eloquent, but less effective display of his associate. "Campbell played off his Apollonian airs ; but they were lost. Marshall spoke, as he always does, to the judgment merely, and for the simple purpose of convincing. Marshall was justly pronounced one of the greatest men of the country. He was followed by crowds, looked upon, and courted with every evidence of admiration and respect for the great powers of his mind. Campbell was neglected and slighted, and came home in disgust. Marshall's maxim seems always to have been, 'aim exclusively at strength,' and from his eminent success, I say, if I had my life to go over again, I would practise on his maxim with the most rigorous severity, until the character of my mind was established." *

Notwitstanding the diligence with which Marshall applied himself to his professional avocations, he found it impossible to withdraw wholly from politics. At that day party spirit ran high in Virginia, and almost every gentleman of talents and standing in the commonwealth found himself arrayed on one side or the other of the great political questions which agitated the public mind. The proclamation of neutrality had resulted in drawing a distinct and visible line of division between the two parties. Marshall, though he had hailed the advent of the French Revolution, in common with the great mass of his countrymen, as the dawn of a brighter day for Europe and the world, did not for a moment hesitate firmly and boldly to place himself on the side of the administration, and vigorously to defend its policy, both in writing and in oral speech. In opposition to the

* 2 Kennedy's Life of Wirt, p. 76.

Wirt was fond of alluding to the intellectual characteristics of Marshall, and of holding them up as an example and incentive to others. "Aim," he says in a letter to a friend, "at the character of *strength*, *cogency*, and *comprehension*, and imitate of all things Judge Marshall's and Locke's simple process of reasoning. The world will ever give its sanction to this as the truest criterion of superior minds."† And again in a letter to his son-in-law : "Observe particularly the *action* of Marshall's mind. * * * Compare it closely and carefully with that of Mansfield, Hardwicke, Kenyon, and Thurlow. These are the great steamships of the law to which we should lash ourselves, till we catch and learn to keep their momentum, and become steamships in our turn.'

† Life of Wirt, Vol. II. pp. 67 and 383.

opinion of some of the first and ablest statesmen of Virginia, he also defended the policy of the mission to England, and the treaty of peace negociated by Mr. Jay. At this critical juncture in the affairs of the nation, men of the highest character and standing stepped aside from their private pursuits and business avocations, to mingle in the primary meetings of the people, with the view of giving direction and energy to the public sentiment. Chancellor Wythe presided at a meeting in Richmond, at which resolutions were passed denouncing the treaty " as insulting to the dignity, injurious to the interests, dangerous to the security, and repugnant to the Constitution of the United States," and Marshall, addressing an assemblage of the same people, in a vigorous and searching speech, succeeded on his part in carrying resolutions approving the conduct of the executive in sanctioning the treaty.

It was about this time that Marshall was again drawn from his profession and forced to accept a seat in the Legislature, contrary to his own wishes and expectations. The circumstances attending his election certainly show him to have been in possession of a very extraordinary degree of personal popularity, and must have been highly gratifying and flattering to his feelings. They are related as follows: From the time of his withdrawal from the Legislature in 1792, two opposing candidates had divided the city of Richmond; the one his intimate friend, and holding the same political sentiments with himself; the other a most zealous partizan of the opposition. Each election between these gentlemen, who were both popular, had been decided by a small majority, and the approaching contest was entirely doubtful. Mr. Marshall attended the polls at an early hour and gave his vote for his friend. While at the polls a gentleman demanded that a poll should be opened for Mr. Marshall. The latter was greatly surprised at the proposal, and unhesitatingly expressed his dissent, declaring that his wishes and feeling and honor were engaged for one of the candidates. At the same time he announced his willingness to become a candidate the next year. He retired from the polls and immediately gave his attendance to the business of one of the courts which was then in session. A poll was, however, opened for him in his absence by the gentleman who first suggested it, notwithstanding his positive refusal. The election was suspended for a few minutes; a consultation took place among the freeholders; they determined to support him; and in the evening he received the information of his election.*

Marshall's election was a most important and timely aid to the administration. He stood now among the leaders of the Federal party in Virginia. The position to which he was elected was precisely the place where his aid was most necessary, and his efforts could be most effectual. The exciting discussion upon Jay's treaty was about to pass from the popular forum into the Legislature. Marshall met and grappled with it there. Anxious friends, it is said, were solicitous that he should avoid engaging in this discussion. It would sacrifice, it was thought, a portion of his well-earned popularity, and might even subject him to rude attacks from the opposition. But Marshall was not a man to shrink from an independent and fearless discharge of duty. The timid Mansfield,† cowering under the haughty glance of Pitt on the floor of the British Parliament, was not the prototype of John Marshall in the Virginia Assembly. In him the firm nerve and steady resolution of the grenadier at Brandywine, had ripened and matured into that higher species of courage, which animates its possessor to risk popularity and reputation, in the discharge of duty, and fearlessly breast the turbulent waves of popular passion. He would not, he said, in answer to the kind remonstrances of his friends, move any measure to excite such a debate; but if the subject were brought forward by others, he should, at every hazard, vindicate the administration, and assert his own opinions.

That moment speedily came. The question of the treaty was soon raised, and the Constitutional objections to it were urged with much force and triumphant confidence. Marshall took the floor, in reply.

* North American Review, vol. XXVI. p. 22.

† "It must be admitted," says Lord Campbell, "that from a want of moral courage he quailed, not only under the ascendancy of Lord Chatham—whom beings of a superior order to our species, might have been afraid to encounter—but of Lord Camden, who was much his inferior in powers of mind and in acquired knowledge. His cry of *Craven!* when the lists had been stretched, and the trumpet had been sounded for a passage of arms on the libel field, lowered his character, and must have been a source of painful remembrance for himself to his dying day. With boldness he might have gained a victory which would have added new lustre to his name."—2 *Lives of Chief-Justices of England*, 576.

He entered the intellectual arena, not encased in the glittering panoply of a splendid eloquence, with the burnished and shining weapons of a gorgeous declamation and an elegant rhetoric—but armed with the Achillean spear, or perhaps it may better be said with the Herculean club of a close, compact, simple, but irresistible logic, which bore down every thing before it. His speech on this occasion was of tremendous power. It has been represented as one of the noblest efforts of his genius. So clearly and so decisively, says one of his eulogists, did he demonstrate the constitutional power of the executive to negociate a commercial treaty—not only from the words of the Constitution and the practice of nations, but from the opinions of Jefferson himself, and the sanction of the whole Virginian delegation in Congress—that the constitutional objection was abandoned, and the Assembly confined itself to passing a simple resolution, disapproving the treaty in point of expediency.

The fame of this admirable argument spread throughout the Union. Even with political opponents it enhanced the estimate of his character; and it brought him into notice of some of the most eminent statesmen who then graced our public councils.* When, therefore, he came to Philadelphia, in 1796, to argue the case of Ware *vs.* Hylton, he had already acquired something more than a provincial reputation—and as a leader of the Federal party in Virginia, he was immediately received by prominent gentlemen entertaining these opinions with a degree of kindness and attention, which not even his subsequent splendid efforts at the bar could enhance. He himself thus speaks of his reception and first acquaintances in Philadelphia:—"I then became acquainted with Mr. Cabot, Mr. Ames, Mr. Dexter, and Mr. Sedgwick, of Massachusetts, Mr. Wadsworth of Connecticut, and Mr. King, of New York. I was delighted with these gentlemen. The particular subject (the British Treaty) which introduced me to their notice, was at that time so interesting, and a Virginian, who supported with any sort of reputation, the measures of the government, was such a *rara avis*, that I was received by them all with a degree of kindness which I had not anticipated. I was particularly intimate with Mr. Ames, and could scarcely gain credit with him when I assured him that the appropriations would be seriously opposed in Congress."

* See Sketch by Judge Story. Miscellaneous Writings, p. 666.

The following year Marshall was again elected to the State Legislature. He did not often take part in its debates, however, and rarely, except when some measure of the Federal government was under discussion. It was during this session that in a debate relative to the general policy of the administration, in which Marshall warmly engaged, a Federal member moved a resolution expressing the high confidence of the House in the "virtue, patriotism, and wisdom" of the President. A gentleman of the opposition, hurried away by the intemperate zeal of party feeling, moved to strike out the word *wisdom.* This motion, as might have been expected, called out an animated and even violent discussion, in which the whole talent of both sides of the House was brought into action. "Will it be believed," exclaims Marshall, indignantly, in a letter to a friend, "that the word was retained by a very small majority. A very small majority in the Legislature of Virginia acknowledging the wisdom of General Washington!" *

About this period the President tendered him the office of Attorney-General of the United States, which he declined, on the ground of its interference with his extensive and lucrative private practice. On the return of Mr. Monroe from France, Washington solicited him to accept this important mission. It was a place whose duties he was preëminently qualified to discharge; for he was thoroughly master of the points involved in the controversy with France, and indeed of the whole subject of our foreign relations. This honorable appointment, too, he thought proper to decline, preferring to continue the practice of his profession, for which, above all public employments, he declared his own preference was decided. He was soon, however, induced to reconsider this determination, and to yield his own inclinations to what he conceived to be the general good of the country. In the summer of 1797, President Adams appointed him, with General Pinckney and Elbridge Gerry, on a special, and it may well be called an extraordinary mission to France,—an appointment which in the critical state of public affairs, and the great interests hanging on the results of the mission, General Marshall did not feel at liberty to decline.

In the preceding sketch of Chief-Justice Jay, I have alluded to the

* Sketch by Judge Story.

foreign relations of the United States at this period, and to the train of events which resulted in the mission to England, and the treaty subsequently made with that power. Mr. Monroe was Minister to France at the time of Jay's treaty, having been appointed to supersede Gouverneur Morris, who had become obnoxious to the French Republic. His reception by the National Convention had been flattering. The Directory, which, in the third year of the Republic, succeeded the Convention, continued an official intercourse with Mr. Monroe, characterized with every appearance of confidence and esteem, until after the consummation of the British treaty, which produced, as might have been expected, great indignation and resentment. Mr. Monroe was soon after recalled by his Government, not without some marks of disapprobation, which his candid disclosures soon dispelled, and General Charles Cotesworth Pinckney of South Carolina, Marshall having declined the nomination, was appointed to succeed him.

Gen. Pinckney was a member of the party which it was supposed was inimical to France. His appointment was not deemed complimentary by the authorities then representing the Republic. The speech of Barras, the President of the Directory, to Monroe on his return from France, in which he declared that the Republic would not "abase herself by calculating the consequences of the condescension of the American Government to the suggestions of her former tyrants" (alluding to the treaty of Jay), had called out severe and just animadversion from President Adams in his message to Congress. The Directory thereupon haughtily refused to receive Gen. Pinckney, or any minister from the United States, "until after the reparation of the grievances demanded of the American Government which the French Republic has a right to expect."

I do not intend here to discuss the question at issue between France and America, in regard to which a wide diversity of opinion existed at that day and perhaps still continues to exist. France complained not only of the neutrality and indifference of America, but of her positive partiality for England, the most formidable of the enemies of the republic ; and this too notwithstanding the treaties of 1778 between the United States and France, and the Convention of 1788. "The United States," said the French minister, "besides having departed from the principles of the armed neutrality during the war for their independence, have given to England, to the detriment of their first allies, the most striking marks of an unbounded condescension." On the other hand the American government replied to these accusations that a constant system of hostility had been kept up on the commerce of our country, under sanction of the decrees of the National Convention. France complained of a breach of treaty stipulations on the part of America, and America complained of depredations on her commerce, committed by France. Neither party perhaps was without some plausible ground of complaint. But while the injuries of France to America were positive, open, and palpable, those of America to France were constructive merely and of a negative character.*

Notwithstanding the haughty conduct of France, and her refusal to receive Mr. Pinckney, President Adams soon after being placed at the head of the government, determined to make another attempt to restore the amicable relations which had existed between that Republic and America, and to make "a fresh attempt at negociation on terms compatible with the rights, duties, interests, and honor of the nation." Mr. Adams desired Jefferson to accept this mission, who declined. Failing in this, it was his intention to appoint Madison, with Hamilton

* A writer in the North American Review for July, 1834, concedes it to be at least a very doubtful question whether we were not actually bound by the treaty to take part with France in her Revolutionary wars, unless we could obtain her consent to our neutrality. Hamilton, and the other advocates of a neutral policy, admitted that the alliance by the treaty of 1778 was a permanent alliance—*dès a présent et pour toujours*—but it was contended that such an alliance could only be construed to apply to a *defensive* war, and that the existing war on the part of France was an *offensive* one. Neither of these positions, however, seems to be strictly correct; certainly not the latter, for if ever there was a defensive war it was that into which the French Republic was forced in 1792. In regard to the former of these positions, it may be said that, if the treaty did create such an obligation, it was released by the positive declaration of the French Government, communicated through its minister Genet on his arrival in this country, who declared that the Republic did not expect the United States to engage with it in actual hostilities. The French minister, Talleyrand, mentions this fact in one of his communications to Pinckney, Marshall and Gerry. "The Republic was hardly constituted," he says, "when a minister was sent to Philadelphia, whose first act was to declare to the United States, that they would not be pressed to execute the defensive clauses of the treaty of Alliances, although the circumstances in the least equivocal manner exhibited the *casus fœderis*."—*See American State Papers.*

as his colleague. But upon merely mentioning the name of Madison to one of his Cabinet, he found, he says, that "it excited a profound gloom and solemn countenance," which after some time broke out in "Mr. President, we are willing to resign."* Fearing that Madison, if nominated, would encounter a veto from the Senate, he abandoned the idea of appointing him, and with him Hamilton also.

Still adhering to his design of appointing some gentleman from the Republican party on this important mission, Mr. Adams, in opposition to the wishes of his Cabinet, but with that spirit of independence and self-reliance which marked all his actions, named Mr. Gerry, who, after some hesitation, consented to accept the appointment, with Gen. Pinckney and Marshall for his colleagues.

It was with great reluctance that Marshall entered upon this important duty. He had a short time before declined the appointment of sole minister to France, having determined to remain for the future entirely in his profession, and he thought, he says, that determination unalterable. His situation at the bar appeared to him more independent and not less honorable than any other, and his preference for it was decided. But public considerations and a high sense of duty finally overcame his scruples and he concluded to accept the appointment.

The history of this mission is one of the most singular that is anywhere recorded in the annals of diplomacy. The envoys met in Paris on the 4th of October, 1797.† It was at a moment peculiarly inauspicious for the success of their mission. The Republic had vanquished its enemies on every side. Spain, Portugal, and Holland had successively yielded. Italy lay prostrate at the feet of the conqueror; and

* See Correspondence of President Adams.

† On their very entry into Paris the envoys were besieged, and obliged to pay the customary tribute. "The morning after my arrival," says Mr. Gerry, "I was waited upon by the *musicians of the Executive*, and the next day by a deputation of *Poissards*, or fishwomen, for presents." These interesting deputations expected fifteen or twenty guineas, which each of the envoys, according to custom, was obliged to give. Mr. Gerry, it seems, negociated with the *Poissards* through the secretary of the legation, Major Rutledge, and thus escaped their kind caresses; but Marshall and Pinckney were not so fortunate:—"When the ladies," adds Mr. Gerry, "get sight of a minister, as they did of my colleagues, they *smother him with their delicate kisses*."

Bonaparte had forced the Emperor of Austria into the celebrated treaty of Campo Formia. The Directory had reached the zenith of its pride and arrogance; and its haughty temper had been already manifested toward America, in such a manner as to leave but slight hopes of a successful and honorable negotiation. The dispatches of the envoys disclose a most revolting picture of the shameless intrigues and corruptions of French diplomacy, under the auspices of the Directory, guided by the subtle genius of that master of the art, Talleyrand. The Americans were informed, not officially, and not even responsibly, that the Directory were exasperated at some part of the President's speech at the opening of Congress, and that they would not probably have a public audience *until their negotiation was finished;* and that, in order to soothe the irritable temper of the Directory, and pave the way to a negotiation, two things were necessary—first to propose a loan by the United States of some millions of dollars for the French treasury, and secondly "in compliance with diplomatic usage" address themselves to the "private gratification of certain high officers of government" by paying, as a sort of corruption fund, the sum of fifty thousand pounds sterling. Without pursuing the intricacies of this semi-official negotiation, if such it may be called, suffice it to say the Americans refused the tribute. The consequence was that they were never officially received; that they remained six months in Paris, not merely unaccredited, but exposed to personal and official mortifications of the most humiliating kind; and were finally obliged to return, without effecting the object of their mission, and even without the common courtesy of an official discussion of it.*

Faithful to their trust, and resolved to leave no means untried to accomplish their object, the envoys remained at their post under all these discouragements and difficulties. On the 17th of January they addressed the government through the Minister for Foreign Affairs in a voluminous and elaborate paper, which contained a full statement and defence of the American policy with regard to France. This masterly communication is found among the published American State Papers.† It needs to be closely and carefully read in order to be fully appreciated. It was draughted by General Marshall, and without doubt

* See Austin's Life of Gerry, for a full and impartial account of this mission.

† State Papers from 1797 to 1801, pp. 219 to 260.

will compare favorably with the ablest diplomatic correspondence in the American archives. The author of the life of Gerry claims for that gentleman the credit of the revision of this admirable State paper, particularly, he says, in regard to its style and manner, and in giving it that "softening and courteous form of address," which everywhere pervades it. However this may be—and the claim is perhaps well founded—one thing is certain, that the style and manner, admirable though these are, may be considered as the least of its merits. In its matter, and the substance of its argument—clear and luminous in its statement, strong in its solid, manly sense, and impregnable in its logic—is found its main title to our admiration. It exhausts the whole subject in controversy; nothing more apparently remains to be said, and at its close one is at a loss to know or conjecture what kind of plausible case can possibly be made out in reply, even by the astute and subtle intellect of a Talleyrand.

To this communication no immediate reply was made. The envoys still remained unrecognized, isolated, cut off from all communication with the government except that arising from the occasional and unofficial visits of Mr. Gerry to Talleyrand, and interviews with certain nameless and mysterious intriguers, who had apparently been commissioned to sound the American Ministers and bring them to terms. On the 19th of February they sent to Talleyrand desiring to know if he had any communication to make in consequence of their letter of the 17th of the previous month. The minister replied that he had no answer to make; the Directory had taken no order on the subject—when they did he would inform the envoys of it. Soon after they again wrote to Talleyrand soliciting a personal interview. He appointed the 2d March, at which time they waited upon him and were received in a private and unofficial capacity. At this interview and another which took place a few days later, the French minister disclosed very clearly the intentions of his government, and gave the envoys to understand in a manner not to be mistaken, that a peace-offering to the wounded feelings of the Directory was necessary in the shape of a loan, as a preliminary to negotiation. To this proposition the envoys unanimously refused to accede. Talleyrand then modified his proposition to the effect that the loan, instead of being immediately advanced, either directly, or by the purchase of Dutch rescriptions which the

Directory then happened to have on hand, should be contracted payable after the war, and in supplies at St. Domingo. On this proposition it is understood a difference of opinion arose among the envoys. Marshall and Pinckney absolutely rejected it, and declined considering the proposal in any form ; Mr. Gerry did not deem it, in this modified form, wholly inadmissible as the basis of a treaty *ad referendum*, reserving to himself the right of a decision on the whole matter when a decision should be eventually necessary.*

This circumstance furnished an occasion to Talleyrand for the employment of one of his characteristic strokes of policy. He attempted to separate the American envoys and to open negotiations with that "one of the three whose opinions, presumed to be more impartial, promise, in the course of the explanations, more of that reciprocal confidence (*plus de cette confiance reciproque*) which is indispensable." This proposition was made in a letter from the French minister under date of March 18th, in which he replies at length to the communication of the American envoys, and with much ingenuity and no little plausibility of argument states the French side of the question.†

It was now evident that all hopes of the successful result of the mission were at an end. Talleyrand's proposition of opening a negotiation with Mr. Gerry alone was of course promptly declined. The envoys, however, deemed it their duty to reply to his communication, which they did on the third of April in a letter drafted by General Marshall, and signed by all three of the envoys.† This calm, temperate and dignified reply fully equals in all respects the original communication of the 17th of January, and fully merits the warm eulogy which it receives at the hands of the biographer of Mr. Gerry. In clear and forcible language, with firmness, frankness, and plainness suited to the character of the United States, it meets, answers, refutes, every topic in succession which was contained in the minister's letter. It denies his accusations, it corrects his misstatements, it overturns his arguments, and presents another splendid instance of the powerful de-

* 2 Austin's Life of Gerry, p. 219. Mr. Austin explains and defends the opinions and conduct of Mr. Gerry on this subject; particularly against the severe and unjust censures of the Secretary of State.

† American State Papers 1797 to 1801, pp. 270 to 278.

‡ American State Papers, from 1797 to 1801, pp. 278 to 304.

fence which integrity, and talents, and learning are capable of making for the injured rights of the country.*

The letter closed with the request that if the Directory should be pleased to order passports for the whole or any of them, such passports would be accompanied with letters of safe conduct, &c. On the same day Mr. Gerry received a note from Talleyrand inviting him to resume their "reciprocal communications," on the supposition, as the minister remarks, "that Messrs. Marshall and Pinckney have thought it useful and proper, in consequence of the intimations given, &c. to quit the territories of the Republic." Thus these two gentlemen received, as President Adams expresses it, their *congé*. Mr. Gerry, though he remained in France after the departure of Marshall and Pinckney, promptly rejected all propositions to proceed to a separate negotiation, maintaining, contrary to the opinion of Talleyrand, that his whole powers ceased with the departure of his colleagues.

So terminated this inglorious, this unfortunate mission. "History," says Marshall, "will scarcely furnish the example of a nation, not absolutely degraded, which has received from a foreign power such open contumely and undisguised insult, as were, on this occasion, suffered by the United States in the persons of their ministers."†

After divers perplexing embarrassments, passports were at length received about the 12th of April, and General Marshall immediately prepared to return to the United States. A difficulty occurred in his obtaining a letter of safe conduct for the vessel in which he proposed to embark, which induced him to express a design, in case it was refused, of returning through England. The same confidential agent of Mons. Talleyrand, with whom Marshall had formerly conversed, said to him on learning this, that it would give great offence to the government of France; and further, that if he should do so, it would be immediately published by the government that he had gone to England to receive the wages he had earned by breaking off the treaty with France! There were men in France, it seems, who could actually be made to believe that Marshall and Pinckney, in refusing to compromise the honor of their country by yielding to the grasping cupidity of the Republic, were the paid stipendiaries of a foreign

* Life of Gerry, Vol. II. p. 225.

† 2 Life of Washington, 427

power! It is not to be supposed that the threat would have deterred the American minister from his design of returning by way of England; but the receipt of his letter of safe conduct soon after removed the necessity of putting any such design into execution; and shaking the dust of Paris from his feet, he embarked from France on the 16th of April, 1798, for his native country.

The high reputation of Marshall suffered no diminution by reason of the inglorious termination of this mission. On the contrary his conduct was everywhere commended and applauded. On the 17th of June, 1798, he arrived at New York, where he was received with the highest marks of respect. His entrance into Philadelphia, two days afterwards, had the eclat of a triumph. Escorted by the military from Frankford to the city, he found himself, on his arrival, surrounded by crowds of citizens anxious to testify their veneration and gratitude. Public addresses were made to him, breathing sentiments of the liveliest affection and respect. A public dinner was given to him by members of both houses of Congress, "as an evidence of affection for his person, and of their grateful approbation of the patriotic firmness with which he sustained the dignity of his country in his important mission," and the country at large responded with one voice to the sentiment pronounced at this celebration; "Millions for defence, but not a cent for tribute."*

It appeared to Marshall that the period had now arrived when he would be able to realize the object of his warmest aspirations, by devoting his time and talents exclusively to the practice of that noble profession to which he was so ardently attached. Solicited to become a candidate for Congress, he promptly declined, and soon found himself again immersed in causes, and surrounded by his old clients. But it seemed his fortune never to be able to escape the demands of public duty. Diligently though he labored to shun them, public employments on every side followed him, sought him out, and pressed themselves upon him.

The circumstances which called Marshall again from his profession, and which separated him from it finally and for ever, are so peculiar and withal so full of interest, that I cannot pass them by in silence. He had been invited by Washington to spend a few days at Mount

* Eulogy by Binney.

Vernon, in company with Bushrod Washington, a nephew of the General. Soon after their arrival the General communicated to his guests the main object of his invitation. It was to urge both of them to enter public life, and become candidates for Congress. The cause of Washington's solicitude upon this occasion is quite apparent. It was, as he believed, a most critical period in the history of the country. The final contest between the Federal and the Republican parties was at hand. His confidence, as I have elsewhere remarked, rested with the former; the latter served only to excite his distrust and awaken his alarm. In the honest sincerity of his heart, he believed it to be a time when good men should come forward and strive to arrest what he regarded as the downward tendency of society and government, whose future filled him with the most gloomy forebodings. There is a sad and touching interest awakened by these last thoughts and actions of this great man, whose mind, full of gloomy apprehensions, was keenly alive to unfounded suspicions of evil; whose vision, darkened by unsubstantial shadows, was unable to penetrate the veil which concealed the brilliant scenes of the future. To him it was not permitted, as to the chosen leader of Israel from Pisgah's top, *to see*, though he might not hope *to enter*, that promised land, destined to be the future inheritance of his people.

These dark apprehensions and forebodings moved Washington to an earnest and pressing effort to induce such men as Marshall and Bushrod Washington to enter the public service for the purpose of attempting to arrest the swelling tide of evil. I have at this moment before me one of his autograph letters, written about the same period—the last year of his life—on the same subject, to Patrick Henry. It is marked in the margin "confidential," and exhibits in every line and letter—in every character of that methodical and somewhat formal, but clear, and bold handwriting, unmistakeable evidence of authenticity.

"It would be a waste of time," he says, "to attempt to bring to the view of a person of your observation and discernment, the endeavors of a certain faction among us, to disquiet the public mind with unfounded alarms; to arraign every act of the administration; to set the people at variance with their government; and to embarrass all its measures. Equally useless would it be to predict what must be the inevitable consequence of such policy if it cannot be arrested." The writer then proceeds to descant upon the gloomy prospects of the country, and to lament the fact that "the most respectable and best qualified characters among us will not come forward" in the public service. "Vain will it be," he continues, "to look for peace and happiness, or for the security of liberty or property, if civil discord should ensue; and what else can result from the policy of those among us, who, by all the means in their power, are driving matters to extremity, if they cannot be counteracted effectually? The views of men can only be known or guessed at by their words or actions. Can those of the *leaders* of opposition be mistaken then if judged by this rule? That they are followed by numbers who are unacquainted with their designs, and suspect as little the tendency of their principles, I am fully persuaded. But if their conduct is viewed with indifference—if there is activity and misrepresentation on one side, and supineness on the other, their numbers accumulated by intriguing and discontented foreigners, under proscription, who were at war with their own government, and the greater part of them with all governments, their numbers will increase, and nothing short of Omniscience can foretell the consequences."*

These serious arguments were now urged upon Marshall and Bushrod Washington. The conference, we are told, was earnest, and full of mutual confidence. The latter gentleman readily yielded to the persuasions of his uncle, but the former hesitated, on the ground of his situation and the necessity of attending to his private affairs. Washington combatted these views, and insisted upon the higher duty of every good citizen to sacrifice his inclinations and interests, and if needs be, to sacrifice himself also on the altar of his country's welfare. To these persuasions Marshall finally yielded—who could resist such an appeal?—and consented to become a candidate for Congress. After a sharp contest he was elected, and took his seat in that body in December, 1799. In the meantime President Adams tendered him a place on the bench of the Supreme Court, vacant by the death of Judge Iredell, which he promptly declined.

* Mr. Henry responded to this earnest appeal, by offering himself as a candidate for the State Legislature, to which he was elected. The letter from which the above extract is taken, is published among Sparks' Collection of the Writings of Washington.

The elections had been eminently favorable to the Federalists. They had a clear majority of twenty in the House of Representatives; still they were not able to carry any strong measure during the session, for the reason, perhaps, alleged by Jefferson, namely, that "many of them were new and moderate men, and soon saw the true character of the party to which they had been well disposed, at a distance."* Of these "new and moderate" men, Marshall was confessedly the leader. It is quite clear, that though politically classed as Federalists, they were not, in the language of the present day, regarded as "reliable," by the partisans of the cabinet and the advocates of strong measures. This will appear by the following passage from a letter of Wolcott, written about the time the session commenced. To the Connecticut secretary, it seems, the mind of the great Virginia lawyer was not cast in a mould large enough, and comprehensive enough to enable him to grasp the full merits of the Hamiltonian policy.

"A number of distinguished men," he says, "appear from the southward, who are not pledged by any act to support the system of the last Congress; these men will pay great respect to the opinions of General Marshall; he is, doubtless, a man of virtue and distinguished talents, but he will think much of the State of Virginia, and is too much disposed to govern the world *according to rules of logic;* he will read and expound the Constitution, *as if it were a penal statute,* and will sometimes *be embarrassed with doubts, of which his friends will not perceive the importance.*"†

These apprehensions of the Secretary were realised during the session.‡ It has been truly said of Marshall, that his course in Congress

* Jefferson's Writings, Vol. III., p. 436.

† Oliver Wolcott to Fisher Ames. Dec. 29th, 1799.

‡ Mr. Adams' discarded Secretary of War, McHenry, some months later, when Marshall had become Secretary of State, even doubted his fidelity to Federal principles. In a letter to Wolcott, under date of November 9th, 1800, he says:—"I have been told Mr. Marshall has signified that he does not mean to resign in the event of Mr. Jefferson being elected President, but to wait most patiently the development of his politics. Will there, my friend, be so great an antipathy between the politics of these two gentlemen, that one of them must fly off from the other?" Wolcott hastens to re-assure his friend on the point:—"The opposition of sentiment" between Jefferson and Marshall, he says, *appears* to be decided, and he believes to be unchangeable.—2 *Gibbs' Wolcott,* 445, 448.

Upon this point, however, Marshall is himself the best authority. "No politi-

was governed solely by his own convictions of right; that if he was a party man he was so by position, and not from temper or partial views; and that he drew from his own convictions even that which went to sustain the efforts and to augment the resources of his party. Nor was he incapable, when the dictates of his own independent judgment required it, to throw off party trammels, and stand aside from party associations. Thus upon a resolution to repeal the obnoxious section of the *Sedition Law*, passed at the previous session, his name is found recorded in the affirmative, while the names of all those with whom he generally acted are on the other side.

Marshall was placed at the head of the committee appointed to prepare an answer to the President's speech; and he participated, influentially, in all the more important discussions and measures of Congress during the session. These measures are a part of the general history of the times which it would be improper in this place to review. One of them, however, is too notable, and too intimately connected with the fame of the Chief-Justice, to be passed over in silence. I allude to the famous debate upon the resolutions of Edward Living-

cal considerations," he says, in a private letter to Hamilton, written soon after this time, and while the presidential contest was pending, and the hard option was thrown on the Federalists to choose between Jefferson or Burr: "No political considerations could induce me to be the Secretary of State while there was a President, whose political system I believed to be at variance with my own." His prejudices against Jefferson were so deeply rooted and inveterate, that he even preferred Burr, until convinced by the persevering and passionate appeals of Hamilton to the contrary. Still, he said, he could not aid Mr. Jefferson lest it might be suspected that a desire to be well with the successful candidate, had in some degree governed his conduct. He regarded him as a man who would "embody himself with the House of Representatives." "By weakening the office of President," he goes on to remark, "he will increase his personal power. He will diminish his responsibility, sap the fundamental principles of the Government, and become the leader of that party which is about to constitute the majority in the Legislature. The morals of the author of the letter to Mazzei cannot be pure."—*Letter to Hamilton.* 6 *Hamilton's Works*, 502.

These early prejudices were increased by subsequent differences and conflicts of opinion, until they resulted, after Burr's trial, in a final cessation of all personal intercourse between these two gentlemen; a course of conduct in which, as I am informed by a venerable gentleman now living, and then at the bar,* the example of Marshall was followed by two or three of his brethren on the bench.

* General Walter Jones.

ston censuring the President for his conduct relative to the extradition of Thomas Nash, otherwise called Jonathan Robbins. Nash was accused of piracy and murder on board a British national vessel at sea, and though claiming to be an American citizen, was, on proof of the offence satisfactory to the Court, surrendered to the British authorities by the District Court of South Carolina, at the desire and request of the President, and was subsequently executed. Livingston's resolutions, which were introduced on the 21st of February, declared the case to be one exclusively of judicial inquiry, and that the decision by the President of the question whether the *casus fœderis* had arisen, and his directions to Judge Bee, were " a dangerous interference of the executive with judicial decisions," and that the compliance of the Judge was " a sacrifice of the constitutional independence of the judicial power and exposes the administration thereof to suspicion and reproach."

These strong resolutions of censure, arousing, as may well be supposed, the warmest party and political feelings, excited one of the most animated and powerful debates which ever arose in the halls of the American Congress. The whole talent of the house—and it was a house distinguished even among the early American Congresses for its splendid ability, genius, eloquence, statesmanship—was drawn out in this magnificent debate. On one side stood Edward Livingston, Gallatin, Macon, Nicholas ; on the other, Otis, Bayard, Harper, Dana, Lee, Rutledge, and last, and greatest of all in the massive strength of his intellect, and the irresistible power of his faculties, John Marshall, of Virginia.

On the 6th of March Gen. Marshall took the floor, and in reply to Livingston and others delivered that elaborate and triumphant argument which, in the language of Judge Story, settled then and for ever the points of national law upon which the controversy hinged.* It was, says the same high authority, one of the most consummate juridical arguments which was ever pronounced in the halls of legislation ; and, like Lord Mansfield's answer to the Prussian Memorial, it was *reponse sans replique*,—an answer so irresistible that

* This celebrated speech was written out by Marshall, and published in full. It may be found in a note to Bee's Reports, 266 ; also in Appendix to the fifth volume of Wheaton's Reports, and in Wharton's State Trials, p. 443.

it admitted of no reply.* A careful perusal of this celebrated speech will satisfy the professional reader that this warm eulogy is not exaggerated, especially if we regard the speech in the light of a great legal and constitutional argument. The lucid order of its topics, the profoundness of its logic, the extent of its research, and the force of its illustration, are indeed unsurpassed, nay, unrivalled. But it is as a constitutional and legal argument alone that it is calculated to strike the attention of the reader. It has no pretensions to eloquence or the graces of rhetoric—there are no striking antitheses to be found in it, no bold figures, no rich flow of diction, no copious fullness of expression, no play of the fancy, no warm gush of the imagination and the feelings. All is an effort of pure ratiocination—of calm, intellectual strength—clear, cold, transparent as the limpid ice beneath which glide swiftly and silently the deep and unfathomable waters of the stream. In the simplicity, and order, and strength of its argument, it is not unlike some of those judicial opinions which its author subsequently pronounced from the bench; indeed, it appears to be precisely such an argument as the Chief-Justice ten years later would have written out after the topic had been thoroughly discussed before him and illustrated by a full display of forensic learning and eloquence. According to the tradition of the time, it is said, that a celebrated statesman, then in Congress, being requested to answer this speech, excused himself on the ground that he deemed it unanswerable.† It appears from the report of the debate that Mr. Nicholas, of Virginia, was somewhat bolder, for he certainly did reply to Marshall, as the record shows. The question was then taken, and the resolutions lost by a majority of twenty-six; some of the opposition members voting against them.

This effort of Marshall is perhaps the best specimen that remains of his style and manner both of forensic and legislative speaking. From it we may infer that he never was what may be called a great orator. The matter rather than the manner, the substance, and not the graces of oratory was the thing which he mainly cultivated. He

* Even Jefferson, so sparing in praise to political opponents, admits the success of Marshall's effort. In a letter to Madison he says: "Livingston, Nicholas, and Gallatin distinguished themselves on one side, and Marshall greatly on the other."—*Jefferson's Correspondence*, Vol. III. p. 434.

† 26 Vol. North American Review, p. 31.

had much of the severe and unadorned simplicity of style which characterizes the speeches of Calhoun, with very little of the copious and Ciceronian flow of Clay, and none of that intense power of language, that gorgeousness of expression in which Webster was sometimes accustomed to clothe a great thought, throwing it out in one of those magnificent sentences, which, once heard, haunt the mind for years. Of his manner of elocution, and his powers as a public speaker, Judge Story says: "In regard to eloquence, if by that be merely meant an ornamental diction, splendor of style, impassioned delivery, and fine flourishes of rhetoric, it could scarcely be said to belong to his forensic addresses. * * * * * But if by eloquence be meant the power to address other men's minds in language expressive and luminous; to present the proper topics of argument in their just order and fullness; to convince the understanding by earnest and sententious appeals; and, by the force of reasoning, to disarm prejudices, to subdue passions, and to dissipate popular delusions; if these be the attributes of eloquence, then, indeed, few men might more justly aspire to such a distinction. I would not claim for him that he possessed the power to seduce men's understandings by persuasive insinuations or honied accents; but I affirm that he withdrew their understandings from the potency of such artifices, so that they fell lifeless at his feet; *telumque imbelle sine ictu*. To him may unhesitatingly be applied the language of Cicero pronounced upon one of the greatest lawyers of Rome, that he possessed a mastery of the highest art of oratory; the art of analyzing, defining, and illustrating a subject; separating the true from the false; and deducing from each other the appropriate consequences." Judge Story, though he had never heard Marshall at the bar, adds that there were times in his private conversation and conferences, "in which he has been roused by the interest of the subject to such a glowing strain of animated reasoning, that I am convinced that he was no stranger to appeals to the heart; and that when he chose he could call up from the very depths of the soul its most powerful feelings."

Congress adjourned on the 14th day of May, bringing to a close Marshall's first and only term of service in the National Legislature. Other and still more responsible duties now sought him out and demanded his attention. As a friend to the administration, he was called upon to give it the most signal proofs of his confidence. The breach between President Adams and his "disjointed cabinet," as it was called in the newspapers of the day, had become irreconcilable,* and immediately on the adjournment of Congress the explosion came. McHenry, the Secretary of War, was the first to retire. His place was immediately filled by the appointment of Marshall. This appointment was entirely unexpected; the first intimation received of it being at the Secretary's office, where he happened on a matter of business preparatory to returning to Virginia. He immediately wrote to Mr. Adams requesting him to withdraw the nomination; but before any action was taken the President's rupture with Col. Pickering resulted in the dismissal of that gentleman, and Marshall was appointed Secretary of State, Mr. Dexter being placed at the head of the War department.

Wolcott asserts that these removals and appointments were made by Mr. Adams in a moment of passion; that the Secretaries were dismissed without any previous designation of their successors; and that it was for a long time uncertain how the vacancies would be filled. He was of the opinion that Marshall, having declined the office of Secretary of War, would decline also that of Secretary of State, but in this he proved to be mistaken. As a consistent friend of the administration, particularly in its foreign policy, which the "British faction," as Mr. Adams termed it, so warmly condemned, he did not feel at liberty to decline the appointment, and there is no evidence that he did not accept it cheerfully and readily. As to the dismissal of the Secretaries, whether done in a moment of passion or not, it can scarcely be denied that the step was both justifiable and necessary. No President, least of all one made of such stern stuff as John Adams, could be expected to keep in his Cabinet, as his confidential advisers,

* Secretary Wolcott, in a letter written at the commencement of the last session, says with much bitterness: "The President's mind is in a state which renders it difficult to determine what prudence and duty require from those about him. He considers Col. Pickering, Mr. McHenry and myself as his enemies; his resentments against Gen. Hamilton are excessive; he declares his belief of the existence of a British faction in the United States."

The reader is referred to what was said *ante*, page 274, in regard to the origin of this misunderstanding between the President and his Cabinet.

gentlemen whom he knew to be personally hostile to his administration. Whatever, therefore, might be the grumblings of the discarded Secretaries, this step of the President cannot but be regarded as judicious and wise. Wolcott thought, too, that General Marshall would "find himself out of his proper element" in his new office.* In this, too, he proved to be mistaken. No man was more familiar with, and thoroughly master of, the whole question of our foreign relations; and these he managed during the year of his administration of the State department, with signal ability and success. His conduct in this respect gave the most entire satisfaction, not to the President only, but to the whole American people. Mr. Adams, in his celebrated Cunningham letters, though so far carried away by his private feelings as to hint the personal incompetency of Col. Pickering, pays a deserved tribute to General Marshall. "Suppose I should tell you," he says, "that the studies of his (Pickering's) early youth, and of his riper years, had not been competent to the profound investigations which his office required. We had discussions of great importance with France, England, and Spain, especially the two former, involving questions respecting neutral rights, respecting British and tory claims, of ante-revolutionary debts. I could get nothing done as I would have it. My new minister, Marshall, did all to my entire satisfaction." The biographer of Wolcott explains this in a manner far from complimentary to Mr. Adams. With regard to Marshall's doing every thing to the President's satisfaction, he remarks with no little asperity—"Every one who knew that great man, (Marshall,) knew that he possessed, to an extraordinary degree, the faculty of putting his own ideas into the minds of others, unconsciously to them. The secret of Mr. Adams' satisfaction was, that he obeyed his Secretary of State without being conscious of it."† But this we are led to believe is also a calumny.

I shall not dwell upon the party discussions and the political history of this period, which, however interesting in itself, will shed no new light on the character of Chief-Justice Marshall. It is sufficient to say that he continued his laborious and useful services as the head of the State department, down to the close of Mr. Adams' administra-

* Letter to Fisher Ames, August 10th, 1800. 2 Gibb's Wolcott, 402.

† 2 Gibbs' Wolcott, 349, 350.

tion, on the 4th of March, 1801, although in the mean time appointed to that high judicial station which he so long adorned. It may also be mentioned, as a fact highly honorable to the character of Marshall, and as exhibiting alike the elevation of his mind and the moderation of his sentiments, that though warmly attached to President Adams, and though the circumstances of his appointment successively to the War and State departments were calculated to excite unpleasant feelings between him and his predecessors, yet in fact they did not awaken the least degree of political rivalry or personal resentment. On the contrary, he soon found himself upon the most friendly and cordial terms with his predecessors, and in the enjoyment of the unlimited confidence of the public.*

Upon the resignation of Chief-Justice Ellsworth, much anxiety was manifested respecting his successor. It was supposed by many that Judge Paterson, then one of the Associate-Justices of the Supreme Court, would be appointed, by others the name of General Pinckney was mentioned. Marshall himself, on being consulted by the President, unhesitatingly recommended Judge Paterson. But Mr. Adams objected to this nomination, assigning as a reason that he could not make it without wounding the feelings of Judge Cushing, who was an old friend and the senior Judge on the bench.† Thereupon he appointed Mr. Jay, who declined. As soon as this fact was known the President promptly sent in the name of Marshall to the Senate, who was unanimously confirmed, and on the 31st January, 1801, commissioned as Chief-Justice of the United States. The appointment was not made, it appears, without some cavilling from those peculiar friends of the President, who manifested so great a proclivity to censure every act of his administration. The Ex-Secretary of War, McHenry, writes with much asperity to Wolcott: "Mr. Adams, it strikes me, has committed another blunder, but, it is true, one not alto-

* "I have often listened," says Judge Story, "to the spontaneous praise bestowed on Mr. Marshall by Col. Pickering, in his own peculiar circle of friends, with unmixed delight. It was full, glowing and affecting. It was a tribute from one of such sincerity of thought and purpose, that praise, even when best deserved, came from his lips with a studied caution of language. His conversation, always instructive, on these occasions rose into eloquence, beautiful, nay touching, with a moral sublimity."

† 26 Vol. North American Review, 32.

gether so rare. I mean in rewarding *dear* friends, and in neglecting *old* ones. Here it was expected by every body that he would have named Mr. Paterson to the vacant seat on the bench, except by Mr. ———, who thought that he should have been appointed, and by me, who thought *the President should have appointed himself.*" * The "blunder" of Mr. Adams proved to be a most fortunate one for the country. Indeed, reflecting men of all parties since that day have been inclined to regard this "blunder" as an act of rare sagacity and intuitive discernment of character. He would be a bold man who should now assert that from among all the able and eminent men who then sustained the administration, or belonged to either wing of the Federal party, (and none other could of course have expected the appointment,) the President might have made a wiser and more judicious selection, or one which would have shed greater lustre upon the judicial history of the country. It was something of this feeling, which after the experience of more than a quarter of a century had demonstrated the wisdom of the choice, prompted the words of President John Q. Adams, who on enclosing a judicial commission to a gentleman of exalted professional reputation, happily alludes to the appointment by his father of Chief-Justice Marshall: "If neither of us," he remarks, "had ever done any thing else to deserve the approbation of our country, and of posterity, I would proudly claim it of both, for these acts, for my father and myself." †

Chief-Justice Marshall took his seat on the bench of the Supreme Court at the February term, 1801. His associates were William Cushing, of Massachusetts, the only remaining member of the Court originally appointed by Washington; William Paterson, of New Jersey, a lawyer of learning and ability, and a statesman of large experience; Samuel Chase, of Maryland, undoubtedly the most vigorous and original intellect next to that of Marshall on the bench; Bushrod Washington, of Virginia, trained in the same school with the Chief-Justice, and bringing with him from the bar of his native State a reputation as well earned as it was afterwards nobly sustained; and Alfred Moore, of North Carolina,‡ then recently appointed to fill the vacancy occasioned by the death of the lamented Iredell.

* 2 Gibbs' Wolcott, 464. † Judge Story's Sketch of Marshall.

‡ Very little appears to be known of this gentleman. He was appointed by

Such was the Supreme Court of the United States at the time Marshall began to preside in it in the winter of 1801. Its sessions were then, for the first, held at the new city of Washington, to which the seat of government had been removed the previous summer. Most of the old members of the bar who figured prominently as advocates at the organization of the Court were still in active practice. The younger race of lawyers, who a few years later composed that brilliant galaxy which centered around the bar of the Supreme Court, such as Pinkney, Wirt, Jones, Hopkinson, Emmett, Webster, and Clay, had not yet entered upon this splendid forum of intellectual effort. Their senior brethren—the veterans of the bar—the men who thronged the precincts of the Court in Jay's and Rutledge's time—Tilghman, Dexter, Lewis, Rawle, Dallas, Martin, Duponceau, Ingersoll—few of whom had yet begun to lag " superfluous on the stage," were the counsel mostly engaged in the earlier causes argued before Chief-Justice Marshall.

Before Marshall came to the bench it had been made a question whether the Judges could be lawfully required, under their commissions, to hold the Circuit Court. The question was disposed of for the time by the new bill for " the more convenient organization of the Courts of the United States," passed among the last acts of President Adams' administration.* This bill relieved the Judges from Circuit duty entirely, and confined them to attendance at the sessions of the Supreme Court, two of which were required to be held annually at the seat of government. The bill had been in operation but little more than a year when it was repealed, under Mr. Jefferson's administration, and the old circuit system restored.† The repeal of the act having assumed a political aspect, an animated and powerful debate sprung up in the House of Representatives, in which the opponents of the repeal maintained with persevering boldness and vigor that by the Constitution Congress could not require the Judges of the Supreme

President Adams toward the close of the year 1799, though the records of the State department do not show the date of his commission. One or two of his opinions are to be found in the reports. He remained but a few years on the bench, and resigning, was succeeded, March 26, 1804, by William Johnson, of South Carolina.

* Act of February, 13th, 1801.

† Act of April 29th, 1802.

Court to sit at the Circuit. This, also, was Marshall's opinion. On the passage of the act of repeal, however, instead of disregarding the act entirely, he adopted a course which, while it perfectly vindicates the independence of his character, exhibits at the same time the extreme caution of his temper. He wrote, it is said,* a circular letter to all the other Judges of the Supreme Court, stating that upon a full examination of the subject, he had come to the conclusion that the Judges of the Supreme Court could not constitutionally be required to hold any other sessions than those of the Supreme Court, or perform any other judicial duty; and he accordingly stated to his brethren, that if they concurred in this opinion, he would decline to sit in the Circuit Court and risk the consequences. The answer returned by his brethren was that they agreed with him in opinion; but considering the question had been settled to the contrary by the acquiescence of the Judges in going the Circuit prior to 1801 they advised that it should not now be disturbed, but should be considered for all practical purposes as finally put to rest. The Chief-Justice thereupon proceeded to hold the Circuit Court for the Virginia district. The question of jurisdiction, and his right to sit as Circuit Judge without a separate commission for that purpose, was raised, and decided by him in the manner indicated by his associates. The case came up for review to the Supreme Court, and the decision, in which Marshall declined taking part, was affirmed; on the sole ground, as stated by Mr. Justice Paterson who delivered the opinion of the Court, that practice and acquiescence, for a period of several years, commencing with the organization of the judicial system, had fixed the construction, and that this cotemporary and practical exposition was too strong to be shaken or controlled.†

I have elsewhere alluded to the immense mass of labors performed by the Chief-Justice, during his service on the bench of the Supreme Court—extending through a continuous period of nearly thirty-five years—and to the number, extent and variety of his decisions. These decisions will be found mostly collected in the nine volumes of Cranch's Reports of the Supreme Court, the twelve volumes of Wheaton, and the first nine volumes of Peters; and his decisions at Circuit in the

* 3 New York Review, 347.

† Stuart *vs.* Laird, 1 Cranch Reports, 299.

two volumes of Brockenbrough. From this mass of material it is of course impossible to do more than call the reader's attention to a few selections of the most important and prominent cases—such as cases of prize and admiralty, cases turning upon questions of great public or national interest, and, above all, those involving principles of constitutional law. In regard to the latter class of cases especially it may with truth be said that the labors of Chief-Justice Marshall have raised an enduring, an imperishable monument to his fame. No jurist, living or dead, can point to a nobler or a prouder record ; and the remark of that one of his associates who knew him most intimately, and who so justly appreciated the value of his friendship,* is nothing but the language of sober truth,—that if all others of his juridical arguments had perished, his luminous judgments, on these occasions, would have given an enviable immortality to his name. From the same excellent authority, we gain something of an idea of the absolute superiority, and the controlling power of Marshall's mind in all these deliberations and decisions upon questions of Constitutional law. "Though we would not be unjust," he says, "to those learned gentlemen who have from time to time been his associates on the bench, we are quite sure, that they would be ready to admit, what the public universally believed, that his master mind has presided in their deliberations, and given to the results a cogency of reasoning, a depth of remark, a persuasiveness of argument, a clearness and elaboration of illustration, and an elevation and comprehensiveness of conclusion, to which none others offer a parallel. Few decisions upon constitutional questions have been made, in which he has not delivered the opinion of the Court ; and in these few, the duty devolved upon others to their own regret, either because he did not sit in the cause, or, from motives of delicacy, abstained from taking an active part." †

One of the most important of these cases of constitutional construction, as it is the earliest in point of time, is the case of Marbury *vs.* Madison,‡ argued and decided at the term of the Court held in February, 1803. In pronouncing the opinion of the Court in this some-

* "There is no one on earth," says Story, in a letter to Miss Martineau, "whose friendship I value more than his ; there is no one whose praise is to me so touching and so dear."

† 26 North American Review, 36.

‡ 1 Cranch Reports, 137.

what noted case, the Chief-Justice clearly and distinctly lays down, and sustains by a chain of irresistible logic, what has ever since been regarded as the fundamental principle, the very sheet anchor of the Constitution, namely, that it is the right and the duty of the judicial department to determine the constitutionality of a legislative act, and if such act be found repugnant to the provisions of the Constitution, to declare it null and void.

This may be considered as the first authoritative exposition of the Court on this subject. The principle had, indeed, been asserted at an earlier period by Judge Paterson at the Pennsylvania Circuit in the case of Horne's Lessees *vs.* Dorrance ;* but it does not appear to have been considered by the professional mind as settled. In the subsequent case of Calder *et ux. vs.* Bull,† it was incidentally drawn into the discussion, and while Judge Iredell intimated the opinion that if an act of Congress, or of the Legislature of a State violated a provision of the Federal Constitution, such act was unquestionably void, and the Court, in a very clear case, had authority so to declare it ; yet, on the other hand, Judge Chase avoided expressing his views on the subject, remarking : "Without giving an opinion, at this time, whether the Court has jurisdiction to decide that any law made by Congress is void, I am fully satisfied that this Court has no jurisdiction to determine that any law of any State Legislature contrary to the Constitution of such State is void."‡

* 2 Dallas Reports, 304.

† 3 Dallas Reports, 386.

‡ This early view of Judge Chase, that the Supreme Court cannot declare a State law void as being repugnant to a State Constitution is sustained by subsequent decisions. "The Court," says Judge Baldwin, delivering the judgment in Jackson *vs.* Lamphire, 3 Peters, 280, "has no authority on a writ of error to a State Court to declare a State law void on account of its collision with a State Constitution, it not being a case embraced within the judiciary act which alone gives power to issue a writ of error to a State Court." A similar opinion is expressed, as the judgment of the Court, by Mr. Justice Washington in Satterlee *vs.* Matthewson, 2 Peters, 413; though, at the same time, he does not deny that a Circuit Court of the United States, sitting to administer the laws of a State, may give to the Constitution of that State a paramount authority over a legislative act passed in violation of it. But this, it seems, is only in case the State tribunals have not themselves passed upon the constitutionality of the law. When they have done so, a rule of decision is furnished to which the Federal tribunals will

The same judge in a subsequent case * had gone so far as to intimate that "the general principles contained in the Constitution are not to be regarded as rules to fetter and control; but as matter merely *declaratory and directory;*" and in the same opinion he adds, that even though it might be alleged that "all acts of the Legislature in direct opposition to the provisions of the Constitution would be void; yet it still remains a question *where the power resides to declare them void.*"

This grave question, lying at the very root of the power and independence of the Federal judiciary, met the Chief-Justice in the case of Marbury *vs.* Madison, and its consideration forms no inconsiderable portion of one of his earliest constitutional decisions. A more momentous question never engaged the attention of that, or any other, tribunal; and its final decision was such as to satisfy the bench, the bar, and the country, and to put the question at rest then and for ever. A brief notice of the case is all that will be given, leaving the professional reader to consult it more fully in the report.

Just before Mr. Adams retired from office he appointed some Federal justices of the peace for Alexandria, in the District of Columbia. The commissions had been signed and sealed, but not *delivered.* Jefferson succeeding to the presidency, found these commissions on the table of the department of state and forbade their delivery. Marbury, named in one of these commissions, applied to the Supreme Court by his counsel, Mr. Lee, of Virginia, for a *mandamus* to the Secretary of State (Mr. Madison) to deliver the commission intended for him.

In the opinion of the Chief-Justice in this interesting case, he discusses in their order the following propositions, and arrives at these conclusions:—

adhere. Though the Supreme Court had repeatedly declared that it would conform to the construction of the statutes of a State made by its own tribunals; yet in the case of Bank of Hamilton *vs.* Dudley's Lessees, 2 Peters, 492, a distinction was attempted to be made by counsel, between the exclusive power of the State Courts to construe legislative acts, and the power to construe the State Constitution by giving effect to an unconstitutional law. But the Chief-Justice refused to recognize such distinction. "The judicial department of every government," he remarks, "is the rightful expositor of its laws; and emphatically of its supreme law."

* Cooper *vs.* Telfair, February Term, 1800. 4 Dallas Reports, 14.

1st. That the applicant has *a right* to the commission he demands.

2d. That this right having been violated, the laws of his country afford him a remedy.

3d. That the case in its nature is one for a mandamus.

4th. But, that being an original process, the Supreme Court has no jurisdiction to issue it, and the act of Congress conferring such jurisdiction, not being authorized by the Constitution, is null and void.*

The application was accordingly denied.

It will be observed that the really important part of the decision is in regard to the constitutionality of the act of Congress and the power of the Court over it. It in reality involved the momentous question whether the Constitution was to be regarded as an absolute limit to

* Mr. Jefferson complained with some degree of asperity of the decision by the Chief-Justice of the first three points above mentioned.

The cause of his complaint seems to have been, that the Chief-Justice really began at the wrong end of the argument. He held that it would have been sufficient to determine the question of jurisdiction alone, without travelling out of the case to determine what the law would have been, if the court *had* jurisdiction. Many years afterwards Mr. Jefferson alludes to this "very irregular and very censurable practice," as he terms it, in a letter to Judge Johnson touching this very case :—"The court determined at once," he says, "that, being an original process, they had no cognizance of it; and there the question before them was ended. But the Chief-Justice went on to lay down what the law *would be* had they jurisdiction of the case; to wit, that they should command the delivery. The object was clearly to instruct any other court having jurisdiction what they should do if Marbury should apply to them. Besides the impropriety of this gratuitous inference, could anything exceed the perversion of the law ?"—See *Jefferson's Correspondence*, Vol. III. p. 372.

I do not regard these inferences of Mr. Jefferson as entirely just toward Marshall, though there may be great reason to doubt the correctness of the decision on these points. Jefferson's argument, and if not sound and conclusive, it is certainly plausible, was, that the commissions being in the executive offices, were deemed to be in the hands of the President, and like a deed were valid and operative only on delivery. The decision of the court on these points he considered "an *obiter* dissertation of the Chief-Justice," and as such, he intimates, that he does not regard it as furnishing a rule to govern his official conduct. The reason of Mr. Jefferson's refusing to deliver these commissions, or sanctioning what he calls Mr. Adams' "midnight appointments," may be drawn from the following hint, contained in a letter to Gerry: "Mr. Adams' last appointments, when he knew he was naming counsellors and aids for me and not for himself, I set aside as far as depends on me."—3 *Jefferson's Correspondence*, 434.

legislative power; or whether it was, as Judge Chase had pronounced it, "declaratory and directory" merely, and, as in England, at the mercy of the legislature;—whether, in short, the judiciary or the legislature were to be the interpreters of the Constitution.* "The powers of the Legislature," says the Chief-Justice, "are defined and limited. To what purpose are powers limited, and to what purpose is that limitation committed to writing, if these limits may at any time be passed by those intended to be restrained? The distinction between a government of limited and unlimited powers is abolished, if these limits do not confine the persons on whom they are imposed. It is a proposition too plain to be contested, that the Constitution controls any legis lative act repugnant to it, or, that the Legislature may alter the Constitution by an ordinary act. Between these alternatives there is no middle ground. The Constitution is either a superior, paramount law, unchangeable by ordinary means, or it is on a level with ordinary legislative acts, and like other acts, is alterable when the Legislature shall please to alter it.

"If the former part of the alternative be true, then a legislative act contrary to the Constitution *is not law:* if the latter part be true, then written constitutions are absurd attempts, on the part of the people, to limit a power in its own nature illimitable.

"Certainly all those who have framed written constitutions contemplate them as forming the fundamental and permanent law of the nation, and, consequently, the theory of every such government must be, that an act of the Legislature repugnant to the Constitution is void.

"This theory is essentially attached to a written constitution, and is consequently to be considered by this court as one of the fundamental principles of our society. It is not, therefore, to be lost sight of in the further consideration of this subject."

This proposition established, the conclusion inevitably and irresistibly follows:

"It is emphatically the province and duty of the judicial depart-

* It involved, perhaps, to some extent the further question presented by Mr. Calhoun in his celebrated nullification resolutions of 1833, namely, whether the general government is "the final judge of the powers delegated to it," or, whether, in the language of these resolutions, "as in all other cases of compact among sovereign parties, *without any common judge*, each has an equal right to judge for itself, as well of the infraction as of the mode and measure of redress."

ment to say what the law is. Those who apply the rule to particular cases must of necessity expound and interpret that rule. If two laws conflict with each other, the court must decide on the operation of each. So if a law be in opposition to the Constitution," &c., &c.

These conclusions have never been shaken, or even doubted, since that day. On the contrary, they have been affirmed and reiterated, and the power of the court extended further; it being held to embrace a jurisdiction, not merely to declare an act of the national legislature void, but also to review, on appeal from the highest court of law or equity of a State, and declare void any statute of such State on the ground of its being repugnant to the Constitution, treaties, or laws of the United States, where the decision of the State court has been in favor of the validity of such statute.*

It is interesting to notice the fact that in the case of Marbury *vs.* Madison—among the earliest of his constitutional decisions—the Chief Justice adheres to a strict construction. Indeed, he might be said, in regard to that particular case, to justify, to some degree at least, the suspicions of the more ardent Federalists as expressed by Wolcott, that he would "construe the Constitution like a penal statute;" that is to say, that he would not hesitate to declare even an act of Congress void unless he read the clear warrant for it in the very letter of the Constitution—a strictness, however, which, it must be confessed, he did not on all occasions so rigidly adhere to.

The general views of Marshall in the exposition of Constitutional law were again expressed in the case of the United States *vs.* Fisher, argued at the February term of the Supreme Court, in 1805.† A

* See the elaborate opinion of Mr. Justice Story in Martin, heir-at-law of Fairfax *vs.* Hunter's Lessees, 1 Wheaton, 304, 323, 352. The Virginia Court of Appeals in that case had refused obedience to the mandate of the Supreme Court of the United States, which reversed the judgment of the State Court, alleging that so much of the act of Congress as gave the Supreme Court appellate jurisdiction over a State tribunal was not warranted by the Constitution.

The constitutional authority of the Supreme Court over the State tribunals was again largely discussed, and reaffirmed by Chief-Justice Marshall in the case of Cohens *vs.* Virginia, 6 Wheaton, 264, which will be hereafter noticed. That case decided that this appellate jurisdiction extended to a suit where a state was a party. And see note, *ante*, page 353, as to the power of the court to declare an act of a State Legislature void, as being repugnant to a State Constitution.

† 2 Cranch Reports, 358.

question had arisen whether the act of Congress giving a preference to the United States over the general creditors of a bankrupt was warranted by the Constitution. In the consideration of this question the Chief-Justice remarks: "That as the court can never be unmindful of the solemn duty imposed on the judicial department when a claim is supported by an act which conflicts with the Constitution, so the court can never be unmindful of its duty to obey laws which are authorized by that instrument. In the case at bar, the preference claimed by the United States *is not prohibited;* but it has been truly said that under a constitution conferring specific powers, the power contended for *must be granted, or it cannot be exercised.*" The Chief-Justice then considers the grant of power, and deduces it from that clause in the Constitution which confers on Congress authority to make all laws which shall be necessary and proper to carry into execution the powers vested by the Constitution in the government of the United States. "The government," he remarks, "is to pay the debt of the Union, and must be authorized to use the means which appear to itself most eligible to effect that object." We shall hereafter have occasion to notice one or two very important decisions affirming the constitutionality of acts, the warrant for which was to be found only in a still more liberal construction of this section.

The case of the United States *vs.* Judge Peters,* at the session of the Court in 1809, afforded the Chief-Justice the opportunity of expressing his views in regard to the independence of the Federal tribunals, of all State legislation. The doctrine which he laid down in that case was that the Legislature of a State could not annul the judgment, or determine the jurisdiction of the courts of the United States, or destroy rights acquired under those judgments. "If it were otherwise," he remarks, "the Constitution itself becomes a solemn mockery; and the nation is deprived of the means of enforcing its laws, by the instrumentality of its own tribunals." The supremacy of the Federal Judiciary over the State tribunals in cases of constitutional construction, and its independence of State legislation, were fixed and prominent ideas in the mind of Marshall, and were always regarded by him as fundamental parts of the Federal system.†

* 5 Cranch's Reports, 115.

† It was afterwards adjudged in McKim *vs.* Voorhies, 7 Cranch, 279, that a

No clause of the Constitution more deeply affects the legislative authority of the states, than that which prohibits a State from passing any law impairing the obligation of contracts. Nor has any been the subject of more protracted litigation, or of more able and learned discussion. One of the earliest of the cases involving this question was the case of Fletcher *vs.* Peck,* brought up on a writ of error from the Circuit Court of Massachusetts, and known by the name of the "Georgia Claim." This cause was twice argued in the Supreme Court, first at the February term, 1809, and again a year afterwards. The ability of the argument was fully commensurate with the novelty and interest of the questions discussed. Not a word need be added in regard to it, further than to mention the names of the counsel who appeared on either side. For the plaintiff in error, on the first argument, was Mr. Luther Martin, and for the defendant, John Q. Adams,† and Mr. Harper of Maryland. On the second argument, Mr. Adams was replaced by Joseph Story, soon about to take his seat in that august tribunal, which he now for the first time addressed.

One of the questions presented by this case involved a discussion of the nature of a public grant of lands, and the effect of a repeal of the grant by a subsequent Legislature. So much of the case as is necessary to understand this question, may be stated as follows: The State of Georgia had granted a tract of five hundred thousand acres of land to the "Georgia Company." The defendant, Peck, claiming title under the company, executed a deed of part of these lands to Fletcher, containing among other covenants, one, that all the title which Georgia ever had in the premises had been conveyed to Peck. The State of Georgia prior to this conveyance had passed an act annulling and declaring void the act under which the grant was made. Fletcher accordingly sued Peck for a breach of covenant, and

State Court has no authority to enjoin a judgment of the Circuit Court of the United States, or stay proceedings under it. It was also determined in Slocum *vs.* Mayberry, 2 Wheaton, 1, that no State tribunal could interfere by process of replevin, injunction, or otherwise, with a seizure of property made by revenue officers under the laws of the United States.

* 6 Cranch's Reports, 87.

† The name of Mr. Adams appears more than once as counsel in the Supreme Court, prior to this period. He was engaged in one or two important causes argued in 1804, and reported in the second volume of Cranch's Reports.

the point presented upon this branch of the case was, whether the Legislature of Georgia could constitutionally repeal the act, so as to rescind the sale made under it.

In pronouncing his decision upon this grave question, the Chief-Justice laid down the doctrine, which it is believed has never since been questioned or shaken, that a grant of lands is a contract within the meaning of the Constitution, and that when a State law was in its nature a contract, and absolute rights have vested under it, a repeal of the law could not divest these rights, or impair the title so acquired. "Since then, in fact," he remarks, "a grant is a contract executed, the obligation of which still continues, and since the Constitution uses the general term contract, without distinguishing between those which are executory and those which are executed, it must be construed to comprehend the latter as well as the former. A law annulling conveyances between individuals and declaring that the grantors should stand seized of their former estates notwithstanding these grants, would be as repugnant to the Constitution as a law discharging the vendors of property from the obligation of executing their contracts by conveyances. It would be strange if a contract to convey was secured by the Constitution, while an absolute conveyance remained unprotected."

Having established the general proposition as regards individuals, the Chief-Justice then proceeds to consider and establish the broader doctrine that a grant from a State is not to be excluded from the operation of the constitutional provision. In regard to this subject he uses the following significant language: "Whatever respect might have been felt for the State sovereignties, it is not to be disguised that the framers of the Constitution viewed with some apprehension, the violent acts which might grow out of the feelings of the moment; and that the people of the United States, in adopting that instrument, have manifested a determination to shield themselves and their property from the effects of those sudden and strong passions to which men are exposed. The restrictions upon the legislative power of the states are obviously founded in this sentiment; and the Constitution of the United States contains what may be deemed a bill of rights for the people of each State." *

* In an opinion delivered by the Chief-Justice in a subsequent case, he enforces

I have observed that Judge Story was engaged in the argument of this interesting cause, the first, and I believe, the only one ever argued by him before that tribunal, of which he soon afterwards became a member. Three years before, he had come to Washington, attracted by business or curiosity, or both, for the first time in his life, and had made the acquaintance of most of the distinguished persons then in the capital. The next winter he repeated his visit. The Supreme Court at that time consisted of the Chief-Justice and six associates, Cushing, Chase, Washington, Livingston, Johnson, and Todd.* Story soon made the acquaintance of most or all of these gentlemen, including the Chief-Justice. A description of the person of Marshall, as he appeared at that time, and the impression which a first interview left upon the mind of Story, will not be without interest to the reader. It is contained in a letter to a friend, written from Washington in the winter of 1808 :

"Marshall is of a tall, slender figure, not graceful nor imposing, but erect and steady. His hair is black, his eyes small and twinkling, his forehead rather low, but his features are in general harmonious. His manners are plain, yet dignified ; and an unaffected modesty diffuses itself through all his actions. His dress is very simple, yet neat ; his language chaste, but hardly elegant ; it does not flow rapidly, but it seldom wants precision. In conversation he is quite familiar, but is occasionally embarrassed by a hesitancy and drawling. His thoughts are always clear and ingenious, sometimes striking, and not often inconclusive ; he possesses great subtilty of mind, but it is only occasionally exhibited. I love his laugh—it is too hearty for an intriguer—and his good temper and unwearied patience are equally agreeable on

similar views, declaring that the State of New Jersey could not, consistently with the Constitution of the United States, pass an act, rescinding a former act, which provided that certain lands which should be purchased for the Indians should not thereafter be subject to any tax, inasmuch as such act was *a contract,* within the meaning of the Constitution. See State of New Jersey *vs.* Wilson, 7 Cranch Rep., 164

* Mr. Brockholst Livingston, of New York, had been appointed in place of Judge Paterson, deceased, on the 10th November, 1806 ; Mr. William Johnson, of South Carolina, in place of Judge Moore, resigned, on 26th March, 1804, and Mr. Thomas Todd, of Kentucky, had been appointed on the 3d March, 1807, under the act then lately passed creating another Circuit, and an additional Justice of the Supreme Court.

the bench and in the study. His genius is, in my opinion, vigorous and powerful, less rapid than discriminating, and less vivid than uniform in its light. He examines the intricacies of a subject with calm and persevering circumspection, and unravels the mysteries with irresistible acuteness. He has not the majesty and compactness of thought of Dr. Johnson; but in subtle logic he is no unworthy disciple of David Hume." *

The artless simplicity of Marshall's manners and conversation seems

* In the same letter we have Story's first impressions of Marshall's associates on the bench:

"Washington is of a very short stature and quite boyish in his appearance. Nothing about him indicates greatness; he converses with simplicity and frankness. But he is highly esteemed as a profound lawyer, and I believe not without reason. His written opinions are composed with ability, and on the bench he exhibits great promptitude and firmness in decision. It requires intimacy to value him as he deserves.

"Livingston has a fine Roman face; an aquiline nose, high forehead, bald head, and projecting chin, indicate deep research, strength, and quickness of mind. I have no hesitation in pronouncing him a very able and independent judge. He evidently thinks with great solidity, and seizes on the strong points of argument. He is luminous, decisive, earnest and impressive on the bench. In private society he is accessible and easy, and enjoys with great good humor the vivacities, if I may coin a word, of the wit and the moralist.

"Of Chase I have formerly written. On a nearer view I am satisfied that the elements of his mind are of the very first excellence; age and infirmity have in some degree impaired them. His manners are coarse and in appearance harsh; but in reality he abounds in good humor. He loves to croak and grumble, and in the very same breath he amuses you extremely by his anecdotes and pleasantry. His first approach is formidable, but all difficulty vanishes when you once understand him. In person, in manners, in unwieldy strength, in severity of reproof, in real tenderness of heart, and above all in intellect, he is the living, I had almost said, the exact image of Samuel Johnson. To use a provincial expression, I like him hugely.

"I ought not to pass by Judge Johnson, though I scarcely know how to exhibit him individually. He has a strong mathematical head, and considerable soundness of erudition. He reminds me of Mr. Lincoln, and in the character of his mind he seems to me not dissimilar. He has, however, less of metaphysics and more of logic.

"This is the first time of Judge Todd's appearance on the bench, and as he is a modest, retired man, I cannot delineate him. He does not appear to want talents."—*Life and Letters of Story*, Vol. I. page 167.

to have been one of the first things to attract the attention of the stranger. All who ever approached him have recorded this as among their earliest and most agreeable impressions. Nothing could be more plain and unpretending than his ordinary intercourse with society. He never talked for the sake of talking, never for display. In his conversation he seemed to forget himself, and be intent only on communicating or receiving pleasurable sensations or information. Conversation with him was a real interchange of ideas, and he was quite as well pleased to listen as to be listened to. " Thus," says the writer of a recent notice of the Chief-Justice, "Nothing could well be wiser than his usual conversation. It was the most artless and yet the soundest sense, rendered agreeable by the greatest amenity of style. Expression he seemed never to have studied—no trick nor even ornament of words, beyond such as were just to the purpose and clearly conveyed his thought : but, of course, to a height of reason and a gentleness of heart like his, there was not wanting an aptness of diction which made their precisely appropriate vehicle, their natural language, and, as such, had its grace in its fitness—the only species of beauty that it could well admit." *

* The same writer has drawn a sketch of his personal appearance, which, to say the least, is not very flattering. Never having seen the Chief-Justice, I am unable to say how near it accords with the truth :

" As to face and figure, Nature had been equally little at pains to stamp with any princely effigy of what pleases, the virgin gold of which she had composed his head and heart. Except that his countenance was thoughtful and benignant, it had nothing about it that would have commanded a second look. Separately, his features were but indifferent; jointly, they were no more than commonplace. Then, as to stature, shape, and carriage, there was nothing in him that was not rather the opposite of commanding or prepossessing : he was tall ; yet his height was without the look of either strength or lightness, and gave neither dignity nor grace. His body seemed as ill as his mind well compacted; he not only was without proportion, but of members singularly knit, that dangled from each other and looked half dislocated. Habitually, he dressed very carelessly ; in the garb, but I should not dare to say in the mode, of the last century. You would have thought he had on the old clothes of a former generation, not made for him by even some superannuated tailor of that period, but gotten from the wardrobe of some antiquated slop-shop of second-hand raiment. Shapeless as he was, he would probably have defied all fitting, by whatever skill of the shears; judge, then, how the vestments of an age when, apparently, coats and breeches were cut for nobody in particular, and waistcoats were almost dressing-gowns, sat upon him."

The trials growing out of the alleged treasonable enterprise of Aaron Burr form one of the most notable events in the political history of the country, as well as one of the most interesting chapters in the judicial career of Chief-Justice Marshall. The connexion of the Chief-Justice with these trials, and his opinions upon the law of treason, as he found it limited and defined in the Constitution of the United States, subjected him to severe criticism and animadversion at the time; but no candid and unprejudiced mind can at this day fail to do full and ample justice, if not to the correctness of his reasoning, at least to the purity of motive, and independence of judgment which prompted those opinions.

Burr was arrested in January, 1807, on the Mississippi; and, having been detained awhile in custody, escaped, and was subsequently again arrested near Fort Stoddart, on the Tombigbee River, making his way, in disguise, to Mobile. From this place he was conducted to Richmond, Virginia, for examination and trial on a charge of high treason. The history of this matter is too well known to render it necessary in this place to enter into the particulars of the transaction, or the details of the evidence. From this evidence it would appear that Burr certainly did at one time entertain visionary notions of his ability to produce a revolution which should result in the dismemberment of the Union and the erection of a Western Confederacy beyond the Alleghanies; and that, finding this enterprise somewhat arduous for his means, he abandoned it, and sought the gratification of his restless and towering ambition in a scheme to invade Mexico and make himself master of those fair dominions.*

Before alluding to the examination and trial of Burr, it will be proper to notice the case of two of his alleged accomplices, brought before the Supreme Court at the February term, 1807, in which the Chief-Justice, after full argument and careful deliberation, delivered his opinion upon the construction of the law of treason as defined by the Constitution. This case is reported under the title of ex parte Bollman and ex parte Swartwout.† It was argued and decided before the preliminary examination of Col. Burr, and the opinion delivered by the Chief-Justice may be taken as his earliest exposition of the law of treason.

* See testimony on Burr's trial.

† 4 Cranch's Reports, 75 to 136.

Dr. Erick Bollman and Samuel Swartwout had been arrested on a warrant issued January 27th, 1807, and committed to prison by order of the Circuit Court for the District of Columbia, on a charge of treason in being concerned in Burr's conspiracy. On motion of the prisoner's counsel, Mr. Charles Lee and Mr. Harper, and after a full argument of the question by these gentlemen, the Supreme Court granted a habeas corpus to bring up the bodies of Mr. Swartwout and Dr. Bollman. The return to the writ was made on the 16th of February, whereupon Mr. Lee moved that the prisoners be discharged or admitted to bail. He was ably supported in this motion by Mr. Harper, Mr. Key, and Mr. Luther Martin, who contended with great force and earnestness, that the commitment was illegal upon its face, and that the testimony upon which it was made, was not sufficient to make out a *prima facie* case of treason. To this argument Mr. Cæsar A. Rodney, the Attorney-General of the United States, and Mr. Jones, the attorney for the District of Columbia, replied with equal vigor and ability. Chief-Justice Marshall delivered the opinion of the Court on the 21st February, granting the motion of the counsel for the prisoners, and discharging them from custody.

I have alluded to this case for the purpose of elucidating more clearly the mode in which the Chief-Justice construed the law of treason; and also as introductory to that important trial at which a few weeks later he was called upon to preside—the greatest trial known to the criminal jurisprudence of our country—which brought to the bar under an indictment for high treason a man who had recently held the second office under the Government, and which called out a display of learning, genius, eloquence, and juridical wisdom, rarely equalled in this or any other country.

The Constitution, the fundamental law of the United States, strictly defines the crime of treason. Sufficiently rigorous for every political necessity, it is scarcely susceptible of being used for the purposes of tyranny and individual oppression. So definite are its provisions that not even a Jeffries could pervert it. No such sanguinary judgments as some of those which have disgraced Westminster Hall have ever been, or ever could be, pronounced from the bench of the Federal Courts The genius of a republic such as ours seeks and establishes another definition of treason from that which consigned a Vane, a Russell, and a

Sidney to the block; and it is really one of the proudest boasts of the republic, that for the whole period of its existence, it has neither asked nor needed any other definition of treason than that contained in the plain, direct, simple constitutional provision—"Treason against the United States shall consist only in levying war against them, or in adhering to their enemies, giving them aid and comfort."

The case of Bollman and Swartwout did not come within this definition. Whatever might have been their connexion with Burr, and the operations set on foot by him, yet, in the view of the Chief-Justice, the essential fact to complete the offence—the *actual levying of war*—was not established. "To constitute that specific crime for which the prisoners now before the Court have been committed," he says, "war must be actually levied against the United States. However flagitious may be the crime of *conspiring* to subvert by force the government of our country, such *conspiracy* is not treason. To conspire to levy war, and actually to levy war, are distinct offences. The first must be brought into operation by the assemblage of men for a purpose treasonable in itself, or the fact of levying war cannot have been committed."

Such was held by Judge Marshall to be the American law of treason. So widely different is it from the English statute of treason—that statute which does not permit the subject to "imagine" the death of the king—that the two do not seem descended from the same parent stem. Russell died for a less crime than even *conspiring* to subvert the government; the unpublished thoughts of a philosopher in his closet caused the head of Sidney to roll from the scaffold. "Such cases can never occur in America," says Chief-Justice Marshall in this opinion. "To prevent the possibility of those calamities which result from the extension of treason to offences of minor importance, that great fundamental law which defines and limits the various departments of our government, has given a rule on the subject both to the legislature and the Courts of America, which neither can be permitted to transcend."

It was not his intention, he remarks, in the same case, to say that no individual can be guilty of treason who has not appeared in arms against his country; on the contrary, if war be actually levied, all who are actually leagued in the general conspiracy and perform any part, however minute, or *however remote from the scene of action*, are to be regarded as traitors.* "To complete the crime of levying war against the United States," he remarks " there must be an actual assemblage of men for the purpose of executing a treasonable design. In the case now before the Court a design to overturn the government of the United States in New Orleans by force, would have been unquestionably a design, which, if carried into execution, would have been treason; and the assemblage of a body of men for the purpose of carrying it into execution would amount to levying war against the United States; but no *conspiracy* for this object, no *enlisting of men* to effect it, would be an actual levying of war."

The session of the Supreme Court at which the case of Bollman and Swartwout was decided had scarcely terminated when the Chief-Justice was called upon to enter upon the trial of Aaron Burr, the principal actor in this gigantic scheme of aggrandizement. Col. Burr had been brought to the city of Richmond on the 26th of March, guarded by a military escort, and on the morning of the 31st appeared with his counsel, Edmund Randolph and John Wickham,

* This part of the opinion of the Supreme Court was the subject of criticism, and much argument, in the discussions on Burr's trial, which I shall presently notice. It was thought by counsel to countenance, in some degree, the odious doctrine of *constructive* treason, which the Constitution in express terms excludes. The Chief-Justice remarks in his opinion on Burr's trial,† that four judges were present at the decision of Bollman and Swartwout's case, and he thought them unanimous; but that he had since reason to suspect that one of them, who was prevented from entering into a full discussion, did not concur in this particular point with his brethren. He adds, that for himself he then thought, and still continued to think, the opinion correct. He qualifies this, however, by remarking that it is not to be understood as adopting the whole doctrine of the English books on the subject of accessories to treason. Such certainly was not the fact. Those only who *perform a part*, and who are *leagued in the conspiracy*, are declared to be traitors. There could be no war levied, and consequently no treason, without the actual embodying of men, and a military assemblage *in force*. All that the Court intended to say was, that in order to convict for treason, it was not absolutely necessary for the accused to be found actually embodied among the treasonable assemblage. He must, however, be proved to have done *some act*, to have *performed some part*, toward the accomplishment of the particular overt act of war laid in the indictment. These were the principles subsequently avowed, as we shall see, by the Chief-Justice on Burr's trial, and it is believed are now to be considered the settled doctrines of the Federal Courts.

† 2 Burr's Trial, page 406. It was insisted by Burr's counsel that this part of the opinion was extra-judicial, and not binding as authority.

Esqrs., before the Chief-Justice, who had already been seated half an hour on the bench. The accused apologized in his blandest manner for the delay, declaring that he had "misapprehended the hour at which he was bound to appear," and the argument, on the motion of Mr. Hay, District-Attorney of Virginia, and Mr. Rodney, Attorney-General of the United States, to commit the accused to answer for a high misdemeanor, and on a charge of treason, immediately commenced. Burr himself, calm, collected, confident in language and manner, addressed the court after his counsel had taken their seats, in opposition to the motion, in one of those plausible and insinuating arguments whose keen and subtle logic was so peculiarly his own. "According to the Constitution," he remarked, "treason consisted in *acts;* that an arrest could only be justified by the suspicion of *acts*, whereas, in this case, his Honor was invited to issue a warrant upon mere conjecture; that alarms existed without cause; that Mr. Wilkinson alarmed the President, and the President alarmed the people of Ohio. He appealed to historical facts," &c.*

The next day the Chief-Justice pronounced his opinion, and after a careful review of the subject, decided to hold Col. Burr to answer the charge of a misdemeanor only, without including the charge of high treason. The offence being bailable, the accused was recognized in the sum of ten thousand dollars.

On the 22nd of May, 1807, Burr was arraigned before Judge Marshall and his Associate, Cyrus Griffin, District Judge of Virginia, at a Circuit Court held for that district at the city of Richmond. The Attorney-General of the United States having withdrawn, Mr. Hay, who conducted the prosecution, was assisted by Alexander McRae and the afterwards celebrated William Wirt, of Virginia. Col. Burr appeared with two additional counsel, Benjamin Botts and John Baker, who were joined soon after by Luther Martin, of Maryland. It is not, however, too much to say—and it is no disparagement to the eminent abilities of either Mr. Randolph, Mr. Martin, or Mr. Wickham—that Burr himself was his own leading counsel, and his the keen and powerful intellect, which originated and directed the admirably arranged proceedings of the entire defence.† Whatever may

* 1 Burr's Trial, p. 7.

† The great ability of Col. Burr as a lawyer has never been denied or ques-

be thought of the guilt or innocence of Col. Burr, or whatever opinions may be entertained of his merits and character as a man, one can scarcely help feeling a degree of interest in his defence, and it may

tioned. The "subtlest practitioner of the times," as he has been significantly termed, he stood for some years, before his elevation to the Vice-Presidency, the formidable rival and competitor of Hamilton at the head of the New York bar. As a mere lawyer, Burr was greater than Hamilton; but as an advocate the latter was no doubt superior. I have heard a gentleman,* who was well acquainted with them both, and had frequently listened to their speeches and arguments at the bar, describe the manner and characteristics of each as a speaker:—Hamilton, rich in declamation, but at the same time cogent and convincing, copious in language, earnest, and sometimes impassioned in manner. Burr, calm, unruffled, almost colloquial, and never attempting anything like declamation or rhetoric, but compact, nervous, and clear as a sunbeam, armed at every point, skillful in defence, adroit in attack. His arguments to the Court, and his addresses to the jury were always brief, but pointed and pertinent; rarely, except upon great occasions, exceeded half an hour, and yet when he closed he seemed to have said everything material to his argument, or which the case required.

After his trial for treason, Col. Burr left the country, a broken and ruined man. Having travelled through England and part of the continent of Europe, he returned to New York in 1812, and opening an office at No. 12 Nassau-street, resumed the practice of the law. It had become too much the fashion, however, to denounce and decry Col. Burr, and he never afterwards regained the confidence of the community. Yet he was engaged upon some causes of great importance, among which may be mentioned the celebrated Eden will case, in the year 1828, reported under the title of Varick *vs.* Jackson, in 2 Wendell's New York Reports, page 166, a case in which the New York Court of Errors, after a most elaborate and exhausting discussion, sustained the positions advocated by Burr, in opposition to the general current of English authorities, namely, that an existing adverse possession against the devisor at the time of making his will and at the time of his death, does not affect the validity of a devise of real estate. It should be remarked, however, that the main argument in the case was made by Burr's associate counsel, Mr. Van Buren, afterwards President of the United States, an argument characterized by more than that gentleman's usual acknowledged legal talent, ingenuity, and great ability. At its close Mr. Burr declined arguing the principal question, which had been so thoroughly discussed by his associate, and merely made a few remarks upon the question of the examination of one of the witnesses.

Burr died on Staten Island, September 14th, 1836, at the advanced age of eighty-five, with scarcely a friend, says one who knew him, "to close his eyes or wipe the dew-drops of death from his brow." He was buried at Trenton, New Jersey. Within a few years a plain monument, with the simplest inscription, has been placed, almost by stealth, at his grave.

* The venerable Dr. Nott, President of Union College.

be something like a sentiment of admiration at the display of keen intellect and eminent skill which he developed on this occasion. Calm and self-reliant, but without arrogance, firm, and perhaps a little haughty in his demeanor, but generally courteous to his adversaries, and respectful to the Court, he displayed throughout the preliminary proceedings of the trial the firm temper of an elevated mind as well as the practiced skill of the veteran lawyer. In his various motions and brief addresses to the Court, not less than in his occasional questions to witnesses on the stand, he exhibited a shrewdness, a depth of observation and a penetration, which certainly develop great capacity and power of mind.* Though Burr may have been a bad man, no one will deny that he was an able one. His scheme to overturn the government or dismember the confederacy, if ever entertained, was an ambition like that of a Cæsar ; the oriental imagination which conceived the plan of an independent empire in Mexico, was not unworthy the genius of a Bonaparte. It would be curious to speculate as to the probable destiny of the Spanish races on this continent, if Burr's dreams of conquest and empire could have been realized ; though he might not have wielded the power of a Napoleon, he had at least all the indomitable will and energy, and more than the ability, of a Francia.

I shall not dwell upon the various circumstances attending this celebrated trial, or review in detail the many grave questions raised and discussed before the Chief-Justice, all of which he considered with an excessive degree of care and caution, and decided in a manner which the accused certainly had no right to complain of. In the prosecution of great State causes in other countries, the influence of the govern-

* Says Mr. McRae, in his able argument on the final and decisive motion in the case : "We blame not the prisoner for exercising any of those rights, which, as a citizen, he is entitled to, and which it were, perhaps, a violation of duty not to exercise ; and no man's talents are more competent to distinguish and assert his rights than those of the accused. We object not to his making any such motion as rightly belongs to his defence. But the prisoner, for the purpose of escaping the effect of the prosecution carrying on against him, has with unexampled dexterity contrived, from the very start, almost invariably, to quit his situation as an accused. On every occasion, from the commencement to the present moment, instead of Aaron Burr defending himself, we find him taking the high ground of public accuser and assailing others."—2 *Burr's Trial*, p. 28.

ment has been usually able to make itself felt through the Court; but the proceedings of this trial bore ample testimony that the American judiciary were in fact, as in name, independent. No government influence could be brought to bear down the accused in that tribunal wherein John Marshall presided, the impersonation of calm, unbending, inflexible justice. Indeed, he did not escape the animadversions of government for some of his rulings on this trial, as I shall presently notice; but none of these served to move him from the strict line of what he regarded as his duty, or to shake his firm purpose. It is, I think, evident throughout, that, while Marshall undertook to determine every question presented to him, by the rule of established legal principles, yet it was his aim in the practical conduct of the trial, to see that the accused at least should not have reason to complain of the slightest act of partiality or wrong. The principle which governed his conduct—and I believe it must be conceded to be not only a liberal and high-minded, but correct rule of action in the trial of a criminal, and especially a capital offence—may be gathered from the last sentence of the following brief passage from his opinion on the motion of Col. Burr for a writ of *subpœna duces tecum*, to the President of the United States, directing him to produce a certain letter of Gen. Wilkinson, a motion fully discussed on both sides, and warmly opposed by the counsel for the government, on the ground, among other things, that the *materiality* of the letter had not been shown. The Chief-Justice, on full consideration, granted the motion. "It is not for the Court," he remarks, "to anticipate the result of the present prosecution. Should it terminate, as is expected, on the part of the United States, all those who are concerned in it should certainly regret, that a paper, which the accused believed to be essential to his defence, which may, for aught that now appears, be essential, had been withheld from him. I will not say that this circumstance would in any degree tarnish the reputation of the Government; but I will say that it would tarnish the reputation of the Court, which had given its sanction to its being withheld. Might I be permitted to utter one sentiment with respect to myself, it would be to deplore most earnestly the occasion which should compel me to look back on any part of my official conduct with so much self-reproach as I should feel, could I declare, on the information now possessed, that the accused is not entitled to the letter in question, if it should really be important to him." *

The grand jury, consisting of some of the most eminent citizens of Virginia,† were empannelled and sworn on the day of the opening of the Court, May 22nd, and the Chief-Justice thereupon delivered his charge to them. But it was not until the 24th of June, and after many adjournments, and protracted discussions, in which Col. Burr and all the counsel employed on either side engaged, that the grand jury brought in indictments against Aaron Burr and Herman Blennerhasset, for both treason and misdemeanor. Burr thereupon

* 1 Burr's Trial, p. 188.

† John Randolph was foreman. Burr claimed the right of challenging the grand jurors for cause, which was allowed. He challenged, however, only two on the panel—Mr. Giles and Col. Wilson C. Nicholas—both of whom had served in the Senate of the United States. The former gentleman, he remarked, had, in his public capacity, formed a decisive opinion on the case. "He is one of the last men," Mr. Burr observed, "on whom I wish to cast any reflections. So far from having any animosity against him, he would have been one of those whom I would have ranked among my personal friends." As to Col. Nicholas, Burr remarked, that "he has entertained a bitter personal animosity against me; and therefore I cannot expect from him that pure impartiality of mind which is necessary to a correct decision." Both these gentlemen, thereupon, by consent, withdrew.

Major Eggleson, one of the jurors, hereupon came forward and remarked that he had expressed great warmth and indignation on the subject, and believed it indelicate for him to serve. Burr, however, declined taking any exception to him, remarking, "There is very little chance that I can expect a better man to try my cause. His desire to be excused, and his opinion that his mind is not free upon the case, are good reasons why he should be excused; but the candor of the gentleman in excepting to himself, leaves me ground to hope that he will endeavor to be impartial."

John Randolph also wished to be excused, declaring that he had "a strong prepossession."

Mr. Burr.—"Really, I am afraid we shall not be able to find any man without this prepossession."

Chief-Justice.—"The rule is, that a man must not only have formed, but declared an opinion, in order to exclude him from serving on the jury."

Mr. Randolph.—"I do not recollect to have declared one."

Mr. Burr did not object to Randolph, and he was accordingly sworn as foreman of the jury.—1 *Burr's Trial*, p. 44.

pleaded not guilty, and was committed for trial. The trial was postponed to the 3rd of August following.

On that day the Court again convened, and the same counsel appeared. Subsequently, and about the time of opening the cause to the jury, Mr. Charles Lee, ex-Attorney-General of the United States, was added to the array of counsel for the defence. Two weeks were consumed in the attempt to obtain a jury, the great mass of those who were summoned exhibiting the strongest prepossessions against the prisoner and his cause.* During these preliminary arrangements and the discussions incident to them, much asperity of feeling was at times exhibited between the counsel on either side. It was observed, however, that the prisoner at the bar preserved, throughout, the most cool and dignified composure, not only avoiding everything like personality himself, but imposing restraint upon his counsel. The veteran Luther Martin, who defended Col. Burr with all the warmth and ardor of friendship,† could not entirely smother those feelings of indignation which the vigorous attacks of the prosecution excited. Being interrupted by one of the counsel for the people, who suggested to him the importance of economizing time, he sharply replied, "I know what

* Most of them were set aside for cause. Occasionally, but not often, Burr exercised his right of peremptory challenge. The first of these peremptory challenges was of a Mr. Hamilton Morrison. After a brief examination, the Court thought that sufficient cause had not been shown against his being a juror, and it appears that he was about to be sworn, when the juror impudently remarked, "I am surprised why they should be in so much terror of me. Perhaps my *name* may be a terror, for my first name is *Hamilton*." Col. Burr quietly observed that "*that* remark was a sufficient cause for objecting to him," and challenged him; whereupon Mr. Hamilton Morrison was set aside.—1 *Burr's Trial*, p. 383.

† Mr. Martin, in offering himself as one of Burr's bail, remarked that he was happy to have this opportunity to give a public proof of his confidence in the honor of Col. Burr, and of his conviction that he was innocent. Indeed, with such warmth and ardor did he enter into the defence, that Jefferson, in one of his letters to the District-Attorney, Mr. Hay, hints at the propriety of *indicting* Martin (whom he denounces as an "impudent Federal bull-dog"), as an accomplice of Burr.

It may be added that Jefferson's denunciations of Martin were repaid with interest. I have been told by an eminent gentleman of the Maryland bar, who was well acquainted, and had practiced with Mr. Martin, that it was one of his common expressions when stigmatizing any person with the strongest terms of opprobrium, to say that he was "as great a scoundrel as Thomas Jefferson."

economy they wish. They wish us to be silent ; they would, if they could, deprive Col. Burr's counsel of an opportunity of defending him, that they *might hang him up as soon as possible, to gratify themselves and the government.*" Mr. McRae denounced the remark as " a most unprincipled and unfounded assertion." Mr. Hay also warmly repelled the charge. The Chief-Justice, in his calm and dignified way, at once restored order. He had hoped " that no such allusions would have been made ; that the government ought to be treated with respect, and that there was a delicacy to be observed on that subject, from which he hoped there would be no departure hereafter." Thereupon Col. Burr remarked : " I rose to stop the progress of such language when up before. I had made sufficient apologies, if any were necessary, for any expressions which had been used, and I had hoped that no allusion would be made to the subject. It will be recollected that I have constantly manifested my displeasure at such expressions. I have carefully avoided such myself, and imposed similar restraints on my counsel ; and urged that the government should be treated with the utmost delicacy, though there was great provocation from the gentlemen on the part of the prosecution, which would have justified harsh terms. I hope these things will cease. On the part of my counsel I am sure they will cease." *

* 1 Burr's Trial, p. 386. I have remarked that Burr preserved an unruffled temper throughout the trial, and rarely suffered himself to be betrayed into anything like warmth of language. Occasionally, however, we notice something of the kind. On his motion that the Court would instruct the jury on certain special points of law, Mr. Hay hoped the Court " would not grant particular indulgences to Col. Burr, who stood on the same footing with every other man charged with a crime."

MR. BURR.—" Would to God that I did stand on the same ground with every other man. This is the first time I have ever been permitted to enjoy the rights of a citizen. How have I been brought hither ?"

The CHIEF-JUSTICE said it was improper to go into these digressions.

Col. Burr thereupon disclaimed any desire to obtain other privileges and rights than those which belonged to every citizen.

On one occasion, too, he expressed himself with much asperity, and with a keen and bitter sarcasm upon what he called " the amiable morality " of the government. Alluding to the arrest of his friends, the seizure of his property and papers, and an order which had been issued, as he says, to kill him while descending the Mississippi, he remarks :

" All this may only prove that my case is a solitary exception from the general

At length, the jury being empannelled and sworn, on Monday, the 17th of August, Mr. Hay opened the case on the part of the prosecution. I shall not undertake to follow the course of the trial, but refer the reader to the printed report of it by Mr. David Robertson, published at the time in two volumes, containing the entire proceedings, including the evidence, the arguments of counsel, and the opinions of the Court upon the various motions made, and questions raised, during the course of the proceedings.

The counsel for the people having adduced their testimony relative to the overt acts alleged in the indictment, namely, the hostile assemblage on Blennerhasset Island in the Ohio river—at which it was not pretended that Col. Burr was present, he being really at the time hundreds of miles distant from the scene of action—now proposed to

rule. The government may be tender, mild, and humane to every one but me. If so, to be sure, it is of little consequence to any one but myself. But surely I must be excused if I complain a little of these proceedings. There seemod to be something mingled in these proceedings which manifested a more than usual inclination to attain the ends of justice. As far as it related to himself perhaps these things were of no account; but what was then to be said of those and other measures, such as the suspension of the *habeas corpus* act, which concerned the whole nation? If, in the Island of Great Britain, such a measure was calculated to produce so much disturbance, what kind of sensation ought it to produce in this country.

"Our President is a lawyer, and a great one, too. He certainly ought to know what it is that constitutes a war. Six months ago he proclaimed that there was a civil war. And yet for six months have they been hunting for it, and still cannot find one spot where it existed. There was to be sure a most terrible war in the newspapers, but nowhere else."

These remarks were made on a motion of Mr. Hay, after the grand jury had been sworn, and before indictment found, to commit Burr to answer a charge of treason—a motion which was denied by the Chief-Justice.—1 *Burr's Trial*, p. 78.

During all the proceedings of the trial, Col. Burr manifested the fearless and firm demeanor of a man who feels himself the object of an unrelenting and unjust persecution. When his accuser, Gen. Wilkinson, entered the Court, the reporter says the countenance of Col. Burr was "marked by a haughty contempt." To his daughter he writes in the tone of an injured and innocent man: "You have read to very little purpose, if you have not remarked that such things happen in all democratic governments. Was there in Greece or Rome a man of independence, and supposed to possess great talents, who was not the object of vindictive and unrelenting persecution?"

connect him with the transaction by collateral testimony. Here the counsel for the prisoner raised the objection, that no such evidence could be given under the indictment. It was at once perceived that the stress of the case lay in this objection, which Wirt, in his speech, very properly characterized as a bold and original stroke in the noble science of defence, marking the genius and hand of a master. The discussion which arose upon it, resulting in a decision by the Chief-Justice, which effectually put an end to the prosecution, was opened by Mr. Wickham. It lasted a week; all the counsel employed on either side having spoken at length upon the question,* and with the opinion of the Court thereon, occupies the last sixty pages of the first, and the whole of the second volume of the report of the trial. I desire to pass no unmeaning or exaggerated eulogy upon this splendid display of forensic genius and eloquence; and therefore shall merely say, that it undoubtedly presents us the fullest and most perfect exposition of the law of treason, both under the common law and statutes of England, and as defined by the Federal Constitution, to be found in the language. Every variety of illustration, every ingenuity of argument, the most ample historical dissertations upon the law of treason, the fullest analysis of cases, the application of the most hidden and recondite principles of the common law—in short materials from all sides and from every source, were pressed into the service of these masterly arguments. Many parts of them are embellished with a richness of language, and an elegance of rhetoric, which serve admirably to relieve the hard and dull outlines of a mere legal discussion. Such especially is the case with the speech of Mr. Wirt, who may be called the Sheridan of the prosecution—a speech which exhibits in a felicitious degree that union of brilliant fancy, eloquence, and legal acumen, which are displayed, though perhaps not in an equal degree, in all the great forensic efforts of that accomplished lawyer. Though it may not deserve the exaggerated encomium which Burke in a moment of ecstacy bestowed on the effort of his eloquent associate on the trial of Hastings, it certainly may claim its full share

* The counsel spoke in the following order: Mr. Randolph followed Mr. Wickham. Mr. McRae and Mr. Wirt for the people replied. Mr. Botts followed for the defence; Mr. Hay for the prosecution; Mr. Lee and Mr. Martin for the defence, and Mr. Randolph closed the argument.

of the compliment extorted from the cold and calm judgment of Marshall on the bench: "A degree of eloquence seldom displayed on any occasion, has embellished a solidity of argument, and a depth of research, by which the Court has been greatly aided in forming the opinion it is about to deliver." *

The Chief-Justice, in his opinion upon the case, decides, that collateral testimony offered to show Col. Burr's connexion with the transactions on Blennerhasset's island is inadmissible. His conclusion upon this point is sustained by a keen and subtle logic, and an almost technical precision of argument, which, however, satisfactory and conclusive to the legal mind, does not leave the case upon that broad and high ground of principle, where the counsel for the defence had placed it; nor does it at once strike the understanding as entirely consistent with the rule, to which the Chief-Justice still adhered, as laid down in the case of Bollman and Swartwout, namely, that if "a body of men be actually assembled for the purpose of effecting by force a treasonable object, all those who perform any part, however minute, or however remote from the scene of action, and who are actually leagued in the general conspiracy, are to be considered as traitors." How then, it might be asked, could the testimony offered to prove Burr's connexion, though remote from the scene of action, be rejected? By a nice, but technical, though doubtless strictly legal distinction. The overt act of treason laid in the indictment was the levying of war in Blennerhassett's Island;—Burr was not present, either in person or in contemplation of law, either actively, or constructively aiding and assisting in the particular act there alleged to have been committed; and whether that act amounted to an act of war or not (which the Chief-Justice intimates he would have submitted to the jury), no proof of any other overt act could lawfully be given in evidence under the indictment.†

The effect of the decision was, of course, to cut off the government counsel from giving any evidence to connect Col. Burr with the transactions on Blennerhassett's Island. The prosecution was at an end. The next day, the jury having retired under the charge of the court,

* 2 Burr's Trial, p. 401.

† See opinion. 2 Burr's Trial, p. 401, *et seq.*

brought in a verdict of not guilty, and a similar fate met the indictment for misdemeanor.

Says Wirt in a letter to a friend: "Marshall has stepped in between Burr and death. He has pronounced an opinion that our evidence is all irrelevant. Burr not having been *present* at the island with the assemblage, and the act itself not amounting to a levying of war." * And again, a fortnight afterwards: "The second prosecution against Burr is also at an end; Marshall again arrested the evidence. A motion will be made to commit him and his confederates for trial in Kentucky, or wherever else the judge shall, from the whole evidence, believe their crimes to have been committed. There is no knowing what will become of the motion. I believe it will be defeated." † In this Mr. Wirt was mistaken. Burr was held to bail in the sum of three thousand dollars to answer in Ohio, for a misdemeanor in setting on foot a military expedition against the territories of Spain.‡ This decision seems to have produced some disgust in the mind of Burr. In a letter to his daughter he remarks: "The opinion was a matter of regret and surprise to the friends of the Chief-Justice, and of ridicule to his enemies—all believing that it was *a sacrifice of principle to conciliate Jack Cade.*" On the other hand the government, or perhaps it may more correctly be said, prominent individuals in public life, connected with the administration, did not fail to animadvert strongly upon the conduct and decision of Marshall during the trial. It was something of this feeling perhaps which induced a distinguished senator from Virginia,§ to introduce a bill at the next session of Congress, *defining* treason, which he claimed the legislative body had a constitutional right to do. Upon this occasion he attacked the opinions of the Chief-Justice with great warmth and boldness, remarking, among other things, "I have learned that judicial opinions on

* Wirt's letter bears date only the day after the decision was pronounced, and he must have misunderstood that part of the opinion. The Chief-Justice did not decide that the transaction on Blennerhassett's Island did not amount to a levying of war. He would have been disposed, he remarks, to leave it as question of fact for the jury, but the point was not to be understood as decided.—2 *Burr's Trial*, p. 422.

† Wirt to Dabney Carr. 1 Kennedy's *Life of Wirt*, p. 205.

‡ He did not appear, and the recognizance was forfeited.

§ Mr. Giles.

this subject are like changeable silks, which vary their colors as they are held up in political sunshine." But arrows like these fell innocuous at the feet of the Chief-Justice. The purity of his motives, the elevation of his mind, and the integrity of his character, were proof against all such attacks. He held no opinions to propitiate the government, none to conciliate the favor of "Jack Cade."

"Why did you not tell Judge Marshall that the people of America demanded a conviction?" was the question put to Wirt, after the trial. "Tell *him* that!" was the reply. "I would as soon have gone to Herschel, and told him that the people of America insisted that the moon had horns as a reason why he should draw her with them."

The law of prize and Admiralty jurisdiction formed one of the most important branches of jurisprudence administered in the Federal tribunals during Marshall's term of service. Hitherto this department of the law had received but little attention either in our own country or in England. Sir William Scott, appointed to the bench in England in 1798, was the first to raise it into respectability in that country, and by his elaborate and luminous opinions, published in Robinson's Reports, he prepared the way for that liberal and enlightened code of American prize law, which the judgments and decisions of Marshall and Story may be said to have created. In the preceding sketches of Marshall's predecessors I have noticed nearly all the important cases of Admiralty and prize law decided in the Supreme Court up to the time he came upon the bench. For several years subsequent to this period, and as late as the argument of the celebrated case of Rose *vs.* Himely,* in the winter of 1808, very few contributions to this branch of law-learning had been made by the American Courts. These contributions were all to be found in the few cases reported in Dallas, and the earlier volumes of Cranch, together with a small volume of decisions in the South Carolina Courts, by Judge Bee. "It is a beautiful science," says Judge Story, two or three years later; but at the same time it was for all practical purposes a new science; for, with the exception of these American cases and the four or five volumes of Robinson's Admiralty Reports then published, very little useful reading

* 4 Cranch's Reports, 241.

was within reach of the lawyer, except one or two treatises or essays, and a few brief notes to collections of Admiralty forms and precedents.

The non-intercourse and embargo acts, as the biographer of Story very correctly observes, created cases confessedly new in their character, and which were not only without precedent, but beyond the reach of established rules. It became, therefore, necessary to build up a new body of law, to open untrodden paths, to reduce general principles to specific form and practice, to apply settled rules to curious and complicated facts, and to educe from conflicting elements clear, just, and practical doctrines. Cases occurred which had never before presented themselves in a similar aspect. The conflicting rights of captors and claimants, of neutrals and belligerents, trading under licenses, or privateering under letters of marque and reprisal, were to be adjusted. And the Court, whose duty it was to decide upon these important subjects, was forced to act comparatively without a guide, and oftentimes to create the law of the case.*

One of the most important of the earlier cases before Chief-Justice Marshall was the case I have just alluded to, Rose *vs.* Himely, which involved the question whether the Courts of this country can examine the authority of a foreign tribunal acting as a prize court, and can disregard its sentence condemning a vessel as prize of war; and if so, whether such sentence of a foreign tribunal is valid, when the vessel at the time is actually lying in an American port. The case received additional importance from the fact that several causes from South Carolina, Maryland, and Pennsylvania depended on the the decision of the same principle. The gentlemen engaged upon all these causes were, therefore, suffered to be heard upon this argument, and a more formidable array of counsel had certainly never appeared at the bar of the Supreme Court. For the appellant were Mr. Charles Lee, Mr. Harper, Mr. S. Chase, Jun., Mr. Dallas, Mr. Rawle, Mr. Ingersoll, and Mr. Drayton. For the respondent—Mr. Duponceau, Mr. E. Tighlman, and Mr. Martin. The argument lasted nine days, three of which were consumed by the speech of Luther Martin alone, as we are assured by a spectator whom Mr. Martin "fatigued almost to death" †

* 1 Story's Life and Letters, 226, 227.

† Judge Story, who, while on his second visit to Washington, was present at this

The decision of the Court was pronounced by the Chief-Justice,—clear, luminous, argumentative, pointed, and brief—travelling not far for illustration—alluding to but few decisions, and these only the de-

argument. In a letter to a friend he has given brief sketches of the counsel engaged in it, which are too interesting to be omitted:

"Harper is diffuse, but methodical and clear; he argues with considerable warmth, and seems to depend upon the deliberate suggestions of his mind. I incline to think that he studies his cause with great diligence, and is to be considered as in some degree artificial.

"Duponceau is a Frenchman by birth, and a very ingenious counsellor at Philadelphia. He has the reputation of great subtilty and acuteness, and is excessively minute in the display of his learning. His manner is animated bnt not impressive, and he betrays at every turn the impatience and the casuistry of his nation. His countenance is striking, his figure rather awkward. A small, sparkling black eye, and a thin face, satisfy you that he is not without quickness of mind; yet he seemed to me to exhaust himself in petty distinctions, and in a perpetual recurrence to doubtful, if not to inconclusive arguments. His reasoning was rather sprightly and plausible, than logical and coercive; in short, he is a French advocate.

"Tighlman is quite an old man, of an unpromising appearance; his face indicates rather a simplicity and weakness of character. Indeed, when I first saw him, I could not persuade myself that he possessed any talent. I heard his argument, and it was strong, clear, pointed, and logical. Though his manner was bad, and his pronunciation not agreeable, every person listened with attention, and none were disappointed.

"Rawle is quite a plain, but genteel man, and looks like a studious, ingenious, and able lawyer. He argues with a pleasant voice, and has great neatness, perspicacity, and even elegance. He keeps his object steadily in view; he distinguishes with care, enforces with strength, and if he fails to convince, he seldom spends his thoughts vainly.

"Ingersoll has rather a peculiar face, and yet in person or manner has nothing which interests in a high degree. He is more animated than Rawle, but has less precision; he is learned, laborious, and minute, not eloquent, nor declamatory, but diffuse. The Pennsylvanians consider him a perfect drag-net, that gathers everything in its course.

"Dallas is a book man, ready, apt, and loquacious, but artificial. He is of a strong, robust figure, but his voice seems shrill and half obstructed. He grows warm by method, and cools in the same manner. He wearies with frequent emphasis on subordinate points; but he cannot be considered as unscientific or wandering.

"Lee, of Virginia, is a thin, spare, short man; you cannot believe that he was Attorney-General of the United States. I heard him speak for a few minutes, but the impression is so faint, that I cannot analyse it."

cisions of Sir William Scott, in the English Admiralty Court—he arrives at his conclusions by a process of that same simple and perspicuous reasoning which characterizes all his juridical arguments. The principles established by it are, that the jurisdiction of a foreign tribunal may be examined in the Supreme Court of this country, and if such tribunal cannot, consistently with the law of nations, exercise the jurisdiction which it has assumed, its sentence is to be disregarded. That in the case at bar, the sentence of the tribunal—a French Court sitting at St. Domingo—was invalid, the captured vessel never having been carried within its jurisdiction, and actually lying in the port of Charleston when the sentence of condemnation was passed. The Chief-Justice further laid down the rule, in which he was sustained by a majority of the Court, that though the rights of war might be exercised by a country on the high seas, yet that the legislation of every country being territorial, its rights of sovereignty in the execution of a mere municipal law must be exercised within its own territory; and therefore that the seizure of a vessel, not belonging to a subject, made on the high seas, for the breach of a municipal regulation, as was the case with regard to the vessel in controversy, was an act which the sovereign could not authorize, and such seizure was totally invalid. To this last proposition Judges Livingston, Cushing, and Chase, though concurring in the general decision, did not accede.

Story next comes to Luther Martin, "that compound of strange qualities," who seems to have impressed him less favorably than either of the others. One can scarcely believe that his description does full justice to that distinguished gentleman:

"He is about the middle size, a little bald, with a common forehead, pointed nose, inexpressive eye, large mouth, and well-formed chin. His dress is slovenly. You cannot believe him a great man. Nothing in his voice, his action, his language impresses. Of all men he is the most desultory, wandering, and inaccurate. Errors in grammar, and, indeed, an unexampled laxity of speech mark him everywhere. All nature pays contribution to his argument, if, indeed, it can be called one. You might hear him for three hours, and he would neither enlighten nor amuse you; but amid the abundance of chaff is excellent wheat; and, if you can find it, the quality is of the first order. * * * * * * He did not strike me at all, and if I were to judge solely from that effort, I should say that he was greatly overrated. But every one assures me that he is profoundly learned, and that though he shines not now in the lustre of his former days, yet he is at times very great."—*Life and Writings of Story*, Vol. I. pages 123,124.

The case of Hudson and others *vs.* Guestier, which was decided the same day, differed from the case of Rose *vs.* Himely in one point, namely, that the captured vessel, the *Sea Flower*, was seized *within* the territorial jurisdiction of St. Domingo, and had been carried into a Spanish port in the isle of Cuba. The question therefore which arose was, whether the Court of the captor lost its jurisdiction over the captured vessel by its being carried into a neutral port. The Court decided in favor of the jurisdiction of the foreign tribunal, holding the possession of the captors in a neutral port, to be the possession of the sovereign. This point was held by a majority of the judges,* and the question was accordingly regarded as settled.

But the principle laid down by the Chief-Justice in Rose *vs.* Himely, that the seizure of a vessel on the high seas *beyond* the jurisdiction of the sovereign, for the mere breach of a municipal regulation, was invalid, and conferred no jurisdiction, was not considered as settled. Accordingly, at the term of the Court, in 1810, the case of Hudson *vs.* Guestier again came up for argument on a new state of facts, from which it appeared that the *Sea Flower* had actually been captured *beyond* the jurisdiction of St. Domingo, and had been carried into the neutral port of Baracoa, in the isle of Cuba. The point, that the French Court had jurisdiction, notwithstanding the captured vessel lay within a neutral port, being considered as settled by the former decision, the sole remaining question was, whether the capture beyond the territorial jurisdiction of St. Domingo was valid. Mr. Justice Livingston delivered the opinion of the Court in favor of the jurisdiction, overruling the doctrine of the Chief-Justice in Rose *vs.* Himely, and in this opinion all the judges except the Chief-Justice concurred.†

* Justice Livingston and one other of the judges dissenting.

† 6 Cranch, 281. The decision in Rose *vs.* Himely is qualified in another respect by the subsequent case of Williams and others *vs.* Amroyd and others, at the term of the Court in 1813. In that case it is said to be settled by the decision of Hudson *vs.* Guestier, that the sentence of a *competent Court* proceeding *in rem.* is conclusive with respect to the thing itself. No Court of co-ordinate jurisdiction can examine the sentence; and though a foreign tribunal should condemn American neutral property under an edict unjust in itself, contrary to the law of nations, and in violation of neutral rights, as declared by the executive and legislative authority of the United States, yet the Courts of this country cannot lend their

This important branch of jurisprudence, namely, Admiralty and Prize law—which subsequently grew up into a system in the Federal tribunals—received a new impulse at the breaking out of the war, and after the accession of Judge Story to the national judiciary.

That eminent jurist took his seat on the bench at the term held in February, 1812,* filling the vacancy occasioned by the death of Judge Cushing. Another vacancy had also recently occurred by the death of Judge Chase, which vacancy had been filled by the appointment of Gabriel Duval, of Maryland. In other respects no change had been made since the appointment of Mr. Justice Todd, in 1807.

From the correspondence of Judge Story at this period, we derive some interesting details relative to the mode of life of the judges at these general terms of the Court, and their manner of dispatching business. They lived together on terms of the most frank and unaffected intimacy: "Our intercourse," he writes, "is perfectly familiar and unconstrained, and our social hours, when undisturbed with the labors of law, are passed in gay and frank conversation, which at once enlivens and instructs." †

The mode of arguing causes in the Supreme Court at that day was excessively tedious and prolix. Long Chancery bills with overloaded documents, and long common law records, with scores of bills of exceptions attached to them, crowded the docket. I have mentioned the three days' speech of Luther Martin in the argument of a single case which lasted nine days. Though this was not, perhaps, a common occurrence, still it was no unusual thing for a cause to consume three or four days in the argument.‡ One lasted five days at the term

aid to the owner to recover such property, because they cannot revise, correct, or even examine the sentence of the foreign tribunal. 7 Cranch Reports, 423.

* He was appointed toward the close of the year 1811, the office having been first tendered to Levi Lincoln, and afterwards to John Quincy Adams, by both of whom it was declined. At the time of Story's appointment he was but thirty-two years of age, and the youngest judge ever raised to the bench of the Supreme Court.

† Letter to his wife. March 5th, 1812.—*Life and Letters*, Vol. I. p. 217.

‡ The Chief-Justice was one of the most patient listeners that ever sat on the bench. "His patience," says Mr. Binney, "was never surpassed;—patience to hear that which he knew already, that which he disapproved, that which questioned himself. When he ceased to hear it was not because his patience was exhausted, but because it ceased to be a virtue. Whether the argument was ani-

when Story first took his seat, and in this case he says a printed *brief* of two hundred and thirty pages was put into his hands in addition. The two hours' rule, subsequently adopted, was not then in vogue to cut short prolixity and arrest dullness. The labor of these heavy causes, however, was much relieved by the mode adopted by the judges, of mooting questions as the argument proceeded, and discussing them step by step, in familiar conversation, at their lodgings. In this way, remarks Story, we often came to a very quick and very accurate opinion in a few hours.

About this period the celebrated William Pinkney, of Maryland, re-appeared at the bar of the Supreme Court, and entered upon that brilliant career, which is almost without a parallel in the history of the profession. With the exception of two years—from 1804 to 1806—Pinkney had been entirely withdrawn from the practice of law for the period of fifteen years, during the greater part of which time he had filled important official stations abroad. Returning to America in 1811, he was soon afterwards appointed Attorney-General of the United States by President Madison, and attended the Supreme Court for the first time at the February term, 1812.*

mated or dull, instructive or superficial, the regard of his expressive eye was an assurance that nothing that ought to affect the cause was lost by inattention or indifference, and the courtesy of his general manner was only so far restrained on the bench, as was necessary for the dignity of office and the suppression of familiarity." An anecdote, related of Marshall I believe by Judge Story, pleasantly illustrates these characteristics. A tedious advocate was drawing out a protracted and wearisome argument, in which he discussed a thousand trivial and unimportant principles, and advanced again and again the most trite and familiar propositions. The Chief-Justice listened to the speaker with profound attention until "patience had ceased to be a virtue," when he interrupted him in his usual placid and affable manner, with the remark: "Mr. ——, I think this is unnecessary. There are some things which a Court, constituted as this is, may be presumed to know."

* The first case argued by Mr. Pinkney, after his appointment as Attorney-General, was a Maryland case—Le Roy *vs.* The Maryland Insurance Company. A crowded audience had assembled to hear him, and Pinkney, who had been keeping the public some time in suspense as to his *début*, exerted himself to the utmost, and with distinguished success. Messrs. Winder and Harper were for the plaintiffs, and Luther Martin, then Attorney-General of Maryland, was associated with Pinkney for the defendants. This, as I have remarked, was the first term of Judge Story on the bench of the Supreme Court. In a letter to a friend, Story

Pinkney was admirably fitted for this appointment at a time when questions of prize law were constantly arising in the Federal Courts. During the six or seven years in which he had officiated in England as one of the commissioners under Jay's treaty, he had acquired an extensive and thorough knowledge of the principles applicable to these subjects, having been almost constantly engaged in the investigation of cases turning upon the law and practice of prize courts, the rights of belligerents and neutrals, the law of contraband, blockade, &c.

One of the earliest causes in which Pinckney was engaged was that of the *Exchange*,* in which the Chief-Justice was called upon to consider and determine some very delicate, as well as intricate questions of international law connected with Admiralty jurisdiction. The *Exchange*, an American merchant ship, had been captured by a French vessel under Napoleon's decree of Rambouillet. Having been commissioned in the French service, and sailing as a French vessel, she had put into the port of Philadelphia, in distress, where she had been proceeded against by the American owners. The French minister thereupon interposed the claim (which was sustained by the Attorney-General, Mr. Pinkney, and Mr. Dallas, the District-Attorney of Pennsylvania), that, being a French national vessel, she was not amenable to judicial process; and that the original seizure was a question of state to be settled by negotiation, and was not a question to be settled in an American Court of Admiralty. These positions, which we are told by the biographer of Pinkney, he sustained with a force of argument, an eloquence, and an extent of learning which raised him in the public estimation to the head of the American bar, were subsequently made the judgment of the Court. The question

alludes to the argument of this case, and gives his earliest impression of Pinkney. Winder, he says, was smart and striking; Harper adroit and able; Martin heavy, unmethodical, and inaccurate; but Pinkney was, to the mind of the young Judge, the Ajax of the argument. "His speech," says Story, after briefly alluding to his defective voice, and vehement manner, "was admirable, his language fluent and select, elegant, glowing, fiery—the *ardentia verba* of oratory—and his logic was conceived with a cogency that bore itself in one continued stream of reasoning:

'Wave followed wave, nor spent its force in vain.'"

* 7 Cranch Rep. 116 to 147.

was a novel one, so far as the Courts of this country were concerned; and, indeed, very little light had been thrown upon it by any adjudged case in England. The Chief-Justice remarks in his opinion that in exploring an unbeaten path, with few, if any, aids from precedents or written law, the Court had found it necessary to rely much on general principles, and on a train of reasoning founded on cases in some degree analogous to this. Following this course of reasoning, and applying these principles, he arrives at a conclusion which is based doubtless upon the highest and most liberal principles of comity and international law—namely, that notwithstanding the vessel might have been the property of the libellants, yet her capture and commission in the service of the French Emperor stamped her with the character of foreign nationality, and having necessarily entered within an American port, and demeaning herself in a friendly manner, she was entitled to be treated in the same manner as any other public armed vessel of the French Emperor, with whom we were at peace, and was exempt from the jurisdiction of the country.

I shall notice but one other of these Admiralty cases argued before, and decided by, the Chief-Justice—namely, the celebrated case of the *Nereide*. This case came before the Court at the memorable session of 1815—a session which called out a more brilliant and imposing display of forensic eloquence and argument, than had ever before or perhaps has ever since, at any one time, been witnessed in the Supreme Court. As a proof of this it is but necessary to mention the names of some of the eminent and able counsel engaged in various causes during the session, such as Pinkney, Dexter, Harper, Jones, Stockton, Emmett, Hoffman, Ogden, Wells, Webster, and Clay. Some of these now appeared for the first time in that august tribunal, among whom was the celebrated Irish exile, Thomas Addis Emmett, of New York.* Mr. Emmett was employed in some important prize causes.

* Mr. Emmett appeared frequently at the bar of the Supreme Court after this period, and in almost every variety of causes. Judge Story, who always expressed the highest respect for his talents and character, speaks of him as follows: "His mind possessed a good deal of the fervor which characterizes his countrymen. It was quick, vigorous, searching, and buoyant. He kindled as he spoke. There was a spontaneous combustion, as it were, not sparkling, but clear and glowing. His rhetoric was never florid; and his diction, though select and pure, seemed the common dress of his thoughts, as they arose, rather than any studied

In two of these—the case of the *Mary*, and that of the *Nereide*—he was opposed by Pinkney. He made his *début* in the first of these cases, in presence of a large and brilliant audience. Embarrassed by the novelty of the scene, and his want of familiarity with the subject, he did not do himself full justice in his argument, and appeared conscious, says Judge Story, who was then on the bench, that he was not making one of his happiest efforts. Pinkney, on the other hand, was thoroughly familiar with the whole range of the discussion, and, excited by the emulation of meeting a new adversary, made one of his most imposing and magnificent speeches. He, of course, won an easy victory, and pressed his advantage with infinite dexterity, but with a harshness of language, and an overbearing manner, which were calculated to wound the sensitive feelings of his opponent.

Soon after, the case of the *Nereide* was called; a brief statement of the facts of which will be necessary in order to enable the reader to understand the positions taken by counsel, as well as the judgment of the Court. Manuel Pinto, a merchant of Buenos Ayres, had chartered the *Nereide*, a British armed vessel, mounting sixteen guns, to transport a cargo belonging in part to himself and others of his countrymen, from London to Buenos Ayres. The *Nereide* had been captured, near Madeira, after an action of about fifteen minutes, by the American privateer, the *Governor Tompkins*. Having been brought into the port of New York, the vessel and cargo were libelled, and both condemned as lawful prize. From this decree Mr. Pinto appealed, under the claim that a neutral might lawfully employ an armed belligerent vessel to transport his goods, and that if such vessel be captured, the neutral property on board is not, by the law of nations, lawful prize, but must be restored to the owner. Mr. Emmett, as

effort at ornament. Without being deficient in imagination, he seldom drew upon it for resources to aid the effect of his arguments, or to illustrate his thoughts. His object seemed to be, not to excite wonder or surprise, to captivate by bright pictures, and varied images, and graceful groups, and startling apparitions, but by earnest and close reasoning to convince the judgment, or to overwhelm the heart by awakening its most profound emotions. * * * * * * His command over the passions of others was an instantaneous and sympathetic action. The tones of his voice, when he touched on topics calling for deep feeling, were themselves instinct with meaning. They were utterances of the soul as well as of the lips."

counsel for Pinto, sustained these positions. He was opposed by Mr. Pinkney. The former was assisted in the argument by Mr. Hoffman, of New York, the latter by Mr. Dallas, of Philadelphia. The question debated, it will be seen, was one of the most important and interesting that could possibly arise in the whole range of that branch of jurisprudence, and the entire discussion was one of surpassing brilliancy and power. Emmett had recovered from his embarrassment, and made one of his happiest and ablest efforts. It was in the exordium to this speech that, after adverting in terms of generous praise to the fame and ability of his opponent, of whose harsh expressions in the previous case of the *Mary*, he had so much reason to complain, Emmett made a touching allusion to himself, and the misfortunes and sorrows of his own life: "My ambition," he said, "was extinguished in my youth; and I am admonished by the premature advances of age not now to attempt the dangerous path of fame." The pathos of the illustrious exile melted the hearts of the audience, and many of them, we are told, were dissolved in tears.*

The atonement of Pinkney in reply was ample as well as appropriate and delicate. Alluding to the opposing counsel, and turning to Mr. Emmett, he remarked: "To one of them, indeed, I have heretofore given unintentional pain by observations to which the influence of accidental excitement imparted the appearance of unkind criticism. The manner in which he replied to those observations reproached me by its forbearance and urbanity, and could not fail to hasten the repentance which reflection alone would have produced, and which I am glad to have so public an occasion of avowing. I offer him a gratuitous and cheerful atonement—cheerful, because it puts me to rights with myself, and because it is tendered, not to ignorance and presumption, but to the highest worth in intellect and morals, enhanced by such eloquence as few may hope to equal—to an interesting stranger whom adversity has tried, and affliction struck severely to the heart—to an exile whom any country might be proud to receive, and every man of a generous temper would be ashamed to offend. I feel relieved by this atonement, and proceed with more alacrity."

The argument of Mr. Pinkney in this great case is admitted to

* Letter of Judge Story to Mr. Sampson.—*Story's Miscellanies*, 806.

have been one of the most able and brilliant which he ever delivered.* It is preserved in Mr. Wheaton's collection of his writings and speeches, and, indeed, is almost the only one of his legal arguments which remains in anything like a tolerable state of preservation. It is certainly a fact, that forensic triumphs are, of all popular triumphs, the most ephemeral. Eloquence of speech, more potent and vivid than the eloquence of written language, is less enduring. It is the flash of the lightning, not the steady effulgence of the noonday sun;—the meteor which dazzles for a moment, not the serene and constant light

* The following extract from this speech may be given, as an example, not of Mr. Pinkney's logic, but of that richness of diction, and gorgeousness of illustration with which he was fond of embellishing his argument. He was criticising the proposition maintained by the counsel for the claimant, that an armed vessel of the enemy might be neutral in respect to her cargo, or, in other words, that a condition of neutrality and war might exist under the same flag. Following up the incongruity of this idea, Mr. Pinkney drew the following bold and striking figure of the *Nereide*.

"I entreat your honors to endeavor a personification of this motley notion, and to forgive me for presuming to intimate, that, if after you have achieved it, you pronounce the notion to be correct, you will have gone a great way to prepare us, by the authority of your opinion, to receive as credible history, the worst parts of the mythology of the Pagan world. The Centaur and the Proteus of antiquity will be fabulous no longer. The prosopopœia to which I invite you is scarcely, indeed, within the power of fancy, even in her most riotous and capricious mood, when she is best able and most disposed to force incompatibilities into fleeting and shadowy combination; but if you can accomplish it, it will give you something like the kid and the lion, the lamb and the tiger, portentously incorporated, with ferocity and meekness co-existent in the result, and equal as motives of action. It will give you a modern Amazon, more strangely constituted than those with whom ancient fable peopled the borders of the Thermodon—her voice compounded of the tremendous shout of the Minerva of Homer, and the gentle accents of a shepherdess of Arcadia—with all the faculties and inclination of turbulent and masculine War, and all the retiring modesty of virgin Peace. We shall have in one personage the *pharetrata camilla* of the Æneid, and the Peneian maid of the Metamorphosis. We shall have Neutrality, soft and gentle, and defenceless in herself, yet clad in the panoply of her warlike neighbors—with the frown of defiance upon her brow, and the smile of conciliation upon her lip—with the spear of Achilles in one hand, and a lying protestation of innocence and helplessness enfolded in the other. Nay, if I may be allowed so bold a figure in a mere legal discussion, we shall have the branch of olive entwined around the bolt of Jove, and Neutrality in the act of hurling the latter under the deceitful cover of the former."

of the same star upon which our fathers have gazed, and which our children shall look upon after us. Many of the brightest ornaments of the legal profession thus live by tradition alone; and the light of that tradition is every day growing more dim as we are gradually withdrawing farther from the generation which witnessed the display of their genius. Even Pinkney himself was no exception to the rule. "After all," exclaims Wirt, in one of his letters, alluding to Pinkney's death, "how long will he be remembered? He has left no monument of his genius behind him, and posterity will, therefore, know nothing of such a man but by the report of others. What should we have known of Hortensius but for Cicero?"

But to return from this digression. Neither the logic nor the eloquence of the counsel for the captors could avail to carry with it the judgment of the Court. The Chief-Justice pronounced the decision, which, though against Pinkney, was coupled with a compliment such as it has rarely fallen to the lot of any advocate to receive:—"With a pencil dipped in the most vivid colors," he says, "and guided by the hand of a master, a splendid portrait has been drawn, exhibiting the vessel and her freighter, as forming a single figure, composed of the most discordant materials of Peace and War. So exquisite was the skill of the artist, so dazzling the garb in which the figure was presented, that it required the exercise of that cold investigating faculty which ought always to belong to those who sit on this bench to discover its only imperfection—*its want of resemblance.*"

The decision of the Chief-Justice in this case has been regarded, and perhaps justly, as one of the least satisfactory ever pronounced by him in this branch of jurisprudence. Starting with the doctrine, which he considers an admitted principle of the law of nations, that a neutral may lawfully place his goods on board an unarmed ship of a belligerent nation, without losing their neutral character, he arrives at the conclusion that the principle is equally sound in its application to an armed belligerent vessel, even though forcible resistance be made by such vessel, and the neutral be on board at the time, provided he does not aid in such resistance. This was carrying the etiquette of international law to its extreme limits; and, whatever reason of dissatisfaction the American captors may have had, certainly foreign nations could have no cause of complaint. The prevailing view of the Court was the more remarkable, inasmuch as it was admitted that it did not rest on any express authority. No similar case could be found ; and only a few scanty materials, made up of inferences from cases depending on other principles, had been gleaned from the books and employed by both parties in the argument.

The conclusions of the Chief-Justice, which were adopted by the majority of the Court, were not concurred in by two of the Judges. One of these, Mr. Justice Story, wrote a very able, and, so far as the argument is concerned, it has been thought, a very conclusive, dissenting opinion. In a letter to a friend, written about the same time, he remarks that he never in his whole life was more thoroughly satisfied that the judgment of the Court was wrong. It may be added that in a similar case, soon after brought to argument in the English high Court of Admiralty,* that court laid down a rule precisely the reverse of the principle established in the Supreme Court of the United States in the case of the *Nereide*, holding, that though neutral property on board a merchant vessel of a belligerent was protected, yet, if placed upon an armed belligerent ship, it would be liable, on just and sound principles, to condemnation along with the captured vessel. The United States Supreme Court, however, adhered to its decision, and though the same point was subsequently raised and argued in another case,† the Court refused to reverse the doctrine established in the case of the *Nereide*, observing that the rule was correct in principle, and the most liberal and honorable to the jurisprudence of this country.

Passing by a variety of interesting and important decisions connected with almost every branch of jurisprudence, made by the Chief-Justice during the last fifteen years of his life, I propose to close this imperfect retrospect of his judicial labors by a brief notice of a few of those more prominent cases involving great questions of constitutional law which passed under his review, and in so doing shall follow the chronological order of these decisions as far as a connected view of the subject will admit.

The opinions of Marshall, it is well known, though not extreme, were nevertheless strongly federal and conservative. The tendency of

* Case of the *Fanny*. 1 Dodson, Admiralty Rep. 443.

† Case of the *Atalanta*. 3 Wheaton's Rep. 409.

his decisions hitherto had been, and steadily continued to be, to sustain the powers of the Federal government, and to vindicate the authority of the Federal judiciary, both over the State tribunals and State legislation. Hence, in the decision of those important cases involving the subject of constitutional restriction on the powers of the separate States, some of which I am now about to notice, he is almost always found sustaining the most liberal constructions in favor of the authority of the Federal government; and, narrowing down, so to speak, within strict limits, the powers of the States. Without undertaking to defend or advocate, upon original principles, the correctness of some of these decisions, particularly one which will presently be noticed,* it is sufficient to say that most of them have been since acquiesced in, and may now be regarded, so far as judicial authority can establish constitutional constructions, as the settled law of our highest tribunal.

I have noticed on a preceding page the case of The United States *vs* Peters,† in which he held that a State legislature could not annul the judgments, or determine the jurisdiction of the Courts of the United States; and also the case of Fletcher *vs.* Peck,‡ deciding that a party could not, consistently with the Constitution, annul his own grant, even if such party were a sovereign State. The case of Terret *vs.* Taylor,§ which was argued at the same term with the *Nereide*, followed, wherein Mr. Justice Story delivered the opinion of the Court, holding that a State legislature could not repeal statutes creating private corporations, or confirming to them property already acquired under the faith of previous laws.

The authority of the Supreme Court to annul State laws as being repugnant to the Constitution, and the powers of the Federal government, was again vigorously applied by the Chief-Justice and his associates, at the memorable session of 1819, in three noted cases,‖ whose vital importance, and intimate connection with the constitutional jurisprudence of the country, render a brief notice of each of them proper and necessary in this place.

* McCulloch *vs.* State of Maryland.

† *Ante*, page 358.

‡ *Ante*, p. 359.

§ 9 Cranch's Reports, 43.

‖ The Dartmouth College case, the case of Sturges *vs.* Crownneshield, and that of McCulloch *vs.* Maryland.

The first of these cases to which I shall allude, is the celebrated Dartmouth College case, reported under the title of The Trustees of Dartmouth College *vs.* Woodward ;* and I notice it first, because, though not the earliest in point of time, of the three great cases decided at the session of 1819, it is closely connected in principle with, and most naturally follows, the cases of Fletcher *vs.* Peck, and Terret *vs.* Taylor, above referred to, and indeed is, in another form, but a branch of the same discussion, namely, the constitutional inhibition upon the States to pass any law impairing the obligation of contracts.

This celebrated case is too well known to need a detailed statement of the facts out of which it arose. Acts of the legislature of New Hampshire, passed in 1816, had invaded the charter of the College, granted by the British Crown before the revolution. A suit was instituted in the State Courts of New Hampshire to test the validity of these acts, and the decision of the highest Court of the State was in favor of their validity and against the College. From this decision the Trustees of the College appealed to the Supreme Court of the United States. The argument of the case was fully commensurate with its great importance, and the unusual interest it had excited. Webster and Hopkinson appeared for the College, and the newly-appointed Attorney-General William Wirt, and Mr. Holmes, on the other side. Of the depth and power, and brilliancy of the arguments, particularly those of Webster and Wirt, it is unnecessary to speak. That of the former, even as it is found in the dry and hard outlines of the reporter's notes, exhibits in its full maturity the greatness and majestic strength of one of those rare intellects that appear at long intervals in the world.† The speech of Wirt, though not fully report-

* 4 Wheaton's Reports, 518.

† Mr. Choate, in his late eloquent eulogy upon Mr. Webster, has supplied the peroration to this argument, together with some interesting reminiscences attending it, from the relation of an eye-witness, Professor Chauncey A. Goodrich, of Yale College. The interest of the narrative, not less than its beauty of expression, furnishes an apology for introducing it in this place :

" The Supreme Court of the United States held its session that winter in a mean apartment, of moderate size—the Capitol not having been built after its destruction in 1814. The audience, when the case came on, was therefore small, consisting chiefly of legal men, the *élite* of the profession throughout the country. Mr. Webster entered on his argument in the calm tone of easy and dignified conversation. His matter was so completely at his command that he scarcely looked

ed, was also of great power and beauty. Indeed, it must have been one of his greatest and most brilliant efforts to have justified the encomiums which his adversary passed upon it. Says Webster in a

at his brief, but went on for more than four hours with a statement so luminous and a chain of reasoning so easy to be understood, and yet approaching so nearly to absolute demonstration, that he seemed to carry with him every man of his audience without the slightest effort or weariness on either side. It was hardly eloquence, in the strict sense of the term—it was pure reason. Now and then, for a sentence or two, his eye flashed and his voice swelled into a bolder note as he uttered some emphatic thought, but he instantly fell back into the tone of earnest conversation which ran throughout the great body of his speech. A single circumstance will show you the clearness and absorbing power of his argument.

"I observed that Judge Story, at the opening of the case, had prepared himself, pen in hand, as if to take copious minutes. Hour after hour, I saw him fixed in the same attitude, but so far as I could perceive, with not a note on his paper. The argument closed, and I could not discover that he had taken a single note. Others around me remarked the same thing, and it was among the *on dits* of Washington, that a friend spoke to him of the fact with surprise, when the Judge remarked :—

"'Everything was so clear, and so easy to remember, that not a note seemed necessary, and in fact, I thought little or nothing about my notes.'

"The argument ended, Mr. Webster stood for some moments silent before the court, while every eye was fixed intently upon him. At length, addressing the Chief-Justice, Marshall, he proceeded thus :—

"'This, sir, is my case! It is the case not merely of that humble institution—it is the case of every college in our land. It is more. It is the case of every eleemosynary institution throughout our country—of all those great charities founded by the piety of our ancestry to alleviate human misery, and scatter blessings along the pathway of life. It is more! It is in some sense the case of every man among us, who has property of which he may be stripped, for the question is simply this : 'Shall our State Legislatures be allowed to take that which is not their own, to turn it from its original use and apply it to such ends or purposes as they, in their discretions, shall see fit?' Sir, you may destroy this little institution : it is weak : it is in your hands! I know it is one of the lesser lights in the literary horizon of our country. You may put it out. But if you do so, you must carry through your work. You must extinguish, one after another, all those great lights of science which for more than a century have thrown their radiance over our land! It is, sir, as I have said, a small college. And yet there are those who love it. [Here the feelings which he had thus far succeeded in keeping down, broke forth : his lips quivered ; his firm cheeks trembled with emotion ; his eyes were filled with tears ; his voice choked, and he seemed struggling to the utmost simply to gain that mastery over himself which might save

letter to him from Boston, soon after: "It is the universal opinion in this quarter, among all who have inquired or heard about the cause, that that argument was a full, able, and most eloquent exposition of the rights of the defendant. I will add that, in my opinion, no future discussion of the questions involved in the cause, either at the bar or on the bench, will bring forth on the part of the defendant any important idea which was not argued, expanded, and pressed in the argument alluded to."

There are those who are still of the opinion that Wirt, if indeed he

him from an unmanly burst of feeling. I will not attempt to give you the few broken words of tenderness in which he went on to speak of his attachment to the college; the whole seemed to be mingled throughout with the recollections of father, mother, brother, and all the trials and privations through which he had made his way into life. Every one saw that it was wholly unpremeditated, a pressure on his heart, which sought relief in words and tears.]

"The court-room during these two or three minutes, presented an extraordinary spectacle. Chief-Justice Marshall, with his tall and gaunt figure bent over as if to catch the slightest whisper, the deep furrows of his cheek expanded with emotion, and eyes suffused with tears; Mr. Justice Washington at his side, with his small and emaciated frame, and a countenance more like marble than I ever saw on any other human being, leaning forward with an eager, troubled look; and the remainder of the court, at the two extremities, pressing, as it were, towards a single point, while the audience below were wrapping themselves round in closer folds beneath the bench to catch each look, and every movement of the speaker's face. If a painter could give us the scene on canvass—those forms and countenances, and Daniel Webster as he then stood in the midst—it would be one of the most touching pictures in the history of eloquence. One thing it taught me, that the pathetic depends not merely on the words uttered, but still more on the estimate we put upon him who utters them. There was not one among the strong-minded men of that assembly who would think it unmanly to weep when he saw standing before him the man who had made such an argument, melted into the tenderness of a child. Mr. Webster had now recovered his composure, and, fixing his keen eye on the Chief-Justice, said, in that deep tone with which he sometimes thrilled the heart of an audience,

"'Sir, I know not how others may feel,' (glancing at the opponents of the College before him,) 'but for myself, when I see my alma mater surrounded like Cæsar in the Senate House, by those who are reiterating stab upon stab, I would not for this right hand have her turn to me and say, '*et tu quoque mi fili!*'''

"And thou, too, my son! He sat down. There was a death-like stillness throughout the room for some moments; every one seemed to be slowly recovering himself, and coming gradually back to his ordinary range of thought and feeling."

had not the better of the argument, was at least on the true side of the question, and that it was going far—indeed to the extreme limit of construction—for the Supreme Court to say, that, by the Constitution of the United States, the legislature of a sovereign State could not alter the charter of a literary corporation resting upon a grant from the British Crown. Such, however, was the decision of the Supreme Court as pronounced by the Chief-Justice, and amplified by the written opinions of Justices Story and Washington, Mr. Justice Duval alone dissenting. The Chief-Justice lays down, broadly and clearly, the propositions, that the charter of the College was a *contract* within the meaning of the Constitution, to which the donors, the trustees of the corporation, and the Crown were the original parties, and that it was made on a valuable consideration, for the security and disposition of property; that the College was a private eleemosynary institution, and that the funds with which it was endowed were bestowed by individuals on the strength of its charter; that contracts of this kind, creating these charitable institutions, are within the purview and protection of the Constitution; that this contract remained unchanged by the revolution, and the duties as well as the powers of the government devolved on the people of New Hampshire; but that the act of the State, complained of, transferred the power of governing the College from the mode expressed in its charter, to the governor of New Hampshire, thus substituting the will of the State for the will of the donors. This, he held, was a subversion of that contract, on the faith of which the donors had invested their property, and the act, therefore, as repugnant to the Constitution of the United States, was null and void.

It is impossible to read this admirably reasoned and luminous opinion of the Chief-Justice without being impressed with the irresistible power of that direct and simple, but acute and subtle juridical logic of which he was so consummately the master.* It is comparatively

* Judge Story notices a favorite mode of reasoning of the Chief-Justice, indicated by his frequent use of the term—"it is admitted." Said Daniel Webster, "when Chief-Justice Marshall says, 'it is admitted, sir,' I am prepared for a bomb that will demolish all my points." Judge Story also remarks that it was a common expression of those who were accustomed to argue before him, "Once grant his premises, and you are forced to admit his conclusions. Therefore deny everything he says."

brief for a case of such magnitude ; but at the same time it is full and comprehensive. He relies upon no authority, and indeed cites no cases. All is an effort of pure ratiocination—of logical deduction. In this respect it contrasts strongly with the more elaborate and striking opinion of Judge Story in the same case—full of illustration, abounding in analogies, overflowing with citations of authorities and adjudged cases. Indeed, so full, and ample, and rich is Story's argument in the abundance of its legal lore, as to throw somewhat into the shade the simple and unadorned, but firm and compact, logic of the Chief-Justice. The two opinions, as has been well remarked, certainly evince the different structure of the two minds of these eminent jurists.*

The next decision at this term which I shall notice was made in the case of Sturges *vs.* Crowninshield,† which established a most important principle relative to the limitation of State sovereignty under the same clause of the Constitution involved in the discussion of the Dartmouth College case, namely, the clause which prohibits a State Legislature from passing any law "impairing the obligation of contracts."

The defendant had been sued in the Circuit Court, on two promissory notes dated in March 1811, and he pleaded his discharge under the Insolvent Act of New York, passed in April 1811. The plaintiff claimed that the act of New York, being retrospective, and assuming, as in this case, to discharge pre-existing debts, was unconstitutional and void. This position was sustained, all the judges appearing to have unanimously concurred in the admirably reasoned and conclusive opinion pronounced by the Chief-Justice—an opinion which deserves to be carefully read by the student of our Constitutional history—establishing the proposition, that a State law assuming to discharge the debtor from his contract to pay an existing debt, by a given time, without performance, and to release him, without payment, entirely from any future obligation to pay, impaired, because it entirely dis-

* The comparison is made by the son and biographer of Judge Story. Its characteristic truth, I apprehend, will be at once recognized. "The argument of the Chief-Justice," he says, "is close, logical, and compact, but somewhat *hard and dry*. The argument of my father is equally convincing, but far more *flowing and learned.*"

† 4 Wheaton's Reports, 122.

charged, the obligation of that contract, and was therefore repugnant to the Constitution of the United States, and void. In another case,* decided at the same time, the Chief-Justice declared as a part of the opinion of the Court, that the circumstance of the State law under which the debt was attempted to be discharged, having been passed *before* the debt was contracted, made no difference in the application of the principle. This proposition, however, was subsequently reviewed, in the case which I shall now notice, and after a full discussion and careful examination, overruled by a majority of the court, the Chief-Justice still adhering to his opinion.

The decision in Sturges *vs.* Crowninshield, as an eminent lawyer has remarked in a recent case involving a branch of the same discussion,† took the States and the profession by surprise. It was a matter of astonishment that up to that time the States had all been wrong. But this surprise was lessened when the case came to be discussed afterwards by the bench as well as the bar in Ogden *vs.* Saunders. This important case, which is considered as having settled the question relative to the constitutionality and extent of State insolvent laws, was brought to argument at the term of the Court held in February, 1824. Mr. Clay and Mr. Webster were the leading counsel on either side, the former supported by Mr. D. B. Ogden and Mr. Haines—and the latter, who maintained the unconstitutionality of the State law, by Mr. Wheaton. The case was afterwards re-argued in connexion with other causes depending on the same question, and the decision of the court pronounced in the winter of 1827.‡ In this latter argument the same gentlemen who advocated the unconstitutionality of the State laws again appeared, and the parties claiming the benefit of these laws were sustained by the eminent

* McMillan *vs.* McNeil, 4 Wheaton's Reports, 209.

† Mr. Reverdy Johnson, in the argument of Cook *vs.* Moffat, 5 Howard, 295. In that case the court reaffirmed the prevailing doctrine in Ogden *vs.* Saunders, holding that a New York contract could not be affected by the discharge of the debtor under the insolvent laws of Maryland. MR. CHIEF-JUSTICE TANEY intimates that he does not regard this part of the decision as in harmony with some of the principles previously adopted by the court, and if the question had not been considered as *res adjudicata*, he would have been in favor of establishing a different rule. See subsequent sketch of Chief-Justice Taney.

‡ 12 Wheaton's Reports, 213.

talents and great ability of the Attorney-General Wirt, and Edward Livingston, General Jones, Mr. Sampson, and Mr. D. B. Ogden.

The case differed from that of Sturges *vs.* Crowninshield in two important particulars, namely, 1st, that in the former case the law acted on a contract which was made before its passage, and in the latter case the contract was entered into after the passage of the law; and, 2d, that the debt claimed to be discharged under the State law was due to a citizen of another State. The first question involved the consideration of the constitutionality of a State bankrupt law applied to contracts made after its passage; the second the very grave question whether the discharge, under such law, of a contract made with a citizen of another State, and where the certificate was actually pleaded in the courts of another State, was a valid discharge of the debt.

It may be here remarked, that this is the only great constitutional question in which the majority of the court are known to have differed from the Chief-Justice. Upon the question of the constitutionality of the insolvent act of New York four of the judges—Mr. Justice Washington, Mr. Justice Johnson, Mr. Justice Trimble, and Mr. Justice Thompson—delivered separate opinions in favor of the validity of the law, and the Chief-Justice—with whom Justices Story and Duval concurred—delivered a dissenting opinion. Upon the second question, Mr. Justice Johnson united with the minority, holding that though a State might constitutionally pass a bankrupt insolvent act to operate upon future contracts and the rights of its own citizens, yet, that a discharge under such act was not a discharge of a debt due a citizen of another State. To the latter part of this proposition Justices Washington, Trimble, and Thompson dissented.*

* The published opinion of Judge Johnson has been since regarded as settling the law in respect to this question. In the case of Boyle *vs.* Zacharie and Turner, at the January term, 1832, Mr. Wirt inquired if the opinion of Mr. Justice Johnson had been adopted by the other judges, when Chief-Justice Marshall said, "The judges of this court, who were in a minority of the court upon the general question as to the constitutionality of State insolvent laws, concur in the opinion of Mr. Justice Johnson in the case of Ogden *vs.* Saunders. That opinion is, therefore, to be deemed the opinion of the other judges who assented to that judgment. Whatever principles are established in that opinion, are to be considered no longer open for controversy, but the settled law of the court."—6 Peters' Reports, 348.

The dissenting opinion of the Chief-Justice on this question of the constitutionality of State insolvent laws, is distinguished by his usual clearness, directness, and logical vigor. Like his previous opinions in the Dartmouth College case, and in Sturges *vs.* Crowninshield, and, indeed, it may be said like all his opinions on constitutional law, it is purely an effort of ratiocination—a piece of simple, logical reasoning and deduction—unsustained by precedent and authority, unaided by analogies, almost severe and hard in its rigid rejection of illustration and ornament. The reasons of Marshall were the suggestive inferences of his own mind; his manner of expression was the natural result of the mode he adopted in the investigation of the subject before him. He was in the constant habit of interpreting the Constitution by itself, of reading it by the steady torch of his own reason, of bringing to bear upon it the illumination of his own clear and strong intellect, of studying it, not in isolated portions and detached sentences, but as a whole. The principles of construction which he applied to it, are admirably summed up by him in the very case under consideration in the following words:—"To say that the intention of the instrument must prevail; that this intention must be collected from its words; that its words are to be understood in that sense in which they are generally used by those for whom the instrument was intended; that its provisions are neither to be restricted into insignificance, nor extended to objects not comprehended in them, nor contemplated by its framers; is to repeat what has been already said more at large, and is all that can be necessary."

Applying these rules of construction, the Chief-Justice arrives at the conclusion that the constitutional inhibition upon the States from passing laws "impairing the obligation of contracts," extends to all contracts prospective as well as retrospective. Had retrospective legislation only been intended, the very word would have been used to convey the idea. Words which directly and plainly express the cardinal intent always present themselves to those who are preparing an important instrument, and will always be used by them. The general

The same doctrine, as I have observed in a previous note, was recognized in the late case of Cook *vs.* Moffat, as a principle too well settled to be shaken, the present Chief-Justice, however, intimating his concurrence, if the question had been still open, in the views expressed by Justices Washington, Thompson, and Trimble.

language used is such as to suggest a general intent to prohibit State legislation on the entire subject—the obligation of contracts—not merely from passing retrospective laws. It must be admitted that it is much easier to deny these conclusions, than to answer or refute the course of reasoning by which they are sustained. All we can say, therefore, in regard to them is that they are not the law of the United States, *because* the majority of the Court did not acquiesce in their correctness.

The last of the three great cases discussed and decided at the session of the Court in 1819, was the well known case of McCulloch *vs.* the State of Maryland,* a case which may be regarded in many respects as the most important ever discussed in the tribunals of the country, involving, as it did, a vital question, and one of the most delicate questions too that can possibly arise, relative to the conflicting powers of the general and State governments, and the supremacy of their respective laws. It was in reality a controversy between the United States and the State of Maryland; and I might here pause a moment, to pay a tribute of admiration to the foresight and wisdom of those statesmen who framed that august tribunal—that "more than Amphictyonic Council," as it was justly styled in the warm and glowing language of one of the most eloquent advocates of the day—the Supreme Court of the United States;—a tribunal vested with authority to sit in judgment not only upon the rival pretensions and claims of sovereign States as among themselves, but also to determine questions of power and right as between the States and the supreme Federal Government;—to determine them finally, and authoritatively, without question and without appeal—without force and even without angry controversy. A tribunal so constituted, with such ample jurisdiction, and yet wisely limited powers, does not find its parallel in history; and it may be added that a tribunal so august, not less on account of its own dignity, than of those vast and unmeasured interests which are committed to its keeping, is nowhere else to be found among civilized nations.

In the present case the controversy between the United States and Maryland was of a very novel as well as of a very interesting character. Each disputed the constitutionality of a law of the other.

* 4 Wheaton's Reports, 316.

Each asserted that the other had transcended the limits of its sovereignty. Maryland had assumed to pass an act laying a tax on the branch of the United States Bank in that State, which law, it was alleged, was repugnant to the constitutional powers of the Federal Government, and void. The State in turn attacked the constitutionality of the law of the Federal Government chartering the Bank. The controversy was deemed of such importance that the government directed the Attorney-General, Mr. Wirt, to appear, and the Court dispensed with its standing rule, which permitted only two counsel to argue on each side. What shall be said of the power and brilliancy of that discussion at the bar which called out the strength of Webster, the culture and erudition of Wirt, and the genius of Pinkney on the one side, and the solid learning and eloquence of Martin, Hopkinson, and Jones on the other *—a discussion that extorted from the presiding judge on the bench the almost involuntary exclamation that it displayed " a splendor of eloquence and strength of argument seldom if ever surpassed ?" Webster opened the debate. Wirt followed Hopkinson. Jones and Martin continued the argument, and Pinkney reserved himself for the reply. The speech of Pinkney occupied three days in the delivery, and is pronounced one of the ablest he ever delivered.† The hall was filled to suffocation by a crowded, but brilliant audience of ladies and gentlemen, and he accordingly addressed himself with more than his usual energy and fire to the discussion of what he somewhat affectedly called the "miserable shreds, the ragged odds and ends, the *tristes reliquiæ*" of what had been left him of the argument. He had hoped to escape, he says, the discussion of the question of the constitutionality of the Bank, and had made it his humble suit to the learned gentlemen on the other side not to conjure up by

* Of this array of counsel, perhaps the strongest and most imposing ever witnessed at the bar of this or any other country, the venerable General Walter Jones, now residing in Washington, is the sole survivor.

† The substance of the argument, from the memoranda taken at the time by Mr. Wheaton, and the imperfect notes subsequently furnished by Pinkney, is all that remains of this great speech. Judge Story, in one of his letters, remarks of it: "I never in my whole life heard a greater speech. It was worth a journey from Salem to hear it. His elocution was excessively vehement, but his eloquence was overwhelming. His language, his style, his figures, his argument, were most brilliant and sparkling."

unhallowed rights the ghost of a departed controversy. If the constitutionality of the Bank could not be assumed, he had hoped, at least, it would have been submitted in respectful silence. But the counsel had thrown down the gauntlet and entered upon the discussion. "The consequence is," he remarks, "that the question of the constitutionality of the Bank has arisen, as it were, from the grave, and in its very shroud presents itself before you, to demand at last the honors of Christian burial, in such sort, that it may hereafter hope to rest in peace beyond the reach of the lawless incantations of those potent sorcerers and their confederates."

This question then met Chief-Justice Marshall at the threshold, in pronouncing the opinion of the Court. He decided it, as is well known, in favor of the constitutionality of the Bank. I do not propose to comment upon or review his argument. The question has been considered as a question of state since that time, and different opinions are entertained in regard to the correctness of this decision. It is perhaps of little practical importance now, as the bank, in the language of one of the counsel for the government, uttered many years afterwards, has become an "obsolete idea." It is sufficient here to say, that the Chief-Justice found no *express* grant for it in the Constitution, but he deduced it from the power to "make all laws which shall be necessary and proper to carry into execution" the powers of government. The substance of his views in respect to this grant of power is expressed in the following passage :—"We admit, as all must admit, that the powers of the government are limited, and that its limits are not to be transcended. But we think the sound construction of the Constitution must allow to the national legislature that *discretion* with respect to the means by which the powers it confers are to be carried into execution, which will enable that body to perform the high duties assigned to it in the manner most beneficial to the people. Let the end be legitimate, let it be within the scope of the Constitution, and *all means which are appropriate, which are plainly adapted to that end, which are not prohibited, but consist with the letter and spirit of the Constitution, are constitutional.*"

The institution of the Bank he believed to be within this definition, and thus arrived at the conclusion that its establishment was not repugnant to the legitimate powers of the general government.

The constitutionality of the Bank being thus established as a "necessary and proper" instrument to carry on the fiscal operations of the government, the Chief-Justice next approaches the delicate, and, if possible, still more important question as to the right of the State of Maryland, in the exercise of its sovereignty, to tax the Bank. The Constitution was found to contain no express provision for the case; it did not in terms prohibit the exercise of such a power by the State· Maryland therefore claimed that this unlimited right of taxation was a portion of her sovereignty which she had never yielded to the general government; and that, though the State might not be at liberty directly to resist a constitutional law of Congress, yet it might exercise its acknowledged powers upon it, and that the Constitution had left the States this right (embracing the unlimited right of taxation,) IN CONFIDENCE that it would not be abused.

The United States, on the other hand, contended that though the States undoubtedly possessed, as an attribute of sovereignty, the power of taxation, to be exercised concurrently with the general government, yet, such was the paramount character of the Federal Constitution, that it would restrain a State from any such exercise of this power as was in its nature incompatible with, and repugnant to, the constitutional laws of the Union. The Bank was a "necessary and proper" instrument to carry out the acknowledged powers of government; the power of taxing it by the States *might* be exercised so as to destroy it; therefore the right of the States to pass such a law was denied. These were the conclusions adopted by Marshall, in that carefully considered and closely reasoned opinion, which he pronounced in the case, and which, it has been thought, contains the clearest and fullest exposition of constitutional law on this subject, and of the nature and extent of the powers of the general and state governments, ever delivered, even by himself, in any one judgment.* The exemption of the Bank from State taxation he rests, to use his own language, "on a principle which so entirely pervades the Constitution, is so intermixed with the materials which compose it, so inter-

* Says Chancellor Kent, "A case could not be selected from the decisions of the Supreme Court, superior to this one of *McCulloch* vs. *the State of Maryland*, for the clear and satisfactory manner in which the supremacy of the laws of the Union have been maintained by the Court, and an undue assertion of State power overruled and defeated."—1 Kent. Com. 427.

woven with its web, so blended with its texture, as to be incapable of being separated from it, without rending it into shreds. This great principle is, that the Constitution, and the laws made in pursuance thereof, are supreme; that they control the constitutions and laws of the respective States, and cannot be controlled by them. From this, which may almost be termed an axiom, other propositions may be deduced as corrollaries, on the truth or error of which, and on their application to this case, the cause has been supposed to depend. These are 1st, That a power to create implies a power to preserve. 2d, That a power to destroy, if wielded by a different hand, is hostile to, and incompatible with these powers to create and to preserve. 3d, That where this repugnance exists, that authority which is supreme must control, not yield to that over which it is supreme." In the application of these propositions to the case under review, he considers the law of Maryland as imposing a tax, not on the real property of the Bank, or on the interest which the citizens of Maryland might hold in the institution in common with other property of the same description throughout the State, but as a tax on the operations of the Bank, as an instrument employed by the government of the Union to carry its powers into execution, and therefore such tax was unconstitutional and void; it being a question not of *discretion* and *confidence* on the part of the State, but a question of ABSOLUTE SUPREMACY as between the powers of Maryland and those of the General Government. Viewed from this position the reasoning and conclusion of the Chief-Justice are too strong to be shaken:—"If the States may tax one instrument, employed by the government in the execution of its powers," he says, "they may tax any and every other instrument. They may tax the mail; they may tax the mint; they may tax patent rights; they may tax the papers of the Custom House; they may tax judicial process; they may tax all the means employed by the General Government, to an excess which would defeat all the ends of the General Government. This was not intended by the American people. They did not design to make their government dependent on the States."*

* These propositions are of course too obvious to be questioned. The danger, however, consists in extending them beyond their proper limits. They evidently are designed to refer to a direct tax upon the means or instrument, not as property

After the searching and elaborate argument in this interesting case, and the deliberate and unanimous opinion of the court thereon, it might well be supposed that the question would have been considered, judicially at least, as settled. Such was not the fact. It was again raised in Osborne *vs.* The Bank of the United States * at the session of 1824, in an appeal from the Circuit Court of Ohio, which court had rendered a decree based upon the assumption that a statute of the State taxing the Bank of the United States, similar to that of Maryland, was unconstitutional.† A revision of the opinion pro-

in the hands of a citizen of the State, but as actually employed in the operations of the General Government. In the case of *Weston* vs. *the City of Charleston*, at the session of 1829, 2 Peters, 449—a case, the argument of which was illustrated by the ornate eloquence of Hayne, and the profound and varied learning of Legaré—the principle laid down in *McCulloch* vs. *Maryland* was carried to a still greater extent. The question was, whether a State tax on government stock issued for loans to the United States was constitutional; but the distinction above alluded to, namely, whether it was a tax upon property merely, or upon the powers of government, was not lost sight of, and indeed seems to have been the only question at issue between the majority and minority of the Court. In pronouncing the prevailing opinion of the Court, the Chief-Justice says: "The tax on government stock is thought by this Court to be a tax on the contract, a tax on the power to borrow money on the credit of the United States, and consequently to be repugnant to the Constitution." The clear and accurate mind of Mr. Justice Thompson, with whom Mr. Justice Johnson concurred, while admitting the general doctrine, drew from it exactly the opposite inference. In his dissenting opinion he says: "Thus, it is said the States cannot tax the Mint; but this does not imply that they may not tax the money coined at the Mint when held and owned by individuals. Again, it is said the States cannot tax a patent right; but if the patentee, from the sale or use of his patent, has acquired property, or is receiving an income, it could not be intended to say that such property or income cannot be taken into the estimate of his taxable property. * * * Congress has power to raise armies; such armies are made up of officers and soldiers, and are instruments employed by the government in executing its powers, and although the army as such cannot be taxed, yet it will not be claimed that all such officers and soldiers are exempt from State taxation. Upon the whole, considering that the tax in question is a general tax upon the interest of money on loan, I cannot think it any violation of the Constitution of the United States, to include therein interest accruing from stock of the United States."

* 9 Wheaton's Reports, 738.

† The Ohio law was passed a few days before the decision of McCulloch *vs.*

nounced in McCulloch *vs.* Maryland was requested, and granted by the court. The Chief-Justice again discusses with great care the questions raised and decided in the former case, particularly that which involved the power of a State to tax the Bank. The conclusions at which he arrives, however, and which are re-established by this judgment, are precisely the same as in the Maryland case, namely, that the creation of the bank was a constitutional exercise of the powers of the General Government, and that the act of the Legislature of Ohio in taxing the Bank was contrary to the Federal Constitution, and void.

This case, it may be remarked, presented another important constitutional question, namely, as to the validity of that part of the act of Congress which authorized the Bank to sue in the Circuit Courts. The question having been raised at the close of the argument, the Chief-Justice and his associates considered it of such vital consequence as to request that the case might be reargued on this point. The case of the Planters' Bank of Georgia * involved the same question, and the two causes came on for argument together. Mr. Harper of Maryland was the leading counsel against the claim of the Bank; and Mr. Clay, Mr. Webster, and Mr. John Sergeant, in favor of the jurisdiction. The opinions delivered by the Chief-Justice in both cases sustain the views of the latter gentlemen, and recognize the right of the Bank to sue in the Circuit Courts of the United States.

At the session of the Court in 1821, another of these interesting cases involving the gravest and most important questions of constitutional law, and of the jurisdiction of the Federal tribunals, was brought to argument. This was the case reported under the title of Cohens *vs.* the State of Virginia.† A judgment had been rendered against the defendants, citizens of Virginia, in the highest court of that State having cognizance of the subject, on an information for selling lottery tickets in a lottery to be drawn in the city of Washington, and the defendants claimed the protection of the act of Congress incorporating the city of Washington. The cause was brought by the

Maryland, and notwithstanding the decision in that case, the Ohio state officers proceeded to levy a tax of $50,000 imposed on the branch Bank of the United States, established in that State.

* 9 Wheaton's Reports, 904.

† 6 Wheaton's Reports, 264.

defendants to the Supreme Court of the United States on a writ of error. The counsel for Virginia, Messrs. Barbour and Smyth, moved to dismiss the writ on the ground that the Court had no jurisdiction, because, 1st, a State is a defendant; 2d, that no writ of error would lie from the Supreme Court to a State Court; 3d, that neither the Constitution nor any law of the United States has been violated by the judgment. Messrs. Pinkney and Ogden sustained the argument on the other side.

The questions involved in the first two points, as was observed by the Chief-Justice, were of great magnitude, and might truly be said, vitally to affect the Union. In the masterly opinion delivered by him, he states these questions in the following clear and precise terms: "They exclude the inquiry whether the Constitution and laws of the United States have been violated by the judgment which the plaintiffs in error seek to review; and maintain that, admitting such violation, it is not in the power of the government to apply a corrective. They maintain that the nation does not possess a department capable of restraining peaceably, and by authority of law, any attempts which may be made by a part against the legitimate powers of the whole; and that the government is reduced to the alternative of submitting to such attempts, or of resisting them by force. They maintain that the Constitution of the United States has provided no tribunal for the final construction of itself, or of the laws or treaties of the nation; but that this power may be exercised in the last resort by the courts of every State of the Union; that the Constitution, laws, and treaties, may receive as many constructions as there are States; and that this is not a mischief, or if a mischief, is irremediable. These abstract propositions are to be determined: for he who demands decision without permitting inquiry, affirms that the decision he asks does not depend upon inquiry.

"If such be the Constitution, it is the duty of the Court to bow with respectful submission to its provisions. If such be not the Constitution, it is equally the duty of the Court to say so, and to perform that task which the American people have assigned to the judicial department."

I cannot hope to present within the limits of this sketch, even an epitome of the profound and unanswerable argument with which the

Chief-Justice sustained the judgment of the Court in this interesting case—an argument, which, to say nothing of its value as a broad and comprehensive and accurate exposition of constitutional law, presents one of the most admirable specimens of juridical logic which ever flowed from the pen of Marshall himself. On a preceding page I have noticed the principles established by, and which followed the decision in the case of Marbury *vs.* Madison, and especially the principle laid down by the Court in the opinion of Justice Story, in the case of Martin *vs.* Hunter's Lessees,* that the appellate jurisdiction of the Supreme Court extends to a final judgment of the highest court of a State, where the validity of a State law is drawn in question as being against the Constitution, treaties, and laws of the United States, and the decision of the State court has been in favor of such their validity. The constitutionality of the same provision was now re-examined, and a flood of light thrown upon the subject by the luminous mind of Marshall, and the principle placed upon a foundation from which it can never again be dislodged. It was held to be no valid objection to the appellate jurisdiction of the Supreme Court, that one of the parties was a sovereign State, and the other a citizen of that State. The Constitution was the supreme law of the land, and the Court the interpreter of that Constitution ; and the judicial power, as originally given, extends to all cases arising under the Constitution or a law of the United States, whoever may be the parties.†

* 1 Wheaton's Reports, 304.

† Mr. Jefferson was never satisfied with this opinion, nor were some others of the most eminent of the statesmen and jurists of Virginia. Judge Roane wrote a very able review of it for the *Enquirer*, under the signature of Algernon Sidney. In reference to this review Jefferson says, in a letter to Judge Johnson, that it appeared to him "to pulverize every word which had been delivered by Judge Marshall, of the extra-judicial part of his opinion ; and all was extra-judicial, except the decison that the act of Congress had not purported to give to the Corporation of Washington the authority claimed by their lottery law, of controlling the laws of the States within the States themselves." Jefferson regarded as extra-judicial the doctrine laid down, as he says, by the Chief-Justice, that notwithstanding the amendment to the Constitution, a State *could* be brought to the bar of the Supreme Court, and that Congress might authorize a corporation of its territory to exercise legislative power within a State, and paramount to the laws of the State. "This doctrine," he observes, "was so completely refuted by Roane, that if he can be answered, I surrender human reason as a vain and useless faculty, given to bewilder, and not to guide us."—4 *Jefferson's Writings*, 371, 372.

Upon the general merits of the case itself, which was afterwards argued by Mr. Ogden and Mr. Pinkney for the plaintiffs, and by Mr. Webster for the defendants, the Chief-Justice delivered a brief opinion, holding that the act of Congress incorporating the city of Washington, under which the sale of the lottery tickets was authorized, was no defence to an indictment for a violation of the statutes of Virginia. The act of Congress did not authorize the corporation *to force* the sale of lottery tickets in states where such sale was prohibited by law.

I am justified in breaking the thread of this hasty review of Chief-Justice Marshall's constitutional decisions, by a brief reference to one case not included under this head, which seems to demand some notice, both on account of its novelty and interest, as well as of its own intrinsic importance. It is the case of Johnson *vs.* McIntosh,* argued and decided at the session of the Court in 1823—a case which opened the entire range of discussion relative to the origin and ground of the title to lands claimed by the European nations in America, and of the right now exercised by the government of the United States over territories occupied by the Indian tribes. The plaintiff claimed title to lands in Illinois, under a grant from the Piankeshaw Indians; the defendant under a grant from the United States. The opinion of the Court, delivered by the Chief-Justice, covers the entire ground, and leaves little room for further discussion. It may be taken as a complete text-book on the subject, and has been held in all subsequent cases to be an ultimate and settled rule of decision. He traces, with a clear and infallible precision of statement, the origin of the right claimed by discovery, the recognition of the principle by the European powers, and its adoption by the United States; he examines the foundation and limitation of the right of conquest, the application of the principle to the case of the Indian savages, and the nature generally of the Indian titles. These titles, as ultimate titles to the fee of the soil, could not now be sustained in America. The fee originally vested in the British government by discovery, according to the acknowledged law of civilized nations, had passed by the Revolution to the United States, and the Indian title was a right of occupancy merely, which the discoverers, or in this case, the government, had the exclusive right of acquiring

* 8 Wheaton's Reports, 543.

The magnitude of the interests in litigation, and the able and elaborate arguments at the bar, rather than any intrinsic difficulty in the subject itself, as the Chief-Justice remarks, had impelled him to a more than usually careful and mature consideration of the subject under discussion.

Returning to a consideration of the constitutional judgments and opinions of Chief-Justice Marshall, the next case that meets us is the famous case of Gibbons *vs.* Ogden,* known as the Great New York Steamboat case, which was decided at the session of the court in 1824. Though belonging to the same class of cases which have been heretofore considered, involving a question of sovereignty between State legislation and the Federal government; yet it presented an entirely new point for consideration, namely, as to the construction and extent of that clause of the Constitution vesting Congress with power to regulate commerce among the several states. The State of New York had granted to Messrs. Fulton and Livingston the exclusive right to navigate all the waters of the State with vessels moved by steam. The plaintiff, Ogden, to whom the right had been assigned, filed a bill for a perpetual injunction against Gibbons, who had infringed upon this right by navigating the river with steamboats, duly enrolled and licensed for the coasting trade, under an act of Congress. The question was, as to the Constitutionality of the law of New York. Chancellor Kent sustained the injunction, and the decree had been affirmed by the New York Court for the Correction of Errors. From this judgment the cause was carried to the Supreme Court of the United States. It has been said, that no cause, up to that date, in the Supreme Court, had ever excited a greater degree of interest and expectation in the country than this, and that none was ever argued with greater ability. The Attorney-General Wirt, and Daniel Webster, were the counsel who contested the constitutionality of these laws; their opponents were Emmett and Oakley, of New York, who, with the zeal natural to citizens of the great State which had granted the exclusive privilege, and with all the resources which the highest legal attainments and the most accomplished skill could supply, vindicated the laws in question. It was a most brilliant pas-

* 9 Wheaton's Reports, 1.

sage at arms, in a forensic tourney ;* a combat, as Wirt had predicted, well worth witnessing. The passage between Wirt and Emmett, which is preserved in the report, and is so familiar as to be repeated in schoolboy declamations,† is certainly one of the finest that is anywhere to be found in the range of forensic discussions, and would alone suffice to relieve a multitude of dull and tedious legal

* See Kennedy's Life of Wirt, Vol. II. p. 142. In a letter to Judge Carr, a few days before the argument Wirt writes: "To-morrow begin my toils in the Supreme Court, and about to-morrow week will come on the great Steamboat question from New York. Emmett and Oakley on one side, Webster and myself on the other. Come down and hear it. Emmett's whole soul is in the cause, and he will stretch all his powers. Oakley is said to be one of the first logicians of the age; as much a Phocion as Emmett is a Themistocles; and Webster is as ambitious as Cæsar. He will not be outdone by any man, if it is within the compass of his power to avoid it. It will be a combat worth witnessing."

† Mr. Kennedy, in his Life of Wirt, says, that the part of the sentence below which is italicised, is interpolated after the reply of Wirt, and when the case was made up for publication. "New York," says Emmett, alluding to the results of the genius of Fulton, "may proudly raise her head and cast her eyes over the whole civilized world; she may there see its countless waters bearing on their surface countless offerings of her munificence and wisdom. She may fondly calculate on their speedy extension in every direction and through every region, from Archangel to Calcutta, and justly arrogating to herself the labors of the man she cherished, and conscious of the value of her own good works, *she may turn the mournful exclamation of Æneas into an expression of triumph*, and exultingly ask—

"'Quæ regio in terris, nostri non plena laboris?'"

The reply of Wirt was one of the happiest efforts of his genius:—

"Sir: it was not in the moment of triumph, nor with the feelings of triumph, that Æneas uttered that exclamation. It was when with his faithful Achates by his side, he was surveying the works of art, with which the palace of Carthage was adorned, and his attention had been caught by a representation of the battles of Troy. There he saw the sons of Atreus and Priam, and the fierce Achilles. The whole extent of his misfortunes, the loss and desolation of his friends, the fall of his beloved country rushed upon his recollection:

'Constitit, et lachrymans, quis jam locus, inquit Achate,
Quæ regio in terris, nostri non plena laboris?'"

Wirt pressed the application in the most felicitous and appropriate language. If the state of things should continue, if the anarchy which New York had sown should not be extirpated, and a war of legislation should follow, the Constitution would ultimately fall, and our republican institutions perish. And what, then,

discussions. Leaving the reader, however, if his curiosity prompts, to study all that remains of the discussion, as it is found in the published report, I shall proceed to notice briefly the final result of the case, and the conclusions laid down by the Chief-Justice in pronouncing the judgment of the court.

The constitutionality of these laws had been maintained in New York by the Legislature, the council of revision, even in Jay's time, and unanimously by the judges of the Supreme Court and the Court for the Correction of Errors. In Livingston *vs.* Van Ingen,* in 1812, the Chancellor had indeed refused to restrain, by injunction, a violation of the right, but rather from serious doubts as to the propriety of the remedy than from any conviction of the unconstitutionality of the laws. This order, however, had been unanimously reversed by the Court for the Correction of Errors, of which the judges of the Supreme Court were ex-officio members, and at a time too when the latter court was presided over by James Kent, and dignified and ennobled by the learning and ability of Smith Thompson, Ambrose Spencer, William W. Van Ness, and Joseph C. Yates.† In the present case, Kent, who had then become Chancellor, had, without hesitation, granted an injunction to restrain the infringement of the right claimed under these laws.‡ "We must be permitted," he remarks in his opinion, "to require, at least, the presence and clear

would be the effect? Despotism would everywhere triumph, and would cover the earth with the mantle of mourning. "Then, sir," he exclaimed, "when New York shall look upon this scene of ruin, if she have the generous feelings which I believe her to have, it will not be with her head aloft in the pride of conscious triumph, 'her wrapt soul sitting in her eyes.' No, sir, no! Dejected with shame and confusion, drooping under the weight of her sorrow, with a voice suffocated with despair, well may she exclaim:

——— quis jam locus ———
Quæ regio in terris, nostri non plena laboris."

* 9 Johnson's Reports, 507.

† Each of these Judges delivered opinions in favor of sustaining the laws of New York, and of their constitutionality, except Judge Spencer, who, being related to one of the parties, declined giving any opinion. The opinions of Chief-Justice Kent and Judge Thompson upon the Constitutional question, are unusually vigorous and able, and should be carefully studied, in connexion with that of Chief-Justice Marshall, by those who desire thoroughly to investigate the subject on both sides.

‡ Ogden *vs.* Gibbons, 4 John. Ch. R. 150.

manifestation of some constitutional law, or some judicial decision of the supreme power of the Union, acting upon those laws, in direct collision and conflict, before we can retire from the support and defence of them. We must be satisfied that—

> Neptunus muros, magnoque emota tridenti
> Fundamenta quatit.

And the Court for the Correction of Errors had unanimously approved the decision.

It required no small degree of moral courage and firmness on the part of the Supreme Court, to unsettle a decision thus sustained; to restrain a power that had been exercised by one of the States, almost without question, from the foundation of the Union; to lop off, with the keen edge of the Constitutional axe, a branch of State sovereignty, which by the growth of years had become so firmly engrafted as to be scarcely distinguishable from the parent trunk; and to assert the supremacy of the Federal authority over State legislation, in a case where its existence had been expressly denied by one of the ablest and most accomplished jurists of that, or any age,* and one who was supposed to some extent at least to share the same opinions, and was a member of the same political school with Marshall himself. But the Chief-Justice was fully equal to the responsibility, though he seems to have encountered it with a deep sense of its magnitude. Referring to the principle contended for by New York, he remarks: "It is supported by great names—by names which have all the titles to consideration, that virtue, intelligence, and office can bestow. No tribunal can approach the decision of this question without feeling a just and real respect for that opinion which is sustained by such authority; but it is the province of this Court, while it respects, not to bow to it implicitly; and the judges must exercise, in the examination of the subject, that understanding which Providence has bestowed upon them, with that independence which the people of the United States expect from this department of government." The result of the examination which the Chief-Justice thus bestowed upon the subject was, that the laws of New York were repugnant to that clause of the Constitution which authorizes Congress to regulate commerce among the several

* Chancellor Kent.

States. This conclusion is sustained by an argument of wonderful acuteness of reasoning, and full of subtle distinctions, but built up and supported by those well-known principles of Constitutional construction which pervade all his opinions. Commerce among the States, he held, cannot stop at the external boundary line of each State, but may be introduced into the interior. The power to regulate commerce, conferred by the Constitution on Congress, comprehends navigation within the limits of every State in the Union, so far as that navigation may be in any manner connected with "commerce with foreign nations, or among the several States, or with the Indian tribes." It may of consequence pass the jurisdictional line of New York, and act upon the very waters to which the prohibition under consideration applies. This power, exercised in pursuance of the Constitution, is supreme, and State laws must yield to it, even though enacted under powers acknowledged to remain in the States. The act of Congress for enrolling and licensing vessels to be employed in the coasting trade, authorizes the navigation of such waters, and embraces all vessels, whether propelled by sails and oars or by steam. After being so enrolled, they are entitled to the same privileges, and can no more be restrained from navigating waters, and entering ports which are free to such vessels, than if they were wafted on their voyage by the winds, instead of being propelled by the agency of fire. The one element may be as legitimately used as the other, for every commercial purpose authorized by the laws of the Union; and the act of a State inhibiting the use of either, to any vessel having a license under the act of Congress, comes in direct collision with the Constitutional powers of the general government, and is void.*

In this opinion, which, though as ingeniously reasoned, is perhaps

* The extent to which it has been attempted to carry this principle, may be seen by reference to the recent case of Veasie *et al.* *vs.* Moor, December Term, 1852, 14 How. 568, in which it was argued that a law of the State of Maine, granting exclusive navigation in the upper part of Penobscot River, to a manufacturing company, who were to improve that part of the river, was contrary to the Constitution of the United States. The river lies entirely within the State of Maine, and the part in which the exclusive privilege was granted was not navigable, being cut off by several dams, erected for manufacturing purposes. This extraordinary proposition, however, found no favor with the Court. The law of Maine was held to be valid; Mr. Justice Daniel delivering the opinion, from which there appears to be no dissent.

less conclusive, than some of those masterly arguments upon which the fame of Marshall as a jurist is built, he make some strictures upon that doctrine of a rigid construction of constitutional power which has been a cardinal theory with some of the ablest and wisest statesmen the country has produced, and especially those of his own State. In the frank exposition of his views upon all constitutional questions which I have designed to give, it would not be proper to pass over or conceal his opinions upon these points. It must be confessed that he was not an advocate of a strict construction of the Constitution, as that doctrine was understood by those illustrious men who formed the republican party. And yet, on the other hand, justice requires it to be also said, that he never assumed or advocated the doctrine that a power could be exercised which was not granted either expressly in the words of the Constitution, or by necessary implication. "What do gentlemen mean by a strict construction?" he inquires in this opinion. "If they contend only against that enlarged construction which would extend words beyond their natural and obvious import, we might question the application of the term, but should not controvert the principle. If they contend for that narrow construction which, in support of some theory not to be found in the Constitution, would deny to the Government those powers which the words of the grant, as usually understood, import, and which are consistent with the general views and objects of the instrument; for that narrow construction which would cripple the Government, and render it unequal to the objects for which it is declared to be instituted, and to which the powers given, as fairly understood, render it competent; then we cannot perceive the propriety of this strict construction, nor adopt it as the rule by which the Constitution is to be expounded." And again, at the close of the opinion, "Powerful and ingenious minds, taking, as postulates, that the powers expressly granted to the Government of the Union, are to be contracted by construction into the narrowest possible compass, and that the original powers of the States are retained, if any possible construction will retain them, may, by a course of well digested, but refined and metaphysical reasoning, founded on these premises, explain away the Constitution of our country, and leave it a magnificent structure, indeed, to look at, but totally unfit for use. They may so entangle and perplex the understanding, as to obscure principles, which were before thought quite plain, and induce doubts where, if the mind were to pursue its own course, none would be perceived. In such a case, it is peculiarly necessary to recur to safe and fundamental principles, and, when sustained, to make them the tests of the arguments to be examined."

It was at this term that SMITH THOMPSON, of New York, took his seat for the first time on the bench of the Supreme Court, in place of Brockholst Livingston, who had died the previous year.* Judge

* The name of LIVINGSTON is conspicuous in the annals of the State of New York. The family is of Scottish origin, and at a very early period seated what is now known as the Livingston Manor, on the Hudson River, in Columbia county, New York. The three brothers, Robert R., Brockholst, and Edward Livingston, were all men of commanding abilities. The Chancellor was the eldest, and figured conspicuously in the revolutionary troubles, and in the early political contests of the State. Edward Livingston, the youngest of these brothers, is too well known as a statesman and jurist to require even a passing notice in this place. Elected in 1794, at the age of thirty years, a member of Congress, he entered upon a brilliant career, which his removal to New Orleans, in 1804, enabled him to pursue with still more eminent and flattering success. Again elected to the House of Representatives in 1823, transferred to the Senate in 1829, appointed Secretary of State in 1831, and Minister to France in 1833, where, thirty years before, his brother, the Chancellor, had preceded him;—all these well-merited honors can scarcely add to the undying fame of the civilian and jurist who framed the code of Louisiana.

BROCKHOLST LIVINGSTON is a name not so well known in our day. He was born about the year 1757, and at the declaration of Independence had just arrived at the age of manhood. He took an active and decided part in behalf of his country in the struggle with Great Britain, and at the close of the war devoted himself to the practice of the law, to which he had been educated. Mr. Livingston was for many years a prominent and successful advocate at the bar. In the earlier New York reports his name frequently appears on the record as counsel. It seems, too, that he engaged in some of the criminal trials of that period, as we find him employed for the defence in the prosecution of Frothingham, before the New York Oyer and Terminer, in 1799, for a libel on General Hamilton. On the 8th of January, 1802, Livingston and Smith Thompson were appointed *puisne* Judges of the Supreme Court of the State, Morgan Lewis being then Chief-Justice, and Kent and Ratcliff *puisnes*. This place he held until 1806, when he resigned it on his appointment as one of the Associate-Justices of the Supreme Court of the United States. Judge Livingston died a few days after the close of the session of the Court, on the 18th of March, 1823, in the sixty-sixth year of his age.

" He had served his country," says Mr. Wheaton, in a brief notice of the death of Judge Livingston, " with distinguished military reputation during the war of

Thompson was Secretary of the Navy at the time of his appointment, and being reluctant to accept the office, the matter was for a little while held in suspense. During the interval the name of Chancellor Kent was brought forward by some of his friends. The main objection to this accomplished jurist seems to have been his connexion with the Federal party, a barrier which even in those times of moderate party heat, could not be entirely disregarded. Notwithstanding this, some of the warmest friends of President Monroe recommended the selection of the Chancellor, in case Judge Thompson should decline, and among them the Attorney-General, Mr. Wirt, who wrote a long and earnest letter to the President, urging the appointment irrespective of party considerations, and as a matter of national, not of mere local interest. It is not certain but that the President might have considered the suggestion favorably, if the acceptance of Judge Thompson * had not rendered further action on the subject unnecessary.

the revolution, and subsequently filled several important civil stations at home and abroad. He was an accomplished classical scholar, and versed in the elegant languages and literature of the southern nations of Europe. At the bar he was an ingenious and learned advocate, fruitful in invention, and possessing a brilliant and persuasive elocution. On the bench his candor and modesty were no less distinguished than his learning, acuteness, and discrimination. His genius and taste had directed his principal attention to the maratime and commercial law; and his extensive experience gave to his judgments in that branch of jurisprudence a peculiar value, which was enhanced by the gravity and beauty of his judicial eloquence. In private life he was beloved for his amiable manners and general kindness of disposition, and admired for all those qualities which constitute the finished gentleman. He died with the deep regret of all who knew him; leaving behind him the character of an upright, enlightened, and humane judge, a patriotic citizen, and a bright ornament of the profession. *Isque et oratorum in numero est habendus, et fuit reliquis rebus ornatus, atque elegans.*"

* Smith Thompson brought to the bench of the Supreme Court the thorough judicial education and experience acquired by a service of seventeen years in the Supreme Court of New York, at a time when that tribunal might claim, in point of dignity, talent, and learning, to rank with any in the civilized world. Educated to the bar, and admitted to practice at an early age, he devoted himself with untiring energy and industry to his profession. A brief service in the State legislature could scarcely be said to interrupt these labors, which were continued with unabated ardor down to the time of his elevation to the bench of the New York Supreme Court. During the period of Thompson's practice, the New York bar was adorned with a galaxy of talent, which, without the least disparagement to

This was the first change that had been made in the Supreme Court since Judge Story's appointment in 1812. I may here properly note the few other changes which occurred during the remainder of

the bar of any other State, may be pronounced wholly unrivalled. Among them were such men as the Livingstons—Brockholst and Edward—Hamilton, Harrison, Hoffman, Burr, Pendleton, and the then junior members of the profession, such as Spencer, Van Vechten, Henry, Ogden, Elisha Williams, and—"the brightest genius of them all"—William W. Van Ness. The first and second volumes of Johnson's cases are the only published New York reports, anterior to the time of Judge Thompson's appointment to the bench. They do not show him to have been at that time engaged in a very extensive counsel practice in the Supreme Court, many, and indeed most of the important cases being committed to the care of the veterans of the profession—Hamilton and Harrison, Livingston and Burr, Pendleton and Troup. That he stood deservedly high is evident, however, from the fact of his being chosen, while still comparatively a young man, from among such a bar, and appointed with Brockholst Livingston to a seat on the bench of the Supreme Court. This appointment was made on the 8th of January, 1802. Morgan Lewis was then Chief-Justice, and James Kent one of the *puisnes*, having been already four years on the bench. On the election of Judge Lewis as Governor of the State, in 1804, Kent became Chief-Justice, and Judge Ratcliff having resigned, Ambrose Spencer and Daniel D. Tompkins were appointed Associates. Such was the New York Supreme Court at that period and for some years afterwards—KENT, LIVINGSTON, THOMPSON, SPENCER, and TOMPKINS—an association of judicial talent, that was never before, and has never since, been seen at any one time in our State. On the appointment of Kent as Chancellor, February 25th, 1814, Judge Thompson succeeded him as Chief-Justice. He presided over the Court until his appointment as Secretary of the Navy, and was succeeded in the Chief-Justiceship by Judge Spencer, February 9th, 1819

Judge Thompson took his seat on the bench of the Supreme Court of the United States on the tenth day of February, 1821, and continued in the discharge of its duties to the time of his death, in 1843. Thus it will be seen that he was on the bench in all nearly thirty-seven years—one of the longest, as it certainly is one of the most honorable, judicial careers on record. His opinions in the United States Supreme Court are to be found in the last four volumes of Wheaton and the sixteen volumes of Peters' Reports; those in the New York Supreme Court, in the first fifteen volumes of Johnson. The author of the eulogy on Judge Spencer very properly characterizes the Reports of Johnson as "by far the most valuable, reliable, and authoritative record of American common law," anywhere to be found. Those containing the opinions of Judge Thompson abundantly show that the record of this common law bears indelibly upon it the impress of his vigorous and logical mind. With Kent and Spencer he may justly claim his full share in the great work which the old Supreme Court entered upon, and so successfully prosecuted—that "of building up and consolidating within this State a system and

the period in which Marshall presided over the deliberations of the Court. On the death of Mr. Justice Todd,* the vacancy was filled by the appointment, May 9th, 1826 of ROBERT TRIMBLE, of Ken-

body of common law, applicable and adapted to the government and institutions of the country."

* THOMAS TODD was born in the State of Virginia on the 23rd of January, 1765. Having lost his parents in early youth, and been deprived of the limited patrimony bequeathed him by his mother, he emigrated with the family of Judge Innis to Kentucky in the spring of 1786. While residing in the family of the Judge he was engaged in teaching the daughters of his friend by day, and at night prosecuting the study of the law by fire-light. He was admitted to the bar soon after he came to Kentucky, and practised for several years with reputation and success. Appointed clerk of the Federal Court for the district of Kentucky, he was soon after, on the erection of the State Government, chosen clerk of the Court of Appeals. This office he held until 1801, when he was appointed Judge of the Court of Appeals, and in 1806, on the resignation of Judge Muter, Chief-Justice. His appointment to the office of Associate-Justice of the Supreme Court of the United States was the first intimation to him that he had been thought of for that station. In making this selection President Jefferson is said to have adopted a mode different from that pursued in later times. He requested each delegate in Congress from the States composing the circuit to communicate to him a nomination of their first and second choice. Judge Todd was the first or second upon the nomination of every delegate, although to some of them he was personally unknown. He was accordingly appointed, and continued in the honorable discharge of the duties of Judge of the Supreme Court until his death, February 7th, 1826.

Judge Story has spoken of the intellectual characteristics of his associate with his usual discrimination: "He had uncommon patience and candor in investigation; great clearness and sagacity of judgment; a cautious but steady energy; a well-balanced independence; a just respect for authority, and at the same time an unflinching adherence to his own deliberate opinions of the law. His modesty imparted a grace to an integrity and singleness of heart which won for him the general confidence of all who knew him. He was not ambitious of innovations upon the settled principles of the law; but was content with the more unostentatious character of walking in the trodden paths of jurisprudence. From his diffident and retiring habits, it required a long acquaintance with him justly to appreciate his juridicial as well as his personal merits. His learning was of a useful and solid cast; not perhaps as various or as comprehensive as that of some men; but accurate, and transparent, and applicable to the daily purposes of the business of human life. In his knowledge of the local law of Kentucky he was excelled by few; and his brethren drew largely upon his resources to administer that law, in the numerous cases which then crowded the docket of the Supreme Court from that judicial circuit. What he did not know, he never affected to possess; but

tucky.* This gentleman died after a service of little more than two years, and his place was filled, March 7th, 1829, by the appointment of JOHN McLEAN, of Ohio, at present one of the Associate-Justices of

sedulously sought to acquire. He was content to learn without assuming to dogmatize. Hence he listened to arguments for the purpose of instruction, and securing examination, and not merely for that of confutation or debate. Among his associates he enjoyed an enviable respect, which was constantly increasing as he became more familiarly known to them. His death was deemed by them a great public calamity; and in the memory of those who survived him, his name has ever been cherished with a warm and affectionate remembrance."

Judge Todd was twice married. Col. C. S. Todd, so honorably known for his gallant military services, was one of his sons by the first marriage. His second wife, whom he married in 1812, was the youngest sister of Mrs. Madison, and widow of Major George Washington, a nephew of the General. He left one daughter and two sons by this marriage.

* The following notice of JUDGE TRIMBLE forms the appropriate introduction to one of the volumes of Peters' Reports:—

"The Honorable Robert Trimble, one of the Associate-Justices of this Court, died at his residence in Paris, Kentucky, in September, 1828.

"Mr. Justice Trimble was born in Augusta County, Virginia, in 1777, and was the son of Mr. William Trimble, one of the earliest settlers in Kentucky—a virtuous man, whose bold, firm, and enterprising character induced him to seek an increase to his fortunes by establishing himself on the frontiers, encountering all the dangers and hardships of a new and advanced settlement.

"Mr. Justice Trimble accompanied his father when he emigrated, and the early years of his life were passed in agricultural industry; and frequently in the amusements and toils of the chase, upon the success of which settlers often depended for food. He was sometimes engaged in defence against Indian invasion, to which the borderers were then constantly exposed. He was distinguished in his youth for his conduct, his courage, and his sagacity; and was acknowledged as a leader by his associates.

"The native and powerful energies of his mind could not be restrained by the situation in which he was placed; and he became desirous of obtaining an education which would fit him for higher duties. By teaching an English school he procured the means of entering Bourbon Academy; and he afterwards was a student in the Kentucky Academy in Woodford county, where he completed his classical attainments. He then studied law, and in 1800 commenced the practice of his profession at Paris, in Bourbon County, where he married. His widow and a numerous family of children survive him.

"Mr. Justice Trimble always enjoyed the highest consideration and confidence of his fellow-citizens. In 1802 he was elected to the House of Representatives of Kentucky; but in the following year he declined a re-election, determining to

the Court. Judge Washington died in 1829, after a service of thirty years, and was succeeded January 6th, 1830, by Henry Baldwin, of Pennsylvania, and on the death of Mr. Justice Johnson, James M. Wayne, one of the present judges of the Court, was appointed, January 9th, 1835. Justices McLean and Wayne are the only present members of the Court who were members also in Marshall's time, the latter having come to the bench the last term at which the Chief-Justice presided.

The decision in the case of Gibbons *vs.* Ogden, relative to the power vested in Congress to regulate commerce among the States,

devote himself to his profession—a duty enjoined upon him by his narrow fortunes. In 1807, his professional reputation and character were such that he was appointed a judge of the Supreme Court of Kentucky; which situation he held for two years with great reputation. He relinquished the office to resume the practice of his profession; and in 1810 he refused the commission of Chief-Justice of the State. In 1813 he again declined the office of Chief-Justice: and having assiduously and successfully devoted himself to the bar until 1817, he was in that year appointed district judge of the United States, for the district of Kentucky. In May, 1826, he received, from President Adams, the commission of Associate-Justice of the Supreme Court of the United States.

"In the performance of his judicial duties in Kentucky, in the state courts, and in the district and circuit courts of the United States, Judge Trimble obtained the respect and esteem of the profession, and of his fellow-citizens. Learned in the law, just and discriminating in his judicial investigations, his decisions were characterized by great legal accuracy, research, and perspicuity; and by an enlarged and liberal equity. In the Supreme Court of the United States, Mr. Justice Trimble maintained and increased the character and reputation which had placed him upon that bench. His opinions were clear and comprehensive, illustrated and enriched by all the legal learning their subjects demanded; and they gave to those who heard them the surest anticipations of increasing usefulness and talents, had it been permitted to him to remain in the performance of the high functions of his station.

"In private and domestic life Mr. Justice Trimble was universally beloved and respected. Gentle, conciliating, and kind in his manners and disposition; honorable and faithful in all his transactions; every one who knew him sought his friendship, and was proud of attaining it. As a husband and a father, his mild and amiable virtues endeared him to those with whom he was connected in these relations; and his home was always the abode of cheerfulness and content. He was a patriot, and a firm republican; and he was devotedly attached to the Union; always maintaining those constitutional principles which have been declared from the tribunal of which he had been an efficient and much honored member."

was followed by the case of Brown *vs.* the State of Maryland in 1827,* involving the question of the extent of the power to regulate foreign commerce. The case was argued with great ability and learning. Mr. Wirt being counsel on the one side, and the present Chief-Justice on the other.† The judgment of the Court, pronounced by Chief-Justice Marshall again swept out of existence, and expunged from the statute-book, the law of a State as being repugnant to the paramount authority of the Federal Government. It was held that the act of the Maryland Legislature, which required every importer of goods, by wholesale, bale, or package, to take out a license, and pay for it, under certain penalties or forfeitures for neglect, was repugnant to the Constitution of the United States, and void; inasmuch as it belonged to Congress to regulate foreign commerce, and the States were prohibited by the Constitution from laying a duty on imports.

It was contended by the counsel for the State of Maryland that the construction of the power of Congress to the extent claimed by the General Government would abridge the acknowledged power of a State to tax its own citizens, or their property within its territory. This proposition was considered by the Court and discussed by the Chief-Justice in his written opinion. He admitted the power to be sacred, but denied that it might be used so as to obstruct the free course of a power given to Congress. Congress was vested by the Constitution with authority to regulate commerce between the States. The power is co-extensive with the subject on which it acts, and cannot be stopped, as had already been decided in Gibbons *vs.* Ogden, at the external boundary of a State, but must enter its interior. It is a component part of the power to regulate commerce, not only to authorize the importation, but to authorize the importer to sell. The right to sell, therefore, is connected with the law permitting importation, as an inseparable incident; and any penalty inflicted on the importer for selling the article, in his character of importer, must be in opposition to the act of Congress which authorizes the importation, and is therefore void. The principle, however, was not carried so far as to deny the right of a State legislature to tax imported goods after they had become mixed with and incorpo-

* 12 Wheaton's Reports, 419.

† See subsequent sketch of Chief-Justice Taney.

rated into the general mass of property of the State. On the contrary, it was admitted that in such case they were liable to State taxation.

The authority of Brown *vs.* the State of Maryland, as well as that of Gibbons *vs.* Ogden, has been thought to sustain the doctrine, repeatedly advanced since Marshall's time, and discussed with great ability, and, it may be added, with no small degree of warmth, both at the bar, and in the consultation room of the judges, that by the grant of power to Congress to regulate commerce, the States are absolutely prohibited from passing any laws on the subject whatever, whether Congress shall have exercised the power or not, the grant to the General Government being in its nature exclusive. In some of these subsequent discussions,* the opinions of Chief-Justice Marshall in the two cases alluded to, have been cited as sustaining this doctrine. A case, however, decided at the session of the Court in 1829, Wilson *vs.* Blackbird Creek Marsh Company,† seems to show that this is not correct. In that case a chartered company was authorized, under a State law, to make a dam across a navigable tide-water creek. A licensed sloop, not being able to pass, broke the dam; and in an action by the company for damages, the defendant insisted that the creek was a navigable highway, over which the power of Congress to regulate commerce, including navigation, extended; and that the State law which authorized an obstruction to this navigation was, therefore, void. The Chief-Justice in delivering the opinion of the

* The subject has been discussed in various cases since that time, and among others in New York *vs.* Miln, 11 Peters, 102; Prigg *vs.* the Commonwealth of Pennsylvania, 16 Peters, 539; and the Massachusetts, Rhode Island, and New Hampshire license cases, 5 Howard, 504; all of which are referred to in the subsequent sketch of Chief-Justice Taney. In the latter cases in particular the whole question was fully considered, and from the opinions of the Chief-Justice, and Judges Daniel, Catron, Woodbury, and Nelson, it seems to be the settled judgment of the Court, that this power is not exclusive, but may be exercised by the States, especially in matters of mere police regulation, except where it comes in conflict with an act of Congress. Mr. Justice Daniel, in his opinion in these cases, enters a vigorous protest against the doctrines contained in the decision of Brown *vs.* Maryland. The question was also raised and discussed in the New York and Boston passenger cases, and in the Wheeling Bridge case. See subsequent sketch of Chief-Justice Taney.

† 2 Peters' Reports, 245.

Court, says: "If Congress has passed any act which bore upon the case, any act in execution of the power to regulate commerce, the object of which was to control State legislation over those small navigable creeks into which the tide flows, and which abound throughout the lower country of the middle and southern States; we should feel not much difficulty in saying that a State law coming in conflict with such act would be void. But Congress has passed no such act. The repugnancy of the law of Delaware to the Constitution is placed entirely on its repugnancy to the power to regulate commerce with foreign nations and among the several States; a power which has not been so exercised as to affect the question.

"We do not think that the act empowering the Blackbird Creek Marsh Company, to place a dam across the creek, can, under all the circumstances of the case, be considered as repugnant to the power to regulate commerce *in its dormant state,* or as being in conflict with any law passed on the subject."*

It will be seen from the foregoing review that the tendency of the decisions of the Supreme Court during the entire period of Chief-Justice Marshall's service on the bench was to sustain the authority of the Federal Government, and to abridge the powers claimed to be exercised by the States. The Court boldly assumed jurisdiction to declare an act of Congress void, as being repugnant to the Constitution, yet this had been actually exercised only in one or two instances, while the power to declare the laws of the States void as against the Constitution of the United States, had been very freely used, and particularly in some of the prominent cases which have already been noticed.†

A case occurred at the session of the Court in 1830, in which it was attempted to carry the principles established in some of these decisions to a very unwarrantable extent. The case referred to was the Providence Bank *vs.* Billings and Pittman.‡ The Providence Bank had been chartered by the Legislature of Rhode Island in 1791;

* See dissenting opinion of Chief-Justice Taney in Wheeling Bridge case, 13 Howard's Reports, 585, 587.

† In a note to the case of Fletcher *vs.* Peck, vol. 2. Cond. Rep., p. 225, the reporter enumerates twenty-six State laws as having been declared unconstitu tional.

‡ 4 Peters' Reports, 504.

and in 1822 the Legislature of that State had passed an act imposing a duty "on licensed persons and others, and *bodies corporate* within the State." The Providence Bank resisted the payment of the tax on the ground that the act of the Legislature was repugnant to the Constitution of the United States, inasmuch as it impaired the obligation of the contract created by the act of incorporation. The cases of Fletcher *vs.* Peck, and of Dartmouth College, it was alleged, had established the principle that a legislative grant to a corporation was *a contract* within the meaning of the Constitution; and the cases of McCulloch *vs.* Maryland, and Weston *vs.* the City of Charleston, had also established the principle that the power of imposing a tax upon the corporation involved the power of destroying it, and was therefore contrary to the provision of the Constitution, which prohibited the States from passing laws impairing the obligation of contracts.

The reasoning in the cases referred to certainly appears to countenance the doctrine advocated by the counsel for the Rhode Island Bank, and, taking these principles as abstract propositions, it would seem difficult to draw the line of distinction. That distinction, however, was drawn by the Court, and the principle very strictly laid down by the Chief-Justice that the power of taxing a bank incorporated by a State legislature was not a violation of the Constitution of the United States. Such a corporation, it was admitted, was a contract. But the act creating the contract contained no stipulation exempting the bank from taxation. The power of taxation was one of vital importance; it was an incident of sovereignty essential to the existence of government, and the relinquishment of such a power was never to be assumed. It might be exercised in all cases by a State, *except when conflicting with a constitutional law of Congress*, the supremacy of which was always to be recognized; and such he contends was the principle recognized in McCulloch *vs.* Maryland, and in Weston *vs.* the City of Charleston. The sovereignty of a State extends to everything which exists by its own authority, or is introduced by its own permission; but it does not extend to those means which are employed by Congress to carry into execution powers conferred on that body by the people of the United States. The law of Rhode Island taxing the Bank, was therefore held to be constitutional and valid.

At the same term of the Court another case of very great interest arose, Craig *et al. vs.* the State of Missouri,* involving the question of the validity of a State law under that clause of the Constitution which declares that no State shall "emit bills of credit." The State of Missouri had passed an act for the "establishment of loan offices," by the third section of which the officers of the treasury of the State, under the direction of the Governor, were required to issue certificates to the amount of two hundred thousand dollars, of denominations not exceeding ten dollars, or less than fifty cents. These certificates were made receivable at the State Treasury of Missouri for taxes, and by all officers of the State, civil and military; certain property of the State was pledged for their redemption; a provision was made for gradually withdrawing them from circulation; and the Commissioners of the loan offices were authorized to make loans of certificates, to citizens of the State, bearing interest at the rate of six per cent, in the manner prescribed by the act. The main question raised by this law was, whether it was a *bona fide* loan, which it was admitted the States have an unlimited power to make; or whether it was an emission of "bills of credit," a power which the States are prohibited from exercising by the Constitution. The Supreme Court of Missouri had decided that the law was valid; and now the State was summoned to appear and defend that law at the bar of the highest tribunal of the Union.

The veteran statesman, who for so many years occupied a seat in the Senate of the United States, and has been recently transferred to the more numerous branch of the National Legislature—Thomas H. Benton—represented the State of Missouri in the Supreme Court, not, as he took occasion to observe in his argument, as the *advocate* of the State, for her acts did not require an advocate to vindicate them, but as "a corps of observation," to watch what was going on. In the commencement of his speech, Mr. Benton complained of the formal language of the writ, which "summoned" the State to appear at the bar of the Court. "In the language of the writ," he remarks, "she is 'commanded' and 'enjoined' to appear. Language of this kind does not seem proper, when addressed to a sovereign State; nor are the terms fitting, even if the only purpose of their process was to obtain the appearance of the State. They impute a fault in the State; they

* 4 Peters Reports, 410.

imply an omission, or neglect by the State. The language of 'commanding and enjoining' would only be well employed if these had occurred."

"The State of Missouri has done no act," he continued, "which was not within the full and ample powers she possesses as a free, sovereign, and independent State. She has passed a law which she considers in the proper and beneficial exercise of her legislative functions; and which had for its object the promotion of the interests of her citizens."

The majority of the Court, however, thought otherwise. In their opinion, pronounced by the Chief-Justice, the certificates of Missouri were "bills of credit," within the meaning of the Constitution, and the judgment of the Court again annihilated the legislative act of one of the States of the Confederacy. "In the argument," remarks the Chief-Justice, "we have been reminded by one side of the dignity of a sovereign State; of the humiliation of her submitting herself to this tribunal; of the dangers which may result from inflicting a wound on that dignity. By the other, of the still superior dignity of the people of the United States, who have spoken their will in terms which we cannot misunderstand. To these admonitions we can only answer, that if the exercise of that jurisdiction which has been imposed upon us by the Constitution and laws of the United States shall be calculated to bring on those dangers which have been indicated, or if it shall be indispensable to the preservation of the Union, and, consequently, to the independence and liberty of the States; these are considerations which address themselves to those departments which may, with perfect propriety, be influenced by them. This department can listen only to the mandates of law, and can tread only that path which is marked out by duty."*

* The case was decided by a divided court. Three of the seven judges—Johnson, Thompson, and McLean—dissented. The precise question again arose at the session of 1834, in the case of Byrne *vs.* the State of Missouri, 8 Peters, 40, in which the decision of Craig *vs.* the State of Missouri, was reviewed and confirmed.

In the case of Briscoe *vs.* the Bank of the Commonwealth of Kentucky, 11 Peters, 257, one of the earliest constitutional cases decided after the appointment of Chief-Justice Taney to the bench, it was held that the act incorporating the Bank of Kentucky was a constitutional exercise of power by the State of Kentucky, and the notes issued by the bank were not "bills of credit" within the meaning of

The session of the Court in 1831 was rendered memorable by the argument and decision of the great Cherokee controversy,* one of the most novel and interesting that had ever occupied the attention of the Court, or, indeed, it may be said, of any tribunal in modern times. It would be impossible within the limits of this sketch to trace the origin, progress, and ultimate issue of the controversy between the State of Georgia and the Cherokee Indians, out of which this singular judicial proceeding arose, and which fills an eventful page in the political history of that period. Nor is this necessary in order to accomplish the sole object I have in view, which is, to state briefly the points at issue, and the decision pronounced upon them by the Court.

From the commencement of the Government the Cherokee Indians, residing within the territorial limits of Georgia, had been recognized as a separate and independent people by the Federal authorities, and a variety of treaties had been negotiated with them, the substance of which it is not necessary to set forth. The Cherokees had made considerable advances in civilization, and had recently adopted a Con-

the Constitution. In the prevailing opinion of the Court the case of Craig *vs.* Missouri was cited, and declared to contain no principle conflicting with the decision in the Kentucky case. Mr. Justice Story dissented, holding, that the principle was the same as in Craig *vs.* Missouri, and that the notes of the Kentucky Bank were "bills of credit" within the decision in that case. The cause, it seems, had been once before argued, in Chief-Justice Marshall's time, and the majority of the Court, including the late Chief-Justice, were of opinion that the act of Kentucky, establishing the bank, was void. In his dissenting opinion on that argument, Judge Story earnestly and warmly vindicated the opinions of Chief-Justice Marshall, and his own, on this subject. At the close of his elaborate argument he observes:—"Mr. Chief-Justice Marshall is not here to speak for himself; and knowing full well the grounds of his opinion, in which I concurred, that this act is unconstitutional, I have felt an earnest desire to vindicate his memory from the imputation of rashness, or want of deep reflection. Had he been living he would have spoken in the joint names of both of us."

The extent to which Judge Story carried his views on this subject is somewhat remarkable. He intimates in his Commentaries on the Constitution, that independent of long continued practice from the time of the adoption of the Constitution, the States would not, upon a sound construction of the Constitution, be authorized to incorporate banks with power to circulate bank paper as currency, in as-much as they are expressly prohibited from coining money as well as emitting bills of credit.

* The Cherokee Nation *vs.* State of Georgia. 5 Peters' Reports, 1.

stitution and form of government. The State of Georgia desired the extinguishment of the Indian title, and the removal of this people out of their territory, which the General Government, in whom the authority to do this has been vested by the Constitution, had hitherto neglected. Georgia, having waited in vain, as she alleged, nearly thirty years, for the accomplishment of this object, now determined to set about obtaining it in her own way, and accordingly passed a series of acts extending the jurisdiction and municipal laws of the State over the Indian territory, and declaring all laws, ordinances, and usages heretofore adopted by the Cherokees to be null and void. Among others was a law prohibiting any white man from residing among the Indians without a special license from the Governor, and taking an oath to support the Constitution and laws of the State. This was the law under which the missionaries Worcester and others were convicted, whose case I shall presently notice. A military guard was also established, and every member of it authorized to arrest any person charged with violating any portion of these laws; and provision was made for a lottery by which the Indian lands were to be divided among the people of the State.

The object of these laws was of course to force the removal of the Indians from the State. The Cherokees complained to the General Government, alleging that the laws were in violation of their treaties made with the United States; they received the answer that there was no help from that quarter, and that the Government would not interfere. In this emergency they took the advice of counsel, and eagerly embraced the last hope that remained, by bringing their case before the Supreme Court of the United States. It was thought that the clause of the Constitution which gives that tribunal jurisdiction in controversies "between a State, or citizens thereof, and *foreign States*, citizens, or subjects," would authorize the Cherokees to sue as a *foreign State*, and, accordingly, a bill was filed in the Supreme Court, in the name of the *Cherokee nation*, against the State of Georgia, praying for an injunction to restrain the State from the execution of these laws, on the ground of their being null and void as against the treaties of the United States. This motion was brought on at the present term, and was argued on behalf of the Cherokees by William Wirt (with whom the late Mr. John Sergeant was associated), with more than his usual earnest and lofty eloquence. Wirt had prepared the case with extraordinary care and fullness; and he entered upon its discussion with intense ardor and enthusiasm. Indeed, discriminating and judicious critics have declared this to be one of the ablest and most admirable speeches ever delivered by that accomplished orator and lawyer. The spectacle was certainly grand and imposing, and the scene such as must have animated and inspired, not the speaker only, but the entire audience that thronged the court-room. "The great interest excited by the controversy," says a writer in the North American Review, "was naturally to be expected from the novelty of the case, the dignity of the parties, and the high importance of the principles in question. The scene wore in some degree the imposing majesty of those ancient debates, in which the great father of Roman eloquence sustained before the Senate the rights of allied and dependent, but still sovereign princes, who had found themselves compelled to seek for protection and redress from the justice of the mighty Republic. We may add that the high and well-earned reputation of the counsel retained by the Indians, added another point of resemblance to the parallel."* The parallel was just both in respect to the cause, the tribunal, and the advocate. If, at that moment, the Supreme

* It must have been at the delivery of the judgment in such a case that Miss Martineau intends her graceful description of a scene in the Supreme Court to apply. "I have watched the assemblage when the Chief-Justice was delivering a judgment," she says; "the three judges on either hand gazing at him more like learners than associates; Webster standing firm as a rock, his large, deep set eyes wide awake, his lips compressed, and his whole countenance in that intent stillness, which easily fixes the eye of the stranger. Clay leaning against the desk in an attitude whose grace contrasts strangely with the slovenly make of his dress, his snuff-box for the moment unopened in his hand, his small, grey eye, and placid half-smile, conveying an expression of pleasure, which redeems his face from its usual unaccountable commonness. The Attorney-General, his fingers playing among his papers, his quick, black eye, and thin, tremulous lips for once fixed, his small face, pale with thought, contrasting remarkably with the other two. These men, absorbed in what they are listening to, thinking neither of themselves nor of each other, while they are watched by the groups of idlers and listeners around them; the newspaper corps, the dark Cherokee chiefs, the stragglers from the far West, the gay ladies in their waving plumes, and the members of either House that have stepped in to listen; all these I have seen constitute one silent assemblage, while the mild voice of the aged Chief-Justice sounded through the Court."—*Retrospect of Western Travel.* Vol. I. p. 165.

Court displayed the imposing and majestic dignity of a Roman Senate, who will deny that its Tully was William Wirt?

The State of Georgia refused to respond, or appear, on the argument. It was currently reported, both at the Capitol and throughout the country, that Georgia would refuse to abide by, or respect, an adverse decision. This report was fully countenanced by the action of the State, which certainly conveyed a significant hint as to her probable course. A Cherokee Indian had been arrested, tried, convicted, and sentenced to be hung, under the authority of the State, for the murder of another Indian. A writ of error was granted to the Supreme Court of the United States on this same question of the validity of the Georgia laws; but the State authorities, without noticing the pendency of the proceedings, caused the sentence to be executed before the appeal could be brought to argument. The difficulty as to how the injunction was to be enforced in case it should be awarded, and the State should refuse to obey, was certainly a formidable one; but Wirt's answer to the objection was both obvious and logical: "It will be time enough," he says, "to meet that question when it shall arise. At present the question is, whether the Court, by its constitution, possesses the jurisdiction to which we appeal: and it is beginning at the wrong end of the inquiry to ask how the jurisdiction, if possessed, is to be enforced."

But this question was never reached by the Court. The motion for the injunction was denied. The opinion of the majority of the judges,* pronounced by the Chief-Justice, though brief, was very carefully prepared, and disposed of the whole case on the question of jurisdiction. The Constitution had conferred upon the Court jurisdiction to determine controversies "between a State, or the citizens thereof, and foreign States, citizens, or subjects." The State of Georgia might unquestionably be sued, but was the Cherokee nation a *foreign State* within the meaning of the Constitution, so as to open to it the doors of the Federal tribunals? This question he decides in the negative. Assenting to that part of the argument of counsel that the Cherokees were *a State*, as a distinct political society, separated from others, capable of managing its own affairs and governing itself, he regards the pecu-

* Justices Thompson and Story dissented; the former of whom wrote an able dissenting opinion.

liar relations of the Indians with the United States, and their dependence upon our government, as entirely precluding the idea that they are to be regarded as a *foreign State* within the purview of the Constitution. The Court, therefore, had no jurisdiction, and the injunction was denied, without entering into a consideration of the merits of the case, or an examination of the validity of the Georgia laws.*

At the next session, a new, and still more interesting phase of the Cherokee controversy was presented. It came before the Court in a different form, and brought up for discussion and decision the whole question as to the validity of the Georgia laws.† The case is doubtless yet fresh in the memory of those whose recollections extend back to that time, and such will remember, too, the interest and excitement which the discussion created throughout the country. I have mentioned the law of Georgia which prohibited, under severe penalties, any white person from residing among the Indians without special permission from the Governor of Georgia, and taking an oath to obey the Constitution and laws of the State. At the time of the passage of the act, Samuel A. Worcester, a citizen of Vermont, was a resident among the Cherokees as a missionary, sent by the American Board of Foreign Missions, and with the license and permission of the President of the United States. He had no license, however, from the Governor of Georgia, and had refused to take the oath required by the act, deeming it incompatible with the duties of his mission. Elizur Butler, and five others, stood in the same category. These gentlemen were indicted in September, 1831, in Gwinnett County, Georgia, convicted, and each sentenced to four years imprisonment at hard labor in the penitentiary. The Governor immediately tendered them a pardon on condition of their conforming in future with the policy of the State. Five of them accepted he pardon, but Worcester and Butler refused, and their cases were brought to the United States Supreme Court on a writ of error. Mr. Wirt and Mr. Sergeant were retained by the Board of Missions, and argued the cause for the missionaries; the State of Georgia did not appear.

* Mr. Wirt, it is said, had great doubts upon the subject of jurisdiction. Some of the most eminent jurists of the country, however, had given their views in favor of it, and among them Chancellor Kent, whose opinion was read on the argument.

† Worcester *vs.* The State of Georgia, 6 Peters' Reports, 515.

A preliminary objection as to the form of the record having been disposed of, and the question of jurisdiction settled in favor of the missionaries, the Court proceeded to inquire into the main question presented by the case, namely, whether the law of Georgia was consistent with, or repugnant to, the Constitution, laws, and treaties of the United States. The Chief-Justice, as was usually the case in the determination of grave questions of constitutional law, pronounced the prevailing opinion of the Court. It is evident that he approached the task deeply impressed with the delicacy as well as the responsibility of the position. But he did not hesitate or shrink from a full discharge of his duties. "The cause in every point of view in which it can be placed," he remarked, "is of the deepest interest. The defendant is a State, a member of the Union, which has exercised the powers of government over a people who deny its jurisdiction, and are under the protection of the United States. The plaintiff is a citizen of the State of Vermont, condemned to hard labor for four years in the penitentiary of Georgia, under color of an act which he alleges to be repugnant to the Constitution, laws, and treaties of the United States. The legislative power of a State, the controling power of the Constitution and laws of the United States, the rights, if they have any, the political existence of a once numerous and powerful people, the personal liberty of a citizen, are all involved in the subject now to be considered. It behoves this Court in every case, more especially in this, to examine into its jurisdiction with scrutinizing eyes, before it proceeds to the exercise of a power which is controverted." Having examined this question, and placed the jurisdiction of the Court upon the clearest basis of both principle and authority, the Chief-Justice next considers the main question presented by the case as to the validity of the Georgia laws under which the missionaries were convicted; and by a train of that simple but masterly and unanswerable reasoning which characterizes all his juridical arguments, arrives at the conclusion that these laws are repugnant to the Constitution, laws, and treaties of the Union. Without following, or attempting to analyze, this argument, I shall merely state his conclusions in his own language: "The Cherokee nation, then, is a distinct community, occupying its own territory, with boundaries accurately described, in which the laws of Georgia can have no force, and which the citizens of Georgia have no right to enter but with the assent of the Cherokees themselves, or in conformity with treaties, and with the acts of Congress. The whole intercourse between the United States and this nation,* is, by our Constitution and laws, vested in the United States. The act of the State of Georgia under which the plaintiff in error was prosecuted, is consequently void, and the judgment a nullity."

In regard to the power of the Court to reverse the judgment, and the right of the plaintiff in error to this remedy, he remarks: "He was seized, and forcibly carried away, while under guardianship of treaties guarantying the country in which he resided, and taking it under the protection of the United States. He was seized while performing, under the sanction of the chief-magistrate of the Union, those duties which the humane policy adopted by Congress had recommended. He was apprehended, tried, and condemned under color of a law which has been shown to be repugnant to the Constitution, laws, and treaties of the United States. Had a judgment, liable to the same objections, been rendered for property, none would question the jurisdiction of this Court. It cannot be less clear when the judgment affects personal liberty, and inflicts disgraceful punishment, if punishment could disgrace when inflicted on innocence. The plaintiff in error is not less interested in the operation of this unconstitutional law, than if it affected his property. He is not less entitled to the protection of the Constitution, laws, and treaties of his country."

The judgment was annulled, Mr. Justice Baldwin alone dissenting; but the formidable question, started by Mr. Wirt in the previous argument, now arose, not indeed in the Court, but in the public mind, how was the decision to be enforced? The State of Georgia treated it as a nullity; the missionaries were still retained in the penitentiary, the Governor declaring, as is said, that he would rather hang them than liberate them under the mandate of the Supreme Court. The General Government gave but little hopes of interfering in the controversy, and no farther judicial proceedings were instituted. Nothing was left for the prisoners but to wait for a day of cooler judgment and more moderate counsels. After some eighteen months this day arrived.

* In the previous opinion, it will be recollected, the Chief-Justice laid down the same principle—that the Cherokees were a separate State or nation; though he held they were not a *foreign* State within the meaning of the Constitution.

The contest had grown hopeless to the weaker party. The missionaries were released ; and here ended this extraordinary chapter in the history of our free government.*

At the session of the Court in 1833, the case of Barron *vs.* The Mayor and City Council of Baltimore † was argued, in which Chief-Justice Marshall delivered one of his last constitutional judgments.‡ The question raised was, whether the provision of the Constitution which inhibits the taking of private property for public use without just compensation, ought to be construed so as to restrain the legislative power of a State, as well as that of the United States ; a question of great importance indeed, but, as the Chief-Justice observed in his opinion, of no very great difficulty. He answers this question without hesitation, and with the unanimous concurrence of his associates, in the negative. "The States, in their several Constitutions," he remarks, "have imposed such restrictions on their respective governments as their own wisdom suggested ; such as they deemed most proper for themselves. It is a subject on which they judge *exclusively*, and with which others interfere no farther than they are supposed to have a common interest. The constitutional provision under consideration, was not intended to secure the people of the several States against the undue exercise of power by their respective State governments, but only against that which might be attempted by the Federal Government ; and the Court was, therefore, of the opinion that the clause of the Constitution which declares that private property shall not be taken for public use without just compensation, is intended solely as a limitation on the exercise of power by the Government of the United States, and is not applicable to the legislation of the States."

The present Chief-Justice of the United States was one of the counsel engaged on the argument in support of the State law—an act of the legislature of Maryland—the validity of which was established by this decision.

* Kennedy's *Life of Wirt.* Vol. II. p. 323.

† 7 Peter's Reports, 243.

‡ He wrote the brief opinion in Byrne *vs.* The State of Missouri, referred to in a preceding note (page 429), at the next session of the Court ; but that case merely re-affirmed the decision in Craig *vs.* Missouri, turning on the same constitutional point.

It may very justly be inferred from this decision, what indeed was indicated in the case of The Providence Bank *vs.* Billings, heretofore noticed,* and some others which might be mentioned, that, however strictly the Chief-Justice was disposed to limit the power of State legislation when that power came in collision with some law of, or authority claimed to be exercised by, the Federal Government; yet, in other cases he was inclined to restrict, rather than to extend, the jurisdiction of the Court, and never assumed to invade the province of State legislation in those matters which, appropriately pertaining to State sovereignty, involve no collision of jurisdiction or power.

Thus we have seen that he regarded the power of taxation to be an inherent attribute of sovereignty, and sacred in all cases *except* when it came in collision with, or *might* be exercised to the destruction of, a rightful power of the General Government, in which case it was void.† So, too, he held, that even the legislative act of a State which divested antecedent vested rights of property, provided always that it did not impair the obligation of contracts, could not be pronounced void by the Supreme Court as against the Constitution of the United States. He had intimated, indeed, in Fletcher *vs.* Peck,‡ that it might well be doubted whether the nature of society and of government does not prescribe some limit to the legislative power; but he nowhere intimates that the Constitution prohibits the States from passing laws derogatory to private rights of property, a power which certainly may be regarded as the highest attribute of sovereignty. This power was asserted to exist in an opinion delivered by one of his brethren, in which the Chief-Justice appears to have concurred.§ The point was again raised in Watson *vs.* Mercer, at the session of 1834, the very last constitutional argument ever made before him.‖ In this case Judge Story, pronouncing the unanimous opinion of the Court, of course including the Chief-Justice, reiterates the doctrine in these broad and general terms: "That the Court has no right to pro-

* On page 426.

† Brown *vs.* State of Maryland, Weston *vs.* City of Charleston, Providence Bank *vs.* Billings.

‡ *Ante*, page 359.

§ Satterlee *vs.* Matthewson, 2 Peters' Reports, 413.

‖ 8 Peters' Reports, 88.

nounce an act of the legislature of a State void, as contrary to the Constitution of the United States, from the mere fact that it divests antecedent vested rights of property ; the Constitution does not prohibit the States from passing retrospective laws generally, but only *ex post facto* laws, and these laws are held to embrace not civil rights, but penal and criminal proceedings and matters only." *

Marshall never fell into the error of his predecessors, that the Federal Courts have a common-law jurisdiction. So, too, he never questioned the exclusive jurisdiction of the State tribunals to interpret their own State statutes, a principle fully established by repeated decisions of the Court. In one case † before him, however, it was contended that the exclusive power of the State Courts to construe their own legislative acts, does not extend to the paramount law, so as to enable them to give efficacy to an act contrary to the State Constitution. Marshall thus deals with the objection, and vindicates the right and authority of the State tribunals over constitutional questions : "We cannot admit this distinction. The judicial department of every government is the rightful expositor of its laws ; and, emphatically, of its supreme law. If, in a case depending before any court, a legislative act shall conflict with the Constitution, it is admitted that the Court must exercise its judgment on both, and that the Constitution must control the act. The Court must determine whether a repugnancy does or does not exist, and in making its determination must construe both instruments. That its construction of one is authority, while its construction of the other is to be disregarded, is a proposition for which the Court can perceive no reason."

I have thus brought to a close this brief review of the judicial life of Chief-Justice Marshall—a review necessarily imperfect, and which I am satisfied cannot give an adequate idea of the extent, the variety, the comprehensiveness, the greatness of his labors. I have not touched upon his decisions at the Circuit, nor have I undertaken, by citing even here and there an isolated case, to indicate the extent of his

* Mr. Justice Johnson, in his dissenting opinion in Satterlee *vs.* Matthewson, considers this doctrine relative to the nature of *ex post facto* laws to be unsound and pernicious.

† Bank of Hamilton *vs.* Dudley's lessees. 2 Peters' Reports, 492.

learning and the value of his labors, in the various branches of commercial and maratime, as well as international law, the law of copyrights, the law of patents, and those other subjects which are peculiarly within the cognizance of the Federal tribunals. These, and a variety of other interesting matters, connected with his judicial services, are necessarily excluded by the limits marked out for this sketch—a sketch which in no sense pretends to the completeness of a full biography. That biography will, doubtless, be written, and the picture filled up by another and more competent hand;—by one having access to his private papers and voluminous correspondence;—and, if done soon, by one perhaps who knew him intimately, and who, from personal knowledge and intercourse, can draw the picture to the life, in the lights and shades of his private as well as his public character—introducing us to his fire-side, his table, his familiar conversation, and every-day life, and illustrating, by personal anecdote and reminiscence, his habits, his peculiar tastes, his mode of life, and even his little infirmities, if any such he may have had. While this, however, has not been attempted, I have yet endeavored to disclose fully and accurately his judicial opinions, upon most of those great questions of constitutional law which, in his capacity of judge, he was called upon to review. In like manner I shall here notice some other views entertained by the Chief-Justice relative to our political and judicial systems, which, though not judicially expressed, he did not hesitate to avow without reserve or concealment.

It is well known that Marshall's opinions upon political questions, as well as upon Constitutional law, were formed in the Federal school, and continued without change and unshaken to the day of his death. A writer in the New York Review, who seems to participate in these views with no little ardor of feeling, declares, that he "abhorred *ab imo pectore* all the modern, new fangled doctrines, so fashionable in Virginia, upon the subject of the Constitution and the principles of the government;"—that is to say, the doctrines contained in and legitimately resulting from the famous resolutions of 1798. Making due allowance for the warmth of this language, the expression, I apprehend, is not far wide of the mark. But, as it has been very properly said, the admiration which one feels for the intellectual powers displayed by the Chief-Justice, in his expositions of the Constitution, is not to be confounded with assent, in all cases, to the results to which he came. Many distinguished men have differed, and still differ from him, in his views of Constitutional law, and even his learned associates upon the bench have not uniformily gone along with him. Thus the resolutions of 1798, it is scarcely necessary to remind the reader, were the work of Madison ; and so far as a mere name may be cited as authority, and aside from the weight to be attached to the judicial character, in questions of constitutional construction, Madison may claim to stand at least on an equality with Marshal ; for he was with the Constitution at its birth, he was its cotemporary expositor, and not only a large portion of its materials, but some of its essential framework, are the contributions of his own hands. It would be no presumption, therefore, were this the proper place to enter upon the discussion, to question, on original principles, the accuracy and soundness of some of the constitutional constructions of the illustrious Judge, so far, at least, as they may be found to differ from those of him, who may, by way of pre-eminence, be called the author of the Constitution. Had James Madison come to the bench in 1801, instead of John Marshall, though the whole current of decisions in questions involving the sovereignty of the states might have been changed, can it, for a moment, be imagined, that such change would have impaired the stability of our institutions, or the liberties of the country ?

It is to be observed, however, that the difference between these two truly great and illustrious minds in regard to the rules of constitutional construction, except perhaps in cases directly involving questions of power between the Federal and State sovereignties, is really less than has been generally supposed. While it must be admitted that Marshall was not a state's rights man (as the term is usually understood), yet his decisions, in a class of cases already referred to, show that he was, in one sense, like Madison, a *strict constructionist;* that no man was less likely than he to *infer* a power in the general government, authorizing an invasion of the rights, and a control of the sovereignty of the State tribunals and legislatures ; and that he by no means shared those loose and indefinite notions which pervaded the Court, and were entertained by prominent Federal statesmen and jurists, in Jay's and Ellsworth's time.

In his political sentiments Marshall was warm and decided ; for, though entirely withdrawn from political life, it is certainly true that he did entertain not only decided, but warm political feelings.* That these feelings may have influenced his judgment in giving construction to great questions of constitutional power is not only probable, but perhaps natural, and unavoidable. Of what avail could argument be to unsettle a principle which had occupied his closest attention, and had been rooted in his mind for years as a fundamental political truth, sustained, as he viewed it, by the letter as well as by the spirit of the Constitution. The argument of such a point must have been to him but another of those dull experiences upon the bench of which Judge Story gives an anecdote in illustration: "That point has been repeatedly decided the other way," remarked the Judge to an advocate who was advancing some new propositions at the end of a long and prosy discourse. "Nevertheless," answered the counsel, "I consider that my duty to my client requires me to argue it." "Very well," replied Story, "you can go on and argue it, if you think your duty requires it. I would not restrict you in the performance of your duty; but I made up my mind on the point and decided it twenty years ago, and have never seen any reason to change it."

While in Congress Marshall voted, as has been elsewhere remarked, for the repeal of the second section of the sedition act, in opposition to his political friends. It is confidently asserted, however, from his own subsequent declarations, that he did not place his vote upon the grounds of any doubt as to the constitutionality of the act, but merely because he deemed the law inexpedient and unsuited to the temper and feelings of the American people.†

He freely expressed to his friends in private conversation his views in regard to the power of Congress to construct roads, and upon the subject of internal improvements generally, recognizing fully the power so far as it was the appropriate means of carrying out the express power given to Congress; as to construct military roads under the

* In a lively letter to Judge Carr, Mr. Wirt, who always entertained for the Chief-Justice the most profound respect, remarks: "I do not believe he has an atom of gall in his whole composition on any other subject than that of politics; or that with him—as with many other great men in the Union, who will never forgive the fall that Mr. Jefferson gave them—*hæret lateri lethalis arundo*."—2 Kennedy's Life of Wirt, 208.

† 3 New York Review, 347.

power to declare war ; to appropriate money for improvements of a national character under the power to regulate commerce between the States, &c., &c.*

He regarded the treaty-making power as extending to cases of cession of territory ; he would not undertake, says Judge Story, to say that it extended to all cases, yet he did not doubt it must be construed to extend to some.†

Passing by these debateable political questions, it would be curious to notice some of his views, not judicially expressed, upon subjects of interest connected with the constitutional jurisprudence of the country, which, controverted in his day, have since been adopted as the settled opinion of the Court. I shall notice but one or two of these.

Under the Constitution the judicial power extends to controversies "between citizens of different States." It had been decided at a very early period by one or two cases in which the Chief-Justice himself pronounced the judgment of the Court, that a corporation aggregate was not "a citizen" within the meaning of the Constitution, and could not sue in the Courts of the United States as such.‡ This opinion, which was adhered to by the Court so late as the session of 1840,§ we are told by Judge Story, was considered by the Chief-Justice, before his death, as incorrect, and as having been given on inadequate grounds.|| It has been subsequently revised by the Supreme Court, and a different rule adopted.¶

Another opinion of Chief-Justice Marshall, which has been considered and adopted by the Supreme Court since his time as correct in principle in opposition to previous decisions, was in relation to the jurisdiction of our Courts of Admiralty. Following the course of the English decisions, the Supreme Court had uniformly held, as the rule was laid down by Mr. Justice Story in the case of the *Thomas Jefferson*,** that the Admiralty had no jurisdiction except upon the sea, or

* 3 New York Review, 347.

† Letter of Judge Story to Edward Everett.—2 Story's Life and Letters, 288.

‡ Strawbridge *vs.* Curtis. 3 Cranch Rep. 267. Bank of the United States *vs.* Devereaux. 5 Cranch Rep. 61.

§ Bank of Vicksburgh *vs.* Slocum. 14 Peters' Rep. 60.

|| Letter to Chancellor Kent. 2 Story's Life and Letters, 469.

¶ Louisville Rail Road Co. *vs.* Letson. 2 Howard's Rep. 497.

** 10 Wheaton's Reports, 428. See also Steamboat Orleans *vs.* Phœbus. 11 Peters' Reports, 175.

upon tide waters within the ebb and flow of the tide. This principle, the Chief-Justice believed, had been misapplied, and was too narrow in its interpretation to be applicable to the great rivers of America, though perfectly correct and reasonable in regard to the jurisdiction in England, where the rivers are short, and none of them navigable from the sea beyond the ebb and flow of the tide. He spoke of this, it is said, as one of the most deliberate opinions of his life,* having no doubt, on a correct application of the principle, that the Admiralty jurisdiction extended over the Mississippi and its branches as far as navigable from the sea, hundreds of miles into the interior ; and also, though he spoke of this with less confidence, over the great inland lakes, which were to be deemed inland navigable seas. Nor did he doubt the constitutional power of Congress to regulate this subject, and confer this jurisdiction, as being within the power to regulate commerce between the States. These deliberate and well considered opinions of the Chief-Justice, though not recognized in his day, have been established in ours, in a recent judgment of the Court, pronounced by the present Chief-Justice,† holding the Act of Congress of 1845, which extends the Admiralty jurisdiction over the lakes and navigable waters connected with the same, to be constitutional. In the judgment of the Court, the act rests, not upon the power of Congress to regulate commerce, but upon the broad and original principle maintained by Marshall, that the Admiralty jurisdiction granted to the Federal government by the Constitution is not limited to tide waters, but extends to all public navigable lakes and rivers, where commerce is carried on with different States or with a foreign nation.‡

The literary labors of Chief-Justice Marshall, and his connection with the Virginia Convention in 1829, are the only incidents of his active life that yet remain to be noted.

* 3 New York Review, 350.

† Genesee Chief *vs.* Fitzhugh. 12 Howard's Reports, 443. See subsequent Sketch of Chief-Justice Taney.

‡ Mr. Justice Daniel, who dissented, must have been mistaken in regard to the views of Marshall on this subject, when, in denying any such extensive ground of Admiralty jurisdiction in this country, or the right of Congress, under the strict provisions of the Constitution, to confer it on the Courts, he claims, if there is any error in the view he adopts, that he is sustained in the view by "the support of Marshall, Kent, and Story." See dissenting opinion of Mr. Justice Daniel.

The private and original papers and correspondence of General Washington, came by his will into the hands of his nephew, Judge Bushrod Washington. Between this gentleman and Marshall, the most intimate friendship existed. Judge Washington, immediately on the death of his uncle, selected the Chief-Justice to write his biography. That work was prepared by Marshall as a religious duty, with all that profound admiration for the character, and reverential affection for the memory, of the man, which he never ceased to entertain, and yet with that severe and almost stern impartiality, and that unsparing critical judgment which concede nothing to friendship, and doubt even the genuineness of those memories which arise unbidden from the warm affections of the heart. The examination of, and selections from, the mass of manuscripts and papers that were placed in his hands was a herculean task ; but the Chief-Justice performed it with scrupulous care and fidelity. The first three volumes of the Life of Washington were published in 1804, the fourth in 1805, and the fifth and last in 1807. These volumes undoubtedly contain the fullest, the most impartial, and the most authentic statement ever written of Washington's military life, and indeed of the entire war.

The author himself was in the army, and was under the immediate command of Washington during the most critical and the most interesting period of his military career ; and it has with truth been said of Marshall that no other man could have brought to this task so many and such various qualifications for its successful accomplishment.

The part devoted to the political history of the times, particularly during the administration of Washington, is also written with singular candor and truthfulness. Of the events he narrates he could speak as matters of cotemporary history. He could speak of them as Æneas might have spoken of Ilium, when, his eye resting upon the pictured representation, in the palace of Carthage, memory brought back to him, in all the vivid distinctness of reality, those scenes of but yesterday. Like the Trojan chief, Marshall had borne his share in the events, and mingled with the men, of the period he describes, and could speak of both with the precision and confidence of personal knowledge. And it is certainly no small praise to say, that entertaining decided and warm party predilections, he has spoken both of men and measures with a moderation, a fairness, and an impartiality, that has left nothing even for political opponents to criticise.*

The merits of the Life of Washington, as an accurate and impartial work of history, are universally conceded. The style might perhaps suggest criticism. It is simple, plain, and unambitious, and perhaps, as is remarked of his judicial opinions, a little "hard and dry." Marshall wrote to communicate facts, to instruct, to convince, not to delight or amuse with the graces of rhetoric. One cannot help thinking, however, that a little more liveliness and warmth of narrative, a little fuller scope of illustration, and a freer play of the fancy, always however within the rigid and strictly circumscribed bounds of historic truth, would have rendered the life of Washington a more readable and popular biography.

The first of these volumes, it should be mentioned, contained a brief

* A note relative to Mr. Jefferson's famous letter to Mazzei, called forth a commentary which forms an unfortunate exception to the above remark. Mr. Jefferson alleges that a paragraph had been interpolated in his Mazzei letter which makes him charge his own country with ingratitude and injustice to France. In a letter written by Jefferson only the year before his death, to Mr. Van Buren, he comments with some severity upon Marshall's reference to this letter, remarking, "And even Judge Marshall makes history descend from its dignity, and the ermine from its sanctity, to exaggerate, to record, and to sanction this forgery." Marshall, in his second edition of the Life of Washington, in 1832, in the note to the Mazzei letter, replies to these comments not without some degree of warmth and asperity.

It is well known that the same reciprocal esteem and good understanding which existed between Madison and Marshall never existed between the latter and Jefferson. It is to be accounted for perhaps not altogether from political differences, but also from that clashing of opinion which arose between the Executive and the Supreme Court during Jefferson's administration. The *extra judicial* opinion, as Jefferson called it, in Marbury *vs.* Madison, was extremely distasteful to the President, and so in a much greater degree, were the rulings and decisions of Marshall in Burr's trial. This is very evident from Jefferson's letters during the trial to Mr. Hay, which are found in his published correspondence. The enemies of Mr. Jefferson have fastened upon him with fierce and almost vindictive animosity, the charge of having attacked the Chief-Justice from feelings of personal as well as political hostility. I do not intend to discuss the merits of the controversy on either side, but merely remark, that so far as the published correspondence of Mr. Jefferson can be taken as a guide, I believe this charge to be greatly exaggerated if not entirely destitute of foundation.

history of the American colonies up to the period of the Revolution. This historical review, after being very fully and carefully revised by the author, was detached from the original work, and republished in 1824 as a "History of the Colonies." In 1832 he republished the Life of Washington, in two closely printed volumes, carefully revised and condensed—the language being, as he remarks in his preface, "in some instances altered—he trusts, improved ; and the narrative, especially that part of it which details the distresses of the army during the war, relieved from tedious repetition of the same suffering."

Chief-Justice Marshall, at the age of seventy-four years, was elected a member of the Convention which assembled early in 1829, to revise the Constitution of his native State. It has been well remarked, that a spectacle of greater dignity than this Convention, has rarely been exhibited. It was composed of the most eminent citizens of Virginia—some of them indeed the most eminent and illustrious of living American statesmen—the record of whose public services reached back to a period before the foundation of the government, and whose histories were interwoven with the history of the republic. Such were the two venerable ex-Presidents of the United States, James Madison and James Monroe. These, with Marshall, might well be called the Nestors of the Convention ; for each of them, like the Pylian sage, amid the Grecian chiefs before the walls of Troy, had survived two generations of men, and was standing now among a third, to enlighten and instruct by the wisdom of years and experience. Among their associates were the late President Tyler, the late Associate-Justice of the Supreme Court, Philip P. Barbour, Henry B. Giles, Littleton W. Tazewell, Abel P. Upshur, besides many other gentlemen, who have subsequently distinguished themselves and earned an honorable fame in the service of their State and country.

It had been intended to call Mr. Madison to preside over the Convention, but his advanced age and physical infirmities induced him to decline. Mr. Monroe was then unanimously selected, and was conducted to the chair by Madison and Marshall. I cannot undertake here to follow the course of the proceedings of the Convention, or to allude even to the prominent subjects of its discussions. The debates were at times very animated, and always exceedingly able. A full report of them has been published, comprising a volume of nine hundred closely printed pages. The Chief-Justice, though not a frequent, much less a tedious, speaker, occasionally mingled in these debates, and spoke with a directness and an earnest sincerity which commanded the respect, if it did not carry conviction to the understandings of his hearers. It is said that one of the most beautiful features of the scene was the reverence manifested for Chief-Justice Marshall. The gentleness of his temper, the purity of his motives, the sincerity of his convictions, and his wisdom, were confessed by all.* Though members might differ from him in judgment, no harshness or asperity of language was suffered to mingle with the reply which his arguments elicited. He spoke upon the two great questions which divided the Convention, namely, the basis of representation, and the tenure of the judicial office, and with especial earnestness and feeling upon the latter. In this debate the judicial act passed by Congress in 1802, restoring the former circuit system, and thereby abolishing the offices of certain judges, was touched upon. The views expressed by the Chief-Justice on this subject were not concurred in by some of the prominent gentlemen in the Convention. His remarks were replied to by Mr. Tazewell and Mr. Giles, but by both with the utmost courtesy and respect, especially the latter, who, forgetting past differences of opinion, expressed the highest personal regard for his venerable associate.

The projected Constitution contained a provision that Judges of the Superior Courts should hold their offices during good behavior. The Chief-Justice proposed to add a clause guarding against such a construction as that of the act of Congress referred to, which by repealing the law establishing the Court, dissolved the tenure of the Judge's office, and discharged him upon the world. In the view of Marshall, this was incompatible with the absolute independence of the Judiciary. He spoke upon this question with earnestness and emphasis —almost, says one, with the authority of an apostle. "The argument of the gentleman," he said, "goes to prove not only that there is no such thing as judicial independence, but that there ought to be no such thing;—that it is unwise and improvident to make the tenure of the Judge's office to continue during good behavior. I have grown old in the opinion, that there is nothing more dear to Virginia, or

* Mr. Binney's Eulogy.

ought to be more dear to her statesmen, and that the best interests of our country are secured by it. Advert, sir, to the duties of a Judge. He has to pass between the government, and the man whom that government is prosecuting,—between the most powerful individual in the community, and the poorest and most unpopular. It is of the last importance that, in the performance of these duties, he should observe the utmost fairness. Need I press the necessity of this? Does not every man feel that his own personal security, and the security of his property depend upon that fairness? The judicial department comes home in its effects to every man's fireside; it passes on his property, his reputation, his life, his all. Is it not to the last degree important, that he should be rendered perfectly and completely independent, with nothing to control him but God and his conscience?"

* * * * * * * *

"I have always thought, from my earliest youth till now, that the greatest scourge an angry Heaven ever inflicted upon an ungrateful and a sinning people, was an ignorant, a corrupt, or a dependent Judiciary."

An incident occurred in one of the discussions in the Convention, that is worthy of being noticed. Among the provisions of the proposed Constitution relative to the legislature, was one restraining the Senate from altering a money bill originating in the other house. The Chief-Justice moved to strike out the clause, and proceeded to express his views upon the subject, remarking, among other things, that the idea was derived from England, where the upper house were hereditary legislators; and however well adapted to their institutions and frame of government, it was not suitable to ours. During his remarks much disorder and confusion prevailed in the house, and his voice was scarcely audible above the tumult. A member sprang to his feet, and addressing the chair, exclaimed: "Wisdom crieth aloud in the street, and her voice is not heard!" The chairman at once called the house to order, and comparative quiet was immediately restored. Marshall continued and concluded his remarks. The question was then taken on the amendment, and carried by a very large majority.

The venerable Chief-Justice presided, for the last time, in the Supreme Court, at the session of 1835. He had now entered upon his eightieth year, and was still in the enjoyment of tolerable health, and in the full possession of his mental faculties. There were some cases pending at this term, involving important questions of constitutional law, and among others that of Briscoe *vs.* The Commonwealth Bank of Kentucky, and Miln *vs.* The City of New York. The Court, however, was not full; for though Mr. Justice Wayne had taken his seat early in the term, in place of Judge Johnson, deceased, yet another vacancy had been created by the resignation of Mr. Justice Duval. In reply to the inquiry of counsel, whether cases involving constitutional questions would be taken up the present term, the Chief-Justice said: "The Court cannot know whether there will be a full Court during the term; but as it is now composed, the Constitutional cases will not be taken up."

The cases accordingly passed over; they passed into the hands of his successor on the bench. For Marshall there was never again "a full court;" he had heard his last argument, and pronounced his last Constitutional judgment. His work was done; the opening of the next session brought with it the eulogy for the departed, in the eloquent words of Clay; and the affectionate and affecting response of Story, who, as senior Judge, occupied the seat of the deceased: "This hall will never again be honored by his presence. But so long as it shall remain devoted to the administration of public justice, so long will it preserve the best records of his fame. He who in future ages shall here seek for his monument, need but look around him and before him. The voices of the eloquent and the learned, which will here pronounce his name, will never fail to breathe forth, at the same time, his most affecting praise."

During this last session of the Court, the venerable Chief-Justice presided with all his accustomed dignified composure, and simple and artless grace of manner. It was a striking and touching spectacle to see the tall, majestic old man, in his robe of office, move with firm step to his usual seat among his brethren. To those especially whose eyes had been accustomed to follow him for years, and whose early admiration for the man had ripened into reverence, the scene was well calculated to awaken the most interesting reminiscences. He stood among them a relict of the past; the last link which connected the government of that day, with the first years of the republic. He had outlived all his former associates. Of the judges who sat with him, during the first ten years of his service, not one remained. Judge Story, the eldest then in commission, had come to the bench a young man, at a period when Marshall might already have been called a veteran, and when his fame as a jurist was well nigh at its zenith. The great lawyers who frequented the Court, and were engaged in argument before him in former years, had, nearly all of them, disappeared. Webster, it is true, remained, then as ever, the leading counsel in the most important causes, and at times the voice of Clay was heard at the bar of the Court; but Wirt had passed away, and Pinkney, and Dallas, and Martin, and Dexter, and Emmett, and Wells. Yet the venerable form of the Chief-Justice, as he stood thus alone among his brethren of the bar and the bench—alone among a new generation of men, excited no painful emotion or compassionate feeling. Men felt in his presence nothing but a serene, a cheerful, almost a lively satisfaction. There were no regrets for the past, nothing to wish for the present, and nothing to fear for the future, for the measure of his fame was full, and with the clear light of his intellect still shining undimmed—still glittering bright and steady over the snows of fourscore winters—it was not likely that that fame could now be impaired. It is stated that Marshall in the latter years of his life feared that he might not retain the full use of his faculties in his old age, and had for some time contemplated a retirement from the bench. He had mentioned the subject to confidential friends, and charged them not to let him remain on the bench a day after they suspected his mind was on the wane. It is also stated that these friends, from a deep reverence and affection for the Chief-Justice, had determined to act upon the suggestion if the time should ever arrive in which it was proper to be done.* That time fortunately never came. The record of the last session of the Supreme Court, at which he presided, and the reports of the opinions he delivered in some of the cases then argued, attest that his faculties remained in their full power to the last. His setting sun, says the authority I have quoted, was seen in its clear, unclouded splendor, beaming as it descended with a larger orb and more softened light, until the very moment when it sunk beneath the horizon, with a beautiful and tranquillizing transparency.

The health of the Chief-Justice began visibly to fail toward the

* 3 New York Review, 340.

close of the term. Early in March, Judge Story writes: "He still possesses his intellectual powers in very high vigor, but his physical health is manifestly on the decline." And yet, notwithstanding bodily weakness, and almost unremitting pain, he continued to bear up with an uncomplaining spirit; and though the loss of his wife visibly and deeply affected him, he maintained to outward view at least, his habitual calmness and serenity of temper.*

At the close of this session of the Court he returned to his residence in Richmond. Here he was seized with a serious and alarming illness. Early in June, however, he got better, and continued to improve, so much so as to receive the visits of his friends, and indeed to inspire temporary hopes of his recovery. Among those who had an interview with him at this period was Chancellor Kent, then on a visit to Virginia.† It was soon apparent, however, that this favorable prospect was delusive. His constitution had become shattered, so that but little hopes were now entertained of anything but mere temporary relief. On the advice of his friends he consented to be taken to Philadelphia, in the hopes of obtaining, as upon a former occasion, some aid from the distinguished medical skill of that city. He was accompanied by three of his sons; and during the brief remnant of his

* Two or three years previous to this period, Judge Story, in a letter to his wife, alludes to the effect on the mind of Marshall of his recent affliction: "On going into the Chief-Justice's room this morning, I found him in tears. He had just finished writing out for me some lines of General Burgoyne, of which he spoke to me last evening as eminently beautiful and affecting. I asked him to change the purpose and address them to you, which he instantly did, and you will find them accompanying this. I saw at once he had been shedding tears over the memory of his own wife; and he has said to me several times during the term, that the moment he relaxes from business he feels exceedingly depressed, and rarely goes through a night without weeping over his departed wife. She must have been a very extraordinary woman so to have attached him; and I think he is the most extraordinary man I ever saw for the depth and tenderness of his feelings."

† I cannot vouch for the accuracy of the following anecdote of the Chancellor's interview with Chief-Justice Marshall, chronicled in the Richmond papers of the day. Kent, it is said, introduced himself, and observing that he had heard of the Chief-Justice's indisposition, added, that not knowing whether he should see him in the next world, he was resolved to have that pleasure in this.

The Chancellor, while in Richmond, visited the "Quoite Club," where his presence attracted very marked attention.

days passed in that city, was attended by them, and by many valued friends, among whom was his brother on the bench, Mr. Justice Baldwin, who, like all his associates, entertained for the Chief-Justice a respect and affection amounting almost to reverence. The death of his eldest son * who was killed at Baltimore by an unfortunate accident, a few days before his father's decease, was concealed from the Chief-Justice, and everything that considerate affection and kindness could prompt, was done to smoothe his passage to the tomb. He was conscious of his approaching end, and with his faculties unimpaired to the last, expired on Monday, the 6th July, 1835, having nearly completed his eightieth year.

The body of the Chief-Justice was brought to Richmond, accompanied by General Scott, Judge Baldwin, and a deputation of the bar of Philadelphia, who on their arrival at Richmond were received as the guests of the city. The ceremonies of the funeral were solemn and impressive. "The city bells," says the Richmond Enquirer, "tolled yesterday nearly the whole day—guns were fired—and, perhaps, no funeral procession, in this city, has ever been more extensive and solemn than the one which yesterday attended him to the grave."

The funeral services were performed by Bishop Moore, according to the ritual of the Episcopal Church, of which the deceased was a member.† On its entrance into the city the corpse was met at the Union Hotel by an imposing procession of the civil authorities, military, clergy, masonic brethren, and citizens, and was taken to his own

* Mr. Thomas Marshall, a gentleman of fine talents and attainments, and at the time of his death a member elect of the Virginia House of Delegates. He was on his way to visit his father at Philadelphia. While walking near the Court-house in Baltimore, a violent thunderstorm arose, and Mr. Marshall with a friend sought shelter from the rain in the hall of the Court-house. A chimney of the building, struck with lightning, as it was thought, fell upon the stairs of the Court-house, and a portion of it in that part of the hall where Mr. Marshall stood, striking him and wounding him so severely that he died early the next morning.

† "Among Christian sects," says Judge Story, "he personally attached himself to the Episcopal church. It was the religion of his early education; and became afterwards that of his choice. But he was without the slightest touch of bigotry or intolerance. His benevolence was as wide as Christianity itself. It embraced the human race. He was not only liberal in his feelings and principles, but in his charities. His hands were open upon all occasions to succor distress, to encourage enterprise, and to support good institutions."

house, according to his request. Thence it was carried to the new burying ground, where it rests near the ashes of his wife.*

The death of Marshall excited a deep sensibility in the public mind throughout the country, and every possible mark of respect was shown to his memory, particularly by the members of the bar and in the various courts of justice. The most eminent of his professional brethren were selected and consented to deliver eulogies upon his services and character—Story, Kent, Webster, Binney, Sargeant. A collection of the proceedings of the different Courts, their resolutions, the addresses of the bar, the responses from the bench, would fill a volume. From all these I select one passage only—a single sentiment—the resolutions adopted by the Charleston bar. It is a sentiment so singularly just and beautiful, so modest, so truthful, and yet so profoundly suggestive, that it deserves to be engraved on the marble bust of the Chief-Justice, which stands on its pedestal in the hall of that tribunal in which he so long presided :—" Though his authority as Chief-Justice of the United States," says the Charleston resolution, " was protracted far beyond the ordinary term of public life, no man dared to covet his place, or express a wish to see it filled by another. Even the spirit of party respected the unsullied purity of the Judge, and the fame of the Chief-Justice has justified the wisdom of the Constitution, AND RECONCILED THE JEALOUSY OF FREEDOM TO THE INDEPENDENCE OF THE JUDICIARY."

It might be expected that having thus followed the Chief-Justice to the close of his career, and sketched, with perhaps a too free pen, his judicial services, his opinions, and his public character, I should speak of his domestic and social virtues, and of that happy combination of faculties which threw a charm around his fireside, and over his intercourse in private life. This would be proper, doubtless, but can scarcely be necessary. I might, indeed, speak of that rare combination of virtue and wisdom which his private as well as his public life manifested —of that wise and considerate propriety of conduct—that natural dignity of deportment—that love of truth and deep sense of moral and religious obligation—that unaffected modesty—that simplicity of character, manners, dress, and deportment—that deep sensibility and tenderness—that ardent love of home and attachment to the pleasures of the domestic

* Richmond Enquirer, July 10, 1835.

circle—that respect, courtesy, and kindness, which he always manifested for the female sex—that absence of all selfish feeling—that benevolence, and that kindly charity, which was not only a principle and rule of his life, but an innate sentiment of his heart. All these might be spoken of in terms of unqualified respect and admiration; but the task has been already done by the hand of another, his intimate companion and friend, for twenty-four years, and in a manner which none may hope to equal or even to imitate.*

In bringing this sketch to a close, however, I cannot refrain from introducing the following tribute to his domestic virtues, from the pen of a venerable kinsman, as preserved by one of his eulogists†—a tribute as full of affectionate tenderness, as it is of a touching simplicity, and genuine truthfulness:

"He had no frays in boyhood. He had no quarrels or outbreakings in manhood. He was the composer of strifes. He spoke ill of no man. He meddled not with their affairs. He viewed their worst deeds through the medium of charity. He had eight sisters and six brothers, with all of whom, from youth to age, his intercourse was marked by the utmost kindness and affection; and, although his eminent talents, high public character, and acknowledged usefulness, could not fail to be a subject of pride and admiration to all of them, there is no one of his numerous relatives, who has had the happiness of a personal association with him, in whom his purity, simplicity, and affectionate benevolence did not produce a deeper and more cherished impression than all the achievements of his powerful intellect."

And to this may be added the last, perhaps the most generous and affecting tribute of that devoted associate, who mourned his loss, not as a friend only, but as a brother—a tribute less to be valued on account of any poetic beauty, than as an evidence of that warm affection, and that undying and reverential admiration, which STORY never ceased to entertain for MARSHALL. The lines, written but a few months after the death of the Chief-Justice, were intended as an inscription for A CENOTAPH.

* Sketch by Judge Story. Miscellanies, pages, 676 to 682.

† Mr. Binney. Address before the Councils of Philadelphia.

"To Marshall reared—the great, the good, the wise,
Born for all ages, honored in all skies;
His was the fame to mortals rarely given,
Begun on earth, but fixed in aim on Heaven.
Genius and learning and consummate skill,
Moulding each thought, obedient to the will;
Affections pure as e'er warmed human breast,
And love in blessing others doubly blest;
Virtue unspotted, uncorrupted truth,
Gentle in age and beautiful in youth;
These were his bright possessions. These had power
To charm through life and cheer his dying hour,
All these are perished? No! but snatched from time
To bloom afresh in yonder sphere sublime.
Kind was the doom (the fruit was ripe) to die,—
Mortal is clothed with immortality."

ROGER B. TANEY.

ROGER B. TANEY.

To the stranger who for the first time visits the Capitol at Washington, there is no more interesting or attractive place of resort than the hall where are held the sessions of the Supreme Court of the United States. It is situated on the ground-floor of the building, in the story below that which contains the chambers where the two branches of the National Legislature assemble. The approach to it, through the main part of the Capitol, is by no means inviting. It is from the dark, damp, cellar-like, circular enclosure immediately under the rotunda, where groups of colossal columns are thickly clustered together for the support of the dome above, conveying to the mind the sole idea of solid, massive, Egyptian-like architectural strength. A hall leading from this enclosure to the south entrance of the Capitol conducts to the Supreme Court room, an apartment of moderate size, which, though neat, is perfectly plain in appearance, and simple in its decorations and furniture. This apartment is lighted by windows immediately behind the seats of the judges—the bar and the audience sitting in front. The consequence of this arrangement is, that so far as the audience is concerned the light is defective, and it is often difficult, and in a dark day impossible, for those sitting immediately in front, to distinguish the features of the members of the Court after they have taken their seats.

If the visitor desires to see the Court in session, he has but to take his seat and wait patiently until the appearance of the Judges. He will ordinarily observe some few members of the bar, other than the counsel engaged in the cause under argument, sauntering in, and taking their seats, and occasionally strangers or other visitors attracted by interest or curiosity ; unless, indeed, some advocate of distinguished reputation is to address the Court, or some cause of more than usual interest is to be called, in which case the Court room is quickly filled, and often by an imposing and brilliant audience of ladies. It may be perhaps a few minutes after the appointed hour of meeting, when, without any flourish of parade, or announcement, the Judges enter in their black silk gowns, in procession, ranked according to the dates of their respective commissions. At the head of the procession you observe a tall, thin man, slightly bent with the weight of years, of pale complexion, and features somewhat attenuated and careworn, but lighted up by that benignant expression which is indicative at once of a gentle temper and a kindly heart. With a firm and steady step, by no means indicating the years which have actually rolled over his head, he approaches to take his seat. His brothers and associates range themselves on either hand, according to their rank, determined by the date of their respective appointments. Immediately on the right Mr. Justice McLean of Ohio, the oldest Judge in commission on the bench, takes his seat ; Mr. Justice Wayne of Georgia on the left ; and so alternately on the right and left Mr. Justice Catron of Tennessee, and Mr. Justice Daniel of Virginia, Mr. Justice Nelson of New York, and Mr. Justice Grier of Pennsylvania, Mr. Justice Curtis of Massachusetts, and Mr. Justice Campbell of Alabama. Presently the crier will open the Court with that quaint and half ludicrous old formula, which has come down to us from the earliest times, commencing, "*O yes—O yes*," and ending, "God save the United States and this honorable Court!" The Court is now in session and you are in the presence of one of the three co-ordinate branches of the Federal government.

If it be a cloudy day, you will not be able to distinguish, beneath the dark mass of hair which overhangs the forehead of the tall, thin, venerable old man who has just taken his seat in the midst of that group of Judges, anything more than the mere outlines of his features; but you will presently hear his voice, in the blandest and most affable of tones: "The Court is ready to hear you, Mr Attorney-General," whereupon the argument of the case at bar immediately proceeds.

The person who has spoken these words is Mr. Chief-Justice Taney, of whose life and judicial career I am now to attempt a sketch. He is just seventy-seven years of age,* and though not in the enjoyment of robust health, as his countenance indicates, yet he continues in the full possession of his vigorous intellectual faculties. The present session completes the eighteenth year of his service on the bench of the tribunal over which he presides, and to which he was appointed as the successor of Chief-Justice Marshall.

Roger Brooke Taney is a native of Maryland, and was born in Calvert County, in that State, on the 17th day of March, 1777. His ancestors, both on the father's and mother's side, were among the earliest settlers of Maryland, having emigrated from England to that colony in Cromwell's time. The name of Taney is of Welsh, or at least of aboriginal British origin, and though not common in England at the present day, is, I am informed, still known there.† The paternal ancestor of Mr. Taney, who came to Maryland about the year 1656, was of the Catholic faith. Like the Puritans of England in the time of Charles I., he sought repose and liberty of conscience in the wilds of the new world ; for the otherwise liberal policy of the Protector, in matters of religious worship and faith, did not embrace the Catholic, and indeed scarcely included the prelatist, within the pale of toleration. While the government of Charles I. drove the Puritan to the shores of New England, that of Cromwell forced the Catholic into the wilderness of Maryland, and thus America became peopled with the bone and sinew of the English nation. The descendants of this gentleman for several generations, Catholics like himself, experienced, even in their secluded retreat in Calvert County, where they tilled the soil in peace with all men, those civil disabilities, and political disfranchisements, which the intolerant legislation of the mother country fastened upon a proscribed church. The Maryland Convention in 1776, however, by its Constitution and Bill of Rights, abolished these arbitrary distinctions, and established full and absolute equality of citizenship and privilege for all religious denominations. Subsequent to this period the father of the present Chief-Justice was repeatedly

* March, 1854.

† Its orthography there seems to have corresponded more closely with its pronunciation. The case of *Tawney vs.* Crowther may be found in 4th Brown's Chancery Cases.

elected to represent his native country in the Maryland House of Delegates.

On the mother's side Chief-Justice Taney is descended from Dr. Roger Mainwaring, Bishop of St. David's, in the time of Charles I., a gentleman of a noble family from Cheshire. The Bishop of St. David's was the friend of Archbishop Laud, and owed his preferment in the church to the good offices of that celebrated but unfortunate prelate. His second daughter, Mary, intermarried with Robert Brooke, Esquire, a gentleman of good family in Sussex, and one of the issue of this marriage was Roger Brooke, the lineal ancestor of the Chief-Justice, from whom his Christian names are derived. The family came to America in 1650, and settled in Calvert County, where the paternal ancestors of the Chief-Justice, after their arrival, also resided.*

Roger Brooke Taney was born in Calvert county in the State of Maryland, on the 17th March, 1777. He was educated at Dickinson College, Carlisle, in the State of Pennsylvania, of which Institution he became a student in the spring of 1792. The College was then under the superintendence of the Rev. Dr. Nesbitt, a Scotch Presbyterian divine, celebrated for his wit and classical attainments. Taney continued a member of this institution three years, and was graduated in the year 1795. He commenced the study of the law in the spring of the following year at Annapolis, where the principal courts of Maryland were then held, in the office of Jeremiah Townley Chase, who two years before had been appointed Chief-Judge of the General Court of Maryland. The bar of this Court, at that time, was ornamented with a brilliant constellation of professional talent, which might compare favorably with that of any other State in the Union. The advantage of mingling with his older professional brethren, and of witnessing their efforts, was not without its influence on the mind of the young student, and excited in his breast a warm and eager

* Robert Brooke, who came to America in 1650, was the first who *seated* Patuxent, about twenty miles up the river, at Delabrooke. Soon after his arrival Lord Baltimore appointed him *Commander* of Charles County, and when the government of Cromwell became established in 1652, he was chosen by the Commissioners for reducing the Plantations, Governor of Maryland. About the same time he removed to the opposite side of the river Patuxent, and dying on the 20th July, 1663, was buried at his seat, Brooke Place Manor, in Calvert County, Maryland.

spirit of professional emulation. During this period, too, he laid the foundation of those solid professional attainments, and acquired those habits of industry and patient investigation which contributed so largely to his subsequent eminent success.

In the spring of 1799, three years after he commenced the study of the law, he was admitted to the bar, and immediately returned to his native county of Calvert to enter upon the practice of his profession. Almost before he had made his *débût* at the bar, however, he was called into political life, being elected in the autumn of the same year a delegate to the General Assembly of Maryland. Mr. Taney was then scarcely twenty-three years of age and the youngest member of the House of Delegates; yet it is said, that amid the stormy debates which occurred in that body, consequent upon the unprecedented popular excitement growing out of the canvass between Adams and Jefferson for the presidency, he displayed an intrepidity of character and an uprightness of motive which gained for him the admiration of his cotemporaries. He was in the house of delegates at the time the announcement of the death of Washington was made to that body, and well remembers the impressive scene. As Charles Carroll of Carrollton, and John Eager Howard, the Committee from the Senate, entered the hall of the House to make the announcement, the members received them standing and in respectful silence; and as Mr. Carroll communicated the afflicting intelligence, the tears streamed down his cheeks, while many an eye around him was also filled in sympathetic sorrow. It was a moment when the voice of faction was hushed, and the din of political strife melted away into profound and reverential silence; for all could unite in heartfelt homage to the memory of the illustrious dead.

Mr. Taney declined a reëlection to the Maryland legislature, with the view of applying himself more closely to the practice of his profession. The following year he removed to Fredericktown, in the county of Frederick, that being regarded as a more eligible and extended field for the pursuit of his professional avocations. Here he remained in the practice of the law with a constantly increasing success and growing reputation, until his removal to Baltimore, a period of twenty-two years. When he entered upon it the scene was entirely new to him. He was comparatively a stranger in that part of the State. A young man of three or four and twenty, with few acquaintances, little personal influence, and but a small stock of experience, his was certainly at the outset no easy and sunshine journey up the steep and rugged ascent which leads to professional eminence, and which requires, even under the most flattering auspices, so large a share of hope, ambition and energy to surmount. "But," remarks the writer of a brief notice of the Chief-Justice* "the wary and reflecting yeomanry of Frederick, Washington, Alleghany and Montgomery counties soon discovered that his industry had no bounds; that he possessed a mind of the highest order; that judgment, acuteness, penetration, capacious memory, accurate learning, steady perseverance in the discharge of duty, a lofty integrity, united with a grave and winning elocution were developed. These qualifications were soon rewarded with an extensive and lucrative practice. As his powers were unfolded with experience, they saw that in the argument of important causes, he disentangled what was intricate, confirmed what was doubtful, embellished what was dry, and illustrated what was obscure."

It was but a few years after his settlement in Frederick ere Mr. Taney by the force of his talents and industry raised himself to a respectable and prominent position at the bar. He was soon employed in many of the most important causes arising in that part of the State. His practice was both lucrative and extensive, not only in the county courts in the judicial district in which he resided, but also in the Court of Appeals. The reports of cases in that Court by Harris and Johnson exhibit abundant evidence of his ability, his industry and his success as an advocate, even before his removal to Baltimore. They show, too, that he was frequently associated with, and opposed by the most eminent and able members of that distinguished and brilliant bar which then assembled in the Maryland Court of Appeals, and that he grappled successfully in intellectual conflict with such men as Pinkney, Winder, Martin, Harper, Williams and Johnson. Thus in 1821, in conjunction with Mr. Harper, he argued in successful opposition to Pinkney, Winder and Williams, the highly important cause of Brown *vs.* Kennedy,† which brought up for discussion, and

* Southern Literary Magazine, June, 1838.

† 5 Harrison and Johnson's Reports, 195.

finally settled, a very novel question relative to the original proprietary title to lands reclaimed from the navigable waters of Maryland; and the following year, associated with General Winder and Mr. Murray, we find him opposed by Harper and Johnson in the argument of a cause eliciting all the learning connected with the intricate law of charitable trusts, an argument which from the brief analysis preserved in the report, seems to have been characterized by an unusual degree of research and ability.

During the period of his residence in Frederick, Mr. Taney's practice at the bar was of the most general and miscellaneous character. It embraced the widest range of subjects and every description of jurisprudence, criminal as well as civil—in the county courts, the courts of equity, the Court of Appeals, before commissioners, before courts martial, and before judicial tribunals of every other character and description. This indeed is the common experience of most advocates who have risen to eminence at the American bar. Unlike the example set us in the courts of England, from which both our equity and common law systems are derived, a division of professional labor or rather of professional pursuit is not very strictly observed among us. The exact conveyancer, the skilful pleader, and the ingenious advocate are not unfrequently found united in the same person—and the framer of a brief is often no other than the very individual who undertakes to unfold and elucidate it before the Court. The door of every tribunal is supposed to be equally open to the American lawyer, and in each he is expected to sustain himself with the same degree of ability and reputation. The practice of Mr. Taney in this respect seems not to have differed from this common professional experience, and the traditional accounts of his successes in these various and diversified professional engagements, certainly exhibit him as the possessor of no inconsiderable versatility of talent.

In 1811, associated with John Hanson Thomas, he defended General Wilkinson, then Commander-in-Chief of the United States Army, before the military court convened at Frederick, to try him on a series of grave and high accusations. The cause was unpopular. Wilkinson had aroused the jealousies of the people when he suspended the *habeas corpus* in 1806, and imprisoned Bollman and Swartwout as accomplices in Burr's treason. We have seen him as a witness on the trial of

Burr,* where he gained little credit and less popularity, many regarding him as having been himself implicated in Burr's designs. The manners of Wilkinson were haughty and unprepossessing. He scorned instead of attempting to conciliate the popular favor; and besides, he was in peculiar odium with a large portion of the people of Frederick, by reason of his having on a former occasion successfully prosecuted, before a court-martial in that town, a gallant and veteran revolutionary officer. Notwithstanding all this, Mr. Taney did not hesitate generously to step forward and render his professional services to the accused, on being selected by him as one of his legal advisers. He himself shared something of the popular feeling against Wilkinson, and the latter was no stranger to the fact. Yet with a full knowledge of Mr. Taney's personal sentiments, so highly did Gen. Wilkinson regard, not his abilities only, but his integrity and honor, that he selected him without hesitation as one of his counsel on this important trial. The notions of Mr. Taney in regard to professional duty were too exalted, and of too chivalrous a nature, to induce him to think of declining the ungracious task. Perhaps the very unpopularity of Wilkinson, and his present helpless and defensive attitude, had more weight with Taney that any other considerations. He undertook the defence of the accused, and fearlessly and without hesitation, braved the public opprobrium. For several months he labored, loyally, faithfully, zealously, and it must be added, successfully, for his client. Wilkinson was acquitted, his sword was restored, and, it is said, his counsel received no other reward than the gratitude of the veteran's heart.

Other instances might be recorded equally honorable to the professional character of Mr. Taney, in which he unflinchingly braved popular censure in the discharge of his duty, and exhibited a like spirit of fearless independence. I shall mention but one of these, which is still well remembered by the older inhabitants of Frederick, where Mr. Taney then resided. A Methodist preacher, well known as Father Gruber, had been indicted for preaching insurrection among the slaves at a camp-meeting of negroes, and Mr. Taney defended him on his trial. The case excited great feeling among many of the inhabitants of that vicinity who were slaveholders, and the court at which Gruber was tried partook of the excitement. On the trial, the

* *Ante*, p. 375.

prosecuting attorney, who was not a very capable man, soon broke down, and one of the Judges, carried away by his private feelings, and perhaps considering that full justice was not done by the prosecutor, took the examination of the witnesses into his own hands. At that time the authority of the Judges with juries was very great, and Father Gruber was thus placed in imminent peril. Mr. Taney suffered the examination to proceed for some time, without interruption, until the Judge, in the heat of his inquiries, asked a question which was clearly improper and inadmissible. Taney had found the opportunity for which he had waited, and springing from his seat, promptly objected to the question as illegal. So well-founded was the objection, that the other judges were forced to rule it against their brother, and from that moment the examination from the bench ceased. The prisoner was acquitted, and for a long period the Methodists of that section of the country entertained the kindest feelings for the Roman Catholic advocate, who had successfully defended their pastor against both popular excitement and judicial power.

In 1816, Mr. Taney was partially diverted from his professional pursuits, by his election to the Maryland Senate. Under the State Constitution, as it then stood, the Senate consisted of fifteen members, whose term of service was five years. They were selected by a body of electors composed of two members chosen in each county by the people, and one from each of the cities of Baltimore and Annapolis. Mr. Taney was chosen one of the electors from the county of Frederick, and appointed by the electoral body a member of the Senate. His connection with this body, and his associations, both personal and political, were of the most agreeable character. I have heard the Chief-Justice himself remark, that if there is one portion of his career which he looked back upon with more satisfaction and pleasure than another, it is the period of his service in the Maryland Senate. His reminiscences of the men and events of that time would no doubt form a highly interesting and agreeable chapter; but these reminiscences, except so far as they relate to public affairs, are mostly within his own memory, and the memories of the few of his associates who may still survive. The habitual reserve of the Chief-Justice, his reluctance to speak of himself, or of his own acts and experiences, and the consequent limited information in regard to them, possessed even by those of his friends who know him best, have rendered my inquiries on the subject fruitless, and prevent me from gratifying any curiosity which the reader might feel, to know something of those personal and private recollections which have left behind them such an agreeable and enduring impression. Of his official services, and the public and political measures in which he was engaged, being mainly of a local or State interest, it is perhaps unnecessary here to speak. Suffice it to say, that he acquitted himself in the Senate, as he had done at the bar, and as he subsequently acquitted himself on the bench, with eminent ability. Having served to the end of the period for which he was elected, he again turned with unremitted industry and application, and renewed ardor, to the exclusive practice of his profession.

Mr. Taney removed to the city of Baltimore in the year 1823. The recent death of Pinkney had left a vacuum in the ranks of the able and talented bar of that city, which no one, even with professional abilities of the very first order, could expect at once to fill. Nevertheless, the field was too tempting alike to professional zeal and ambition, to be shunned. Taney entered upon it in the full vigor of his faculties, with an established reputation, and with talents and attainments that fitted him to maintain it against all opposition.

The death of Martin, of Harper, and of Winder, would have left him not only confessedly at the head of the Baltimore bar, but almost without a rival, had not William Wirt removed to that city in 1829, to dispute with him the sceptre of professional eminence. Within the year of Wirt's settlement in Baltimore, he and Taney were all that remained of the older members of the bar in that city. They stood, says Kennedy in his Life of Wirt, among a younger generation—Meredith, Johnson, Glenn, M'Mahon, Mayer,—and at their head, "instructors to guide, models to be imitated, gifted with all qualities to stimulate the ambition of generous minds striving after an honorable fame."

On his removal to Baltimore, he entered upon that more enlarged sphere of practice to which the Federal Supreme Court introduced him. From this period down to the time of his resigning the office of Attorney-General of the United States, he was frequently engaged in the argument of causes in the Supreme Court at Washington, his name being found upon the record, as counsel in almost every case of importance, arising from the Maryland district. In 1825, we find him engaged in the case of Manro *vs.* Almeida*—an admiralty case from the Circuit Court of Maryland—in which some very important questions relative to the jurisdiction and practice of courts of Admiralty and maratime jurisdiction are discussed. This branch of the law, it is well known, was a favorite study with Judge Story; and the argument of Taney, though he was upon the losing side of the case, seems to have attracted the attention of that eminent judge. At the very next session of the court, in a private letter to a friend at home, Story remarks: "The Court has been engaged in its hard and dry duties with uninterrupted diligence. Hitherto we have had but little of that refreshing eloquence which makes the labors of the law light; but a case is just rising which bids fair to engage us all in the best manner. Webster, Wirt, Taney—a man of fine talents, whom you have probably not heard of—and Emmett, are the combatants, and a bevy of ladies are the promised and brilliant distributors of the prizes."†

The case referred to was that of Etting *vs.* The Bank of the United States.‡ It was a suit involving a large amount of property. One of the questions raised and discussed was a principle of legal ethics, namely: What concealment or suppression of material facts in a contract, where both parties have not equal access to the means of information, will avoid the contract? Taney was associated with Webster, for the plaintiff in error, who sought to avoid, on the ground of fraud, the contract on which the Bank had recovered judgment, and Emmett, with the Attorney-General Wirt, appeared for the Bank. What the argument must have been when such "combatants" entered the intellectual arena, the reader will judge for himself. The Chief-Justice, in his opinion, speaks of the "great efforts which have been bestowed upon the case," and the "very elaborate arguments which have been made at the bar." But all these efforts and arguments were wasted, as the case went off upon a mere question of practice, leaving the principles of law, which had been discussed, unsettled. Morally it might have been considered a drawn battle, but for all practical purposes the

* 10 Wheaton's Reports, 473.

† Life and Letters of Story.

‡ 11 Wheaton's Reports, 59.

Bank achieved a complete victory, inasmuch as the Court, being divided in opinion, judgment was *affirmed*.

Mr. Taney was engaged at the same term—the Attorney-General Wirt being his associate, and Webster one of his opponents—in the argument of the interesting case of Cassell *vs.* Charles Carroll of Carrollton.* It was a claim made, under the original proprietory title of Maryland (which had been confiscated during the revolution), to certain quit rents reserved on a large tract of land granted by Lord Baltimore to the father of Charles Carroll. The whole question, as to the right of the heir of Lord Baltimore to these quit rents (which the people of Maryland had repudiated since 1773,) was argued with great learning and ability on both sides; Mr. Taney sustaining the defendant against the proprietary claim. Judge Story in his opinion speaks of the "important and difficult points" discussed, and the "great ability and care" of the argument, but the decision did not determine the more important and complex question discussed, as to the validity of the proprietary claim, it having been placed entirely upon a collateral question, namely, that the interest under which the plaintiff claimed, had been long since transferred and divested by a valid assignment. The judgment in favor of Charles Carroll, Mr. Taney's client, was accordingly affirmed.

In the preceding sketch of Chief-Justice Marshall, I have alluded to the case of Brown *vs.* The State of Maryland,† argued at the January term, 1827, which involved in the discussion, and finally settled, a principle of constitutional law, of a character so vital and important, as to make this a leading case, always cited as authority and for illustration, in every future discussion in which the question was raised. Here Taney again met his former antagonist, William Wirt. Each of them was associated with a junior member of the Baltimore bar, the former with Johnson, and the latter with Meredith. The power and brilliancy of the discussion was equal to the magnitude and importance of the question presented. That question was as to the constitutionality of a law of the Maryland legislature, which required the importers of foreign goods to take out and pay for a license under certain penalties and forfeitures; an act which it was claimed was repugnant to the

* 11 Wheaton's Reports, 134.

† *Ante*, page 424.

provisions of the Constitution which vested Congress with power to regulate commerce, and which prohibited the States from levying imposts. Taney sustained the State law—the Attorney-General opposed it. The latter succeeded, but the former came out of the contest with untarnished laurels, and undiminished reputation. Though in the warmth of professional excitement and emulation, he was at first inclined to regard the decision of the Court with disfavor, yet his cooler and more matured judgment fully approved it. Twenty years afterwards, in one of those frequent discussions of the same constitutional provision, to which he listened on the bench, he gave his full assent, as a judge, to the correctness and propriety of the decision.*

Taney encountered the Attorney-General in two other cases at this session of the Court. In the first of these, The United States *vs.* Gooding,† an indictment for a violation of the Slave Trade act, he was successful, Judge Story delivering the opinion of the Court, which declared the indictment fatally defective ; in the latter, Drummond *vs.* Prestman,‡ presenting a question of commercial law, he failed, Judge Johnson delivering the judgment. These cases, however, present nothing worthy of note, except to the professional reader, by whom they may be consulted in the reports.

The following May Mr. Taney was engaged in opposition to his renowned antagonist, Mr. Wirt, on the argument of the celebrated mandamus case against the Rev. Mr. Duncan, which the graphic pen of Mr. Kennedy has so felicitously described in his life of Mr. Wirt. Mr. Duncan was a Presbyterian clergyman of Baltimore, and the proceeding seems to have been to oust him, and the portion of the congregation who adhered to him, from the possession of the church property. This gavè Mr. Wirt the opportunity of making one of

* In the decision of the License Cases, 1847, referring to the case of Brown *vs.* Maryland, he remarks : "I at that time persuaded myself that I was right ; and thought the decision of the Court restricted the powers of the State more than a sound construction of the Constitution of the United States would warrant. But further and more mature reflection has convinced me that the rule laid down by the Supreme Court is a just and safe one, and perhaps the best that could have been adopted for preserving the right of the United States on the one hand, and of the States on the other, and preventing collision between them.

† 12 Wheaton's Reports, 460.

‡ 12 Wheaton's Reports, 620.

those pointed and happy quotations, which, in the hands of that master of rhetoric, often carried with them a more potent conviction than the subtlest argument or the clearest demonstration. We can well imagine what must have been the effect, upon the thronged audience crowding the Court-room, of that splendid burst of declamation with which Wirt concluded his speech, especially, when turning to the excellent Mr. Duncan, modestly shrinking at the sound of his own praises, "he exclaimed," says Mr. Kennedy, "with the most graceful elocution,—

> 'Besides, this *Duncan*
> Hath borne his faculties so meek, hath been
> So clear in his great office, that his virtues
> Will plead like angels, trumpet-tongued against
> The deep damnation of his taking off.' "*

What may have been the merits of Mr. Taney's argument, or the force of his reasoning, in comparison with that of his gifted antagonist, we are left to conjecture. Certain it is he failed in his application, and Mr. Duncan and his friends were left in possession of the field, or, more literally, the church property. The trial being before the Court—an audience proverbially unimpressible, and deaf to eloquent appeals and rhetorical figures—it is but reasonable to suppose that Mr. Wirt owed his victory as much to the solidity and fire of his argument as to the felicity and aptness of his illustrations.

During the same year that this trial occurred—the year 1827—Mr. Taney received the appointment of Attorney-General of Maryland. This appointment was made by the Governor and Council; and it is a fact worthy of mention, as it is equally honorable to both parties, that Mr. Taney was at that time politically opposed to the body which conferred upon him the office. The latter were the ardent supporters of Mr. Adams, who was then President, and the former was equally decided and open in his preference for General Jackson. Yet, notwithstanding it was a time when party feelings ran high, and the contest had become animated, the Maryland Council did not hesitate to confer the appointment upon Mr. Taney, thus evincing in a most marked manner their high appreciation of his personal character as well as of his distinguished professional abilities. This office he held

* 2 Kennedy's *Life of Wirt*, page 199.

until June, 1831, when he resigned it, upon receiving the appointment of Attorney-General of the United States.

In the mean time Mr. Taney continued his extensive and lucrative practice in the Federal Courts. Among the important cases in which he was employed intermediate the date of his appointment as Attorney-General of Maryland and as Attorney-General of the United States, may be mentioned the following: McLanahan *vs.* The Universal Insurance Company,* at the session of 1828, in which some highly interesting questions on the law of marine insurance arose, and in which he successfully encountered the Attorney-General Wirt, and that eminent and able lawyer, Mr. David B. Ogden, of New York. The interesting and important case of Van Ness *vs.* The City of Washington and the United States,† at the session of 1830, eliciting a splendid forensic discussion, in which Mr. Taney, the then Attorney-General Mr. Berrian, Mr. Wirt, Mr. Webster, and Mr. Jones participated. The cases of Tiernan *vs.* Jackson, The Petapsco Insurance Company *vs.* Southgate, and Shepherd *vs.* Taylor, at the session of 1831,‡ in the two former of which Mr. Taney was opposed by Mr. Wirt, and in the latter, involving an interesting question of Admiralty jurisdiction, was associated with that eminent counsel. In all these discussions Mr. Taney acquitted himself with marked ability, and fully vindicated his claim to stand with Webster, and Wirt, and Berrien, in the very front rank of advocates at the American bar.

During all this period Mr. Taney was engaged in an extensive and constantly increasing practice in the Maryland State Courts, and especially in the Court of Appeals. I have already alluded to the seven volumes of Harris and Johnson's reports—extending over a period of twenty-six years, commencing at the year 1800—as exhibiting abundant evidence of the professional talent of the Chief-Justice prior to his removal to Baltimore. After this period the field of his labor was enlarged, and his services were sought, on one side or the other, in nearly every controversy of great magnitude litigated in the highest tribunal of the State. The professional reader who has the curiosity to look through the two volumes of Harris and Gill's reports, extend-

* 1 Peters' Reports, 170.

† 4 Peters' Reports, 232.

‡ 5 Peters' Reports, 580, 604, 675.

ing from 1826 to 1829, and the first two or three volumes of Gill and Johnson's, bringing the reported cases down to the time of Taney's appointment as Attorney-General of the United States, will perceive that he was employed in most of the cases of importance argued during this period in the Maryland Court of Appeals. These cases embrace every variety of controversy known to the law, both legal and equitable, the Court having appellate jurisdiction over the Court of Chancery as well as the Common Law Courts. To show the diversified character of his professional avocations, and the extent and variety of his labors, it may not be amiss in this place briefly to allude to some of the more prominent of these cases. They are taken almost at random from the volumes of reports above alluded to.

The case of Ringgold *vs.* Ringgold,* a case of great magnitude and interest, drawing out a discussion of the whole equitable doctrine of trusts, and the relative rights, duties, and responsibilities of trustees and their *cestuis que trust*, was decided in 1826. Mr. Taney was associated in the argument with Wirt, Jones, and Magruder, and opposed by Berrian, Hoffman, and Mayer.

Betts *vs.* The Union Bank of Maryland,† at the June term 1827, called out from him an admirable argument in support of the common law principle, that although a particular consideration is mentioned in a deed, yet proof of another consideration, which is not repugnant to the one mentioned, may be given to support the deed.

At the same term, in the case of Oliver *vs.* Gray,‡ he discussed with marked ability the doctrines of the statute of limitations, and particularly that branch of it relative to the nature and character of the acknowledgment required to take a case out of the statute.

The Union Bank of Maryland *vs.* Ridgley,§ a case which occupies more than a hundred pages of the report, presented some interesting questions relative to the law of corporations, but the decisive point in the discussion seems to have turned upon one or two technical questions of pleading, the argument of which shows the mind of Taney to have been as acute and subtle in the analysis of what may be

* 1 Harris & Gill's Rep., 11.

† 1 Harris & Gill's Rep., 175.

‡ 1 Harris & Gill's Rep., 204.

§ 1 Harris & Gill's Rep., 324.

called the metaphysics of the law, as the most enthusiastic disciple of Saunders or Chitty might wish to encounter.

In Osgood *vs.* Lewis,* at a term of the Court in 1829, he had Wirt for his antagonist, and succeeded against that renowned advocate in a discussion which laid open the whole of that interesting branch of legal ethics which embraces the doctrines of the law of warranty, and of implied fraud or deceit in the sale of chattels.

The highly important case of Pawsons' Administrators *vs.* Donnell,† presenting some grave questions of maritime law, and involving interests of great magnitude, followed, in which Taney was again opposed by Wirt. The case was submitted on written arguments, that of Taney, together with his reply to the brief of Mr. Wirt, comprising sixty pages of the report, covers the entire range of the controversy, and thoroughly exhausts the discussion on his side of the question.

The following year he distinguished himself in the argument of two highly important cases of Marine Insurance, Allegre Administrators *vs.* the Maryland Insurance Co ,‡ and the Chesapeake Insurance Co. *vs.* Allegre's Administrators.§ These cases involved the examination of a branch of the law lying rather beyond the ordinary circle of professional study, except to the practicing advocate of a large commercial city, and until the removal of Mr. Taney to Baltimore, his attention of course had not been very closely directed to it. The result, however, was highly honorable to his reputation, exhibiting as it did the versatility of his genius, its comprehensiveness and generality, and its perfect adaptation to the entire range of legal investigation and forensic debate. It should be added that the whole argument, in both cases, as shown by the report, was uncommonly able, Wirt, Meredith, and Mayer, being engaged with Taney in the discussion.

Many of the cases in which Taney was engaged were long, intricate, and tedious chancery suits, requiring, in their successful management, not only an exact and comprehensive knowledge of the principles of equity jurisprudence, but a plodding perseverance, a laborious industry, and a patient investigation, to which genius, in its lofty aspirations,

* 2 Harris & Gill's Rep. 496.

† 1 Gill & Johnson's Rep., 1.

‡ 2 Gill & Johnson's Rep., 136.

§ 2 Gill & Johnson's Rep., 164.

will rarely stoop, and the advocate of established reputation too often regards as an irksome and ungracious task. As specimens of this class of cases the professional reader may consult the following, argued by Mr. Taney at the bar of the Court of Appeals: Hudson *vs.* Warner and Vance,* involving a discussion of the reciprocal duties and liabilities of mortgagor and mortgagee, and the rights of creditors in and to the mortgaged property; McCubbin *vs.* Cromwell,† requiring an examination into the nature and character of chancery jurisdiction and practice in cases of dower, &c.; Williams *vs.* Carman,‡ presenting some interesting questions in regard to equity jurisdiction and practice in granting relief by injunction, &c., &c. For the management of this class of cases Mr. Taney seems to have been peculiarly well fitted, as well by temperament, as by habit and diligent study. He entered upon them relying upon patient industry, perseverance, and labor, rather than upon the inspirations of genius, and he came out of them, if not always with success, at least with reputation and honor.

To complete the diversified character of his professional toils during this period, Mr. Taney, as will be recollected, had upon his hands the labors of the Attorney-Generalship of Maryland. Among a multitude of private professional engagements, it not unfrequently happened that his attention was occupied by important State causes, which found their way into the Court of Appeals. Thus we meet, in the second volume of Gill and Johnson, the cases of State of Maryland *vs.* Wayman, and Wayman *vs.* The State,§ raising a very grave question under the Maryland Constitution, as to the tenure of office in that State; also The State *vs.* Scribner and Baker,‖ presenting a technical, but novel point, on an indictment for selling a lottery ticket, in a lottery not authorized by the State; and various other cases, which perhaps it would be neither useful nor interesting to allude to in this place.

It should be added, before dismissing this branch of the subject, that even his appointment as Attorney-General of the United States, did not entirely withdraw Mr. Taney from practice in the Maryland Court

* 2 Harris & Gill's Rep., 415.

† 2 Harris & Gill's Rep. 443.

‡ 1 Gill & Johnson's Rep., 184.

§ 2 Gill and Johnson's Reports, 246.

‖ 2 Gill and Johnson's Reports, 254.

of Appeals. His name appears as counsel in several suits of the first magnitude and importance, argued while he was Attorney-General, and a member of the Cabinet of Gen. Jackson; as the case of Chalmers *vs.* Chalmers, on the equity side of the Court, in 1832; that of Clagett *vs.* Salmon, the following year; and the great insurance case of Maryland and Phenix Insurance Company *vs.* Bathurst, in which, with Johnson and Glenn for his associates, he encountered a formidable array of counsel on the other side, headed by William Wirt.

The frequent professional encounters of the Chief-Justice with Mr. Wirt, have already been noticed. Wirt had lost none of that lofty professional ambition, that intense and eager spirit of emulation, which had characterized his efforts ten or fifteen years earlier, when, entering himself upon the Attorney-Generalship, he was accustomed to meet Pinkney, at the bar of Baltimore, and in the Supreme Court at Washington. A debate with Pinkney he then deemed "exercise and health," and to foil him, in fair fight, a crown so imperishable, that he felt a kind of youthful pleasure in preparing for the combat.* Wirt now sustained to Taney the same position that Pinkney had sustained to Wirt. He stood on the topmost round of the professional ladder, and had reached the very summit of his lofty ambition; and Taney could with justice say of his eminent rival, as Wirt did not hesitate to say of Pinkney, that his reputation was so high as to render it no disparagement in being foiled by him, and great glory in even dividing the palm.†

The perpetual professional antagonism existing between them, never engendered animosity, or degenerated into personal ill-feeling, but on the contrary, served only to increase the mutual esteem and respect which each entertained for the talents of the other. Mr. Wirt, though in general chary of his compliments, did not hesitate to do ample justice to the great abilities of his rival. On one occasion, in a suit in the United States Court, with that rare felicity of expression, so characteristic of his elegant genius and classic taste, he alluded to Taney, who was his opponent in the cause, as "the man of moonlight mind;—

* Letter to William Pope, Oct. 18th, 1818.

† Ibid. 2 Kennedy's *Life of Wirt*, 74.

I mean," he added, "the moonlight of the Arctics, where you have all the *light* of day without its *glare!*"

No comparison perhaps ought to be made between these distinguished advocates. Their professional talents were as diverse as their manner at the bar, and their style of elocution. Wirt was the polished orator, elegant and exact, both in matter and manner, highly ornate, always warm, sometimes impassioned. Taney, the logician, clear, calm, and argumentative, directing his simple and unostentatious discourse to the reason, rather than the impulsive feelings and passions. His manner at the bar, however, has been described as highly impressive. "When his slow and solemn form was seen rising in Court," says an observer, "every ear was open, and all eyes were fixed upon the speaker—the audience insensibly taken captive, and borne away by the weight of his argument and the tones of his eloquence. He moved along like the majestic Mississippi, full, clear, and magnificent. Whenever the late Mr. Wirt was opposed to Mr. Taney, he would facetiously say, that he dreaded nothing so much as his 'apostolic simplicity.' So soft and amiable was his deportment, that even amidst the heat and turmoil of *nisi prius* litigation, he was never known to offend the feelings of any of his brethren. His conversation was never roughened by austerity or pedantry; and when his gallant bearing extorted from all the most unfeigned praise, he would almost hide himself from public admiration, with the unaffected modesty of his native character."*

The office of Attorney-General of the United States, always filled with commanding ability, had been, for the twenty years immediately preceding Taney's appointment, adorned with the most splendid talent which the country has produced. Pinkney, who held the office a little over two years, resigned it, in 1814, into the hands of Richard Rush. That gentleman, on his appointment as Minister to England, in 1817, was succeeded by William Wirt, whose classic intellect and genius, during a period of twelve years, threw a new lustre around this dignified and responsible station. Mr. Berrian, of Georgia, to whose great capacity in the legislative, as well as the judicial forum, the whole country will bear honorable testimony, followed Mr. Wirt, and held the office two years, through the sessions of 1830 and 1831.

* "Southern Literary Messenger," June, 1838.

To follow predecessors like these, and to fill the sphere they had occupied, without suffering by the comparison, required a mind of no common mould, and abilities of the very highest order. Mere respectability of talent would have had occasion to esteem it a singular piece of ill-fortune that such an honor should be thrust upon it, at such a time; while mediocrity must have irretrievably and hopelessly sunk at the very threshold.

The resignation of Mr. Berrien, who retired with the other members of General Jackson's Cabinet, opened the way for Taney's appointment to the vacant Attorney-Generalship. He came into office on the reconstruction of the Cabinet, in June, 1831. The new Cabinet comprised a mass of intellect, and a collective strength and energy, never surpassed at any period in the history of the government. Besides the new Attorney-General, its members were, Edward Livingston, Secretary of State; Louis McLane, Secretary of the Treasury; Lewis Cass, Secretary of War; Levi Woodbury, Secretary of the Navy; and Amos Kendall, Postmaster-General. Mr. Duane subsequently succeeded to the place of Mr. McLane, in the Treasury Department, when the latter was appointed Secretary of State, on the resignation of Mr. Livingston, who was sent as Minister to France.

It has been truly remarked, that the office of Attorney-General has nothing to recommend it to an indolent man. Its incumbent is, *ex officio*, a member of the Cabinet, and his duties, prescribed by the law, are "to prosecute and conduct all suits in the Supreme Court, in which the United States are concerned, and to give advice and opinions upon questions of law, when required by the President, or when requested by the heads of any of the departments, touching matters which may concern their departments." These opinions, as Mr. Southard very correctly remarks in his eulogy upon Mr. Wirt, are official; "not merely persuasive upon the judgment of other officers, but, so far as the construction of the law is concerned, regarded as binding; and if error be committed, the responsibility is, in a great degree, taken from them and cast upon him—a responsibility by no means light to a sensitive and well-organized mind." Mr. Taney's official opinions are to be found in the volume of "Opinions of the Attorney-Generals," published by order of the Twenty-sixth Congress. They comprise nearly one hundred pages of the volume, and though generally brief, they are all of them distinguished by that clearness and perspicuity which characterize the mind of their author.

In the other branch of his official duty, that of prosecuting and conducting, in the Supreme Court, the suits in which the United States were concerned, the records of his labors during the two years in which he held the Attorney-Generalship, is to be found in the sixth and seventh volumes of Peters' Reports. This record shows a great number and variety of cases argued by Mr. Taney, in his official character, and furnishes ample testimony of his professional ability, industry, and success. I shall not trespass upon the reader's patience by attempting a review of these cases. They embrace, for the most part, controversies turning upon questions of a purely legal character, and may therefore be properly passed by without further remark. It should be said, however, in justice to Mr. Taney, that some of these arguments were uncommonly able, and were noticed at the time by the bench, as well as by his brethren of the bar, as being among his best and happiest efforts. This was especially the case at the session of the Court in 1833—a session not so remarkable for interesting cases and brilliant arguments, as some which had preceded it. "The cases hitherto argued," writes Judge Story,* "have been of no general interest; and the arguments have not been striking. We have however had some fine arguments from Binney and Sargeant, of Philadelphia, and Mr. Attorney-General Taney."†

* Letter to Judge Fay, February 10th, 1833.

† Among the cases at the session of 1832, in which the Attorney-General distinguished himself, may be mentioned The United States *vs.* The State Bank of North Carolina, 6 Peters' Reports, 29; McLane *vs.* The United States, ibid. 404; and The United States *vs.* Nourse, ibid. 470. The first of these cases, one of the earliest arguments of Taney after his appointment to the Attorney-Generalship, laid open an interesting discussion relative to the origin and nature of the right of priority of payment of debts due to Government, and whether this right, under our system, as in England, rested upon sovereign prerogative, or was wholly founded on positive statute. The Court held, in accordance with the reasoning of the Attorney-General, that though a statutory, and not strictly a prerogative right, yet it was to be traced to the same broad principles of public policy which governed the royal prerogative, namely, the securing of an adequate revenue to sustain the public burdens, and discharge the public debt, and therefore the statute should receive a fair and liberal, and not a strict and narrow construction. Among the important cases argued by the Attorney-General, at the subsequent

As a member of the Cabinet, and one of the constitutional advisers of the President, Mr. Taney shared his full proportion of responsibility in that series of strong and energetic measures which the administration of General Jackson originated and carried out, and which make so marked a figure in the political history of the country. The nullification controversy, the question of the recharter of the United States Bank, the removal of the deposits, and other subjects of the deepest moment, at that time, agitated the public mind, and divided the national councils. It is scarcely necessary to add, that, throughout all the stormy contests growing out of these discussions, the Attorney-General stood firmly and unflinchingly by the side of the President, and rendered to the measures of his administration an energetic and effective support. He was, from the beginning, a decided and earnest opponent of the Bank; and he coöperated so heartily with the President in his system of prompt and vigorous action against that institution, as to call down upon his own head, not the censure only, but the active animosity, pushed to the verge of proscription, of that powerful majority which then controlled the Senate and opposed the administration.

I do not design to trace fully the political history of Mr. Taney during his connection with General Jackson's Cabinet. It was a period of stormy debates, heated party discussions, and intense popular excitement. The great question of the day—overriding and absorbing all others for the time being—was the Bank controversy, a controversy too memorable in the political annals of the country to be soon forgotten. Mr. Taney was reluctantly drawn into it, and by the force of circumstances, rather than by any volition of his own, was, for a brief period, placed in a position to test fully the temper of his mind and the firmness of his courage. The history and details of this controversy, in which Mr. Taney acted a part so prominent as to call down upon himself personally the bitter and unmeasured denunciations of the most eminent leaders of the opposition, may be consulted more at large by the reader in the political annals of the day. Reminded that I am sketching the career of the jurist, and not the politician, I

session of 1833, may be mentioned, The United States *vs.* Macdaniel, 7 Peters' Reports, 1; Sampeyrac *vs.* The United States, ibid. 222; Barron *vs.* The Mayor and City of Baltimore, ibid. 243; and Scholefield *vs.* Eichelberger, ibid. 586.

shall pass it by with such brief notice only as the subject seems necessarily to require.

The question of the removal of the deposits from the United States Bank, arose while Mr. Taney was Attorney-General. We have the highest authority for the fact, that in every stage of that question he had been in favor of the removal; so that his conduct, when made Secretary of the Treasury, was the result of his previous judgment and convictions of duty.* The measure, we are assured on the same authority, originated with the President himself, and was emphatically his own. Taney, with a single other member of the Cabinet, the Postmaster-General, warmly approved it; the rest were either indifferent to the project, or opposed it.† Mr. Duane, the Secretary of the Treasury, absolutely refused to carry out the measure, whereupon the President, with characteristic promptness, decision, and independence, removed him from office, and appointed Mr. Taney in his place. Though he had neither courted nor desired the post, he did not shrink from its acceptance, or endeavor to shun the responsibility. His entry upon the office at such a time, and under such circumstances, with the certainty of making himself a prominent mark for the arrows of the opposition, and staking, as he did, his reputation and character upon the issue of the controversy, evinced not only a fearless independence, and firmness of purpose, but a generous devotion and disinterested friendship, which no one could more fully appreciate, or was more ready to acknowledge, than General Jackson himself. In his letter to Mr. Taney, when the latter retired from the office of Secretary of the Treasury, he expresses these acknowledgments, in language whose warmth and earnestness attest its genuine sincerity: "Knowing that such a station was not desired by you," says the President, alluding to the Attorney-Generalship, "and was in opposition to your course of life, I could not but feel grateful to you, when, in compliance with my invitation, you exchanged the independence of your professional pursuits for the labors and responsibilities of the office of Attorney-General of the United States. This sentiment was greatly and deservedly increased during the last year, when becoming acquainted with the difficulties which surrounded me, and with my earnest desire

* Senator Benton's *Thirty Years' View*, p. 414.

† Ibid.

to avail myself of your services in the Treasury Department, you generously abandoned the duties and avocations to which your life had been devoted, and encountered the responsibility of carrying into execution those great measures which the public interest, and the will of the people, alike demanded at our hands. For the prompt and disinterested aid thus afforded me, at the risk of personal sacrifices, which were then, probably, and which have now been, realized, I feel that I owe you a debt of gratitude and regard which I have not the power to discharge."*

The appointment of Mr. Taney to the Secretaryship of the Treasury, was made in September, 1833. Mr. Benjamin F. Butler, of New York, was selected to succeed him as Attorney-General. On the 22d of the same month, was issued the famous order, signed by the new Secretary of the Treasury, for the removal of the deposits from the Bank—or more correctly speaking, directing the collectors of revenue thereafter to cease making their deposits in the Bank, leaving the amount actually in it to be drawn out at intervals, and in different sums, according to the course of the government disbursements. The measure was at once assailed by the opposition press with rancorous vehemence and acrimony ; and the attack thus commenced was transferred to the legislative forum at the opening of the celebrated " Panic session " of Congress, in December, 1833.

The day after the meeting of Congress, the Secretary of the Treasury communicated his reasons for the removal of the deposits, in an able and luminous report, which covered the entire ground of the controversy. The propriety and necessity of the act were placed mainly on the ground of the misconduct of the Bank, and the insecurity of the public revenue placed in its keeping. As was to have been expected, the report called out prompt action in the Senate, which then contained a decisive majority against the President and his measures. Mr. Clay took the initiative in this action. Soon after the commencement of the session, he called the attention of the Senate to the report of the Secretary, and submitted two resolutions on the subject. One of these was a resolution of censure upon the action of the President ; the other declared the reasons assigned by the Secretary of the Treasury, to be " unsatisfactory and insufficient." After a protracted and

* 46 Niles' Register, p. 326.

animated discussion, in which all the leading members of the Senate took part, the resolution was finally passed, on the 5th April, 1834, by nearly a strict party vote, twenty-eight in the affirmative, to eighteen in the negative. On the same day, the famous resolution of censure on the conduct of General Jackson, subsequently expunged from the Journal by order of the Senate, was carried by a vote of twenty-six to twenty.*

The passage of these resolutions, and the unusual degree of obloquy which had been cast upon Mr. Taney during the course of the debate, indicated pretty clearly the temper of the Senate, and the probable result of his nomination before that body. Anticipating this result, the President delayed sending in his nomination until near the end of the session. In the mean time, in obedience to the resolution of the Senate, the Secretary prepared and sent in a carefully digested and elaborate report upon the state of the finances. The report, "replete with plain facts and luminous truths," as Mr. Benton expressed it, was not apparently what the majority of the Senate had expected, for, instead of showing a financial decline and embarrassment of the government resources, it disclosed, notwithstanding "the Bank panic" was then at its height, an increase in every branch of the public revenue. Mr. Webster attempted to arrest the reading of the report, and moved its reference to the Finance Committee; but the minority were determined that it should go forth to the country, and the reading was insisted on. "It is not what was expected," said Mr. Benton, in the course of a powerful speech on the subject; "but it is what is true, and what will rejoice the heart of every patriot in America. A pit was dug for Mr. Taney; the diggers of the pit have fallen into it;

* The yeas and nays on the resolution declaring the reasons of the Secretary of the Treasury unsatisfactory and insufficient, are as follows:—

YEAS.—Messrs. Bibb, Black, Calhoun, Clay, Clayton, Ewing, Frelinghuysen, Hendricks, Kent, King (of Georgia), Knight, Leigh, Mangum, Naudain, Poindexter, Porter, Prentiss, Preston, Robbins, Silsbee, Smith, Southard, Sprague Swift, Tomlinson, Tyler, Waggaman, Webster.

NAYS.—Messrs. Benton, Brown, Forsyth, Grundy, Hill, Kane, King (of Alabama), Linn, McKean, Moore, Morris, Robinson, Shepley, Tallmadge, Tipton, White, Wilkins, Wright.

On the passage of the resolution of censure upon the President, Mr. Hendricks and Mr. King, of Georgia, voted with the minority.

the fault is not his; and the sooner they clamber out the better for themselves. The people have a right to know the contents of this report, and know them they shall; and if there is any man in this America, whose heart is so constructed as to grieve over the prosperity of his country, let him prepare himself for sorrow; for the proof is forthcoming, that never, since America had a place among nations, was the prosperity of the country equal to what it is at this day!"*

The report of the Secretary was communicated to the Senate about the middle of June. On the 23d of that month his nomination was sent in, and the next day he was rejected by the same majority which had declared his "reasons" for the removal of the deposits unsatisfactory—eighteen to twenty-eight.† The Senate also refused to confirm the nomination of Mr. Stevenson, Speaker of the House, as Minister to England. "These results," says the 'Weekly Register,' "were unanimously expected. The Senate had already pronounced its judgment on Mr. Taney in declaring that his reasons assigned for the removal of the deposits were insufficient."

Mr. Taney immediately placed his resignation in the hands of the President, and soon after returned to Baltimore. His entrance into that city had rather the appearance of a triumph than of a defeat. Escorted by a numerous cavalcade to the Columbian Gardens, which had been previously arranged for his reception, he there met a large assembly of his friends and the citizens of Baltimore, whom he addressed in vindication of his character and conduct. A public dinner was given to him soon afterwards at the same place, at which Mr. Benton, of the Senate, and Mr. Allen, of the House of Representatives, were present. Nor were these demonstrations of approval confined to the city of Baltimore. They were manifested elsewhere, and indeed all over the State of Maryland. On the 6th of August he was entertained at a public dinner by a numerous assemblage of his old neighbors and friends of Frederick, where he had so long resided. In the deeply impressive address which he made on that occasion—

* Senator Benton's *Thirty Years' View*, pp. 462, 463.

† Though the majority was the same, there was a trifling alteration in the character of the vote: thus, Mr. Hendricks, of Indiana, and Mr. King, of Georgia, who on the former occasion had voted with the majority, now voted in favor of confirmation. Mr. McKean did not vote, and Mr. Moore voted against the confirmation.

speaking of his rejection by the Senate, of the studied defamation which had been heaped upon him, and of the ultimate vindication of his character from the aspersions of his opponents—he beautifully alluded to his former residence and associations in Frederick :—

"Having, as I have already said, had no connexion until recently with the General Government, I was altogether unknown to the great body of the citizens of the other States, and cannot, therefore, in reply to the assaults made upon me, appeal to their knowledge of my principles and conduct. But in Maryland it is othewise. Born in the State, my life has been passed in the midst of its citizens, until age is now coming upon me. To them I can confidently appeal, for they have known me from my childhood. To the citizens who now surround me, I can still more confidently, for among them I passed twenty-two years of the prime of my life, taking an active part during all that time in their public concerns. It is from the people of Maryland that the citizens of other States must in a great measure learn my character and my principles—and of none more justly can the inquiry be made than of the citizens of this county—who have so long and so intimately known me."

In a speech delivered by Mr. Taney at Elkton, on the 4th September, 1834, at a public dinner given to him by the Jackson Republicans of Cecil county, he took occasion very fully to vindicate his own conduct, and to repel the assaults which had been made upon him. Some recent expressions of Mr. Webster, who, in a late public address, had alluded to Mr. Taney as the "pliant instrument" of the President, called out from him on that occasion a sharpness of reproof and a severity of language which he was not often accustomed to use. "It is well understood," he remarks, "that when my nomination was before the Senate for their decision, no charge was brought against me—not a word of accusation was uttered, and I was rejected by a silent vote. If there was supposed to be anything in my character and conduct which justified my rejection, then was the time to have brought it forward. The charge could then have been investigated. But this was not done. And I had, therefore, a right to expect that no senator who had given a silent vote for my rejection, would, after the close of the session, follow me, with the spirit of hostility, into private life. In one instance, and but one, as far as my knowledge extends, has this expectation been disappointed. And I find that at a public dinner at Salem, some time ago, Mr. Webster of the Senate took occasion to speak of me as the 'pliant instrument' of the President, ready to do his bidding." Mr. Taney then meets and answers the imputations thrown out by Mr. Webster; and, having fully replied to him, and corrected him in some of his statements of facts, he makes the following tart and caustic personal application. "Neither my habits nor my principles lead me to bandy terms of reproach with Mr. Webster or any one else. But it is well known that he has found the Bank a profitable client, and I submit to the public, whether the facts I have stated do not furnish ground for believing that he has become its 'pliant instrument,' and is prepared on all occasions to do its bidding, whenever and wherever it may choose to require him. In the situation in which he has placed himself before the public, it would far better become him to vindicate himself from imputations to which he stands justly liable, than to assail others." *

Attempted political proscription rarely fails to re-act upon its authors and to advance the fortune of the person unjustly proscribed. Two or three years before this period Mr. Van Buren had been rejected by the Senate as Minister to England; and now, as Vice-President of the United States, he was the presiding officer in that very body which had condemned him. Mr. Taney had been rejected by the same body, and his name was now mentioned in some quarters for the Vice-Presidency, in connexion with that of Mr. Van Buren for the Presidency. It is by no means improbable that such might have been the result of the condemnation of Mr. Taney by the Senate, had it not been for his entire withdrawal from politics on being nominated by the President to fill a position more congenial to his tastes and habits, and the pursuits and studies of his whole previous life.

In January, 1835, the venerable Gabriel Duval † one of the Asso-

* The entire speech is published in Niles' Register. Vol. XLVII. pp. 105–108.

† Gabriel Duval, an eminent lawyer of Maryland, was appointed by President Madison an Associate-Justice of the Supreme Court in the year 1811, in place of Judge Chase. Judge Duval had been long and honorably known to the Maryland bar. In April, 1796, on the promotion of Judge Goldsborough to be chief Judge of the General Court, Mr. Duval was appointed one of the Associate-Jus-

ciate-Justices of the Supreme Court of the United States, resigned his office in consequence of the infirmities of age, and President Jackson immediately appointed Mr. Taney to supply the vacancy. The great legal ability and high professional character of Mr. Taney rendered this appointment eminently and obviously proper. Since the death of Wirt he stood confessedly without a rival at the Maryland bar. An unblemished personal as well as professional reputation, and a character whose purity no man, not blinded by political animosity, could venture to assail, might, it was thought, rise above all political considerations, and disarm even the opposition of party spirit itself. But it was not so. The majority of the Senate declined to entertain or act upon the nomination, for the reason, as was alleged at the time, of the contemplated new arrangement of the judicial system as to the circuits. At the last moment of the session the subject was brought up and *indefinitely postponed*, a vote which was no doubt intended, and was understood, as equivalent to a rejection.

tices. This place he retained until 1802, when he accepted the Comptrollership of the Treasury of the United States. On the passage of the act of the Maryland Legislature, in 1806, abolishing the General Court, and re-organizing the Court of Appeals and the County Courts, Judge Duval was successively appointed to the office of Chancellor, Judge of the Court of Appeals, and Chief-Judge of the County Courts of the first Judicial District, all of which stations he declined. Accepting the appointment of Associate-Justice of the Supreme Court of the United States in 1811, he continued in the discharge of the duties of this place for a period of nearly a quarter of a century, when, resigning his seat on account of the infirmities of age, he was succeeded by Philip P. Barbour, on the 15th March, 1836.

Judge Duval died in 1844. His colleague, Judge Story, presiding at the ensuing session of the Court in the temporary absence of the Chief-Justice, bears the following honorable testimony to his worth and virtues: "His urbanity, his courtesy, his gentle manners, his firm integrity and independence, and his sound judgment, so eloquently and truly stated at the bar, are entirely concurred in by all of us who have had the pleasure of knowing him. His revolutionary and patriotic acts belong to the general history of his country. For myself, having had the honor of an appointment to this bench on the same day he received his, we were during his whole judicial life, for about a quarter of a century, cotemporaries, although he was advanced in years far beyond myself; I can, therefore, bear my own testimony to the justice of the eulogium which has been pronounced at the bar upon his social and judicial qualities. They will long be cherished in our memories with grateful satisfaction."

Thus matters stood when Chief-Justice Marshall died, in the summer of 1835. As had been the case on previous occasions, much speculation was indulged in relative to the succession. From cotemporary newspapers I find the names of Judge M'Lean, Henry St. George Tucker, President of the Virginia Court of Appeals, and other distinguished citizens, besides that of Taney, mentioned for the office. But the President "kept his own counsel," as Washington had done, and delayed making the appointment until the next meeting of Congress. In the mean time the rumor that Mr. Taney had been, or was about to be, appointed during the recess, called out some sharp comments from the press. I find in the National Intelligencer a communication signed "Causidicus," in which the writer, after alluding to the fact that an appointment in the recess of the Senate would be temporary only, and held at the will of the Senate, or of the President, who might change his mind, goes on to remark: "No man of delicacy would act as Judge under such an appointment. I have a high respect for Mr. Taney as a man and a lawyer, and do not know whether in the present state of parties, we can expect to obtain a better Chief-Justice, but I do not believe he will take upon himself the functions of a Judge of the Supreme Court until his nomination shall have been confirmed by the Senate." This was certainly a very singular suggestion. Just forty years before, Washington had appointed Judge Rutledge, in the recess of the Senate, under precisely similar circumstances, and no one had ventured to suggest that delicacy required him to abstain from taking his seat for that cause, and until after his confirmation by the Senate. But whatever might have been the propriety of a nomination in the recess, it was not made, and the consequence was that the Supreme Court was left without a Chief-Justice during its session in the winter of 1836.

On the 28th December, 1835, President Jackson sent in to the Senate the name of Roger B. Taney, for the office of Chief-Justice of the Supreme Court, and the name of Philip P. Barbour, of Virginia, for the office of Associate-Justice. Notwithstanding the political complexion of the Senate had changed, the nomination encountered a warm and vigorous opposition. At the head of this opposition stood the acknowledged chiefs of their party, Messrs. Clay and Webster. The former of these, in particular, with the impulsive ardor of his nature, labored zealously to defeat the nomination, and signalized his assaults upon the nominee by an uncommon degree of asperity and bitterness of remark. I am informed by an eminent member of the Maryland bar,* who, though of opposite politics, was at the time warmly in favor of the confirmation of Mr. Taney, that Mr. Clay, not many years after, with the open and generous frankness of his nature, made the *amende honorable* to the Chief-Justice, in a manner creditable alike to the characters of both. He frankly admitted to Judge Taney, that at the time of the nomination, he had used some harsh expressions, and made many unkind remarks in regard to him, which he sincerely regretted, adding, with a cordial shake of the hand, that he regarded him as a worthy successor of Chief-Justice Marshall. It would have been difficult even for Mr. Clay to have framed a higher or more delicate compliment.

The nomination of Mr. Taney was not acted upon until the 15th March, 1836, when it was ratified by a majority of fourteen votes.† Soon after, he was sworn into office by Judge Glenn, District-Judge of Maryland. He took his seat, for the first, on the bench, in the beginning of the following month, April, at a Circuit Court held in Baltimore, for the District of Maryland. On this occasion he made some brief remarks to the Grand Jury, in place of the customary charge, and for the purpose of giving his reasons for the course he intended to pursue in dispensing with anything of the kind thereafter: "He had a few words to say to them," he remarked, "not so much in compliance with the usage which had prevailed, of charging grand juries, of which he disapproved, and would in future dispense with altogether ;‡

* The late Attorney-General of the United States, Mr. Reverdy Johnson.

† The following is the vote :—

AYES.—Messrs. Benton, Brown, Buchanan, Cuthbert, Davis, Ewing (Illinois), Grundy, Hendricks, Hill, Hubbard, King (Alabama), King (Georgia), Linn, McKean, Moore, Morris, Nicholas, Niles, Prentiss, Rives, Robinson, Ruggles, Shepley, Swift, Tallmadge, Tipton, Walker, Wall, Wright—29.

NAYS.—Messrs. Black, Calhoun, Clay, Crittenden, Ewing (Ohio), Leigh, Mangum, Naudain, Porter, Preston, Robbins, Southard, Tomlinson, Webster, White—15.

Messrs. Moore and Prentiss, who now voted aye, had voted against Mr. Taney's confirmation as Secretary of the Treasury.

‡ This determination was constantly adhered to by the Chief-Justice from that time onward. It has never been his practice to deliver charges to the grand juries empanneled in his courts.

but more for the purpose of giving his reasons for departing from it, and his present charge would necessarily be brief. He thought the Court should enter at once with promptness and industry upon the discharge of its duties, disconnected from all *unnecessary forms*. The age had passed by, which called for particular instructions from the Court; the public mind had become enlightened, and the intelligence of juries was adequate to the discharge of their duties. The District-Attorney was ready to counsel them in all matters of law. It was unnecessary that the Court should enter the wide field of jurisprudence, when the attention of the jury would be called but to few infractions of the criminal laws of the land." The Chief-Justice then advised the jury, that it was their duty carefully to examine the testimony laid before them, and find no bill, except upon the clear conviction of the guilt of the accused.

Judge Taney took his seat on the bench of the Supreme Court in January, 1837. Judge Barbour, who had also been confirmed by the Senate, took his seat at the same time. There were then before the Court three cases, of very great interest, each of them involving the question of the validity of a State law, and of course opening the whole field of discussion as to the conflicting powers of the State and general governments. These cases had been discussed, but not decided, in Chief-Justice Marshall's time, and the opinion of that eminent jurist seems to have been, in each case, that the State law was repugnant to the Constitution of the United States, and void. In this opinion, Mr. Justice Story, who dissented from the final judgment of the Court, in all three of the cases, concurred. No little curiosity was manifested in regard to these cases, by the profession, as well as by the public men of that time, who had watched the current of constitutional decisions in the Supreme Court. The great point of interest and anxiety seemed to be to know whether the Court, as then constituted, would apply, by judicial construction of the Constitution, the same strict limits to the powers claimed to be exercised by the States, as had been established in Marshall's time. The public, however, were not kept long in suspense. Judgment was rendered in all three cases, *sustaining the State laws*.

The first of these cases was from New York, and is reported under the title of City of New York *vs.* Miln.* The opinion of the Court was pronounced by Judge Barbour, and was to the effect, that the Legislature of New York might, without violating the Constitution of the United States, pass an act concerning passengers arriving in vessels in the port of New York, requiring the master of every vessel arriving, under certain penalties, to make a report, in writing, respecting his passengers, within twenty-four hours after his arrival. It was argued by counsel in this case, and so Mr. Justice Story appears to have thought, in his dissenting opinion, that the principles of the case fell directly within the decisions in Gibbons *vs.* Ogden, and Brown *vs.* State of Maryland, heretofore noticed.† The majority of the Court, however, including the Chief-Justice, were of a contrary opinion, regarding the act of New York, as not a regulation of *commerce*, but of *police*, and that therefore it was passed in the exercise of a power which rightfully belonged to the State. *Persons*, it was said, are not the subjects of *commerce;* and, not being imported goods, they do not fall within the reasoning founded upon the construction of a power given to Congress to regulate commerce, and the prohibition of the States from imposing a duty on imported goods.‡

* 11 Peters' Reports, 102.

† *Ante*, pages 412, 424.

‡ This doctrine is controverted by the cases of Smith *vs.* Turner, and Norris *vs.* City of Boston, which I shall presently notice, reported in the seventh volume of Howard's Reports. In these cases, which attracted so much attention and interest at the time, the discussion seems to have passed from the bar into the consultation-room of the Judges, and resulted finally in declaring, by a vote of five judges to four, that a State law imposing taxes upon the masters of vessels bringing passengers and emigrants into the ports of such States, was contrary to the Constitution of the United States, and void, because the exclusive power to regulate commerce is, by the Constitution, in Congress; and the term commerce, comprehends the intercourse of persons or passengers. Mr. Justice Wayne, who upon this question sided with the majority of the Court, gives a very interesting history of the discussion in the consultation-room, and the conflicting views of the Judges in the case of New York *vs.* Miln, though his recollections of some of the facts differs from that of the Chief-Justice, as stated by him in his dissenting opinion. Judge Wayne avers that nothing but the conclusion arrived at by Judge Barbour in New York *vs.* Miln, was the judgment of the Court, namely, that the New York law "does not assume to regulate commerce between the port of New York and foreign ports," and was therefore constitutional. In other words, that it was a mere police regulation, but that the Court did not concur in the proposition of

Briscoe *vs.* The Bank of the Commonwealth of Kentucky,* was the next of these cases. The validity of the act of the Kentucky Legislature, establishing a bank "in the name and behalf of the Commonwealth of Kentucky," was here drawn in question, under the constitutional provision which restrains the States from emitting bills of credit. The case had been formerly argued before the Court, and Mr. Justice Story says, that a majority of the Judges who then heard it, including Chief-Justice Marshall, were decidedly of the opinion that the act of Kentucky was unconstitutional and void, and that it fell precisely within the principle adjudged by the case of Craig *vs.* The State of Missouri, in Chief-Justice Marshall's time.† A reargument was ordered, and the case was again discussed with consummate learning and ability, Henry Clay being one of the counsel in behalf of the validity of the Kentucky law,‡ followed by that able and accomplished lawyer, the late Senator Southard, of New Jersey, in opposition. The judgment of the Court, pronounced by Mr. Justice

Judge Barbour, that "persons are not subjects of commerce." Four of the Justices out of the seven who heard that case, he says, namely—himself, Story, McLean, and Baldwin, thought that commerce did comprehend the intercourse of persons or passengers; and a fifth, Mr. Justice Thompson, declined expressing an opinion on that point. The case of New York *vs.* Miln, he thinks, is perfectly consistent with the cases of Gibbons *vs.* Ogden, and Brown *vs.* Maryland, and was not intended to modify, in the slightest particular, what had been the judgments in the latter cases. These views of Mr. Justice Wayne, should, of course, be considered in connexion with what is said in the very able dissenting opinion of the Chief-Justice, with whom Judges Daniel, Woodbury, and Nelson concurred.

The late case of Cooley *vs.* The Wardens of Philadelphia, December term, 1851, 12 Howard's Reports, 300, is another decision upon this vexed question of the power to regulate commerce. It decides that the grant of this power to Congress does not deprive the States of the power to legislate on the subject of pilots, and regulate pilotage fees and penalties demanded for neglect or violation. From this decision Justices Wayne and McLean dissented.

* 11 Peters' Reports, 257.

† *Ante*, p. 428.

‡ The closing remarks of Mr. Clay's speech were deeply impressive: "The day will be disastrous to this country," he exclaimed, "when this Court shall throw itself upon the ocean of uncertainty and adopt an interpretation of the prohibition of the Constitution, which will apply to a constructive bill of credit. The large and prosperous commercial operations of our country are carried on by bills of exchange, notes, and bank notes, redeemable in specie, and on which suit

McLean, sustained the validity of the law. The case of Craig *vs.* Missouri, was held not to be authority, on the point that the bills of the Kentucky Bank were bills of credit within the meaning of the Constitution, as the decision in that case applied to obligations of an entirely different character. Though a State was prohibited from emitting bills of credit—that is to say, such paper as was denominated bills of credit, before and at the time of the adoption of the Constitution,—yet there was no limitation in the Constitution, on the power of a State to incorporate banks. A State might therefore grant acts of incorporation for the attainment of those objects which it deems essential to the interests of society. Such a power is necessarily incident to sovereignty.

The last, and perhaps most important of these cases, is the celebrated case of Charles River Bridge *vs.* Warren Bridge.* It had been argued at a former term, before Chief-Justice Marshall, and after being held under advisement by the Court, for a year, was, on a difference of opinion among the Judges, ordered to be reargued. In this case, the Chief-Justice delivered his first constitutional judgment—a judgment in which he sustained,—in opposition to the powerful reasoning of Daniel Webster, who appeared as counsel for the plaintiffs,—the validity of the Massachusetts' law, incorporating the Warren Bridge. As the question itself is one of great interest, and the judgment of the Court has been the subject of much criticism, it may be proper here very briefly to notice this case.

The Charles River Bridge held its franchises under acts of the State and colonial Legislatures of Massachusetts. It claimed that these acts vested in the Company, in perpetuity, an exclusive right of erecting and maintaining a bridge over the Charles River, and receiving the tolls; and being a grant, or *contract*, within the meaning of the

may be brought should they not be paid according to their tenor. The credit of all such bills may be brought into question, should the Court decide this case against the defendants. KEEP TO THE PLAIN MEANING OF THE TERMS OF THE CONSTITUTION, and do not seek, BY CONSTRUCTION, to include in its prohibitions such paper as that which is brought into question in this case, and all will be safe."

* This case is reported at length in the 11th volume of Peters' Reports, comprising about one-third of the entire volume. Over sixty pages are devoted to the elaborate and very able dissenting opinion of Judge Story.

Constitution, as settled by former decisions of the Court, the Legislature had no power to impair the obligation of this contract, by authorizing another bridge, and especially a free one, by the side of the Charles River Bridge. This the Legislature of Massachusetts had assumed to do, by incorporating the "proprietors of the Warren Bridge," which, after having paid its expenses, within a period not exceeding six years, was to be surrendered to the State. The Charles River Bridge filed a bill to obtain an injunction, to prevent the erection of the Warren Bridge. The decision of the State Court being in favor of the validity of the law, the case was brought into the Supreme Court of the United States, on the ground that the act of the Massachusetts Legislature violated the Constitution of the United States, which prohibits any State from passing laws impairing the obligations of contracts.

The Chief-Justice delivered the opinion of the Court, sustaining the validity of the law, and sustaining it, as we conceive, upon the highest principles of public policy, as well as the most obvious, and indeed necessary constitutional construction. The plaintiffs' claim, of course, rested mainly upon that class of cases, noticed in the sketch of Chief-Justice Marshall, which hold that a legislative grant is a contract, such as Fletcher *vs.* Peck, Terret *vs.* Taylor, and especially the Dartmouth College case; and therefore the sovereign power of the State is inhibited from passing any act which, even constructively, may tend to destroy the value of, or *impair*, that contract. The extent to which these doctrines were attempted to be carried, will be seen by reference to the case of Providence Bank *vs.* Billings and Pittman, heretofore cited,* in which it was insisted that a State had no power to tax a banking corporation chartered by the State. This proposition, however, received no favor at the hands of the Court, whose decision sustained the sovereignty of the State in the exercise of such a power, even though it might be used to impair the value of the charter, or *contract.* The present case involved a principle entirely similar; and so, indeed, it is considered in the opinion of the Chief-Justice. He regards the Providence Bank case as precisely analagous to the present, and places his decision on the same grounds. "The case now before the Court," he remarks, "is, in principle, precisely the

* *Ante*, page 426.

same. It is a charter from the State. The act of incorporation is silent in relation to the contested power. The argument in favor of the proprietors of Charles River Bridge, is the same, almost in words, with that used by the Providence Bank; that is, that the power claimed by the State, if it exists, may be so used as to destroy the value of the franchise they have granted to the corporation. The argument must receive the same answer; and the fact, that the power has been already exercised, so as to destroy the value of the franchise, cannot in any degree affect the principle. The existence of the power does not and cannot depend upon the circumstances of its having been exercised or not." The power which the State had claimed to exercise in the Providence Bank case, was the taxing power; the power which it claimed to exercise in this case, was, the power to make internal improvements, and regulate public travel; and the Chief-Justice considers them both alike as elements of sovereignty, and as essential to the existence of government. "A State ought never to be presumed to surrender this power," he says, "because, like the taxing power, the whole community have an interest in preserving it undiminished. And when a corporation alleges, that a State has surrendered, for seventy years, its power of improvement and public accommodation, in a great and important line of travel, along which a vast number of its citizens must daily pass, the community have a right to insist, in the language of this Court, above quoted, 'that its abandonment ought not to be presumed, in a case, in which the deliberate purpose of the State to abandon it, does not appear.'"

The opinion of the Chief-Justice, dismissing the bill, was concurred in by Judges Wayne, Baldwin, and Barbour. Judge McLean concurred in the judgment, on the ground that the Court had no jurisdiction; the State law, in his view, acting not upon the contract, but upon the property, and Judges Story and Thompson dissented.

The decisions in these cases were of course not suffered to pass without remark and criticism. An elaborate commentary upon them appeared in the "New York Review," for April, 1838, in which the writer, adopting, of course, the doctrines of Judge Story, in his dissenting opinions, handles the judgments of the Supreme Court with no little severity. "In reading these decisions," he remarks, "we perceive at once an altered tone, and a narrower spirit, not only in Chief-

Justice Taney, but even in some of the old associates of Chief-Justice Marshall, when they handle constitutional questions. The change is so great, and so ominous, that a gathering gloom is cast over the future. We seem to have sunk suddenly below the horizon, to have lost the light of the sun, and to hold on our way *per incertam lunem sub luce maligna.*" One can scarcely refrain from a smile at the evident earnestness with which the writer expresses his desponding fears and doubts. The reflections that these decisions gave rise to, were, to his mind, of the most painful character, inducing, he says, the conviction that the Constitution was seriously impaired; that the clause restraining a State from passing any law impairing the obligation of contracts, was essentially expunged from the Constitution, so far as concerns legislative grants; that the grant to Congress of power to regulate commerce, was impaired; and that the prohibition, that "no State shall emit bills of credit," was in effect repealed; and the writer's dismal apprehensions are summed up with this sad reflection: "In short, when we consider the revolution in opinion, in policy, and in numbers, that has recently changed the character of the Supreme Court, we can scarcely avoid being reduced nearly to a state of despair of the Commonwealth!"

These apprehensions were, in some degree, shared by others, and even by Judge Story himself, who was so much dissatisfied with the decisions of the cases referred to, that he was upon the point of resigning his seat on the bench. Writing to Judge McLean, he says: "There will not, I fear, ever, in our day, be any case in which a law of a State, or of Congress, will be declared unconstitutional, for the old constitutional doctrines are fast fading away, and a change has come over the public mind, from which I augur little good. Indeed, on my return home, I came to the conclusion to resign. But my friends have interposed against my intention, and I shall remain on the bench, at least for the present."* Story remarks, in this same letter, that the opinion delivered by the Chief-Justice, in the Bridge

* 2 Story's Life and Letters. It may be added that Judge Story's chagrin arose mainly from the decision in the Bridge case, and that it was entirely disconnected from anything like personal feeling toward the Chief-Justice and the majority of the Court. In a letter written during the same term he remarks: "The Judges go on quite harmoniously. The new Chief-Justice conducts himself with great urbanity and propriety," &c.

case, was not deemed satisfactory, and that a great majority of the ablest lawyers in Massachusetts were against the decision of the Court. This no doubt was so, and he might have added, that able lawyers elsewhere, as had been, and is, and always will be the case in the decision of all delicate and important questions of constitutional law, differed in opinion in regard to the decision.* It is thought unnecessary, however, now to vindicate the propriety and correctness of that judgment. It has been generally acquiesced in, and, I believe, approved, by some of the best legal minds in the country. It might very well be, that the position of Judge McLean was entirely correct, and that the case on the merits was with the plaintiffs ; it might be, that Judge Story was also correct, when he stated in one of his letters, that "a case of grosser injustice, and more oppressive legislation, never existed ;" and yet all this had really very little to do with the merits of the question as it was presented on the record. That question was, whether, even admitting the State law to have been oppressive and unjust, and an interference with vested rights, the Federal tribunals could annul it, it being conceded that this could not be done, under former decisions of the Court, unless the act incorporating the Warren Bridge should be deemed a violation of the contract *implied* in the legislative grants to the Charles River Bridge. This question was met and decided in the negative. Indeed, the time seemed to have come, when it was absolutely necessary to assign some further limit to this doctrine of implied contract in legislative acts—as had once before been done in the Providence Bank case—a doctrine which, pushed to its last consequences, would absolutely prohibit a State Legislature from authorizing the construction through its territory of two collateral turnpikes, or lines of canal, and perhaps from passing general acts for the incorporation of bridge or railroad companies, such as may now be found on the statute-books of some of the States. On this point, the reasoning of the Chief-Justice is so clear and pointed, that it is not easy to see what answer can be given to it. "If this Court should establish the principles now contended for, what is to become

* Even Chancellor Kent expresses his dissatisfaction in a letter to Story, adding, "I have lost my confidence and hopes in the constitutional guardianship and protection of the Supreme Court."— 2 Story's *Life and Letters*, 270. The Chancellor, it will be remembered, was not satisfied with the decision of Chief-Justice Marshall in Gibbons *vs.* Ogden, which over-ruled his own judgment.

of the numerous railroads established on the same line of travel with turnpike companies, and which have rendered the franchises of turnpike corporations of no value? Let it once be understood that their charters carry with them these implied contracts, and give this unknown and undefined property in a line of travelling, and you will soon find the old turnpike corporations awakening from their sleep, and calling upon this Court to put down the improvements which have taken their place. The millions of property which have been invested in railroads and canals, in lines of travel which had been before occupied by turnpike corporations, will be put in jeopardy. We shall be thrown back to the improvements of the last century, and obliged to stand still until the claims of the old turnpike corporations shall be satisfied, and they shall consent to permit these States to avail themselves of the light of modern science, and to partake of the benefit of those improvements which are now adding to the wealth and prosperity, and the convenience and comfort, of every other part of the civilized world."

The judicial opinions and decisions of Chief-Justice Taney are collected in the last six volumes of Peters' Reports, and the fourteen volumes of Howard's Reports of the Supreme Court. They comprise altogether a collection of which any jurist might have reason to be proud. It will, of course, be impossible to do more in this place than barely to glance at a few of the more important and interesting of these cases, and in making my selections I shall confine myself mainly to that class of cases which involve the decision and settlement of questions of constitutional law.

One of the most interesting of these questions was that which arose at the very next term after the decision in the Charles River Bridge case, in the controversy between Rhode Island and Massachusetts, relative to the boundary line between these States. This case attracted much attention at the time, both on account of the novelty of the question, and the character of the parties litigant. The State of Rhode Island had summoned the State of Massachusetts to the bar of that "more than Amphictyonic Council"—the Supreme Court.

The complainant, without claiming any right to the soil to the exclusion of the actual occupants under the laws of Massachusetts, claimed political sovereignty and jurisdiction over about one hundred square miles of territory, containing a population of about five thousand souls, which sovereignty and jurisdiction then were, and always had been, exercised and possessed by Massachusetts. Rhode Island alleged a mistake in the original location of the boundary line between the two States, and demanded that this boundary line might now be established by the judgment of the Court, and that Rhode Island might be restored to and confirmed in the sovereignty and jurisdiction of the disputed territory. The counsel for the State of Massachusetts moved to dismiss the bill for want of jurisdiction ; first, because of the character of the respondent, independent of the nature of the suit ; and secondly, because of the nature of the suit, independent of the character of the respondent. The discussion was conducted with distinguished ability, as it could not well fail to be when such counsel as Daniel Webster, of Massachusetts, and Samuel L. Southard, of New Jersey, entered the lists on opposite sides, and grappled in intellectual combat. The opinion of the Court, delivered by Mr. Justice Baldwin, was adverse to the motion of Mr. Webster, and sustained the jurisdiction in all points. It may be found at length in the report of the case.*

All the members of the Court who heard the discussion, appear to have concurred in the result, except the Chief-Justice, who delivered a dissenting opinion.

This opinion is brief, but clear and pointed. It discloses, at a glance, the conceptions entertained by the Chief-Justice in regard to the jurisdiction of the Court in matters of controversy between States, and is another evidence of that habitual caution, and it may be said, repugnance, which he has always manifested in wielding the power of the Federal judiciary to control or coerce State legislation—a power, it may be added, which was viewed with the most extreme jealousy in the earlier years of the republic. He does not doubt the jurisdiction of the Court, under the Constitution, to hear and determine a controversy between States, where the suit is brought to try a right of property in the soil, or any other right which is properly the subject of judicial cognizance and decision ; but this power does not extend to a suit brought to determine political rights, as he held the present to be. Sovereignty and jurisdiction are not questions for judicial decision ; for the allegiance in the disputed territory cannot be a matter of pro-

* 12 Peters' Reports, 713.

perty. "Contests for rights of sovereignty and jurisdiction," he observes, "between States, over any particular territory, are not, in my judgment, the subjects of judicial cognizance and control, to be recovered and enforced in an ordinary suit, and are therefore not within the grant of judicial power contained in the Constitution." It was therefore his opinion, against the unanimous opinion of his associates, (except Mr. Justice Story, who did not sit in the cause,) that the bill ought to be dismissed for want of jurisdiction.

It is worthy of remark, that this opinion of Chief-Justice Taney was so deliberately formed, and so firmly maintained, as to be made the grounds of his final decision in the cause. After a variety of proceedings in the case, which are fully preserved in the reports,* the

* The history of this case exhibits the curious and novel spectacle of a controversy between two independent States on a question of sovereignty and territorial jurisdiction, assuming in the Federal Courts all the features of an ordinary equity suit, and governed throughout not only by the principles, but by the practice, of the English Courts of Chancery. The motion to dismiss the bill, at the term of 1838, being overruled, Mr. Webster moved, on behalf of Massachusetts, and obtained leave, to withdraw the plea and appearance which had been entered for the State. The State of Rhode Island at the same time obtaining leave to amend her bill of complaint. At the next term Rhode Island asked for a rule on the State of Massachusetts to answer, which was granted, the time to answer being extended until the next term. (Rhode Island *vs.* Massachusetts, 13 Peters' Reports, 23.)

In conformity with this rule, Massachusetts filed a plea and answer, and the cause was brought before the Court on the sufficiency of the plea and answer, at the January term, 1840. (14 Peters, 210.) After a very elaborate and able argument, the Chief-Justice delivered the opinion of the Court, overruling the plea of Massachusetts, on the ground of its violating the rules of pleading in Chancery Courts—it being, in technical parlance, *multifarious*, that is, containing two separate and distinct defences. Leave was granted to Massachusetts, however, to demur or answer, and accordingly she came in at the next term with a general demurrer to the bill, alleging that it contained no case for the interference of the Court, with the line of division actually existing, as stated in the bill itself, between two independent States, fixed by treaty, compact, or agreement between them, and acquiesced in for a century or more. After another able and learned argument, the Chief-Justice delivered the opinion of the Court, overruling the demurrer on established principles of equity jurisprudence, granting leave to the defendant, however, to answer the bill. (15 Peters, 233.) Finally, after more than ten years of legal warfare, the case was brought to argument on its merits, and Massachusetts, defeated in so many preliminary combats, was signally and com-

matter was at length brought to argument, on the merits, in the winter of 1846. The opinion of the Court, delivered by Mr. Justice McLean, was against the claim of Rhode Island, on the ground that the alleged mistake in running the boundary line was not clearly established, and even if such mistake were proved, it would be difficult to disturb a possession of two centuries by Massachusetts under an assertion of right, with the claim admitted by Rhode Island, and other colonies, in the most solemn form. The Chief-Justice, concurring in the judgment of the Court dismissing the bill, declined expressing any opinion upon the merits of the controversy, but places his decision solely on the ground of a want of jurisdiction. "We are to determine," he says, "whether Rhode Island is in this Court entitled to the relief she asks for Entertaining upon this subject the opinion heretofore expressed, and which has been confirmed by subsequent reflection, I think she has not; and that this Court has no constitutional power to decide the question in dispute between the States, and consequently that the bill ought to be dismissed."*

Chief-Justice Taney delivered the opinion of the Court in the Bank of Augusta *vs.* Earle, and the two other cases depending on the same principle, argued at the same time, at the January term, 1839.† This opinion contains some interesting doctrines relative to the nature and character of corporations created by statute, and the rights and powers of the corporations of one State acting within the territorial jurisdiction of another. The law of comity among nations, permitting corporations created by one sovereignty to make contracts in another, and to sue in its courts, is declared to prevail among the several States of this Union. For, the States of the Union "are SOVEREIGN STATES; and the history of the past, and the events which are daily occurring, fur-

pletely victorious. The strategy and skill of the lawyers throughout these various campaigns would certainly lose nothing in comparison with that displayed by a Frederick or a Napoleon. At all events, we are forced to the reflection, that whether the Constitution authorizes it or not, this is really a more sensible and satisfactory, as well as a more equitable way of settling questions of sovereignty and political differences, than that usually adopted for maintaining the "balance of power" between the States of Europe.

* Rhode Island *vs.* Massachusetts. 4 Howard's Reports, 639.

† 13 Peters' Reports, 520.

nish the strongest evidence that they have adopted towards each other the laws of comity in their fullest extent."

During the session of the Court in 1841, Judge Barbour died.* On

* The following discriminating tribute to the memory of Judge Barbour is from the pen of his brother and associate, Mr. Justice Story. A brief sketch of his life and services may also be found in the introduction to the last volume of Peters' Reports.

"The family from which Judge Barbour was descended, was one of the oldest and most respectable in Virginia. His great-grandfather was a merchant of Scotland, who immigrated to this country. His grandfather was the pioneer and first settler of the country lying between the eastern base of the Blue Ridge and the South-west mountains. His father, Thomas Barbour, inherited considerable wealth, and was a member of the old House of Burgesses, from the then very large county of Orange. He was one of those who, in 1769, signed the 'Non-Importation Act' between this country and Great Britain. After the formation of the Union, he was elected to the Legislature. Richard Henry Lee, in a letter to his brother, Arthur Lee, bore testimony to his worth, to the effect, 'that he was glad that Thomas Barbour was in our State Councils, for he was a truly intelligent and patriotic man.'

"On the maternal side, as his name indicates, Judge Barbour was related to the Pendleton family, his grandmother having been the aunt of the distinguished Judge Pendleton. Philip Pendleton Barbour was born on the 25th of May, 1783. Owing to his great hospitality, and a long series of disasters, his father was unable to afford him that liberal education which his talents and early promise would have justified. He was, however, sent early to school, where he soon developed many of those qualities for which he was afterwards so justly distinguished. He exhibited great aptitude for the acquisition of languages; and, with a correct taste and strong memory, sought out and retained through life the beauties of the Greek and Roman classics. Even in the performance of the tasks of a country school, he manifested that precision of information and depth of research, which, on a broader theatre, and carried to higher subjects, won for him a wide-spread and enduring reputation. He remained at school until the end of 1799. During the early part of 1800 he studied law at home; but, in October, he determined to visit Kentucky, where, under great difficulty and embarrassment, he commenced the practice of law. In the summer of 1801, he yielded to the persuasions of his friends to return to Virginia; and, having borrowed the necessary funds, spent one session at William and Mary College. In 1802, he resumed the practice of law in Virginia. In October, 1804, he was united to Frances T. Johnson, daughter of Col. Benjamin Johnson, of Orange county, Virginia. During the next eight years he applied himself unceasingly to his profession. In 1812 he was elected to the Assembly, where he continued two sessions. In 1814, he was elected to Congress, where he continued until 1825. While there, he was chairman of the Naval and Judiciary Committees; and in 1821,

the opening of the Court after the adjournment caused by this event, the Attorney-General, Mr. Gilpin, presented the proceedings of a meeting of the bar on the occasion of the death of Judge Barbour,

was chosen Speaker of the House of Representatives. About the year 1825, the University of Virginia went into operation. He was offered the professorship of law in that institution, and was pressed by Mr. Jefferson to accept it. He refused this station, however, and was appointed a Judge of the General Court of Virginia. In 1827, at the written request of a majority of his old constituents, he resigned his seat on the Bench, and was rëelected, without opposition, to Congress. In 1829, together with the illustrious Madison, he was chosen to represent the county of Orange in the convention, called to amend the Constitution of Virginia. He presided over the deliberations of this body in a manner which elicited the approbation of its members. He was also president of the Anti-Tariff Convention, which met in Philadelphia. In 1830, he retired from the practice of a profession which had yielded him considerable wealth, and of which he had been one of the brightest ornaments, and accepted the station of Federal Judge for the eastern district of Virginia. The chancellorship was offered to him and declined; as was also the post of Attorney-General. He refused the nomination for a seat in the Court of Appeals, the Gubernatorial Chair, and the Senate of the United States. As Federal Judge, he won new honors, and showed himself worthy of the high and enviable station to which in 1836 he was called, that of Associate-Judge of the Supreme Court of the United States. Having thus reached the height of the profession which he had chosen, he was unweariedly striving, with a virtuous ambition, to win that fame which great ability can only give when joined with pure principles, when death cut him off in his useful career, and robbed our country of one of its most distinguished sons.

"It remains for us to take a brief notice of the professional attainments and judicial character of Mr. Justice Barbour. It has been already seen that no inconsiderable portion of his life was employed in active political duties and pursuits, which if not incompatible with, are (to say the least) by no means favorable to the cultivation of juridical knowledge, or to found a solid reputation in the law. He did not, however, at any time relax his vigilance in his professional studies, or become indifferent to professional success. On the contrary, he had the ambition to acquire all the knowledge which might be useful in his practice at the bar, and the persevering firmness to surmount every intervening obstacle. His mind was in a remarkable degree acute, sound, and discriminating, inclining to subtilty in disquisition, but not misled by it. He was earnest, candid, patient, and laborious in all his investigations; quick to discern the real points and merits of a case; but slow in arriving at his own conclusions. His talents were of a high order; but he was distinguished less for brilliancy of effort, than for perspicacious, close, and vigorous reasoning. He sought less to be eloquent than to be accurate; less to persuade by declamatory fervor, than to convince by clear and logical

and moved that they be entered on record. Chief-Justice Taney responded in the following appropriate and affecting remarks: "I speak in the name of the Court, and by its authority, when I say that we have scarcely yet recovered from the unexpected blow which has fallen upon us. Our deceased brother, for weeks past, has been daily with us in the hall, listening to the animated and earnest discussions which the great subjects in controversy here naturally produce; and he has been with us, also, in the calmer scenes of the conference room, taking a full share in the deliberations of the Court, and always listened to with the most respectful attention. It was from one of these meetings, which had been protracted to a late hour of the night, that we all last parted from him apparently in his usual health; and in the morning we found that the associate whom we so highly respected, and the friend we so greatly esteemed, had been called away from us, and had passed to another, and we trust a better world. The suddenness of the bereavement, the character of the Judge we have lost, and his worth as a man, made it proper to suspend the business of the Court until to-day. The time was necessary, not only to pay the honors due to his memory, but to recollect and fit ourselves for renewed labors.

"Judge Barbour was a member of this Court but a few years; yet he has been long enough here to leave behind him, in the published

deduction. The learning, therefore, that he brought to the discussion of every cause, was pertinent, exact, and illustrative. It had point and force, and not merely remote or loose analogies to give it effect. When he was elevated to the Bench, he felt a deep and conscientious sense of his new duties; and was solicitous to master all the learning appropriate to discharge them in the best manner; and especially, after his appointment to the Bench of the Supreme Court, he devoted his leisure, with strenuous diligence, to attain all the various knowledge demanded for eminence in that station. Few men ever labored with more entire success in such a noble pursuit. During his brief career in that Court, he widened and deepened the foundations of his judicial learning to an extraordinary extent; his reputation constantly advanced, and his judgments were listened to with increased respect and profound confidence. If he had lived many years with good health, he could not have failed to have won the highest distinction for all those qualities which give dignity and authority to the Bench. It might be truly said of him, that he was not only equal to all the functions of his high station, but above them—*par negotiis, et supra*——. His country has lost by his death a bright ornament, and a pure and spotless patriot."

proceedings of the Court, striking proofs of the clearness and vigor of his mind, and of his eminent learning and industry. But those only who have been intimately associated with him as members of the same tribunal, can fully appreciate the frankness of his character, and the singleness and purity of purpose with which he endeavored to discharge his arduous duties. By those who have thus known him, his memory will always be cherished with the most affectionate remembrance; and we will cordially unite with the bar in the honors they propose to pay his memory."

Judge Barbour, it will be recollected, came to the bench at the same term with the Chief-Justice; and his death was the first that had occurred since Judge Taney had taken his seat. He was succeeded by Mr. JUSTICE DANIEL, of Virginia, who is still a member of the Court. It may be here properly remarked, that by the act of Congress of March, 1837, two additional justices were added to the Court, making the whole number nine, instead of seven. Under this act Mr JUSTICE CATRON, of Tennessee, and Mr. JUSTICE MCKINLEY, of Alabama, were appointed, and took their seats at the session of 1838. The latter gentleman having recently died, his place has been filled by the appointment of Mr. JUSTICE CAMPBELL, of Alabama, now the junior Judge on the bench, a gentleman who brings to the high station he occupies, an exalted reputation for learning and ability, and who bids fair to do honor to a tribunal that can point to such names on the roll of its members, as a Washington, a Livingston, a Story, a Thompson, and a Woodbury.

I may also here properly notice the few other changes made in the Court during the period of Chief-Justice Taney's service. SAMUEL NELSON, for many years Chief-Justice of the Supreme Court of New York, a name well and honorably known in the judicial history of a State whose judges, in point of character, learning, and ability, may claim to rank with those of any other State in the Union, was appointed to succeed the venerable SMITH THOMPSON, on the 13th February, 1845. That eminent and enlightened statesman, and sound constitutional jurist, LEVI WOODBURY, of New Hampshire, succeeded to, and it is not too much to say, filled, the place of Judge Story, by appointment of President Tyler, 20th September, 1845. Dying a few years after, BENJAMIN R. CURTIS, of Massachusetts, was appointed to succeed him, on the 27th January, 1852. Robert C. Grier, of Pennsylvania, was appointed on the 4th August, 1846, in place of Judge Baldwin, deceased. Both Justice Grier and Justice Curtis, are still members of the Court.

The session of 1841 was memorable for the discussion and decision of several cases of great magnitude and interest. Among them were the Florida land claim, reported under the title of Mitchell *vs.* United States ;* the case of the Amistad,† in which the venerable ex-President Adams, after a period of nearly forty years, reappeared at the bar of the Supreme Court as one of the counsel ;‡ and the case of Groves *vs.* Slaughter,§ on the determination of which, it is said, more than three millions of dollars depended—a case which, says Judge McLean, was "argued with surpassing ability on both sides," as no one will doubt, who recollects that the counsel for one of the parties were Attorney-General Gilpin, and Senator Walker, of Mississippi, and for the other, Clay, Webster, and Jones. I shall not dwell upon these cases, as the Chief-Justice did not deliver the judgment of the Court in either of them. It may be observed, however, that in the one last mentioned, an important question of constitutional law was discussed, namely, whether the grant of power to Congress to regulate commerce among the States, vests in Congress the power to regulate the traffic in slaves among the different States; and if so, whether it does not carry with it an implied prohibition on the States from making any regulations on the subject ;—but the question was not adjudicated, the decision being placed on other grounds.

At the same term of the Court, a case from New Jersey was brought to argument, which attracted great attention at the time, both on account of the novelty of the claim, and the immense value of the interests depending on its decision. The territories and government of East Jersey, originally held by the Duke of York, by grant from Charles II., King of England, became subsequently vested in twenty-

* 15 Peters' Reports, 52.

† 15 Peters' Reports, 518

‡ Judge Story, in one of his private letters, speaks of the "extraordinary argument" of Mr. Adams in this case ; adding—"extraordinary I mean for its power, for its bitter sarcasm, and its dealing with topics far beyond the record and points of discussion."

§ 15 Peters' Reports, 450.

four persons, called the East Jersey proprietors, who having surrendered up to the crown the powers of government, remained the admitted proprietors and owners of the entire soil and territory of East Jersey. This proprietary body survived the troubles of the revolution, and has continued to exist, from that day to the present, in unbroken succession, under its ancient organization, and recognized by the laws of the State, as the undisputed owner of all vacant and ungranted lands within the territorial limits of East Jersey. Under a proprietary grant of a certain portion of the bed of the Raritan river and bay, the grantee, who claimed an exclusive right of fishing for oysters, under his grant, brought an action of ejectment against a defendant, claiming a similar right under a lease from the State. On the trial, in the Circuit Court, Judge Baldwin sustained the proprietary title, against that of the State. And the defendant thereupon brought the case into the Supreme Court. It was deemed to be of so great consequence, that the Legislature of New Jersey passed a special act, directing the Governor of the State to attend the sittings of the Court, at Washington, on the argument. The most eminent and able counsel were employed on both sides, and the arguments, as may be seen from the report of the case,* were characterized by the highest degree of professional learning and ability. Judge Barbour's death prevented a decision of the question at this term, and a reargument was ordered. This took place at the session in January, 1842. Mr. George Wood, and General Wall, then one of the senators from New Jersey, appeared for the State; and Mr. Ogden, and Mr. Silas Wright, then a senator in Congress from New York,† for the proprietary claimant. The Chief-

* Martin et al. *vs.* Waddell. 16 Peters' Reports, 367.

† This, I believe, was the first, and, I am not sure, but the only argument, ever made by that eminent citizen at the bar of the Supreme Court. It was prepared with extraordinary and most laborious care and industry, and like every other product of the mind of its author, was clear, compact, and logical. It was not regarded at the time, however, as one of his happiest efforts, and from the closeness with which he confined himself to his brief, it was evident that he himself felt the embarrassment of being suddenly transferred from the Senate Chamber to the judicial forum. Mr. Wright was not engaged in the first argument. The counsel for the proprietors on that occasion were Southard, of New Jersey, and Sherwood, of New York.

Justice delivered the opinion of the Court, which was adverse to the proprietary title. The navigable waters of New Jersey, he held, passed to the Duke of York, and to the proprietors, but they passed as part of the prerogative rights annexed to the political powers conferred on the Duke, and not as private property, to be parcelled out and sold to individuals; and the right of fishery was a part of these prerogative rights, or, in other words, one of the royalties incident to the powers of government. When the proprietors surrendered up the government, the navigable waters of New Jersey went back to the crown; and when, at the revolution, the people of New Jersey took possession of the reins of government, the prerogatives and regalities, which belonged either to the crown or the parliament, became immediately and rightfully vested in the State. The proprietary claim to an exclusive fishery, in the navigable waters of New Jersey, was therefore declared to be unfounded, and the judgment of the Circuit Court reversed. Mr. Justice Thompson, with whom Judge Baldwin concurred, delivered a very able and closely written dissenting opinion.*

In the well know Pennsylvania slave case,† argued and decided at this term, Mr. Justice Story had the opportunity, which, a few years before, he had feared would never again occur in his time, of declaring a State law unconstitutional and void, and that too, by the unanimous

* The decision in this case was thought not to have settled the question as to the proprietary title, or *fee*, in the soil of the navigable waters of New Jersey, but merely that a right of exclusive fishery did not exist in the proprietors. Accordingly, to test this question, an action of ejectment for certain city lots at Jersey city, reclaimed from the bed of Hudson River below low-water mark, was afterwards commenced under the proprietary title against the persons in possession. This case was brought to argument at the late session of the Supreme Court. The judgment of the Court, pronounced by the Chief-Justice, was adverse to the proprietary claim, it being held that the former decision was substantially a disposition of the present question, and that the fee of the soil, as well as the public uses of the navigable rivers of New Jersey had passed out of the proprietors to the Crown, and at the revolution had passed back from the Crown to the people of New Jersey. The author speaks with knowledge of the facts of this case, as he was one of the counsel engaged on the argument in behalf of the proprietary title. It will be found reported in the 15th Volume of Howard's Reports, under the title of Den ex dem Russell *vs*. The Associates of the Jersey Company.

† Prigg *vs*. Commonwealth of Pennsylvania. 16 Peters' Reports, 543.

judgment of the Court. It is to be remarked, however, that while all the Judges agreed in the actual decision rendered in the case, namely, that the Pennsylvania law was unconstitutional, yet the Chief-Justice, and two or three of his associates, did not concur in the reasonings and principles laid down in the prevailing opinion of the Court. The case was this: Prigg, a citizen of Maryland, had taken a fugitive slave, by force and violence, from the State of Pennsylvania, without the certificate required by the act of Congress, of 1793, and brought such slave to the State of Maryland. For this act, Prigg had been indicted under a law of Pennsylvania, entitled, "An act to give effect to the provisions of the Constitution of the United States, relative to fugitives from labor, for the protection of free people of color, and to prevent kidnapping;" one section of which act provided, that the taking and carrying away of any negro or mulatto, by force and violence, &c., out of the State, should be deemed a felony, punishable by fine and imprisonment. The act which had been passed by the Pennsylvania Legislature, for the purpose of meeting the supposed wishes of Maryland, on the subject of fugitive slaves, provided a mode for their rendition by the State authorities. The fugitive slave had been brought before the Pennsylvania magistrate, by virtue of the law, but that functionary refused to take cognizance of the case, and Prigg thereupon, without further license or warrant, carried her and her children away into Maryland. By an amicable arrangement between the two States, judgment was entered against Prigg in the Court below, and the case was thereupon brought to the Supreme Court of the United States, by the coöperation and sanction of both States, in the most friendly and courteous spirit, with a view to have the grave question presented by it, finally adjudicated.

The opinion delivered by Judge Story, with whom Mr. Justice Wayne and some other members of the Court concurred, maintained, among other things, that the Pennsylvania law was unconstitutional, because the section of the Constitution which provides that fugitives "shall be delivered up," places the remedy *exclusively* in Congress, and therefore that the States are prohibited from passing any law on the subject, whether Congress had or had not legislated on it. From this proposition, the Chief-Justice, while concurring in the main with the conclusions arrived at by Judge Story, dissents. He holds that not only are the States not prohibited from legislating on the subject, but, on the contrary, it is enjoined on them as a duty to protect and support the owner when he is endeavoring to obtain possession of his property found within their respective limits. Upon this point he expresses these views :

"The language used in the Constitution does not, in my judgment, justify the construction given to it by the Court. It contains no words prohibiting the several States from passing laws to enforce this right. They are in express terms forbidden to make any regulation that shall impair it. But there the prohibition stops. And according to the settled rules of construction for all written instruments, the prohibition being confined to laws injurious to the right, the power to pass laws to support and enforce it, is necessarily implied. And the words of the article which direct that the fugitive "shall be delivered up," seem evidently designed to impose it as a duty upon the people of the several States to pass laws to carry into execution, in good faith, the compact into which they thus solemnly entered with each other. The Constitution of the United States, and every article and clause in it, is a part of the law of every State in the Union, and is the paramount law. The right of the master, therefore, to seize his fugitive slave, is the law of each State ; and no State has the power to abrogate or alter it. And why may not a State protect a right of property acknowledged by its own paramount law? Besides, the laws of the different States, in all other cases, constantly protect the citizens of other States in their rights of property, when it is found within their respective territories ; and no one doubts their power to do so. And in the absence of any express prohibition, I perceive no reason for establishing, by implication, a different rule in this instance ; where, by the national compact, this right of property is recognized as an existing right in every State of the Union."

Judges Thompson and Daniel also delivered opinions to the same effect, namely, that the constitutional power vested in Congress was not exclusive ; nor did it prohibit the States, in the absence of a law of Congress, from legislating to protect and enforce this right guaranteed by the Constitution. They concurred, however, in the judgment of reversal, on the ground that the act of Congress of 1793 was a constitutional exercise of power, and that the Pennsylvania law conflicted with it, and was therefore null and void.

At the session of 1843, Chief-Justice Taney delivered the judgment of the Court in the case of Bronson *vs.* McKinzie, *et. al.*,* annulling and declaring void a law of the State of Illinois, on the ground that it violated the provision of the Constitution which prohibits a State from passing any law impairing the obligation of contracts. The act of the Illinois Legislature, passed subsequent to the contract, provided that the equitable estate of a mortgagor should not be extinguished for twelve months after a sale under a decree in Chancery, and that there should be no sale unless two-thirds of the amount at which the property has been valued by appraisers should be bid therefor. Neither Judge Story nor Judge McKinley was present at this discussion, the result of which furnished another evidence that the apprehensions expressed by the former were entirely unfounded. The opinion of the Chief-Justice is a clear, luminous and most able exposition of the law on this subject, and has generally been regarded by the profession as entirely satisfactory. Judge McLean dissented, taking the somewhat subtle, if not technical, distinction, that the State law acted upon the *remedy*, and not upon the *contract.*

This case was followed at the next term of the Court by McCracken *vs.* Hayward,† which fully confirmed the decision in Bronson *vs.* McKinzie in all its points, re-affirming the doctrine that the valuation and stay laws of Illinois were inoperative upon existing contracts, and void. The Chief-Justice does not appear to have been present at the argument and decision of this cause. Very early in the session he was attacked by severe indisposition, and was prevented from taking his seat during the remainder of the term, and from participating in the decision of the very important cases brought on for argument. Among these may be mentioned the great case of the Girard will, so elaborately and splendidly argued by Webster and Jones, on the one side, and by Binney and Sergeant on the other, the opinion in which was delivered by Justice Story, sustaining the will,—an opinion concurred in unanimously by his brethren, without altering (says Story, with some appearance of self-satisfaction), "a single sentence as I

* 1 Howard's Reports, 311.

† 2 Howard's Reports, 608.

originally drew it up ;" also the celebrated Gaines case, which has excited so great a degree of public interest, not so much perhaps on account of the large amount of property involved in the controversy, as by reason of the romantic nature of the history upon which it turned—the history of Zulime Carriere, and her daughter, Myra Clark Gaines ;* and also the case of the Louisville, Cincinnati and Charleston Rail Road Company *vs.* Letson, which established the very important principle that a corporation is to be deemed an inhabitant of a State, capable of being treated as a citizen, for all purposes of suing and being sued, a principle not only denied by former decisions of the Court, but the opposite of which had been considered by the profession as too well established to be again unsettled.† And lastly, the case of Bank of the United States *vs.* United States,‡ in which the Government was held liable to pay fifteen per cent. damages as the drawer of a foreign protested bill, under a statute

* Gaines et ux. *vs.* Chew et. al. 2 Howard's Reports, 619. Another branch of this interesting case is reported under the title of Patterson *vs.* Gaines et ux.. 6 Howard, 650 ; and another under the title of Gaines *vs.* Relf et al., 12 Howard, 473. The Chief-Justice did not sit in these causes, as a near family relative was interested in the event. The decision in the last of these cases, at the session of 1851, finally decided the claim adversely to Mrs. Gaines.

† Only four years before, the Supreme Court, in the case of Commercial Bank of Vicksburgh *vs.* Slocum, 14 Peters 60, following the cases of Strawbridge *vs.* Curtis, 3 Cranch 267, and Bank of the United States *vs.* Deveaux, 5 Cranch 84, had decided that a corporation, as such, was *not* a citizen of the United States ; and at the same term, in Irvine *vs.* Lowry, 14 Peters 293, it was declared that the decisions had been uniform upon this subject, and must be followed. Mr. Justice Wayne, who delivered the opinion of the Court in the present case, overruling these decisions, remarks, however, that the Vicksburgh Bank case was most reluctantly decided on the authority of the two former cases above alluded to, and that not only were these cases never satisfactory to the bar, but they were also unsatisfactory to the Court that made them. No one, he adds, questioned them more than the Chief-Justice (Marshall) himself, who gave these two decisions, and he repeatedly expressed his regret that they had been made. In a letter of Judge Story, in which he expresses his satisfaction that the Supreme Court had at last adopted a more correct rule, he makes a similar remark in regard to Chief-Justice Marshall, adding that Mr. Justice Washington was also of opinion that these decisions were wrong in principle, as they must be admitted to be inconvenient in practice.

‡ 2 Howard's Reports, 711.

of Maryland, allowing that amount to the holder of such protested bill. In this case, the Chief-Justice prepared a carefully considered dissenting opinion, which will be found in the Appendix to this volume of the reports. The case had been before him as Attorney-General, and his opinion then, as now, was, that the Bank had no claim in law or equity to the damages in question. It is proper here to add that in a subsequent case decided at the session of 1847,* the Court ruled, that the Government was not liable to the Bank for these consequential damages. The Chief-Justice, though he withdrew from the bench, for the reason that he had given an official opinion as Attorney-General, concurred entirely in this judgment of the Court. Judges McLean and Wayne dissented, regarding the question as having been substantially decided in the former case.

At the session of the Court in the winter of 1845, several cases involving questions of constitutional law were brought to argument. Those in which the Chief-Justice delivered the opinion of the Court are the cases of Kendall *vs.* Stokes, Searight *vs.* Stokes, Niel, Moore & Co., *vs.* the State of Ohio, and the State of Maryland *vs.* the Baltimore and Ohio Rail Road Company, all of which are contained in the third volume of Howard's Reports. The first of these cases was a suit brought against the Post-Master General for damages, in consequence of acts which the Court held to be official, but not ministerial acts; and the principle was recognized that a public officer, acting from a sense of duty, in a matter where he is required to exercise discretion, is not liable to an action for an error of judgment.

In the second of these cases the question was, as stated by the Chief-Justice, whether the State of Pennsylvania can lawfully impose a toll on carriages employed in transporting the mail of the United States over that part of the Cumberland road which passes through that State. In the judgment of the Court—Justices McLean and Daniel dissenting—a carriage, whenever it carries the mail of the United States, must be held to be laden with the property of the United States within the meaning of the compact between the Federal Government and the State of Pennsylvania, and therefore exempt from payment of tolls. But the Court did not construe the exemption as extending to other property in the same vehicle, or persons travelling

* United States *vs.* Bank of the United States. 5 Howard's Reports, 382.

in it, unless in the service of the United States, nor to more carriages than were *necessary* for the safe and convenient conveyance of the mail. The case was thought to come within the principle established in McCulloch *vs.* the State of Maryland, "that a State Government has no right to tax any of the constitutional means employed by the Government of the Union to execute its constitutional powers."*

Neil, Moore & Co., *vs.* the State of Ohio, presented a similar question, and the Chief-Justice, in his opinion, carried the rule still farther. Under the compact of surrender between Congress and the State, it was held that toll could not be charged upon passengers travelling in the mail stages on the Cumberland road, without being also charged upon passengers travelling in other stages, and that such a tax was against the contract, and void.

The case of Maryland, *vs.* the Baltimore and Ohio Railroad Company, presented the question whether a law of the Maryland Legislature was void on the ground that it impaired the obligation of a contract. The State had directed a subscription of $3,000,000 to the Railroad Company, with the proviso that the Company should locate the road through the towns of Cumberland, Hagerstown, and Boonsborough, or, in default, should forfeit $1,000,000 for the use of Washinton County in Maryland, where the two towns last mentioned are situated. The Company, having assented to the law, refused to locate the road through these towns, and a suit was accordingly commenced for the penalty. Subsequently the Maryland Legislature passed a law repealing so much of the act as required the location of the road through these towns, and remitting the forfeiture of the $1,000,000. This act, it was alleged, was unconstitutional and void, inasmuch as the penalty had become due to Washington County by *contract.* The Court, however, the Chief-Justice delivering the opinion, ruled otherwise. The original act was not a contract within the meaning of the Constitution. It was merely a penalty inflicted on the Company as a punishment for disobeying the law, which the State had a right to release, the whole scope of the law showing that it was a legislation for State purposes, and a measure of State policy, which the State had a right to change at its pleasure ; and that neither the County nor any of its citizens acquired any private interest under it which could be main-

* See *ante*, page 402.

tained in a court of justice. The case was argued with marked ability by Mr. Sergeant and Mr. Jervis Spencer, and by the Attorney-General, Nelson, and Mr. Reverdy Johnson in opposition.

This was the last term of Judge Story upon the bench of the Supreme Court. At the opening of the Court at the next session, in the winter of 1846, Chief-Justice Taney was called upon to perform the melancholy duty of responding to the announcement of the death of his eminent associate. The brief and touching sentences he pronounced on the occasion are beautiful alike for their simplicity, and their sincerity and their tenderness.

"It is difficult for me," he remarked, in reply to the Attorney-General, who had moved the usual testimonials of respect, "to express how deeply the Court feel the death of Mr. Justice Story. He had a seat on this bench for so many years, and was so eminently distinguished for his great learning and ability, that his name had become habitually associated with the Supreme Court, not only in the mind of those more immediately connected with the administration of justice, but in that of the public generally throughout the Union. He had indeed all the qualities of a great judge ; and we are fully sensible that his labors and his name have contributed largely to inspire confidence in the opinions of this Court, and to give weight and authority to its decisions.

"It is not, however, in this country only, that the name of Justice Story is respected and honored. His works upon various branches of jurisprudence have made him known to eminent men wherever judicial knowledge is esteemed and cultivated ; and wherever he is known, his opinions are quoted with respect, and he is justly regarded as one of the brightest ornaments of the age in which he lived. But it is here, on this bench, that his real worth was best understood, and it is here that his loss is most severely and painfully felt. For we have not only known him as a learned and able associate in the labors of the Court, but he was also endeared to us as a man, by his kindness of heart, his frankness, and his high and pure integrity. We most truly and deeply deplore his death, and cordially unite with the bar in paying appropriate honors to his memory.

"The proceedings of to-day will therefore be entered on the records of the Court, as a lasting testimony of our respectful and affectionate remembrance of our departed brother."

The intercourse between this eminent Judge and the Chief-Justice was always of the most agreeable character. Though at times they differed in opinion *toto cœlo*, and especially upon questions of constitutional construction, yet they habitually cherished for each other feelings of mutual kindness and esteem. Story always spoke respectfully of the abilities and attainments of Taney, even before the latter came to the bench. Further acquaintance ripened into reciprocal esteem. When, at the close of his career, Judge Story had become dissatisfied with his position on the bench, we find him frankly acknowledging to a friend that his personal intercourse with the Chief-Justice and his associates had always been pleasant.* And on his part the Chief-Justice never failed to express for Judge Story that respect and esteem, which were so justly due to the virtues and worth, as well as

* Letter to Hon. Ezekiel Bacon. April 12th, 1845:

"I have been long convinced that the doctrines and opinions of the "Old Court" were daily losing ground, and especially those on great Constitutional questions. New men and new opinions have succeeded. The doctrines of the Constitution, so vital to the country, which in former times received the support of the whole Court, no longer maintain their ascendancy. I am the last member now living of the old Court, and I cannot consent to remain where I can no longer hope to see those doctrines recognized and enforced. For the future I must be in a dead minority of the Court, with the painful alternative of either expressing an open dissent from the opinions of the Court, or, by my silence, seeming to acquiesce in them."

Under the influence of these sombre views, Judge Story came to the conclusion definitely to resign his seat in the Supreme Court, and to fall back on his law professorship at Harvard College, a station which he had occupied for several years; and with this view he returned from his last term of service at the session of 1845. His death, however, occurred before he had an opportunity of accomplishing this design. He died on the 10th of September, 1845, at the age of sixty-six years, thirty-three of which had been passed in the discharge of his duties of Judge of the Supreme Court. The Life of Judge Story, in two volumes, by his son William W. Story, presents a full and complete record of his private, his judicial, and his professional career. It is marked throughout by a pious, filial, and almost reverential admiration for the character of the man whose memory it embalms; but this by no means detracts from its rare value as the narrative of a life drawn from the amplest materials, and illustrated by minute description, as well as copious detail. The student will find it a book to be read with profit as well as pleasure.

the profound and comprehensive learning, of one of the most illustrious jurists this country, or the world, has produced.

The Massachusetts, Rhode Island, and New Hampshire License cases,* reported at January term, 1847, brought before the Court a constitutional question of great magnitude and interest. The questions in these cases arose under that much-discussed clause of the Federal Constitution, which vests Congress with power to regulate commerce. In the first two cases the precise point was, whether a State might assume to regulate or prohibit the retail of wines and spirits, the importation of which from foreign countries has been authorized by act of Congress ; and in the last case, whether a State might prohibit by law the sale of liquor imported from another State, there being no act of Congress to regulate such importation. In the decision of these cases the judges unanimously determined that the laws under review were all valid and constitutional.

In these opinions, however, there appears to be much diversity as to the principles on which the cases are decided. Six of the judges, including the Chief-Justice, expressed their views at length, and the whole subject of the power of Congress over foreign and internal commerce, and the conflict between the authority of the General and State Governments is considered, with a copious fullness of argument, and with an accuracy and closeness of deduction, that leaves very little to be said in any future discussion. I do not propose to notice any of these arguments except that of the Chief-Justice, which is certainly very able, and, I believe, has generally been regarded as entirely satisfactory to the profession. No one, I apprehend, can read it without being satisfied that it places the decision of these cases—particularly the New Hampshire case—upon true and correct grounds, if not the only grounds upon which they can permanently stand.

The Chief-Justice does not deny, but, on the contrary, fully admits the proposition, that if these State laws were in collision with an act of Congress, they would be unconstitutional and void. If, in the Massachusetts and Rhode Island cases, the law had obstructed the importation, or prohibited the sale of the article in the original cask

* Thurlow *vs.* Massachusetts, Fletcher *vs.* Rhode Island, and Pierce et al. *vs.* New Hamphire. 5 Howard's Reports, 504.

or vessel, *in the hands of the importer*, it would have been void ; because the importation was permitted by Congress in the exercise of its constitutional power to regulate foreign commerce. But this he held was not the case. The State laws were framed to act upon the article after it had passed the line of foreign commerce into the hands of the dealer, and had become a part of the general mass of the property of the State. This, he contended, was precisely the principle recognized in Brown *vs.* Maryland, and to which he gave his entire assent.

The New Hampshire case was different. The law prohibited the sale, in any quantity, without license ; and the sale, in that case, had been made by the importer, in the cask in which the liquor had been imported from Massachusetts into New Hampshire. The case therefore, in his view, turned upon the question, whether, in the absence of a law of Congress regulating commerce between the States, all State laws on the subject are null and void. In other words, whether a mere grant of power to the General Government, can be construed as an absolute prohibition to the exercise of any power over the same subject by the States. Upon this question a diversity of sentiment had existed among the members of the Court, as was evident in the judgment in Prigg *vs.* Pennsylvania. The Chief-Justice had there distinctly expressed the opinion, that a mere grant of power to Congress, was not exclusive, or prohibitory upon the States,* and this doctrine he not only reiterates, but makes the main ground of his judgment. "The controlling and supreme power over commerce with foreign nations, and the several States," he observes, "is undoubtedly conferred upon Congress. Yet, in my judgment, the State may, nevertheless, for the safety or convenience of trade, or for the protection of the health of its citizens, make regulations of commerce for its own ports and harbors, and for its own territory ; and such regulations are valid, unless they come in conflict with the law of Congress. Such evidently, I think, was the construction which the Constitution universally received at the time of its adoption, as appears from the legislation of Congress and of the several States ; and a careful examination of the decisions of this Court, will show, that, so far from sanctioning the opposite doctrine, they recognize and maintain the power of the

* *Ante*, p. 509. In the Wheeling Bridge case, the dissenting opinion of the Chief-Justice is placed upon the same grounds. See post.

States."* This construction he believes is legitimately to be drawn from what was really intended to be decided in Gibbons *vs.* Ogden, as well as in Brown *vs.* Maryland, and is fully and authoritatively sanctioned in the case of Wilson *vs.* The Blackbird Creek Marsh Company, heretofore noticed among the cases decided in Chief-Justice Marshall's time.†

The case of Cook *vs.* Moffat,‡ decided at this term, brought under review and reëxamination, the question of the effect of a debtor's discharge under the insolvent laws of one State, on a contract made in another State, so much discussed in Chief-Justice Marshall's time, and which was settled by the decisions in Ogden *vs.* Saunders, and Boyle *vs.* Zacharie.§ The judgment of the Court was in accordance with these decisions. The Chief-Justice, though acquiescing in that judgment, on the ground that the question was *res adjudicata*, expressed his disapprobation of the principle on which the case turned. He considered the true doctrine to be, that the bankrupt law of one State, should receive in the tribunals of a sister State, the respect and comity which the established usages of civilized nations extend to the bankrupt laws of each other.

At the same term, the very important Admiralty case of Waring *vs.* Clark,‖ was decided, in which the attention of the Court was, for the first time, called to the question, whether the Admiralty jurisdiction, conferred by the Constitution, was to be limited to, and interpreted by, what were cases of Admiralty jurisdiction in England, when the Constitution was adopted by the States of the Union ; or, whether that jurisdiction in a public navigable river extended beyond the ebb and flow of the tide. The collision, in this case, had taken place on the Mississippi River, near the bayou Goulah, and there was much doubt whether the tide flowed so high. The majority of the Court, however, thought there was sufficient proof of tide there, and consequently it was not necessary to consider whether the Admiralty jurisdiction extended higher. This subject will presently be noticed again,

* In these views the Chief-Justice is sustained by the opinions of Judges Catron, Daniel, Woodbury and Nelson.

† *Ante*, p. 425.

‡ 5 Howard's Reports, 295.

§ *Ante*, p. 399–400.

‖ 5 Howard's Reports, 441.

when I come to speak of the case of *the Genesee Chief*, in which the Chief-Justice delivered the opinion, asserting the bold and comprehensive doctrine, that the Admiralty power of the Court extends beyond the flow of the tide in public navigable waters, and over the great fresh-water lakes.*

I pass over several important cases, at this and the next ensuing term, and come down to the session of the Court in 1849, which brought to final argument and adjudication, the New York and Boston Passenger cases.† They arose upon the same constitutional provision involved in the discussion of the Licence cases which I have just noticed, namely, that which vests in Congress the power to regulate commerce. The argument involved a review of the same principles which were examined in the former discussions on this subject, and the report of the cases occupies no inconsiderable portion of the entire volume which contains the decisions made at the session of 1849. These celebrated cases, either one or both, had been under argument at four several terms of the Court, commencing with the argument of Smith *vs.* Turner, at the December term, 1845. The question presented by the record in that case, was, whether a law of the State of New York, laying a tax upon the masters of vessels arriving from a foreign port, of one dollar for every steerage passenger, and one dollar and fifty cents for every cabin passenger, and upon the masters of coasting vessels, of twenty-five cents for each passenger such vessels might contain, for "hospital moneys," was repugnant to the Constitution of the United States, and void. The Massachusetts case, Norris *vs.* the City of Boston, turned upon a similar question.

The decision of these cases presented these two distinct points for adjudication. 1st. Is the power to regulate commerce, *exclusively* vested in Congress? 2d. Is a tax upon persons or passengers, a regu-

* The case of Waring *vs.* Clark, it may be added, is distinguished for the extraordinary and singularly powerful dissenting opinion of Judge Woodbury, in which, upon both reason and authority, he denies that the Admiralty jurisdiction extends within the body of a county even upon tide waters—an opinion whose learning and research, whose close and vigorous logic, and whose bold and original, and comprehensive, deductions, leave it in doubt whether the capacity of its author as a jurist was not greater than a long life of public service had proved it to be as a statesman.

† Smith *vs.* Turner, Norris *vs.* City of Boston. 7 Howard's Reports, 283.

lation of commerce? Both of these points, it was claimed, on the argument, had been heretofore settled by repeated and solemn judgments of the Court. In support of the affirmative of the first proposition, the decisions in Brown *vs.* Maryland, and Gibbons *vs.* Ogden,* were confidently cited. To sustain the negative of the latter proposition, the authority of the city of New York *vs.* Miln, was, with equal confidence, invoked. The result of the deliberations of the consultation-room, and the judgment of the Court, seem to have left both questions in an uncertainty still more perplexing, and an obscurity still more profound, than when the discussion began. The State laws, it is true, were declared null and void, by the votes of five Judges, against four.† And thus far there was a decision of the cases; but everything else was left unsettled. Such was the diversity and conflict of views even among the Judges who concurred in the prevailing opinion, that the reporter himself seems to have been perplexed, and very frankly declares that "there was no opinion of the Court, as a Court."

The Chief-Justice led off on the other side in a dissenting opinion, which met the full concurrence of his brethren, Judges Daniel and Nelson, and in which he was most powerfully sustained by Judge Woodbury, in one of those masterly, comprehensive, and elaborate constitutional arguments upon which the fame of that eminent man, as a jurist, rests—the most elaborate, perhaps, and, some have thought, the ablest ever delivered by him while upon the bench—one of those full, and rigid, and exhausting arguments, whose object is not to demonstrate a theory merely, but to establish a principle, and literally to overwhelm and annihilate what he regarded as the errors which combated it.

The opinion of Judge Taney is comprised within thirty pages of the reported case, and is well worthy of attentive and careful study by any one desirous of becoming master of the principles involved in the discussion. I shall not, of course, attempt to give even an analysis of it in this place. It is sufficient to remark, that he adheres throughout to those same constitutional views and constructions which he had expressed on previous occasions, and among them, that the power to regulate commerce is not *exclusive* in Congress; and also, that *persons,*

* *Ante*, p. 412.

† For Reversal—Judges McLean, Wayne, Catron, McKinley, and Grier.
For Affirmance—The Chief-Justice, and Judges Daniel, Nelson, and Woodbury.

not being the subjects of *commerce*, a tax upon passengers or emigrants could not be considered a commercial regulation. The latter proposition had apparently been directly held in the case of City of New York *vs.* Miln, the authority of which, upon this point, was now attacked in the conference-room of the Judges, as it had been at the bar. Mr. Justice Wayne, who sat in that case, denied that it established any such principle, or that the expression there used was sanctioned by the majority of the Court; and in support of this view he gives a statement of his own recollections of the circumstances connected with the opinion delivered in that case. The Chief-Justice differs from Judge Wayne somewhat in these recollections, and insists that the dictum in City of New York *vs.* Miln, was to be regarded as the judgment of a majority of the Court; but as I have already alluded to this subject on a previous page, it is unnecessary, in this place, to pursue it further.*

The cases of Luther *vs.* Borden *et al*, † decided at this term, brought before the Court for discussion some of the gravest questions which can possibly arise relative to political rights, and the origin and ground of government. These cases grew out of the unfortunate controversy in Rhode Island in regard to the "People's Constitution," framed, as it was admitted, without the forms of law, but, as it was claimed, by the votes of a majority of the people of the State. I allude to these cases not for the purpose of tracing the origin and progress of the controversy, or of reviewing the discussions which grew out of it; but for the purpose barely of citing another instance going to show the extreme repugnance of Chief-Justice Taney in assuming an authority, or extending the jurisdiction of the Court beyond those well defined and strict limits which the Constitution had marked out. Upon a former occasion, in the case of Rhode Island *vs.* Massachusetts,‡ we have seen him standing alone in opposition to all his brethren, declining to take cognizance of what he regarded as a purely political question lying beyond the judicial authority. On the present occasion, with the assent of all his brethren who participated in the argument,§ he stands nearly

* See note, *ante*, page 492.

† 7 Howard's Reports, 1.

‡ *Ante*, page 499.

§ Judge Woodbury dissented upon the sole point as to the authority of the State to declare martial law. His elaborate and masterly opinion upon this question is

upon the same ground. The question which of the two opposing governments was the legitimate one was purely a question of political power ; the political department of the State had determined it, and the State courts had recognized and acted upon this determination. Whatever might be the propriety of that decision, it was not for the Federal tribunals to overstep the boundaries of their known jurisdiction, and to invade the proper domain of the political department. " Much of the argument on the part of the plaintiff," he remarks, " turned upon political rights and political questions, upon which the Court has been urged to express an opinion. We decline doing so. The high power has been conferred on this Court of passing judgment upon the acts of the State sovereignties, and upon the legislative and executive branches of the Federal Government, and of determining whether they are beyond the limits of power marked out for them respectively by the Constitution of the United States. This tribunal, therefore, should be the last to overstep the boundaries which limit its own jurisdiction. And while it should always be ready to meet any question confided to it by the Constitution, it is equally its duty not to pass beyond its appropriate sphere of action, and to take care not to involve itself in discussions which properly belong to other forums."

The scrupulous caution of the Chief-Justice in confining the exercise of the judicial power within its well-defined and circumscribed limits, and his repugnance to assume an authority not warranted by the strict terms of the Constitution, are manifest not in the foregoing cases only, but in nearly all the constitutional cases which came before him. One or two exceptions, however, have occurred, and among them the most prominent, perhaps, and boldest, is that extending the admiralty jurisdiction of the Court beyond the flow of the tide on navigable waters, and over the great lakes.

The Constitution of the United States provides that the judicial power shall extend " to all cases of admiralty and maratime jurisdiction ;" and the question whether Congress could ever grant the Federal Courts, or the courts could ever constitutionally exercise, power to hear and adjudicate cases which were not of " admiralty and maratime jurisdiction" at the time of the adoption of the Constitution,

the *reponse sans replique* of juridical argument, and leaves the subject very nearly exhausted.

might well be considered a question of no slight importance. In the earlier discussions in the old Supreme Court, it had been settled contrary, as it was very ably argued, to the English admiralty cases, that the jurisdiction extended within the body of a county on tide waters ;* and the doctrine seemed too well settled to be shaken, although in the recent case of Waring *vs.* Clark, to which I have referred on a preceding page, Judge Woodbury, with whom Judge Daniel concurred, endeavored, unsuccessfully, to bring the Court back to what he regarded as the more strict and legitimate constitutional construction.† It was, however, considered as equally well settled that if the jurisdiction did extend *infra corpus comitatus*, it was also, as in England, *limited* by the ebb and flow of the tide. The doctrine was so laid down by Judge Story as the unanimous opinion of the Court in the case of the Thomas Jefferson, in 1825,‡ and was recognized and followed by subsequent cases.

I have alluded in the preceding sketch of Chief-Justice Marshall to the opinion entertained by that distinguished Judge, that these cases had been decided upon wrong principles, and that the admiralty jurisdiction of the Federal Courts ought to be held to extend over the lakes, as well as over our great rivers as far as navigable beyond the flow of the tide.§ No convenient opportunity, however, ever occurred to him to express these views in a judicial decision. The task passed into the hands of his successor upon the bench, by whom it was performed in precisely the same manner that it would have been done by Marshall himself.

The case which elicited this important opinion of Chief-Justice Taney is that of *The Genesee Chief*, at the December term of 1851.‖ The collision and loss had happened on Lake Ontario, and the vessel had been libelled in the District Court for the Northern District of

* See remarks on this subject, ante page 250, and note.

† Judge Daniel has always consistently and firmly adhered to these views. See his dissenting opinions in New Jersey Steam Navigation Co. *vs.* The Merchants Bank, 6 How. 344. Newton *vs.* Stebbins, 10 How. 586. Genesee Chief *vs.* Fitzhugh, 12 How. 443.

‡ 10 Wheaton's Reports, 428. And see Steamer Orleans *vs.* Phœbus, 11 Peters, 175. United States *vs.* Combs, 12 Peters. 72.

§ *Ante*, page 444.

‖ Propellor Genesee Chief et. al. *vs.* Fitzhugh et. al., 12 Howard, 443.

New York. In 1845 Congress had passed an act extending the admiralty jurisdiction over the lakes and the navigable waters connecting, and the important question now presented was, whether this act was authorized by the Constitution. The question had never yet been directly presented or decided. For though the attention of the Court had been directed to it in Waring *vs.* Clark,* and also at the next subsequent term in the New Jersey Steam Navigation Company *vs.* The Merchants' Bank,† yet nothing upon this point was definitely settled. The Chief-Justice now met the question boldly, and finally disposed of it. The judgment of the Court was pronounced by him. He sustained the act of Congress, and the jurisdiction, upon the broadest and most extended principles. The prior decisions of the Court limiting the jurisdiction to tide waters, commencing with the case of the *Thomas Jefferson*, are all swept away. As to that decision, he remarks, that, as it was "founded in error, and the error, if not corrected, must produce serious public as well as private inconvenience and loss, it becomes our duty not to perpetuate it." The validity of the act of Congress is placed upon the original and inherent jurisdiction of the Court. "It is evident," he says, "that a definition that would at this day limit public rivers in this country to tide water rivers is utterly inadmissible. We have thousands of miles of public navigable waters, including lakes and rivers, in which there is no tide. And certainly there can be no reason for admiralty power over a public tide water, which does not apply with equal force to any other public water used for commercial purposes and foreign trade. The lakes and the waters connecting them are undoubtedly public waters; and we think are within the grant of admiralty and maratime jurisdiction in the Constitution of the United States."

The only dissenting voice to this judgment of the Court, as appears from the report, was that of Mr. Justice Daniel. Judge Woodbury was no longer there to enter a protest against the adoption of a principle, analogous to that which, on a previous occasion, he had so powerfully combated. He died during the preceding vacation, and the customary honors had been offered to his memory at the opening of this session of the Court.‡

* 5 Howard Reports, 441.

† 6 Howard Reports, 344.

‡ The public career and eminent services of Judge Woodbury are too well

At the ensuing session, the same melancholy tribute was rendered to the memory of Judge McKinley, of Alabama, who had died since the last adjournment.*

known to require even a passing notice in this place, and indeed it would be doing him injustice to attempt it within the brief limits of a note. Governor of the State of New Hampshire, Secretary of the Navy, and afterwards of the Treasury, and for many years one of the ablest and most eminent members of the United States Senate, his last and greatest distinction—in the eloquent words of Attorney-General Crittenden—was that of "Judge of the Supreme Court of the United States, whose jurisdiction is more extended than any other upon the continent, and whose mandate is obeyed from Boston to San Francisco." He was but six years on the bench, but he was there long enough to leave behind him, in the language of the same eloquent speaker, "a fame which is immortal."

In response to the brief address of the Attorney-General on the death of Judge Woodbury. Chief-Justice Taney remarked: "His life had been passed mainly in the public service, before he became a member of this Court. And in the various and important offices, judicial and political, to which he had been appointed, he was always found equal to the duties imposed upon him, and never failed to distinguish himself by the extent and accuracy of his information upon every subject connected with his official duties, or upon which he was at any time called upon to act. The same learning, and the same untiring industry, marked his brief course on this bench. We all feel that we have lost in him an able, upright, and learned associate, and most truly and sincerely deplore his death."

The judicial and constitutional opinions of Judge Woodbury are to be found in Howard's Reports from the 4th to the 11th volume inclusive. His speeches and other works have been recently published, and furnish a valuable addition to the political history of the country.

* Judge McKinley had been a member of the court for fifteen years, having been appointed by President Van Buren in the spring of 1837, under the act increasing the number of judges to nine. He had been a distinguished member of both houses of Congress, and at the time of his appointment as judge, had just been elected a senator from Alabama for the full term of six years. His death was accelerated, it is thought, by the efforts he made to attend the last session of the Court, when his health had become too infirm to encounter the fatigue of a journey to Washington. The character of Judge McKinley, both as a jurist and a man, is very appropriately summed up by Attorney-General Crittenden in his brief address to the Court, on moving the customary resolutions: "I had the good fortune," he remarks, "to be acquainted with Judge McKinley from my earliest manhood. In the relations of private life he was frank, hospitable, affectionate. In his manners he was simple and unaffected, and his character was uniformly marked with manliness, integrity, and honor. Elevation to the bench of the

The present sketch would be extended to undue limits, were I to enter upon a particular review of the various constitutional and other important questions which have occupied the attention of the Supreme Court for the last three or four years, and in the discussion and final determination of all of which the vigorous and still active mind of Judge Taney has participated. I may mention, however, in passing, that at the session, commencing December, 1850, he pronounced the judgment of the Court, in the case of The Philadelphia and Wilmington Railroad Co. *vs.* Maryland,* re-affirming the doctrine which had, on more than one occasion, been held, that the taxing power of a State is never presumed to be relinquished, or, unless the intention to relinquish, is declared in clear and unambiguous terms; and therefore that a railroad corporation, chartered by the State, is not presumed to be exempted from State taxation.† Also, that at the subsequent term, commencing December, 1851, he delivered an able dissenting opinion in the celebrated Wheeling Bridge case, a controversy still fresh in the public mind, and too well known to require more than a passing notice.‡ Also, that at the following session, commencing December,

Supreme Court made no change in him. His honors were borne meekly, without ostentation or presumption.

"He was a candid, impartial, and righteous judge. Shrinking from no responsibility, he was fearless in the performance of his duty, seeking only to do right, and fearing nothing but to do wrong."

Chief-Justice Taney adds that "He was a sound lawyer, faithful and assiduous in the discharge of his duties, while his health was sufficient to undergo the labor." And that, "He was frank and firm in his social intercourse, as well as in the discharge of his official duties; and no man could be more free from guile, or more honestly endeavor to fulfil the obligations which his office imposed upon him."

* 10 Howard's Reports, 377.

† The principle was similar to that laid down by Chief-Justice Marshall, in Providence Bank *vs.* Billings, heretofore noticed. It was also based upon similar grounds with those assumed by Chief-Justice Taney in his earliest constitutional judgment, in the Charles River Bridge case. It is proper here to remark that the principle of the latter case was fully sanctioned by the Court at this term, in the case of East Hartford *vs.* Hartford Bridge Co., 10 How. 511, the opinion being given by Judge Woodbury, in which he cites with approbation a portion of the reasoning of the Chief-Justice in the Charles River Bridge case.

‡ 13 Howard's Reports, 519.

In this case, it will be recollected, the Court declared the bridge a nuisance, and that the act of Virginia authorising the structure, so as to obstruct navigation,

1852, he dissented from the judgment of the Court, in a brief opinion, in the important case of The Vincennes University *vs.* The State of Indiana, holding, in opposition to the majority of his brethren, that a reservation of public lands by Congress, for the use of a seminary of learning, was not like a grant or donation to a private individual, or for private purposes, but that the State, on the organization of its government, succeeded to the land as trustee, and could constitutionally dispose of it, and appropriate the fund to the uses for which it was dedicated.* At the same time he delivered the judgment in Kennett *et al. vs.* Chambers,† a case arising in the Texas district, in which is re-affirmed the safe, and wisely conservative, principle, that it belongs exclusively to the political department of the government to recognize a new government in a foreign country, claiming to have displaced an old and established one, and until such recognition, the Judiciary are bound to consider the old order of things as having continued. The legal consequence of this rule, in its application to the particular case, was held to be, that a contract to advance money to a General in the Texan army, after the declaration by Texas of its independence, but before recognition by the United States, was void, as being in contravention of the public policy and laws of the Union.

In bringing to a close this review of the judicial labors of Chief-Justice Taney, I might with propriety apologize for its incompleteness and imperfection. Looking back upon the extensive field which has been passed over, I am satisfied that but little more has been done in his case, as in the case of his predecessor, than to gather, here and there,

would afford no protection to the company, inasmuch as the Ohio, being a navigable stream, was subject to the commercial power of Congress. On the latter point the Chief-Justice thought the case fell precisely within the principle of the Blackbird Creek Marsh Company, decided in Chief-Justice Marshall's time. *Ante*, page 425. And he could not perceive, he says, "how the mere grant of power to the legislative department to regulate commerce, can give to the judicial branch the power to declare what shall and what shall not be regarded as an unlawful obstruction." Mr. Justice Daniel, in a strong and well reasoned opinion, also dissented from the majority of the Court. It is proper to add that the judgment of the Supreme Court was practically nullified by a subsequent act of Congress, declaring the Wheeling Bridge a *post road* of the United States.

* 14 Howard's Reports, 269.

† 14 Howard's Reports, 39.

a sheaf, leaving a rich and abundant harvest behind. To gather that little has been no easy task, for the profusion of the material renders it the more difficult to make a proper and discriminating selection. I have aimed to confine the review mainly to the most important constitutional questions, which, from time to time, have come before him. In doing so, it has been unavoidably necessary to pass over without notice a mass of interesting cases, comprehending almost every branch of civil jurisprudence, connected, not only with those subjects which belong exclusively to the Federal tribunals, but embracing, also, the entire range of legal and equitable remedies. A thorough and accurate study of these subjects is the province of the professional man alone; and a critical review of them would not, therefore, be expected in this place. Perhaps enough has been done, however, to indicate something of the extent, the variety, and the usefulness of the labors performed by the subject of this sketch during a period of eighteen years' uninterrupted service on the bench, and to convey to the reader some adequate notion of those rare endowments of character, of intellect, and of temperament, which must combine in the man, who, as has been the good fortune of Judge Taney, is able to fill with honor to himself, and profit to his country, the office of Chief-Justice of the United States.

Judge Taney married, in early life, a daughter of John Ross Key, and has seen a numerous family growing up around him. He has now reached a ripe old age, but is yet, as his later judgments abundantly manifest, in the full possession of his mental faculties.

He still presides with ease and dignity over the deliberations of the Supreme Court. The past session has been one of more than ordinary labor. An uninterrupted term of three months was followed by a brief recess during the month of March, the session again commencing on the first of April. Several causes of great magnitude and intricacy were brought before the Court. Among these, the Spanish land title case, Choteau *vs.* Malony, involving property to the amount of many millions of dollars, the result of which was looked for with intense interest, and which has been decided against the validity of the Spanish grant; also the McDonough will case, on which depended property to the amount of from five to eight millions of dollars, devised mainly for charitable purposes to the cities of Baltimore and New

Orleans.* The importance of some of these cases was such as to induce the Court to relax the two hour rule, and this of course protracted the labors of the session. The argument of the McDonough Will case alone occupied the greater portion of a week—an argument, it may be added, distinguished by an uncommon display of forensic ability, eloquence, and learning.

And during all these discussions, from the commencement to the close, the venerable Chief-Justice was to be seen in his seat, day after day, vigilant, patient, attentive, and carefully listening to every word uttered, and apparently weighing each sentence, and every proposition, as it fell from the lips of the advocate. Every day, at the usual hour of opening the Court, whoever else might be absent, he was sure to be seen, heading the procession of Judges, and with slow and measured, but firm step, approaching his customary seat. Whatever impatience or indifference others might manifest at the dullness or prolixity of an argument, no sign or look upon his countenance indicated anything else than the most careful attention. You might watch him by the hour, and it was the same. You might be sure that he suffered no word to escape him ; that he heard every thing worth hearing ; that his mind was fixed upon the subject ; and that he remembered whatever might be material to the merits of the argument. I have elsewhere remarked that the patience of Chief-Justice Marshall was proverbial, and that he was one of the best listeners who ever sat upon the bench. In this respect, Chief-Justice Taney emulates the example of his illustrious predecessor. No one who, with respectful address, invokes the Court where he presides, fails to obtain a full and attentive hearing. I believe there are no qualities of the Judge which more strongly win upon the favor of the profession, than that amenity of temper and equanimity of mind which lead him, on all occasions, to a calm, earnest, respectful, and (even though *apparent* only) unabstracted attention to the arguments addressed to him. The best listener, other things being equal, has generally the strongest hold upon the affections of the bar ; for an attentive and respectful hearing is a spontaneous compliment to eloquence, it is a delicate flattery to modest mediocrity, and a kind of benevolence even to dullness itself. Many an advocate at

* Mr. Justice Campbell delivered the opinion of the Court in this case, sustaining the will.

the bar, no matter whether with a bad or a good case, has felt the risings of that hot and passionate indignation which prompted the exclamation of the Athenian: "Strike, but HEAR ME!" But it has not been at the bar of the Court where Marshall presided, and where Taney presides. To the elevated and pure minds of Judges like these, an attentive hearing of the case is not merely the exercise of an empty compliment, but it is a solemn obligation. To HEAR is, with them, a part, and no inconsiderable part, of judicial duty; and this duty is discharged with a full appreciation of the deeply significant truth embodied in that delicate and classic conception which associates the bandaged eyes of Justice, with the ever open and attentive ear.

The present is not perhaps the proper time or occasion to speak of the private and social virtues of the eminent man whose public career I have thus endeavored to trace. That task will be more appropriately performed hereafter. A sense of delicacy forbids any attempt to speak the eulogy of the living; in a few more years it may be done with freedom, with discriminating impartiality, and without reserve. It is the province of the cotemporary observer to note facts, and to record the actions of those eminent men who still remain upon the stage, and of posterity to pass upon their merits after they shall have gone from among us. It is sufficient here to say, what all who know Chief-Justice Taney, will regard as but a simple act of justice, that in the domestic relations, and in the private and social intercourse of life, he is as much beloved as he is respected in his public and judicial character. A reputation beyond reproach or the breath of calumny, a purity of life that no man can assail, a frank, independent, manly uprightness of conduct which knows no guile, are united with that benignity of temper, those generous sympathies of the heart, and those solid household virtues which brighten the social circle, and gladden the domestic hearth. In his intercourse with others there is a warmth of kindly feeling, united with an unaffected simplicity of manner, that irresistibly wins upon all who approach him; but it is blended with a natural dignity of carriage that commands respect, and represses undue familiarity.

We may point to Judge Taney as one of our best specimens of the American lawyer and jurist. His whole life, from earliest manhood, has been professional. He is one of the few really eminent men of the country who have scarcely any political history. With the single exception of the brief period, during which he filled the office of Secretary of the Treasury, in the Cabinet of General Jackson, he was never at any time entirely withdrawn from the studies connected with his profession. The few years of his service in the Maryland Legislature, temporarily diverted his attention, but did not entirely interrupt his legal pursuits. His appointment as Attorney-General of the United States introduced him merely to a wider theatre of professional action. He came to the bench, a deeply read, and profoundly learned lawyer—a master of the principles, and thoroughly skilled in the practice, of the law. He brought with him large acquirements, and the fruits of a ripe experience, and the result has been, that he has sustained himself with ability and honor, as the head of the Federal Judiciary, and has proved himself, in the words of Mr. Clay, "a worthy successor of Chief-Justice Marshall."

Long may he continue to fill that place, and to enjoy that merited distinction. To one like him, we may address, in no spirit of unmeaning adulation, the words of the Roman bard—

Serus in cœlum redeas.

www.ingramcontent.com/pod-product-compliance
Lightning Source LLC
LaVergne TN
LVHW021257110826
845150LV00003B/413